THE ILLUSTRATED ENCYCLOPEDIA OF
AMERICAN
INDIAN
MYTHOLOGY

THE ILLUSTRATED ENCYCLOPEDIA OF
AMERICAN INDIAN MYTHOLOGY

LEGENDS, GODS AND SPIRITS OF NORTH, CENTRAL AND SOUTH AMERICA

DAVID M. JONES
AND BRIAN L. MOLYNEAUX

LORENZ BOOKS

I would like to dedicate this book, with thanks, to three teachers and lifelong friends: Bess Sewelson, Ernie Avellar and (the late) Roald Wick. (DMJ)

For my mother, Mary, in memory of my father, Fred, and for my own family: Wendy and our children Fred, Alexandra and Lily. (BLM)

This edition is published by Lorenz Books,
an imprint of Anness Publishing Ltd,
Hermes House, 88–89 Blackfriars Road,
London SE1 8HA;
tel. 020 7401 2077; fax 020 7633 9499

www.lorenzbooks.com; www.annesspublishing.com

Anness Publishing has a new picture agency outlet for images for publishing, promotions or advertising. Please visit our website www.practicalpictures.com for more information.

UK agent: The Manning Partnership Ltd
tel. 01225 478444; fax 01225 478440;
sales@manning-partnership.co.uk
UK distributor: Grantham Book Services Ltd
tel. 01476 541080; fax 01476 541061;
orders@gbs.tbs-ltd.co.uk
North American agent/distributor:
National Book Network
tel. 301 459 3366; fax 301 429 5746;
www.nbnbooks.com
Australian agent/distributor:
Pan Macmillan Australia
tel. 1300 135 113; fax 1300 135 103;
customer.service@macmillan.com.au
New Zealand agent/distributor: David Bateman Ltd
tel. (09) 415 7664; fax (09) 415 8892

Publisher: Joanna Lorenz
Editorial Director: Helen Sudell
Senior Editor: Claire Folkard
Design: Mario Bettella, Artmedia
Map Illustrator: Stephen Sweet
Picture Researchers: Veneta Bullen (UK),
␣␣␣␣ita Dickhuth (US)
␣␣␣rial Reader: Richard McGinlay
␣␣␣␣ion Controller: Steve Lang

ETHICAL TRADING POLICY
Because of our ongoing ecological investment programme, you, as our customer, can have the pleasure and reassurance of knowing that a tree is being cultivated on your behalf to naturally replace the materials used to make the book you are holding. For further information about this scheme, go to www.annesspublishing.com/trees

© Anness Publishing Ltd 2001, 2009

Previously published as *Mythology of the Americas*

Page 1: DANCERS ON THE NORTHWEST COAST OF NORTH AMERICA
Frontispiece: INCA TUPAC AMARU
Title page: CHIBCHA GOLD PECTORAL (top); AZTEC GOD, XÓLOTL (bottom)
This page: THUNDERBIRD ON A TOTEM POLE

PUBLISHER'S NOTE
The entries in this encyclopedia are all listed alphabetically. Names in italic capital letters indicate that that name has an individual entry. Special feature spreads examine specific mythological themes in more detail. If a character or subject is included in a special feature spread it is noted at the end of their individual entry. Although the advice and information in this book are believed to be accurate and true at the time of going to press, neither the authors nor the publisher can accept any legal responsibility or liability for any errors or omissions that may be made.

CONTENTS

PREFACE

This encyclopedia concerns the continents of America, from the Canadian Arctic to the last landfall above the Antarctic seas. These are lands of great contrast – frigid tundra, cool and searing deserts, vast grasslands and forests, lush woodlands, dense, humid jungles, and immense mountain ranges.

The native peoples' mythologies, as diverse as these landscapes, are explored in three sections, starting with North America and the linguistic and tribal groups of Canada and the United States, whose legends reflect ways of life based variously on hunting and gathering, agriculture and fishing. The section on Mesoamerica (broadly, Mexico and the countries of the isthmus to the south) includes the great Aztec Empire in the uplands and the Maya states to the east and south, as well as their predecessor cultures. The South American section covers cultures from Colombia to Chile and from the Pacific Coast across the high Andes to the Brazilian rainforests – including the Inca Empire and its progenitors.

Humans entered America when it was joined to Asia by an Ice Age land bridge over what is now the Bering Strait, migrating south and east, along the coasts and into the interiors, reaching Tierra del Fuego by 9000 BC or earlier. The first peoples were nomads: gathering, fishing and hunting in seasonal rounds. By about 5000 BC, some people had discovered how to cultivate some of the plants they gathered and how to domesticate some of the animals around them. Tending these involved settling in one place; then – as trade in surplus food began to develop in the ensuing millennia – villages were able to support specialist craftsmen who produced objects and services over and above

DANCE *was an important part of ritual for many tribal peoples, and invariably had both a spiritual and practical significance. These dancers are assuming the spirit of the bear, giving them the power and wisdom necessary for successful hunting.*

the barest necessities of life. Some societies became yet more complex, and towns developed, ultimately growing into city-states, kingdoms and empires, with powerful dynastic rulers and organized priesthoods.

But most cultures did not evolve steadily from nomad group to empire, or abandon their natural spirituality, focused on earth and sky, for great corporate religions intertwined with the power structures of a state. In some environments – too harsh, remote, impenetrable or infertile to support the denser populations from which complex societies could develop – the inhabitants continued to gather, fish and hunt, or work small garden plots near their camps or villages, or tend animals. And some complex societies developed too far – collapsing as they exhausted the environment that had sustained them – while others fell to climatic change or natural disaster, or were conquered by neighbours.

Yet each of these diverse cultures had one thing in common: the need for a mythology to explain not only the vastness and power of the cosmos and the wonders of nature, but also the mysteries of the human mind, with its desires, its fears and its capacities for good and evil, creation and destruction, and selfishness and altruism. This mythology enabled these cultures to find meaning, balance and a sense of place in the world they inherited.

Mythology is not just a miscellaneous collection of old tales and legends; it embraces all of what we now call religion, science and philosophy (natural, moral and metaphysical). It asks fundamental questions – how the world began, how it will end, where humans fit in and how they can influence it, and how individuals and communities should interact. Since the questions are the same, we see common threads running through the mythologies described here: heavens above and nether worlds below; the critical importance of the sun, moon and stars; gods, heroes and monsters creating, transforming and destroying successions of nascent worlds; the sacred significance of the landscape itself, and of particular elements within it.

Even so, answers to these questions vary with the societies that ask them. The Choctaw ancestors, emerging out of the hill of Nanih Waiya from their previous world, looked out on a landscape very different from the ones that greeted the first Aztecs leaving the caves of Chicomoztoc, or Manco Capac and the Inca ancestors appearing

GOLD and other metals were highly valued by many Ancient American cultures, perhaps most famously by the Incas, and were used for religious and decorative purposes. This gold and copper jaguar head was discovered in the Lambayeque Valley in Peru.

from Tambo Toco mountain. In the fertile Mississippi Valley, the Choctaw became sun-worshipping agriculturalists; the Aztecs left harsh Aztlán for the Basin of Mexico and built an empire fuelled by war (and sacrifice) to garner from elsewhere the resources they needed; and from highland Peru the Inca Empire, America's largest, redistributed the wealth of the Pacific coast, the high *pampas* and the dense rainforest fringes of the Andes along a fantastic network of roads. Yet, similar myths can appear in the most diverse of societies and environments: the "bird nester" theme (one of two competitors persuades his rival to make a perilous climb to gather birds' eggs, then removes the ladder and maroons him) is found among the Yurok of the Californian coast and the Kayapo in the Brazilian rainforest; the common prominence of serpents and jaguars in religious imagery throughout Mesoamerica and South America; or the popularity of the trickster coyote among many North American and Mesoamerican peoples. It is these contrasting threads of similarity and difference, confirmation and contradiction, and the search for basic truths about life, that make the fabric of the mythology of the Americas so fascinating.

TEOTIHUACÁN was one of the most important city-states in ancient Mesoamerica. The Aztecs believed that the huge pyramid-temples, such as this one depicting images of the gods Quetzalcoátl and Tlaloc were burial mounds for gods and giants.

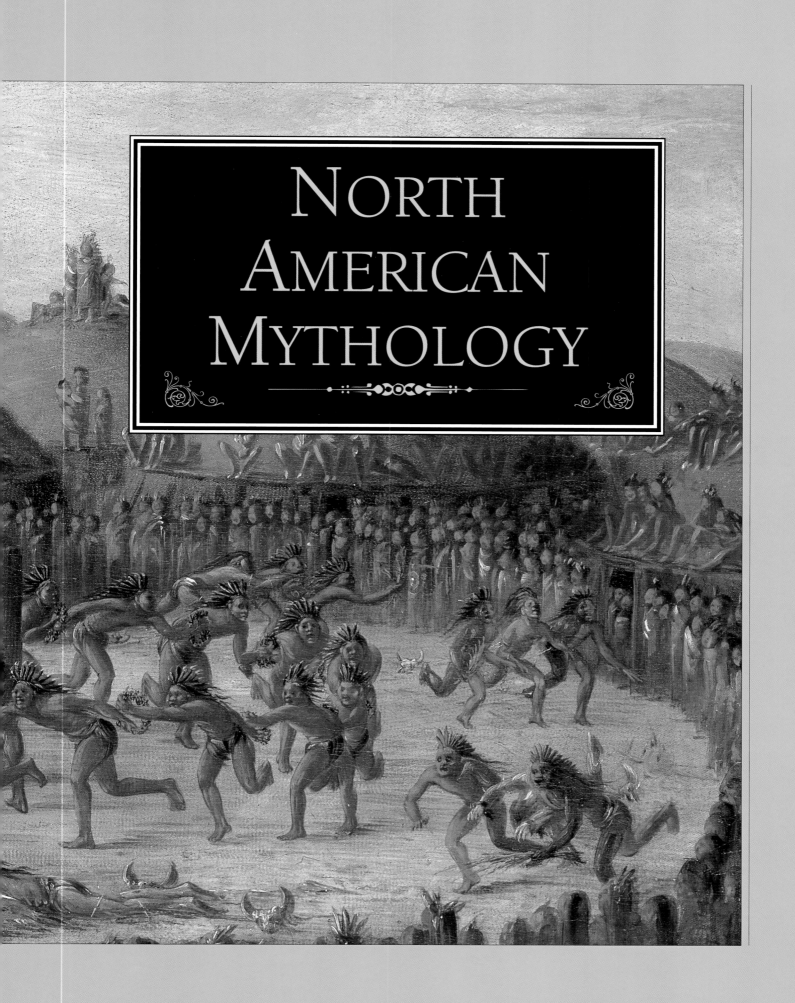

NORTH AMERICAN MYTHOLOGY

INTRODUCTION

THE CULTURAL HERITAGE of North American aboriginal peoples includes oral traditions remembered and preserved in mythologies. Story-tellers over thousands of years of Native North American culture have been unconstrained by literary form, which can transform inspiration into rigid canons of belief and practice. They have been free to listen to their own heritage and speak with voices that reflect individual vision and the wisdom of the ages. Personal insight, sought through dreams, vision quests and other forms of inspiration, is a critical aspect of spirituality in most North American aboriginal cultures. It makes the mythology as mutable – and fragile – as the story-teller's world. Yet, by living in the spoken word, the song and the dance, the spirits of the imagination survive across generations, passing on the essence of what it takes to be a human being.

The Spiritual Life

People of all cultures define the world as they experience it, so their mythologies must account for what they see. Every part of a landscape has the potential for spiritual identity. This is often literal: high places are close to the sky and the remote gods; caves provide entry into the earth and its hidden spiritual forces. Other, less dramatic, places and objects involved in mythological events only have meaning if a narrative survives. All material things have spiritual potential – from tiny stones worn down in birds' gizzards, kept by some tribes as powerful medicine, to the great trees used to construct ceremonial lodges. Moreover, in many cultures, every living thing harks back to a time when all creatures spoke with a common voice and pursued similar social lives. This mythological age is not lost in the deep past defined by science, for aboriginal concepts of time are both linear and cyclical: linear as the steps and stages of a human life, and cyclical as the generations that renew all life and the

earth itself. This endless spiral means that the past never recedes into the distance; even the time of creation is only just beyond the reach of the story-teller. The mythological narratives of a culture are thus an eternal present, renewing social identity with every telling.

Native North Americans once shared the most ancient of patterns of life – moving from place to place, following the seasonal shifts of nature to gather wild plants and hunt game – and the religious beliefs and mythologies of hunters and gatherers reflect this. Their search for spiritual knowledge and understanding was seen in terms of a journey, a quest for vision, that took them away from the protection of their familiar surroundings into a natural world containing the mysterious forces that brought life and death, famine and plenty.

When many centuries of harvesting native plant species gradually developed into a formalized agriculture – sparked by the spread of corn (maize) from Mexico well over 2,000 years ago – some peoples adopted a more sedentary life. These horticultural groups adapted their belief systems to the rhythms of lives spent in one place and measured by the structured routines of planting, tending and harvesting corn (maize), beans, squash and other crops in gardens and fields. Unlike nomadic hunters and gatherers – who, through personal quests or with the help of shamans, gained access to the spirits wherever they moved – farming people most often focused their worlds in the ceremonial centres of their villages, enclosed by a familiar landscape, and tended to develop organized priesthoods and religions.

The European Invasion

Immediately after the first contact with Europeans in the 17th century, the introduction of their trade goods and domesticated animals to cultures reliant on natural substances – such as stone, bone, plant fibres and clays – had a dramatic impact on North American cultures.

DEVIL'S TOWER, Wyoming, known to the Lakota as Mato Tipila, has drawn people to it for at least 10,000 years. It figures in the mythologies of the Arapaho, Cheyenne, Kiowa, Sioux and other regional tribes. In ancient times, the great mass of volcanic rock provided shelter for practical and spiritual needs, and gave hunters excellent views across the Belle Fourche Valley. Its rock-strewn flanks are now important sites for vision quests and other personal rituals, while the surrounding grasslands are the settings for Sun Dances and other significant tribal ceremonies.

CEREMONIES forge the link between the land, human life, and the creative and nurturing powers of nature. In this representation by a Zia Pueblo artist of a mythical corn ceremony, the broad leaves of the plant shelter drummers who sing sacred songs while dancers, under the life-giving rain, offer gifts to the creative essence above the sky. (PAINTING BY IGNACIO MOQUINO, 1938.)

Horses, metal, glass, firearms – all seemed at first magical and then essential, disrupting cultural routines that had taken centuries to develop. When white soldiers, missionaries, traders and settlers followed, they set in motion what was to become a devastating and irreversible process of social disintegration that had a disastrous effect on tradition. Except for those in the remotest forest regions of the north and in the Arctic, almost all tribes were decimated or eliminated by force of arms or disease, and distracted from their traditional hunting-and-gathering or farming economies by the fur trade and the lure of European material goods that it brought. By the mid-19th century they had been driven from their homelands to distant reservations. These new lands were generally infertile, rugged and remote, with little perceived economic potential to Europeans. Yet hunter-gatherers were expected to take up farming, and farmers were meant to raise crops, on the poor, often arid, soils. On many reservations, individual tribes were forced to cohabit with others, speaking

different languages and following different traditions. They were assaulted by governments intent on destroying indigenous culture through Western education, the substitution of English for native tongues, and indoctrination in Christianity – which included systematic attempts to eliminate ancient religions.

The cultural dissonance was intense because native people held concepts of land use and property, of time, of the nature of the world itself, that were dramatically different from those of white people. When Sauk and Fox chiefs, plied with lavish gifts and liquor, signed away their lands in the Treaty of 1804 for a meagre sum of money, the great Sauk chief Black Hawk explained his actions thus: "My reason teaches me that land cannot be sold. The Great Spirit gave it to his children to live upon. So long as they occupy and cultivate it they have the right to the soil. Nothing can be sold but such things as can be carried away." Only on the Northwest Coast, where families and clans held

rights to virtually all aspects of life, from myths to shellfish beds, and among some northern Californian tribes, did hunters and gatherers regard land as property. The absolute loss of land was inconceivable to most chiefs, even when they actually signed it away. American Indians were also baffled by Western concepts of time. The rigorous segmentation of life into equal fragments imposed a strange and different rhythm, one that responded to mathematical logic rather than reflecting the changing patterns of nature.

The American Indians drew their identity from the intertwining of the natural world around them and the spiritual world that was their philosophy, science and religion. From the reservations, the view of the spiritual and

THE MISSION was a familiar sight in Southern California by the early 19th century. Starting at San Diego in 1789, Franciscan friars founded 21 missions along El Camino Real ("the Royal Road") to Sonoma, in order to bring Christianity to the region's native tribes. The techniques of the missionaries were both subtle and aggressive, leading many people to question the wisdom of their own spirituality. This view of San Gabriel Mission, near present-day Los Angeles, shows an American Indian dwelling in the foreground. (PAINTING BY FERDINAND DEPPE, 1832.)

THE HARSH LANDSCAPE of the Great Basin desert in Nevada is lit by afternoon sun following a storm, throwing the juniper, sage and scattered piñon pines into sharp relief. Culture thrived in this stark, arid land, despite the cruel climate and sparse resources – a testimony to the strength and creativity of the aboriginal peoples.

physical world was not the same as it had once been. Traditional sacred sites and landscapes – the very foundations of tribal culture – were no longer accessible, because they were on white-controlled private land. Many elders, the keepers of traditional knowledge, were among the staggering numbers that died following the move to reservations. Others lost touch with ancestral roots as a result of the pressures of assimilation, and many younger people were unable to maintain their cultural identities. By the mid-20th century, mythologies, and the narratives and rituals that made them vital, reflected this dissolution of cultural integrity, surviving in many places as half-remembered fragments, or disappearing altogether.

There were some groups among whom the strong core of native beliefs persisted. Some occupied lands unattractive to whites, such as the Arctic and Subarctic, interior mountain regions and the deserts of the Southwest. Some maintained a relatively independent economy, including a few of the seagoing cultures of the Northwest Coast. Others retained significant land bases within their traditional homelands. Ultimately, as environmental awareness began to strengthen in the second half of the 20th century, aboriginal philosophies of respect for,

and sensitivity to, the earth and its resources rose to prominence. In this atmosphere of new-found respect, mythologies were no longer the quaint stories of disappearing cultures, but ideas and beliefs that made a direct connection between human life and the surrounding world. The depredations of 400 years of domination by Western culture had left an indelible mark; nonetheless, the new relevance of these ancient mythologies inspired spiritual regeneration, rediscovery and re-creation of the knowledge that was almost lost. The growing cultural strength of North America's first nations continues to this day, with new narrative forms – literature, theatre and electronic media – growing beside the traditional arts of story-telling, visual arts, drama and dance. These new visions look forward, at the same time respecting tradition and recalling the lessons of the past. They express, as the ancient elders did, the realities of the present for the sake of the future.

Mythology Today

With such a dramatic and complex background, North American mythology is not easily organized or presented. The individual nature of American Indian religions, the generations of story-tellers, and the difficulty of using one

language to explain another's vision, as well as the loss of traditional culture by assimilation, and the sparse, fragmented collection of oral traditions that remain, all mean that the names (and spellings) and exploits of mythological beings may be highly variable. We draw from many different kinds of sources: anthropological texts, collections of myths, and contemporary Indian narratives. We use traditional names for some characters, and their English translations for others – sometimes the traditional name is already well-known, and sometimes the English name provides a description that would be obscured if the native word was used. The naming of tribes is equally complex. Many tribes were given their names by whites, either because they did not know the tribe's own name for itself or because it did not anglicize easily. Sometimes these names were actually pejoratives used by rivals or enemies. Other tribes never had, or used, a collective name until anthropologists or other whites gave them one. In recent times, some tribes have demanded that their chosen names be used in place of the ones conferred on them by others – the Inuit, for example, rejecting the universally familiar term "Eskimo". In this book we use the names most commonly recognized, while adding variant spellings and the names that tribes may prefer themselves in parentheses or, if the new name is gaining acceptance, in the main text.

Given the significance of the natural environment to cultural adaptation and expression, we divide tribal groups according to the regions in which they last lived freely: the Arctic, the Subarctic (northern, or boreal, forests), the Northeast, the Southeast, the Great Plains, the Southwest, California, the Great Basin, the Columbia Plateau, and the Northwest Coast. The distinct environmental character of each of these regions strongly influenced its peoples, determining, for example, whether an individual group had the potential to amass food resources or move from hunting and gathering to horticulture and, thus, the pattern of beliefs that would develop within the group as a result.

Environment, and the proximity of tribes to each other, has a much greater influence on the form a culture takes than language does, but knowledge of the language of one's traditions is crucial to cultural identity. Language also gives us an understanding of tribal origins and relationships, for the languages that exist today all developed over thousands of years from roots in Asia. Languages change and diversify over time, especially if the population is highly dispersed and isolated. However, through identifying similar words and grammatical constructions used by different groups, linguists can identify

many language-family relationships although a few languages defy analysis, perhaps because their origins lie so deep in the past that the shared words and grammatical constructions are now obscure.

The study of North American native languages shows that tribal groups within a language family tend to cluster in certain regions – the Algonquian peoples in the northern part of the continent, and the Uto-Aztecan peoples in the south, for instance – but there are also outlying groups speaking a language unrelated to those of the cultures around them. Since language relationships may persist in spite of dramatic changes in a culture, anomalies in the distribution of languages may reveal evidence of ancient migrations. Perhaps the most dramatic example in North America is the Navajo. These herders and farmers of the Southwest region are identified with sand paintings and a complex mythology focused on corn. Yet they speak an Athapascan language related to the languages of groups living as far north as Alaska and the Northwest Territories, who spend their lives hunting and fishing in the northern forests.

North American mythologies were once as diverse as the languages and environments of its original inhabitants.

CHILDREN offer the best chance to keep alive the spirit of a culture. Among Indian peoples, the interaction between elders and the very young provides the spiritual strength that young people need as they grow. The Navajo children gathered here listen to an elder, whose stories of history, legendary heroes and the events of creation ensure that future generations keep their cultural identity through the dramatic changes they will experience in their lifetimes.

But in our modern "information society", native voices often speak of a common reality: putting the case that individual groups must work together to achieve the strength they need to regain lost rights and lost lands. This is reflected in a spread of common religions, common rituals and common mythologies among once diverse tribes. Nevertheless, the vitality of surviving mythologies teaches that there is also strength in diversity. By keeping the link between peoples and their homelands, a wealth of unique cultural heritage can flourish, and its narratives carry the life experiences and wisdom of thousands of generations into the future.

The past 400 years in North America are a history of cultural and linguistic decline and extinction. Now the challenges to native cultures include the revival of tradition and the renewal of mythology to accommodate new political and social realities.

THE CREATIVE ARTS are flourishing today, reflecting a renewal of pride among aboriginal peoples. Cedar wood-carving along the Northwest Coast carries on a tradition extending several thousand years into the past, but with a new freedom, generated by a changing society and access to new technologies. In a modern depiction of the Haida origin story, the formal symmetry of the traditional style gives way to a more dynamic expression (left), as Raven opens the clam shell and releases the first humans on to the muddy flats left by receding primordial waters. (CEDAR CARVING BY BILL REID.)

LANGUAGES OF THE TRIBES

A language is not merely a way of speaking: it is a way of seeing and explaining the world. English translations of stories told in native tongues can only reveal the surface of the deep emotional and philosophical insights that the original words embodied. Even so, such translations give us an opening into an intellectual world that extends back thousands of years. Although we cannot *hear* the words in which these stories were first spoken, study of the languages reveals subtle relationships among the tribes of the North American aboriginal family that help to account for the sharing of mythological characters, events and themes.

This study, which explores the development of languages by tracing them back to common roots, is highly complex. the thousands of languages and dialects spoken during prehistoric times are now a few hundred, many of which are on the verge of extinction, so that linguists have little to work with. Classification is therefore always hypothetical and, since research continues, in a state of flux.

This table provides a very general organization of languages and dialects spoken by the people of the tribes mentioned. Some language phyla and families and many languages and dialects are therefore left out. The left column contains the language family name under which all related languages are grouped, and each succeeding column to the right represents a more detailed group, subgroup, language or dialect. Isolate languages are those thought to be unconnected to any other group. As languages develop and diversify over time, the left-to-right shift is also (putatively) a shift in time, from past to present, across the centuries of aboriginal life in North America. Since the classification is intended as a rough sketch, we have omitted more detailed language relationships at the tribal level, as many of these are still subject to scholarly debate.

Readers who wish to pursue this fascinating subject further may consult the sources used for the following scheme:

Joseph E. Grimes and Barbara F. Grimes (eds), *Ethnologue Language Family Index* (13th ed.), Dallas TX: Summer Institute of Linguistics, 1996 (also see www.sil.org/ethnologue/families).

Alvin M. Josephy, jr. (ed.), *America in 1492*, New York: Vintage Books, 1993.

Carl Waldman, *Atlas of the North American Indian*, New York: Facts on File, 1985.

The *Ethnologue* classification, which is generally adhered to here, follows the classification scheme of William O. Bright (ed.), *International Encyclopedia of Linguistics*, Oxford and New York: Oxford University Press, 1992.

LANGUAGE FAMILIES

Language subgroup(s):
Language/dialect name Tribe name

ALGIC:
Algonquian:
Central:
Cree (5 dialects)	Cree
Kickapoo	Kickapoo
Menominee	Menominee
Mesquaki	Fox
Montagnais	Montagnais
Ojibwa (4 dialects)	Ojibwa
Potawatomi	Potawatomi

Eastern:
Abnaki-Penobscot	Abenaki, Penobscot
Delaware	Delaware
Maliseet-Passamaquoddy	
	Malecite-Passamaquoddy
Micmac	Micmac
Naskapi	Naskapi

Plains:
Arapaho	Arapaho
Blackfoot	Blackfoot
Cheyenne	Cheyenne
Gros Ventre	Gros Ventre
Wiyot isolate	Wiyot
Yurok isolate	Yurok

CADDOAN
Northern:
Arikara	Arikara
Pawnee	Pawnee
Wichita	Wichita

ESKIMO-ALEUT
Aleut	Aleut
Inuit	Inuit

HOKAN
Esselen-Yuman:
Mohave	Mojave

Northern:
Karok	Karuk

Salinan-Seri:
Chumash	Chumash

IROQUOIAN
Northern:
Cayuga	Cayuga
Mohawk	Mohawk
Oneida	Oneida
Onondaga	Onondaga
Seneca	Seneca
Tuscarora	Tuscarora
Wyandot	Wyandot

Southern:
Cherokee	Cherokee

KERESCAN
Cochiti	Cochiti Pueblo
Keres	Keres Pueblo

KIOWA-TANOAN
Kiowa-Towa:
Jemez	Towa Pueblo
Kiowa	Kiowa

Tewa-Tiwa:
Tewa	Tewa Pueblo
Tiwa (northern and southern)	
	Tiwa Pueblo

KUTENAI isolate
	Kootenay

MUSKOGEAN
Eastern:
Alabama	Alabama
Muskogee	Creek, Tuskegee
Seminole	Seminole

Western:
Choctaw	Choctaw

NA-DENE
Athapascan:
Apachean:
Jicarilla Apache	Jicarilla Apache
Kiowa Apache	Kiowa Apache
Lipan Apache	Lipan Apache
Mescalero-Chiricahua Apache	
	Mescalero-Chiricahua Apache
Navajo	Navajo
Western Apache	Aravaipa Apache

Canadian:
Beaver	Beaver
Chipewyan	Chipewyan
Dogrib	Dogrib
Han	Han
Hare	Sahtu
Sarsi	Sarcee
Slavey	Slavey
Yellowknife	Yellowknife

Ingalik-Koyukon:
Degexit'an	Degexit'an
Koyukon	Koyukon

Pacific Coast:
Hupa	Hupa

Tahltan-Kaska:
Tahltan	Tahltan

Tanana-Upper Kuskokwim:
Haida isolate	Haida
Tanana	Tanana
Tlingit isolate	Tlingit

PENUTIAN
California Penutian:
Maidu (4 dialects)	Maidu
Miwok (6 dialects)	Miwok, Yosemite
Wintun	Wintu

Chinookan:
Chinook	Chinook

Plateau Penutian:
Klamath-Modoc	Klamath, Modoc
Nez Perce	Nez Perce
Yakima	Yakima

Tsimshian:
Nass-Gitksian	Niska, Gitksan
Tsimshian	Tsimshian
Zuni isolate (incorporation under Penutian is hypothetical)	Zuni

SALISHAN
Bella Coola	Bella Coola
Central Salish	Coast Salish

Interior Salish:
Flathead-Kalispel	Flathead
Okanagan	Okanagan
Sanpoil	Sanpoil
Colville	Colville

Tsamosan:
Lower Chehalis	Lower Chehalis
Upper Chehalis	Upper Chehalis

SIOUAN
Central:
Assiniboine	Assiniboine
Dakota	Mdewakanton, Wahpekute, Sisseton and Wahpeton
Iowa-Oto	Iowa
Lakota	Teton
Mandan	Mandan
Nakota	Yankton, Yanktonai
Omaha-Ponca	Omaha
Quapaw	Quapaw
Stoney	Stoney
Winnebago	Winnebago

Missouri Valley:
Crow	Crow
Hidatsa	Hidatsa

UTO-AZTECAN
Northern:
Comanche	Comanche
Hopi	Hopi
Luiseño	Luiseño
Northern Paiute	Northern Paiute
Serrano	Gabrielino
Shoshoni	Shoshoni
Ute-Southern Paiute	Ute, Southern Paiute

Southern:
Papago-Pima	Papago, Pima

WAKASHAN
Northern:
Kwakiutl	Kwakiutl

Southern:
Makah	Makah
Nootka	Nootka

YUKI
Wappo	Wappo
Yuki	Yuki

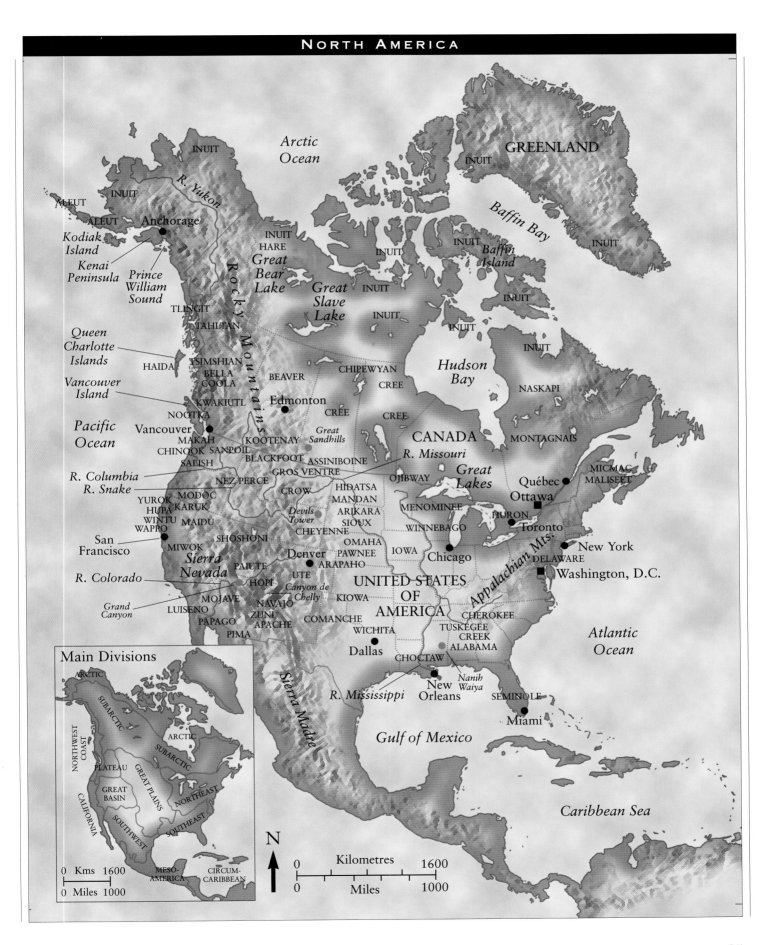

NORTH AMERICA

INUIT

Arctic Ocean

GREENLAND

INUIT

R. Yukon

Baffin Bay

INUIT

ALEUT

INUIT

ALEUT

Anchorage

INUIT

HARE

INUIT

INUIT

Baffin Island

Kodiak Island

Great Bear Lake

INUIT

INUIT

Kenai Peninsula

Prince William Sound

Great Slave Lake

INUIT

INUIT

TLINGIT

INUIT

TAHLTAN

INUIT

Queen Charlotte Islands

Rocky Mountains

HAIDA

TSIMSHIAN

BELLA COOLA

BEAVER

CHIPEWYAN

Hudson Bay

NASKAPI

Vancouver Island

KWAKIUTL

Edmonton

CREE

CREE

CREE

Pacific Ocean

NOOTKA

Vancouver

MAKAH

KOOTENAY

Great Sandhills

CANADA

MONTAGNAIS

CHINOOK

SANPOIL

BLACKFOOT

ASSINIBOINE

R. Missouri

MICMAC

MALISEET

R. Columbia

SALISH

GROS VENTRE

OJIBWAY

Great Lakes

Québec

R. Snake

NEZ PERCE

CROW

HIDATSA

Ottawa

YUROK

MODOC

MANDAN

MENOMINEE

HURON

Toronto

HUPA

KARUK

ARIKARA

WINNEBAGO

Appalachian Mts.

New York

WINTU

MAIDU

Devils Tower

SIOUX

Chicago

DELAWARE

WAPPO

CHEYENNE

IOWA

Washington, D.C.

San Francisco

SHOSHONI

OMAHA

MIWOK

Denver

PAWNEE

Sierra Nevada

PAIUTE

ARAPAHO

UNITED STATES OF AMERICA

R. Colorado

UTE

Canyon de Chelly

KIOWA

Atlantic Ocean

HOPI

CHEROKEE

Grand Canyon

MOJAVE

NAVAJO

COMANCHE

LUISENO

ZUNI

TUSKEGEE

PAPAGO

APACHE

WICHITA

CREEK

PIMA

ALABAMA

Dallas

CHOCTAW

New Orleans

Nanih Waiya

R. Mississippi

SEMINOLE

Gulf of Mexico

Miami

Sierra Madre

Caribbean Sea

Main Divisions

ARCTIC

SUBARCTIC

NORTHWEST COAST

ARCTIC

PLATEAU

SUBARCTIC

CALIFORNIA

GREAT PLAINS

GREAT BASIN

NORTHEAST

SOUTHWEST

SOUTHEAST

MESO-AMERICA

CIRCUM-CARIBBEAN

| 0 Kms 1600 |
| 0 Miles 1000 |

N

| 0 | Kilometres | 1600 |
| 0 | Miles | 1000 |

A

THE ABENAKI

THE ABENAKI (Abnaki) is a group of Algonquian-speaking tribes who ranged throughout the Atlantic maritime regions of southern Canada and the northeastern United States. The centre of their traditional homeland was present-day Maine, where the eastern Abenaki (including the *PENOBSCOT*, the *PASSAMAQUODDY*, and the *MALISEET*) hunted moose, deer and other game, fished the many lakes and rivers, and gathered wild plants. The western Abenaki, who occupied the milder inlands across Vermont and New Hampshire to the eastern shores of Lake Champlain in New York, subsisted mainly by horticulture and fishing.

The wars of the 18th century, which prompted the Abenaki and *MICMAC* to form the *WABANAKI* confederacy, forced many Abenaki to flee into Quebec, where they continue to live today. The rest occupy reservations in northern Maine (Penobscot, Passamaquoddy and Maliseet) and reserves in New Brunswick (Maliseet) or are scattered across the non-Indian lands and communities of the region.

THE AFTERLIFE

THE AFTERLIFE is, for most peoples, a journey to the land of the dead, a place of spiritual repose and comfort, if not happiness.

For the *INUIT*, the Land of the Dead lies above the sky. The sky itself is solid, pierced by holes that let in light and sometimes spill celestial fluids that fall as snow or rain into the land of the living. Above the sky the ghosts of the dead may find rest, for the air is warm, the sky is bright, and land animals are abundant. As if in reaction against the often hard life by the ocean, only a few variants of the Inuit myth mention seals, walruses and other sea creatures.

Sometimes, the desire to prolong the familiar in the afterlife reflects the harsher realities of life in the recent past. The Chiricahua *APACHE* people believe that the dead fall through a trapdoor

AN INUIT MOON MASK from western Alaska. The board around the face represents air, the hoops symbolize levels of the cosmos, and the feathers are stars. Inuit believe that the souls of the dead first rise into the heavens. After regaining their spiritual energy they travel with the moon down to earth again, where they may take human or animal form.

hidden by tall grass and slide down a great mountain of sand to the underworld. This world is similar to the Apache's own, extending, in one account, to the presence of white people.

AH-AH-NEE-NIN

see *GROS VENTRE*.

THE ALABAMA

THE ALABAMA people lived originally in what is now Alabama and Mississippi, growing corn (maize), beans and other crops in the warm, fertile river valleys, and hunting and gathering when necessary. They are close relatives of the Coushatta, who speak a similar Muskogean language. The two nations fragmented during the European conquest and were uprooted in the 19th century, when the United States government forcibly removed all southeastern tribes to Oklahoma. Just three small groups have survived: the Coushattas of Louisiana, the Alabama-Coushatta Tribe of Polk County, Texas, and the Alabamas and Quassartes of Oklahoma.

THE ALEUT

THE ALEUT consist of several Arctic cultures occupying the north Pacific and Bering Sea regions between North America and Asia. The Alutiiq inhabit the coastal areas of south-central Alaska, including Prince William Sound, Kodiak Island (which has the largest concentration of villages) and the Kenai and Alaska Peninsulas. The Aleut peoples of the western Aleutian Islands and the Commander Islands (Russia) have a distinctive language and culture. All Aleuts resemble the *INUIT* in their way of life, exploiting the abundant resources of land and sea (especially sea mammals, such as otters, and caribou). They lived in semi-subterranean houses, built of timbers and banked with earth. The effects of the trade in sea-otter fur and sealskin, beginning with Russian exploitation in the 19th century, were devastating, but the Aleuts' survival was ensured by their fierce resistance by their remoteness from centres of white American culture, and by the 20th-century decline in the fur trade.

ALINNAQ

see *MOON MAN*.

ALWAYS-LIVING-AT-THE-COAST

ALWAYS-LIVING-AT-THE-COAST (*KWAKIUTL*) became the progenitor of killer whales after a dramatic encounter with *COYOTE*.

Always-Living-at-the-Coast had a notoriously unmarried daughter named Death-Bringing Woman.

She had received many suitors, but their reward had been death, and their bones were piled high. Coyote decided to paddle his canoe down to the coast to court her. Some people along the way mocked his effort, and he transformed them into birds and then into the first deer; others encouraged him, so he created rich salmon and shellfish grounds on the spot. Then, a young woman whose sight he restored told him Death-Bringing Woman's terrible secret: she had a toothed vagina. She gave him a stone chisel and instructed him to blunt the teeth when the time came. Coyote did, and, with her weapons gone, Death-Bringing Woman happily accepted him as her husband. Angered, her father Always-Living-at-the-Coast tried several times to kill Coyote, but he always failed.

One day Coyote and his wife joined the old man in his canoe. As they paddled across the sea, Coyote chewed a piece of wood until it was soft, formed it into the shape of a killer whale and threw it into the water, exclaiming that the old man would be the killer whale of future generations. At that moment, whales rose out of the sea and dragged Always-Living-at-the-Coast under the waves.

THE ALASKAN SEA OTTER (Enhydra lutris lutris), was hunted to near extinction in the 18th and 19th centuries because of its luxurious fur. It is once again thriving.

ANISHINABE see *OJIBWAY*.

THE APACHE [Jicarilla, *KIOWA*, Lipan, Mescalero-Chiricahua, Aravaipa] speak an Athapascan language. As the Athapascan home-land is the Subarctic, it is clear that the Apache migrated from these northern regions to their present homelands in the southwestern United States and in northern Mexico. They put their hunting and gathering skills to good use in the rugged south-western landscapes and, where appropriate, took up farming and herding. Five main tribal groups exist today: the Jicarilla Apache, Kiowa Apache, Lipan Apache, Mescalero-Chiricahua Apache and Aravaipa (Western) Apache. The Kiowa Apache, during the original migration, joined up with and were influenced by the Kiowa, an unrelated people moving south from the mountainous regions of the upper Missouri who spoke a Kiowa-Tanoan language. They eventually settled in the southern Great Plains, south of the Kiowa proper, and now live in Oklahoma. The Chiricahua people, also known as the Fort Sill Apache Tribe, live mostly in Apache, Oklahoma; the Jicarilla people live in northern New Mexico; and the Lipan live with the Mescalero and a group of Chiricahua people on the

SHARP NOSE was a great Arapaho leader. Facing the destruction of his people, he travelled to Washington, DC, in 1877 with two other Shoshoni leaders, Black Coal and Friday, and negotiated successfully for the establishment of an Arapaho reservation.

Mescalero Reservation in New Mexico. The Aravaipa occupy lands in central southern Arizona.

APOONIVI (*HOPI*) is a prominent rise with a whiteish top that lies southwest of the Oraibi mesa (plateau), one of the major Hopi settlements in northeastern Arizona. When a person dies, his or her spirit climbs steps up the slope of this hill on its way to Maski, the Home of the Dead.

THE ARAPAHO [Northern, Southern] originated as one of the Algonquian-speaking peoples of the Great Lakes region. Some time in the last few thousand years they migrated to the Great Plains to pursue a life of nomadic buffalo-hunting. They once occupied territories from southeastern Wyoming, through southwestern Nebraska and eastern Colorado, to northwestern Kansas.

The Northern Arapaho live on the Wind River Reservation in Wyoming, and the Southern Arapaho are scattered all across

non-reservation land allotments throughout Oklahoma.

ARCHITECTURE, in the form of shelters, is often conceived as a microcosm of the supernaturally created earth and its sheltering sky.

In a Skidi *PAWNEE* account of the origin of the earthlodge, *TIRÁWAHAT*, the creator, planned the structure to take care of earth children born of stars. From their place in the sky, each of the star gods put a post in the ground, and Tiráwahat marked his own place in the centre with an ash tree. The *LODGE* opened to the east – the direction of warmth and light, thought and planning – and up to the sky. The Chief's Council (the constellation Corona Borealis) got the Sun to send down fire to burn the tree. It became the first hearth,

APACHE HEADWARE depicting a meteor or shooting star. It may represent a powerful, protective spirit perceived in a dream.

and, from this time on, its coals got their light from the Morning Star and the Sun. As the smoke-hole faced the sky, the abode of the creator and the source of all wisdom and instruction, smoke became the carrier of messages to the gods.

THE ARIKARA were Caddoan-speaking horticulturalists and buffalo hunters who lived along the Missouri River in central South Dakota. After falling prey to disease, inter-tribal warfare and other depredations caused by the incursions of white people into the region, they moved with two allied tribes, the *MANDAN* and the *HIDATSA*, into North Dakota. This group, known as the Three Affiliated Tribes, now occupies the Fort Berthold Reservation in North Dakota. They live on the remnants of their land not flooded after the damming of the Missouri in the 1950s.

B

ARROW BOY (*CHEYENNE*) was a hero who brought the sacred *MEDICINE* bundle ceremonies to his people from the spirit world, ensuring their prosperity. He had an exceptional origin and quickly revealed great supernatural powers.

A woman became pregnant, but four years passed before the child was born. Soon after the birth, his parents died, and the boy went to live with his grandmother. He began to walk and talk almost immediately and, foreshadowing supernatural feats to come, he took his buffalo-calf robe and turned it hair side out, just like a *SHAMAN*. One night, when the shamans gathered to reveal their power, the boy appeared and asked them to cover him with a robe. He then went through an amazing sequence of transformations. The first time the shamans removed the robe, the boy's head was severed; the next time, he was an old man; the next time, a pile of bones; and lastly, he was a boy again. Through these acts, he showed the shamans that he was truly one of them, having mastered the essence of the shamanic process, being able to die and come back to life again.

Since he was still a boy, however, he remained outside the realms of power until a tragic act transformed the lives of his people. He slew a chief, Young Wolf, in a fight over a buffalo he had killed and, when the people learned of this they resolved to kill him, considering him a danger to the tribe. But the boy escaped and, as if by coincidence, all the buffalo disappeared, causing a great famine. Meanwhile, the boy travelled to the high mountains and stumbled upon one with a large opening. When he entered the mountain, he found a council of elders representing each of the tribes. Each man held a sacred bundle – and there was one empty place with a bundle beside it. The elders told him that, if he took this place, he could carry the bundle

BUFFALO (Bison bison) *roamed the grasslands and forest margins of the Great Plains and Rocky Mountain foothills in vast herds, and were an irresistible lure to hunting and gathering tribes such as the Assiniboine.*

back to the Cheyenne and restore their strength. For four years they taught him the bundle ceremony, with its songs and rituals, and revealed the power of the four medicine arrows within the bundle. He also learned how to divine the future and make magic to help in warfare and hunting.

When he returned to his people, he took the name Arrow Boy, as a sign of his spiritual transformation, and he began to exercise his new-found abilities. To ease the famine, he took some buffalo bones and transformed them into fresh meat, and then he began to instruct the people in the proper way to appease the spirits. They camped in a circle and erected a large *TEPEE* in the centre. He called the shamans to bring their rattles and pipes, and, in the shelter of the tepee he sang the four songs of the sacred arrows. As he sang the fourth song, a great roar shook the whole camp – the thundering hooves of a great herd of buffalo! Because Arrow Boy brought the medicine arrows and showed his tribe the way to use them, they never wanted for food again.

THE ASSINIBOINE people are a Siouan tribe that migrated on to the Great Plains from the western Great Lakes region after the introduction of the horse in the 17th century. They occupied a large territory in present-day southern Saskatchewan and adjoining parts of Montana, North Dakota, and Manitoba, following the vast buffalo herds that provided them with

food, clothing and other essentials of daily life. They were historic allies of the *GROS VENTRE*, with whom they now share the Fort Belknap reservation in Montana. Bands also live at the Fort Peck reservation, shared with the *SIOUX*, and several reserves in Canada, including Carry the Kettle and Mosquito Grizzly Bear's Head in Saskatchewan.

AWONAWILONA (*ZUNI*) was an androgynous presence, the "all-container", that created mist out of thoughts when all was dark and empty. As the mist grew thick, it fell as rain and filled the void with a vast ocean, and the creative presence became the Sun. The Sun then took some of its flesh and laid it on the water as a green scum. When it was firm, the mass separated into two great beings, forever locked in an embrace: *MOTHER EARTH* (Awitelin Tsita) and *FATHER SKY* (Apoyan Tachu). These two conceived all life in the four wombs of Awitelin Tsita.

THE BEAR is a powerful animal that intrigues native thinkers because it is at once fearful of humans, a fierce and dangerous adversary and a shambling beast with speed and great physical agility. Its most curious and significant aspect, however, is that when

it is skinned it looks startlingly human – proof to them of the ancient mythical age when the animal people walked the earth.

In an Eastern *SHOSHONI* account, a man tells of witnessing bears performing a *SUN DANCE*. While on a buffalo hunt, he came upon a trail marked with many bear tracks and followed the tracks to an open place, where he saw the bears gathered around a pine tree. Hiding downwind, so that they would not smell him, he watched the strange ceremony. The pine tree was painted yellow, red and green, and the bears danced in four measured steps forwards and backwards, all the time looking at the pole and singing. Their *puhagant* (*SHAMAN*) had also built a sacred fire. The hunter somehow knew they were praying for the health of their children.

The bear is especially important to the Algonquians of the northern forests. The *MIDEWIWIN* society of the *OJIBWAY* regarded the bear as the most powerful *MANITOU*. When initiates learned the complex songs and rites of the Midé, they were said to follow the bear path in their learning. Among the Eastern

THE GRIZZLY BEAR (Ursus horribilis) *can change from lumbering grace to charging ferocity in a matter of seconds. With its great size and speed, it can easily outrun a human being.*

CREE, the master of the bears is Memekwesiw. When shamans conduct divination rites in the small cylindrical or conical structure called a "shaking tent", they sometimes call on him to grant success at hunting. When this great spirit comes into the tent, he fights with the shaman, dragging his massive bear claws against the hide or canvas, clearly visible to those gathered outside. The fight is crucial to the band, for, if the shaman wins, Memekwesiw grants them bears during the next hunt.

To the Lakota SIOUX, the bear has the power to cure, so their shamans seek the help of the bear spirit and use medicinal herbs given their efficacy by it. The HUPA explain how the bear brought them a MEDICINE for controlling complications in pregnancy. Bear got pregnant, but she got so big she had problems walking. As she sat troubled, she was startled by a voice behind her. It was the voice of a redwood sorrel plant, and it told her to pick and eat it. She did, and the next day she was able to walk again. She knew the humans to come would have the same problem, so she decided to pass the medicine on. She imbued the herb with her power so that people could talk to her through it.

The bear is also rightly portrayed as dangerous by American Indian story-tellers. The ALEUT have a moralistic tale of a white-faced bear that was once a man. He was a good hunter who became a bear with white face and feet because he was too successful (a hunter must be prudent when taking game; taking too much is a sign of greed). When other hunters submit to their own greed and try to kill him, he chases them back to their village and tears them apart. The OJIBWAY believe that some powerful shamans court evil by transforming themselves into bears and stalking humans in the night – they are called bear-walkers. (See also SPIRITS OF THE EARTH)

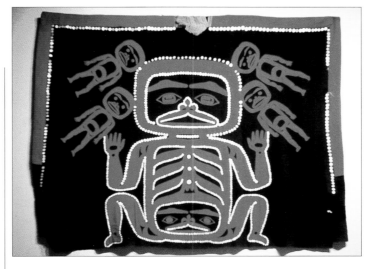

BEAR MOTHER is depicted on a modern Haida button blanket. The design is appliquéd and then the buttons are sewn along the edges.

BEAR MOTHER

BEAR MOTHER is a popular story in the Northwest Coast and Plateau areas. A woman is abducted by a BEAR and has his children. She ultimately betrays the bear to her brothers, who kill him, and she returns home.

In a HAIDA version, accounting for the origins of the Raven CLAN crest, two young lovers were prevented from marrying because they both belonged to the Raven clan. They ran away to the woods, but a bear abducted the girl, and the boy fled. He lost hope of finding her, and so she remained with the bear and had his children. After years of desperation, however, the young man returned to the forest, rescued his lover and they were allowed to remain together. The KOOTENAY variation on this version again ends with betrayal and the bear's death at the hands of the girl's brothers.

BEAR RITUALS

BEAR RITUALS are important to the CREE, who prepare carefully for a BEAR hunt because the bear spirit is so powerful. Every aspect of the process, from the way the hunter dresses to the dividing and eating of the meat, is marked by detailed ritual prescriptions, prayers and offerings. The feast takes place in a feast lodge, accompanied by much ritual and enjoyment. The hunter, always mindful of the need to respect the bear spirit, cuts a piece of meat from the bear's heart and throws it in the fire, praying to Memekwesiw to grant more bears. At the end of the feast, the LODGE is opened, and the spirit of the bear escapes into the forest and returns to its master. If the people have followed the rituals correctly, the bear will revert to its animal form, so that the hunters may kill it again.

The story of a young Cree hero who saves his band from starvation supports this belief. A powerful hunter called Nenimis had captured all the animal spirits and locked them away in a box in his lodge, causing great suffering throughout the land. The young Cree volunteered to find the animals and free them. After travelling far, he came upon Nenimis's lodge. Nenimis told the youth he would offer him food, but unless he ate everything offered, he would die. It was a difficult test (and one looked upon with relish when times were hard), for Nenimis gave him one of every kind of animal, cooked whole, but the youth ate them all. Defeated, Nenimis abandoned the lodge and disappeared. The young hero then broke open the box, released the spirits and cut a hole in the lodge so that they could return once again to the forest.

The Cree are particularly careful to respect the skull and bones of the bear (as they are with the bones of all the animals they kill). Sometimes the successful hunter will keep the skull in his lodge overnight, to induce DREAMS of bears that will give him luck in the future, but then the group dispose of the remains in ritual fashion. They do not allow dogs near them, because dogs are unclean, so they hang the bones from a specially prepared tree. They strip the tree of most of its bark and branches, leaving only a small tuft of new growth at the top, and they paint it from the bottom up in ochre or vermilion, with horizontal red stripes. Then they paint circle and bar designs in vermilion on the bear's skull, stick tobacco in the jaw, tie ribbons of hide and cloth to it, and lash it to the tree.

DANCE is used to celebrate the practical and spiritual significance of the bear by many tribal peoples. As they move to the sound of drums, the dancers assume the spirit of the bear, giving them the power and wisdom necessary for successful hunting.

THE BEAVER [Dunne-za] tribe is an Athapascan-speaking hunting and gathering people who live in the forests and parklands of the Peace River region of north-western Alberta and adjoining British Columbia. They traditionally hunt moose, deer, buffalo and small game, and gather roots, berries and other wild plants. At least half the 600 members of the tribe continue to speak the native language.

BEAVER WIFE (*OJIBWAY*) is a story that teaches respect for animals. A long time ago, a young woman was fasting to help resolve her emotional problems, when a strange man appeared to her and asked her to live with him in his home at the edge of a lake. It was a wonderful place, with everything she could want in food and clothing and shelter. She soon became pregnant and – strangely – bore four children. Life was pleasant, she wanted for nothing, and she busied herself making reed mats and bags. It was only when a man came by that she realized she had married a beaver!

Over the years she bore many young, and every spring she would send them out into the world. Often her husband and children would go with the man and return with trade goods: kettles and bowls, knives and tobacco. It was a time when people and beavers lived in harmony – the people took beavers for their pelts, but the spirits quickly returned in an endless cycle of renewed life. When the couple grew old, the husband told the wife that she must return to her human home, as he had to return to his own spirit master.

After he was gone, she stayed in her house and continued her work until one day a man tried to break into the beaver lodge, and she cried out. The man feared she was a *MANITOU*, but when he reached down through the hole and felt her head, he knew she was neither that nor a beaver. She climbed out of the lodge, an old woman with beautiful white hair, a wonderful cloth skirt, a beaded cloak, pretty moccasins and earrings. She lived a long time among her people and taught them to respect the beaver always, so that they would never be without its wonderful pelt. (See also *SPIRITS OF THE EARTH*)

BEGOCIDI (*NAVAJO*), "One-Who-Grabs-Breasts", a *TRICKSTER* who represents the darker side of the human spirit. In some situations he has a rapacious sexual appetite, causing women who submit to his unnatural and improper advances to give birth to monsters, and in others he is a transvestite. He is also the first potter and in some versions is a creator (as he was a child of the Sun).

THE BELLA COOLA are Salishan speakers who occupy a section of the rugged coastal region of British Columbia, just to the north of Vancouver Island. This is a region with a mild climate, coastal seas teeming with sea mammals and fish, vast beds of shellfish

A BELLA COOLA MASK, collected in 1913, representing one of the ancestors of humankind. The creator employed four carpenters to carve these beings in the form of birds and animals. This ancestor flew to earth as an eagle.

along the shores, rivers with an abundance of salmon and trout, and deep forests with deer and other game and a wide variety of plants. It provided sufficient resources for hunters and gatherers to develop an affluent way of life more akin to that of agriculturalists. Their stratified society of elites, commoners and slaves was organized by family and clan. They lived in permanent villages of cedar-plank houses, and developed a complex and striking visual art, including monumental *TOTEM POLES*, intricately carved household goods and woven baskets, that evoked the ancestral animal beings believed to be responsible for their origins.

THE BEAVER creates a safe and secure home by using construction techniques that are surprisingly human. Since it spends most of its time in the water, the beaver builds a dam to flood an area of sufficient depth to build a lodge of mud and sticks with an underwater entrance.

BIBLE STORIES were a potent weapon in the hands of missionaries, as their simple narratives had themselves emerged from mythological traditions in the Middle East. Biblical teachings influenced some story-tellers to the extent that they adapted Bible stories into the context of native situations.

The *CHOCTAW*, for example, relate a version of the Tower of Babel. There was originally only one race of people, the Choctaw, fashioned by the Creator out of yellow clay (this is a different version of creation from the Choctaw emergence myth of *NANIH WAIYA*). They were content, but they were curious about what the blue sky and clouds might be, so they decided to build a tower to reach the sky. After the first day of piling rocks to build the mound, a wind came in the night and blew it down. They started again the next day, but that night the winds blew it down again. On the third night, the wind was so strong that the whole structure came crashing down upon them. Strangely, they survived, but when they came up from beneath the rocks and tried to speak to one another, they found that they spoke different languages and could no longer understand one another. The people who still spoke Choctaw remained, but the others scattered across the continent and formed all the different tribes that exist today.

BIG BLACK METEORIC STAR (*PAWNEE*) is a star northwest of the Morning Star. It controls all animals, especially the buffalo, and is responsible for the coming of the night.

BIRD NESTER is a widespread theme reflecting the psychological tensions related to family life. A father and son compete for the same woman. The father sends the son to climb to a high nest but, so that he can take the woman, he removes the ladder and maroons

the boy. Ultimately, however, the son is rescued by supernatural beings and takes revenge on the father. For a *YUROK* version of this theme, see *COYOTE*.

THE BLACKFOOT (or Blackfeet) [Blackfoot, Blood, Northern Piegan, Piegan] consist of four related Algonquian-speaking tribes occupying lands in northwestern Montana and southern Alberta: the Piegan in Montana, and the Northern Piegan, Blood and Blackfoot in Alberta. They seem to have moved westwards from Saskatchewan during the 18th century and ranged widely in the Northern Plains, following the great buffalo herds, which provided them with food, clothing and other essential resources. They were traditional allies of the *SARCEE* and the *GROS VENTRE* in the Blackfoot Confederacy. (See also *TRANSFORMATION, SPIRITS OF THE EARTH*)

BLESSINGWAY (*NAVAJO*) is a collection of stories and rituals re-enacting the creation of the present world after the emergence of people from the underworld. It includes the birth of *CHANGING WOMAN* and the founding of the Kinaalda (girls' puberty ceremony). Involved with childbirth rites, weddings and house-blessings, it is intended to secure a good, healthy life.

BLOOD CLOT (*BLACKFOOT*) is the *CULTURE HERO* Kutoyis, the

PLAINS TRIBES used a simple but effective method to transport goods and people unable to ride. The travois consists of heavy poles hauled by horses. This hand-coloured photograph shows a Blackfoot family in the foothills of the Rocky Mountains c. 1900.

adopted son of First Man and First Woman. He was the miscarried foetus of a buffalo cow (hence his name, which refers to the placenta). In heroic fashion, he slew giant animals and monsters – *BEARS* and rattlesnakes, for example, and Wind-sucker (a tornado), who ate people passing by – and successfully outwitted evil women.

His last mission was to destroy a monster, Blood-sucker, on the shore of a large lake. He fought with it in the water until Thunder killed it with lightning and threw it on the prairie. When his work was done, Blood Clot died and took his place, like all the dead, as one of the stars. The lake is no longer to be found, but on its dry bed lie Blood Clot's bones, and the blood-red rocks that record the battle.

BLUE JAY (*CHINOOK*) is an important *TRICKSTER* in Northwest Coast tradition. To the Coast *SALISH* he is a mere clown, but in the interior, the Salish and Penutian people of the forests regarded him more highly. The Chinook honoured him with a Blue Jay dance. *SHAMANS* would dance until overwhelmed by Blue Jay's power, at which point they would run

madly around the village, imitating the raucous call of the bird until they were brought back to the medicine lodge by their fellow tribesmen. After regaining their senses, they had gained the power to perform cures and grant wishes.

BRIGHT EYES (*PAWNEE*) was a spurned suitor in a moral tale who, after his rejection, went off and married a prairie dog (and became one). The couple eventually returned to the village, became human and led a good life, until the man once again met the woman who had rejected him. She apologized, and, in a moment of weakness, they had intercourse. Because of this transgression, the man's wife and children returned to the prairie dog town, and he died of a broken heart.

THE PRAIRIE DOG (Cynomys ludovicianus) is a small, hamster-like rodent of the plains and plateaux of the west. It is a social animal that lives in a network of burrows and tunnels in warrens, called "towns", with distinct social units called coteries. When an intruder enters the area, the prairie dog gives out a sharp barking alarm that quickly alerts the colony. In 1901, one extended town in the plains covered an area of 160 x 386 km (100 x 240 miles) and contained 400,000,000 prairie dogs. They have been exterminated in most of their territory by ranchers.

TRANSFORMATION

A HUMAN LIFE IS SO BRIEF that the face of the earth seems absolute and unchanging. No living being has seen the billions of years of tectonic shifts, overwhelming seas and ice ages that have scarred the land, so the idea of a decaying world is almost unimaginable. Someone with superhuman power must have made the rivers, as we might trace a line in the sand. And someone must have given us the gifts of nature that we use to sustain our lives. In aboriginal thought, the time when powerful beings transformed creation's dark, empty lands into the familiar, sheltering earth is only just out of reach of memory. Life at that time was fluid. Those first ancestors shifted and changed form at will between humans, animals and objects as they carried out their formative tasks – bringing daylight and fire, hewing out the shape of the land and creating the stuff of cultural life. Raven, Coyote and the other trans-formers are not the props of a simple animal worship, but emerged from the elders' awareness that the super-naturals had withdrawn from the world they created – just as the knowing raven and the sly coyote circle on the edges of human culture today.

A SHAMAN (right) needed contact with the spiritual forces of nature to ensure the health and wellbeing of a tribal society. To attract, entice or control these forces, shamans sought out worldly objects with special qualities that gave them great medicine power. Here, a Blackfoot shaman, dressed to cure illness, wears the pelt of a bear and is festooned with the skins of snakes, and other talismans of the animal beings at the core of life. (19TH-CENTURY PAINTING BY GEORGE CATLIN.)

SHAMANS (below) moved among the beings of the spirit world, so people feared and respected them. In a modern pencil drawing by a Baker Lake Inuit artist, the spirit of a dead shaman comes back to provide food for her descendants. Inuit people believe that the spirits of shamans remain in the land, so they avoid their gathering places. The people of Baker Lake talk of two small islands where these restless spirits seem to dwell, as hunters who have camped there have lost valuable equipment, supplies and dogs. (DRAWING BY RUTH ANNAQTUUSI TULURIALIK, 1985.)

A FAMILIAR LANDSCAPE (above) transformed from a featureless world is a great story that is preserved in the contours and features of the earth. Raven created the Queen Charlotte Islands, the land of the Haida, because he was tired of flying and had no place to rest on the primordial waters. He created the land by dropping stones in the water or, in another version, by splashing the water and turning the spray into rock.

TRANSFORMATION (right) was not only a spiritual concept, but also a practical necessity, especially before the introduction of the swift-footed horse. In prehistoric times, hunters had to stalk game on foot, so they often adopted the guise of animals in order to move close enough to shoot them with their arrows. In this woodcut, two hunters draped – perhaps surprisingly – in wolf skins crawl towards a herd of buffalo. (EDUARD VERMORCKEN, AFTER A PAINTING BY GEORGE CATLIN, 1848.)

C

BRIGHT-CLOUD WOMAN (*TSIMSHIAN*) is the provider and protector of salmon. She married the trickster *RAVEN*, with predictable consequences: Raven got greedy, gambled away his salmon stocks, and she abandoned him.

BROTHER GODS (*MOJAVE*) were creator-*TRANSFORMERS* who formed (along with all other creatures) when earth and sky touched. One, Matavilya, led the people to the centre of the world, built the first house and, after unintentionally making sexual overtures to his daughter, sickened, died and became the first cremation (during which *COYOTE* stole his heart). The other, Mastamho, after making the Colorado River and causing a flood, led the people to a sacred mountain (Avikwame) where he taught them Mojave culture and imbued their *SHAMANS* with dream power.

THE COLORADO RIVER was created by one of the Brother Gods. Its turquoise-green ribbon is a miraculous sight in the deserts of Arizona, providing life-giving water and a mirror that joins the earth and sky.

THE BUFFALO CAP (*CHEY-ENNE*) is a very sacred object associated with the *SUN DANCE* origin myth. Seeking to end a terrible famine, a young *SHAMAN* (eventually to be named Erect Horns), entered an opening in the middle of a mountain and encountered Great Medicine. This spirit taught him the

Sun Dance and gave him the buffalo cap to wear during the ritual. When he returned to his people and instructed them in the ceremony, they were able to overcome the famine and ensure a plentiful supply of buffalo in the future.

BUFFALO HUSBAND (*BLACK-FOOT*) is a story that relates the origins of the Ikunuhkahtsi (Bull Dance). A bull buffalo took a woman as a wife. When her father tried to rescue her, the buffalo killed him. However, the woman brought her father back to life, so the bull husband taught him the Bull Dance ceremony (intended to propitiate the buffalo spirit), and the father and daughter were allowed to return to their home.

BUFFALO WIFE figures in a widespread Plains myth which accounts for the origin of the buffalo-hunting tradition. The people hunted buffalo with little success until a man married a buffalo woman. She took him to her

THE GRAND TETONS rise abruptly into the skies above the lush grasslands of the Snake River valley in Wyoming. For the native peoples who hunted buffalo on the plains, these great landmarks were important parts of their sacred lands.

homeland and taught him how to use a bow to kill the animal, as well as how to prepare the meat. He brought the knowledge back to his people, and forever afterwards they hunted and caught buffalo with great ease.

BUFFALO WOMAN (*CHEY-ENNE, PAWNEE*) is involved in a Great Race theme, in which animals and birds once raced between Mato Tipila (*DEVIL'S TOWER*) and the Teton Mountains (both in Wyoming) in order to prove which was the greatest. In an arrogant move, a buffalo woman was chosen to represent her species, but Hawk (prairie falcon) defeated her, ensuring that humans and birds would always rule over other animals.

THE BUFFALO was hunted before the introduction of the horse, when hunters had to outwit it to capture it. They would ambush the animals as they grazed in gullies or arroyos, or travelled along narrow valley edges, and in some places they stampeded the animals over steep cliffs.

BUKWUS (*KWAKIUTL*) is a monstrous spirit who dwells in the dark rainforests of the Pacific coast. Although he is repulsive, he has a fierce longing for companionship. With his beautiful singing voice, he attracts to his home the spirits of those who have drowned.

CARIBOU MOTHER (Central and Eastern *INUIT*) is the mistress of the caribou. In an Iglulik account, there were no caribou

A MODERN BUKWUS MASK records the strong, fierce qualities of this wild monster of the forests.

until an old woman went inland and fashioned them from her breeches. The original caribou was dangerous, as it had sharp fangs and tusks. After one of these monsters killed a hunter, the old woman went back inland, gathered them all together, knocked out the sharp front teeth and changed the tusks into antlers. Then she gave them each a kick on the forehead, creating the hollow that can still be seen to this day, and they ran off. Unfortunately, hunters still had difficulty killing the caribou, because the hair on the woman's breeches all lay in one direction, and the streamlined caribou ran like the wind. So she gathered them together again and made the hair lie in different patterns, slowing them down enough to be hunted. Her work done, the old woman went to live with the caribou and never returned to the human world.

CAYUGA see *IROQUOIS*.

THE CELESTIAL CANOE
(*ALABAMA*) relates to the movement of stars through the seasons and the effects these movements have on the natural world. The Alabama refer to the bowl of the Big Dipper (the Plough) as the Boat Stars. To their *CREEK* neighbours, it is a distinct constellation: Pilohabi, meaning "image of a canoe". It is a potent seasonal marker, as it first

falls to the horizon and rises again in late July. This is the time of the Green Corn (Maize) Ceremony celebrated by these southeastern peoples, when the first corn ripens. Among the Alabama, the supporting myth contains elements also found in the Green Corn Ceremony, including dancing, feasting and a *STICK-AND-BALL GAME*.

Visitors from the sky descended to the earth in a canoe to play stick-ball on a prairie, then ascended again into the sky. A man witnessed this daily occurrence, and one day captured one of the women and took her as his wife. She bore children and had a pleasant life, but she yearned for her home in the sky, so she went out to the prairie with her children and climbed into the boat as it rested there. However, the attempt failed, because her husband returned from hunting unexpectedly and pulled them back to earth. Then the mother secretly built a second, smaller, canoe for her children, and she tried again. This time she succeeded, rising into the night sky in the big canoe, but her husband managed to grab and hold back the smaller canoe with the children in it. Eventually the father agreed to take the now-grieving children into the sky to find their mother. An old woman in her sky *LODGE* fed the children squash and corn cobs, and then directed them to another house where they found their mother dancing. Once again they all returned to earth, but after a time the still-unhappy woman finally took her children in the big canoe and left the earth forever. The husband tried to follow in the smaller canoe, but when he looked down he fell to earth and was killed.

THE GREAT BEAR, Big Dipper or Plough is one of the most striking constellations in the northern sky. Because the arrangement of stars is so clear, and it rises and sets in a predictable cycle through the year, it was an important marker of seasonal change among many northern peoples.

CHANGING WOMAN (Estsánatlehi) (*NAVAJO*) was so named because she has the power to grow old and become young again, following the rhythm of the earth's seasons. First Man ('Altsé Hastiin) and First Woman ('Altsé 'Asdzáá), two of the beings from the First, or Black, World (*SPIDER WOMAN* was another), discovered her in a raincloud on top of a mountain. They fed her on pollen and dew, and she grew rapidly. After puberty, she exposed her body to sun and water and conceived the *TWIN* war gods, *NAYENEZGANI AND TOBADJISHTCHINI*. After her sons had made the world safe from monsters, she went to live on an island beyond the western sea. By dancing on the four directions, she produced rain clouds (east), fabrics and jewels (south), plant life (west) and corn (maize) and animals (north). She figures prominently in the Navajo ritual complex called *BLESSINGWAY*. For an *APACHE* version of this myth, see *WHITE-PAINTED WOMAN*.

THE CHEHALIS [Lower, Upper] are two small tribes who once occupied a territory that stretched along the Chehalis River in present-day southwest Washington State. They speak closely related Salishan languages.

The Upper Chehalis lived among the headwaters of the river, and so pursued a traditional interior hunting and gathering life, whereas the Lower Chehalis lived at the river's mouth, where they could also exploit the resources of the sea. They now occupy the Colville Reservation in northeast Washington State, along with the remnants of a number of small regional tribes.

CHÉMSEN see *RAVEN*.

THE CHEROKEE, an Iroquoian-speaking people, once controlled a vast territory that spread across the southeastern United States. It included the Carolinas, the Virginias, Kentucky, Tennessee, Georgia and Alabama. They grew corn (maize) and other crops in the fertile river valleys, and hunted and gathered according to the seasons.

After various treaties in the 18th and early 19th centuries restricted them to infertile mountainous areas, the US government forced them to leave their ancestral lands in 1838 and 1839 to journey over 1,600 km (1,000 miles) to Indian Territory (in present-day Oklahoma). Many Cherokee perished, while others refused to leave, and took refuge in the mountains. Although the majority of Cherokee now live in northeastern Oklahoma, they still retain a small but vital presence in North Carolina. (See also *NEW GODS*)

THE CHEYENNE [Northern, Southern] people are an Algonquian-speaking tribe that probably originated in the prairies and mixed woodlands of the upper Mississippi Valley region and gradually spread into the northeastern Great Plains. After the horse was introduced to the region in the 18th century, they took up the traditional Plains buffalo-hunting life, following the herds and using the animals for food, clothing and other material necessities. Their territory at this time was so vast, stretching from the Yellowstone River in Montana to the upper Arkansas River in Colorado and Kansas, that they became separated into northern and southern groups.

The Northern Cheyenne now live on the Tongue River Reservation in Montana, and the Southern Cheyenne occupy land allotments in Oklahoma.

CHIBIABOS (FOX, POTAWATOMI) was the wolf brother of the culture hero WISAKEDJAK (or NANABUSH). He was the ruler of the dead.

DULL KNIFE (1810–1883), a Northern Cheyenne chief, tried to lead his people 2,400 km (1,500 miles) back to their ancestral homeland in Montana after being forcibly removed to Oklahoma. When their struggle roused public sentiment, the government granted them a reservation.

CHILD-OF-THE-WATER (Chiricahua APACHE) is a CULTURE HERO who was born after WHITE-PAINTED WOMAN conceived a child by letting the rain fall on her navel or vagina (note the similarity here to the NAVAJO stories of CHANGING WOMAN and NAYENEZGANI AND TOBADJISHTCHINI). The boy slew the monsters responsible for killing human beings – a giant (see LANDSCAPE), an antelope that killed with its eyes, monster eagles and a buffalo. Two narrative fragments give different versions of the creation of human beings. In one, Child-of-the-Water created them out of mud figures; in the other, he enveloped himself in a dark cloud and disappeared, leaving in his place the first two human beings.

THE CHINOOK were members of a large Penutian-speaking tribe that once occupied coastal lands in Washington State and the Lower Columbia River basin in Oregon and Washington. They fished, hunted and gathered the marine life along the Pacific coast and journeyed up the inland rivers to take salmon and trout. Their language developed a pidgin form, Chinook Wawa, which became a trading language along the coast from Oregon to Alaska. Disease and dislocation drastically reduced their numbers after white settlement. They now live on allotments at Quinault, on Washington's Olympic Peninsula.

THE CHIPEWYAN live in the vast northern forests to the west of Hudson Bay, from the Churchill River in Manitoba to Lake Athabasca in northern Saskatchewan and Alberta to Great Slave Lake in the Northwest Territories. They are the largest of the DENE, a group of closely related Athapascan peoples, which also include the Slavey (or Slave), the Dogrib, Yellowknife and Sahtu. These semi-nomadic groups travelled in small bands in a seasonal round along the innumerable rivers and lakes of the boreal forests

A CHOCTAW HOUSE fashioned from palmetto leaves attached to a pole frame. The loose construction allowed air to circulate in the hot and humid climate.

and the edge of the treeless Arctic barrens, hunting caribou, moose, deer, bear and other game animals, catching waterfowl and gathering berries and other plant foods. While the fur trade established a dependency on a Western economic system, their remoteness from centres of modern culture has enabled them to retain many of their traditional practices and beliefs.

CHIPPEWA see under OJIBWAY.

THE CHOCTAW people are a Muskogean-speaking tribe that lived in the area of present-day Mississippi. The river valleys provided an abundance of plant and animal life, deer, waterfowl, turkeys, nuts and grasses, and the fertile soil supported corn (maize), beans and other crops. The agricultural base of these and other Mississippian peoples supported a well-organized society. It has many of the religious features associated with Mesoamerican influences, such as sun worship, raised earthen ceremonial plazas, burial mounds, and common iconographic elements in art and religion.

Between 1830 and 1836, the government removed most of the tribe to Indian Territory (in present-day Oklahoma), causing great loss of life. Today, the Mississippi Choctaws live in small rural settlements scattered across the state, whereas the Oklahoma Choctaws are centred in Tuskahoma.

CHRISTIAN TEACHINGS have worked their way into the structure and content of ancient oral traditions. Although beliefs about singular creators, primeval waters and great floods may predate the Biblical epics, it is impossible to differentiate these very ancient resonances from the intense ideological impact of more than 500 years of missionary activity in North America.

One unfortunate consequence of this religious proselytizing was the demotion of traditional CULTURE HEROES in favour of the Christian repertoire. This is strikingly clear in a modern narrative of the BEAVER tribe's culture hero Saya. He transformed the animal people into the animals we see today, and he was the first hunter. When Saya travelled to the land of the dead, he followed a long path around the rim of the world (like YAMANHDEYA, the culture hero of the Beaver's northerly neighbours, the *DENE*) but now, as the story explains, this travail is no longer necessary. *JESUS* has made a straight cut (short cut) directly to heaven.

THE CHUMASH people are
a small tribe that once occupied the offshore islands and coasts of southern California in the area of present-day Santa Barbara, where they prospered on the abundant deep-sea and coastal food resources of the Pacific Ocean. Spanish influence almost overwhelmed their rich culture, and the last known speaker of any of the five Chumash languages (of the Hokan family) died in 1965. Work by an anthropologist in the first half of the 20th century, however, provided enough ethnographic evidence to help support a Chumash cultural revival that has taken place in the past 20 years.

CLANS, like all tribal institutions,
have origins within the belief systems of their people. A clan is a group of related families in a tribal culture that traces its origins to a specific mythological ancestor. Clan origins are therefore an important part of narratives about events that took place when the world was taking shape.

When the *HOPI* people began emerging from the First World, for example, they started to hunt for

A MORALISTIC TABLEAU, set at the Spanish Mission of the Alamo in Texas, shows a group of Spanish men gambling outside the mission. They contrast starkly with the devout Indian people kneeling in the background.

the rising sun. The first band came upon a dead *BEAR*, so it became the Bear Clan, the second came upon the same skeleton but found gopher holes around it and became the Gopher Clan. Other Hopis, who travelled much more slowly, as they had many children, found a nest of spiders and named themselves the Spider Clan. This particular clan made a fortuitous choice, for they gained the protection of the wise and powerful grandmother, *SPIDER WOMAN*. To help them in their journey, she took dust from their bodies and fashioned the first burro to carry their heaviest loads. The Bear Clan, which arrived first and quickly established its village, remains a powerful group. Although the Spider Clan was the last to arrive, it became the biggest Hopi clan because of the large number of children its ancestors brought with them on their journey.

THE COCHITI, a Keresan-
speaking *PUEBLO* culture, live along the Rio Grande in north central New Mexico. In order to farm in

this dry region, they practise irrigation. They retain their traditional social structures, including two moieties (an anthropological classification for the two halves into which all the *CLANS* are divided), the Turquoise Kiva and the Pumpkin Kiva, about a dozen clans, and numerous *SECRET SOCIETIES*, but they are mainly practising Catholics.

THE COLVILLE people are a
small Salishan tribe living in the rugged Plateau region of northeastern Washington State. Before the coming of the *WHITE MAN*, they fished the local rivers for salmon, and supplemented their diet with deer and other small game and plant foods. They were uprooted during the 19th century, when a motley collection of prospectors, miners, loggers and settlers invaded their territory, and they are now consolidated in an extremely complex organization of at least 16 tribes in the Colville Reservation.

THE COMANCHE (Nemene)
were once a nomadic hunting and gathering people, speaking an Uto-

PUEBLO tribes strongly resisted the incursions of Spanish and American peoples, even as Catholic missionaries spread Christianity among them. Pecos Mission church, at Pecos Pueblo, New Mexico, was the seat of the Pueblo Revolt of 1688, when the tribe rose up against the Spanish.

Aztecan language, who ranged from the Rocky Mountains into the interior of Mexico. In 1867, the US government compelled them to sign the Medicine Lodge Treaty, which removed them to a reservation in southwest Oklahoma, but in 1887 the General Allotment Act dissolved the reservation, allotted 65 ha (160 acres) of land to each adult, reserved a small amount of land for future tribal members, and distributed the remaining thousands of acres to non-Indian settlers. In spite of their lack of territory, the Comanche retain many aspects of their traditional culture and are especially noted for their elaborate dance costumes, which contain fine feather and beadwork.

COPPER WOMAN (CHIPE-
WYAN, DENE) figures in a story related to the origins of native copper, found in the north on the Copper and Coppermine Rivers.

Once an *INUIT* abducted a woman, but she escaped and, while fleeing home, discovered yellow nuggets. She guided a hunting party back to the spot to see these strange stones, but the men could not resist molesting her. Her honour violated, she sank into the ground in shame, and the men left offerings of meat to make up for their transgressions. Now known as Copper Woman, she transformed these offerings into copper.

THE LIVING SKY

T HE SKY MUST BE THE REALM OF GODS. Well beyond the reach of even the highest mountains, the greatest powers reside there – light and darkness, the changing seasons, furious storms and life-giving rains – and it is the source of many creations.

Some remote creators used the dark cosmos as a staging ground for their work, but in most narratives the sky was a world with its own physical and social dimensions, not an airless void. In an Iroquois version, for example, a young woman fell through a hole in the sky world, and the birds and water animals had to create dry earth to support her. The heavens may also be a final resting place for supernatural beings who are transformed into stars. The sky is crucial to cultural identity, because it defines the land and sets the rhythm of the world. The cycles of the sun, moon and stars evoke a sense of time, marking the passage of human lives. As a measure of space and time, the sky therefore unites the mythical and the actual in an eternal flow of darkness and light.

THE MOON MASK (above) *of a Tlingit shaman reflects the common perception of the moon as a being with human attributes. For the Tlingit and other Northwest Coast tribes, the significance of the moon was not simply in its cosmological origins, but in its control of the rising and falling of the tides crucial to life on the edge of the Pacific Ocean. The mask, carved in cedar c. 1840–70, enabled the shaman to draw some of the power of this great sky being.*

THE FURY OF STORMS (above) shows the overwhelming power of the beings in the sky world. The idea of thunder and lightning as the work of a giant thunderbird makes sense in an animate universe. The dark storm line, edged with lightning, rampages over the land and is gone, just like a hawk or eagle in flight, hunting for food.

THE PLEIADES (above), known to astronomers as Messier 45, is an open star cluster (top right) approximately 410 light years from earth . It plays an important role in many tribal mythologies, often as seven maidens, one of which (the dimmest star) is veiled or has fallen to earth. For the Pawnee, these stars symbolize unity.

THE GRANITE CEILING (above) of an Algonquian shaman's cave near the Lake of the Woods in northwestern Ontario is painted with red ochre images of stars and forms that may represent celestial beings. In prehistoric times, the night sky was crucial as a knowledge resource – a device for thinking about history and the world of the spirit.

THREE CORN MAIDENS *are depicted emerging from the cobs they personify, in this modern Hopi painting. Farming cultures commonly attribute corn to the work of a Corn Mother or Corn Maidens.* (PAINTING BY MILLAND LOMAKEMA.)

CORN MAIDENS

CORN MAIDENS (*ZUNI*) are personifications of corn (maize), whose role in Zuni agriculture is re-enacted in the Corn Dance.

In one version of the narrative, Corn Maidens accompanied the first people to the surface of the earth, but they were invisible until two witches, the last people to emerge, perceived them. Recognizing their power, the witches gave them corn and squash seeds. The first people continued their journey, leaving the maidens at Shipololo (place of mist and cloud) where they lived in a cedar bower roofed with clouds. There they danced. When the Ahayuta (warrior *TWINS*) discovered the maidens, they brought them back to the people, whom starvation always threatened. The maidens danced in a courtyard decorated with cornmeal paintings of clouds. After the butterfly and flower god Payatami lusted after Yellow-Corn Maiden, however, the maidens fled back to Shipololo. A terrible famine ensued, until at last the Ahayuta brought them back to the settle-ment. The Corn Dance ensures that these important gods are properly respected, so that they will always remain among the Zuni.

CORN MOTHER

CORN MOTHER, as the mistress of corn (maize), is associated with all aspects of the cultivation of this important crop.

To the Keresan and Isleta *PUEBLO*, she is one of two sister deities born in the underworld. In one version of the myth, before the emergence of human beings into the present world, Thought Woman gave the two sisters baskets of seeds and images representing all future beings; in another, Corn Mother planted bits of her heart in the ground, and the corn sprouted up. In the *IROQUOIS* version, the corn stalks spring from Corn Mother's breasts. Western *ABENAKI* people say that corn tassels are yellow because the Corn Mother has yellow hair.

A *CHEROKEE* story explains why corn requires special cultivation and matures slowly over a single season each year. The Cherokee corn mother is Selu, the wife of the *MASTER OF ANIMALS*, Kanáti. After her two sons, Good Boy and He-Who-Grew-Up-Wild, released all their father's game animals, and the family had nothing but corn and beans to eat, the boys noticed that their mother's storehouse had an endless supply. One day they followed her and discovered that she produced corn by rubbing her abdomen, and beans by rubbing her legs (or, in another version, armpits). Fearing that she was a witch (or offended by the source of the food), the boys refused to eat. With her secret out, Selu told her sons that she would soon die. To cushion their loss, she instructed them to clear a patch of ground, drag her clothes over the surface and watch by night; in the morning they would find a field of corn. Unfortunately, when she died, the boys cleared only seven small patches. Consequently, corn does not grow everywhere. And, because they tired of the nightly vigil, the corn stopped maturing quickly, and now takes an entire summer season to grow.

COTSIPAMAPOT

COTSIPAMAPOT (Moapa), the old woman creator, scattered earth around her island, making all the creatures of the world – including one man. Her daughter could not mate with this man because she had a toothed vagina, but Cotsi-pamapot told him how to grind down the teeth. The couple eventually had children – the first people – and the old woman had them placed in the centre of the Moapa world.

COTTONTAIL

COTTONTAIL (Great Basin) is a *TRICKSTER* who lacks any of the redeeming features of the *CULTURE HEROES*, causing havoc even for that inveterate trickster *COYOTE*. Cottontail once made war on the sun, either to reduce its excessive warmth or put it higher in the sky, regardless of its effects on the people. His rather brutal nature is made clear in a northern *PAIUTE* version of the story, in which he went to the home of the North Wind, seduced its daughter and burned her alive with all her brothers.

A COUNCIL OF ANIMALS

A COUNCIL OF ANIMALS constitutes the common decision-making process in mythologies. When there is a problem to resolve, the supernatural animal people hold a council, just as humans do. This reflects the common native belief that animals have societies resembling human ones, with similar forms of social organization. This democratic approach contrasts with the Christian idea of a single omnipotent creator.

The most widespread example of an animal council at work is in the *EARTH DIVER* creation story. For the *TUSKEGEE*, the entire creation was the result of a debate. Some of the birds – the only creatures who

CULTIVATORS *during prehistoric times had a highly sophisticated understanding of the biology of corn (maize), using selection to develop strains suitable for their habitats, even while they conceived of the process in mythological terms.*

could live in a world of air and water – wanted land, in order to increase their food supply, but others wanted things to remain the same. To resolve the issue, they appointed EAGLE as chief, and asked him to decide. He supported the argument in favour of land, and asked for a volunteer to search for some. Dove accepted the challenge, but he flew across the skies and saw nothing but endless water. Then Crawfish dived deep into the water and returned with a bit of mud in his claws. Eagle took this mud and made an island. As the waters began to fall, the island got bigger and bigger, until other islands emerged to join into a single earth.

COYOTE is a complex and fascinating CULTURE HERO, varying from tribe to tribe between wise TRANS-FORMER and bumbling TRICKSTER. Agriculturalists tend to regard him as a crude and dispensable pest.

In a typical HOPI story, for example, Coyote was a sheep-stealer who harassed their flocks until they drove him into NAVAJO lands, where

THE ANIMAL GUARDIANS of tribal peoples keep council about the trials of life as do their human relatives. In this work by an Onondaga artist, the animal ancestors of Iroquois clans gather by the Tree of Peace, the symbol of unity of the Iroquois peoples. (PAINTING BY ARNOLD JACOBS.)

a Navajo shepherd outwitted him and burned him alive in a SWEAT-LODGE. The Hopi use the epithet "ihu", which means both coyote and sucker, for a person easily fooled.

To hunters and gatherers, however, Coyote is a resourceful creature, with a strong will to survive – but, just like humans, he is sometimes the victim of his own devious ways. This contradictory status is evident in a Navajo CRE-ATION story, re-enacted during a nine-day ceremony, in which one of his pranks ended up causing the emergence of the Navajo into the present world. He lived in Black World, an island-like place floating in mist. Only ants and other insect-people inhabited it until the touching of two clouds created First Man and First Woman. As the population grew, the group began to

quarrel, and eventually moved to a second world, where they discovered bigger insects and monstrous animals. When they escaped into a third world, Coyote inexplicably kidnapped a water monster's baby, causing a great flood. To save the people, First Man planted a reed that rose into the sky; the people climbed it and emerged into the present world.

In California, the coastal MIWOK say that Coyote created the earth by shaking his blanket over the primeval waters, causing them to dry up, while the MAIDU rank him with EARTH-MAKER as one of the two original beings. To the Maidu, Earth-maker represented an abstract potential for creation. Coyote carried it out, and caused DEATH in the real world. Coyote is responsible for human death in a CHINOOK story with an Orpheus-like theme, in which he and EAGLE travelled to the land of the dead to retrieve their wives. They came upon an enormous lodge, where they discovered that the dead only appear when an old woman creates darkness by swallowing the moon. To rescue their wives, Coyote killed the woman, swallowed the moon and gathered up all the dead in a box. When the two heroes started back, Coyote was so anxious to see his wife, whose voice he heard, that he lifted the lid, and all the dead

rose up in a cloud and disappeared. If he had been patient and waited until they had returned home to open the box, there would be no death in the world today.

For all his weaknesses, Coyote is the consummate transformer. In the Great Basin, he created earth by pouring sand on the primeval waters, created light, stole fire, stole pine nuts and released impounded game animals. The WAPPO of California credit him with the origin of language, as he stole the bag of words from Old Man MOON. In the Plateau region, the SANPOIL believe he releases the salmon.

In a YUROK myth, he is even responsible for the money supply (the Yurok, like many coastal peoples, having a strong sense of property and its value in exchange). In this scenario, Coyote was a sinful father who stranded his son in a nest high up a tree so that he could seduce the young man's two wives (a version of the universal BIRD NESTER theme). When the son finally climbed down, he was so angry that he stole all the wealth of the tribe (DENTALIUM SHELLS), but Coyote managed to get it back, and redistributed it.

THE COYOTE lives and hunts close to areas of human settlement, but it is seldom seen except by its tracks, like these in the desert sands of Nevada.

CREATION accounts attribute the origin of the earth and sky, humans and other living things to the actions of supernatural beings. While accounts of a singular creator, a Great Spirit, are now relatively common across the continent, this fundamentally hierarchical religious structure is most consistent with the structured agricultural societies of the Southwest. The ZUNI creator, for example, is the sun (Yatokka taccu, the Sun Father), the most powerful object in the sky.

The drama of creation, unique for each tribal group, resolves into several general scenarios. In the EARTH DIVER theme, the emphasis is not on the origin of the cosmos, but on the practical need to create some land on which to live. In a CHEROKEE version, the original world, made of solid rock, sat above the sky, but its inhabitants had a problem: it was getting overcrowded, and there was nothing but water below. After much discussion, the water beetle, called Beaver's Grandchild, agreed to go down, and eventually came back with some soft mud, which began to grow and formed the earth. For an ARAPAHO version, see FLAT PIPE.

Another approach has supernatural beings constructing the world and its features through actions analogous to those in the human world. In an INUIT story from Kodiak Island, when RAVEN got light from the sky, a bladder descended containing a man and a woman. As they struggled, they stretched the bladder until it formed the world, with hills and mountains rising up where they pushed at the walls with their hands and feet. The man's hair became the forest and all its animals, the woman made seas by urinating, and rivers and lakes by spitting into ditches and holes, and when the man used one of the woman's teeth as a knife to carve wood, the woodchips became fish. The most crucial transformation of all took place when one of the

couple's sons played with a stone that became an island. The TRANSFORMER put another son and a female dog on the island and set it afloat. When it came to rest, it was Kodiak Island, and the boy and his dog wife became the ancestors of all the Kodiak Island people.

The concepts of impregnation, gestation and birth also figure in a variety of accounts. In one Great Basin narrative, a young woman and her mother lived on a small island, perhaps the only people in the world. It was a lonely life, so the mother sent the daughter out to find a mate, and she eventually came back with COYOTE. As there is no life without struggle, Coyote first had to overcome one serious obstacle. His new wife had a toothed vagina. Fortunately, he was able to jam it with a stick of wood and impregnate her. She gave birth to many tiny babies, and as she did, she dropped them into a wicker pitcher. When the pitcher was full, Coyote scattered them over the land.

The emergence theme, typical of the Southwest, has within it an ancient resonance of the original hunting and gathering life. The process of creation is a long and arduous journey through a series of underworlds wracked by turmoil

and danger. The first beings in HOPI creation lived in the deepest of three cavernous worlds beneath the present surface. This first world was dark, crowded and filthy. As the suffering was so great, two brothers (TWIN warrior gods) pierced the roof of the cave and planted a cane below; it grew through the opening into a second underworld, and the people climbed up on its ladder-like joints. This second cave was also dark, and after a time it too became crowded and filthy. When the people became distressed and began to fight amongst themselves, the Twins planted another cane and they climbed into the third (highest) cave. There they had a measure of peace, for they found fire and, by the light of torches, were able to build shelters (KIVAS) and travel from place to place. But this world soon turned contrary. Women neglected their families so that they could dance and, in the ensuing chaos, wives mixed with wives so the husbands could not tell one from another – promiscuity reigned. Fathers even had to care for the abandoned children. To rid the world of this evil, the people finally climbed into the fourth world, the present one, in the Grand Canyon, Arizona. After much wandering, they eventually

THE CREE, when they are on their hunting grounds, make use of only those modern tools and materials that help them in their daily lives. Canvas, for example, provides a strong and lightweight shelter ideal for camps, such as this one near the eastern shore of Hudson Bay.

settled in villages, now seen as ruins in isolated places high in the mountains, in caves or in the sides of deep canyons.

The rest of creation is usually in the hands of TRANSFORMERS, who arrive in a barren land and leave it filled with landscapes and living things when their work is done. To the MAKAH, for example, the new earth consisted only of sand, grass and animal people. Then the two brothers of the Sun and Moon, the Hohoeapbess (Two-Men-Who-Changed-Things), came to earth to make it ready for the Makah. They changed the creatures according to their behaviour in the mythic age. One, a thief, they changed into a seal, so that he could not steal with his shortened arms. A great fisherman became the great blue heron; another fisherman, one who could not resist stealing other's catches, they changed into the kingfisher. And two creatures with huge appetites they changed into RAVEN and his wife CROW.

THE CREE are an Algonquian-speaking nomadic hunting and gathering people who range in small bands through vast, lake-strewn forests surrounding Hudson Bay – from Quebec in the east to Saskatchewan in the west – as well as the northern margins of the Great Plains. Caribou and other game, fish and wildfowl provide most of their sustenance. The main tribal groups are the Plains Cree, Western Wood Cree and Swampy Cree in the west, and the Mistassini Cree and Tête de Boule Cree in the east. (See also *LANDSCAPES OF MEMORY*)

THE CREEK (Muskogee) were a farming people who lived in towns and villages in what are now the states of Georgia and Alabama. Their agricultural base enabled them to develop a stratified society with considerable wealth and extensive trading networks. Their religion showed influences from Mesoamerica in the construction of earthen ceremonial plazas, religious iconography, and burial mounds. During the 18th century, they formed the Creek Confederacy, which incorporated many smaller Muskogean-speaking tribes uprooted by European settlement. Later, during the 1830s, the government forcibly moved most of these tribes to Indian Territory (Oklahoma). While most Muskogee people live in Oklahoma, the descendants of Creek groups who resisted are scattered from Florida to Alabama.

CROW (*DENA*) is a *CULTURE HERO* and *TRICKSTER*, interchanged in narratives with *RAVEN*. The crow is a watchful, crafty scavenger, drawn to human settlement for what it can forage. It can be loud and quarrelsome but, while hunting, it soars silently or scans the world from a perch high in a tree. The conflation of Crow with Raven may be the result of variations in story-telling, but it is also possible

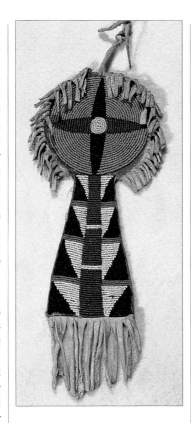

A BEADED ORNAMENT was attached by a Crow warrior to his horse's bridle. The cross design represents the four sacred directions and quarters of the world.

that the two similar birds were joined more closely in traditional mythology than they are in their modern biological classifications.

THE CROW tribe are a Siouan-speaking Plains people that migrated to the Great Plains from south of the Great Lakes and took to a buffalo-hunting way of life after the introduction of the horse in the 18th century. They followed the herds and used the animals for food, clothing and other material necessities. They are historically associated with the *HIDATSA*, village horticulturalists who lived along the Missouri River. They now occupy a reservation in south-central Montana.

DEATH is thought of as just part of the creation cycle. This heart-shaped wooden charm is used in the Naxnox dance of the Tsimshian. The owl symbolizes the soul of someone who has recently died.

CULTURE HEROES are supernatural beings who inhabited the earth throughout the mythic age. As *TRANSFORMERS*, they prepared it for the everyday needs of humans. This was a time of creative ferment, so culture heroes had characteristics of humans and animals, both idealized and observed through the experience of generations of story-tellers. This combination of the real and ideal meant that the heroes varied in their behaviour from altruism to lust, deceit and other baser human instincts. Although personalities of such great complexity are not easily classified, they are often described according to where their exploits fit in this range of human aspects. A supernatural being is heroic when involved in the tasks that define the culture to come, but a *TRICKSTER* when subject to baser human desires.

DAGWANOENYENT (Seneca) is a dangerous spirit, represented by the whirlwind. The Seneca

believe she was the daughter of the North Wind.

DAKOTA See *SIOUX*.

DEATH, as well as every living thing, has a place in *CREATION* myths. The *APACHE* view the origin of death as a deliberate act, the result of a debate between *RAVEN* and *COYOTE* as to whether humans should be immortal. To decide the matter, each threw an object in the water and proclaimed that if it sank, people would ultimately die; one threw a stick, but the other threw a stone, and that is why there is death. The Jicarilla and Lipan Apache say that Raven threw in the stone; the Chiricahua Apache blame Coyote. The *UTE* see the decision as a power struggle between two *CULTURE HEROES*, Wolf and Coyote. Wolf wanted the dead buried in anthills and revived the next day, but Coyote decreed that they would be put in the ground, their families would cut their hair in mourning, and that they would never return.

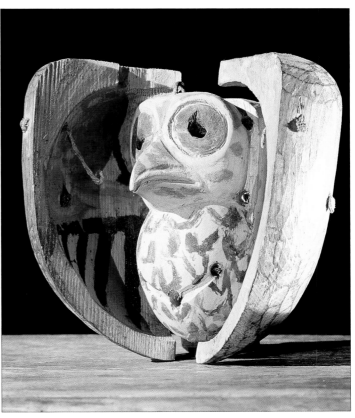

D

DEGANAWIDA

DEGANAWIDA (Seneca) was the mythical founder of the *IROQUOIS* Confederacy. In the Seneca version he was born to a Huron virgin, matured rapidly, then crossed Lake Ontario in a white stone canoe to reform the warring Iroquois. It is said that he planted the Great Tree of Peace that is symbolic of the League of the Iroquois. This tree has four great long white roots running outwards in the four directions to guide all the people to its shade, and it has an *EAGLE* at the top to warn the nations in case of outside attack.

THE DELAWARE (Lenni Lenape) [Munsi, Unami] once occupied the Atlantic coast in the Delaware River region, where they grew corn (maize) and other crops and hunted and gathered according to the season. Colonial settlement forced them out before 1700. The two original groups, speaking two related Algonquian languages, scattered westwards, stopping in Pennsylvania, Ohio, Indiana, Missouri and Kansas. Some of the Munsi people live in Wisconsin and Kansas, but most have now settled on the Six Nations of the Grand River Reserve of the *IROQUOIS*. The Unami live in a Federal Trust Area set aside for the Delaware in western Oklahoma.

DENA (formerly Tena) [Degexit'an, Koyukon, Tanana] is an anthropological classification for three related Athapascan tribal groups with similar ways of life who live in the Yukon River drainage in Alaska: the Tanana, the Koyukon and the Degexit'an (formerly known as Ingalik). These are typical subarctic peoples, who live by travelling the innumerable waterways and lakes in the boreal forests, hunting caribou, moose, deer, *BEAR*, beaver and other small game, catching wildfowl and fish, and gathering roots and tubers.

THE DENE are a group of closely related Athapascan peoples – including the Slavey (or Slave), Dogrib, *CHIPEWYAN*, Yellowknife and Sahtu – who live in the boreal forests of northern Canada from Great Bear and Great Slave Lakes east to Hudson Bay, in the Northwest Territories and south into northern Alberta, Manitoba and Saskatchewan. They travel with the seasons in small bands along the multitude of rivers and lakes in their vast territory in search of caribou, moose, *BEAR*, beaver and other game, fish, wildfowl and wild plants.

HIAWATHA (above), the hero of Henry Wadsworth Longfellow's narrative poem The Song of Hiawatha, *was a character mainly derived from stories of the Ojibway culture hero and trickster Nanabush, as he is fancifully pictured here. The Hiawatha of the tribes of the Northeast was actually Deganawida, the Mohawk founder of the Iroquois Confederacy.*

A SIOUAN WOMAN (above) in ceremonial costume displays her most precious possession: an elaborate necklace of dentalium shells, beads and silver coins.

DENTALIUM SHELLS (*KARUK*) represent an important symbol of wealth across the continent. Dentalium is a small, tusk-shaped mollusc that lives along the Pacific Coast from Alaska to California. The shells have been an important trade item in much of North America for thousands of years; the most desired variety was the pure white *Dentalium pretiosum* or "precious dentalium".

Dentalium Shell (Pisivava) lived alone in Upriver Ocean. He bore many young and, as they continued to grow, he decided to convert them into wealth for the people who were to come. He made strings from iris fibres and arranged the dentalia in necklaces of five sizes, the largest being the most valuable. To dress the shells up, he took the skin of a red-bellied snake, pulled it over them and decorated the top with a woodpecker crest. Then he made purses out of elk-horn, deerskin and turtle-shell. With the necklaces finished, he created a human village out of his hair and instructed the people how to use the shells as a form of money – for buying women, paying blood money (compensation for murdered relatives) and gambling.

DEVIL'S TOWER, a large, grey volcanic core composed of igneous rock hardened into massive vertical columns and exposed by erosion, rises to a height of more than 366 m (1,200 feet) above the Belle Fourche River valley in northeast Wyoming. This striking monolith is held sacred by all the tribes of the region, including the *KIOWA, ARAPAHO, SHOSHONI, CROW, CHEYENNE* and Lakota *SIOUX*.

The Kiowa name, Tso-aa, or tree rock, relates to a story of its origin. Seven young girls were playing outside their village when a *BEAR* attacked them. They fled back towards the village, but had to take refuge on a small rock, and, as the bear came closer, they prayed to the rock to save them. The rock began to grow upwards until the girls were out of reach of the bear, who scratched in vain at the sides. The rock grew so high that the girls were pushed into the sky, where they became the seven stars now known as the *PLEIADES*.

DEVIL'S TOWER is a volcanic mass, one of its most striking aspects being its enormous ribs, formed from the cooling of the magma. They stand out starkly in late afternoon sunlight.

E

DIRTY BOY is the protagonist of a widespread theme involving the failure of people to appreciate true worth. He is commonly a boy so unattractive that most people shun him but, when someone treats him kindly, he transforms into a handsome young man, who returns the generosity shown him through his spiritual powers.

In a *BLACKFOOT* story cycle, Dirty Boy (also called Found-in-the-Grass) began life as *LODGE BOY*. He was one of two monster-slaying brothers. When his brother, Thrown Away, climbed a tree into the upper world and disappeared, Lodge Boy declined into the pathetic and unappealing Dirty Boy. A kindly old woman took him in and made him arrows, with which he won a shooting contest for the daughter of the chief. As his spirit grew stronger, he proved himself in further tests of strength and prowess, and grew into a handsome man. After saving his tribe by gathering up buffalo and ensuring their continued prosperity, he rose into the sky where he joined his brother in the constellation we now call Castor and Pollux.

DJILÁKONS
see *WEEPING WOMAN*.

DJOKÁBESH (*MONTAGNAIS, NAS-KAPI*), who figures in one of the first North American myths to be recorded (in the Jesuit Relations of 1634, by Father Paul le Jeune), is a *CULTURE HERO* and monster-slayer. In one of his exploits, he killed a monstrous *BEAR* that had eaten his mother. Unlike many roaming heroes, Djokábesh kept close to home, returning to his sister after each adventure. She had her own heroic qualities, once rescuing him when he was swallowed by a fish.

DOG HUSBAND (Iglulik *INUIT*) is a narrative theme that resolves the problem of how to maintain the integrity of the mythic world after human beings and animals are

separated. This particular version also explains the origins of non-Inuit groups.

A father, frustrated by a daughter who would have no husband, cursed her by ordering her to marry his dog. A man soon appeared wearing a dog amulet, and married her. He was a dog in human form. The woman became pregnant and gave birth to a large litter – half of them human beings and the other half dogs. Since the dog-husband could not hunt like other Iglulik husbands, the woman's father had to provide meat. Because this went against all proper conduct, he resolved to kill his son-in-law. One day, the dog-husband swam from the father's camp with the meat, but it was weighed down with stones, and he drowned. Angry at her father for the curse that had caused this unnatural marriage in the first place, the woman called on her dog-children to kill the father. They mauled him, but he escaped and ceased to bring her food. With no one to supply meat, the young woman transformed her clothing (and/or her boots) into boats and sent the children out into the world to fend for themselves.

To the Inuit, these dog and human children became the ancestors of Indians (or spirits) and white people.

DOGRIB see *DENE*.

DJOKÁBESH killed a bear that had eaten his mother. Bears often feature as fierce adversaries in North American myths.

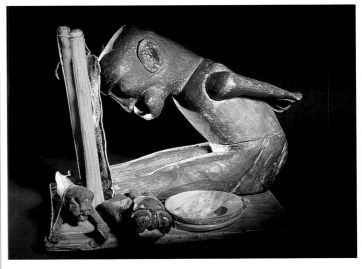

DREAMS are an essential aspect of a person's social identity and spiritual growth. They may have great import, especially at times of crisis or transition. At the birth of a child, a parent or elder may provide a name given in a dream; a youth undergoing the transition to adulthood may be expected to dream the presence of a guardian spirit; and dreams may guide people through hunting, travel, warfare or other important cultural events. *SHAMANS* use dreams as a means of gaining wisdom and understanding, using their experience, just as modern psychologists do, to help resolve problems in daily life. As the dream world is the world of spirits, it involves powerful forces that the dreamer must always respect; to ignore or misuse the wisdom of dreams can be dangerous.

DUNNE-ZA see *BEAVER*.

EAGLES, as large birds of prey with a commanding presence and the ability to soar high into the sky, are often associated with militaristic power and great hunting ability.

To the *WICHITA*, eagles were created when the father of *CULTURE HERO* Young-Boy-Chief (Waiksedia), weary of conflicts, asked the people of his village to abandon their village and their human forms. Some families turned into birds, others into animals of the forests and plains. For his part, the old chief poured a gourd of water over the fire in his lodge; as the steam and smoke enveloped his family,

SHAMANS USE dreams and trances to take them into the spirit world. In this Alaskan Inuit carving, a shaman sits in a trance, accompanied by two animal-like spirit helpers. The drum he uses to conjure the spirits lies beside him.

including Young-Boy-Chief, they rose into the sky as eagles. The *HOPI* relate how Eagle helped *COYOTE* steal a box of light – the sun and the moon – from the *KACHINAS*, while the *CROW* tribe associate eagles, especially bald-headed ones, with thunder. In *INUIT* beliefs, eagles dwell in the land above the sky, and so *SHAMANS* may place eagle down on the tops of ceremonial staffs during hunting rituals, to aid the hunters in their quest for game. For a *TUSKEGEE* creation myth, see *COUNCIL OF ANIMALS*.

THE EAGLE, largest of the hunting birds, soars high in the sky, scanning the landscape below with a keen vision that can spot the smallest of prey. Its size, strength and sharp senses make it one of the most powerful of the animal beings.

LANDSCAPES OF MEMORY

THE HEROIC EVENTS OF CREATION AND TRANSFORMATION do not depend only on the recollection of ancient traditions. They live on in the shape of the land itself: every towering rock or twist in a river records the acts of the culture heroes who changed the earth as they lived on it. In some places, the marks of creation are still fresh. Thus, the Choctaw can still gaze upon the very place they emerged, a mound called Nanih Waiya, near present-day Philadelphia, Mississippi. Other land forms preserve individual supernatural acts. The Penobscot, for example, can speak of a time when Gluskap killed a moose at Moose-tchick, for the bones and entrails of this giant creature are still visible around Bar Harbor, Maine.

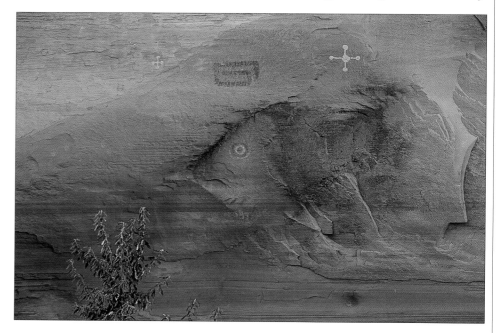

The story-teller's landscape also provides an effective mental map of a tribal homeland, coloured and textured with the places where supernatural events occurred (the ability to visualize environmental detail was crucial for people who often had to travel great distances over vast, trackless environments during their seasonal rounds). Since aboriginal people intertwine oral tradition and geography in this way, they still have a spiritual hold on their lost lands, a bond that they can verify and renew as long as those lands exist.

ANCIENT ROCKS (left) seem to bear the weight of eternity on their weathered heads. These pink granite domes thrust above the dry lands of central Texas, near a formation known as the Enchanted Rock. By night, the rock seems to recoil from the coolness of the air, for it emits strange cracking sounds, like voices from the depths of the earth.

A FISH (above) emerges from the jagged scars of a weathered layer of sandstone on the face of a cliff in Canyon de Chelly, Arizona. Aboriginal artists saw the natural earth as a place of transformation, where the essence of the ancestor creators remained, hidden in stone. With a touch of paint or some carving, these beings emerge, creating a place of worship for generations to come.

THE ROCKS (left) that form the skeletal structure of the earth are alive, as they have distinctive shapes and substance, exhibit change and decay, and hold within them the memories of the events of creation. In a small clearing in the woods of Pennsylvania, near the Delaware River, a host of weathered rocks carries a strange quality that made them sacred to the Unami and Munsee people who once lived here – when they are struck, they give off a bright, ringing sound. Wherever they are found, ringing rocks serve to confirm the subtle powers of even the most inanimate of earthly objects.

A GREAT SERPENT (right) was fashioned more than 2,000 years ago by the people of the Adena or Hopewell cultures, on a narrow promontory above Brush Creek, in Adams County, Ohio. The mound, built up with yellow clay and stones, is 440 m (400 yards) long. The serpent's tail is coiled, and it appears to be holding an egg in its mouth. Serpents figure in mythologies across the world, as they have the extraordinary power, reflected in their unique locomotion on the physical plane, to move between the surface of the earth and the underworld abodes of the spirits.

A PLACE (left) with great spiritual power may be marked by something startling, unexpected, that seems to remove it from the surrounding landscape. In the broad, flat prairies of Saskatchewan, there is an island of golden sand that rises into dunes covering 190,000 ha (470,000 acres). Here in the Great Sandhills, the Plains Cree believe that the Memekweciwak, or little people, dwell, making the chipped-stone artefacts that people still find along its margins.

F

EARTH DIVER is a *CREATION* theme, in which the earth is shaped from mud that an animal retrieves from the depths of the primeval waters. It has continuous distribution throughout Europe, Asia and most of North America. While most narratives keep to the conventional story of struggle by various animals to reach the bottom of the ocean and retrieve the mud (see *COUNCIL OF ANIMALS*), a northern Alaskan version has *RAVEN* diving under the water, spearing a clod of earth and raising it to the surface. And the *YAKIMA* peoples relate the story of Wheememeowah, the Great Chief Above, who completes the task himself, scooping mud from the shallows. For an Algonquian version, see *WISAKEDJAK*.

EARTH-MAKER is a creator who is found in the stories of several different tribal groups.

The *MAIDU* say that he floated on the primeval waters with *OLD MAN COYOTE*, and that the two of them decided to make land. They floated until they found what appeared to be a bird's nest (it was Meadowlark's nest). First they stretched the nest out to the rim of the world using ropes, then they painted it with blood, so that all kinds of creatures would be born (some rocks are still blood-red today, as proof of this event). By stretching it even further, they made it big enough to travel in. Earth-maker then went around making creatures, countries and languages, while Coyote maintained the ropes. When there is an earthquake, the people know that it is Coyote trying to stretch the world a little more.

The *PIMA* Earth-maker created people out of clay, but they were misshapen, and, after arguing with *ELDER BROTHER*, he sank into the earth. The *WINNEBAGO* relate that Earth-maker, after creating the earth, made *HARE* in the image of a man, and sent him into the world where he was born of a virgin. He

later founded the *MIDEWIWIN* society in order to secure human immortality.

ECHO (*UTE*) figures in an origin story that combines ribald humour with theorizing about a mysterious natural phenomenon.

Echo was a jealous, demanding woman who kidnapped Dove's child and raised him to be her husband. One day, the young man was out hunting when he came upon his mother. She was overjoyed to see him again, and they devised a plan so that he could escape from Echo. The next time he killed a buffalo, he piled the meat high in a cedar tree, forcing his wife to devise a way to get it down. While Echo struggled with the meat, the youth and his mother put a tree stump in his bed and ran away. When Echo returned with the meat, she saw the outline of her husband in the bed and, thinking she saw his erect penis above the blanket, had intercourse. When she discovered the ruse, she rushed after the two, who had flown up to his grandfather's home on a cliff. The grandfather, Rattlesnake, hid them outside the entrance to his cave and crawled back into the darkness. When Echo entered the cave, she saw an erect penis in the dim light and began to have intercourse. As she did, the cave got smaller and smaller, until there was just enough room for Rattlesnake to escape, leaving Echo trapped forever in the cliff.

ELDER BROTHER (*PIMA*), Siuuhu, was a son of sky and earth and the creator of the Hohokam (a prehistoric culture that disappeared *c.* 1450). After molesting some maidens at a puberty ceremony, he was killed. Four years later, he revived and followed the setting sun into the underworld. From there, he guided new people on to the earth, the present Pima, whom he led in battle against the Hohokam, driving them away. After creating the game animals and ceremonies necessary to propitiate the gods, he retired again to the underworld. He remains the patron of the war rite.

ESKIMO see *INUIT*.

ESTSÁNATLEHI
see *CHANGING WOMAN*.

FATHER SKY
see *MOTHER EARTH*.

A WESTERN DIAMONDBACK rattle-snake, featured in the Echo story, will shake its tail angrily to warn away predators.

FIRE is essential to human life, so its creation and control were among the most important tasks of *CULTURE HEROES*. Because of its value and its highly magical properties, fire was usually controlled by supernatural beings, and it was up to the heroes to steal it. Possessing fire is not enough, however. Fire-making tools must have the power to release the fire from the wood.

In a *YUROK* account, the animal heroes joined together to steal both fire and daylight from the sky people. At first the world was in darkness, and the animal people found this tiresome, so Megwom-ents (the dwarf food-giver) went to the sky and discovered that the sky people had abundant light. He came back to earth and then guided the *TRANSFORMER* Wohpe-kumeu, *EAGLE*, Pigeon, Sandpiper, Hummingbird and some other beings to the sky lodge where the light was kept. The sky people would not open the door, so *WOH-PEKUMEU* decided to impersonate a beautiful woman to get in. He tied his hair, took his blanket, a burden basket filled with acorns

FIRE is both terrible and wonderful – destructive as it rages through a northern California sequoia forest, but life-giving too, because the forest will revive with new vigour when the next spring arrives.

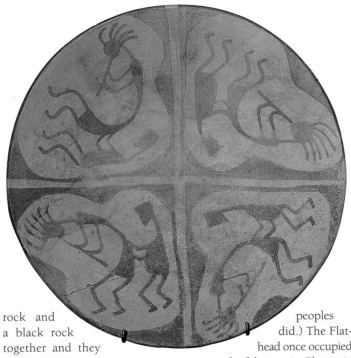

and salmon (they were actually pitch and alder bark) and a basket dipper, and easily gained entrance. Inside, the sky people were feasting, and he saw two baskets hanging, one holding fire and the other daylight. The revellers took no notice of him and, when they had finished their meal, they left him there alone (it was night, and they were busy with the night sky). Just before daylight, Wohpekumeu stole the baskets, but the sky people discovered the theft and pursued him. They had almost caught him when he gave the baskets to Eagle, who carried them further, and they were then passed in succession to Pigeon, Hummingbird, Sandpiper and, finally, Water Ant, who escaped into the water. When the sky people abandoned the chase, Water Ant came out of the water, daylight flooded the land, and he breathed the fire out of his mouth on to a willow tree – which is why fire drills are always made from willow.

The heroes in a SANPOIL version must make some sort of ladder to get into the sky, so they try to shoot an arrow into it and then make a chain of arrows down to the ground. All the animals fail except Woodpecker, who made his bow and arrows from superior materials – the bow of an elk rib, arrows from service-berry bushes and eagle feathers, and the points from flint (which he obtained by inducing Flint Rock and Hard Rock to fight). With the chain made, the animals bring the fire from the sky, and Horsefly and Hummingbird carry it to all parts of the Sanpoil country.

In the Yurok and Sanpoil narratives, culture heroes brought fire to the earth. In a DENA story it was humans that invented fire-making, spurred on by the selfish actions of a trickster. Long ago, when people had no fire, they watched CROW simply reach into the water and hook out burning coals, but they could never duplicate the feat. Then one day a boy struck a white

rock and a black rock together and they sparked. He lit some grass, but the spark always died. Then another boy made a bow drill and surrounded the tip with the dried, rotten heartwood of a birch (punk). When he created a spark (a glowing coal), he lifted it with a bone knife into the grass, and it burned.

FLAT PIPE, the sacred PIPE of the ARAPAHO, is central to tribal identity. It is imbued with powerful MEDICINE and so must always be wrapped in a bundle and protected by a pipe-keeper.

Flat Pipe is, in essence, the force that created Arapaho culture. Its role is only revealed in the Flat Pipe ceremony, but several simplified accounts are recorded. Flat Pipe (the pipe is personified) floated on four sticks on the primeval waters. He bade the animals dive down into the waters and retrieve mud so that he could use it to make land, and finally Duck succeeded. There was not sufficient clay, however, so Turtle went down and got enough for Flat Pipe to create the earth.

THE FLATHEAD tribe are hunters, fishers and gatherers. They speak a Salishan language closely related to that of their northwestern neighbours, the Kalispel. (They were so named by whites under the misapprehension that they flattened their heads, as some coastal

peoples did.) The Flathead once occupied much of the interior Plateau in western Montana and Idaho. After giving up their rights to this land in the Hellgate Treaty of 1855, they joined other Salish and Kootenay tribes on the Flathead Reservation in western Montana. Two unrelated tribes, the CHINOOK and CHOCTAW, were once also called Flatheads earlier in the historic period.

FLINT (IROQUOIS) is the evil one of TWIN brothers born to the daughter of WOMAN-WHO-FELL-FROM-THE-SKY, While Sapling, the good twin, transformed the landscape, slew monsters and created culture, Flint, with the aid of his grandmother, attempted to undo the good. Sapling created animals, but Flint kept them in a cave, and Sapling had to release them. Flint attempted to build an ice bridge to the land of the monsters, so that they could cross over and kill humans, but Sapling sent Bluebird to frighten Flint, and the ice melted. The flint (chert) used to make weapons is believed to be drops of Flint's blood, shed in fights with his brother.

FLUTE LURE is a mythological story-type in which the sound of a flute or other wood instrument plays a significant part. In a moralistic PAPAGO story, an outcast woman who has spent her life

struggling painfully through the mountains, used music (the sound of the flute) as a seductive device. She gave birth to TWIN boys who – magically – matured quickly and, to help them get married, she showed them how to make flutes from canes, so they could lure Buzzard's two daughters. After marrying the daughters, they went to visit Buzzard, but were killed by his henchman, Blue Hawk.

FLYING (OR ROLLING) HEADS feature as monsters in many oral traditions. For the IROQUOIS, the disembodied Flying Head is a creature of storms, four times as tall as the tallest man. Its thick skin is so matted with hair that no weapon can pierce it. The head has huge fangs, and two vast bird wings growing out of its cheeks, enabling it to fly.

THE MOON, the mother of twin boys in a Blackfoot account of creation, is beheaded for falling in love with a rattlesnake. Now a monstrous flying head, she chases the boys, but they will be saved when mountains spring up to protect them.

G

FLYING SHIELDS (*HOPI*) were made from woven cotton, and were used by supernatural beings for transportation.

FOAM WOMAN (*HAIDA*) was one of two mythic mothers of the Haida moieties (halves), into which the society was divided (the other was *WEEPING WOMAN*). Foam Woman was the ancestor of the Raven *CLANS*, and appeared at the time of the world flood. She had 20 breasts, ten on each side, and at each breast she nursed the future grandmother of one of the Raven families.

FOUND-IN-THE-GRASS
see *DIRTY BOY*.

THE FOX (Mesquaki), or Red Earth People, are an Algonquian tribe who ranged widely in the prairies west of Lake Michigan, where they hunted, fished, gathered and grew maize (corn), beans and other crops in season. After being nearly exterminated in the early 18th century, they joined forces with their traditional allies, the Sauk (or Sac), forming the Sac and Fox Nation. They removed to Iowa in 1804 after an unjust treaty gave them a pittance – about $2,000 and an annuity in goods worth approximately $1,000 – in exchange for all their lands east of the Mississippi (a large part of present-day Illinois, Missouri, and Wisconsin). In 1827, they rebelled

KEOKUK, Sauk and Fox chief, c. 1848. Unlike the heroic resistance leader Black Hawk, Keokuk co-operated with the whites, and was eventually responsible for signing away most tribal land.

when the Federal government decided to remove all native people from Illinois. The Sauk leader Ma-ka-tai-me-she-kia-kiak (Black Sparrow Hawk), known popularly as Black Hawk, and his people (warriors, women and children) were eventually crushed in 1832 at the Massacre of Bad Axe, on the Mississippi River. The Sauk chief Keokuk eventually signed away all but 16 ha (40 acres) of the remaining tribal lands. In 1857, the survivors purchased a small plot of land along the Iowa River in central Iowa, and they remained there after the Sauk were forced to move to Kansas in 1861. This land, which is not a government-controlled reservation, is called the Mesquaki Indian Settlement.

THE GABRIELINO, speaking an Uto-Aztecan language, was a small hunting and gathering tribe that occupied lands in southern California around present-day Los Angeles. They were especially skilled deep-sea fishers, taking their plank boats well offshore in search of sea lions, seals, otters and a wide variety of fish, including swordfish, halibut and tuna. They were once considered extinct, but the resurgence of pride in Indian identity caused a number of Gabrielinos to reassert their tribal affiliation. They have no land base, but several groups are actively trying to regenerate their traditional culture.

GAHÉ (*APACHE*) are the supernatural beings who are represented by gahé dancers (corresponding to the Pueblo *KACHINA* dancers). The Chiricahua Apache believe that the gahé live inside certain mountains and wear costumes and decorate their faces in ways that Chiricahua learn through visionary experience,

and subsequently recreate in their dances. The gahé dancers appear at curing rituals and at girls' puberty rites. The gahé also act as protectors of the Chiricahua people. One narrative describes how they rescued an Apache war party, equipped only with traditional weapons, that was being pursued by Mexican cavalry. A man prayed to the gahé of a nearby mountain, who poured out and surrounded the soldiers. They opened a cave in the rocks and drove them all inside, then closed it forever. It is said that one can still see the soldiers' shoes piled up at the mouth of the cave.

GLUSKAP is the principal *CULTURE HERO* and *TRANSFORMER* of northeastern Algonquian coastal peoples, also known as Glooskap. He is similar in essence and character to a hero of Algonquian tribes in northeastern woodlands, *NANABUSH*, and to a hero of Algonquian tribes south of the Great Lakes, known as *WISAKEDJAK*. Like Wisakedjak, Gluskap has no clearly defined animal attributes.

Gluskap's origins are obscure, since most narratives focus on his exploits. In a Christianized myth of the western *ABENAKI*, he formed himself out of the dust left over from the creation of Adam.

In a recent *MICMAC* version, lightning created Gluskap when one bolt struck the sand and formed the image of a human body, and a second strike gave him life. At first, he was stuck to the ground

THE GAHÉ, or spirits of the mountains, are represented here by Apache dancers. The dancers are also sometimes called Mountain Spirit Dancers or Fire Dancers. They dance to ward off evil spirits and illness during the Apache girls' puberty ceremonies.

with his head facing the rising sun, his feet towards the setting sun, and his arms pointing north and south. After watching animals, birds and plants thrive around him, he asked Nisgam (Sun) to free him. At that moment a third bolt of lightning raised him to his feet so that he could walk the earth.

Gluskap explored the land in all directions, travelling west until he came to an ocean, south until the land narrowed and he could see an ocean on each side, and north to the land of ice and snow. Eventually he returned to the lands of his creation, and stayed there.

A *PENOBSCOT* story cycle captures some of his heroic deeds. He freed all the *HARES* of the world after fighting through blizzards when they were imprisoned by the Great Hare; he killed a monster frog that had drunk all the world's water, causing a drought; he rescued his brother Wolf from the serpent Atosis; and he tamed the giant wind bird (known to the *PASSAMAQUODDY* as Wuchowsen, or Wind-Blower, who sits on a great rock at the north end of the sky). Traces of his exploits can still be seen across the Atlantic region, from agates in the Minas Basin of Nova Scotia – jewels that he made for his grandmother's necklace – to mountains and rock outcrops all along the coast.

GREAT SPIRIT

is the name commonly given to a singular creator. Such a being probably existed in the ancient beliefs of some tribes, but it is generally inconsistent with the spirit of egalitarianism and democracy that characterizes most tribal groups. It is likely that some creators of this type have emerged through the influence of Christianity.

GRIZZLY BEAR WOMAN

(*NEZ PERCE*) exemplifies the unpredictable nature of *BEARS*, as benign foragers and fierce and aggressive adversaries, which makes them difficult beings to control in the spirit world.

The Nez Perce believe that when a woman becomes involved with a grizzly bear spirit, its strength overwhelms her, and she takes on its monstrous character. They relate the story of a young girl kidnapped from her family by bears. When her brother, Red-headed Woodpecker, found her after a long search, she complained that they mistreated her: she was degraded and humiliated in shocking ways – they forced her to eat naked, as was their custom, and they wiped their buttocks on her. To rescue her, Woodpecker gained entry to the bears' lodge by taking the form of a handsome

A GRIZZLY BEAR'S uncontrolled rage, when provoked, makes it one of the most dangerous of forest animals and feared by all the North American tribes.

THE GREAT SPIRIT, or creator, is invoked by a warrior in a Plains Indian earthlodge. He lies beside the sacred fire beneath the smokehole which is open to the heavens. (PAINTING BY GEORGE CATLIN, C. 1830.)

youth. He ate with them (they hastily covered themselves in his presence) and then kept them up so late that they fell into a deep sleep. He then tied each one by its hair to a tent pole and set fire to the lodge. He urged his sister to flee, but, strangely, she asked him to wait and watch the bears burn. When the fire was over, she secretly picked up the bears' teeth from the ashes as they began the journey home. While they were walking home, the brother heard a growling noise behind him, and he discovered that his sister had changed into a bear. She began to chase him, hoping to catch and eat him, but he was saved by a group of women out digging roots. He took these women as his wives, and his sister was condemned to roam the forests in search of human prey.

THE GROS VENTRE,

unaccountably given this name ("Big Bellies") by French explorers, call themselves Ah-ah-nee-nin, which

means White Clay People. They are an Algonquian tribe, related to the *ARAPAHO*, who migrated long ago from the edge of the boreal forest near Lake Winnipeg to join other forest peoples on the Great Plains. After the introduction of the horse to North America, the Gros Ventre people began to specialize in buffalo-hunting, and they followed the vast herds across the broad plains of Montana and Saskatchewan. They eventually gave up their claims to their traditional territory in 1888, and were removed to a reservation at Fort Belknap, in Montana, which they share with the *ASSINBOINE*. They were traditionally allied with the *BLACKFOOT* and the *SARCEE* in the Blackfoot Confederacy.

THE HAIDA

[Coastal, Island] occupy the Queen Charlotte Islands (Haida Gwaii) off the coast of British Columbia and small section of the Alaska mainland. Along with their northern neighbours, the *TLINGIT*, they speak a Na-Dene language. As the warm Pacific waters teem with life, and the forests are deep and lush, the Haida obtained sufficient resources from fishing, hunting and gathering to support a social structure more typical of complex agricultural societies, with ranked social classes and private property. The exuberant outpouring of heraldic art strongly manifests the hierarchical nature of the society. Representations of the animal ancestors of *CLANS* and families are carved or painted on virtually all formal objects, including *TOTEM POLES*, house-fronts and

THE HAIDA inhabit the Queen Charlotte Islands. This 19th-century photograph shows how their cedar plank houses and totem poles followed the edge of the sea.

house support posts, masks, headdresses, boxes, dishes, basketry and many other material goods.

Both island and coastal Haida were subject to strenuous efforts by governments and missionaries to assimilate them, but they have kept much of their culture, and remain in the area of their original homelands. (See also *TRANSFORMATION*)

H

SPIRITS OF THE EARTH

THE EARTH IS INFUSED WITH SPIRITUAL ENERGY. When supernatural beings shaped the lands during the age of transformation, all material things had the potential to live as humans and animals do. Because of this legacy, aboriginal thinkers see the earth as a living spiritual realm where supernatural beings still reside. Every territory has its special places. A large hill near the junction of the Snake and Grande Ronde rivers (in present-day Idaho), for example, figures prominently in a Nez Perce fire story. Of the supernatural protagonists, Cedar, old and half dead, remained on the top of this hill for generations around the turn of the 20th century. The visual impact of this tree, craggy, ancient, and etched against the sky, created a spiritual link that many other sacred places share. High mountains and prominent rock formations, caves and crevices, waterfalls and springs are all spirit dwellings. Whether the earthly spirits live, ever-watchful, above the land or are hidden away, to be suddenly encountered on a path or waterway, they always remain powerful, even dangerous, in their abodes.

A TALL BLOCK (left) of ancient sediment stands like a sentinel among the mountains along the border between Alberta and Montana. Because of its solitary, commanding presence, it is known as Chief Mountain. The Blackfoot regard it as a highly sacred place, where people may seek dreams and visions, and draw spiritual power.

THE DARK OPENING (above) of Danger Cave, in the western desert of Utah, looks over barren salt flats. The first humans to live here, 11,000 years ago, walked through grasslands and pine forest but, several thousand years later, the land had become too inhospitable to support them. To Native American people, such sites are sacred places, as they contain the spirits of all those ancestors who lived and died there.

MOUNTAINS (left) reach so high into the sky that the forces controlling the weather move among them. Here the snows cover the Sandia Mountains, near Albuquerque, New Mexico. Climbing to such heights is a journey into the realms of the spirit world, done carefully and with respect.

BEAVERHOUSE LAKE (below left), in northwestern Ontario, is dominated by a massive, domed granite formation resembling a beaver's lodge. At the highest point, reached by a steep climb up the cliffs, a single smear of red ochre indicates the site of a vision quest. It was an ideal spot, secluded and yet close to the sky and the immense sweep of the lake.

FANTASTIC WATER CREATURES (below), can be seen carved on a rock cliff along the shore of Sproat Lake, in Nootka territory on western Vancouver Island. They may have figured in mythological interpretations of the lake and its resources or in origin stories related to an important tribal ancestor.

AN ETHEREAL DAWN (right) breaks over brooding waters near the Lake of the Woods, Ontario. This view is from a large, square room cut by nature into a massive granite formation covered with red ochre rock paintings. The walls inside this strange opening are bare, suggesting that it was perhaps too filled with spirit power to be sullied by paint. Here, a shaman would have conducted rituals to obtain the visions and dreams necessary for contact with the manitous in the rocks and the waters below.

A HIDATSA warrior, dressed for the Dog Dance. (*ILLUSTRATION AFTER A 19TH-CENTURY PAINTING BY KARL BODMER.*)

THE HAN (Han-Kutchin) are an Athapascan-speaking people who live in the boreal forests of eastern Alaska and adjoining parts of Yukon Territory in Canada. They live in isolated settlements along rivers and lakes, where they continue to pursue some of their traditional hunting and gathering activities, including moose hunting, salmon fishing and berry picking.

THE HARE tribe is a nomadic Athapascan hunting and gathering tribe concentrated northwest of Great Bear Lake on the northern edge of the boreal forests. They lived in small bands and travelled through their vast territory along the many rivers and lakes, subsisting on caribou, moose, deer, beaver and other small game, fish, wildfowl and seasonal berries and roots. Because of their remoteness, they have been able to retain many of their traditional ways.

HARES and rabbits figure in many oral traditions as *CULTURE HEROES* and *TRICKSTERS*. Great Hare (Winabojo, *NANABUSH*) is the principal culture hero of northeastern and Subarctic Algonquian cultures; and Hare (called Mastshingke, or rabbit, by the *OMAHA*) is a hero and trickster who delivers the Siouan peoples of the Great Plains from man-eating *BEARS*, rolling heads and other monsters.

Rabbit (Mahtigwess) is known to the *MICMAC* and *PASSAMA-QUODDY* as a trickster with great magical powers. In a tale set during historic times, he throws a chip of wood into the water and transforms it into a three-masted ship, complete with coloured flags, three rows of heavy cannon and a crew – with himself as the captain, resplendent in a large, gold-trimmed cocked hat with great white plumes.

HASTSHIN (Jicarilla *APACHE*) were beings who existed in the beginning, when there was only Darkness, Water and Cyclone. They created the earth and the underworld, and then the sky.

HEROIC CHILDREN are very common characters in mythologies. They embody a range of cultural values common to most societies: innocence, which makes them closer than adults to an idealized spiritual condition; potential, in their energy for moral and spiritual growth as they mature; and continuity, in their significance as members of an emerging generation. Given their nearness to creation and its resources of spiritual power, it is not surprising that heroic children may mature unusually quickly, or are wise beyond their years. Heroic children are also an effective dramatic device, as there may be a great disparity between the child and its adversaries. They must often slay a host of fearsome monsters, for example, or undergo tests of character and determination, or outwit adults of a much higher social status, but perhaps fewer virtues. Children are naturally imbued with the promise of a better world, and perhaps this, more than anything, makes their heroic deeds during the mythical age reasonable and appropriate. Examples of heroic children are *MUSP AND KOMOL*; *LODGE BOY AND THROWN AWAY*; *STAR BOY*; and Sweet Medicine (see under *HOOP-AND-POLE GAME*).

THE HIDATSA are a Siouan people who once lived along the Missouri River in western North Dakota. They had come from the woodlands and prairies south of the Great Lakes long ago, and their traditions say they emerged from Devil's Lake in eastern North Dakota. They were sophisticated horticulturalists, who not only grew corn (maize), squash and five varieties of beans, but practised seed selection and controlled plantings. They also hunted buffalo when necessary. After being distracted by the fur trade and severely reduced in the mid-19th century by smallpox and inter-tribal conflicts, induced by the westward spread of white culture, they joined other tribes on the Fort Berthold Reservation in North Dakota.

THE HOOP-AND-POLE GAME is a game with religious overtones, played across the continent. Players attempt to throw sharpened poles through a hoop. The enclosed space is generally divided into sections with twine or rawhide, and the score is calculated according to which section of the hoop the pole goes through.

The Northern *CHEYENNE* attribute the origins of the game to the *CULTURE HERO* Sweet Medicine. A young virgin of a good family bore a child after hearing a voice, for four nights in succession, telling her that a spirit man named Sweet Root

SAN CARLOS APACHE youths play the hoop-and-pole game. The San Carlos tribe live in the rugged semi-desert lands of southeastern Arizona, close to where Mt Graham, their most sacred place, rises into the sky out of the flat desert sands.

would visit her. Shamed by her unexplained pregnancy, she abandoned the baby she delivered. An old woman nearby heard the baby's cries and took it home. She named the boy Sweet Medicine, because she found him where MEDICINE roots grew that helped make mothers' breast milk flow.

The boy grew unnaturally quickly and became a highly skilled hunter, even though still a child. Yet no one paid attention to him because he lived with an aged grandmother in a poor TEPEE. So he directed his grandmother to make a hoop wrapped with buffalo hide and prepare four cherry sticks. When she had done so, he began to throw the pointed sticks through the hoop. This new game attracted the people, and they gathered around. He threw the last stick, and when it went through the hoop, it changed into a fat buffalo calf. This calf was magical: no matter how much meat the people cut off, there was always more. This accounts for the promise in every hoop-and-pole game that the playing will ensure an abundance of buffalo.

A YOUNG HOPI girl wears her hair in the squash-blossom (or butterfly) style, indicating that she is available for marriage. After marriage, she will wear a simple braid.

THE HOPI [Hopituh Shi-nu-mu] are a western *PUEBLO* people who live in the area of Black Mesa in northeastern Arizona, surrounded by the territory of their regional rivals, the *NAVAJO*. They speak an Uto-Aztecan language, which reveals a southern affiliation quite distinct from that of the Athapascan Navajos. They lived in large community houses, built of stone or *adobe* (mud bricks), in towns established well before the historic period. The Hopi practised the small-scale horticulture typical of southern tribes, growing corn (maize), beans, squash and cotton. Through careful selection of their corn crops, they developed a plant with a tap root long enough to endure the arid conditions of their fields, and they also selected varieties in their four sacred colours – red, white, blue and yellow. They expanded into cattle-ranching after the arrival of Europeans.

HORSES transformed native cultures, practically and spiritually, during the historic period, especially in the Great Plains. They escaped into the wild in 1540, during the first Spanish expedition into the Southwest. Numbers increased dramatically when the Spanish retreated after the Pueblo rebellion in 1680. The use of the horse quickly spread from the *PUEBLO* across the deserts and grasslands of the continent; records of French traders in Kansas indicate that the *CHEYENNE* were using the horse by 1745. The Indians had no word for "horse", so they created one out of words they used for other animals: for example, Elk Dog, Spirit Dog, Sacred Dog or Moose Dog. As all religions strive to account for mysteries within the specific experience of the culture, there are origin stories that regard the horse as a gift of the supernaturals.

According to the *BLACKFOOT*, the *CULTURE HERO* Long Arrow brought the first horses to the tribe. Long Arrow was an unfortunate orphan boy: deaf, treated like a mangy dog and unloved by everyone but his sister. When the people broke camp, they simply abandoned him, but a kindly old chief named Good Running eventually adopted him. The boy recovered

BEFORE THE WHITE MAN divided up the vast open plains with barbed wire, the Indian people let their horses range wild, catching and taming them as they were needed. (19TH-CENTURY PAINTING BY GEORGE CATLIN.)

his hearing, learned to speak and eventually grew up to be a fine hunter. When he asked his adopted father how he could repay him for his kindness, the chief told him that there was talk of powerful spirit people living at the bottom of a faraway lake. They had mysterious animals to do their work – swift and strong and bigger than elk, but able to carry burdens like dogs. He called them Pono-Kamita (Elk Dogs). Every fourth generation, young warriors had gone in quest of one of these wonderful creatures, but they had never returned.

Long Arrow took up the challenge and, after a long journey and encounters with many spirits, found a giant lake surrounded by snowy peaks and waterfalls of ice. After falling asleep in a meadow, he was awoken by a beautiful spirit boy-child, who took Long Arrow to his grandfather's lodge at the bottom of the lake. The grandfather lived in a large *TEPEE* of tanned buffalo hide, decorated with images of two strange animals in vermilion paint and with a kingfisher perched on top. Since Long Arrow had braved the journey into the depths of the lake, the grandfather rewarded him with one of the Elk Dogs. When he discovered that the grandfather himself was an Elk Dog and the master of these animals, Long Arrow asked for three things:

the grandfather's rainbow-coloured quilled belt, his black *MEDICINE* robe and a herd of Elk Dogs. If he wore the robe, Long Arrow would be able to prevent the animals from running away, and if he learned the dance song and prayers carried by the belt, he would always maintain the animals' respect. He then caught one of the Elk Dogs with a magic rope woven from the hair of a white buffalo bull, and rode home with the herd, never looking back along the way. He brought the animals to his tribe, and they never again had to struggle on foot to move their travois or hunt the buffalo. (See also *THE STRANGERS*)

I

THE HUPA are an Athapascan people of hunters and gatherers who once lived in the Hoopa Valley along the lower Trinity River in northwest California. Their most important foods were salmon and acorns, both abundant at different times during the year. Like the Northwest Coast peoples, they had concepts of wealth and private property, related to fishing grounds and oak groves. The tribe now occupies a small reservation within its ancient homeland.

HURON see under *WYANDOT*.

IKTOMI (*SIOUX*) is a *TRICKSTER*, the first son of *INYAN*. His mischief figures in a Dakota Sioux *CREATION* account. Waziya (Old Man) and his wife Wakanka, who lived beneath the earth, had a daughter, Ite, who was married to Tate (the Wind). Iktomi convinced her parents that, if they helped him play a prank on the other gods, Ite's beauty would rival that of Hanwi (the Moon). Iktomi gave Ite a charm that caused her to dwell more and more on her appearance and less and less on her sons (the Four Winds). Then, at a feast of the gods, Ite captivated Wi (the Sun) so much that he gave up his wife Hanwi's seat to her. Hanwi was humiliated. After a council, Skan (the Sky, and judge of gods and spirits) ruled that the Sun would lose the comfort of his wife, the Moon; he would rule in the day and she at night, and whenever they were together she would cover her face in shame.

IN THE JUMP DANCE, or Redheaded Woodpecker Dance, a world renewal ceremony, Hupa dancers wear headdresses of red woodpecker crests edged with deerskin and topped by a fringe of deer hair, large strings of dentalium shells, and deerskin robes, worn as kilts. The function of the straw-stuffed cylinders they carry is no longer known by modern Hupa. (PHOTOGRAPH BY E. S. CURTIS, C. 1896.)

THE INUIT [Alaskan, Central, Greenland], commonly known to outsiders as Eskimos (a pejorative Algonquian term meaning "eaters of raw meat"), occupy the Arctic regions of the continent, from Alaska to Greenland. They spread by sea from Siberia much later than other North American peoples, perhaps 5,000 years ago.

Inuit culture is relatively uniform, as all its peoples speak Eskimo-Aleut languages and share a harsh, mainly treeless environ-ment bordering the North Pacific Ocean, the Bering Sea and the Arctic Ocean. These regions all experience short summers and very long, dark and cold winters. Cultural differences relate to the proximity of Inuit groups to other peoples, including *ALEUTS* and North American Indians, and to variations in habitat, from the extreme northern polar regions to the edges of the boreal forest.

Alaskan groups include the Kodiak Island peoples, the Tikigaq and the Iñupiat. The Kobuk are a band of Iñupiat who live in western Alaska. The Nunamiut are an inland people subsisting mainly on caribou.

Central groups, occupying the Arctic mainland and island regions of Canada, include the Mackenzie, the Copper, the Netsilik, the Iglulik and the Baffin Island Inuit. They are the classic "Eskimos", who lived in igloos during the long Arctic winters and hunted for seal at breathing holes in ice floes, travelling by dog team and sled. The Caribou are an inland people who hunted caribou and fished the freshwater lakes and rivers northeast of Hudson Bay.

A GROUP OF INUIT ELDERS are wearing labrets (lip plugs). Alaskan and Mackenzie Delta Inuit carved these plugs in ivory, stone or other materials, and wore them as decorations.

The Greenland people include the Polar Inuit, who live along the Greenland coast north of Baffin Island. (See also *NEW GODS, NEW MYTHOLOGIES, THE DARK SIDE*)

INYAN (*SIOUX*), or Rock, is the ancestor of all things. Inyan was a soft, unformed mass, imbued with power, but alone. So he opened his veins and created Maka, the earth. As his blood was blue, it flowed over Maka, making the sky and the waters. The loss of blood made Inyan shrink and become hard, and he lost his power.

THE IOWA (Paxoje), a Siouan culture, originated in the region south of the Great Lakes, but eventually joined the tribal movement west as buffalo hunting became a major form of subsistence. Their tribal name is Paxoje, which means Dusty Noses, but they refer to themselves in English as Ioway. During the 1870s, the tribe split in two: some members accepted individual allotments near the Missouri River along the Kansas–Nebraska border (now a reservation) while others travelled to Indian Territory (now Oklahoma) and lived on common land. The latter group gained a reservation in 1883 but, after the Dawes Act of 1887, the government opened it up to white settlers as part of the 1889 Oklahoma Land Run. Today they control approximately 80 ha (200 acres) of Federal trust lands, scattered in north-central Oklahoma. The two groups are now separate and, like all other Native American nations, are threatened by assimilation – through decline in the number of native speakers, a small and frag-mented land base, intermarriage with whites and the ideological and economic impact of the dominant American culture.

IQIASUAK (Nunamiut *INUIT*) was a man who willingly transformed himself into a caribou

K

because he was lazy and could not face the responsibilities of human life. He was eventually killed by an equally lazy hunter who failed to butcher him properly, forgetting to detach the skull from the atlas vertebrae. This imprisoned his soul in the skull, and he could only watch helplessly as the spirits of the other caribou escaped so that they could be reincarnated. Eventually, another hunter came along and, attracted by the rack of antlers, detached the vertebrae, so freeing Iqiasuak's soul.

THE IROQUOIS [Haudeno-saunee] are five Iroquoian-speaking tribes – Mohawk, Oneida, Onondaga, Cayuga and Seneca – who controlled a large territory east of Lakes Ontario and Erie in the north-east woodlands. They were horticulturalists, who raised corn (maize), squash and beans, supplemented by hunting and gathering, in the temperate open woodlands of the region. Their habitations were distinctive communal longhouses, made of bent saplings covered with bark, which extended up to 91 m (300 feet).

In the 17th century, they were allied in a confederacy given supernatural sanction by the unifying exploits of the CULTURE HERO

A CARVED WOODEN MASK with braided horsehair was used by members of the False Face Society of the Iroquois during curing (world renewal) ceremonies. Dancers wore such masks to invoke the spirits and gain protection for the tribe.

CARIBOU (genus rangifer), which feature in the Iquiasak story, live in the tundra and boreal forest margins of Canada and Alaska.

DEGANAWIDA. The Tuscarora, a related tribe occupying present-day North Carolina, joined the alliance in the 18th century, creating the Six Nations Confederacy. The alliance fell apart during the American Revolution, as the tribes could not agree which side to support. Many Iroquois settled after the war on the Six Nations Reserve near Brantford, Ontario, while the rest moved to the Buffalo Creek Reservation in New York State. Each group has its own confederacy council. (See also *DEATH AND AFTERLIFE, THE STRANGERS*)

JESUS CHRIST (Chiricahua *APACHE*) and his Resurrection have influenced an account of the departure of the culture hero *CHILD-OF-THE-WATER* from the earth. At the end of his journeys, Child-of-the-Water visited his mother's birthplace, where he was killed and put in a cave blocked by a big stone; he had a large spear wound in his left side. His mother, *WHITE-PAINTED WOMAN*, cried outside the cave, and heard him say that he would see her again. On the third day he rose into the sky and, when the people moved back the big stone, the cave was empty.

JESUS THE TRAVELLER (interior *SALISH*) is a substitute for the traditional *TRANSFORMER*, Hwan, in one *CHEHALIS* story-teller's narrative. Jesus the Traveller teaches people to make wedges and mauls for splitting wood, better ways to catch salmon, transforms monsters, and drops fish bones into rivers, creating salmon, suckers and trout.

KACHINAS (*HOPI*) are the gods who live unseen and participate in human affairs. They are similar to spirits of the dead, for the Hopi believe that those who have led a proper life come back as Kachinas. They usually reside at springs and travel about in the clouds, and, because of their association with water, the people pray to them for rain. Hopis say that they must represent the Kachinas by masked dancers and votive dolls because the real Kachinas have abandoned them, the result of Hopi transgressions.

KÁNEKELAK (*KWAKIUTL*) is a character who figures in a variation of the widespread mythological theme of *HEROIC CHILDREN*.

Kánekelak and his younger brother had selfish parents who mistreated them. While the children starved, the parents feasted on ever larger catches of salmon. When Kánekelak discovered their

secret, he threw his father into the air, turning him into a heron, and transformed his mother into a red-headed woodpecker. To protect his brother, now named Only One, he built him an enormous house, left him four whales to eat, and went out into the world. He slew monsters, transformed the dangerous animal people into the animals of today,

KACHINA DANCERS carve small replicas of the kachina gods called tihu and give them to females, especially girls nearing marriage. The effigies are invested with Kachina spirit, so they are kept in the house, where they are attached to the walls or rafters.

met the ancestors of the Kwakiutl *CLANS*, and at last returned to the house to find that his brother had long ago starved to death, leaving only a pile of dry bones. Kánekelak revived Only One with the water of life and then sent him to live out his days in the north, while he himself retired to the south.

KARARIWARI see *POLARIS*.

THE KARUK (Karok) people are a Hokan-speaking tribe who occupied the central part of the Klamath River basin in northwestern California, subsisting by salmon-fishing, hunting and gathering. They gradually dispersed under pressure from incoming white settlers, losing almost all their territory. Today, they have a very small land base in the region, but continue to pursue aspects of their traditional culture.

KATS (*TLINGIT*) is the protagonist in a Tékwedi *CLAN* crest origin myth. Kats, a member of the Tékwedi clan, married a grizzly-*BEAR* woman, and they had both human children and bear children. When he refused to feed his bear children, the bears killed him, and the Tékwedi, in response, claimed the grizzly crest to display on their *TOTEM POLES* and houses.

KERES see *PUEBLO*.

THE KICKAPOO people are an Algonquian tribe who originated in the woodlands south of the lower Great Lakes. Here, they carried on a typical seasonal round of hunting, fishing, gathering and some horticulture. In 1819, many bands of Kickapoo were pushed out of their homelands, between the Wabash and Illinois rivers in Illinois and Indiana, to accommodate veterans of the War of 1812. Several bands resisted, however. Among them, the chief Mecina and his band fought back, but they were forced across the Mississippi by the military after months of fighting. Another chief, Kennekuk (who was also a prophet, preaching a return to traditional ways), managed to resist peacefully until the end of the Black Hawk War in 1832. The forced migrations and dispersals scattered tribal groups across the states of Indiana, Illinois, Missouri and Texas.

KIOWA GIRLS and a baby are all prepared for an important ceremony. The girls wear fringed, painted deerskin, and the baby carrier is elaborately decorated with quillwork and trade beads.

By the turn of the 20th century, the Kickapoo were divided into two groups, one in Oklahoma, Texas and Mexico, the other in Kansas. The Kansas Kickapoo, removed there from Illinois in 1832, occupy a reservation that the government gradually reduced from 310,000 to 8,100 ha (768,000 to 20,000 acres), less than half of it under tribal control. The Kickapoo to the south live on small land allotments. Although now politically separated, the tribes continue to maintain a common religion.

THE KIOWA tribe are a hunting and gathering people who speak a Kiowan-Tanoan language. They migrated to the southern plains from the mountainous regions to the northwest, near the headwaters of the Yellowstone River in present-day Montana, attracted by the vast buffalo herds. After fierce resistance to

white settlement in the 1860s and 1870s, the survivors were removed to the Kiowa-Comanche-Apache Reservation in southwest Oklahoma but, in 1900, the government broke up this reservation and allotted less than 20 per cent of the land to the tribes. They continue to occupy these Federal trust lands.

KIVAS (*HOPI*) are semi-subterranean chambers, usually circular, used for ceremonies and as gathering places. In the kiva is the *SIPAPU*, the symbolic centre of the world. The kiva is a focus of community activity. *KACHINA* dancers practise there and hold dance performances, and the Flute and Snake societies (see *SECRET SOCIETIES*) hold meetings. Men and boys may weave there and make kachina dolls and bows and arrows, and women hold their own special rites.

THIS ANCIENT PETROGLYPH
(rock carving) is said to represent the hunchbacked flute-player Kokopelli. It is located near Galisteo, New Mexico.

A CIRCULAR MASONRY structure at Pueblo del Arroyo, Chaco Canyon, New Mexico. The Anasazi people, ancestors of modern Pueblo tribes, built the pueblo between c. 1065 and 1140. Although no evidence remains of use, the structure probably served as a kiva (a Hopi word meaning "ceremonial house").

KLAMATH See under *MODOC*.

KOKOPELLI (*PUEBLO*), the so-called humpbacked flute player, is widely represented in prehistoric rock art and on pottery. Since his phallus is often prominently displayed in such depictions, he is speculatively associated with fertility, and has become a popular symbol outside traditional native religion. Among the *HOPI* he has also become a contemporary *KACHINA*, associated with seduction, procreation and hunting.

KOMOL See under *MUSP*.

THE KOOTENAY (Kutenai), whose name means "water people", lived along the eastern flanks of the Columbia Plateau, to the east of the Rocky Mountains, where they fished for trout and sturgeon in the lakes and rivers, hunted elk, deer and other forest game, and gathered food plants in season. Linguists generally regard their language as an isolate (meaning that it is unconnected to any other known language group), but some theorize that it may possibly be related to Algonquian. The Kootenay now occupy small reservations and

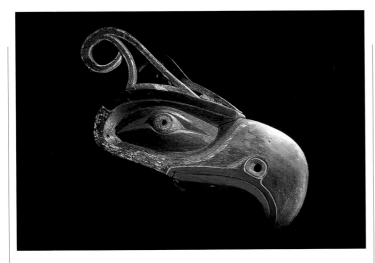

allotments in southeast British Columbia and adjoining parts of Montana, Idaho and Washington.

KUTOYIS see BLOOD CLOT.

THE KWAKIUTL (Kwakwa-ka'wakw) are a Wakashan-speaking people who occupy northern Vancouver Island and the adjoining mainland. As inhabitants of the Pacific coast, with its rich diversity of deep-sea, coastal and inland food resources, the Kwakiutl developed a social structure more typical of a complex agricultural society, with ranked social classes and private property. They underwent the depredations typically suffered by tribes in the region, being decimated by smallpox and other diseases and harassed by missionaries. They remain, however, in parts of their original homeland and continue to pursue many of their traditional cultural practices, including a dramatic art style, expressed in the carving of TOTEM POLES, masks and other ceremonial objects, and elaborate ceremonials, all celebrating the mythological heroes and events of their past. (See also THE DARK SIDE)

KYÁLKO (ZUNI), the messenger god, brings to the people the story of emergence from out of the underworld every four years. He acts through the Kyálko impersonator, who recreates this central narrative as part of a young man's puberty ceremony.

KWAKIUTL artists create deeply carved and brightly painted wooden masks that lend great drama to the dances of the winter ceremonial season. This thunderbird headdress, dating to before 1920, is identified by its down-turned beak and horns. A dancer used it in the "Tsayeka" or red cedar bark dance series.

LAKOTA see SIOUX.

LANDSCAPE and the shape of the physical world reinforces the reality of traditional ideas about the past and acts as a permanent storage place for tribal memories.

When the Chiricahua APACHE CULTURE HERO CHILD-OF-THE-WATER killed a giant who was encased in four jackets of flint, the monster fell over four mountain ridges. The rocks still show where he fell – probably in the form of outcrops of flint (actually chert), which prehistoric peoples valued highly as a source of raw material for their tools. One can ride a horse through Child-of-the-Water's bones, and the ashes of the fire that he and his companion, Killer-of-Enemies, made when the giant disturbed them are still visible on the ground.

THE GRANITE MONOLITH of El Capitan in Yosemite National Park, California, stands like a massive sentinel at the entrance to the Yosemite Valley. Its sheer cliffs drop more than 915 m (3,000 feet). The effect is visually and spiritually overwhelming, making this an important part of the cultural landscape of the Sierra Miwok who settled here.

Mountains are very commonly the subject of origin stories. The YOSEMITE (Sierra Miwok) explain the origin of Tutokanula (today known as El Capitan, a large mountain in Yosemite National Park) as a supernatural event triggered by two young and curious adventurers who often ranged far from home. One day these boys found a new lake, so they decided to swim across to a large rock on the other side. They climbed the rock and fell asleep in the sun on the top, but, strangely, continued to sleep through the night and the next day, and for a long time after that. As they slept, the rock grew higher and higher until it became a huge granite mountain that brushed the sky. The boys eventually awoke to find themselves trapped. When the animals heard of the plight of the boys, they decided to try and save them. Each tried to jump to the mountain top: the mouse jumped a foot, the rat two feet, the raccoon higher, and the grizzly BEAR and mountain lion higher still, but none of them could succeed. Then the tiny measuring-worm decided to give it a try. Little by little, he inched up the mountain until at last he reached the summit. He found the boys, and led them on a great slide down the snowy slopes back to their tribe.

LENNI LENAPE see DELAWARE.

LITTLE PEOPLE are most commonly dwarfish beings who inhabit places outside camps and settlements and tend to cause mischief.

OJIBWAY travellers may see little people (the Maymaygwaysiwuk) paddling their stone canoes or playing along large cliffs. They live in the rocks and come and go through cracks and crevices, and one must always be on guard for them. The WYANDOT say they are old enough to remember the Flood, and the PASSAMAQUODDY believe they were here before GLUSKAP. In a MICMAC tale, the little people (Pukalutumush) are identified as the creators of petroglyphs.

The Tewa PUEBLO envisage their TWIN war gods, who were monster-slayers, as Towa É, which translates as "little people".

LODGE is a general term used to describe a permanent native dwelling. In the Great Plains, the earthlodge is a dome-shaped structure with a log frame. It is covered with earth or sods, and its floors are dug below ground level. The term may also be used to refer to other similar dwellings, such as tepees, which are covered with bark, skins or woven mats, and certain ceremonial structures.

L

THE DARK SIDE

MONSTERS EXIST in mythology to give shape and meaning to the unknown, the dangerous and the unwanted. Many story-tellers describe how, when the earth was still young, terrible creatures raged across the land, threatening the fragile harmony of human and animal beings in the new world. By the act of destroying these monsters, supernatural beings created the heroic, defined the limits of good and evil, and established supernatural power as an overwhelming force. But, while cosmic beasts disappeared, other dangerous creatures retreated only to the margins of the world, lurking just beyond familiar horizons, in the darkness or deep under water. Some of these are fearsome apparitions and the stuff of nightmare: bodiless heads or hideously deformed animals. Others, including many of the "little people" that travellers encounter, cause accidents and other irritations in daily life. Still others, such as the great horned serpents who live under lakes and rivers in Algonquian territory, have the capacity for positive as well as negative acts. This acknowledgement of life's dark side resolves the fundamental contradiction of nature – that it is at one time both a nurturing and a destructive force.

A THUNDERBIRD sits atop a modern Kwakiutl totem pole. The association of thunder and lightning with giant birds may come from the way a thunderstorm soars across the sky, spreading dark squall lines across the horizon under a dark central mass, pierced by flashing light.

MISHIPIZHEU (left), the great horned serpent, is painted in red ochre on a sheer granite cliff overlooking Agawa Bay, Lake Superior. Travellers appeased this powerful manitou with prayers and offerings so that he would keep the waters calm as they passed.

A PLUMED SERPENT (below left) rises from the desert rocks of the Galisteo Basin, south of Santa Fe, New Mexico. Tewa people inhabited this region from the late 13th century until the Pueblo Revolt in 1680. Their abundant rock art still speaks of the powerful spiritual forces in the desert landscape.

THE IMAGE (below) of a mountain lion is etched into a slab of sandstone in northeastern Arizona's Painted Desert by an unknown prehistoric artist. The most dangerous forces in the spiritual world usually took the form of the most dangerous animals in real life.

PALRAIUK (below) the sea monster, gorged with the partly dismembered remains of one unfortunate victim, chases a kayak, seeking more prey. This Yupik walrus ivory engraving expresses the wariness of the Inuit whale hunter in the unpredictable Arctic seas.

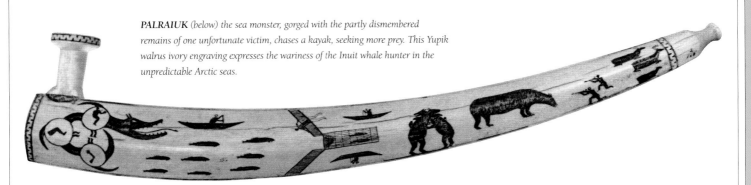

M

LODGE BOY AND THROWN AWAY

LODGE BOY AND THROWN AWAY are the main characters in the *HIDATSA* version of a story cycle about heroic *TWINS* that is told throughout the Plains.

The cycle begins with a pregnant woman inviting a stranger into her *LODGE* while her husband is away. In some versions the stranger is Double Face, a monster with eyes, nose and mouth on the back of his head. The woman offers to serve food to her guest, and he convinces her that he must have it served on her abdomen. When she complies, he cuts through the meat into her body, killing her and delivering her twin sons. He throws one in a spring and keeps one in the lodge. When the woman's husband returns, the monster flees, leaving one child and the body of the wife behind. The man buries his wife and raises Lodge Boy. The other child, Thrown Away, only comes in to eat while the father is away. At last, the man captures Thrown Away, and takes the wildness out of him by burning incense in his nose. The twins then go about slaying monsters, including Double Face. In a *WICHITA* version, the father goes to live in the sky, and the twins follow when their work is done. The *SARCEE*, *BLACKFOOT*, *GROS VENTRE* and *ARAPAHO* join this story with another on the life of *DIRTY BOY*.

LONE MAN

LONE MAN (*MANDAN*) was the companion of First Creator, who was responsible for the beginning of the cosmos. The two creators made the earth from mud brought from the primeval sea by Duck, and populated it with all living things. Lone Man's later exploits included the release of buffalo from the control of Speckled *EAGLE*, the rescue of the Mandan from a world flood by building a watertight stockade around the village, and the imprisonment, in a tomb of black rock, of the monster-slayer Foolish Doer, who was too frightening to remain in the company of human beings.

IN A COMING OF AGE ceremony in a Mandan earthlodge village, the young initiates, dragging bison skulls attached to their flesh, are each supported by two dancers as they run around a sacred "ark". This was the end of the Okipa, a four-day religious ceremony that renewed tribal spirit and ensured a plentiful supply of buffalo for the year. (PAINTING BY GEORGE CATLIN, 1832.)

When his work was done, Lone Man left for the south, whence he communicates as the south wind.

LOON WOMAN

LOON WOMAN, according to a myth among peoples of northern California, attempted to commit incest and, in so doing, caused a world fire. One day, she saw a long hair floating on the water (or found it in a comb) and was enthralled by it. In order to discover its owner, she compared it to the hair of her ten brothers and, finding that it was from the eldest brother's head, fell hopelessly in love with him. She secretly lay with him while camping and he, horrified, freed himself and put a rotten log in his place. To escape the horror of her act, he ran home and ordered his family to jump into a basket that would carry them into the sky. But the sister awoke, saw the rising basket and set fire to the family's lodge. Unfortunately, while the basket was still rising, *COYOTE*, who had happened by, peered over the edge; the basket fell and the family perished in the flames. The sister gathered up the victims' blackened hearts and wore them as a necklace – seen as the black neck-band of the common loon (great northern diver).

LOST-ACROSS-THE-OCEAN

LOST-ACROSS-THE-OCEAN is a *CULTURE HERO* of the *YUROK*, *HUPA*, *KARUK* and *WIYOT* of northwestern California.

The Hupa say he sprang from earth, released deer and salmon, instituted childbirth, created landscape features and instituted the Jumping Dance to counteract disease. After killing cannibals and transforming cannibal soap-roots into food, he created tribes by defecation. When his work was done, he crossed the ocean, and lives beyond the end of the sky.

THE LUISEÑO

THE LUISEÑO people are an Uto-Aztecan-speaking tribe that once occupied a large area of coastal southern California within the San Luis Rey and Santa Margarita River basins. They lived on the abundant marine life of the warm Pacific coastal waters and harvested acorns from the oak-covered coastal hills. In 1891, the Act for the Relief of the Mission Indians established five Luiseño reservations, some of which included traditional farmland. Today, the people living near the rivers run successful orchard operations, and have market gardens and domesticated animals. Those in the drier inlands, where water is very often scarce, are limited by their surroundings to relying on subsistence farming.

MAHTIGWESS

MAHTIGWESS see *HARES*.

THE MAIDU

THE MAIDU [Northeast, Northwest, Valley], speakers of Penutian languages, live in the northeastern interior of California. The Northeast Maidu, Northwest Maidu (once known as the Digger), and Valley Maidu all speak separate languages. They are fishers, hunters and gatherers who share cultural traits with the more northerly Northwest Coast peoples, as well as with adjacent Plateau and Great Basin groups. Although they were dispersed before the 20th century, they now have a small land base within their traditional territory.

THE MAKAH

THE MAKAH live on the Olympic Peninsula, south of Vancouver Island. They are the most southerly of the Wakashan-speakers, and so are related to the *NOOTKA* and *KWAKIUTL*. Like other Northwest Coast peoples, they hunted, fished and gathered in the midst of abundant natural resources. The Makah were highly skilled hunters of sea mammals, pursuing whales and fur seals in the open sea. The Treaty of Neah Bay established the Makah Reservation in 1855. One of their original village settlements, at Ozette, near the northwestern tip of the Olympic Peninsula, was partly buried in a mudslide some 500 years ago and rediscovered in the 1960s. The mud had preserved the remains of the cedar-plank houses in the village, and all the tools and other material goods used in the course of daily life.

THE MALISEET

THE MALISEET (Malecite) are an Algonquian people who hunted, fished and gathered along the rivers of southern New Brunswick and adjoining parts of northern Maine. The seasonal rhythm took them

THIS MEDICINE BUNDLE and small whistle was worn by a warrior of a Great Plains tribe around his neck to give him spiritual power.

from interior to coast, giving them access to a great diversity of food resources, including moose, deer and beaver, fish and waterfowl, clams and other shellfish, and seals and porpoises. During the 18th century, they joined the WABANAKI confederacy. They now occupy reservations in New Brunswick, Maine and Quebec.

MANABUSH, MANABOZHO
see NANABUSH.

THE MANDAN
are a Siouan people who lived along the Missouri River, near its confluence with the Knife River in North Dakota, in large villages of earthlodges (see LODGE). They raised squash, corn (maize), sunflowers and tobacco along the fertile and moist flood plains of the river and its tributaries. They also hunted buffalo, which provided them with essen-

MÁTO-TÓPE, or Four Bears (c. 1795–1837), was a highly respected military and religious leader among the Mandan. He was given his name after a skirmish with the Assiniboine, in which he fought with especially great ferocity.

tial meat and hides for clothing. Along with their traditional allies, the HIDATSA and the ARIKARA, the Mandan share the Fort Berthold Reservation in North Dakota.

MANITOU
is an Algonquian term, used primarily by the OJIBWAY to describe the most powerful supernatural beings, as well as the all-pervasive spiritual essence they symbolize. This personification, from the great spirit Gitchi-Manitou (or Kitchi-, or Chi-) to the numerous spirit-beings who dwell in the Ojibway landscape, sets it apart from the other Native American concepts of immanent power,

such as the SIOUX "wakan" and the IROQUOIS "orenda".

MASAWU
(HOPI) is the KACHINA who greeted the first people as they emerged from the underworld. The kachina dancer charged with impersonating this god does so by wearing a skeleton mask with enormous white eye sockets.

MASTAMHO
see BROTHER GODS.

THE MASTER/MISTRESS OF ANIMALS
is a god or spirit who controls animals (see also MOTHER OF ANIMALS). This being may be a central figure in the culture's belief system (such as Sedna, the SEA MOTHER of the INUIT) or a malicious spirit who captures either all the animals or a crucial game animal species, thus causing the people to starve until a hero sets the animals free.

In an UTE scenario, all the animal people were short of food except for the Crows, who always seemed to have plenty to eat. No one knew where the buffalo had gone, but the Crows had a vast tent that they would not let anyone else look into. As soon as someone peeped in, CROW would poke something in their eye. Finally, Darning Needle went to look; he was so slim that, when Crow poked something through the peephole, it went right by, and Darning Needle discovered Crow's secret: he had captured all the buffalo. The animals had a council and made a plan for releasing them. Weasel transformed himself into a dog and remained in the area, while the rest of the people broke camp and left; the Crow children found the dog and took it back to their camp. When the Crows were asleep, Weasel let all the buffalo out.

As the plenitude of animals depends on the will of gods or heroes, people ever after must pay due respect to the animal spirits in order to be sure of a continuing

supply of food. This is why hunters set aside time before, during and after the hunt to ensure that the proper rituals, prayers and procedures are carried out, as the CREE do in their BEAR RITUALS.

MASTSHINGKE
see under HARES.

MATAVILYA
see BROTHER GODS.

MEDICINE
is a translation of various concepts related to spiritual efficacy. Medicine is invested in an object or substance used in curing or in some other beneficial way. Native people do not attribute its power to its pharmaceutical properties – it may have none – but to its capacity to harness and direct spiritual forces. Hence, a herb or other substance, or a sacred smoking PIPE or other object, may provide, or be, good medicine.

THE MENOMINEE people are an Algonquian tribe who lived in the forests between Lake Michigan and Lake Superior, where they hunted deer, bear and other forest game, fished the lakes and rivers, and gathered wild rice, roots, berries and other plant foods. Their name means "wild rice people". The tribe once occupied over 3.6 million ha (9 million acres) of land in present-day central and mideastern Wisconsin and part of the Upper Peninsula of Michigan. Their reservation was established in 1854, leaving the tribe with only 94,700 ha (234,000 acres) of land.

MESQUAKI see FOX.

THE MICMAC (Mi'kmaq) are a hardy seagoing people who originally occupied most of present-day Nova Scotia, northern New Brunswick, part of northern Maine, and southern Newfoundland. They were among the first tribes to be contacted by Europeans and their missionaries, at the beginning of the 17th century. During the 18th century, they joined the WABANAKI confederacy. They pursued the nomadic hunting, fishing and gathering life typical of maritime Algonquian tribes, moving in a seasonal round between the interior, where they hunted moose, deer and other small game, and the coast, where they paddled their ocean-going canoes in the open waters of the Atlantic in pursuit of whales and porpoises. The tribe has a number of small reservations in Nova Scotia, New Brunswick, Maine, Quebec and Newfoundland. (See also THE STRANGERS, NEW GODS)

THE MIDÉWIWIN, or Grand MEDICINE Society, was an organization of SHAMANS devoted to curing disease. It flourished among the OJIBWAY and other Great Lakes Algonquians during the 19th and early 20th centuries. It was a

THE MILKY WAY is an important astronomical configuration for a number of different tribes. Many believe it is the pathway to another world.

SECRET SOCIETY, open to men and women, who worked their way through a number of degrees (levels of attainment), which incorporated beliefs, rituals and curing techniques of increasing complexity. Midé shamans engraved or painted birch-bark scrolls with pictographic records of their origin myths, ceremonies and songs. There are still adherents to the Midéwiwin philosophy practising today, though the organization is no longer central to the religious activities of the people.

THE MILKY WAY, the white arch of stars that dominates the moonless night sky, has inspired many theories about its origin.

The Mescalero APACHE, who call it the Scattered Stars, believe that one of the TWIN War Gods dropped a container of seeds during a fight with his brother, and the seeds scattered across the sky. Many peoples believe that the Milky Way is a pathway to a sky world or to the land of the dead. The SEMINOLE explain that their creator, Breath-maker, blew into the sky, and the vapour from his breath made a pathway leading to the City of the West. This is where the good souls go, carried there by the Big Dipper. (See also THE LIVING SKY)

MINK, a rather disreputable TRICKSTER popular in Northwest Coast narratives, is a useful foil for RAVEN. He is generally involved in sordid intrigues with women, most of which end in disaster.

MISHIPIZHEU (OJIBWAY), a horned serpent, lives under lakes and rivers. Mishipizheu (literally, "Great Lynx") is a very important spiritual presence in Ojibway culture. Unlike many other monsters, his status is closer to that of a god, for he exercises power over the vast network of lakes and rivers within Ojibway lands in the Canadian Shield (north of the Great Lakes).

In some accounts, he was responsible for the primordial flood. He occupies caverns and tunnels beneath the lakes, so he is able to travel easily anywhere in the region. He is said to stir up the waters of lakes and turn rivers into dangerous rapids to drown people – it is therefore wise to leave a bit of tobacco or some other small offering when one enters a lake that might be one of Mishipizheu's many lairs. When he travels on the land, he crawls like a giant leech,

saturating the ground and leaving swamps and quicksand behind.

The Ojibway of the Lake Temagami region of northern Ontario describe him as the source of all snakes. When he was crossing a lake, a bolt of lightning shattered him, and all the pieces turned into small snakes: the ancestors of all the snakes of today.

He may also provide MEDICINE, but is so dangerous that his power can even overwhelm SHAMANS. In one incident, a shaman dreamed that if he struck the water with a stick and sang a special song the spirits would reward him. He did so, but, as he struck the water, it erupted into a violent whirlpool, and the great serpent rose up to confront him. The man boldly (and greedily) asked the creature for medicine to make him healthy, rich and prosperous. Mishipizheu lowered his head, and the shaman saw a bright red substance similar to red ochre (or copper – Mishipizheu was the guardian of native copper mines on the shores of Lake Superior) between his horns. The man scraped this medicine into a piece of birch bark, and the serpent told him how to use it. For a time, the medicine worked, and the man prospered, but in fact he paid a terrible price – eventually his wife and children died, and he lived out his wretched life poor and alone. (See also THE DARK SIDE)

THE MIWOK (Me-wuk) [Coastal, Lake, Valley] are a Penutian-speaking people who lived in three distinctive ecological zones in central California. The Coastal Miwok settled on the central California coast, while the Lake and Valley Miwok (including the Sierra Miwok, who live in the mountains to the east) occupied the interior. They had a sophisticated preservation technology, storing the masses of acorns they gathered in granaries of woven branches and grass, suspended above the ground. The coastal people had the most diverse food supply, as they had access to shellfish and other sea creatures, in addition to the freshwater fish, deer, other small game, acorns and other plant foods along the lakes and rivers. They were heavily affected by European contact from the 16th century onwards – in 1578 they encountered the English explorer, Sir Francis Drake.

Over the centuries, the Miwok suffered disease, missionizing and, after the discovery of gold in the region in 1848, death at the hands of prospectors and settlers. They resisted for a short time, but their rebellion was crushed in 1851, and they were forcibly removed to several *rancherias* (small reservations) in their traditional territory.

MOAPA see under *PAIUTE*.

THE MODOC, speakers of a Penutian language, once occupied the rugged mountains of the Cascade Range along the Oregon–California border, where they fished the rivers for salmon, gathered roots in the drier uplands, and hunted small game. The regionally important sacred site, Mt Shasta, was once part of their homeland.

The Modoc lost their lands as a result of the Council Grove Treaty of 1864, and were removed to the Klamath Reservation in Oregon, which they shared with the Klamath (a closely related and culturally similar tribe) and the *PAIUTE*. In the late 1860s, discontent with their treatment by the Klamath provoked a group of Modoc under Kintpuash (known as Captain Jack) to leave the reservation and return to their homeland. The United States military crushed the renegades in 1872–3. They executed Kintpuash and three of his followers, and exiled the rest to the Quapaw Agency in Indian Territory (the Quapaw being an unrelated tribe who once lived in the area of present-day Arkansas). Soon after the

execution, grave robbers disinterred Kintpuash's body and displayed the remains in a carnival in the eastern states. The two Modoc groups, based in Oregon and Oklahoma, are now politically and culturally separate.

MOHAWK see *IROQUOIS*.

THE MOJAVE (Mohave), speakers of a Yuman language, live along the Colorado River and in the Colorado basin in Arizona and California. They grow corn (maize) and beans on river flood plains, net fish and gather mesquite and other plant foods. Unlike most other aboriginal groups, the Mojave continue to occupy part of their traditional homelands – largely because their semi-desert environ-

A MOJAVE female doll is decorated with face paint and wears trade bead earrings and necklaces.

ment had little economic value for the incoming white people, but also because the tribe resisted relocation to reservations.

MOMOY (*CHUMASH*) is a grandmother who gives help to child monster-slayers. The word is the same as that for the hallucinogenic drug, toloache, made from datura, or jimsonweed. In one account relating to the use of the drug in a tribal rite, the grandmother washed her hands in a bowl of water and gave it to her grandson to drink so that he could become braver.

MONDAMIN (Southern *OJIBWAY*) is the male corn spirit, who generates corn from his body.

THE MONTAGNAIS [Innu], an Algonquian hunting and gathering people, live in the vast boreal forests of central Quebec, where they range in small bands, following the seasonal patterns of moose, deer and other game, fish, wildfowl and wild plants. They were heavily involved in the French fur trade,

THE MOON is portrayed on this wooden mask which is carved in the typical Tsimshian style of smooth, restrained facial modelling, with subdued colours and a lifelike finish.

beginning in the 17th century, and hence were one of the first tribes to be described by Europeans. While the fur-trade economy forever altered the tribe's way of life, their remoteness has helped them to retain much of their traditional culture. They are now joined with the *NASKAPI* and collectively known as the Innu.

MONTEZUMA see *POSAYAMO*.

THE MOON, with its prominence in the sky, its predictable phases and its relationship with the sun, has inspired a wide variety of mythical interpretations.

To the Coast *SALISH*, Moon is a *TRANSFORMER*, born of the union of a woman and a star, who gave the people salmon, and other fish and game (see *STAR HUSBAND*). To the *MAIDU*, he is a rather villainous *TRICKSTER* who steals children.

THE TRICKSTER

THE CREATIVE BEINGS responsible for the complex texture of North American cultures established methods for living that enabled people to thrive over thousands of years. Yet humans must always face the tension between appropriate and inappropriate thoughts and actions, reflecting the vagaries of a natural world that both sustains life and takes it. Mirroring this reality, transformers and culture heroes were quixotically human, with the same lusts, desires and foibles as the people they would create. Raven brought daylight to the Tsimshian, for example, by tricking an old chief who kept it in a box on the Nass River. Raven became a spruce needle, entered the chief's daughter in a drink of water, impregnated her, was born,

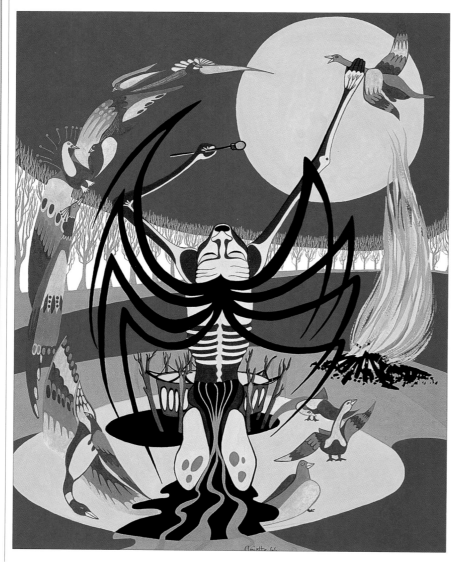

and then, as a small child, took the box at an unguarded moment, quickly changing back to his original self and flying off with his prize. This was no altruistic act: he released the daylight in anger, after some fishing people refused him a feed of *oolichan* (a smelt-like fish, very high in fat). By giving the tricksters human capacities and imperfections, and by treating creation as the incidental acts of great beings pursuing their own agendas, the story-tellers wisely create realistic parallels between life as it is lived and its origins.

THE SPIDER-LIKE TRICKSTER *Iktomi is part of the essence of the Siouan world, at once graceful like the sweep of birds though the sky and jagged as a leafless tree, a singer of songs and a crafty predator. (PAINTING BY OGLALA LAKOTA ARTIST ARTHUR AMIOTTE.)*

THE WOLVERINE (left), the largest member of the weasel family, is a ferocious scavenger that feeds mainly off dead animals. It can quickly devastate the food caches crucial to the survival of the northern forest peoples. To fit its reputation as a glutton, it may also attack and kill other mammals and even caribou – especially if such animals are injured or weakened by winter hunger.

RAVEN (above) releases the sun from its box. The raven is a worthy trickster – black, portly and strutting, with large beak and bright, black eyes. In settlements, he is a crafty thief, like his cousin the crow, and he rules his patch of forest aggressively, watching for intruders from high in a tree. (SILK-SCREEN PRINT BY THE KWAKIUTL ARTIST CALVIN HUNT.)

THE COYOTE (left), grey and short-haired, is a creature ever-watchful on the boundaries of humankind, loping along a beach or skulking at the edge of a field by day, a ghostly shadow at dusk, and an eerie howl in the night.

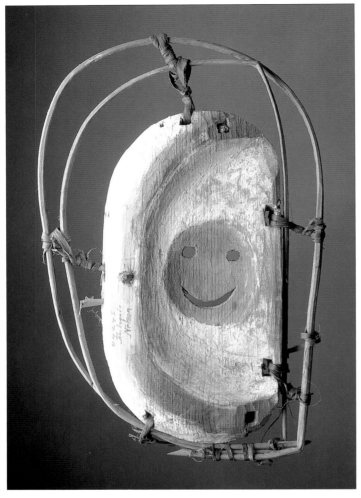

AN INUIT MASK represents a half moon. The hoops are the surrounding sky, and the face reveals the inua, *or spiritual essence, of this supernatural being.*

MOON MAN

MOON MAN (Alinnaq) (*INUIT*) interprets the close relationship of sun and moon as a dramatic tale of forbidden love and eternal longing.

A man, Alinnaq, secretly lusted after his sister. One night he slipped into her bed and had sex with her, and she, discovering the identity of the lover, cut off her breast, demanded that he eat it, and fled into the darkness with a torch of lamp moss. The brother followed with another torch, but he fell in the snow and the light was almost extinguished. They both rose into the sky, the sister becoming the sun and her brother the moon. He pursues her still and, when there is an eclipse, they say that he has caught her.

Alinnaq is the major deity in the western Arctic, among the Tikigaq and other Alaskan Iñupiat. He controls the game (replacing Sedna, the *MISTRESS OF ANIMALS* in the central and eastern Arctic), keeping a vast tub of whales and seals, and running herds of caribou around the inner walls of his igloo. *SHAMANS* confront Alinnaq in person when food is scarce. The most important ritual takes place during the spring, when whale hunters seek Alinnaq's help. During the climax of the ceremony, the women stand on their igloos as the moon rises, shout at the moon and raise pots of water blessed by the shaman towards the hole in the sky that connects the earth to the moon. If Alinnaq gets the water, he drops whale effigies made of lamp tar into the pots, and these become powerful hunting amulets.

MOON WIFE

MOON WIFE (*ALEUT*) is a character used to explain the different phases of the moon.

Two young women, fascinated by the moon, spent their nights making symbolic love to him by basking in his light in the shelter of a skin boat. Then one night he appeared to them as a young man. He told them that he would take the most patient of the two into the sky to be his wife – patience being necessary because the work in the sky was hard. As the three rose into the sky, one could not resist looking down, and she fell back to the boat. The other, who went to live in Moon's house (a *barrabara*, a timbered, earth-banked pit house), was frustrated and lonely. Her husband usually slept during the day and worked all night, but she could never be sure when he would come home, and he always refused her request to accompany him during his nightly tasks.

One night he permitted her to leave home so that she could amuse herself, but he warned her not to go into two particular *barrabara*, for each had a curtain under which she must never look. Predictably, she could not resist going into these forbidden places. In the first one, she raised the curtain and saw a half-moon, quarter-moon and a sliver of moon; in the second, she found a full moon, one almost full, and one more than half full. They were like masks, and when she tried to put one over her face, it stuck – so she could not hide her transgression from her husband. As the secret was out, he decided to let her help him. He would do his rounds with the full moon, and then she would take over, wearing the different phases, while he rested.

THE MOTHER OF ANIMALS

THE MOTHER OF ANIMALS gives birth to game or produces it from her body. Many cultures in the Arctic and Subarctic refer to animal mothers in their mythologies – examples of the universal mythological theme of the *MASTER/MISTRESS OF ANIMALS*.

The Kodiak Island *ALEUT* believe that a single young woman gave birth to all animals, one after another. The *HARE* tribe relate the story of Egg Woman who, after being abused by human males, became mother of the hares. In a *TAHLTAN* narrative, a pregnant woman, abandoned, gave birth to moose, caribou and other animals, thus becoming Atsentmá (meat mother). Sedna, the *SEA MOTHER* of the *INUIT*, begins as an unwanted woman. A man (commonly her father) throws her out of his boat and then chops off her fingers as she clings to the

MOTHER CORN and other earth deities were revered by the Navajo. This 19th-century rug depicts yei figures, earth spirits associated with the fertility of corn. Such images are properly made as sand paintings, but they are too sacred to be exposed to public view. Hence, Navajo artists translate the sand painting motifs into weavings and paintings.

N

gunwale. The fingers change into seals and walruses, and she sinks to the bottom and becomes the ruler of the animals of the sea. There she awaits the attention of *SHAMANS* seeking a plentiful food supply.

MOTHER CORN is the personification of the important corn (maize) plant as a goddess.

NISHANÚ NATCHITAK first made giants, but he eventually killed them because they mocked him. He planted some as corn kernels and drowned the rest in a world flood. He also planted corn in the sky; when it matured, he took an ear and turned it into Mother Corn, who came down from the sky world to lead the new people (the *ARIKARA*) up out of the ground. A badger and a mole helped Mother Corn by burrowing upward through the earth. When they emerged, she led them westward past three obstacles (a chasm, a thick forest and a lake) and then departed for the sky. The people lacked order, however, and ended up fighting and killing one another, so Nishánu sent Mother Corn back with a man to be their leader. While she taught the people the proper rituals, the new leader showed them how to make war.

MOTHER EARTH and FATHER SKY (*NAVAJO*) are two cosmic beings, stretched out like a man lying on top of a woman. The space between them has several layers (air and then stars), and the stars are either attached to the sky or are hanging down from it. The concept of a Mother Earth and Father Sky, once absent from the oral traditions of many cultures, is now an integral part of modern pan-Indian religions.

MUDHEADS (*PUEBLO*) are sacred clowns. During mainly solemn ceremonials, the mudheads break the tension with ridiculous antics and silly pantomimes. They are not trivial characters, but rather holy people who play an integral role in the sacred rites.

In one *ZUNI* characterization, the Mudheads are not very bright, so a man tries to teach them a few simple tasks. When they try to climb a ladder, they get all tangled up. When they try to work out how

A YUPIK SEALSKIN MASK possibly used in a Bladder Festival (Nakaquik) to show respect to seals so that they would continue to let hunters kill them. The Yupik traditionally destroyed their dance masks after use – returning them to nature.

MUDHEADS, or koshares, are depicted tumbling madly down a ladder, upsetting the sober tone of a Hopi religious ceremony. Their general silliness opens the audience to important moral lessons, as they inevitably pay for their impudence. (THE DELIGHT MAKERS, PAINTING BY FRED KABOTIE.)

to sit on a chair, they attempt every way but the right way: one sits on top and tumbles off, another sits underneath, another backwards and another upside down. When they try to build a house, they start with the roof and then have to try to build downwards with several Mudheads holding it up. Then they build one from the inside, but it has no doors or windows, so they become trapped.

MUSP AND KOMOL (*CHINOOK*) are *TRANSFORMER TWINS* whose origin is explained in a variation of the *BEAR MOTHER* story.

A young woman abducted by a grizzly *BEAR* gave birth to a son and a daughter. Her brothers rescued her, and she eventually married a village chief. Unfortunately, since she happened to be a laughing monster and a devouring monster, she accidentally swallowed the whole village. When she coughed up her husband, he had lost his legs, so she hung him on the wall in a basket. Incredibly, she managed to conceive with him and bore two sons, the heroes. They seized their terrifying mother, shook her bones out of her skin and turned these into a dog, their faithful companion. After teaching people how to catch salmon, dig shellfish and hunt whales, the *TWINS* turned into boulders that are still visible today.

NAKAQUIK (*INUIT*), the Bladder Festival, is a winter solstice ceremony in which the bladders of animals killed during the year are ritually returned to the sea (and to Sedna) to ensure abundant game.

NAKOTA see *SIOUX*.

NANABUSH is the principal *CULTURE HERO* and *TRANSFORMER* of the *OJIBWAY*. He is known by several different names, including Manabush, Manabozho, Nanabozho, Wenebojo and Winabojo. This is the result of dialect variation across Ojibway culture. The *MENOMINEE*, close relatives of the Ojibway, call him Menapus, or "Big Rabbit" (see *HARES*). He shares many attributes and story types with the hero of Algonquian tribes south of the Great Lakes, known as *WISAKEDJAK* or Wisaka, and the hero of north-eastern coastal Algonquians, *GLUSKAP*. He also appears in the *WALAM OLUM* of the *DELAWARE* peoples.

Nanabush is a highly complex figure, combining the attributes of culture hero, transformer and *TRICKSTER*. He gave the northern landscape its character and created many living things, fought evil *MANITOUS* and brought to the Ojibway the defining elements of their culture. In a *MIDÉWIWIN* society story of *CREATION*, Nanabush made men from earth, but they disappeared – stolen by evil manitous – until he created Thunderers to watch over them. In a Wisconsin Chippewa (southern Ojibway) account, in which he is called Wenebojo, he came into this world from blood clots that a cold and starving old woman picked from the carcass of a moose and stored in a mitten. As soon as he emerged, he transformed himself into a small rabbit, crossed a great ocean and stole fire from the people living there for his grandmother.

Some of his transformations combine ribald antics and, perhaps, some rather darker sexual undertones. He once turned himself into a caribou, feigned death and allowed all the birds and animals to consume him until only his anus was left. When a turkey buzzard flew down to eat this and, in so doing, stuck its head up the anus, Wenebojo tightened his rectum and captured the bird. The

buzzard escaped when Wenebojo joined a game of lacrosse – but it scraped its head pulling it out, which is why this bird is red and scabby and smells bad.

For all his antics and noble acts, Wenebojo was subject to lust, envy, greed and the other foibles of humankind – and generally suffered for his temptations. In another southern Ojibway story that carries a serious lesson about incest, Wenebojo tricked his daughters into marrying him, and eventually felt so ashamed that he crawled into the open mouth of a muskie (a species of predatory fish) and remains there to this day.

NANIH WAIYA (*CHOCTAW*) is a hill in Winston County, Mississippi, near the headwaters of the Pearl River. This is the place where the Choctaw and several related tribes emerged from the underworld. The first to emerge were the Muskogees (*CREEKS*), who then travelled east; next came the *CHEROKEES*, who moved to the north; then, the Chickasaws, who followed the Cherokee trail and settled near them in the north; and finally, the Choctaws, who stayed on the lands around Nanih Waiya.

NAVAJO WOMEN are preparing wool and weaving a carpet. The Navajo learned how to weave with native grasses and cotton from the Pueblos. In the 17th century, they obtained Spanish Churro sheep and began to work with wool, making fine blankets with simple but striking geometric designs. They began to make carpets during the late 19th century.

Some believe that Grasshopper Mother, who led the people through the shaft to the top of the hill, was killed when she stayed behind. To avenge her death, Aba, the creator, closed the entrance and transformed the murderers into ants. Others believe that the shaft remains open.

THE NASKAPI [Innu] live in the boreal forests of northern Quebec and Labrador. They follow the typical northern Algonquian cultural pattern, travelling through their lands in small bands, hunting caribou, moose, deer, bear, beaver and

THIS HIDE COAT is in the typical Naskapi decorative style, which consists of intricately painted linear and curvilinear geometric patterns. Such patterns were part of the Naskapi religious iconography. They first appeared on clothing during the early 18th century.

other large and small game, taking fish and waterfowl from the innumerable lakes and rivers, and gathering seasonally available food resources. Like the *CREE* and their other Algonquian neighbours, they especially prize the *BEAR* and conduct *BEAR RITUALS* to ensure success in the hunt and the propitiation of the species. They are now joined with their *MONTAGNAIS* neighbours to the south, and are known as the Innu.

THE NAVAJO [Dine] are an Athapascan-speaking people who gradually migrated south from the Athapascan homeland in the northwestern Subarctic, and arrived in the Southwest about 1,000 years ago. When they arrived in this land of semi-arid mountains and plains,

O

they pursued their traditional hunting and gathering, but learned from the neighbouring *PUEBLO* tribes how to plant corn (maize). Early Spanish accounts record fields of corn surrounding Navajo settlements. This reliable food supply dramatically changed their lifestyle and became the focus of their religious beliefs, as it provided a powerful metaphor for the course of human life. Their economy changed again when they obtained sheep, goats and horses, and herding became their primary activity. They were aggressive, asserting their hold over a large territory impinging on the traditional homelands of the *HOPI* and other Pueblos. They drew much from these tribes, including weaving, sand painting, and aspects of religious belief. The Navajo Reservation is the largest in the US (more than 7.29 million ha/18 million acres).

NAYENEZGANI AND TOBAD-JISHTCHINI (*NAVAJO*), equating to the *APACHE* Monster-Slayer and *CHILD-OF-THE-WATER*, are the Navajo versions of the *TWIN* war gods conceived by *CHANGING WOMAN* after she exposed her body to the sun and dripping water.

NEZ PERCE, a Penutian-speaking tribe, had their homeland on the Columbia Plateau, in present-day Idaho, Washington and Oregon, where they hunted, fished and gathered along forested rivers. After they obtained horses, however, they began to live off the great buffalo herds that ranged throughout the northwestern Great Plains.

In 1855, the US government forced them to cede several million acres of territory. In 1863, the tribe lost most of its remaining 3.24 million ha (8 million acres) when they were forced into signing another treaty. This led to a war in 1877, during which Chief Joseph and some of his people tried to flee to Canada. The US military captured them just short of the border, after

a trek of 2,735 km (1,700 miles), and the chief never saw his homeland again. The poignant figure of Chief Joseph in surrender came to represent one of the most powerful symbols of the terrible, shameful destruction of the American Indian people. Today, the Nez Perce own or control 37,510 ha (92,685 acres) in north-central Idaho.

NISHANÚ NATCHITAK (Nesaru, Chief-Above) (*ARIKARA*) was the creator of human beings. He first made giants, who proved too unruly and disrespectful. After saving a few smaller people by transforming them into grains of corn (maize) and storing them in a cave, he caused a flood to rid the world of the giants. He then planted corn in the heavens and transformed an ear of this corn into a woman, *MOTHER CORN*. She eventually led the people out of the underworld and gave them their culture.

THE NOOTKA [Nuu-Chah-Nulth] is a Wakashan-speaking tribe that occupied the western and southwestern shores of Vancouver

CHIEF JOSEPH was the tragic, heroic resistance leader of the Nez Perce. To avoid incarceration at the Fort Lapwai, Idaho, reservation in 1877, he fled north with a small band of followers, seeking freedom. The US Cavalry cornered the demoralized remnants of his band just 64 km (40 miles) from sanctuary in Canada. Chief Joseph spent the rest of his life in exile.

THIS NOOTKA HAT is made of woven cedar bark and decorated with whales and other clan symbols. Only a chief with whaling privileges could wear it, as the symbols are both displays of chiefly power and representations of important clan ancestors.

Island. Like their Pacific Coast mainland relatives, they lived in coastal villages of large communal cedar-plank houses and harvested the abundant resources of the coastal waters and forests. Skilled hunters of sea mammals, they braved the open waters of the Pacific in large cedar canoes to pursue whales and seals. As a coastal people, they were contacted early by European explorers, including the Spanish explorer Juan de Fuca (1592) and the English explorers James Cook (1776–8) and George Vancouver (1792). While they suffered the depredations typically caused by European contact (disease, loss of traditional culture through missionary activity and trade, and loss of territory), their structured maritime society has allowed them to retain the essence of their cultural identity.

NORELPUTUS (*WINTU*) was a prophet who composed a new set of myths in the late 19th century. He created an elaborate mythology that revolved around the high god Olelbis (One-Who-Is-Above) and his consort Mem Loimis (Water Woman).

NUSMATTA (*BELLA COOLA*) is a house in the sky that contains all the mythical narratives related by story-tellers.

OBSIDIAN (*YUROK*) personifies the black volcanic glass that was the best and most sought-after raw material for prehistoric stone tool-making.

A young man became obsessed with catching a fiery mass that he saw floating down a river. After failing several times, he fell into a deep depression and wept uncontrollably. Finally, after setting a net in the river and a snare on the bottom, he caught his elusive prey, a fish-like creature. He told it that he was lonely and had no one to talk to, and it told him that it kept moving down the river because it wanted to leave its home. The man had been kind and respectful, so the creature, Obsidian, told him that, from then on, it would be beautiful and valuable, and would endure as long as people continued to respect it through rituals. Obsidian revealed to the man where it grew up and then never spoke again. Thereafter, the people were always able to find obsidian for their tools.

DEATH & AFTERLIFE

DEATH IS NOT ABSOLUTE in a world where nothing is inanimate, and time does not retreat endlessly into extinction; people withdraw from bodily existence, just as the culture heroes did after the age of transformation. Those supernatural beings were responsible for the fact of death, usually because of some heroic failing. Among the Modoc, for example, a chief named Kumokums allowed people to go to the Land of the Dead because his village was overcrowded – unfortunately, he did not reckon on losing members of his own family. The path of the dead may lead into an underworld, into a remote land beyond the horizon, or into the sky. Most cultures hope that it will be a place of physical and spiritual ease: thus, some tribes in the rugged Northwest Coast interior speak of a welcoming refuge, a wonderful flat land of sweet-smelling flowers that they refer to as Prairie Town. The longing for the return of the dead to life is expressed in stories of living people who, Orpheus-like, journey to the land of the dead to retrieve a loved one. During the terrible suffering caused by the white invasion, this longing occupied entire tribes on the Great Plains; by dancing the Ghost Dance, they hoped to revive their ancestors and return the world to its original state.

THE STARS were the souls of all the people who had died, in some tribal philosophies. This belief persists in accounts of the origin of specific constellations, such as the Pleiades, which are commonly held to be six or seven sisters, transported from the earth into the sky.

DANCERS (above) on the Northwest Coast wear masks that display their clan status and heritage, and imbue them with the power of the clan ancestors they represent. The renewal of spiritual links through ceremony helps the tribe to maintain its cultural identity.
(*PAINTING BY PAUL KANE, 19TH CENTURY.*)

THIS TABLEAU (left) represents life and death among the Sioux residing near Fort Pierre, Dakota Territory (present-day South Dakota). The platform burial exposed the deceased to the life-giving elements and to the sky, allowing the spirit to rejoin the air from which it came.
(*ENGRAVING, 1844, FROM A PAINTING BY KARL BODMER.*)

OLD BEAR (above) was a Mandan shaman. The shaman's spiritual powers and knowledge of ceremony ensured that the dead received the respect necessary to release the soul back into the spirit world.
(*PAINTING BY GEORGE CATLIN, 1832.*)

TANANA INDIAN SPIRIT HOUSES (above) lie in a cemetery at Tok, southern Alaska. St Timothy's Episcopal Mission was established in 1912 on the north side of the Tanana River, several miles from the present-day community of Tok. Because of the influence of Christianity, the Tanana people blend traditional and Christian themes in their burials.

OFFERING SITES are places associated with supernatural beings and events, where supplicants wishing for some good fortune leave offerings. Offering rituals are a common part of worship at sacred places.

In an example from the Plateau region, a large, upright boulder, more than 2 m (6 feet) tall and roughly in the shape of a human body, used to stand in the homeland of the Kalispel tribe, near the present border with Canada (it was eventually destroyed by settlers or by construction activity).

To the *OKANAGAN* and *COLVILLE* peoples, this rock was Camas Woman, or Wishing Stone – the name is associated with camas root (Camassia esculenta), a powerful *MEDICINE*. A woman named Blue Flower journeyed to the Okanagan valley in search of a young man she hoped to marry, the eldest of three brothers. She carried a basket filled with camas bulbs. When she met the brothers, the two younger ones started fighting over her, just as *COYOTE* happened by. He began to laugh at the spectacle, which annoyed Blue Flower so much that she spoke sharply to him. Insulted, Coyote turned the lower part of her body into stone, transformed the three young men into three mountains, and abandoned her. When he happened to come back that way again, he discovered that she had thrown the camas bulbs back to her home in the Kalispel region – she did not want camas to grow in the Okanagan valley – and used her own power to transform herself completely into stone. Impressed by her strength and perseverance, Coyote gave her special power as a wishing stone.

In another Okanagan version, probably influenced by Roman Catholic teachings, the name came during a time of great sickness, when the Great Chief Above instructed a *SHAMAN* to gather all the people at the Wishing Stone. When the sun reached its height, a

bright light appeared and a beautiful woman floated down. She gave the people camas bulbs, with instructions on planting them, and told them that in the spring the blue flowers would be so thick they would look like a lake. They were to gather the roots in the autumn, use them as medicine, and they would never again have the sickness. Suddenly, a breeze lifted her into the sky, and she disappeared into the clouds. From that time on, the people left gifts for her at the Wishing Stone.

THE OJIBWAY (Anishinabe) [Northern, Plains, Southern], who now prefer their traditional name Anishinabe, are a large Algonquian tribe that once controlled a vast, rugged territory around the shores of Lake Superior.

They may be generally divided into three groups: the Northern Ojibway (including the Salteaux), who occupy the boreal forests north of the upper Great Lakes; the Plains Ojibway, who live at the edge of the eastern Great Plains; and the Southern Ojibway (commonly called the Chippewa), who lived in the mixed deciduous and coniferous forests and prairies south of the upper Great Lakes. Each group adapted to its surroundings. The northern Ojibway were hunters and gatherers similar to the *CREE* and other northern

peoples; the Plains Ojibway moved out of the forests to pursue a buffalo-hunting way of life; and the southern Ojibway supplemented their hunting and gathering with horticulture. The Ojibway of the boreal forests produced one of the most striking and enduring forms of art and religious expression on the continent: red-ochre rock paintings, scattered across the great granite cliffs lining the endless waterways of the Canadian Shield, from northwest Manitoba to eastern Ontario. Because the Ojibway avoided removal, they continue to occupy their traditional homelands in a large number of reservations and other communities in Ontario, Manitoba, Saskatchewan, Michigan, Wisconsin, Minnesota, North Dakota and Montana. (See also *NEW MYTHOLOGIES, THE DARK SIDE*)

THE OKANAGAN are a Salishan-speaking people who lived in the Plateau region of southern British Columbia and northern Washington. Okanagan dialects include those spoken by the northern and southern groups and by neighbouring *SANPOIL*, *COLVILLE* and Lake tribes. The Okanagan were a forest people who fished for salmon, trout, sturgeon and other species along the many lakes and rivers draining the rugged mountain ranges of the area. They hunted deer and other game, and

ROCK PAINTINGS at Darky Lake, in the Quetico region of northern Ontario, capture the essence of traditional and recent Ojibway life. In one scene, several canoes, probably carrying moose hunters, cross the lake in the grip of Mishipizheu. On another part of the rock, a stick figure representing a hunter fires a gun – the puff of smoke suggests that it is an old muzzle-loader. Most importantly, there is a diminutive, but powerful, image of a turtle, which, the Ojibway believe, holds up the earth.

gathered berries, roots and other plants. Some continue to live on ancestral lands, but others fled to the Colville Reservation in Washington to escape harassment by the miners who poured into the area in the late 19th century in search of gold and other metals.

OLD MAN, the *TRANSFORMER* of the *HAN*, Dogrib and *CHIPEWYAN* peoples, outwitted giants, monsters and various animals, including *BEAR* and *WOLVERINE*, who all wanted to trap and eat him. *RAVEN* was his great adversary.

OLD MAN COYOTE is a *CROW* name for the creator.

THE OMAHA people are a Siouan-speaking tribe who migrated from the prairies and woodlands south of the Great Lakes to settle in the eastern Great Plains, between the Mississippi and Missouri Rivers. They lived in earthlodges (see *LODGE*) in large villages along the rivers and streams, and grew corn (maize), beans and squash on the region's fertile flood plains, hunted buffalo and other game, and gathered wild plants as the seasons provided. They were traditional allies of the *PAWNEE*. The Omaha was always a small tribe, with approximately 2,800 members in 1780 but, by 1802, disease and warfare had reduced this already number to 300. Today they occupy a small reservation in northeastern Nebraska, within the limits of their original territories.

P

IN A HEROIC tale, told by an Omaha story-teller about 100 years ago, two warriors were chasing some Pawnee who had stolen their horses, when they encountered and killed a monstrous rattlesnake. When they ate the monster, they turned into harmless grass snakes that, ever after, came into Omaha camps in the summer.

ONE-WHO-GRABS-BREASTS

see *BEGOCIDI*.

ONEIDA, ONONDAGA

see *IROQUOIS*.

THE ORPHEUS MYTH is a

universal theme in which a man (Orpheus, in the original Greek tragedy) journeys to the land of the dead to retrieve his loved one, finds her and begins to lead her out, but loses her to the dead again when he breaks a rule that he must not look at her or touch her on the way back (see under *COYOTE*).

The Chiricahua *APACHE* believe that a critically ill person may enter the underworld and find where their dead ancestors dwell but, if it is not yet their time, they will not eat any food offered to them, and so will return to the world above and recover.

THE OTTAWA people are a

Great Lakes Algonquian tribe who lived around Lake Huron, where they hunted game, fished and gathered in a rugged land of granite-edged lakes and rivers, covered by forests. They are close relatives of the *OJIBWAY*, with whom they share a history of migrating from

the Atlantic to their present home. Their great chief Pontiac fomented a rebellion in 1763, influenced by a seer known only as the Delaware Prophet, who preached a rejection of the *WHITE MAN* and a return to traditional ways. With the collusion of the French, Pontiac organized all the tribes of the region into a confederacy and overwhelmed many British forts that year, but a long and unsuccessful siege at Detroit eventually proved his downfall. The Ottawa peoples in Canada share two reserves in their traditional lands in Ontario with the Ojibway, whereas the Ottawa in the United States were first removed to northeastern Oklahoma, and were then resettled on a small reservation in northern Michigan.

THE PAIUTE [Northern, South-

ern] are an Uto-Aztecan hunting and gathering people who once occupied a vast territory extending all the way from central Oregon through parts of California and eastwards across the Great Basin as far as southeastern Wyoming.

The Northern Paiute, also called Paviotso, ranged across the desert steppes east of the Cascade Mountains in the north to the Sierra Nevada in the south. Those groups who lived along the shores of lakes subsisted mainly on fish (which they netted and trapped) and waterfowl, along with wild plants, while other bands hunted antelope, deer and other game, and gathered piñon nuts. Miners, loggers and settlers gradually forced them off their lands during the 19th century, although not before there had been a series of battles with the United States military between 1858 and 1868. The tribe finally settled on reservations established in Nevada and Oregon. Many members, however, remained on their ancestral lands in northeastern California, where their descendants now have several small land-holdings. These Cali-

AN IMAGINARY SCENE of prehistoric life in the deserts of the Great Basin, the home of the Paiute. In a world without boundaries, these hardy people chose to remain in this arid, rocky land, and developed a culture successful enough to spread over the present-day states of Nevada, Utah, Arizona and New Mexico.

fornia people, the Owens Valley Paiute, had a similar hunting and gathering way of life in this arid region, but they were able to use irrigation along the Owens River to improve the growing conditions of wild plants that they harvested for their bulbs.

The Southern Paiute are speakers of a language closely related to that of the *UTE*. They once hunted and gathered in a large territory that included parts of present-day California, Arizona, Nevada and Utah. In this harsh and rugged land of semi-desert scrub, they lived mainly on small game and desert plants. The Southern Paiute are culturally distinct from their Northern relatives, and the two groups' languages are mutually unintelligible. After losing most of their population and lands during the late 19th-century occupation of the region by miners and ranchers, the Southern Paiute dispersed into a number of small tribal groups, including the Moapa, and now live in southern Nevada.

PALÖNGAWHOYA see under

POQANGWHOYA BROTHERS.

THE PAPAGO, or Tohono

O'Odham, were desert pastoralists who traditionally occupied the interior of the Sonoran Desert in southwest Arizona. They successfully adapted to the rigours of a hot and dry land by harvesting cacti and other plants, supplemented by hunting birds and other small game. They speak an Uto-Aztecan language closely related to that of the *PIMA*, who live along the nearby Salt and Gila Rivers. Both groups may be descended from the Hohokam, a sophisticated prehistoric culture with the engineering skills needed to construct networks of irrigation canals for their dry valley fields. The Tohono O'Odham now live on three reservations within their aboriginal territory.

A PAPAGO woman. (PHOTOGRAPH BY EDWARD CURTIS, 1907.)

PÁPAKALANÓSIWA (*KWAKI-UTL*), a cannibal being associated with the origin of the Hamatsa, a Kwakiutl *SECRET SOCIETY*. The Hamatsa conduct one of the most important dance rituals of the Tsetseka, an extended period of winter ceremonials.

In one version, this fierce monster kidnapped a chief's wife and forced her into an unholy marriage. The chief's three sons eventually found her in Pápakalanósiwa's house, and discovered that she had given birth to a monster son. They fled, but their mother alerted the cannibal, and he chased after them, blowing his whistle and shouting "Hap! Hap! Hap!" (the traditional cry of the Hamatsa dancer). The young men attempted to slow down Pápakalanósiwa with various obstacles. One threw down a stone, which became a mountain; another dropped a comb, which turned into a thicket; a kelp bladder of oil that became a lake; and a stick that became a huge cedar. When they reached the safety of their house, the chief promised the cannibal he would kill his three sons and serve them as food if the monster brought back his wife. When Pápakalanósiwa returned home, he and his son fell into a fire trap and were consumed. With Pápakalanósiwa's death, the chief's wife came to her senses, fanned the ashes and created mosquitoes – condemned to seeking human blood. All that remained of Pápakalanósiwa was the whistle, which has become an important part of the Hamatsa dance.

THE PASSAMAQUODDY people are an Algonquian tribe who once lived along the coastal rivers of north-eastern Maine and adjoining parts of New Brunswick. Theirs was a typical maritime life, fishing and gathering shellfish along the Atlantic shore, and hunting moose, deer, fish and other game on inland rivers and lakes. Once Europeans occupied the coasts, however, they were forced inland. They were part of the *WABANAKI* confederacy during the 18th century, but they surrendered title to their lands in 1794 and now have a very small reservation (91 ha/225 acres) on Passamaquoddy Bay and a larger parcel of reservation and Federal trust lands in the interior.

PAVAYOYKYASI (*HOPI*) is a being who walks about sprinkling the plants in Hopi fields early every morning with dew. He is envisaged as a handsome youth who always dresses nicely.

PAVIOTSO see under *PAIUTE*.

THE PAWNEE [Chaui, Kitkahahki, Pitahawirata, Skidi] are a Caddoan-speaking people who once ranged through the central Great Plains in Nebraska, Kansas and Oklahoma. They were skilled horticulturalists, growing many varieties of corn (maize), beans and squash, and they hunted buffalo.

A SKIDI PAWNEE chief is wearing a fine buffalo robe, emblazoned with the sacred star symbols that infused all aspects of Pawnee life.

The four Pawnee bands were driven from their lands to a reservation in Oklahoma but, in 1893, the reservation was dissolved in favour of individual land allotments. This shattered a people who, a century earlier, had numbered some 10,000, and by 1906 there were only 600 Pawnee left. The return of some tribal lands in Oklahoma and an improving economic picture has brought the tribe back from the brink of extinction, although its once rich ceremonial culture is now lost. (See also *THE LIVING SKY*)

PAXOJE see *IOWA*.

THE PENOBSCOT people are an Algonquian tribe who, like their more northerly neighbours, the *PASSAMAQUODDY*, lived along coastal rivers in Maine. It is a varied environment, with forests in the north and grasslands in the south. The tribal name is a shortened version of what they call themselves, which translates as "people of the white rocks country". They moved from interior to coast in a seasonal rhythm, hunting moose, deer, beaver and other game, fishing for salmon, sturgeon and other species, gathering shellfish, collecting maple sap and digging the roots of wild plants. Although hundreds of years of acculturation have severely reduced the number of those who speak the native language and practise traditional ways, the tribe continues to protect and nurture what remains. The tribe joined the *WABANAKI* confederacy during the 18th century, but lost most of its territory in 1796, and most of what it had left

THE PEYOTE cactus (Lophophora williamsii), seen here at a site near Huizache, San Luis Potosi, Mexico.

in 1833. It fought back in the courts and, in 1980, a land-claim settlement provided the money to buy property to augment its small reservation and other land-holdings.

PEOPLE MOTHER (Northern *PAIUTE*) figures in a Great Basin human-origins story.

During the time of animal people, a monster that killed with its gaze invaded a village, leaving everyone dead except a small boy and a woman who was living in seclusion outside the village because she was menstruating. She fled with the child, but when she made camp, a giant kidnapped and killed the boy, and displayed the child's body on its belt. The woman sought shelter with Gopher Woman and prepared food for her continuing journey, gathering and grinding seeds into meal. Next, a monstrous *FLYING HEAD* attacked her, but Wood Rat hid her in his cave. Finally, she found the boy, revived him, and they reached the mountain-top home of a hunter, who became her husband. Their union created all the people of the world.

PEYOTE is a hallucinogenic cactus used as a sacrament by the Native American Church.

In a Brule *SIOUX* account of its origin, the *COMANCHE*, a tribe living far to the south in a land of deserts and mesas, suffered from a deadly disease. An old woman dreamed she would find a

MEDICINE herb that would save her people and so, with her granddaughter, she went into the desert to find this magical plant. As night fell, and they huddled together, tired and hungry, she heard the wing-beats of a giant bird. It was an EAGLE, flying on a path from east to west. She prayed to the eagle for wisdom and power, and then, near dawn, she saw a man floating in the air above them. He pointed to a peyote plant, and they discovered that the juice was refreshing.

The second night, he came again, and she prayed for help to get back to her people. This time he told her she would return after two more days with the power to cure. The grandmother and child ate more of the sacred medicine, and power entered the grandmother through it, giving knowledge, understanding and a sacred vision. Although they stayed awake all night, when the sun rose and shone upon the hide bag with the peyote, the woman felt strong. She told her granddaughter to pray to the herb, as it was telling her many things.

On the third night, the spirit came again, and taught her how to show her people the proper way to use the medicine. As she began to wonder how she would find more of this powerful herb, she heard small voices calling – it was all the peyote growing around them. They gathered the peyote buttons and filled the bag. The next night, at sunset, they saw the spirit again, and he pointed the way home. Amazingly, the woman and child had taken no food or drink for four days, yet the peyote kept them strong.

When they returned to their village, they taught the men how to use the herb. The knowledge and wisdom they gained showed them how to gather the sacred things needed for the first peyote altar – the peyote buttons, drum, gourd, fire, water and cedar – and how to make the symbols and conduct the ceremony. They soon conquered the disease, and word of the peyote

ceremony and its great power spread quickly across the continent.

THE PIMA

THE PIMA, a horticultural people speaking an Uto-Aztecan language, live along the Gila and Salt Rivers in the Sonoran Desert of southwest Arizona. As with their relatives, the Tohono O'Odham (see PAPAGO), they are probably descendants of the Hohokam, a prehistoric culture who irrigated the desert to grow their crops (see ELDER BROTHER). They raised cotton, corn (maize) and other crops and supplemented their diet with small game and desert plants, including prickly pear, saguaro and other cactus fruits. They are now well known for their fine coiled baskets. The Pima moved to reservations on each of the two rivers in the late 19th century.

PIPES

PIPES used for smoking tobacco in ritual contexts are treasured sacred objects among many hunting and gathering tribes, as their use manifests the personal and collective relationship between people and the spirit world. The "Peace Pipe", described in historical sources and popular accounts, records only one of the pipe's functions, as a gesture of conciliation and a symbol of common purpose and agreement. To the ARAPAHO, the world as we know it rests on a pipe (see FLAT PIPE) and, to some other Plains cultures, the most powerful spirits gave the pipe as a gift to human beings, as WHITE-BUFFALO-CALF WOMAN gave hers to the

A PIMA BASKET TRAY, woven from willow rods, bleached yucca and, for the black fibres, devil's claw (Proboscidea parviflora), a common cactus-like herb. The design was not mere decoration: it would have had a name and symbolic significance expressing some aspect of Pima religious iconography.

Lakota SIOUX. Loss or neglect of these pipes would be so disastrous that each tribe has keepers who very carefully protect them.

THE PLEIADES

THE PLEIADES is a small, compact constellation of stars visible in the northern hemisphere. Because it appears in the winter, northern tribes associate it with food shortages and other stresses. Central and southern tribes, on the other hand, tend to focus on its origins.

The IROQUOIS incorporate the stars in a lesson about giving respect to your elders. During a pleasant autumn, seven children met daily in a quiet spot on a lake to dance. An old man had warned them that to continue with their

dancing would cause evil, but they persisted and eventually danced into the sky. In a variant, one of them falls back (hence the dim seventh star) and grows as a pine tree, which is why Iroquois relate pine pitch to starlight. The CHEROKEE have a similar story. The YUROK see the stars as six maidens who dance across the sky. The PAWNEE call them the Seven Stars and see them as a symbol of unity.

A NEZ PERCE account offers another explanation for the dim seventh star. One of the seven sister stars, called Eyes-in-Different-Colours, loved an earth man, even after his death, and she mourned so much for him that her eyes became dim with grief and shame. To hide herself away, she took the veil from the sky and covered her face with it.

The NAVAJO depict the PLEIADES (dilyéhé) in string figures. SPIDER WOMAN taught them this art to help them learn to concentrate. The Navajo make this particular figure in order to maintain the clarity necessary to keep things stable and beautiful – the ingredients of a long and fruitful life. (See also THE LIVING SKY, DEATH & AFTERLIFE)

THE PLEIADES is a star cluster in the constellation Taurus. Seven stars are visible to the naked eye, and under clear, very dark conditions, this number increases considerably. Because the cluster is so distinctive, it features in the astronomical observations and mythologies of peoples across the northern hemisphere.

POKANGS is the English name for the *POQANGWHOYA BROTHERS*, the *HOPI* version of the *TWIN* war gods.

POLARIS (Skidi *PAWNEE*), the North Star, is called Karariwari in the Pawnee language – "the star that does not move". Because all the other stars revolve around Karariwari, they consider it to be the Chief Star. He is able to communicate with the chief of the people, ensuring the stability and control necessary to be a strong leader. Near Karariwari is a circlet of stars (the Corona Borealis) known as the Chief's Council.

To the *NAVAJO*, Polaris is the symbolic centre of the hogan (the traditional Navajo home, a conical structure made of logs and sticks and covered with mud, sods or *adobe*); it represents the central fire. They also recognize the Male Revolver (the Plough or Big Dipper) and Female Revolver (Cassiopeia) as elders who set a moral example for earth people. Just as they revolve around Polaris, so people should always be near their homes to carry out family responsibilities.

POLARIS remains fixed in its northern abode, whereas other stars appear to move through the heavens as the earth goes through its seasons. Since the earth moves through a 26,000-year cycle called precession, the true north celestial pole shifts among the northern stars. In ancient times, Thubian was the northern star and, in the distant future, it will be Vega.

THE ACOMA PUEBLO, perched on a massive sandstone mesa that rises a long way above the desert plains of New Mexico, is said to be the oldest inhabited settlement in the United States. Archaeological evidence suggests that the Pueblo built it in the 12th century. The Spanish explorer Coronado visited the site in 1540.

POQANGWHOYA BROTH-ERS (*HOPI*), grandsons of *SPIDER WOMAN*, are the *TWIN* war gods responsible for ridding the world of monsters. The common name is also the elder twin's name; the younger is Palöngawhoya. They tend to be described as ragged and mischievous, and are ardent shinny players (a popular *STICK-AND-BALL GAME*). They normally reside near a Hopi village, although they can roam the world. Their present task is to hold the Earth tightly on each side. If they let go, it will spin wildly.

POSAYAMO, also known as Montezuma, figures in millenarian cults that sprang up after centuries of oppression by whites in Arizona and New Mexico. In some pueblos, people kept sacred fires burning in anticipation of his return to deliver the people from the conquering whites. The Tewa *PUEBLO* say he was born to a virgin who got pregnant while she was eating pine nuts. Although an outcast as a child, he had a spirit father who told him he would one day rule all the Indians, but he left for the south and has not yet returned.

The *PIMA* people had a *CREATION* story in which Montezuma replaced the traditional supernatural, *ELDER BROTHER*.

THE POTAWATOMI once shared the woodlands and prairies south of the Great Lakes with other Algonquian tribes, growing corn (maize), beans and squash, hunting, fishing and gathering wild foods. White occupation of the region in the 18th century devastated the tribe, and they were forcibly relocated to reservation lands in the southern plains of Kansas and Oklahoma. Some groups resisted the removal and instead scattered through northern Indiana, Michigan, northern Wisconsin and Ontario, where they still live. The Potawatomi are traditionally regarded as the "Keeper of the Fire", representing the sacred fire of traditional religion, in the "Three Fires", an alliance with two other related Algonquian tribes. The southern *OJIBWAY* (Chippewa) are the "Keeper of the Faith", and the *OTTAWA* (or Odawa) are the "Keeper of the Trade".

THE PUEBLO [Eastern, Western] people are a diverse group of agrarian cultures who occupy desert regions of the southwest in Arizona and New Mexico. They derive from prehistoric cultures who began cultivating corn (maize) approximately 4,000 years ago and had village sites at least 2,000 years ago. Their other major crops are beans, squash and cotton. The name "Pueblo" derives from a Spanish term meaning "village", describing their characteristic single-storey surface dwellings and multi-storey cliff dwellings of *adobe* (mud brick) or stone. They also build a distinctive underground chamber, the *KIVA*, within which the most important religious rites take place.

The Western Pueblos are the *HOPI*, an Uto-Aztecan tribe, and the *ZUNI*, who speak a language isolate (unrelated to any other known language) that some linguists theorize may be part of the Penutian family. The Eastern Pueblos, settled in the Rio Grande Basin, are the Keres-speaking Keres and *COCHITI*, and the Kiowa-Tanoan groups Tewa, Tiwa and Towa (the Isleta and Taos

Pueblos are Tiwa groups). The Spaniards profoundly influenced the Pueblos, who first came into contact with them in the 16th century, but their well-structured societies and strong defensive force were fairly resistant to assimilation. They continue to live on reservations constituting a small portion of their original homelands. (See also *THE DARK SIDE*)

PULEKUKWEREK (*YUROK*) translates as "of downstream (end of world)" and "sharp (horn on buttocks)". A hero and monster-slayer, he introduced the people to true tobacco. Previously they had smoked bay leaves.

A RAINBOW is often assumed to be a positive phenomenon, as it is in Christian iconography. Yet agricultural peoples may see it as a negative sign. The *HOPI*, for example, say it is an evil force, with a stench so terrible that clouds are afraid of it. If a rainbow arches under clouds on their way to water Hopi lands, the clouds retreat, causing drought.

RAVEN, the major supernatural figure across the northwestern part of the continent, is a hero, *TRANS-FORMER* and *TRICKSTER*.

For the Alaskan *INUIT*, Raven created the mainland by harpooning a giant sea animal, without a beginning or end, which then turned into land. The Kobuk say that Raven created land after a great flood by spearing a floating sod of earth, which then sank. He managed to haul it back up into his boat and kill it, at which point it turned into earth.

On the northern Northwest Coast, Raven is the primary hero among the *TLINGIT*, *HAIDA* and *TSIMSHIAN*. In the southern part of the area, his role as transformer is more important. Raven tended to be preoccupied with hunger, and his selfish obsession often led to events crucial to the survival of

ACOMA PUEBLO rainbow dancers wait to perform at an inter-tribal ceremonial in Gallup, New Mexico. At Acoma, the rainbow dance is held during the Christmas season.

humankind. In a Tsimshian narrative, Raven came down from the sky to a village on the southern tip of the Queen Charlotte Islands to complain about the intense mourning of a couple grieving for their dead son. He appeared as a young man, bright as fire, above the boy's bed. The parents hoped that he had come to replace their boy, but – strangely – he did

A TLINGIT RAVEN rattle, collected c. 1850. A kingfisher sits on the top of the rattle, sticking its tongue into the mouth of a human with a bear's head (possibly a mask), and a frog-like creature clings to the raven's belly. Chiefs used these rattles during coming-of-age ceremonies to confer intellectual light, wisdom and the power of the clan on the initiates.

not eat. Then he saw two slaves who ate great quantities of food: a male and female, both named Mouth at Each End. They served the youth a dish of whale meat with a scab in it (which is how the slaves got so hungry), and this made him so ravenous that he ate up all the village's provisions. Ashamed of being unable to satisfy his guest, the chief named him Wigyét (giant), gave him a bladder filled with seeds and told him to fly to the mainland and sow berries on the hillsides and fish-eggs in the streams, so that he would always have something to eat. On the way, he dropped a round stone into the water so he could rest, and it became an island that is seen to this day. After scattering fish-eggs and berries, Wigyét decided it would be easier to get food if the sky was not so dark. The account ends with a theft-of-daylight story (see *FIRE* for other fire-theft accounts). Thereafter,

people called him Chémsen (raven).

In another Tsimshian narrative, Raven is responsible for *DEATH*. He came upon Stone and Elderberry, arguing over who should give birth first. He touched Elderberry, and that is why people die and elderberries grow on their graves. If he had touched Stone first, people would exist for ever, just as stones do.

In another story, he provides a lesson in the need to follow ritual correctly. In human form, he took a beautiful woman as his wife. She was the Mistress of Salmon for, when she dipped her fingers into the water, salmon appeared. Raven made a big mistake, using salmon vertebrae as a comb (they must be returned to the water to ensure the immortality of the species) and, when it got stuck in his hair, he cursed the comb. Offended, the salmon wife swam away, forever making the salmon more difficult to catch. (See also *TRANSFORMA-TION, THE TRICKSTER.*)

RAVEN AMULETS are worn by *INUIT* to encourage success in hunting. The inland Netsilik and the Iglulik make amulets of raven claws for male children and attach them to the back-pouches where mothers carry babies. The Iglulik sometimes stitch raven skins into male infants' clothing.

ROCK see *INYAN*.

THE STRANGERS

EVENTS THAT SHAKE UP THE WORLD are preserved in oral tradition. The Micmac tell of a strange, floating "island" that suddenly appeared in the sea. From a distance, the people could see animals climbing in the branches of several trees. When the island drew close the animals became men, and soon a shore party arrived that included a man in the long robes of a priest. These strangers had other wonders in store, such as guns, iron and copper kettles, and woollen blankets. Despite the European origin of such things, each tribe developed stories to explain them within its own traditions. So the Navajo thank their Creator for bringing horses, cattle and sheep from the Spanish in Mexico. As Europeans became more numerous, story-tellers absorbed them into their tales – for example, involving them in the antics of Coyote and other tricksters. But it was the deadly impact of these invaders, and the heroic resistance of native people,

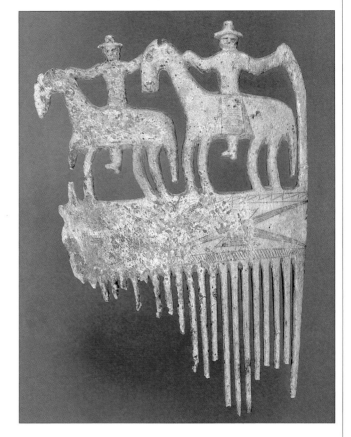

that preoccupied the story-tellers. Thus, the Kiowa culture hero Saynday tricked Smallpox, the bringer of death, into first visiting their traditional enemy, the Pawnee. Before Smallpox could return, Saynday created a ring of fire to protect his people from this terrible scourge.

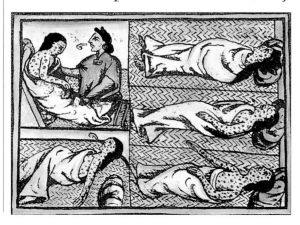

AN IROQUOIAN ornamental hair comb (above) was made from bone by a Cayuga carver in the late 17th century. Traditionally, the decorations were figures associated with Iroquoian life, so this craftsman duly recorded the coming of the white man – probably two European traders arriving at his village in upstate New York.

THE MOST DEVASTATING IMPACT (left) of the European expansion into North America occurred before most native people had ever seen a white man. In 1520, some of the soldiers in the expeditionary force of the Spanish explorer Cortés suffered from smallpox, a disease that had ravaged the Far East and then Europe for at least 2,000 years. As the native people had no resistance against this and other common European diseases, it moved quickly through the Aztec population in Mexico and then spread across North America, killing millions. (ILLUSTRATION BY A 16TH-CENTURY AZTEC ARTIST.)

A MILITARY EXPEDITION (left) in 1874, led by General George Armstrong Custer, discovered gold in the Black Hills of Dakota Territory, land sacred to the Sioux. The predictable flood of prospectors and miners on to Sioux lands precipitated a series of bitter conflicts with the military who, despite treaty obligations, defended white interests. On 25 June 1876, Custer's Seventh Cavalry attempted to put down a force of Sioux, Northern Cheyenne and Northern Arapaho warriors along the Little Big Horn River. Famously, they failed, and were completely wiped out. This coloured pencil drawing, made by one of the Sioux combatants, records the action in the heat of the battle.

THE INTRODUCTION of the horse *(right)* was responsible for the transformation of Great Plains culture. Because of the vast distances across the grasslands, most groups living in the region were river-bound horticulturalists. When hunting and gathering tribes from the South, the Great Lakes region and the western mountains obtained the horse, however, they were able to move across the plains and hunt the buffalo. In this picture, Osage warriors round up wild horses. (PAINTING BY GEORGE CATLIN, 19TH CENTURY.)

THE MICMAC (below) were skilled sea hunters who pursued whales and porpoises in canoes specifically designed for ocean travel. When the French and English introduced sailing vessels into the region, the Micmac adapted them easily to their own use. Micmac, hunting and fishing along the shores of Kejimkujik Lake, in south-central Nova Scotia, engraved the smooth slate shoreline rocks with images of their culture – here, two seagoing canoes with masts and sails, are steered by men wearing European top hats, which were a popular trade item in the 19th century.

A DETAIL (left) of the Sioux drawing of the battle of the Little Big Horn River, showing a warrior striking down a Seventh Cavalry trooper.

S

SAC see *FOX*.

SAHTU see *DENE*.

THE SALISH [Coast, Interior] are named after their Salishan language. The Coast Salish occupy the coastal areas of southern British Columbia and southeastern Vancouver Island, and the northern coasts of the Olympic Peninsula in Washington. They had no agriculture, but the warm Pacific coastal environment provided them with an abundance of sea and forest resources, including whales and other sea mammals, salmon, oolichan and other salt-water fish, trout, clams, mussels, sea urchins and other shellfish, deer, bear and other game of the temperate rainforests, and a wide range of wild plants. Since they had a food surplus, they adopted a sedentary lifestyle, living in villages of cedarplank houses, and developed a complex social organization – including a stratified society with nobles, commoners and slaves – resembling those of agricultural peoples. They produced art in abundance, mainly depictions of mythological ancestors representing *CLAN* and family crests, on carved and painted cedar *TOTEM POLES* as well as on a wide range of ceremonial and household goods. Although they now have only a small portion of their original territory, they continue to live in the lands of their ancestors. For more information about the Interior Salish, see *FLATHEAD*.

SALMON BOY (*HAIDA*) offended salmon and was taken to the land of the salmon people. He learned the rituals that fishers must use when they catch salmon, returned briefly as a human to teach his people these rituals, and then went back to live with the salmon for ever.

SALT WOMAN (*COCHITI*) created salt from her flesh and mucus.

As salt is crucial to Southwestern peoples, those seeking it must conduct detailed rituals and observe strict taboos.

SALTEAUX see under *OJIBWAY*.

THE SANPOIL people are an Interior Salishan tribe, speaking a dialect of the *OKANAGAN* language, who live in the Columbia Plateau region of northern Washington. Like other tribes that inhabit this rugged region of grass-covered valleys, forested hills and mountain ranges, the Sanpoil were mainly fishers and hunters. They now share the Colville Reservation in northeastern Washington (established in 1872) with a bewildering mix of other small Plateau tribes.

SAPLING see under *FLINT*.

SALMON, when they are ready to spawn, swim up the fast-flowing rivers in vast numbers until they reach the place of their own birth, a bed of freshwater gravel. During this journey, they can be speared as they leap through rapids and narrow channels on their way upstream, as this modern impression of a Chinook fisherman shows. (PAINTING BY ERNST BERKE.)

THE SARCEE, who prefer to be known as the Tsuu T'ina, are an Athapascan people of the northern Great Plains, occupying southern and central Alberta. They were traditionally allied with two Algonquian tribes, the *BLACKFOOT* and the *GROS VENTRE*, in the Blackfoot Confederacy. They pursued the traditional Plains life of buffalo hunting until disaster struck. First, a smallpox epidemic devastated them in 1869 and 1870. Then, white hunters began to slaughter the buffalo for their hides, leaving few for the Sarcee. After a drought in 1878, when the buffalo migrated to better grasslands south of the US border, white hunters set prairie fires to prevent their return north again. This caused the virtual extinction of the buffalo in Canada by 1879, and collapse of the buffalo-hunting cultures soon afterwards. Having lost their livelihood and source of food, the Sarcee were at the mercy of the Canadian government. They now occupy a small reserve in southern Alberta.

SAUK see *FOX*.

SAYA see *YAMANHDEYA*.

SAYNDAY is the *KIOWA CULTURE HERO* and *TRICKSTER*. In one of his most notable exploits, he arranged the theft of the sun from the far side of the world to quell the eternal darkness among his own people. He first kept the sun in front of his *LODGE*, where it burned too brightly, and then inside, where its light was so intense it shone through the walls, and finally on the roof, above the smoke-hole. This caused a fire that destroyed the lodge, and so he threw the sun away, into the sky.

SEA MOTHER (*INUIT*) is generally known as Sedna in the central

A SHAMAM of the Southern Ojibway tribe incised this plan view of part of a Midéwegan, the sacred Midé lodge, on a birch-bark scroll at Leech Lake, Minnesota. It depicts Mishipizheu and the other manitous through whom the shamans draw their curing power.

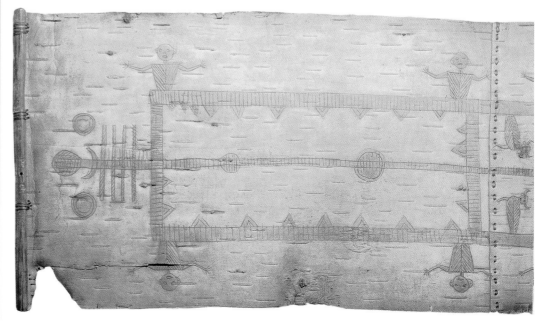

and eastern Arctic, among the Mackenzie, Copper, Netsilik, Iglulik and Baffin Island groups. Present in the sea and all its animals, she is the MISTRESS OF ANIMALS and MOTHER OF ANIMALS.

Story-tellers sometimes recount her origin in a singular narrative, and sometimes in an extension of the DOG HUSBAND story. A woman, the "one who would have no children" married, but she was miserable. As the winter ended, her father visited and decided to take her back. When her husband discovered what had happened, he turned into a seabird (identified as a petrel or fulmar) and flew after them. As he neared the fleeing pair, he caused a great storm that tossed the boat around so violently that the girl fell overboard. She clung to the gunwale, but the father cut off her fingers. They fell into the water and became different animal species: seals, walrus, whales, salmon and polar bears (depending on the version). The fingerless woman then sank to the bottom of the sea and became Sea Mother.

People respect her through hunting ritual, taboos and the ritual disposal of sea-mammal and fish remains. When they observe the proper rituals, she responds by providing abundant game and fish, and when they neglect the rituals, she takes away those resources. In order to counter the threat of star-

vation, SHAMANS then have to go into trances to comb Sedna's hair, infested with the vermin of broken taboos – as she is without fingers, she cannot comb it herself. When they finish, she is grateful, and sets the game animals free again.

SECRET SOCIETIES are social organizations with an exclusive membership (most often determined by sex, age and social status), a hierarchical structure and a set of esoteric beliefs and rituals, which are generally devoted to religious matters responsible for the health and welfare of the group. They are most commonly found in agrarian cultures (and, in modern times, industrialized ones), where the economic and power structures exist to maintain a system in which individuals may be differentiated by social status. The Flute and Snake societies of PUEBLO peoples are examples of the many secret societies among agricultural groups in North America. The prosperous hunters and gatherers of the Northwest Coast have secret societies in which membership is confined to élites and may be inherited. The MIDÉWIWIN of the OJIBWAY and other Algonquians of the Great Lakes region was a secret curing society of SHAMANS.

SEDNA See under SEA MOTHER.

SEMINOLE DANCERS, wearing traditional dress of multicoloured cotton, perform in front of a chickee, a stilt house open on all four sides and thatched with palmetto leaves.

THE SEMINOLE consist of members of related Muskogean tribes dispersed by waves of European incursion and expansion beginning in the 15th century.

These tribes hunted, fished, gathered and grew crops in the richly varied environments of Florida. Most Seminole are descended from the CREEK, who once occupied a vast territory in the southeast. The present tribal character and distribution came about during and after the Seminole Wars, a protracted resistance to forced removal fought in the Everglades between 1835 and 1842. In 1830, President Andrew Jackson signed the Indian Removal Act, which forced the removal of all tribes west of the Mississippi River. The CHEROKEE won a United States Supreme Court case defending their right to remain, but the President simply ignored the verdict and ordered the United States Army to evict all the affected tribes, including the Seminole, from their ancestral lands. In the ensuing removal and long forced march to Indian Territory (now Oklahoma) known as the Trail of Tears, cruelty by the Army, starvation, disease, harassment by bandits and by hostile western tribes caused

wholesale suffering and the decimation of the peoples involved. The Seminole were able to resist because they could hide deep in the swampy reaches of the Everglades, but eventually most were relocated to Oklahoma. Despite the dominance of white society, the tribe maintains its traditional culture in both Florida and Oklahoma.

SENECA see IROQUOIS.

SHAMANS are the religious specialists of hunting and gathering tribes, using spiritual techniques extending back to Palaeolithic times. Theirs is a highly individual ability, involving some form of transcendence to carry them into the spirit world. They may be healers (hence the common term "MEDICINE man"), seers (essential in hunting and warfare), or keepers of sacred knowledge. Although agriculturalists tend to have organized priesthoods, their cultures usually maintain shamanic elements, especially in matters of fertility, hunting magic, and the seeking of visions. (See also TRANSFORMATION, SPIRITS OF THE EARTH, DEATH & AFTERLIFE, THE DARK SIDE.)

SHAMANS on the Northwest Coast conduct a ritual outside a cedar plank house. They wear woven cedar bark blankets. (PHOTOGRAPH BY E.J. CURTIS, 1914.)

THE SHOSHONI [Western, Eastern], a large tribe of Uto-Aztecan speakers, hunted and gathered over a vast territory that included parts of the Great Basin, Plateau and Great Plains, in what is today eastern California, eastern Oregon, central Nevada, southern Idaho, northern Utah and western Wyoming. The Western Shoshoni pursued an exacting seasonal round in their relatively arid and resource-poor territory. They trapped groundhogs and other rodents, sage grouse and other birds, gathered pine nuts, grass seeds and berries, and, in the autumn, organized large communal antelope hunts. They now occupy reserves in Nevada, Idaho and California. The Northern, or Wind River, Shoshoni took to the Plains way of life, subsisting mainly on buffalo. They were settled in the Wind River Reservation in west central Wyoming in 1868.

THE SNAKE RIVER in Wyoming derives its name from an earlier historic name for the Shoshoni people. The Mandan, Omaha and Teton Sioux referred to them as "Snakes" because their tribal sign was a serpentine gesture.

SIERRA MIWOK see *YOSEMITE*.

SILA (*INUIT*) is the supreme being of the physical universe, responsible for the winds.

THE SIOUX [Dakota, Lakota, Nakota] people are made up of 14 Siouan-speaking tribes (known

LOW DOG was a warrior chief of the Oglala Sioux, who fought General Custer at the Battle of the Little Big Horn in 1876. He is wearing a bone breastplate and bone necklaces to protect him in battle.

popularly as the Sioux) and had a territory that once extended across the prairies and Plains from Wisconsin to the foothills of the Rocky Mountains in Montana. With their central location in the Plains, they became fully adapted to buffalo hunting, which provided most of their food resources, clothing and other material necessities. The name "Sioux" is no longer preferred, because it derives from an Algonquian pejorative "nadowe-siuh", meaning "snakes".

There were originally seven nations in three dialect groups in this territory. The Lakota, known as the Teton, were in the west; the Nakota, comprising the Yankton and Yanktonai, in the centre; and the Dakota, comprising the Mdewakanton, Wahpekute, Sisseton and Wahpeton, were to the east. The Brule people are a subdivision of the Lakota.

These Siouan peoples suffered the fate of all native people in the region, after a heroic resistance against the military lasting for almost 50 years. This included the legendary Battle of the Little Big Horn (often called Custer's Last Stand) on 25 June 1876, when a force of Sioux, Northern *CHEYENNE*, and Northern *ARAPAHO* wiped out General George Armstrong Custer and his Seventh Cavalry. The resistance ended with the Seventh Cavalry's catastrophic massacre of Big Foot and his mainly unarmed band of men, women and children at Wounded Knee Creek, in South Dakota, on 29 December 1890. In spite of such depredations, the tribe fiercely retains the essence of its traditional culture and controls significant territory in its homeland, especially in South Dakota. (See also *DEATH AND AFTERLIFE, THE STRANGERS, NEW MYTHOLOGIES*)

SIPAPU (*PUEBLO*), the opening into the underworld, is often believed to lie under a lake. The Taos Pueblo emergence lake may be Blue Lake, north of the Taos pueblo itself. The *HOPI* emerged at Ongtupqa (the Grand Canyon) at a site known as Sipaapuni. They believe that, when people die, they return there. For them, this most

sacred part of Ongtupqa is the dwelling place of *KACHINAS*, and the source of clouds.

SLAVE, SLAVEY see *DENE*.

SOLITUDE-WALKER see *TAIKOMOL*.

SPIDER ROCK (*NAVAJO*), the home of *SPIDER WOMAN*, is located in Canyon de Chelly, Arizona.

SPIDER WOMAN is a supernatural being who is common to many oral traditions.

When the first ancestors of the *NAVAJO* emerged, monsters roamed the lands. Spider Woman (Na ashje'ii 'Asdzáá) gave power to her grandsons, *NAYENEZGANI AND TOBADJISHTCHINI*, to search for the sun, their father, and ask him for help. When they found him, he showed them how to destroy the monsters. Grandmother Spider eventually became one of the most important Navajo deities, responsible for many of the essential cultural features, including weaving on a loom. When her tasks were finished, she chose the top of *SPIDER ROCK* for her home.

The *HOPI* say she was created before animals. She led the first people up from the underworld.

She has two forms – a small spider and an aged, but ageless, grandmother. As a spider, she lives in the ground in a small *KIVA*-like chamber, and emerges from a hole likened to the *SIPAPU*. Like all grandmothers, she is wise and compassionate, coming to the aid of people in need or danger.

STAR BOY is a hero (known by various names) among the *CROW, ARAPAHO, BLACKFOOT, IOWA* and other Plains tribes. His story

generally begins with the tale of the *STAR HUSBAND*.

An old woman, known as Grandmother, Old-Woman-Night, or Old-Woman-Who-Never-Dies adopted the boy. Like *LODGE BOY AND THROWN AWAY*, he was a monster-slayer. At the climax of his adventures, he went through death and resurrection. A snake entered his body, stayed until the boy died, and remained even as he became a pile of bones. Since the snake prevented him from returning to life, he rose into the sky and became the Morning Star. To the Blackfoot, he is the tribal hero, Scarface. The *KIOWA* say that early on the hero divided into two Split Boys. One eventually disappeared under a lake, while the other transformed himself into the *tsaidetali MEDICINE*, which are the sacred bundles, or portable altars, of the Kiowa.

STAR HUSBAND is a popular

narrative, found everywhere south of the Arctic, about women who take stars as husbands.

In a Coast *SALISH* version, two sisters who fell in love with the stars rose into the sky, and one bore a son. While digging roots, the sisters accidentally punched a hole in the sky and, seeing the earth below, made a ladder out of twisted cedar boughs, and descended, taking the baby with them. The child was *MOON*. The sisters asked Toad to look after Moon, but she was blind, so Dog Salmon took Moon off to his country at the edge of the world. Moon grew up and had sons of his own. Meanwhile, the sisters created another child from Moon's cedar-bark nappy (diaper). Then Moon began his journey home, accompanied by Dog Salmon. On the way, he transformed beings into stone and into animals and landscape features. When he reached his sky home, he joined his brother, who became the Sun.

STARS and all the major celestial

bodies figure in oral traditions. The *ZUNI* join the origin of several stars in an account of the battle between the *TWIN* war gods and Cloud-swallower, who is taking all the clouds from the sky and causing droughts. They cannot defeat him head on, so they join forces with Gopher, who takes them into the earth and tunnels up beneath Cloud-swallower's heart. They shoot the monster and fling his various parts into the sky. His heart flies into the east and becomes the Morning Star, his liver flies west and becomes the Evening Star, his lungs rise as the Seven Stars (*PLEIADES*), and his entrails lie across the sky as the *MILKY WAY*.

STICK-AND-BALL GAMES

originated deep in North American prehistory. They were already being played with numerous variations by peoples all across the continent when the first Europeans arrived.

MYRIAD STARS light the dark deserts of Arizona, forming timeless patterns that gave native intellectuals a way to chart the rhythms of life and the vastness of their lands.

CHOCTAW WARRIORS, with playing sticks in each hand, move in a seething mass around the elusive ball, in a stick-and-ball game observed in the early 19th century. (PAINTING BY GEORGE CATLIN.)

Stickball is set on a playing field with goals (posts) at either end. Players – sometimes hundreds – each carry a stick with a small net at the top (the *CHOCTAW*, according to the painter George Catlin, who observed a game in 1836, held a stick in each hand) and attempt to carry, or throw, the ball across the opposing goal line. The modern game of lacrosse, brought to European colonists by the *IROQUOIS*, is a variant of stickball. The sky people play games of stickball in the *ALABAMA* story of the *CELESTIAL CANOE*.

Shinny was another game with a similar structure, except that, in this one, the sticks were curved at the end in order to strike, rather than catch, the ball. It was played by the *HOPI CULTURE HEROES* the *POQANGWHOYA BROTHERS*.

Such games could be fiercely competitive, and indeed they were sometimes violent, but they helped to release tensions between or within tribes, just as sports do in modern cultures. The religious ceremonies that attended such games reveal the seriousness of their intent.

NEW GODS

WHEN THE FIRST CHRISTIAN MISSIONARIES set foot on the North American continent, they found peoples they could not fit into the Biblical history of the world. While these aboriginal cultures had millennia of wisdom and experience, the newcomers saw them as primitive, virtually non-human and in need of correction. As the Europeans explored and occupied native lands, the flood of alien ideas and material goods they generated quickly overwhelmed native cultures already decimated by invasion, the spread of foreign diseases and forced removal from their homelands. These depredations caused drastic changes in their world view. No longer intertwined with their own earth and sky, the natives of the land listened and learned – sometimes avidly, but more often helplessly – about a single god and a morality fashioned on a distant continent. In some places they were also prey to conflicting ideas, as missionaries of different faiths competed for converts. Some groups resisted by creating new narratives to counter Christian teachings. Others attempted to avoid the total loss of their mythologies by appropriating Christian elements, especially a single creator or a Jesus-like transformer who took the place of the traditional culture hero. But, even though more than 400 years of aggressive missionary work has forever altered oral tradition, the spiritual remoteness of the Christian drama allowed the survival of fundamental native beliefs about the spiritual essence of the landscape and its knowing creatures.

WHEN MISSIONARIES *moved into an Indian settlement, they ran the risk of being killed for their aggressive assaults on religious traditions that were many thousands of years older than Christianity. Spanish Franciscan monks built this mission at Isleta Pueblo, New Mexico, in 1629, and fortified it heavily against Indian attacks. Two Franciscan missionaries had been murdered nearby in 1581, and the threat of Pueblo resistance was always tangible.*

RELIGIOUS *paraphernalia (above) that had a distinctive Micmac style developed after most of the Micmac were converted to Christianity by French Catholic missionaries in the 18th century. Altarpieces in particular were elaborately decorated, as in this petroglyph example, carved in slate at McGowan Lake, in central Nova Scotia.*

AN ALTARPIECE *(above), painted by Father Guy-Mary Rousselière in a small wooden church on the shore of Pond Inlet, in the Canadian Arctic territory of Nunavut, shows Inuit having a vision of Jesus Christ.*

IN A HIDE PAINTING *(right), commemorating a late-19th-century Sun Dance, participants gather around a large Christian cross. As Christian beliefs and rituals spread through Indian communities across the continent, they were often integrated into traditional ceremonies as one of the host of powerful forces that had to be respected.*

T

THE SUN DANCE, a sacred renewal ceremony,

THE SUN DANCE, a sacred renewal ceremony, is held throughout the Plains in late spring or early summer. It generally involves four days of complex ritual with allusions to boy heroes such as Scarface for the *BLACKFOOT*, and *LODGE BOY AND THROWN AWAY* for the *HIDATSA*.

The *ARAPAHO* place a special knife on the Sun Dance altar, said to be the one Double Face used when performing a caesarean section on the mother of their *TWIN* heroes (see under *LODGE BOY*). They also honour the mother of *STAR BOY*, identifying her with the centre pole in the Sun Dance lodge. In the Arapaho version of the *STAR HUSBAND* tale, the young heroine climbs a tree into the sky following a porcupine (usually the sun or moon in disguise). (See also *NEW GODS.)*

SWEATLODGE rituals are, even today, an essential part of religious worship in many American Indian cultures. They serve two primary purposes: for ritual cleansing and for the intensification of sensual experience through the effects of intense heat and darkness, which can lead to heightened states of awareness. The most common type of sweatlodge is a small hut, fashioned from curved saplings and covered with skins or bark. The participants bring hot rocks into the structure from a fire outside and pour water over them, producing the steam. As sweating is a ritual, the construction of the lodge and the carrying out of the sweat follow religious prescriptions and may be attended by songs, prayers and other rituals. In the Great Plains, for example, a sweat is an essential part of the *SUN DANCE* ceremony.

SWEET MEDICINE see *HOOP-AND-POLE GAME.*

THE TAHLTAN are an Athapascan people who lived in the Stikine River region of northern British Columbia, hunting, fishing and gathering in a seasonal round through their remote boreal-forest environment. They continue to pursue many of their traditional ways, but they are now centred in the towns of Telegraph Creek, Dease Lake and Iskut.

TAIKOMOL (*YUKI*) or Solitude-walker, the creator, began as a voice in sea foam, then rose up in human form and established the earth by laying a cross over the water.

TENA see *DENA.*

A SWEATLODGE site may be located in an area imbued with spiritual power, such as the edge of a sacred mountain.

TEPEES (Tipis) are conical tents of skin (or bark) covering a frame of poles, erected in a circle, that support each other at the apex. An uncovered area at the top serves as a smoke-hole for the tent. Tepees were the characteristic dwellings of the nomadic buffalo-hunting peoples of the Great Plains, but were used by many different North American peoples.

TEWA, TIWA see *PUEBLO.*

THROWN AWAY
see under *LODGE BOY.*

THUNDERBIRD, a giant bird often identified as responsible for thunder and lightning, is a powerful spirit, demanding respect among many peoples.

The *PASSAMAQUODDY* tell of two men who tried to discover the origin of thunder. They travelled north to a high mountain and saw a cave-like opening, which they tried to enter. One made it through but, as the other crossed the threshold, the mountain closed in, and he died. The survivor walked into a large plain with an encampment of tepees (huts of arched poles covered with bark, animal skin or woven mats, typical of Algonquians of the northeast) and people playing a ball game. As he watched, they finished their game, sprouted wings and flew south – they were thunderbirds. He came upon some old men left in the village, and told them that he wanted to know where thunder came from. They put him into a large mortar and pounded him until he was soft enough to be shaped into a new body: a thunderbird. Then they gave him a bow and arrows, and sent him on his way. Although he was now a thunderbird, he never forgot his homeland, and so he became a powerful protector of the Passamaquoddy tribe. (See also *THE LIVING SKY, THE DARK SIDE*)

ON A PAWNEE ceremonial drum, the dark leading edge of a prairie storm takes the shape of a giant thunderbird. As the thunderbird's eyes and wings flash with lightning, the winds, rushing into the coming storm, stir up a flock of swallows.

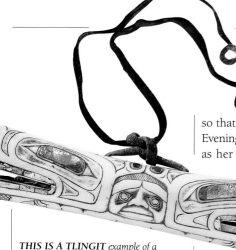

THIS IS A TLINGIT example of a typical shamanic device. Northwest coast shamans sometimes diagnosed an illness as the loss of the patient's spirit or soul. To bring the spirit back they used a small, polished bone carved in the shape of a two-headed animal (usually the sisiutl, a two-headed sea monster) and engraved with a third, central face. The shaman would catch the spirit in this device and then blow it back into the patient's body. This example is inlaid with abalone shell.

TIIKUYWUUTI (*HOPI*) died giving birth, hence her name, Child-Sticking-Out Woman. She is the mother of all game animals. She is beautiful, daubs her face with a white pigment, and wears a mask and a ruffled collar. Unsuccessful hunters pray to her to have intercourse with them, so that they can be better hunters. She leaves behind the tracks of a jack rabbit.

TIRÁWAHAT (*PAWNEE, ARIKARA*), the creator (whose name translates as "expanse") is a powerful, unseen presence residing at the zenith, who puts the gods in their proper places. The Sun occupies the east, the *MOON*, the west. The Morning Star is the warrior who drives *STARS* towards the west, where the Evening Star presides as the mother of all things.

Tiráwahat made a North Star, a Southern Star and other stars to help hold up the sky; then the four elements – Clouds, Winds, Lightning, Thunder (given to the Evening Star to put in her garden); and then the earth. The creator fashioned the earth by first dropping a pebble in a large stormy cloud; water was formed, then the sky-supporters struck the water with their war clubs, separating it so that earth appeared. When the Evening Star took the Morning Star as her consort, they produced a girl who would be the mother of humanity, and the Moon and Sun produced a boy to be her husband. The new husband learned from Evening Star how to make the sacred *MEDICINE* bundle, and the elements taught him the songs of all the ceremonies.

TLAGU (*TLINGIT*), translated as "of the long ago", is the term Tlingit story-tellers use to refer to stories of the past, including core beliefs and all the forms of story-telling related to the ancients.

THE TLINGIT, speakers of a Na-Dene language, once controlled the coasts of southeast Alaska and northern British Columbia, and the southeastern edge of Yukon Territory. They led a sea-going life, hunting whales and other sea mammals, salmon, halibut and other salt-water fish, clams, mussels and other shellfish, and deer and other forest game. Their culture was similar to the complex and highly structured societies of the *HAIDA* and *TSIMSHIAN* to the south, with an intricate and abundant art and ceremonialism devoted to the display of the mythological ancestors of *CLANS* and families. They occupied areas exploited heavily by Russians, British and Americans during the heyday of the fur trade, but successfully resisted the aggressive and often murderous traders until the purchase of the territory by the United States in 1906. Contact with European and American cultures, however, caused debilitating disease, dislocation and acculturation in the same way that it did among other coastal peoples. Many Tlingit are assimilated into the dominant society, but some continue to pursue their traditional culture. (See also *TRANSFORMATION, THE LIVING SKY, NEW MYTHOLOGIES*)

TOBACCO see *WYANDOT*.

TOBADJISHTCHINI see *NAYENEZGANI*.

TOHONO O'ODHAM see *PAPAGO*.

TOTEM POLES are monumental cedar poles erected by northern Northwest Coast peoples to display family and *CLAN* crests, denoting their legendary descent from animal ancestors.

The *KWAKIUTL* recount the appearance of the first totem pole. Wakiash was a chief, but he did not own a dance as the other chiefs did, so he went into the mountains to fast in the hopes of gaining one. After four days, a little green frog appeared and told him to lie still, as he was on the back of a raven that would fly him around the world for four days. Among the wonderful things he saw was a house with a beautiful totem pole in front. He wanted to take it home. The frog read his thoughts and told the raven to stop. When the chief came to the entrance of the house, he heard singing. Wakiash caught a little mouse-woman who ran outside, and gave her a piece of mountain-goat fat. When she asked him what he wanted, he demanded the pole, the house and the dances and songs. He then surprised the animals in their dance, which caused them great shame because they were masquerading as humans. To compensate, they taught him their songs and dances, and showed him their masks, including the Echo mask. The Beaver Chief added a special pole he named Kalakuyuwish, meaning sky pole. Beaver folded the house up like a little bundle, gave Wakiash a headdress, and instructed him to throw down the bundle when he reached home and all would reappear.

Wakiash did as he was told, and the house was wonderful, as all the creatures on it moved. The whale painted on the house front was blowing, the carved animals on the pole spoke in their own languages, and all the masks inside the house talked and cried aloud. This raucous behaviour woke up Wakiash's people. When they came to the chief's house they told him it was not four days but four years that he had been away. Wakiash danced for the people, taught them the songs he had learned and showed them how to use the masks. When at last the dancing stopped, the house disappeared, back to the animals. All the chiefs were envious because Wakiash had the best dance of all. He then made a house and masks and a great totem pole out of wood, which all the people honoured with a new song. This was the first pole – Kalakuyuwish, or the pole that holds up the sky. (See also *NEW MYTHOLOGIES, THE DARK SIDE*)

THIS TOTEM is known as the "Hole-in-the-Sky" pole. It was originally used as the ceremonial entrance point for a house in Kitwancool village, a Tsimshian settlement situated along the banks of Skeena River in British Columbia.

TOWA see *PUEBLO*.

TRANSFORMERS are an essential element of American Indian religious philosophy, as these supernatural beings are responsible for the *CREATION* of the world as it is now, in the age of the story-tellers. During the formative age, all beings had the capacity to transform both themselves and things around them, as the entire world was fluid and changing. Hence, both *CULTURE HEROES* and villains took part. Some transformations were intentional, such as the creation of humans and animals, but some others were incidental, produced in the course of supernatural events. Transformers ensured that all of nature and culture had an origin that fitted logically into the beliefs and traditions of the tribe, securing a clear and powerful sense of social identity. Examples of transformers are the culture heroes *COYOTE*, *RAVEN*, *TIIKUYWUUTI* and *TRAVELLER*. (See also *TRANSFORMATION*)

TRAVELLER (*DENA*), a *CULTURE HERO* also known as "the Man-who-Went-Through Everything" or "the One-who-Travelled-Among-all-the-Animals-and-People", canoed into Dena territory from the headwaters of the Yukon River. Dena peoples living along the Koyukuk River call him "Betohoh", because he became a Pine Grosbeak when he died. His adventures contrast somewhat with *RAVEN*'s because he tended to avoid mischief.

He was a canoe maker. In a Dena version, he experimented until he successfully made a birch-bark canoe. He killed a spruce grouse, took out the breastbone and fitted the bones together for the frame. Then he cut up a sheet of birch bark and got some women to sew it together around the canoe and seal the joins with pitch.

TRICKSTERS are beings with supernatural powers who introduce a strong sense of reality into myths, as they manifest the whole range of human foibles, counterbalancing the often idealized and rarefied personalities of gods and *CULTURE HEROES*. Some beings, such as the culture heroes *COYOTE*

THE TRAVELLER was a canoe maker. The birch-bark canoe was the preferred method of travel across the northern forests of North America, as it was easily made, ran swiftly and silently, and was light enough to carry from lake to lake or along river rapids too rough to paddle. (INDIAN CANOE, PAINTED BY FRANK SCHOONOVER, 1922.)

and *RAVEN*, may combine both heroic virtues and a predilection for playing silly, selfish or evil pranks. Others, such as *COTTONTAIL*, never quite rise to the level of the heroic, acting instead as foils or sidekicks to their braver and more gallant companions. (See also *TRANSFORMATION, THE TRICKSTER*)

THE TSIMSHIAN [Gitksan, Niska, Tsimshian] consist of three Penutian-speaking tribal groups who occupy the northern coast of British Columbia, extending up the Nass and Skeena River basins into the Coast Mountains. Since their territory included both coasts and mountains, they had access to an enormous variety of natural resources, whales and other sea mammals, salmon, halibut and other salt-water fish, mussels, sea urchins, clams and other shellfish, and deer and other game in the coastal forests. As the Niska and Gitksan lived along the flanks of the Coast Mountains, they were able to hunt mountain sheep and goats, from which they obtained wool that they traded with their coastal relatives in return for oil from the oolichan fish (also known as the candlefish because, when dried, it could be lit like a taper). With a sedentary lifestyle and the ability to

produce and trade surplus food and materials, the tribe developed social structures and traditions more consistent with agriculturalists than hunters and gatherers. They produced magnificent carvings in cedar, from monumental *TOTEM POLES* to intricately fashioned boxes and other ceremonial wares, and also carved, painted and engraved horn, copper and other materials, and wove fine baskets. Typical of Northwest Coast peoples, they produced masks depicting their mythological animal ancestors, but they also created portrait masks of stunning realism. Protected by their resource base, the Tsimshian have survived the worst depredations of European culture, and continue to maintain many of their cultural traditions.

THE TRICKSTER AND TRANSFORM-ER RAVEN finds humankind in a cockle shell, as on this chest lid. It is carved in argil-lite, a dense, dark slate, by Charles Edenshaw, the premier Haida carver of the late 19th century.

TSÚNUKWA (*KWAKIUTL*) is a cannibal, one of the Winter Dance spirits. She can bring the dead to life, but story-tellers represent her as dim-witted.

In one Winter Dance origin story, a young man helped her recover the body of her dead son. After reviving him with her water of life, the grateful mother gave the hero a supply of the water and a mask representing herself, which he later wore in performing the first Tsúnukwa dance.

TSUU T'INA see *SARCEE*.

TUSCARORA see *IROQUOIS*.

THE TUSKEGEE people were a small southeastern tribe, subsisting on hunting, gathering and horticulture, who lived in what is now north-central Alabama and adjoin-

A SHAMAN'S MASK is carved with the subtlety and fine finishing characteristic of the Tsimshian. The combination of human and animal attributes reflects the shaman's ability to transcend the present world and commune with the animal ancestors.

ing parts of Tennessee. They seemed to have adopted the *CREEK* language and customs during the late 18th century, and are now extinct.

TWINS are a very common character type in Native American mythology. In the Southwest, the *NAVAJO*, *APACHE*, *PUEBLO* and other tribes characterize warrior twins as *CULTURE HEROES*, working together to transform the world and slay monsters. *LODGE BOY* and his twin brother, Thrown Away, fulfil the same role for the *HIDATSA* in a story cycle of heroic twins that is found throughout the Plains.

Twins can also be used to serve as a metaphor for opposition – such as between good and evil, as in the Iroquoian stories of Sapling and his evil brother *FLINT*.

UPRIVER-OCEAN GIRL (*YU-ROK*) was the provider of water for the Yurok world.

COYOTE searched for water, because the country had none, and he knew humans would need it. He travelled everywhere looking for water, all across the sky, and then decided to go upriver. He crossed the sky, descended to earth on a ladder and met Upriver-Ocean Girl. He told her that there was no water, so she created it out of her body. She entered the dry river bed and the water began to flow into a lake. Coyote pointed out that the water would be no good without fish, so she created salmon and trout.

THE UTE [Ute, Chemehuevi] are speakers of an Uto-Aztecan language who at one time hunted and gathered across a vast territory in the Great Basin, through Utah and Colorado and into parts of southern Wyoming and northern New Mexico. Having access to a variety of environments beyond the arid desert steppes, they were able to supplement their hunting of antelope and rabbits with deer, elk, buffalo and mountain sheep. Where available, they also caught fish and reptiles, trapped wildfowl, and gathered edible insects. After numerous forced removals, relocations and the eventual loss of most of their reservation lands, the three dialect groups, the Ute, Southern *PAIUTE*, and Chemehuevi, are now settled on reservations in southeast Colorado and eastern and northeastern Utah.

THE WABANAKI ("daybreak land people") confederacy, was an alliance of several eastern Algonquian hunting and gathering tribes inhabiting the Atlantic coasts and the interior from Nova Scotia to

Maine: the *MICMAC* and several of the *ABENAKI* peoples, the *MALISEET*, *PASSAMAQUODDY*, and *PENOBSCOT*. They joined together in order to make peace with the aggressive Mohawk, an *IROQUOIS* people, and their allies, the Algonquian-speaking *OTTAWA*, during a period of strife in 18th century that was fuelled by European political rivalries and by competition in the fur trade. The western Abenaki, a horticultural people occupying the most southerly part of this region, also joined for a brief time.

WALAM OLUM (*DELAWARE*) is an account of Delaware *CREATION* and migration, painted and engraved in 183 red pictographic characters on wooden sticks. The authenticity of this artifact has been debated by academics since it was first brought to light by the French scholar Constantine Samuel Rafinesque in 1836. An analysis of Rafinesque's original papers, undertaken in 1998, suggested that he had first written the document in English and then translated it into Delaware.

"ALWAYS RIDING" was a Ute leader of the Yampah band. Federal officials brought Ute leaders to Washington in 1868 for treaty negotiations. The government broke the treaty in 1873 and, within a few years, the Ute had lost most of their remaining lands.

NEW MYTHOLOGIES

NATIVE NORTH AMERICANS must fight to preserve the knowledge and wisdom of their ancestors in a world dominated by Western culture. But thousands of years of adaptation have also taught them to look ahead to the welfare of future generations. Ritual practices once confined to specific tribes and culture areas, such as the sweatlodge and the sundance, have spread across the continent, helping to reinforce the spirits of peoples threatened by extinction. New religions, such as the Native American Church, have rites that seem to resonate with the ancient past, while admitting some elements of Christianity. These groups give strength to native identity and provide a traditional path towards the future. Many other native people are Christians and, although some of

A VISITOR leaves the Clan House at Totem Bight State Park, Ketchikan, Alaska. While the original Northwest Coast villages were almost completely abandoned during the late 19th century, new housebuilding and carving are beginning to revive the ancient crafts.

their churches accommodate traditional beliefs and practices, others resolutely reject non-Christian symbolism, ritual paraphernalia or ceremonies. For all that, the spirits of the earth are alive outside organized religion, since the rich narrative tradition thrives in

AN INUKSUIT, a stone figure constructed by Inuit hunters to drive caribou, stands snow-covered on an Arctic winter day. What was once practical is now sacred, as aboriginal people treasure every surviving trace of their original life, before the coming of white people.

the creative arts. Native artists, dancers, writers and musicians use modern media as a new form of story-telling, one that shows respect for the old and yet gives life to the new. This creative energy is helping to change the face of native culture, yet it is still in keeping with the ancients. Mythology is a way of expressing the rich and wondrous texture of life as it is lived, and so it is appropriate that the old culture heroes live on in new worlds of expression.

OJIBWAY ARTIST (above) Blake Debassige is part of a generation of painters who have followed the lead of Norval Morriseau in translating traditional ideas into a modern idiom. In his surreal Bear Driving a Cadillac (above), Debassige imagines what it would be like if this powerful ancestor lived in the world of modern capitalism.

SIOUX ARTIST (left) Oscar Howe (1915–1983) used the symbols of the circle and Tahokmu, or spider web, to create swirling interplays of colour and form on traditional themes. Woman Scalp Dancer (left) depicts a Sioux ceremony, when enemy scalps were taken for protection from the spirits of those they had killed.

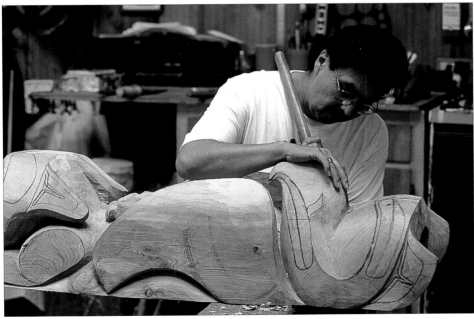

AT BEAR BUTTE (above) western South Dakota, one of the most important sacred places of the Sioux, traditional religion dovetails with tourism, as the site is also a park. Near the sign warning away recreational visitors are prayer flags and bundles left by Native American worshippers.

A TLINGIT CARVER works on a new totem pole at Ketchikan, in southeast Alaska. The great tradition of Northwest Coast art survived the depredations of the historic period and flourishes once again. While it continues to have profound cultural meaning to the tribes along the coast, the outpouring of wood and stone carvings, paintings, prints and jewellery is also recognized as an important part of the world's artistic heritage.

THE WAPPO, speakers of a Yuki language, once lived among the mountains of northern California, hunting small game, fishing and gathering acorns and other wild plants. Like most of the California tribes, the Wappo were either eliminated or forced from their lands by incoming white people, and there were none left in their aboriginal home in the Napa Valley in 1908. The descendants of the surviving Wappo now occupy small land-holdings in the region.

WATER SERPENTS are creatures that figure in mythologies across North America.

Among the *HOPI*, Paalölöqangw is both feared and respected. He resembles a giant rattlesnake, with a round, greenish head, protruding eyes, a mouth studded with sharp teeth, a large horn and a crest of ochre-stained feathers. These attributes, resembling those of Quetzalcóatl, the feathered serpent god of the Toltecs and Aztecs, reflect the Mesoamerican influences on Hopi culture. He also sports a fan of eagle tail-feathers and a seashell necklace. He is master of the ocean, and he lives in springs that he creates by vomiting up water. The Hopi pray to him for

THE IMPACT of the White Man is evident on this Cherokee man's fine ceremonial costume. Along with traditional features – quilled sash, nose ring, long ear loops and earrings – he sports a large silver trade breastplate and a silver medallion.

THIS SOUTHERN Ojibway ceremonial drumstick is made of an animal jawbone carved in the shape of Mishipizheu, the great horned water serpent who lives in deep lakes and rivers.

rain. In one tradition, the serpent lies across the oceans, with the *TWIN* war gods straddling him, keeping watch over the Hopi. If the people begin to falter in their observance of proper ritual, the twins, along with their grandmother, *SPIDER WOMAN*, will cause the serpent to writhe and drown the entire earth.

The Chiricahua *APACHE* regard some springs as abodes of water monsters, and so they are afraid of using them. In one account, a young girl went to fill her water jar and disappeared. Her mother sought out a *SHAMAN*, who conducted ceremonies for four nights and called in a spirit who told the girl's father to go to the spring. There, the father saw a strange man, with long hair and eyes as bright as the stars, rise out of the water with the daughter at his side. She told him that the man was her husband, and that she now preferred her new underwater home. To compensate her father for his loss, the couple foretold that as long as he stayed in his own country, he would be a great hunter and kill many deer. Unfortunately, he eventually decided to leave his home and his people, and ultimately died in a war with the invading Spanish.

WEEPING WOMAN (*HAIDA*) or Djilákons, is one of the mythic mothers of the Haida moieties, the two halves into which Haida *CLANS* are divided (the other is *FOAM WOMAN*). In one version, she takes the form of a frog whom some hunters have offended. In retaliation, she destroys all humans in a volcanic eruption – except for one girl, who becomes the ancestor of the *EAGLES*. In another version, she gives birth to all the clans herself.

WENEBOJO see *NANABUSH*.

WHITE-BUFFALO-CALF WOMAN (Lakota *SIOUX*) is the great supernatural being who is credited with providing the most powerful tribal *MEDICINE* of the Lakota, the Calf Pipe.

In one account, the Lakota once lived beside a lake far to the east, but, after a hard winter, they were forced to migrate. Two scouts sent ahead suddenly encountered a beautiful maiden dressed in sage, holding a buffalo-skin bundle. One of them rushed at her lustfully, but she brought down rattlesnakes, and he was reduced to bones. She instructed the other to construct a circle of green boughs, and told him she would reappear in front of the entire tribe. Before the people she unwrapped the *PIPE* and instructed them in the songs and prayers of the five great ceremonies: the Foster-parent Chant, the *SUN DANCE*, the Vision Cry, the Buffalo Chant and the Ghost-keeper. She told them that they would always be a nation if they revered the pipe. Then she disappeared, and the people saw only a white buffalo calf on the prairie.

WHITE CLAY PEOPLE see *GROS VENTRE*.

WHITE MAN's first dramatic appearance to the Native Americans is preserved in several oral traditions. The *CHINOOK* tell of the sighting of the first ship. A woman gazed out to sea and saw a strange object that looked like a whale, except that it had two spruce trees standing upright on it. She moved closer and saw that it was clad with copper and had ropes tied to the trees. When a bear came out of this strange object, she saw that it had the face of a human being. Terrified, she ran to the village, crying, and the people rushed back to confront this monster. The two strange men they found there held out copper kettles and put their hands to their mouths, asking for water. After capturing them as slaves, the Chinook burned the vessel.

Oral traditions needed to account for the presence of Europeans in *CREATION*. In two accounts, *COYOTE* is held responsible.

In the *PIMA* version, Coyote pestered the creator as he attempted to fashion human beings out of clay. When the creator went out for wood to fire the clay, Coyote took the clay figures out of the kiln and moulded them into dogs. Now suspicious of Coyote, the creator placed a further batch of clay humans in the kiln and fired them. However, he then foolishly believed it when Coyote told him that the batch was done. The figures turned out pale and underdone: the first white people.

In the *FLATHEAD* version, Old-Man-in-the-Sky, the creator, had to placate *OLD MAN COYOTE* (Coyote as a first being) by creating human companions for him, because he was so lonely that his weeping threatened to cause a new world flood. The creator sent him off to fill a parfleche (rawhide bag) with red earth. Coyote was so tired after filling the bag that he fell asleep. While he slept, Mountain Sheep happened along and decided to trick him. He emptied the bag, filled the bottom with white earth, topped it up with red and put it back. When Coyote finally returned to the creator, it was almost dark. The creator took the soil out of the bag and began to shape two

men and two women – the first people – and Coyote took them down to the land and gave them breath. Only in the morning light did he discover that one of the two pairs was white.

A Chiricahua APACHE narrative resolves the problem of accounting for the creation of the material culture of Europeans via two CULTURE HEROES, CHILD-OF-THE-WATER and Killer-of-Enemies (a brother or other relation). The connection is made between Killer-of-Enemies and European culture because he received corn (maize) from Yusn, the creator. Corn and all other domesticated plants and animals, guns and other trade goods are therefore under his purview. Child-of-the-Water is associated with traditional weapons and foods, since he and his mother first collected wild plants.

WHITE-PAINTED WOMAN (Chiricahua APACHE) was mother of the CULTURE HERO CHILD-OF-THE-WATER. She supported her child hero and instructed the Chiricahua in the girls' puberty rite and other important ceremonies.

THE WICHITA, a Caddoan-speaking people, raised corn (maize), beans, squash and other crops in the river basins of the southern Great Plains. They lived in grass-thatched conical huts,

surrounded by their crops. In 1872, they were relocated to reservation lands in Indian Territory (which eventually became Oklahoma); however, the United States Congress never ratified the agreement and, in 1901, most of the original Wichita lands were opened for allotment to white settlers. Today, the tribe controls a mere 4 ha (10 acres), although it shares 972 ha (2,400 acres) with two other tribes, the related Caddo and the DELAWARE.

A WICHITA lodge consists of a dome-shaped pole framework, thatched with grass, with a smoke-hole in the centre.

A WINNEBAGO woman weaves a basket using thin splints of oak. Traditional basket designs had names and meanings, often associated with beings and events held sacred by the tribe.

WIDOWER-FROM-ACROSS-THE-OCEAN see WOHPEKUMEU.

WINABOJO see NANABUSH.

WÍNDIGO (northern Algonquians) is a cannibal giant with a heart of ice, a personification of madness associated with either winter starvation or extreme gluttony.

The OJIBWAY see the Wíndigo as a giant MANITOU, in the form of a man or woman, who is afflicted with a never-ending hunger. This ghastly monster resembles a body removed from a grave – withered, skeletal and with the smell of death. When the Wíndigo prepares to attack a person, a dark snow-cloud rises up, the air turns so cold that the trees crack, and the wind causes a blizzard. The monster tears its victims apart, eating their flesh and bones, and drinking the blood, and some people die of fright when they see it or hear its shriek. Yet, the more the creature eats, the hungrier it gets,

and so it perpetually rages through the dark forests in search of new prey. One lesson of the Wíndigo, therefore, is moderation – it teaches of the need for people to manage critical food supplies so that they can avoid winter famine.

THE WINNEBAGO [Ho-Chunk] are a Siouan-speaking people who originated in present-day Wisconsin, to the south of the Great Lakes, where they hunted, fished, gathered wild rice, and grew corn (maize) and other crops.

In 1826–7, they rose up against encroaching settlers, and then, in 1840, they were forcibly removed from their homeland to northeast Iowa. In the following decades, they were relocated several times: first to central Minnesota, then to South Dakota and finally, in 1863, to the Winnebago Reservation in northeast Nebraska. During the 1880s, when half of their members moved back to Wisconsin, the Winnebago tribe separated into the two distinct groups that exist today: the original Hochungra ("People of the Big Voices") in Nebraska, and the returnees, the Wonkshieks ("First People of the Old Island"), in Wisconsin.

WINTU, or Wintun, are a small Penutian-speaking northern California people who once hunted and gathered in the Sacramento Valley. They suffered greatly during the invasion by white people, losing their lands and approximately 80 per cent of their population. They retain some small land-holdings, and continue to struggle to keep their traditional way of life.

WISAKEDJAK (Wisaka) (Algonquians, including *KICKAPOO, CREE, FOX,* and *POTAWATOMI*) is in many characteristics analogous to the *OJIBWAY* hero *NANABUSH*.

A Plains *CREE* account begins with a variation of the monstrous *FLYING HEAD* theme. A woman gave birth to two sons, the eldest being Wisakedjak. One day, her husband discovered her consorting with snakes, so he ordered his sons to run away, and in a rage killed the snakes, fed his wife their blood, chopped off her head and fled into the sky. The furious woman sent her buttocks after the boys and her head after the husband. The buttocks caught up with the children at a river, but a crane picked them up and flew them across to safety. The crane then picked up the mother (she was now whole again) and dropped her into the water, where she changed into a sturgeon.

THE WOLVERINE of the mythological age took on the traits of the humans he would harass in the present world. In a Dena tale, Wolverine traps and eats people until he is outwitted by Traveller, the Dena culture hero, who kills the entire family except one wolverine daughter. Her revenge is to make all wolverine thieving and destructive to humans, stealing animals from traps and breaking into caches of meat.

Free from his mother, Wisakedjak left his younger brother and set off on monster-slaying adventures. While he was away, the brother turned into a wolf and was eventually killed by *WATER SERPENTS*, who used his hide as a door flap. On hearing of his brother's fate, Wisakedjak stormed the serpents' den and killed their chief but, in the struggle, the serpents caused a world flood. The hero survived, however, by building a raft, and then sent a loon (great northern diver) down to fetch some earth, and created the world anew.

THE WIYOT, an Algic-speaking culture, once fished, hunted and gathered along the coast of northwestern California. They were almost wiped out by incoming white people, most notably in 1860, when a large ceremonial gathering was massacred by citizens of the town of Eureka – a traumatic event that influences the lives of Wiyot to this day. They now have three small land-holdings (*rancherias*) in the region.

WOHPEKUMEU (*YUROK*), the Widower-From-Across-the-Ocean, is a *CULTURE HERO, TRICKSTER* and *TRANSFORMER* whose various achievements include stealing salmon and acorns for humankind, regulating the rivers and instituting natural childbirth (instead of violent caesarean births).

WOLVERINE, an important *TRICKSTER* and *TRANSFORMER*, may destroy traps and furs like his animal counterpart, but he also has powers of healing.

The *DENA* believe that he made all flint tools by gnawing rocks to shape them. In a parable for children, Wolverine teaches the importance of trust and prudence. Near the beginning of the world, Wolverine stole two children and kept them in a tree cache. In another cache below, he kept his food; there were all sorts of food in

WOMAN-WHO-FELL-FROM-THE-SKY falls through a hole made by an uprooted tree in the sky world, and plunges towards the primeval waters covering the earth. A flock of geese prepares to break her fall while a turtle provides a landing below. (OUR EARTH, OUR MOTHER, *BY SENECA ARTIST ERNEST SMITH.*)

his cache, but he fed the children only fat. One day, the curious children decided to look in Wolverine's cache. When they discovered all the food, they stole some meat and then confronted Wolverine, demanding to know why he kept it to himself. He told them that he had been saving the meat for the future, when they were out on their own – but, because they had betrayed his trust, they would become thieves and liars instead.

WOMAN-WHO-FELL-FROM-THE-SKY (*IROQUOIS*) figures in an explanation of the *CREATION* of the world.

In a land above the sky, a young woman became the bride of an older man but transgressed (in some versions committed adultery), and this caused the tree of life to be uprooted. (In another version, she married a chief and fell ill. In a *DREAM*, the chief was advised to lay her beside the tree that sup-

plied corn [maize] to the people, and to dig it up.) The pregnant woman fell (or was pushed or kicked) through the hole where the tree had been and plummeted towards the water below, but some ducks (or geese) cushioned her descent and held her in the air. Then, to make her a permanent resting place, the assembled animals agreed to create land. Muskrat volunteered to dive under the water for some mud, but he drowned and floated to the surface. Fortunately, Beaver found enough mud in Muskrat's claws and mouth to fashion some land, and Turtle volunteered to support it. The new earth and Turtle grew larger, and the woman gave birth to *TWINS*, the *CULTURE HERO* Sapling and his evil contrary, *FLINT*.

THE WYANDOT are the descendants of two Iroquoian tribes, the Huron and the Tobacco, who lived in what is now southern Ontario, between Lake Simcoe and Georgian Bay, on Lake Huron. They were organized in a loose confederacy called the Wendat. The *IROQUOIS* drove these two horticultural tribes from the region in the middle of the 17th century and scattered them east along the St Lawrence River and south of the Great Lakes. A small number of the Huron eventually settled in Quebec, but the rest of the group escaped to the west end of Lake Erie, where they became known as the Wyandot. In 1843, they were forcibly removed to Kansas, from where most of them were driven out again by 1857 and settled in northeastern Oklahoma.

THE YAKIMA are an amalgam of once-independent tribes and bands, speaking several different languages, who occupied the Plateau region in south-central Washington State. They were predominantly salmon fishers and gatherers along the Columbia River and its tributaries.

After acquiring horses in 1730, they took up buffalo hunting and adopted some cultural traits of Plains tribes. They were forcibly removed to a reservation in the region in 1855, but did retain

THE RECONSTRUCTED Sainte-Marie among the Hurons is a mission founded by French Jesuits in 1639 in the land of the people known then as the Huron (in present-day southern Ontario). In 1649, the Iroquois attacked it in the course of their destruction of the Huron, Tobacco and Neutral tribes, and killed Fathers Jean de Brébeuf and Gabriel Lalemant along with many Wendat. The survivors scattered, and the descendants of one group became the Wyandot Nation of Kansas.

sufficient land (approximately 567,000 ha/1.4 million acres at present) to survive economically and maintain their cultural identity.

YAMANHDEYA (*DENE*), also known as He-Went-Around-the-Edge, was a *CULTURE HERO* who travelled around the rim of the earth in his pursuit of monsters. The *BEAVER* know him as Saya.

YELLOWKNIFE See *DENE*.

THE YOSEMITE (Sierra Miwok) people are the most southerly of the Sierra *MIWOK*, and are one of the groups belonging to the Miwok language family. They were hunters and gatherers, and they occupied the Sierra Nevada foothills of central California. They suffered the depredations typical of California tribes during white settlement – disease, killing and dislocation – but the tribe nonetheless continues to inhabit small land-holdings within its traditional territory.

THIS YAKIMA BOY (left) wears traditional costume at the Ellenburg Rodeo, Washington State. Pow-wows and rodeos provide Native North Americans with a public outlet for their proud cultures, seen most dramatically in their ceremonial dances.

THE YUKI people are a small northern California hunting and gathering tribe, named after the language they speak, who were almost eliminated during the 19th-century settlement of the region by whites. Along with the *MAIDU, WINTU* and other aboriginal groups in the area, they were relocated during the 1860s and 1870s on the Round Valley Indian Reservation within traditional Yuki territory. Their language is now extinct, but they maintain their cultural identity.

THE YUROK, an Algonquian people, lived in northwestern California around the mouth of the Klamath River. They subsisted primarily on the abundant salmon, small game and acorns of this area. Having managed to resist white incursions during and after the Gold Rush of 1849, they were forced into the Klamath River Reservation (which ran along 32 km/20 miles of the river) in 1855, and the Hoopa Valley Reservation in 1864. After further land reductions, the tribe now hold approximately 3,645 ha (9,000 acres) of reservation land and allotments.

THE ZUNI people are a Western *PUEBLO* tribe, speaking a language isolate (unrelated to any known language family) that some linguists classify under the Penutian family. They once occupied the Zuni and Little Colorado River valleys in New Mexico and Arizona. They grow corn (maize) and other crops and, since the coming of Europeans, herd sheep and other animals. Their philosophical organization and their world view are structured on an intricate system of spatial domains, incorporating the seven original villages and the four corresponding cardinal directions plus zenith, nadir and centre. All social, religious and environmental patterns are oriented within this system, managed by an organized priesthood. The Zuni refer to each of their villages as *itiwana*, meaning "the middle place". The original Zuni reservation was established in 1877, but the United States government reduced this holding substantially in the 20th century. Although they remain in their ancestral lands, and have very successfully resisted the incursions of European and American culture, the Zuni now control less than 3% of their original territory.

A ZUNI MAN stands beside an eagle on its cage. As the eagle is a great hunter and powerful ancestor, its feathers are highly valued in ritual and ceremony by many different tribes.

Z

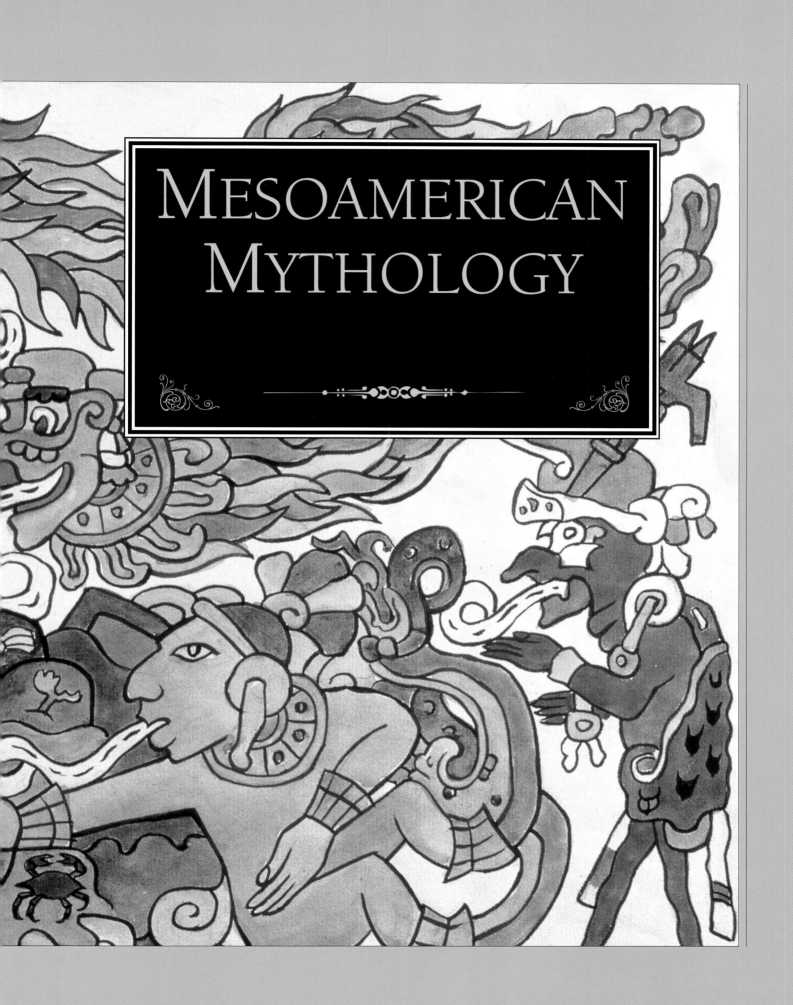

MESOAMERICAN MYTHOLOGY

INTRODUCTION

MESOAMERICA IS BOTH a cultural concept and a geographical area. The geographical area includes both drier highlands and more humid lowlands, and is defined by mountain chains and plateaux within, deserts to the north, and tropical rain forests, grasslands and marshes to the south and east, and by the Pacific Ocean to the west and the Caribbean Sea and Atlantic Ocean to the east. The ancient native peoples of this vast area shared a general cultural cohesion that has been defined and refined by archaeological evidence – comprising artifacts, architecture, technology, economy, settlement patterns and social organization – since the term Mesoamerica first came into use in the 1920s.

A long list of cultural traits is recognized as common to peoples and cultures who lived in what are now central, southern and eastern Mexico, Guatemala, Belize and El Salvador, and parts of Honduras, Nicaragua and Costa Rica. One principal trait was an economy based on corn (maize) agriculture (both irrigation and slash-and-burn). The northern limit of Mesoamerica was defined by the limit up to which irrigation agriculture was possible, corresponding approximately to the Sinaloa, Lerma and Pánuco rivers in northern Mexico. This boundary shifted somewhat over the course of time, especially in the northwest region, as climatic change limited or expanded the area in which agriculture was possible with the technology of the time. A southward shift of the northern boundary in the Postclassic Period (see below) was a major cause for the migration of peoples southwards into central Mesoamerica, and of much military conflict.

The southern boundary of Mesoamerica is less well defined. Nevertheless, there is a noticeable "fading" of the full set of Mesoamerican traits, although individual characteristics were present in parts of the isthmus of Central America. Conversely, this area was the northern limit of the penetration of some South America cultural traits and therefore constituted a cultural "buffer zone".

Within its vast area, the peoples and cultures of Mesoamerica had distinct characteristics and languages, both through history and as co-existing cultures and civilizations. At the same time, they also shared a wealth of primary cultural characteristics and comprised a "diffusion sphere", within which important events in one region eventually affected the whole area. Making use of natural communication routes between regions, intricate networks of long-distance trade were established, which endured through the development and passing of civilizations. In addition to corn agriculture and long-distance trade, the principal Mesoamerican cultural traits included ball courts with ring goals, stepped pyramid-platforms, *codices* (books of bark paper and deerskin), hieroglyphic writing, human sacrifice, position numerals and an acute understanding of mathematical principles, a solar year of 18 months of 20 days each plus 5 extra days, and sophisticated socio-political structures encompassing complex social hierarchies, market systems, urbanism on a vast scale and complex religious beliefs with a large pantheon of gods, goddesses and concepts.

As in the southern intermediate zone, the diffusion of certain Mesoamerican cultural traits accompanied long-distance trade contacts, both in commodities and as a result of Mesoamerican prospecting for raw materials, particularly into the far north. The most prominent examples are the adaptations of the ball game in the Southwestern cultures of the US and in the Caribbean Antilles, and the construction of ceremonial complexes of earthen mounds in the Southeastern cultures of the US.

THE CREATION of the world and its creatures and inhabitants, inspired by the mid-16th-century Quiché Maya text of the Popul Vuh. (PAINTING BY DIEGO RIVERA, 1886–1957.)

Languages and writing

Before about 4000 BC all Mesoamerican languages were probably closely related. Soon after that, several large language groups developed. In central and northwestern Mesoamerica numerous Uto-Aztecan languages were spoken, the most important of which are Nahua, its close

relative Nahuatl, and Cora and Uto-Aztecan dialects to the far northwest. Nahuatl was the language of the Aztecs, and almost certainly of the Toltecs before them, but was probably not spoken by the still earlier Teotihuacanos. As the Aztecs built their empire in the Late Postclassic Period, they spread the use of Nahuatl as a sort of *lingua franca*. Another language group in the north was Otomí, several dialects and languages of which were spoken by peoples north and west of the Basin of Mexico.

A second group was Macro-Mayan, comprising numerous related languages spoken throughout the Gulf Coast lowlands and the Yucatán Peninsula and highlands to the far south. It includes Huastec in the northeast Gulf Coast region, Totonac in the central Gulf Coast, and various Maya languages east and south of these. Lowland Maya languages include Mixe, Zoque and Chontal in the southern Gulf Coast region, Yucatec Maya in the Yucatán Peninsula, and Mame, Pipil and Quiché in the far southern highlands east of the Isthmus of Tehuantepec.

A third language group was the Mixtecan languages in the highlands to the south of the Basin of Mexico, west of the Isthmus of Tehuantepec. The most important are Mixtec and Zapotec, which, with several other languages, developed from a more ancient Oto-Zapotecan stock.

One language, Tarascan, represents a sort of "Basque" among these groups. It is unrelated to any of the Uto-Aztecan or other languages, although it sits in the midst of the former, and was spoken by the arch-rivals of the Aztecs on their northwestern frontier.

Several writing systems were developed by ancient Mesoamericans. For the most part these consist of hieroglyphs carved on stone monuments, stelae and walls, carved in plaster, and on bone, shell and jade objects, sometimes on wood, and painted on murals and in the *codices*. Thus most early Mesoamerican writing did not progress beyond pictographs.

Aztec and Maya writing, however, was more sophisticated. Aztec writing in the *codices* and other media comprised a close association of text and images, combining pictographs directly depicting objects with ideograms (glyphs, "ideographs", with meanings of a more abstract concept or action). The Aztecs employed some phoneticism by using homonyms, and were on the verge of a truly phonetic writing system at the time of the Spanish conquest of Mesoamerica in 1519.

Maya hieroglyphs are even more advanced. They were carved primarily on stone, but also on stucco and wood, and were painted on pottery and cloth as well as in *codices*. They could be read fully only by an educated elite. Like Aztec writing, Maya hieroglyphs must be used

in combination with pictographic images and with the entire pictorial scene to fully appreciate the "embedded text". For example, the verb or the activity might be provided by the image, while the nouns and objects are provided by the glyphs. Many glyphs were phonetic, for while some represent whole words, others represent single syllabic sounds – a consonant plus a vowel. Thus Maya writing was nearly fully phonetic, and was certainly fully functional as a writing system.

Cosmology

Mesoamerican "mythology", a somewhat suggestive term from a Western religious point of view, was based on religious naturalism. Ancient American peoples, like all peoples, felt compelled to explain the important things in their universe, beginning with where they came from and their place in the larger scheme of things. They developed accounts of their observable cosmos to help them to understand what things were important, and how and why things were the way they were. These beliefs constituted their religion.

These accounts, which we refer to here as "myths", did for the ancient peoples of Mesoamerica what science and/or the Christian religion does for Western society today, or indeed any other religion or belief structure does elsewhere in the world: they provided people with a conceptual framework for living and for the comprehension of, and relation to, the mysteries of their observable universe. Their myths sanctified the universe and humankind's place within it, at the same time eliciting or inciting direct experience of the sacred.

Religion permeated virtually every aspect of Mesoamerican life, and cosmology was completely bound up within Mesoamerican religious concepts. Religious themes were important from very early times, and ritual symbolism was made manifest in art and architecture. Physical expressions of religious practices became prominent first among the Olmecs of the central-southern Gulf Coast, and only a little later in the central and southern highlands. As well as architecturally complex ceremonial centres, there were many figurines and symbols on pottery, and carved stone stelae. The details of the nature of worship at these early ceremonial precincts are unknown, but many of the deities can be identified.

Several themes can be detected within Mesoamerican religion, more detail on which is given in the feature pages and alphabetical entries. These include the concept of duality, death and the underworld, a large pantheon of gods and goddesses with specific characters, functions and manifestations for different occasions and meanings, sacrifice – including animal, human, and autosacrifice – and cyclical time, together with a progression of creation episodes.

Mesoamerican worship was focused on public display and a certain amount of communal participation. At the same time there was a distinct élite body of trained priests, and the most sacred rites were performed only by them. In addition, there were cults and semi-secret societies, such as those of the Jaguar and Eagle Warriors. The function of ceremonial centres and their precincts was public display, to which the populace of the cities and of the surrounding countryside could gather on religious festival dates. Private and small-group worship was also practised to images of the major deities and to lesser household deities. There were also many sacred sites, such as caves or mountains, some of which had temples. Some locations were clearly sacred from a very early time, even

though, much later, the actual original site was hidden under the multi-layered building episodes of a huge temple-pyramid. Perhaps the two most famous examples are the cave and spring beneath the Pyramid of the Sun at Teotihuacán and the Sacred Cenote (a natural water hole) at the Maya site of Chichén Itzá, into which sacrifices and offerings were made over a long period of time.

Sources of information

There are many sources of Mesoamerican religious beliefs, verbal, written and archaeological. Native verbal accounts were recorded by Spanish chroniclers and priests, and much information about their cultures and religions was written down by native Mesoamericans who had been taught by Spanish missionaries. In addition to such written sources, there are the monuments and artefacts of the cultures themselves. Gods, goddesses, religious themes and ceremonial rites were depicted in stone – and in a few cases wooden – sculptures (both as free-standing figures and as architectural embellishment), on ceramics and in jewellery, in wall murals, in featherwork and textiles and in metalwork. Temple edifices and ceremonial precincts can also tell us something about the nature of religious worship through their layout, room divisions, and the use of open and

JAGUARS were an essential and prominent feature of Mesoamerican religious iconography. They were painted in murals and on pottery, carved in plaster and stone, and depicted in the codices. These stone jaguar heads decorate a platform at Maya-Toltec Chichén Itzá. (EARLY POSTCLASSIC PERIOD.)

enclosed, sunken and raised spaces between and within them.

For Mesoamerica, only 18 native screenfold *codices* that pre-date the Spanish conquest, survive. From central Mesoamerica a group of five manuscripts, often referred to as the "Borgia Group", are concerned primarily with the sacred ritual calendar and divination: the codices *Borgia*, *Cospi*, *Fejérváry-Mayer*, *Laud* and *Vaticanus B*. Nine other central Mesoamerican codices describe the myths and historical legends of the Aztecs and their Late Postclassic Period near neighbours. From the Maya area, only four Late Postclassic codices survive: the *Dresden*, *Grolier*, *Madrid* and *Paris* codices. Like the Borgia Group, they are principally manuals of divination for use with the ritual calendar.

The most important sources of Aztec and late Maya mythology are post-Spanish-conquest manuscripts written by Spanish priests and Spanish-trained natives. Some of these manuscripts even appear to be transcriptions of lost pre-conquest books. Two of the most famous examples of the former are by the priests Fray

Bernardino de Sahagún and Fray Andrés de Olmos. From the prolific efforts and studies of Sahagún we have the massive *Historia General de las Cosas de Nueva España*, an encyclopedia of Aztec culture, written in both Nahuatl and Spanish in 12 books and with more than 1,850 pictures. From Olmos we have the *Historia de los Mexicanos por sus Pinturas*, one of the most complete accounts of the Aztec creation myths. Perhaps the most important example of a transcription from a lost ancient book is the highland Guatemalan Quiché Maya *Popul Vuh*, an account in three sections of the origins of the Maya world, the mythical tale of two sets of hero twins and of the origins of humans and corn, and the legendary history of the Quiché people.

Archaeological material speaks for itself in as much as it represents the physical manifestations of Mesoamerican beliefs – how they depicted their gods and goddesses, and the physical spaces within which they practised their religion. Our knowledge of Aztec and Maya religion from the written sources provides the backdrop on to which we project a picture of the religious practices of their contemporary neighbours, and into the past. The Aztecs and Maya had an all-embracing religious philosophy, and the Aztecs especially, in their empire building, maintained an open capacity for absorbing the deities and ceremonies of their predecessors and contemporaries. Similarities between the artifacts of Aztec and Maya religion and earlier ones provide a sound basis for deducing the strong themes in Mesoamerican religion that began with the Olmecs and most ancient Maya, and were developed, added to and remoulded by the civilizations that followed.

Mesoamerican history

Archaeologists organize the chronology of Mesoamerica into several periods. The first, the Palaeoindian or Archaic Period, began with the migration of humans into the New World across the Bering Strait land bridge, provided by a lower sea level when much water was locked up in glacial ice. Evidence for this migration is dated about 15,000 years ago, but migrations might have taken place as early as 40,000 years ago. The earliest incontrovertible evidence of humans in Mexico is dated *c*. 7500 BC at Iztapan.

Incipient agriculture and the development of early village life began in the sixth millennium BC and continued in some areas into the first millennium BC.

SERPENT IMAGERY, alongside that of the jaguar, permeated Mesoamerican religious iconography. Many ceremonial precincts – as at the pyramid-platform of Tenayuca, north of the Aztec capital at Tenochtitlán – were defined by a Coatepantli ("serpent wall") of writhing stone serpents.

MONTE ALBÁN, the Zapotec capital, was established deliberately by the expanding, and probbaly rival, urban centres in the valleys overlooked by the plateau. The ceremonial precinct was built on the partly artificially levelled ridge between two hilltops.

The first cultural developments to warrant the term civilization began in the Preclassic Period or the Formative Period (*c*. 2500 to 100 BC). Villages grew in size and population, and the construction of special buildings among ordinary dwellings indicates the beginnings of religious ceremony. In about 1200 BC the Olmecs of the central and southern Gulf Coast began to construct ceremonial architecture and to erect monumental sculptures with iconography that depicted deities, cosmology and symbols of rulership. A little later, similar activities began among the Zapotecs in the southern highlands, where calendrical symbols were used from 600 BC, and in the Maya area of the Isthmus of Tehuantepec, Yucatán, Guatemala and Belize. The Zapotec mountain city and ceremonial centre of Monte Albán was established about 500 BC, apparently as a deliberately co-operative effort by the towns of the valley.

In the Protoclassic Period (*c*. 100 BC–AD 300), complex urban-based cultures began to flourish all over Mesoamerica. Long-distance trade and diplomatic and military contact spread pan-Mesoamerican religious themes, raw materials and artefacts among these cultures. In the Basin

of Mexico, the sites of Cuicuilco in the south and Teotihuacán in the northeast Basin began to grow at increasing rates. In the Oaxacan highlands, Zapotec civilization remained focused at Monte Albán. At Maya sites such as Izapa, Kaminaljuyú, Abaj Takalik, El Mirador, Tikal and Uaxactún, monumental architecture and art were erected in large centres loosely spread over large areas. At Izapa, in particular, stone monuments were carved with mythological scenes.

In the succeeding Classic Period (c. AD 300–900), Maya ceremonial cities flourished throughout eastern and southern Mesoamerica. Maya hieroglyphic writing reached a high level of complexity and, now that it has been deciphered, reveals the names of Maya cities, rulers and deities. Classic Period Maya cities were never united into a single empire or confederation, but hieroglyphic inscriptions record the conquests and temporary alliances of numerous rulers and cities (for example Uxmal, Río Bec, Palenque, Yaxchilán, Tikal, Copán and Kaminaljuyú). Their calendrical system, writing, art, architecture and religious iconography were shared. In Oaxaca, Monte Albán continued to dominate the southern highland region.

In the Basin of Mexico, Teotihuacán grew under a strict authoritarian plan to cover more than 20 sq km (8 sq miles), with some 200,000 inhabitants, around an immense ceremonial centre whose main avenue stretched 2 km (1.5 miles) north to south. Near the centre, the walls of élite palaces were painted with religious scenes, gods and goddesses. Teotihuacán's rulers were ambitious and dominated the whole of central Mesoamerica economically, if not militarily, and traded and prospected for raw materials far into the northern regions. Teotihuacán and Monte Albán rulers established and maintained diplomatic and economic contacts, and even kept enclaves of their respective peoples in each other's cities. Diplomatic and economic ties were also maintained between Teotihuacán and Maya Tikal and Kaminaljuyú, both of which might have been conquered by Teotihuacán.

Other Classic cities included Gulf coast El Tajín and, around the Basin of Mexico, Teotenango, Cholula and Xochicalco dominated local regions, but seem to have been restricted by the power of Teotihuacán. At Xochicalco, the iconography of the Pyramid of the Serpents and other monuments indicates that, in the seventh century, there appears to have been a gathering of priests and "astronomers" from the Maya, Zapotec and central Mesoamerican cities to synchronize and standardize their calendars.

The Postclassic Period (c. AD 900–1521) began with the virtual abandonment of many Classic Period Maya cities, and Monte Albán and Teotihuacán, many of which had suffered periods of decline in the century and a half before AD 900. In the Early Postclassic Period (c. AD 900–1250) new cities arose to dominate the regions of Mesoamerica. Northwest of the Basin of Mexico,

Tula (ancient Tollán) dominated northern and central Mesoamerica, as climatic change shifted the northern limits southward. About the same time, Chichén Itzá in Yucatán rose as a ruling city remarkably similar to Tollán in what appears to be a sort of Toltec "Empire" of strong military alliance between north and south. Nevertheless, in the intervening area, cities such as Teotenango, Cholula and Xochicalco reasserted their local power, and new centres, such as Mitla and Yagul, Tututepec and Tilantongo were established in the Oaxacan highlands to replace Monte Albán.

In the final, Late Postclassic Period (c. AD 1250–1521), Toltec and Chichén Itzán powers waned, while the Aztecs rose to power in the Basin of Mexico from their capital at Tenochtitlán, and began their conquests of central Mesoamerica. At the same time, new Maya city-states, such as Mayapán and Tulum, were established throughout Yucatán. Northwest of the Basin of Mexico, the Kingdom of the Tarascans, from their capital at Tzintzuntzan, held out staunchly against Aztec attempts to conquer them. Similarly the Tlaxcaltecan state, to the east of the Basin, resisted and held the Aztecs at arms length.

In 1519 Hernán Cortés and about 500 Spanish soldiers, with a few firearms, cannon and horses, landed at Veracruz on the Gulf Coast. Despite its wealth and power, the Aztec Empire was only about a century and a half old. Many of its subjects resented Aztec domination and were eager to rebel. Taking advantage of this internal ferment and using knowledge of the predicted return of Quetzalcóatl, the plumed serpent god, in the guise of a bearded man from the east, Cortés was able to ignite this turmoil into open rebellion, to gain hundreds of thousands of native allies and overthrow the Aztec Empire.

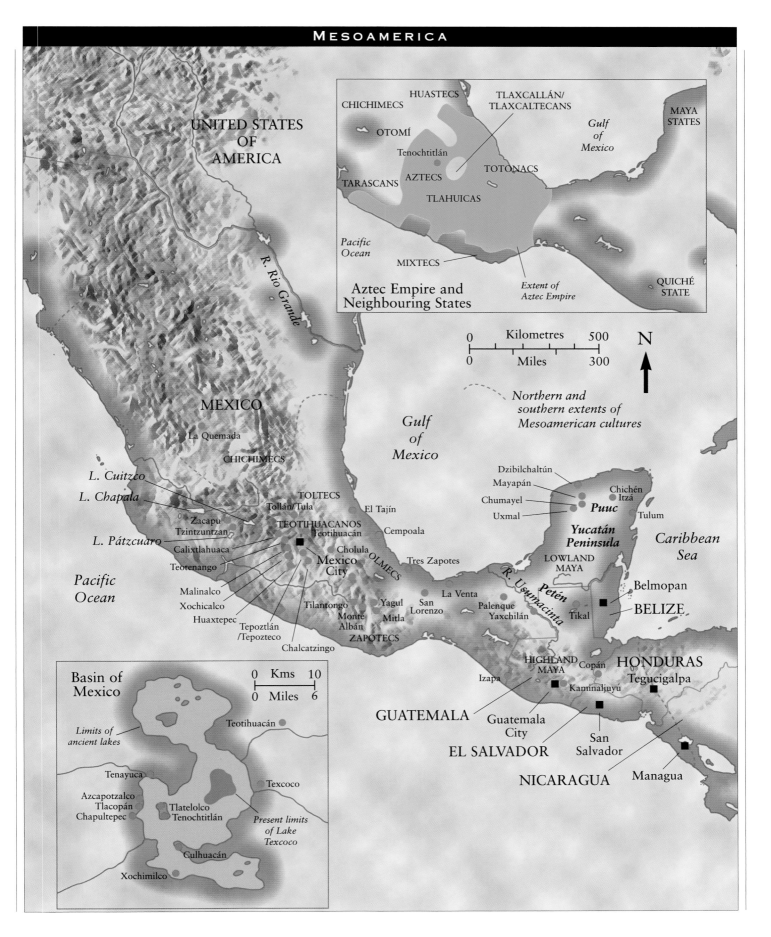

MESOAMERICA

Aztec Empire and Neighbouring States

CHICHIMECS

HUASTECS

OTOMÍ

TLAXCALLÁN/
TLAXCALTECANS

Gulf
of
Mexico

MAYA
STATES

Tenochtitlán

TARASCANS

AZTECS

TOTONACS

TLAHUICAS

Pacific
Ocean

MIXTECS

Extent of
Aztec Empire

QUICHÉ
STATE

Kilometres 500
Miles 300

N

Northern and
southern extents of
Mesoamerican cultures

UNITED STATES
OF
AMERICA

R. Rio Grande

MEXICO

La Quemada

CHICHIMECS

L. Cuitzco

L. Chapala

Zacapu

Tzintzuntzan

L. Pátzcuaro

Calixtlahuaca

Teotenango

Malinalco

Xochicalco

Huaxtepec

Tepoztlán
/Tepozteco

Chalcatzingo

TOLTECS

Tollán/Tula

TEOTIHUACANOS

Teotihuacán

Cholula

Mexico
City

Tilantongo

Monté
Albán

Mitla

Yagul

ZAPOTECS

El Tajín

Cempoala

OLMECS

Tres Zapotes

San
Lorenzo

La Venta

Palenque

Yaxchilán

R. Usumacinta

Gulf
of
Mexico

Dzibilchaltún

Mayapán

Chumayel

Uxmal

Puuc

Chichén
Itzá

Tulum

Yucatán
Peninsula

LOWLAND
MAYA

Petén

Tikal

Belmopan

BELIZE

Caribbean
Sea

Pacific
Ocean

HIGHLAND
MAYA

Izapa

Copán

HONDURAS

Tegucigalpa

GUATEMALA

Kaminaljuyú

Guatemala
City

EL SALVADOR

San
Salvador

NICARAGUA

Managua

Basin of Mexico

Kms 10
Miles 6

Limits of
ancient lakes

Teotihuacán

Tenayuca

Azcapotzalco
Tlacopán
Chapultepec

Tlatelolco
Tenochtitlán

Texcoco

Present limits
of Lake
Texcoco

Culhuacán

Xochimilco

A

THE ACANTUN were four demons, each one associated with a colour and a cardinal direction. They figured in *MAYA* new year rites and in ceremonies associated with the carving of idols. They are frequently mentioned in the *RITUAL OF THE BACABS*.

ÁCATL ("reed") was the 13th of the 20 *AZTEC* day-names and one of the year-bearing days – there were 13 *Ácatl* years in a 52-year cycle (see also *CALLI*, *TÉCPATL* and *TOCHTLI*). It had an unfavourable augury and its patron deity was *TEZCATLIPOCA* or *ITZTLACOLIUHQUI*; its orientation was east. The *MAYA* and *ZAPOTEC* equivalent days were *BEN* and *QUIJ*.

It is depicted in the codices as a bundle of cane arrows bound with leather straps. Calendrical dates and deity associations included: *1 Ácatl*, the mythical birth date of *QUETZAL-CÓATL*; *2 Ácatl*, the mythical death date of Quetzalcóatl; *7 Ácatl*, the dedication date of the Templo Mayor in *TENOCHTITLÁN*; and *13 Ácatl*, for the calendrical representation of the sun.

ACHE ("lizard") was the fourth of the 20 *ZAPOTEC* day-names; the *AZTEC* and *MAYA* equivalent days were *CUETZPALLIN* and *KAN*. (See also *BEYDO*)

ACPAXACO was an *OTOMÍ* water goddess, an aspect of or equivalent to Aztec *CHALCHIÚHTLICUE*.

AH CHICUM EK was an alternative name for *XAMEN EK*, the *MAYA* god of the North Star.

AH KINCHIL see *KINICH AHAU*.

AH MUCEN CAB was the *MAYA* "honey" god, patron of bee-keeping. Honey figured prominently in Mesoamerican cuisine and was an important item in Maya trade, along with *cacao* (see *EK CHUAH*). (See also *THE BACABS* and *XMULZENCAB*)

AH MUN, *MAYA* God E, also known as Yum Kaax, was the corn (maize) deity and god of agriculture in general. His alternative name Yum Kaax meant "Lord of the forests". He is always represented as a youth, to personify growth and well-being, and frequently has a corn plant sprouting from his head, or a corn-ear headdress. In the Maya codices he is portrayed with a deformed head, the forehead sloping or flattened.

He was patron of *KAN* ("ripe corn"), the fourth day of the Maya 20-day month, and associated with the south and with the colour yellow. He was symbolized by the number eight, and his name glyph is his own head merging into a conventionalized corn ear and leaves. He was a benevolent god and, as such, was associated with, or under the protection of, *CHAC*, god of rain, but was also controlled by wind, drought and famine; he is sometimes shown in combat with *AH PUCH*, god of death. In the Classic Period, Maya rulers were sometimes depicted in the guise of Ah Puch/Yum Kaax scattering grains of corn. (See also *CREATION & THE UNIVERSE*)

AH MUN, Maya god of corn (maize) (God E), is typically portrayed as a beautiful youth to personify ripe corn, the silk tassel forming his hair. (LATE CLASSIC PERIOD, COPÁN TEMPLE 22.)

AH PUCH, *MAYA* God A, also Hun Ahau, also Yum Cimil, was the god of death and principal rival of *ITZAMNÁ*. In the Yucatán he was frequently called *YUM CIMIL* ("Lord of Death"). He was portrayed with a death's-head skull, bare ribs and long spine with projecting vertebrae, or sometimes as a bloated figure, with black spots on his clothing, suggestive of decomposition, and sometimes adorned with bells (see *CIZIN*).

As a principal deity – Hun Ahau – he ruled *MITNAL*, the lowest level of the nine Maya underworlds. He was patron of *CIMI* ("death"), the sixth day of the Maya 20-day month, and of the number ten, and was associated with the south and with the colour yellow. His connection with death made him a close ally of the gods of war and of sacrifice, and he was often accompanied by a dog, a tropical *Muan* (or *Moan*) bird and/or an owl – a bird generally associated with unfavourable events and a portent of death in Mesoamerica. Glyphs that signify him included a sacrificial flint knife and a motif that resembled a % sign. In form and domain he was the equivalent to Aztec *MICTLANTECUHTLI*.

The Maya in particular, and in contrast to central Mesoamericans, were highly fearful of death, and the bereaved expressed extreme mourning, weeping silently by day and giving out shrieks of grief at night. For them, Yum Cimil stalked the houses of the sick in search of more victims. Ordinary members of society would be buried beneath house floors, or behind the house, their mouths filled with ground corn (maize) and their hands holding jade bead "money". Nobles were cremated and their ashes deposited in special urns; sometimes shrines were built over them.

AHAU ("lord") was the last of the 20 *MAYA* day-names; it was the day of the sun god *KINICH AHAU* and was associated with the number four. *1 Ahau* was the Maya calendrical name for the planet Venus as the morning "star" and *7 Ahau* was the name for Venus as the evening "star". The *AZTEC* and *ZAPOTEC* equivalent days to *Ahau* were *XÓCHITL* and *LAO*.

AHAU KIN see *KINICH AHAU*.

AHUIATÉOTL, or Ahuíatl, the *AZTEC* god of voluptuousness, was one of the five *AHUIATETEO*. He was one of several manifestations of *XOCHIPILLI* and an alternative name for *MACUILXÓCHITL*.

THE AHUIATETEO were the five *AZTEC* spirits of the south, who were companion deities of voluptuousness. *AHUIATÉOTL* was one of their number.

AHUÍATL see *AHUIATÉOTL* and *MACUILXÓCHITL*.

AH PUCH, the Maya death god (God A), or Yum Cimil ("Lord of Death") is depicted in this unprovenanced stone relief as having skeletal features and projecting vertebrae. He is also clutching an umbilical cord.

AKBAL ("darkness") was the third of the 20 *MAYA* day-names; it was associated with darkness and the night. The *AZTEC* and *ZAPOTEC* equivalent days were called *CALLI* and *GUELA*.

ANALES DE CUAUHTI-TLÁN, also known as the *Codex Chimalpopoca* or as the *Historia de los Reinos de Culhuacán*, is a late 16th-century source of Aztec history, myth and legend written in *NAHUATL*, the language of the Aztecs. In particular, it relates the story of how corn (maize) and other edible plants were given to humankind in the world of the Fifth Sun.

APE ("cloud") was the 19th of the 20 *ZAPOTEC* day-names; the *AZTEC* and *MAYA* equivalent days were *QUIÁHUITL* and *CAUAC*.

ARARÓ, the Springs of, see *SICUINDIRO*.

ATEMOZTLI ("the water falls") was the 17th (or, in some sources, 16th) of the *AZTEC* 18 months in the solar year. The rain god *TLÁLOC* was the principal deity worshipped during this month.

ATL ("water") was the ninth of the 20 *AZTEC* day-names; it had an unfavourable augury and its patron deity was *XIUHTE-CUHTLI*. The *MAYA* and *ZAPOTEC* equivalent days were *MULUC* and *NIZA* or *Queza*. Calendrical dates and deity associations included: *1 Atl*, for *CHALCHIÚHTLICUE*; and *4 Atl*, for the Fourth Sun of the Aztec *CREATION MYTH*.

ATLATONAN, an earth and water goddess, was one of four *AZTEC* goddesses who were impersonated by virgins and were symbolically married to a young warrior, himself impersonating the god *TEZCATLIPOCA*. For a year Atlatonan and her companions – *HUIXTOCÍHUATL*, *XILONEN* and *XOCHIQUETZAL* – served and attended to the warrior, until the festival of *TÓXCATL*, the sixth of the 18 Aztec months, held in honour of Tezcatlipoca. At the end of the month, the warrior was abandoned by his wives and all five were then ritually sacrificed.

ATLCAHUALO ("they leave the water") was the second (or, in some sources, the first) of the 18 months in the *AZTEC* solar year, in which the rain deities, especially *TLÁLOC* and *CHALCHIÚHTLICUE*, were propitiated by the sacrifice of children. *QUETZALCÓATL*, who, as *ÉHECATL* ("wind"), blew the rains away, was also honoured. It was also called *Cuauhuitlehua* ("raising of the poles") and *Xilomanaliztli* ("offering of the tender corn/maize ears"). (See also *ETZALCUALIZTLI*)

AZCATL, the red ant, was the messenger who led *QUETZALCÓATL* to his grain store inside *TONACATÉ-PETL* ("sustenance mountain"). As told in the *ANALES DE CUAUHTITLÁN*, he was running along the ground carrying a corn (maize) kernel, when he was discovered by Quetzalcóatl, who was searching for food to feed the newly created human race of the Fifth Sun (see *CREATION MYTHS*). Quetzalcóatl asked where such wonderful food could be found, but only after much bullying would Azcatl agree to reveal the source. He led Quetzalcóatl to Tonacatépetl, where Quetzalcóatl transformed himself into a black ant and followed Azcatl through a narrow entrance deep into the mountain. Inside Azcatl had stored corn and many other types of seeds and grains, some of which Quetzalcóatl took back to *TAMOANCHÁN*, where the gods chewed the corn and fed some of the resulting mash (*maza*) to the infant humans, giving them sustenance for growth and strength.

THE AZTECS were comprised of seven tribes, usually recognized to be the Acolhua, the Chalca, the México, the Tepaneca, the *TLALHUICA*, the *TLAXCALTECA* and the Xochimilca, all of

THE MÉXICA Aztecs were the last to arrive in the Basin of Mexico. Several codices depict the scene of the "sign" sent to the México priests through their war god Huitzilo-pochtli, to settle on the island where they witnessed an eagle sitting on a nopal cactus devouring a serpent, here depicted in the Codex Aubin.

whom migrated into central Mesoamerica from somewhere in the northwest of present-day Mexico. The México were the last to make their way into the Basin of Mexico, and were the tribe that is now generally referred to as "the Aztecs".

After serving other tribes in the Basin as mercenaries, they angered the Culhua-Toltec tribe by sacrificing to *HUITZILOPOCHTLI* a Culhua-Toltec princess offered to them in a marriage alliance. Banished to an island in the westernmost lake of the Basin, they built their capital city, *TENOCHTITLÁN*, from which they proceeded, through alliances and conquests, to built their empire. In the mid-15th century their ruler Moctezuma I Ilhuica-mena formed and led the Triple Alliance between Tenochtitlán, Texcoco and Tlacopán against the states of Tlaxcala and Huexotzingo east and southeast of the Basin. Later, as Aztec ambitions increased, they began to subdue their allies and other city-states throughout the Basin and beyond.

They were eventually overthrown by the Spanish adventurer Hernán Cortés in 1521, who used their legend of *QUETZALCÓATL*'s return against them.

B

The Aztec gods formed a large pantheon, which was acquired both by inheritance from, and participation in, a long tradition of deities in earlier Mesoamerican civilizations, and also through the propensity of the Aztecs to adopt the deities of peoples they conquered. The mythologies of the Aztec tribes and their contemporaries included some 1,600 deities, many with overlapping attributes and functions. They can be grouped into several general thematic categories.

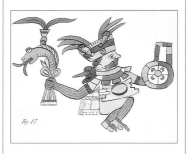

TWO OF the most important Aztec deities were one of most ancient in the Mesoamerican pantheon and one of most recent: Tláloc (above), the ancient god of rain and agriculture was vital to Mesoamerican existence; and the war god Huitzilopochtli (left), unique to the Aztecs and the god who sent a sign to the México priests about where to found their capital, Tenochtitlán.

The *Principal deities* were HUITZILOPOCHTLI, QUETZALCÓATL, TEXCATLIPOCA and TLÁLOC.

Creator deities included CIPACTONAL and OXOMOCO, OMECÍHUATL and OMETECUHTLI, OMETEOTL, TLOQUE NAHUAQUE and Tonacacíhuatl and Tonacatecuhtli.

Deities of fertility included AHUIATÉOTL, Ahuiatl, CENTÉOTL, CHALCHIUHCÍHUATL, CHICOMECÓATL, CIHUACÓATL, COATLÍCUE, ILAMATECUHTLI, IXCUINAN, MACUILXÓCHITL, QUILAZTLI, TETEOINNAN, TLAZOLTÉOTL, TOCI, TONANTZIN, Xilmen, XIPE TOTEC, XOCHIPILLI and XOCHIQUETZAL.

Fire deities included AHUIATETEO, CHANTICO, CUAXÓLOTL, HUEHUETÉOTL and XIUHTECUHTLI.

The *PULQUE deities* included CENTZÓNTOTOCHTIN, MAYÁHUEL, OMETOCHTLI, PATÉCATL, TEPOZTÉCATL and TEZCATZONTÉCATL.

Sky or heavenly deities included CAMAXTLI, the CENTZONHUITZNAHUAC, the CENTZONMIMIZCOA, CITLALICUE, CITLALINICUE, CITLATONA, COYOLXAUHQUI, ITZPAPÁLOTL,

MEZTLI, MIXCÓATL, NANAHUATZIN, OMEYOCÁN, PILTZINTECUHTLI, TECUCIZTÉCATL, TLAHUIZCALPANTECUHTLI, TONATIUH and the TZITZIMIME.

The *Deities of the underworld* included CHALCHIUHTECÓLOTL, CHALMECATECUHTLI, Huahuantli, MICTECACÍHUATL, MICTLANTECUHTLI, TEOYAOMIQUI, TEPEYOLOHTLI, TLALTECUHTLI and YOHUALTECUHTLI.

The *Weather deities* (rain, wind, storm) included CHALCHIÚHTLICUE, ÉHECATL, HUIXTOCÍHUATL, NAPPATECUHTLI, the TEPICTOTON and the TLÁLOCS.

Miscellaneous other deities are ATLATONAN, CHALCHIUHTOTOLIN, CHIMALMAN, the CIHUATETEO, HUEHUECÓYOTL, ITZTLACOLIUHQUI, ITZTLI, IXTLILTON, MATLALCUEITL, Matlalcueye, OMÁCATL, OPOCHTLI, PAYNAL, TLALCHITONATIUH, TLALTÍCPAC, XÓLOTL, YACATECUHTLI and YÁOTL.

AZTLÁN ("place of the cranes"), was the legendary land in northwest Mesoamerica in which the caves of CHICOMOZTOC were located,

and from which the seven Aztec tribes originated; sometimes associated with La Quemada in Zacatecas.

THE BACABS were the sons of the supreme god ITZAMNÁ. They supported the four corners of the earth in the MAYA cosmos. (In another version of the myth, they were said to have been placed at the four corners of the earth by HUNAB KU to hold up the sky.) Each Bacab was named, was a "year-bearer" in the Maya calendar, and was associated with a world colour and a cardinal direction: thus Can Tzional was white (*zac*), associated with north, and bore MULUC years; Hozanek was yellow (*kan*), associated with south, and bore CAUAC years; Hobnil was red (*chac*), associated with east, and bore KAN years; and Zac Cimi was black (*ek*), associated with west, and bore IX years. (See also THE CHACS and THE PAUAHTUN.) As year-bearers they influenced the luck of the year. In addition, the Bacabs were the patron deities of bees and of apiaries (see also AH MUCEN CAB).

The Maya sacred book, the CHILAM BALAM of Chumayel, describes the creation of the world, when the 13 Lords of the Sky (the OXLAHUN TI KU) were defeated by the nine Lords of the Underworld (the BOLON TI KU) and the four Bacabs were set to support the four corners of the earth. At the Toltec-Maya site of Chichén Itzá, small, carved stone "atlantean" figures

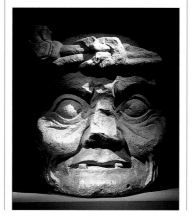

with upheld arms, that support stone shelves, lintels and benches, are thought to represent Bacabs.

THE BAT-GOD figures prominently in the ZAPOTEC, MAYA and AZTEC pantheons. At Zapotec Monte Albán, the Bat-god was portrayed as a god of corn (maize) and of fertility generally. In the Maya pantheon bats were especially associated with the underworld (see CAMA ZOTZ, XIBALBA and ZOTZ). The Aztec Bat-god, Tlacatzinacantli, is shown with similar associations in several codices.

BEN ("growing corn/maize") was 13th of the 20 MAYA days and was associated with growing corn (maize) plants. The AZTEC and ZAPOTEC equivalents were ÁCATL and QUIJ or Ij or *Laa*.

BENELABA, or Pilalapa Caache, with his wife Jonaji Belachina, were the special deities of Southern ZAPOTEC Coatlán. Benelaba was the sun god and god of war, while his wife was goddess of the dead and of the underworld. A *relación* (native history) tells us that these deities were brought to the city by one of its rulers after a visit to the MIXTECS, and that he also brought back with him the Mixtec practice of animal and human sacrifice, which had not been practised previously in Coatlán. Worship of Benelaba was exclusive to men, who sacrificed dogs, turkeys, quail and male war captives. Worship of Jonaji Belachina was exclusive to women, who offered similar sacrifices to her. The alternative name for Benlaba was – Pilalapa Caache ("seven rabbit" in Zapotec), and for Jonaji Belachina, Xonaxi Peochina Coyo ("three deer").

BETAHOXONA was the Sierra ZAPOTEC creator god; see COZAANA.

THE BACABS supported the sky at the four corners of the Maya cosmos. They were frequently depicted as old men.

(CLASSIC PERIOD COPÁN TEMPLE 11)

BETAO YOZOBI was the Sierra *ZAPOTEC* for the corn (maize) god *PITAO COZOBI*.

BEYDO ("seeds" or "wind") was a *ZAPOTEC* deity of the southern highlands of Mesoamerica. He was fourth of the nine Southern Zapotec day names (known as *ACHE* to the Central Zapotec), associated with objects considered to be sacred, and with natural forces.

BEZELAO see *COQUI BEZELAO*.

BOLON DZ'ACAB, or Bolon Tz'acab ("he of the nine generations"), *MAYA* God K, also called Kawil, was the Maya god of lineage and descent. Sculptures and depictions of him in the codices portray him with a reptilian face and an extended upper lip, or with a long upturned snout – and he is therefore called the "long-nosed god" by archaeologists – usually with an axe or smoking cigar in his forehead, holding a mirror, and sometimes with serpent feet. In carvings on stone stelae the image of Bolon Dz'Acab often appeared on a manikin sceptre, the symbol of rulership and power, grasped by Maya kings. For example, at the Maya city of Palenque (on the Usumacinta River in Chiapas, Mexico), Bolon Dz'Acab's mythical birthdate is carved on the Temple of the Foliated Cross, which itself was built to commemorate the birth and origins of the authority of the ruling lineage of the city.

In Classic Period Maya texts he is also called Kawil. Like the *BACAB* Hobnil, he was associated with the east and with years that began with the Maya day *KAN* ("ripe corn/maize"). He is frequently shown in association with *ITZAMNÁ* or with *CHAC*, and is possibly the equivalent of Aztec *TEZCATLIPOCA*.

THE BOLON TI KU were the nine *MAYA* Lords of the Underworld, identified as distinct glyphs but whose names are otherwise

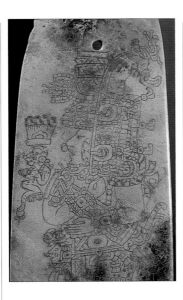

BOLON DZ'ACAB, Maya God K of descent and lineage, is the incised effigy at the end of this ceremonial stone bar of rulership, depicted with his characteristic extended upper lip.

unknown. They were arch rivals of, and were beaten by, the 13 Lords of the Sky (*OXLAHUN TI KU*) at the creation (see *CREATION MYTHS*). Their Aztec equivalent were the Yohualteuctin (see *LORDS OF THE NIGHT*).

BOOK OF THE DAYS see *TONALAMATL*.

BULUC CHABTÁN ("11 faster"), *MAYA* God F, was an earth deity, a god of war and of human sacrifice (see also *EK CHUAH* and *ETZ'NAB*). In the Maya codices he is distinguished by a black line partly encircling his eye and extending down his cheek. The glyph for 11 appears at his head, and he was patron of the Maya day *Manik* (a grasping hand). Sometimes he is shown accompanying *AH PUCH* – or Yum Cimil – but he is more often depicted on his own as a god of war, torching houses with one hand and stabbing people with a spear in the other.

CABAN ("earth") was the 17th of the 20 *MAYA* day-names; it was associated with the number one

and with the young earth goddess, the moon and corn (maize). The *AZTEC* and *ZAPOTEC* equivalent days were *OLLIN* and *XOO*.

CABRACÁN, giant and mountain destroyer in the Maya *POPOL VUH*, was the second son of *VUCUB-CAQUIZ* and brother of *ZIPACNÁ*, and was destroyed with them by hero twins *HUNAHPÚ* and *XBALANQUÉ* in *XIBALBA*. The twins offered him a dish of poisoned fowl, which made Cabracán so weak that they were able to bury him alive.

CALLI ("house") was the third of 20 *AZTEC* day-names and one of the year-bearing days – there were 13 *Calli* years in a 52-year cycle (see also *ÁCATL*, *TÉCPATL* and *TOCHTLI*). It had a favourable augury and its patron deity was *TEPEYOLOHTLI*; its orientation was west. The *MAYA* and *ZAPOTEC* equivalent days were called *AKBAL* and *GUELA*.

Calendrical dates and deity associations included: *1 Calli*, one of the *CIHUATETEO*; *2 Calli*, for *XÓLOTL*; *3 Calli*, for the gods of fire; *4 Calli*, for *MICTLANTECUHTLI*, god of death; *5 Calli*, god of lapidaries and husband of *9 Itzcuintli* as *CHANTICO*, patroness of metalworkers; *6 Calli*, also for Mictlantecuhtli; *7 Calli*, regarded as a good day for merchants; *8 Calli*, for the year of the creation of the *macehual* (Aztec commoners); and *10 Calli*, the mythical birth date of the wind god *ÉHECATL*.

A TERRACOTTA figurine of a warrior from the island of Jaina, off the Gulf Coast, is probably meant to represent Buluc Chabtán, Maya God F of war and human sacrifice.

CAMA ZOTZ, portrayed with a sharp obsidian knife, was the killer *BAT-GOD* of Maya *XIBALBA*, the underworld. As described in the sacred *POPOL VUH* text, Cama Zotz challenged the hero twins *HUNAHPÚ* and *XBALANQUÉ* in *ZOTZ-IHÁ* (the "House of Bats", one of the levels of *XIBALBA*), and tried to prevent their passage. In the fight that ensued, Hunahpú was beheaded by Cama Zotz, but later retrieved it through a ruse during a ball game against the gods who ruled the underworld.

CAMAXTLI was the *TLAXCALTECAN* god of the hunt and of war. He had aspects corresponding to Aztec gods *MIXCÓATL*, *HUITZILOPOCHTLI* and *TEZCATLIPOCA*.

CAN TZIONAL see *THE BACABS*.

THE CANEQUES, probably of *OLMEC* origin, were *MAYA* dwarf-like "poltergeists" and minor rain and thunder deities, possibly the assistants of the Maya god *CHAC*. They lived in the forests and caused mischief to residents and travellers.

CANNIBALISM was a religious act in Mesoamerica, undertaken only by priests and nobles after ritual sacrifice. This gruesome scene from the Codex Magliabecchiano *shows the death god Mictlantecuhtli presiding over such a feast.*

CANNIBALISM in Mesoamerica, although widespread among the cultures, was neither casual nor common. It was a solemn undertaking and a religious act only engaged in by selected, high-ranking members of society, usually priests, but also kings and nobles. The practice is well attested in Spanish Colonial native documents.

There is some suggestion of ritual cannibalism among the Preclassic Period *OLMECS* at the site of San Lorenzo, where fractured human bones were found in special deposits. The best evidence for cannibalism, however, is confined to the Postclassic Period. Among the *MAYA* the flesh of human sacrifice was considered sacred food; among the *TARASCANS* the bodies of sacrificial victims were divided between the gods and the chief priests – the portion for the gods being sacrificially burned and the remaining parts eaten by the priests. For the *AZTECS*, the consumption of the flesh of human sacrificial victims constituted a communion with the gods. The gods demanded human sacrifice and were "fed" the bodies of the victims in ritual burnt offerings. At the same time, the victim was perceived to embody the god (through deity impersonation), and therefore consumption of the victim's flesh was a partaking of divine being.

CAUAC ("rain" or "storm") was the 19th of the 20 *MAYA* day-names and one of the year-bearing days – there were 13 *Cauac* years in a 52-year cycle (see also *IX, KAN* and *MULUC*). It was associated with the south cardinal direction and the colour yellow, with the number three, and it had an unfavourable augury. *AZTEC* and *ZAPOTEC* equivalents were *QUIÁHUITL* and *APE*. (See also *DUALITY & OPPOSITION*)

CE ÁCATL TOPILTZIN QUETZALCÓATL ("One Reed Sacrificer Plumed Serpent"), to the *AZTECS*, was both a manifestation of the god *QUETZALCÓATL* and the legendary human founder and ruler of ancient Tollán (modern Tula), the new *TOLTEC* capital to the north-west of the Basin of Mexico. In his human guise, he was the son of the Toltec-*CHICHIMEC* tribal ruler *CE TÉCPATL MIXCÓATL* and a Nahua woman (other versions suggest that he was the son of Mixcóatl and the goddess *CHIMALMAN*), born after his father's death at the hands of a rival faction. The boy was raised in exile and brought up to revenge his father. Later, after becoming ruler of the Toltecs, he led them out of the Basin of Mexico and founded Tollán (in AD 968, according to Aztec tradition). He was himself defeated in further factional rivalry, however, and departed Tollán with his followers for the Gulf of Mexico.

Intriguingly, the Maya traditional date of AD 987 for the establishment of Maya-Toltec Chichén Itzá by the invading leader *KUKULKÁN* coincides roughly with the traditional Aztec dates for the departure of Quetzalcóatl from Tollán (see also *TEPEU*) – although there is incomplete agreement with the historical and archaeological evidence. The Aztecs regarded the Toltecs as the fount of civilization and strove to emulate them in their warlike and expansionist demeanour, so there is ample reason to suspect that they tampered with Toltec legend themselves. Indeed, we have several renditions in three principal post-Spanish conquest documents: the *ANALES DE CUAUHTITLÁN*, the *Relación de Genealogía*, and the *Memoria Breve de Chimalpahin*. Some scholars even argue that the events in the Toltec legends have been compressed, and therefore record in a formal way events and situations that occurred more than once during Toltec history.

For more on this complicated figure, see under *KUKULKÁN, MIXCÓATL, QUETZALCÓATL* and *TAMOANCHÁN*.

CE TÉCPATL MIXCÓATL ("One Flint Cloud Serpent") was the legendary *TOLTEC-CHICHIMEC* tribal ruler whom the Aztecs regarded as the founder of the Toltec dynasty. He led his people from somewhere in northwest Mesoamerica into the Basin of Mexico, where they established the city of Culhuacán. After his murder by a rival faction his son, the future king *CE ÁCATL TOPILTZIN*, was born to his wife, a Nahua woman from the Basin, but she died giving birth to him. Ce Técpatl Mixcóatl was subsequently deified as *MIXCÓATL*.

CENTÉOTL, or Cintéotl, was the central Mesoamerican god of the corn (maize) plant; he also had several feminine forms. He was the son of the earth goddess

CENTÉOTL, the Aztec corn (maize) deity, is seen here in feminine form as a young maiden wearing a corn-cob headdress. (LATE POSTCLASSIC PERIOD.)

TLAZOLTÉOTL and possibly originated in the Olmec *GOD II*. He was often portrayed wearing a headdress of corn ears and, in contrast to *XILONEN* (young, tender corn) and to *ILAMATECUHTLI* (old and dried-up corn), represented the mature, ripe plant. He was fourth of the nine Aztec *LORDS OF THE NIGHT* and, in the guise of Xochipilli-Centéotl ("corn-flower prince"), seventh *LORD OF THE DAY*.

In some sources he was the son of *CHICOMECÓATL* and closely related to *XOCHIPILLI*, the flayed flower god of souls. Thus, penitence to Centéotl was thought to ensure a regular supply of corn. In April he was given offerings of blood, dripped on reeds and placed at the doors of the houses, to solicit a favourable planting season. Also in connection with the spring planting, Centéotl was protected by *TLÁLOC*, god of water.

CENTZONHUITZNAHUAC AND CENTZONMIMIZCOA (both from *NAHUATL centzontli*, "400"), were the stars of the southern and northern constellations respectively, and the brothers and sisters of *HUITZILOPOCHTLI*, the *AZTEC* god the sun and of war. The Centzonmimizcoa were the "cloud serpent" (the Milky Way; see also

CITLALÍCUE, CITLATINÍCUE and MIX-CÓATL). Both of the groups were dispersed into the sky by Huitzil-opochtli as a punishment for plotting to kill their mother (some-times named as OMECÍHUATL, and sometimes as COATLÍCUE) who they thought had conceived them in sin.

THE CENTZÓNTOTOCHTIN

("400 rabbits (tochtli)") is a collec-tive term in NAHUATL for the gods of PULQUE and drunkenness. The maguey plant goddess MAYÁHUEL and the pulque god PATÉCATL were their figurative mother and father.

CHAC, MAYA God B, was the god of rain, and the equivalent of Aztec TLÁLOC, Mixtec DZAHUI, Totonac TAJÍN and Zapotec COCIJO, and possibly also to Tarascan CHUP-ITHIRIPEME. He was portrayed with a long, hanging nose, often up-turned at the tip, a lolling tongue and scrolls (probably tears) beneath his eyes. He was sometimes fanged, sometimes toothless. Chac was depicted singly and in stacks of heads at Copán and at Chichén Itzá, and at many other Maya sites throughout the Petén and Puuc regions of Yucatán.

Despite his somewhat fierce appearance, Chac was benevolent and brought rain and fertility to crops, but also wind, thunder and lightning. He was symbolized by the number six and patron of the day IK ("wind"). In some texts Chac has four manifestations who, like the BACABS, were each associated with a cardinal direction and a colour – north/white, south/yellow, east/red and west/black. Other texts refer to these CHACS as his four assistants.

CHAC PAUAHTUN

see PAUAHTUN.

CHAC XIB CHAC

see THE CHACS.

CHACMOOL, a life-size or near-life-size reclining carved stone figure, was associated with temples.

CHAC was the Maya rain god (God B). His stone head, with curled nose, decorated the platforms and buildings of numerous Classic Period Puuc-style sites, as here at Kabah in central Yucatán.

Its legs are half bent and its head is turned to one side, and the figure grasps an open stone box, resting on its abdomen, to receive offer-ings. The name – MAYA for "red jaguar" – was applied to this type of figure by archaeologists because the first example was discovered at the Maya-Toltec city of Chichén Itzá in Yucatán, but the origins of such figures were in fact in north-central Mesoamerica, at the TOLTEC capital of Tollán (Tula). Chacmool figures have also been found at sites in the Basin of Mexico, in the TARASCAN cities to the northwest of the Basin, and among the TOTONACS in the central Gulf Coast.

Some scholars consider the chacmools to be representations of TEZCATZONTÉCATL, who was one of the Aztec PULQUE gods of drinking

and inebriation. (See also DEATH & SACRIFICE)

THE CHACS, in some MAYA texts, are portrayed as the four assistants of the rain god CHAC. Each ruled a cardinal point, or corner, of the earth and a colour: Zac Xib Chac was white (zac) and ruled the north; Kan Xib Chac was yellow (kan) and ruled the south; Chac Xib Chac was red (chac) and ruled the east; and Ek Xib Chac was black (ek) and ruled the west. They are closely related to the four year-bearing BACABS. (See also THE PAUAHTUN)

CHALCHIHUITLICUE

see CHALCHIÚHTLICUE.

CHALCHIUHCÍHUATL was an AZTEC goddess of the harvest.

CHALCHIUHTECÓLOTL

("precious owl") was, appropri-ately, the AZTEC god of the night, one of the many aspects of "black" TEZCATLIPOCA, a major deity of the Postclassic Period.

CHACMOOL figures, designed to receive offerings in the "box" held on their abdomens, were first found at Maya-Toltec Chichén Itzá, but their origin was later realized to be from the Toltec culture of north-central Mesoamerica.

CHALCHIÚHTLICUE ("she of the jade skirt"), or Chalchihuit-licue (an alternative spelling), the AZTEC goddess of water, was the sister and female counterpart of TLÁLOC. Her name incorporates the NAHUATL term chalchíhuitl, meaning "jade" or "green stone", and, thus by extension, anything precious; and by further analogy still to the colour of jade, it also means "water".

Chalchiúhtlicue was the god-dess of rivers, oceans and floods, patroness of the fifth day Cóatl ("serpent"), third of the 13 LORDS OF THE DAY and sixth of the nine

CHALCHIÚHTLICUE, the Aztec water goddess, suitably bedecked with jade – the symbol of water – depicted in the pre-Spanish conquest Codex Vaticanus B.

LORDS OF THE NIGHT. She presided over the Fourth Sun of the Aztec CREATION MYTH. She was often portrayed as a river, beside which grew a nopal (prickly pear) cactus bearing fruit which symbolized the human heart. The Gulf of Mexico, whose coastal waters were so important in Mesoamerican trade, was known as Chalchi-uhcueyecatl, meaning "water of the goddess Chalchiúhtlicue" in Nahuatl. She was related to the goddesses CHICOMECÓATL and XILONEN.

CHALCHIUHTOTOLIN ("precious turkey") was an aspect of the *AZTEC* god *TEZCATLIPOCA*. As such he was a deity of the night and of mystery. He ruled the Aztec day *TÉCPATL* ("flint knife").

CHALMECATECUHTLI, an *AZTEC* god of sacrifice and of the underworld, was an alternative for *MICTLANTECUHTLI* as the 11th of the 13 *LORDS OF THE DAY*.

CHANTICO was an *AZTEC* earth goddess and special deity of Xochimilco, in the Basin of Mexico. She was goddess of the hearth (see also *CUAXÓLOTL*) and patroness of metalworkers, especially of goldsmiths. She bore the calendrical name *9 ITZCUINTLI* and was related to *MICTLANTECUHTLI*, god of death.

CHEBEL YAX see *IX CHEBEL YAX*.

CHICCAN ("serpent") was the fifth of the 20 *MAYA* day-names; it was associated with the number nine and with the rain god. The *AZTEC* and *ZAPOTEC* equivalent days were *CÓATL* and *ZEE* or *Zij*.

CHANTICO, the Aztec goddess of the hearth and of metalsmiths, is depicted in the early post-Spanish conquest Codex Borbonicus *wearing a jade nose ornament.*

CHALCHIUHTOTOLIN, the "precious turkey" god of night and mystery – one of the many manifestations of Tezcatlipoca – is depicted in the early post-Spanish conquest Codex Borbonicus.

CHICCHAN, *MAYA* God H, was the rain god of the Chorti Maya of eastern Guatemala, Honduras and El Salvador. He was patron of Chicchan ("serpent"; the fifth day of the Maya 20-day month) and symbolized by the number nine.

CHICHÉN ITZÁ see *TOLTECS*.

CHICHIMECA was the general term used by the *AZTECS* to refer to the nomadic hunter-gatherer peoples of the northern deserts, beyond the fringes of the civilized societies of Mesoamerica. They were regarded as "barbarians".

The term was also applied to all groups who originated in the north and migrated south after the fall of Tollán (Tula), including the *TOLTECS*, whom the Aztecs regarded as the fount of civilization.

One of the most important Chichimec groups entered the Basin of Mexico in the 12th century AD, led by the legendary chief Xólotl. They founded the city of Tenayuca in the north Basin, and their descendants later joined the Acolhua Aztecs on the eastern lake shores to establish a capital city at *TEXCOCO*. In keeping with their background, a prominent Toltec-Chichimec god was *MIXCÓATL*, god of the hunt.

CHICOMECÓATL, or Chicomolotzin, ("seven serpents", derived from *chicome* "seven" and *cóatl* "serpent") was a central Mesoamerican goddess of corn (maize) and vegetation generally, who was closely related to *CENTÉOTL*. She was usually portrayed in the codices with a red face and body, and wearing a paper mitre-like headdress adorned with rosettes, or, in sculpture, holding ears of corn in each hand. She was also known as Chicomolotzin or "seven ears of maize" (*olotl*) and, in her manifestations as a goddess of fertility, as *CHALCHIÚHTLICUE* and *XILONEN*. Her feast day was 7 *Cóatl*, and she was honoured at the festival of *OCHPANITZLI*, an *AZTEC* harvest festival held during the 12th month of the 18 months that made up the Aztec solar year.

CHICOMOLOTZIN
see *CHICOMECÓATL*.

CHICOMOZTOC ("seven caves") were the legendary caves from which the seven *AZTEC* tribes originated. They were located in *AZTLÁN*, a land somewhere to the northwest of the Basin of Mexico. The seven tribes are usually recognized as the Acolhua, the Chalca, the México, the Tepaneca, the Tlal-

huica, the Tlaxcalteca and the Xochimilca, all of whom migrated southeastwards to settle in or near the Basin of Mexico.

CHICOMOZTOC, the seven caves located in Aztlán ("place of the cranes") – somewhere in the northwest of Mesoamerica; in legend the seven Aztec tribes emerged from them, depicted here as an island in the Codex Boturini.

THE CHILAM BALAM (literally "prophet jaguar") are 18 post-Spanish-conquest Yucatecan *MAYA* sacred texts, written in European script. They relate the Maya calendar, traditional histories and myths (including the Maya *CREATION MYTH*), along with advice and medicinal recipes. The most informative texts are the so-called *Pérez Codex* and those that came from the Yucatecan towns of Chumayel, Tizimín, Maní, Kaua and Ixil.

CHILLA ("crocodile") was the first of the 20 *ZAPOTEC* day-names; the *AZTEC* and *MAYA* equivalent days were *CIPACTLI* and *IMIX*.

CHIMALMAN was the *AZTEC* personification of female divinity, expressed in several ways. The term was applied to the human female bearers (counterpart of the *TEOMAMAQUE*) of tribal cult objects during the Aztec migration stories. In one myth Chimalman was the Nahua wife of the *TOLTEC-CHICHIMEC* tribal ruler *MIXCÓATL*, who impregnated her with an arrow from his bow. As a result she became the mother of *CE ÁCATL TOPILTZIN QUETZALCÓATL*, the legendary founder and ruler of Tollán (Tula). In other myths she is portrayed as either the mother of *COATLÍCUE*, the Aztec earth goddess, or sometimes of *HUITZILOPOCHTLI*.

CHINA ("deer") was the seventh of the 20 *ZAPOTEC* day-names and one of the year-bearing days – there were 13 *China* years in a 52-year cycle (see also *PIJA, QUIJ* and *XOO*). The *AZTEC* and *MAYA* equivalent days were *MÁZATL* and *MANIK*.

CHICOMECÓATL, or "seven serpents", the Aztec corn (maize) and fertility goddess, is depicted wearing an elaborate headdress decorated with rosettes and a phallic-like serpent belt, and holding a corn plant and ears. (LATE POSTCLASSIC PERIOD.)

CHINAMPAS, misnamed "floating islands", were not floating at all. Rather, they were artificial rectangular fields, separated by canals, built out from the shores of the southern lakes and around the island capital of Aztec *TENOCH-TITLÁN* in the Basin of Mexico. In the course of more than a century

aligned rows of *chinampas* extended from the southern lake shores roughly halfway across lakes Xochimilco and Chalco, connecting the island city of Cuitláhuac (modern Tláhuac) and the island of Xico to the mainland. Around Tenochtitlán they extended up to about 500 m (545 yards) from the island's shores towards the mainland.

They were created by constructing a frame of wood and reeds, then filling this with mud from the lake bottom. Trees were planted on the plots to anchor them and to help hold the soil with their roots. New lake mud was dredged periodically and spread onto the islands to maintain fertility.

The use of *chinampas* enabled the scores of city-states throughout the central and southern Basin of Mexico to support dense populations, and encouraged regular trade through market gardens.

CHUEN ("monkey") was the 11th of the 20 *MAYA* day-names; it was associated with the arts and crafts, and with the *MONKEY-FACED GOD* (Maya God C). The *AZTEC* and *ZAPOTEC* equivalent days were called *OZOMATLI* and *LOO* or *Goloo*.

CHUPITHIRIPEME was the *TARASCAN* rain god. He was probably the equivalent in aspect and importance – especially in the semi-arid lands of the Tarascan state – to the *AZTEC TLÁLOC*, the *MAYA CHAC*, the *MIXTEC DZAHUI*, the *TOTONAC TAJÍN* and the *ZAPOTEC COCIJO*.

CIB ("wax") was the 16th of the 20 *MAYA* day-names; it was associated with the *BACABS*, patrons of beekeeping. The *AZTEC* and *ZAPOTEC* equivalent days were *COZCACUAUHTLI* and *LOO* or *Guiloo*.

CIHUACÓATL (meaning "serpent woman") was an *AZTEC* earth goddess associated specifically with the west. Cihuacóatl represented a

passive principle in Aztec religious pluralism: as *TONANTZIN* she was the mother of humankind; as *COATLÍCUE* she was the venerated mother of *HUITZILOPOCHTLI*, god of war; as *QUILAZTLI* she raised the legendary ruler *CE ÁCATL TOPILTZIN QUETZALCÓATL*, founder of the Toltec capital at Tollán (Tula), after his mother, *CHIMALMAN*, died while giving birth to him. Thus Cihuacóatl became the patroness of the *CIHUATETEO*, the spirits of woman who died in childbirth. In reference to her role as companion, Cihuacóatl was the title the Aztecs gave to the co-ruler alongside the *tlatoani* or Aztec king. Following the conversion of the Aztecs to Christianity she became "La Llorana" ("the weeping woman") in Mexican folklore.

Cihuacóatl's role in the creation of humankind followed the escape of *QUETZALCÓATL–ÉHECATL* from the devious attempts of *MICTAL-NTECUHTLI* to stop him in the underworld. Having fetched the bones of the inhabitants of the previous world, turned into fish bones in the destroying deluge, Quetzalcóatl–Éhecatl brought them to Cihuacóatl in *TAMOANCHÁN*, the place of miraculous birth. She ground them up into a flour-like meal and placed the meal in a special clay pot, around which the gods gathered, and into which they shed drops of their blood (or, in another version, just Quetzalcóatl's blood, from his penis). From this paste, men and women were moulded to populate the newly created world.

CIHUAPIPILTIN was the general term used for the souls of deceased *AZTEC* women; see also the *CIHUATETEO*.

THE CIHUATETEO were the spirits of *AZTEC* women who died while giving birth. Their patroness and protector was the earth goddess, *CIHUACÓATL*. They lived in the west in a paradise known as

CIHUACÓATL, "serpent woman" – note her serpent belt – is manifested here as the earth-mother goddess Coatlícue, mother of the war god Huitzilopochtli. (LATE POSTCLASSIC PERIOD AZTEC STONE SCULPTURE.)

Cincalco (*NAHUATL*, meaning "the house of corn/maize"), from which their role was to come to the aid fallen warriors and eventually to convey them to the world of the dead, which was in the east. The warriors were borne across the morning sky by the sun and were met at noon by the Cihuateteo. Death in childbirth was considered to be the equivalent of a man's death in battle, the latter being believed by the Aztecs to be the most honoured way to die. Portrayed with skulls for heads, and feet bearing fierce claws, the Cihuateteo were venerated by sorcerers and witch doctors, but they sometimes descended to earth in order to create mischief and harm amongst humans.

CIHUATLAMPA is the western quadrant of the earth in *AZTEC* cosmography. It was represented by the year sign *CALLI* ("house"), and by the day signs *MÁZATL* ("deer"), *QUIÁHUITL* ("rain"), *OZOMATLI* ("monkey"), *CALLI* and *CUAUHTLI* ("eagle"). Within it, Cinalco was the western paradise for women who died in childbirth; they met warriors from the eastern paradise, who had fallen in battle, accompanying the sun across the sky. It was generally associated with misfortune.

CREATION & THE UNIVERSE

T HE AZTECS AND THE MAYA both recorded an elaborate sequence of creations preceding their own world. The Aztec creation myth comprised five successive worlds and suns, the first four ending in cataclysm; the Maya creation story comprised three worlds, the first two, being imperfect, also ending in destruction. In both of these cultures the final creation myth ended with humans being formed from corn (maize) dough, the ultimate gift of the gods being the knowledge of how to grow corn and other edible plants for human consumption and survival.

Similarly, virtually all Mesoamericans perceived the earth as the back of a huge reptilian being, a crocodile or cayman, lying in the water. The other parts of the cosmos were above and below the earth, and in both Aztec and Maya sources are described as multi-layered. Maya sources also describe a second concept, in which the earth is a huge iguana house, a reptilian structure whose sides (walls), roof (sky), and floor (earth) were formed by the bodies of iguanas.

The Aztec universe – Teyollocualoyán – comprised a vertical stratification of thirteen celestial and nine underworld layers, with the earth in between as the first layer in both directions. The levels were each ruled by a deity, and the celestial deities were each associated with a bird.

AZTEC CREATION was based on the idea of four successive worlds (left), created and destroyed before the Aztecs' own world, that of the Fifth Sun. Four of these "suns" or "epochs of nature" are depicted here: the people of the Second Sun – destroyed by winds – were turned into monkeys (upper left), those of the Third Sun – destroyed by fire – into birds (lower right), those of the Fourth Sun – destroyed by floods – into fishes (upper right), and those of the Fifth Sun given the gift of agriculture (lower left). (ILLUSTRATION FROM RESEARCHES CONCERNING THE INSTITUTIONS AND MONUMENTS OF THE ANCIENT INHABITANTS OF AMERICA BY FRIEDRICH ALEXANDER BARON VON HUMBOLDT, 1814.)

QUETZALCOÁTL (left), the "plumed serpent", was sent by the gods after the creation of the Fifth Sun, in his guise as the wind god Éhecatl, to collect the bones of the fishes of the Fourth Sun's inhabitants from the underworld. Having completed this task, and humans having been created from a paste of the ground-up bones and blood of the gods, Quetzalcóatl-Éhecatl discovered corn (maize) kernels and seeds of other edible plants in Tonacatépetl ("sustenance mountain"). He gave humans the knowledge of agriculture, scattering the seeds across the land for the rain god Tláloc to water.

THE VIENNA CODEX (below) or Codex Vindobonensis shows a "world tree" with the gods Tezcatlipoca (left, with "smoking mirror" figure above his left arm) and Quetzalcóatl (right, with quetzal bird head above his right arm) to either side of it. Rooted in the earth, the branches of the tree spread into the heavens to support the sky. The concept of a "world tree", planted at the centre of the universe and constituting the fifth of the cardinal directions, was central to both Aztec and Maya thought.

THIS PANEL (above), painted by the artist Diego Rivera (1886–1957), was one of a series inspired by principal episodes in the sacred text – known as the Popul Vuh – of the Guatemalan highland Quiché Maya. The Maya believed in a universe that was the result of a succession of creations. From a world of darkness and water, the gods created the earth and all the creatures on it, and the fish of the seas. Then the gods Tepeu and Gucumatz (or Kukulkán) attempted to fashion humans out of mud, as Rivera shows.

AH MUN (right) or Yum Kaax, the god of agriculture and corn (maize) plants, featured prominently in architectural and portable artefacts, such as this incense burner in the form of the god holding a potted corn plant in his right hand. Maya civilization was as dependent on corn as its contemporaries in central Mesoamerica. The crop was grown in cleared plots of rain forest and on raised, irrigated fields around the ceremonial centres of Maya cities.

(ARTEFACT FROM THE POSTCLASSIC PERIOD MAYA CITY OF MAYAPÁN, YUCATÁN.)

CIMI ("death") was the sixth of the 20 *MAYA* day-names; it was represented by the owl, portent of death, and its glyph resembles a % sign. The *AZTEC* and *ZAPOTEC* equivalent days were *MIQUIZTLI* and *LANA*.

CINCALCO see *CIHUATETEO*.

CINTÉOTL see *CENTÉOTL*.

CIPACTLI ("crocodile") was the first of the 20 *AZTEC* day-names; it was a lucky day, a symbol of birth, life and sustenance; its patron deity was *TONACATECUHTLI*. The *MAYA* and *ZAPOTEC* equivalent days were *IMIX* and *CHILLA*.

Cipactli was the Earth Monster, the crocodile on whose back the world sits. Calendrical dates and deity associations included: *4 Cipactli*, for the fire god *XIUHTECUHTLI*; *6 Cipactli*, for the earth goddess *TLAZOLTÉOTL*; and *9 Cipactli*, for *MICTECACÍHUATL*, goddess of death.

CIPACTONAL was the "first man" in the *TOLTEC* and *AZTEC CREATION MYTH*. He and his wife *OXOMOCO* were regarded as the first sorcerer and sorceress, who together invented astrology and the calendar. His *MAYA* equivalent was *XPIYACOC*.

They were also instrumental in bringing corn (maize) and other edible plants to humankind. When *QUETZALCÓATL* was unable to shift *TONACATÉPETL* (literally "sustenance mountain") the two old diviners cast lots to determine how to do this. The signs told them that the weakly and diseased god *NANAHUATZIN* should do this, by splitting Tonacatépetl open. To do so, Nanahuatzin called upon the help of the four *TLÁLOCS*, the directional gods of the winds, rain and lightning. The mountain was duly split and the winds blew the grains and seeds across the land while the rains watered them so that they grew where they fell. Humans were quick to take advantage of this renewable source of food.

los q̃ nacian aqui nãcen de borrachos

CITLALÍCUE, or Citlalinícue, literally the "star-skirted" or "she of the skirt of stars" in *NAHUATL*, was goddess of the heavens and one of the *AZTEC* names for the Milky Way (see also the *CENTZONMIMIZCOA* and *MIXCÓATL*). As Citlalícue she was the ruler of the third of the 13 celestial levels in the Aztec universe (but see also *OMECÍHUATL*). As the female counterpart of *CITLATONA* she was one of the feminine aspects of *OMETEOTL*.

CITLALINÍCUE, another name for *CITLALÍCUE*; the *AZTEC* name for the Milky Way. See also *THE CENTZONMIMIZCOA* and *MIXCÓATL*).

CITLALTEPEC ("Hill of the Star") was one of the *AZTEC* names for Cerro de la Estrella in the Mexico City precinct of Ixtapalapa near the ceremonial centre of *TENOCHTITLÁN*, and the venue for *TOXIUHMOLPILIA*, ("the tying of the years") ceremony.

CITLATONA was the masculine aspect of *OMETEOTL*, the Aztec concept of duality (see *OMETECUHTLI*).

CIZIN, from *ciz*, is the *MAYA* word for flatulence and, by extension, the putrescence of the underworld (see also *AH PUCH*).

CITLALÍCUE, "star-skirted", was goddess of the heavenly firmament, seen here on the right, below the Milky Way. Opposite her sits Mayáhuel, goddess of the maguey plant. (EARLY POST-SPANISH-CONQUEST AZTEC CODEX BORBONICUS).

CLOUD SERPENT
see *MIXCÓATL*.

COAÍLHUITL
see *TLACAXIPEHUALIZTLI*.

THE CÓATL ("serpent") figured prominently in Mesoamerican imagery stretching from the earliest times through to the Postclassic Period. Serpents were associated with both male and female deities and *cóatl* forms an element of many of their names, for example

CHICOMECÓATL, CIHUACÓATL, COATLÍCUE, MIXCÓATL, QUETZALCÓATL and XIUHCÓATL.

Along with feline features, fangs and forked tongues they formed an important element in the art of every Mesoamerican culture. Examples that attest to the endurance and ubiquitous use of serpent imagery include the "Greek Key" patterns that form stylized, sinuous snakelike architectural decorations seen on *ZAPOTEC* and *MIXTEC* walls, the writhing serpents on the Temple of Quetzalcóatl at *TEOTIHUACÁN*, the Pyramid of the Serpent at Xochicalco, the *coatepantli* (serpent walls) around *TOLTEC* and *AZTEC* ceremonial precincts, and the "cloud serpent" image of the Milky Way.

Cóatl was also the name of the fifth of the 20 Aztec day-names; it had a favourable augury and was associated with the number nine; its patron was *CHALCHIÚHTLICUE*. The *MAYA* and *ZAPOTEC* equivalents were *CHICCHAN* and *ZEE* or *Zij*.

COATLÍCUE ("serpent lady"), was the *AZTEC* supreme earth goddess. She was the mother of *HUITZILOPOCHTLI* (god of war), of *COYOLXAUHQUI* (moon goddess)

CÓATL, the serpent, appeared from the earliest of times in Mesoamerican iconography alongside feline imagery. Here, the roof of the Temple of the Jaguars at Postclassic Period Maya-Toltec Chichén Itzá is supported by serpent columns, their heads on the ground, rattles in the air.

COATLÍCUE, "serpent lady", the supreme Aztec earth goddess, embodied the earth-monster. She is shown here with a serpent tongue and fangs, snake-headed arms and a writhing mass of serpents for a skirt.

and of the CENTZONHUITZNAHUAC and CENTZONMIMIZCOA (the southern and northern stars). She ruled the rainy season and was associated generally with agriculture and sustenance. In one myth she is the daughter of CHIMALMAN; other manifestations include CIHUACÓATL, TETEOINNAN, TOCI and TONANTZIN.

Coatlícue was wife of the cloud serpent MIXCÓATL (god of hunting) but was magically impregnated with Huitzilopochtli by a feathery ball that descended to her as she swept her house. She tucked the ball into her bosom, but later could not find it. It was said that this was what impregnated her "without sin". Nevertheless, her sons and daughters plotted to kill her for her disgrace. They would have succeeded had not Huitzilopochtli been born just in time, fully armed, to decapitate his sister Coyolxauhqui, by mistake, and to kill his other brothers and sisters, dispersing them into the heavens as stars.

The most famous sculpture of Coatlícue (at the Museo Nacional de Antropología in Mexico City) shows her as a hideous monster with a massive head covered in scales, two beady, staring eyes and a wide, scaly mouth complete with four huge fangs and a forked serpentine tongue. Two great spurts of blood, in the shapes of snake heads, issue from each side of her block-like torso to form her arms, and are thought to be representations of Tonacatecuhtli and his consort Tonacacíhuatl (Lord and Lady Flesh), or perhaps less graphically OMETECUHTLI and OMECÍHUATL (Lord and Lady of Duality). She wears a necklace of alternating severed human hands and hearts, setting off a skull pendant in the middle – all symbolic of the need for blood and human sacrifice to sustain the sun. A scaly snake encircles her waist and her skirt writhes with serpents (the two largest form the ties of her waist band and dangle below the skull of her pendant), the whole symbolizing the human race of which she was Mother. Down her back fall 13 tresses to represent the 13 heavens or levels of Aztec cosmography as well as the gods who control the earth's natural forces. The tresses also symbolize the 13 months of 20 days in the 260-day calendrical cycle – and possibly of the normal human gestation period – and the 13 LORDS OF THE DAY. Another skull, the counterpart of that on the front, dangles below her tresses. Beneath her skirt, her legs are covered with plumage and end in "feet", each of which have four vicious talons.

In such hideous guise Coatlícue represented both the womb and the grave of humankind.

COCHANA was an alternative name for HUECHAANA, a valley ZAPOTEC mother goddess.

COCIJO ("lightning"), or Pitao Cocijo, also called Gozio and Lociyo, was the southern highland Valley ZAPOTEC rain god. The evidence of archaeology, and of native histories (relaciones) indicate that Cocijo was a principal deity of the Valley Zapotec cities, who ruled the four cardinal directions and the Zapotec fifth direction, the zenith. He was portrayed with a composite body of human, jaguar and serpent features and a forked tongue to symbolize lightning. So numerous were representations of Cocijo, especially on funerary urns accompanied by "companion" urns set in a semi-circle around his effigy, that it is thought that there was a special cult devoted to him. One relación (from the Southern Zapotec city of Sola) states that rites performed to PITAO COZOBI (god of corn/maize) were also offered to Cocijo at the harvest cutting of the first chilli plant.

To the Southern Zapotec he was Lociyo and, to the Sierra Zapotec, Gozio. Other Mesoamerican equivalents deities were MAYA CHAC, MIXTEC DZAHUI, TOTONAC TAJÍN and AZTEC TLÁLOC, and possibly also TARASCAN CHUPITHIRIPEME (see also COQUENEXO).

Cocijo (or tobicocij) was also the name for a period of 65 days, a full quarter of the Zapotec ritual calendar (piye), which served as the Zapotec equivalent to the Aztec Tonalpolhualli (see ORDERING THE WORLD). Each cocijo was further subdivided into five periods of 13 days each.

CODEX CHIMALPOPOCA

see ANALES DE CUAUHTITLÁN.

COPIJCHA, or Pitao Copijcha, also sometimes called Xaquija, was the Valley ZAPOTEC sun god and the god of war, and was the patron deity of the city of Xaquija (modern Teotitlán). He was associated with the macaw, a sun bird, who was believed to fly down from the sky to enter his temple. He was equivalent to the Aztec TONATIUH.

COQUEBILA was the ZAPOTEC lord of the centre of the earth. His name glyph was apparently the same as that for QUIABELAGAYO ("five flower").

COQUECHILA, who was the Southern ZAPOTEC Lord of the Underworld, was an alternative name for COQUI BEZELAO.

COQUEELAA was the Southern ZAPOTEC god of the cochineal harvest, and a deity worshipped especially in the city of Sola. Fowl were sacrificed to him at the planting of the nopal cactus, which harbours the insect, and at the cochineal harvest.

COQUENEXO was the "Lord of multiplication" (probably a permutation of COCIJO), and was the principal deity to the Sierra ZAPOTEC city Zoquiapa.

COCIJO was the Zapotec god of rain. This stone sculpture from the southern highlands of Oaxaca shows him with a human body, jaguar face and forked tongue to represent lightning.

COQUI BEZELAO was the Mixtec god of death. His inclusion as the handle of a utilitarian object such as this drinking vessel served as a constant reminder that death was inescapable.

made the journey to the top of a nearby mountain in order to practise autosacrifice, by piercing and letting blood from their tongues and ears, and to pray for the city's well being and prosperity. These rites were always begun at night, when the sacrifices were performed, and ended at the same hour of the following night.

To the Southern Zapotec Coqui Bezalao was known as Bezalao, Pezalao or Pitao Pezalao – in the city of Ocelotepec – and Leta Ahuila.

COQUI XEE, also called Leta Aquichino, Liraaquitzino, Pijetao and Pije Xoo, was the Valley *ZAPOTEC* abstract concept of infinity, the unknowable – "the he (or it) without beginning or end" – and in this sense the creator god. He (it) was the supreme "force", the "above" and, as Pije Xoo, "the source of time". All the seemingly baffling and complex pantheon of Zapotec gods and goddesses were in essence merely aspects, attributes, manifestations, permutations, or refractions of this supreme being. In this, he was similar to the Aztec concept of *TLOQUE NAHUAQUE*. The Southern Zapotec knew him as Leta Aquichino or Liraaquitzino.

COQUIHUANI, a *ZAPOTEC* deity, was god of light, and was special to the city of Tlalixtac in the Mesoamerican southern highlands. Men and boys were sacrificed to him, along with offerings by the priests of quetzal feathers, dogs and blood. These rites were accompanied by excessive *PULQUE* drinking and dancing before the idol.

COQUIXILLA see *COQUI XEE*.

COSANA NOSANA see *COZAANA*.

COQUI BEZELAO, or Bezalao, also called Coquechila, Pezalao, Pitao Pezalao and Leta Ahuila, was the special god of the Valley *ZAPOTEC* city of Mitla, along with his wife *XONAXI QUECUYA*. They were the gods and goddesses of death and of the underworld and were worshipped throughout the Oaxaca Valley around

Mitla, sometimes under their Southern Zapotec names of Coquechila and Xonaxi Huilia, respectively. Mitla itself was known among the Zapotecs as the "city of death", "place of rest", or "the underworld" and, indeed, passages and tombs beneath palaces and monumental staircases at the site lend credence to this epithet.

Coqui Bezelao was also a patron deity to the Sierra Zapotec city of Teocuicuilco, and only the priests were permitted to enter the temple in which his idol was kept. Special rites were held every 260 days; the residents brought quail, brightly coloured feathers and precious green stones to the priests, who

COYOLXAUHQUI was the Aztec moon goddess. Her name means "golden bells" and she was frequently shown, as here, with bell ornaments on her cheeks and also depicted on her cap.

COYOLXAUHQUI ("golden
bells") was the *AZTEC* moon goddess and daughter of *COATLÍCUE*. She is easily recognized in sculpture and various portrayals in the codices by her ornaments of bells. According to the Aztec myth, her brothers and sisters the stars (see *CENTZONHUITZNAHUAC* and *CENTZONMIMIZCOA*) conspired to kill their mother, because they believed that Coatlícue had conceived a child in sin. Coyolxauhqui attempted to warn her mother but, as she approached ahead of her brothers and sisters, her new brother *HUITZILOPOCHTLI* (sun and war god), who emerged fully armed from his mother's womb, decapitated her in his haste to defend his mother. Only afterwards was Coatlícue able to tell Huitzilopochtli of his sister's good intentions. Huitzilopochtli threw Coyolxauhqui's head up into the heavens to become the moon, where the bells on her cheeks still shine in the night sky. In Aztec myth, the scene of her decapitation recurs each day as the moon sets and the sun drives away the darkness, and this daily brother-sun/ sister-moon struggle symbolized the day and night, the battle of light against the darkness, and good against evil.

One of the most spectacular finds in recent Mexican archaeology, discovered in 1978 at the Templo Mayor in Mexico City, was that of a huge circular carved stone portraying the dismembered body of Coyolxauhqui. Her head, which was decorated with bells on the cheeks, her torso, her arms and legs, and also a skull and other symbols of death are all depicted. Together they represent her destruction by Huitzilopochtli.

COZAANA ("the begetter"), or
Cosana Nosana, or Noçana, or Pitao Cozaana, was the Valley and Southern *ZAPOTEC* creator god. He was the male counterpart of *HUECHAANA* and was associated especially with the city of Chichicapa and with children. As the creator god he was associated with animals and humans, and, in various aspects, with ancestors and with hunting and fishing. The Sierra Zapotec people knew him as Betahoxona.

COZCACUAUHTLI ("vulture")
was the 16th of the 20 *AZTEC* day-names; it had a favourable augury and its patron deity was the "obsidian butterfly" *ITZPAPÁLOTL*. The *MAYA* and *ZAPOTEC* equivalent days were *CIB* and *LOO* or *Guiloo*.

Because it was bald, the *cozcacuauhtli* was perceived to be the representative of old age.

COZICHA COZEE was the
principal deity of the Southern *ZAPOTEC* city of Ocelotepec. He was the god of war, and was portrayed as a fierce warrior clutching his bow and arrows. Native histories (*relaciones*) related to the Spanish chroniclers tell us that Ocelotepec was constantly at war with its neighbours, which made this special relationship between god and city appropriate. Cozicha Cozee was closely associated with *COPIJCHA*, the sun god.

THE CREATION MYTHS of
both the *AZTECS* and the *MAYA* were highly elaborate. Their essential elements were no doubt shared with the other peoples of Mesoamerica. A common component was the concept of a succession of worlds, in which one world was replaced by another after the first had been destroyed. Destruction was usually by natural forces sent by the gods, but sometimes also involved supernatural forces. The myths of each are explored in more detail on the following pages.

IN THE CREATION MYTHS, after the destruction of the Fourth Sun, the gods convened at Teotihuacán, "City of the Gods". The sun and moon of the Fifth World were created and set into motion through the sacrifice of the gods.

Aztec Creation Myth

The Aztec creation story was of five successive Suns. The First Sun (Night; glyph *Nahui Océlotl*; "Four Jaguar"), was ruled by *TEZCAT-LIPOCA* ("Smoking Mirror"). It was inhabited by giants, but ended when Tezcatlipoca's brother *QUET-ZALCÓATL* ("Plumed Serpent") caused the giants to be devoured by jaguars. The Second Sun (Air; glyph *Nahui Éhecatl*; "Four Wind"), was ruled by Quetzalcóatl. It was destroyed by winds, and its "people" were turned into monkeys. The Third Sun (Rain of Fire; glyph *Nahui Quiáhuitl*; "Four Rain") was ruled by the rain god *TLÁLOC*. It was destroyed by a rain of fire, and its inhabitants were transformed into birds. The Fourth Sun (Water; glyph *Nahui Atl;* "Four Water"), was ruled over by Tláloc's sister *CHALCHIÚTLICUE*. Floods destroyed this world, and surviving inhabitants were turned into fish. The Fifth Sun (glyph *Nahui Ollin*; "Four Movement/Earthquake"), that of the Aztecs, was ruled over by the sun god *TONATIUH*. It was predicted that it would end in cataclysmic earthquakes.

The Fifth Sun was created by the gods in an assembly at *TEOTI-HUACÁN* (literally "city of the gods") after the destruction of the Fourth Sun. A composite myth can be compiled from several sources, including details about the creation of the earth, sun and moon, the creation of humans, and the provision of essential elements in Aztec life, such as corn (maize) agriculture and the basis for the practice of human sacrifice.

Despite their earlier rivalry, Quetzalcóatl and Tezcatlipoca co-operated in the creation of the earth of the Fifth Sun. The great Earth Monster *TLALTECUHTLI* provided them with the raw materials. Quetzalcóatl and Tezcatlipoca descended from the sky to see Tlaltecuhtli astride the world ocean. She greeted them ferociously and craved flesh to eat. Her jaws were

fanged, and her elbows, knees and other joints had gnashing mouths. Quetzalcóatl and Tezcatlipoca were appalled at the sight of her, and concluded that the world could not possibly exist while such a monster survived, so they plotted to destroy her. Transforming themselves into two great serpents, one seized Tlaltecuhtli by the right hand and left foot while the other seized her by the left hand and right foot. In the ensuing struggle they succeeded in ripping her asunder – and Tezcatlipoca lost a foot. Her upper body became the earth and other portions were thrown into the sky to create the heavens. The other gods, however, were not pleased with these actions, and consoled the spirit of Tlaltecuhtli by decreeing that all plants essential to the wellbeing of humans must arise from parts of her body.

Eight gods divided this world into four quadrants by making four roads to the centre, and raised the heavens above it. To support the sky, Tezcatlipoca and Quetzalcóatl transformed themselves into two huge trees – the tree of Tezcatlipoca decorated with obsidian mirrors and that of Quetzalcóatl with emerald-coloured *quetzal* feathers. In appreciation, Tonacatecuhtli ("Lord of Sustenance") made them lords of the heavens and the stars.

THE PYRAMID OF Quetzalcóatl and Tláloc at Teotihuacán symbolizes the importance of two of Mesoamerica's earliest deities. Masks of Tláloc and Quetzalcóatl alternate on the pyramid tiers.

The Milky Way became their road and, in one variation, Tezcatlipoca was transformed into the Great Bear constellation.

The world was still dark, however, so the gods built a huge fire. The headstrong and haughty god *TECUCIZTÉCATL* boasted that he would sacrifice himself in this "funeral" pyre and rise again as the sun. But when faced with the flames he lost his nerve and it was his weak, humble and allegedly cowardly brother *NANAHUATZIN* who jumped first, thus persuading Tecuciztécatl to jump. Consequently Nanahuatzin rose as the sun while Tecuciztécatl emerged as the moon. Both shone equally brightly at first, until one of the gods obscured the light of the moon by throwing a rabbit (*tochtli*) into its "face" (see *MEZTLI*).

The sun and moon were set in motion by *TLAHUIZCALPANTECUH-TLI* – one of Quetzalcóatl's many guises. Nanahuatzin, who was now

THE PYRAMID of the Moon at Teotihuacán, framed by the bulk of the sacred mountain Cerro Gordo, was dedicated to the Great Goddess or Teotihuacán Spider Woman.

the sun god *TONATIUH*, demanded blood sacrifice and fealty. Outraged at such arrogance Tlahuizcalpan-tecuhtli hurled a dart at the sun with his *atl-atl* (spear-thrower), but he missed. Tonatiuh retaliated, piercing Tlahuizcalpantecuhtli through the head and transforming him into stone – as the god of coldness, *ITZTLACOLIUHQUI* – an episode said to explain the dawn chill. So the gods and goddesses concluded that they must sacrifice themselves. Quetzalcóatl was called upon to cut out their hearts with a sacrificial obsidian blade – thus establishing the manner in which humans also had to be sacrificed to feed Tonatiuh, ironically perceived as "the life-giving sun", with the blood of life.

The Fifth Sun lacked inhabitants so the gods conferred again, and again called on Quetzalcóatl, this time in his guise as the wind god *ÉHECATL*. He was tasked to travel to the underworld, *MICTLÁN*, to retrieve the bones of the people of the former world. When he reached Mictlán, Quetzalcóatl announced his mission, but the suspicious *MICTLANTECUHTLI*, Lord of the Underworld, and his wife, *MICTE-CACÍHUATL*, asked him why the gods wanted the bones. Quetzalcóatl explained that the gods felt compelled to people the newly created earth, but Mictlantecuhtli agreed to give up the bones only if Quetzalcóatl would perform an apparently easy task: travel around Mictlán four times while sounding a conch-shell trumpet continuously. In place of a conch-shell trumpet, however, the devious Mictlantecuhtli gave him a plain conch shell, with no finger holes. Quetzalcóatl saw through the ruse, and called upon worms to eat through the shell to make holes, and upon bees to fly into the shell and make it roar with their buzzing.

When he heard the blast of the conch Mictlantecuhtli reluctantly agreed to give up the bones, then changed his mind as Quetzalcóatl was taking them away. He ordered his servants to dig a huge pit to block Quetzalcóatl's escape. Quetzalcóatl fell into the pit when a quail burst into flight and startled him; he appeared to be dead, and the bones, scattered in the pit, were broken and pecked by the quail. But he eventually revived, collected up the broken bones and made good his escape to TAMOANCHÁN, the place of miraculous birth. (The different sizes of people were explained by the different sizes of the broken bones after they were used to fashion new humans.) Quetzalcóatl delivered the bones to the old goddess CIHUACÓATL, who ground them and mixed them with the blood of the gods (or in another version, with blood from Quetzalcóatl's penis) to mould into men and women.

In another version of this story, Quetzalcóatl was accompanied on his journey to the underworld by XÓLOTL ("dog animal"), who acted as his guide. In this variation it was Xólotl who brought back a bone to the gods, who then sprinkled it with blood and caused it to give birth to a boy and a girl. Xólotl then raised the children on thistle milk and thus peopled the world of the Fifth Sun.

Yet another variation describes how Tezcatlipoca attempted to preserve two people from the Fourth Sun. He told the man, Tata, and his wife Nene to hide in the hollow of a tree, where he cared for them. He told the couple to eat only one ear of corn (maize) each while they waited for the flood waters to abate. When it was safe to descend from the tree, however, they saw a fish, one of their transformed former brethren, and, unable to overcome their temptation they caught the fish, made a fire, and cooked and ate it. The smoke was noticed by the gods CITLALÍCUE and CITLATONA, who cried out in rage, whereupon Tezcatlipoca descended upon the hapless couple in fury. His plan undone, he cut off the couple's heads and placed them on their buttocks, thus creating the first dogs. Clearly this story, recorded after the Spanish conquest, has an element of Christian influence in its "first couple" and "first disobedience" themes.

The next task was to supply the new race with sustenance. The gods and goddesses set about searching for a suitable food for humans, and, once again, it was Quetzalcóatl who played a crucial role. His attention was drawn by a red ant, AZCATL, scurrying along the ground carrying a grain of corn. He asked the ant where such a wonderful food was to be found, but Azcatl refused to tell him. After much threatening, however, Azcatl agreed to reveal the source, and led Quetzalcóatl to Mount TONACATÉPETL (literally "mountain of sustenance"). There Quetzalcóatl changed himself into a black ant and made his way through a narrow entrance passage to follow Azcatl deep into the mountain,

THE FOUR QUADRANTS *and directions of the universe, centred on the "Old Fire God" – the creator god Xiuhtecuhtli – are pictured on the first page of the early post-Spanish-conquest Codex Fejérváry-Mayer.*

where there was a chamber filled not only with grains of corn, but also with many other types of seeds and grains. Quetzalcóatl took some of the corn kernels back to Tamoanchán, where the gods chewed it and fed some of the resulting mash (*maza*) to the infant humans, whereupon they gained strength and grew.

Then the gods asked, "What is to be done with Tonacatépetl?" Quetzalcóatl attempted to haul the entire mountain, by slinging a rope around it, to a more convenient place on earth, but it proved too heavy even for him to move. So, rather than try to bring the mountain and its grains and seeds to the humans, it was decided to scatter the grains and seeds from the mountain over the earth. The old diviners OXOMOCO and CIPACTONAL cast lots to determine how this was to be done, and the signs told them that it was the god Nanahuatzin who should do this, by splitting Tonacatépetl open. Nanahuatzin, in turn, called upon the help of the four gods of the directional winds, the rains, and lightning – the TLÁLOCS. Tonacatépetl was duly split asunder and the black, blue, red and white (or yellow) winds

blew the grains and seeds across the land, while the rains watered them so that they took root and grew where they fell. Humans were quick to take advantage of this renewable source of food.

Finally, the gods concluded that something further was needed to provide humans with pleasure and to cause them to sing and dance in their honour. The ever obliging Quetzalcóatl, in his manifestation as the wind god Éhecatl, persuaded the beautiful young virgin MAYÁHUEL to leave her abode in the sky and accompany him to the earth, where the two became lovers and embraced in the form of two entwined branches of a tree. Mayáhuel had been pursued by her guardian, the fierce "grandmother" goddess TZITZIMITL, but the latter was too late to stop the union. In her wrath she split the tree in two, destroying the branch representing Mayáhuel and feeding the shreds to her demon servants, the TZITZIMIME. Éhecatl, however, remained unharmed and, after resuming his former shape, gathered Mayáhuel's bones and planted them in a field where they grew, and lived on, as the *maguey* that produces the white drink known as PULQUE.

111

Maya Creation Myth

Maya creation stories also describe a succession of worlds, created by *HUNAB KU*. The first world was inhabited by the *SAIYAM UINICOB* ("adjuster men"), a race of dwarfs who, so the Maya believed, had built the ruined cities of the past. This work had been done in darkness because the sun had not yet been created but, when the sun rose on the first dawn, the Saiyam Uinicob were turned to stone. This world was destroyed by the first great flood, *haiyococab* ("water over the earth"). The second world was inhabited by the Dzolob ("offenders"), a mysterious race. It, too, was destroyed by flood waters, which poured from the mouth of the great sky serpent. The third world, that of the Mazehualob (the ancient Maya), would also end in a flood, and a fourth world come about in which would live a mixture of all the inhabitants of the previous worlds. In due course the fourth world will also end in flood. The sacred book *CHILAM BALAM* of Chumayel explains that the third Maya world came about after the 13 Lords of the Heavens (the *OXLAHUN TI KU*) were defeated by the nine Lords of the Underworld (the *BOLON TI KU*) and the *BACABS* were set to support the four corners of the earth.

This cyclical universe of creation and destruction mirrored Maya daily life and reflected their concept of duality, in which the rain god *CHAC* brought forth new corn (maize) shoots and plants each year, while *AH PUCH*, god of death, attempted to nip off the buds and tender new leaves.

The creation myth of the Guatemalan Quiché Maya also survives in their sacred text, the *POPUL VUH*. In the beginning, "all was in suspense, all calm, in silence; all motionless, still, and the expanse of the sky was empty. . . There was nothing standing; only the calm water, the placid sea, alone and tranquil. . . Then came the word. *TEPEU* and *GUCUMATZ* conferred.

They talked then, discussing and deliberating; they agreed, they united their words and thoughts."

There was only water and darkness on this new earth. Then the gods created the animals, and Gucumatz and Tepeu attempted to fashion humans out of mud, but were disappointed because these humans could not speak or worship their creators. When the mud dried they crumbled to dust, so the world was destroyed by flood. Next the gods made men of wood and women of rushes. They were stiff and unable to move, although they could speak and multiply. But they lacked brains, and could not recognize their creators. They became wicked and had to be destroyed, as before, by flood. The survivors became monkeys.

Finally, the gods made beings from yellow and white corn dough. When the sun rose on the first day of this creation, the humans were flesh. They had brains, recognized their creators and worshipped them, but were too knowledgeable, so the gods clouded their eyes to keep them focused on day-to-day events. Unlike the other Maya sources, the *Popul Vuh* mentions no anticipated fate for this world.

CUAUHTLI ("eagle") was the 15th of 20 *AZTEC* day-names; it was unfavourable and its patron deity was *XIPE TOTEC*, the "flayed one". The *MAYA* and *ZAPOTEC* equivalents were *MEN* and *NAA*. The *cuauhtli* was the mascot of the Eagle Warriors (see *WARRIOR CULTS*).

CUAUHUITLEHUA see *ATLCAHUALO*.

CUAUHXICALLI ("eagle house") were carved stone receptacles in which the hearts and blood of sacrificial victims were placed after being torn from the victims' bodies. The earth lord *TLALTECUHTLI* was often carved on the underside of the box.

CUAXÓLOTL was the *AZTEC* goddess of the hearth and an alternative name for *CHANTICO*. She was portrayed with two heads, to symbolize both the good and evil potentials of fire.

CUERAUÁPERI, or Cueraváperi, "she who causes to be born", was the *TARASCAN* creator goddess (or the feminine creation principle), goddess of birth and agriculture and, curiously, patroness of sewing. Her consort was *CURICAUERI*, the sun god, in union with whom she produced the moon goddess *XARATANGA*. While Xaratanga was the new moon, Cuerauáperi represented the old moon.

As sworn enemies of the México *AZTECS*, the Tarascans were almost constantly at war, and prisoners were a ready source of sacrificial victims for their gods. At the feast of *SICUINDIRO*, prisoners were sacrificed to Cuerauáperi, and priests dressed and danced in the victims' flayed skins (see also *XIPE TOTEC*). The hearts of the victims were thrown into the thermal springs of Araró, from which it was believed Cuerauáperi drew water to create clouds to water the crops.

CUAUHTLI, the eagle, was a powerful symbol in Meso-american cosmology and a symbol of the Aztec nation.

CUETZPALLIN ("lizard") was the fourth of 20 *AZTEC* day-names; with a favourable augury; its patron was *HUEHUECÓYOTL*, the trickster. The *MAYA* and *ZAPOTEC* equivalents were *KAN* and *ACHE*.

Cuetzpallin represented creative natural forces, dying and regeneration. In the codices it is depicted as a lizard, the front half painted blue (for night), and the rear half painted red (for day). Calendrical dates and deity associations included: 1 *Cuetzpallin*, as a calendrical name of the god *ITZTLACOLIUHQUI*; and 6 *Cuetzpallin*, for *MICTLANTECUHTLI*, the god of death.

CULHUACÁN see under *CE TÉCPATL MIXCÓATL*.

CURICAUERI, or Curicaveri, was the *TARASCAN* creator god (or masculine creation principle), sun god, fire god and god of corn (maize) as *QUERENDA-ANGAPETI*. He and his consort, the creator goddess *CUERAUÁPERI*, produced the moon goddess *XARATANGA*.

The centre of his cult was at the great fivefold temple complex of *YÁCATAS* at Tzintzuntzan. It was essential to honour him by keeping perpetual fires burning in the Yácatas and, for this purpose, there were five special priests called *curihtsit-acha* ("lord who is in charge of the fire"). Smoke was considered especially significant and believed to be a special form of contact between humans and gods. Tobacco was thrown into sacred fires to give fragrance, and only priests were allowed to smoke it. A group of women was also assigned to honour Curicaueri by weaving rich blankets and making corn bread to be burned on his fires.

War prisoners were sacrificed to Curicaueri and their blood offered to the sacred fires at the feast of *SICUINDIRO*. The priests dressed and danced in the flayed skins of the victims (see also *XIPE TOTEC*), and the victims' hearts were thrown into the thermal springs of Araró.

CURITA-CAHERI was the messenger of the *TARASCAN* gods.

DUBDO was another name for the *ZAPOTEC* god of corn (maize) and the Zapotec fifth *LORD OF THE NIGHT*. (See also *PITAO COZOBI*)

DZAHUI, or Tzahui, was the *MIXTEC* god of lightning and rain, equivalent to *AZTEC TLÁLOC*, *MAYA CHAC*, *TOTONAC TAJÍN* and *ZAPOTEC COCIJO*, and probably also to the *TARASCAN CHUPITHIRIPEME*.

DZOLOB, a mysterious race, were the "offenders", the inhabitants of the second world in Maya creation; see *HUNAB KU* and *CREATION MYTHS*.

EARTH MONSTER
see *TLALTECUHTLI*.

EB ("bad rain") was the 12th of the 20 *MAYA* day-names; associated with the malignant rain god who sent mist, dew and dampness that caused mildew on the corn crop. The *AZTEC* and *ZAPOTEC* equivalent days were *MALINALLI* and *PIJA*.

ECOZTLI see *PACHTONTLI*.

ÉHECATL, *NAHUATL* for "wind", was possibly of *HUASTEC* origin and became the god of winds throughout central Mesoamerica, and was associated with the cardinal points and colours. He was a manifestation of *QUETZALCÓATL*, the plumed serpent, and was often known as Quetzalcóatl-Éhecatl or Éhecatl-Quetzalcóatl. He was honoured, especially by the Huastecs, with round or round-ended temple-platforms in many cities – allegedly to offer less resistance to prevailing winds. In the codices and sculpture Éhecatl was shown wearing a bird-beak or duck-billed mask, most famously in the statue excavated at the Temple of Quetzalcóatl-Éhecatl in Calixtlahuaca, a city of the Matlazinca (in the Toluca Valley west of the Basin of Mexico). He ruled the second of the 20 Aztec days (*Éhecatl*; Maya *IK*; Zapotec *QUIJ* or *Laa*; all meaning wind).

Éhecatl was a rather enigmatic deity, with numerous guises and roles, many auguring unfavourable events. Calendrical references include: *1 Éhecatl Iztac Tezcatlipoca* – "white Tezcatlipoca", the equivalent of Quetzalcóatl; or *4 Éhecatl*

DUBDO, the Zapotec corn god, is depicted in this carving wearing a corn cob headdress. (CLASSIC PERIOD.)

Xólotl – Quetzalcóatl's twin. As *6 Éhecatl* he was the sun. As *7 Éhecatl* he was associated with the day of the creation of humankind by Quetzalcóatl, and as *9 Éhecatl* he represented the winds from the four quarters. As Quetzalcóatl, he was instrumental in the creation of the Fifth Sun, and in the origin of humans (see *CREATION MYTHS*).

The gods decided that people were needed to populate the world and sent Quetzalcóatl, as Éhecatl, to *MICTLÁN* (the underworld) to retrieve the bones of the people of the former world. He arrived and announced his mission, at which the ruler *MICTLANTECHUHTLI* and his wife declared that Éhecatl-Quetzalcóatl could have the bones only if he would carry out an ostensibly easy task – travel around Mictlán four times while blowing on a conch-shell trumpet. In place of a trumpet, however, Mictlantecuhtli gave Éhecatl-Quetzalcóatl a conch shell with no finger holes. Spotting this deficiency, Éhecatl-Quetzalcóatl called upon worms to drill holes and upon bees to fly into the shell and make it roar with their buzzing. Mictlantecuhtli reluctantly gave up the bones, but attempted several times to get them back, each time being outwitted by Éhecatl-Quetzalcóatl. The bones were delivered to the old goddess *CIHUA-CÓATL*, who ground them and mixed them with the blood of the gods to mould men and women (or in a different version, mixed the ground bones with blood from Éhecatl's penis).

At their assembly at *TEOTI-HUACÁN*, the gods called upon Éhecatl-Quetzalcóatl again. The twin brothers *NANAHUATZIN* and

ÉHECATL, Huastec-Aztec god of the wind, was one manifestation of Quetzalcóatl (the "plumed serpent"). He was most frequently portrayed with a buccal or duck-bill mask.

TECUCIZTÉCATL leapt into the sacrificial fire and emerged as the sun and the moon. They remained motionless, however, until Éhecatl blew upon them, setting them on their journeys across the sky.

In yet another myth, Éhecatl brought physical love and the *maguey* or *agave* (*Agave americana*; from which the intoxicating drink *PULQUE* is made) into the world, by persuading the beautiful virgin *MAYÁHUEL* to leave her abode in the sky and descend to the earth with him. They became lovers by embracing each other as a tree of two entwined branches, but were pursued by *TZITZIMITL*, Mayáhuel's fearsome "grandmother" guardian. When she arrived too late to stop the union, in her wrath she split the tree in two, destroying the branch representing Mayáhuel and feeding the shreds to her demon servants. Éhecatl, however, remained unharmed and, resuming his former shape, gathered Mayáhuel's bones and planted them in a field where they grew into the *maguey* plant. (See also *COLOURS & THE CARDINAL DIRECTIONS*)

ORDERING THE WORLD

THE CONCEPT OF CYCLICITY permeated the entire fabric of Mesoamerican culture and society. From the daily journey of the sun across the sky, through the monthly cycles of the moon and the annual pattern of the seasons, to the super-annual countings of days and months according to the motions of the planets and stars, virtually every Mesoamerican act or task was believed to occur under the auspices of celestial movements. Cyclical time directed both men and the gods and goddesses, and regulated all thought, from people's everyday decisions to their world view to social evolution. Even the world itself had been created in a series of episodes and would ultimately end in a closing of the cycle by the destruction of the Fifth Sun.

Such belief in unremitting cyclicity was intimately connected to Aztec collapse in 1519–21, and helps to explain their complex and enigmatic reaction to the Spaniards. The Aztecs believed that Moctezuma II Xocoyotzin's reign, and the world of the Fifth Sun, would end upon the return of Quetzalcóatl the man-god, from the east, to claim his rightful rule and to create a new world order. The celestial movements ominously coincided with the arrival of Hernán Cortés, who cannily used the knowledge of this belief to his advantage.

THE INTRICATELY CARVED STONE (above) popularly known as the "calendar stone", found in Mexico City in 1790, represents the sun god Tonatiuh or his counterpart, the night sun Yohualtecuhtli. The sun and cosmic symbolism are manifest. A central image is surrounded by a series of ring-panels. In the centre is the sun, represented by a stylized human face with a sacrificial stone knife protruding from the mouth. The first ring contains, to right and left, two rounded claw-arms clutching human hearts, and four glyph panels representing each of the four previous suns – Jaguar, Wind, Rain (of Fire) and Water. The second ring contains the glyphs of the 20 Nahuatl day-names. A third (narrow) ring comprises repetitive, decorative designs, and is followed by a fourth ring with repeated symbols representing turquoise and jade, the colours for the heavens and symbols of the equinoxes and solstices. The outer border comprises two Xiuhcóatl (turquoise, or fire, snakes) symbolizing cosmic order, cyclicity and the present world.

THE TWENTY AZTEC day-names (right, shown bottom right to top left) are crocodile, wind, house, lizard, serpent, death, deer, rabbit, water, dog, monkey, grass, reed, jaguar, eagle, vulture, movement, flint knife, rain, and flower. There were three chronological systems in Mesoamerican lives: the 365-day cycle, the 260-day cycle and a Venusian cycle of 584 days. The first two were combined by the Aztecs to form the Xiuhmolpilli, a 52-year cycle. The 365-day cycle was made up of 18 months of 20 days each, plus five extra, ill-omened days at the end of each year. Each month had special rites associated with it. The Aztecs also divided each day into 13 "hours" of daytime and 9 "hours" of nighttime. The sequence of days in each month was fixed, and therefore the day-name on which a new solar year began shifted by five days each year. (ILLUSTRATION FROM RESEARCHES CONCERNING THE INSTITUTIONS AND MONUMENTS OF THE ANCIENT INHABITANTS OF AMERICA BY FRIEDRICH ALEXANDER BARON VON HUMBOLDT, 1814.)

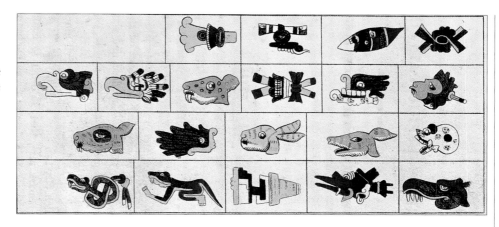

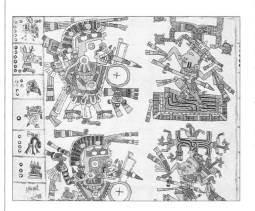

THE PYRAMID of the Niches (right) at the Totonac site of El Tajín emphasizes the importance and widespread use of the 365-day calendar throughout Mesoamerica. The six tiers and temple of the pyramid-platform include 88 niches on the base tier, then successively 76, 64, 52, 40, 28 and 17 at the top.

THE IMPORTANCE of Venus (above), known as the god Tlahuizcalpantecuhtli – the morning and evening "stars", is demonstrated by his depiction in the codices and his influence over daily lives. During the periods of the Venusian synodical orbit he was believed to rule and attack the different social orders, his power over them being symbolized by the darts he hurls at them in these scenes. (PRE-SPANISH CONQUEST CODEX COSPI.)

DAY-NAMES

	AZTEC (Cempolhualli) glyph	patron deity	augury	MAYA (Uinal) glyph	ZAPOTEC glyph
1	Cipactli (crocodile)	Tonacatecuhtli	good	Imix (earth-monster)	Chilla (crocodile)
2	Éhecatl (wind)	Quetzalcóatl;	evil	Ik (breath, wind)	Quij or Laa (wind)
3	Calli (house)	Tepeyolohtli	good	Akbal (darkness)	Guela (night)
4	Cuetzpallin (lizard)	Huehuecóyotl	good	Kan (ripe corn/maize)	Ache or Beydo (lizard)
5	Cóatl (serpent)	Chalchiúhtlicue	good	Chicchan (serpent)	Zee or Zij (serpent)
6	Miquiztli (death)	Tecciztécatl or Meztli	evil	Cimi (death)	Lana (blackness)
7	Mázatl (deer)	Tláloc	good	Manik (hand)	China (deer)
8	Tochtli (rabbit)	Mayáhuel	good	Lamat (Venus)	Lapa (rabbit)
9	Atl (water)	Xiuhtecuhtli	evil	Muluc (water)	Niza or Queza (water)
10	Itzcuintli (dog)	Mictlantecuhtli	good	Oc (dog)	Tella (dog)
11	Ozomatli (monkey)	Xochipilli	neutral	Chuen (monkey; craftsman)	Loo or Goloo (dog)
12	Malinalli (grass)	Patécatl	evil	Eb (bad or poor rain)	Pija (draught)
13	Ácatl (reed)	Tezcatlipoca or Itztlacoliuhqui	evil	Ben (growing corn)	Quij or Ij or Laa (reed)
14	Océlotl (jaguar)	Tlazoltéotl	evil	Ix (jaguar)	Gueche (jaguar)
15	Cuauhtli (eagle)	Xipe Totec	evil	Men (moon; wise one; eagle)	Naa (eagle)
16	Cozcacuauhtli (vulture)	Itzpapálotl	good	Cib (wax)	Loo or Guiloo (crow)
17	Ollin (movement, earthquake)	Xólotl	neutral	Caban (earth)	Xoo (earthquake)
18	Técpatl (flint knife)	Tezcatlipoca or Chalchiuhtotolin	good	Etz'nab (cutting edge)	Opa (cold)
19	Quiáhuitl (rain)	Tonatiuh or Chantico	evil	Cauac (rain; storm)	Ape (cloud)
20	Xóchitl (flower)	Xochiquetzal	neutral	Ahau (lord)	Lao (flower)

G

EIGHT DEER TIGER CLAW (AD 1011–63) was the legendary 11th-century ruler of the *MIXTEC* cities of Tilantongo (founded about AD 875) and Tututepec, whose exploits are recorded in the *Codex Nuttall*, the *Codex Colombino* and the *Codex Becker 1*.

He founded Tututepec in the early 11th century near the Pacific coast and co-ruled (AD 1030–63) Tilantongo with his half-brother, with whom he established that city's second dynasty. From Tututepec he conquered the surrounding Mixtec towns in Mixteca de la Costa and Mixteca Alta. The codices describe his five marriages, his murder of his half-brother and seizure of power in Tilantongo, and the end of his rule when he offered himself up for sacrifice. In the *Codex Nuttall* he is shown in *TOLTEC* dress, while his courtiers wear Mixtec costume, which has led some scholars to argue that he sought Toltec affirmation of his power. Some even argue that he visited the Toltec capital at Tollán (Tula) to receive his turquoise nose plug as a symbol of rank.

EK CHUAH, *MAYA* God M and known as "black war leader", was a Yucatecan god of war in his malevolent aspect, and simultaneously god of travellers, merchants and prosperity in his benevolent aspect (see also *THE OLD BLACK GOD*). As the latter he was usually portrayed as a merchant, with a bundle of merchandise on his back and staff in hand. In Yucatecan Maya "Ek" means both "black" and "star", and Ek Chuah was often associated with *XAMEN EK* ("north star"). At least one depiction shows him with the head of Xamen Ek, and thus the North Star and guide of merchants. As the "black scorpion", the god of merchants and as "black war leader" he was portrayed with a large, drooping lower lip, and was painted black, with black rings around his eyes. As war leader he was, of course, a special god of those who died in battle. (See also *BULUC CHABTÁN*.)

Ek Chuah was also the patron of *cacao* (Theobroma cacao; cocoa; chocolate), which, with honey (see *AH MUCEN CAB*), was one of the most important items of Maya trade. Mesoamericans also used *cacao* beans as a currency to purchase small household items; and in post-Spanish Conquest times *cacao* beans were even used to pay labourers' wages. Owners of *cacao* plantations held a ceremony in honour of Ek Chuah in the month of *Muan* (15th of the 18 months of the year). As god of merchants, his Aztec equivalent was *YACATECUHTLI*.

EK PAUAHTUN see *PAUAHTUN*.

EK CHUAH, Maya God M, was the "black scorpion" merchant god and "black war leader". He carries a merchant's staff and bundle on a tumpline, and has a typically drooping lower lip and ringed eye.

EK XIB CHAC see *THE CHACS*.

EL TAJÍN see *TAJÍN*.

ETZALCUALIZTLI ("meal of corn/maize and beans") was the seventh (or, in some sources, sixth) of the 18 months in the *AZTEC* year. As with *ATLCAHUALO*, the principal deities honoured were the god and goddess of water, *TLÁLOC* and *CHALCHIÚHTLICUE*.

ETZ'NAB, *MAYA* God Q, was god of evil, and probably of human sacrifice (see also *BULUC CHABTAN*). He was symbolized by the number two.

Etz'nab ("cutting edge") was also the 18th of the 20 *MAYA* day-names; it was associated with the number two and with God Q, who probably presided over the sacrifices. In the codices it is represented by a pressure-flaked obsidian knife, the sort used in performing human sacrifices. The *AZTEC* and *ZAPOTEC* equivalents were *TÉCPATL* and *OPA*.

THE EVIL GOD see *ETZ'NAB*.

THE FAT GOD, a pan-Mesoamerican deity of the Preclassic to Classics periods, was especially worshipped in the Classic Period city *TEOTIHUACÁN* and its "empire", and at Classic Period *TOTONAC* sites of the central Gulf Coast. His importance recedes towards the end of the Classic Period, corresponding to the waning of Teotihuacán. He is thought to have represented prosperity and sensuous pleasure, and his role appears to have been subsumed by the cults of *XOCHIPILLI* and *MACUILXÓCHITL* in the Postclassic Period.

FIRE CEREMONY see *TOXIUHMOLPILIA*.

THE FLOWERY WAR see *XOCHIYAÓYOTL*.

GOD I was the *OLMEC* god of the earth, sun, water and fertility. He is depicted as a "dragon" – a monster creature with flaming eyebrows, a prominent nose, L-shaped or trough-like eyes and a host of composite features, including a serpentine forked tongue, crocodilian limbs or eagle talons, jaguar fangs and human attributes. His prominence in the Olmec pantheon suggests a link to royal power and dynastic succession, political institutions that were nascent in Olmec civilization. His associations with earth, sun, water and fertility indicate that this was possibly a creator deity, ancestral to several later Mesoamerican gods and goddesses, in particular pan-Mesoamerican *HUEHUETÉOTL*, Maya *ITZAMNÁ* and Aztec *XIUHTECUHTLI*.

GOD II was the *OLMEC* corn (maize) god, identified as such by corn cob symbols sprouting from a cleft in his head, and the god of agriculture in general. Figures of God II depict a toothless infant – presumably a manifestation of youth and life – with a were-jaguar countenance of almond-shaped eyes, a wide, flat nose and a plump, flaring upper lip, and often a decorated band across his forehead. He was presumably antecedent to all Mesoamerican corn deities, in particular the Aztec god *CENTÉOTL*.

GOD III was the *OLMEC* deity associated with celestial matters, particularly with the sun, and agricultural fertility. For reasons not completely understood, God III is also connected with chinless dwarfs. He was a bird-monster, with combined avian and reptilian features: a raptor's beak with conspicuous cere (sometimes with a single, cleft upper fang), paw-like wings ending in talons and, in some figures, the head bears a harpy-eagle's crest. Like *GOD I*, he has L-shaped or trough-like eyes and flame eyebrows.

GOD IV was the *OLMEC* god of rain, and, by extension, of agricultural fertility. Like *GOD II*, he is depicted as an infant were-jaguar,

with almond-shaped eyes, a flattened, pug nose, flaring upper lip and an easily identifiable toothless mouth turned down at the corners. He is usually shown wearing a distinctive, sectioned headband, crenellated ear ornaments and a pectoral badge with crossed bands. Because of his special association with clouds, rain and fertility, he is thought to be ancestral to *MAYA CHAC* and *AZTEC TLÁLOC*.

GOD V is a designation no longer used by archaeologists.

GOD VI was a mysterious *OLMEC* deity thought to have represented spring and the concept of annual renewal or resurrection. He is portrayed as a disembodied cleft head with almond-shaped eyes, the open one of which has a distinct band or stripe across it. As with other Olmec gods, his toothless mouth has prominent gum ridges and is shaped in a hideous grin. Some of these attributes seem to suggest that God VI might have

GOD VI or X was the Olmec composite jaguar-monster god, with cleft head, almond-shaped eyes and a toothless, pouting mouth. The flame shoulders and "torch" are attributes of God I – earth, sun, water and fertility.

been antecedent to *XIPE TOTEC*, the *HUASTEC* and central Mesoamerican god of spring, whose priests dressed in the flayed skins of their human sacrificial victims.

GOD VII, sometimes referred to as the Olmec "dragon", was another less well-defined *OLMEC* deity, possibly an early "feathered serpent". Although he can be distinguished from them, his features are similar to those of *GOD I* and *GOD III* – a serpentine head and body with avian head crest and wings.

GOD VIII was the *OLMEC* fish-monster, associated with oceans, and with standing (as opposed to flowing) bodies of water in general. Appropriately, he has a fish body with a forked tail, crocodilian teeth

and shark-like features, but crescent-shaped eyes and a human nose. His decoration often consists of crossed bands or stripes along the body.

GOD IX is a designation no longer used by archaeologists.

GOD X was yet another *OLMEC* were-jaguar deity who had attributes similar to those of *GOD VI* – a cleft head, almond-shaped eyes and a toothless, prominent gummed mouth – but he is identifiable through the figure-of-eight motifs in his nostrils and the lack of eye bands or stripes. He was normally shown as a disembodied head and, in composite imagery, invariably occupied a position secondary to the other gods.

GOD A see *AH PUCH*.

GOD B see *CHAC*.

GOD C see *XAMEN EK*.

GOD D see *ITZAMNÁ*.

GOD E see *AH MUN*.

GOD F see *BULUC CHABTÁN*.

GOD G see *KINICH AHAU*.

GOD H see *CHICCHAN*.

GOD K see *BOLON DZ'ACAB*.

GOD L see *THE OLD BLACK GOD*.

GOD M see *EK CHUAH*.

GOD N see *PAUAHTUN*.

GOD Q see *ETZ'NAB*.

GODDESS I see *IX CHEL*.

GODDESS O see *IX CHEBEL YAX*.

GOLOO ("dog") see *LOO*.

GOZIO was the Sierra *ZAPOTEC* name for *COCIJO*.

GREAT GODDESS see *TEOTIHUACÁN SPIDER WOMAN*.

GUCUMATZ was the Quiché *MAYA* name for *KUKULKÁN*, the "feathered serpent". He is described in the Quiché sacred text of the *POPUL VUH*, in which the gods Gucumatz and *TEPEU* created the earth and all of the living things on it, although it took them many attempts before they were satisfied with their efforts to create humans (see *CREATION MYTHS*).

GUECHE ("jaguar") was 14th of the 20 *ZAPOTEC* day-names; *AZTEC* and *MAYA* equivalent days were *OCÉLOTL* and *IX*.

GOD VII, possibly the Olmec precursor to Quetzalcóatl the "plumed serpent", was depicted (above the serpent-masked human figure) on Monument 19 at the Gulf Coast site of La Venta.

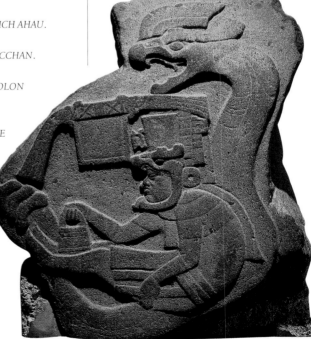

H

GUELA ("night") was the third of the 20 *ZAPOTEC* day-names; the *AZTEC* and *MAYA* equivalent days were *CALLI* and *AKBAL*.

GUILOO ("crow") see *LOO*.

HISTORIA DE LOS REINOS DE CULHUACÁN see *ANALES DE CUAUHTITLÁN*.

HOBNIL see *THE BACABS*.

HOZANEK see *THE BACABS*.

HUAHUANTLI see *TEOYAOMIQUI*.

THE HUASTECS lived in northeast Mesoamerica, along the northern Gulf Coast. They spoke a *MAYA* or related language but, from about 1400 BC, had become split off from the more southerly Maya by the intervention of other groups into the central Gulf Coast. Indeed, Maya chronicles refer to their Huastec ancestry. Influences from *TEOTIHUACÁN*, especially architectural, and from the central Gulf Coast *TOTONAC* are evident at Classic Period Huastec sites. In the Postclassic Period the Huastecs were conquered by the México *AZTECS*.

Several Mesoamerican deities and religious concepts appear to be of Huastec origin. During the late Classic Period, the *TOLTEC* cult of *QUETZALCÓATL* might have originated among them, particularly the worship of him as *ÉHECATL*-Quetzalcóatl; a distinctive Huastec architectural form associated with this cult was round or round-ended temple platforms.

Another important central Mesoamerican god of Huastec, or earlier, origin was *XIPE TOTEC*, flayed god of spring (see also *GOD VI*). Other deities possibly of Huastec ancestry are the earth goddesses *TOCI*, *IXCUINAN* and *TLAZOLTÉOTL*, and the concept of *TAMOANCHÁN*, a terrestrial paradise.

HUAUHQUILTAMALCUAL-IZTLI see *IZCALLI*.

HUECHAANA, or Huichaana, also Cochana, *HUICHANATAO*, Nohuiçana, Nohuichana and Pitao Huichaana, was a Valley *ZAPOTEC* mother goddess associated, alongside her male counterpart *COZAANA*, with children. She was also associated with hunting and fishing – hunters and fishers offered her sacrifices for help in their endeavours. In addition, like *PICHANTO*, she was the intermediary for humankind with *PICHANA GOBECHE*.

HUEHUECÓYOTL, or Ueuecóyotl ("old coyote" – *cóyotl*), was the central Mesoamerican god of cleverness and trickery, the wily old coyote who wreaked spontaneous mischief, especially that associated with sex. He enjoyed a widespread cult among ancient Mesoamerican cultures, and might have been of pre-Nahuatl origin, possibly *OTOMÍ*. He was patron of the Aztec day *CUETZPALLIN*, and featherworkers (called *amantecas*) worshipped a god with a coyote companion (*cóyotl inahual*).

His unpredictability made the ordered and severe *AZTECS* especially suspicious and watchful of him. As the trickster coyote figured so prominently in southwest North American myth, it is tempting to speculate that this deity was an ancient accoutrement pre-dating Aztec migration from the northwest into the Basin of Mexico, and that the association continued to be reinforced by trading contacts between central Mesoamerica and northern peoples.

HUEHUETÉOTL, also called *XIUHTECUHTLI*, *OTONTECUHTLI* and Xócotl, was the name for an ancient Mesoamerican deity, literally the "Old One", the *OLD FIRE GOD*, possibly descended from the Olmec *GOD I*. He was usually portrayed as an old man, with wrinkled skin and toothless mouth, supporting an incense brazier on his head. He was first among the nine Aztec *LORDS OF THE NIGHT* and the 13 *LORDS OF*

THE DAY. The *AZTECS* called him Xiuhtecuhtli, as the god who presided over the New Fire Ceremony (see *TOXIUHMOLPILIA*).

HUEYMICCAILHUITL ("great feast of the dead") was the 11th (or, in some sources, the 10th) of the *AZTEC* 18 months, in which the fire god, *XIUHTECUHTLI*, and *YACATECUHTLI*, patron of merchants, were worshipped. Sacrificial victims were drugged, then roasted before their hearts were cut out. In the codices the month is represented by death symbols and mummy bundles. It is also called *Xocotlhuetzi* ("honouring of the fruit tree").

HUEYPACHTLI ("much hay") was the 14th (or, in some sources, 13th) of the *AZTEC* 18 months, in which the *TLÁLOCS* and *TEPICTOTON* were propitiated.

It is also called *Pillahuana* ("the children drink") and *Tepeílhuitl* ("feast of the mountains").

HUEHUETÉOTL, or the Old Fire God, was represented as an old, bearded man, supporting a brazier for ritual fires and incense burning, as here in this late Classic Period terracotta from Veracruz.

HUEYTECUILHUITL ("great feast of the lords") was the ninth (or, in some sources, eighth) of the *AZTEC* 18 months. It was a ritual feast day in which the corn (maize) god *XILONEN* and the "serpent woman" earth goddess *CIHUACÓATL* were honoured, and in which the Aztec lords feasted the commoners with food, song and dance, and sacrificed male and female impersonators of the two deities.

HUEYTOZOZTLI ("great watch") was the fifth (or, in some sources, fourth) of the *AZTEC* 18 months, a month in which sacrifices were held to propitiate the god and goddess of corn (maize) *CENTÉOTL* and *CHICOMECÓATL*, the purpose being to bring on the tender young corn plants (*toctli*). The ceremonial climax was a procession of virgins to the Temple of Chicomecóatl, where seeds were blessed and a corn-goddess impersonator was sacrificed. Children were offered to the rain god *TLÁLOC* for the success of crops.

HUICHAANA see *HUECHAANA*.

HUICHANATAO was a *ZAPOTEC* goddess of the city of Chichicapa who, like *HUECHAANA*, was associated with children; her male counterpart was *PITAO COZAANA*. She might have been the same as *PICHANTO*, who acted as the intermediary in appeals between people and *PICHANA GOBECHE*.

HUITZILOPOCHTLI ("Hummingbird of the South" or "Blue Hummingbird on the Left" – Mesoamericans regarded the west as "up", making the south the left) was an exclusively *AZTEC* deity who had no identifiable predecessors in earlier Mesoamerican cultures. His symbolic "brothers" in the Aztec pantheon were *QUETZALCÓATL*, *TEZCATLIPOCA* and *XIPE TOTEC*. In one legend he is the son of the creator couple *OMECÍHUATL* and *OMETECUHTLI*. In another he is the son of *COATLÍCUE*, whose life he saved by defeating his brothers and sisters *THE CENTZONHUITZNAHUAC* and *THE CENTZONMIMIZCOA*, who had plotted to kill her, although he first killed his sister *COYOLXAUHQUI* by mistake. (Coyolxauhqui was, in fact, attempting to warn Coatlícue of the plot but, as she approached ahead of them, her new brother Huitzilopochtli emerged fully armed from his mother's womb and did not realize this. He decapitated her in his haste and threw her head into the heavens to become the moon. In Aztec myth, this event recurs daily as the moon sets and the sun drives away the darkness – symbolic of the struggle between day and night, light and dark, good and evil.)

Huitzilopochtli was the sun god and the god of war (hummingbirds

were regarded as the souls of fallen warriors), the tribal god of the México Aztecs (the "people of the sun"), the last Aztec tribe to arrive in the Basin of Mexico and the one that created the empire, and the patron of the Aztec capital, *TENOCHTITLÁN*. As the sun, he was accompanied in his daily journey across the sky, from daybreak until noon, by the souls of warriors fallen in battle – the Aztecs regarded death in battle to be the most honourable way to die – then, from noon to sunset, by the *CIHUATETEO* in their descent into the west, symbolizing a falling eagle. Through the night he illuminated the underworld of the dead.

Huitzilopochtli was given equal status beside *TLÁLOC*, the life giver, and in Tenochtitlán their twin temples stood atop the Templo Mayor pyramid-platform, with a magnificent double stone staircase ascending to them. Huitzilopochtli's temple was plastered and painted blood red for war, while Tláloc's was painted in brilliant blue (representing water) and white, and the priests of both gods were afforded equal rank in Aztec society.

In legend, Huitzilopochtli led the México from a cave in *AZTLÁN*, in the deserts of the northwest, into central Mesoamerica. In their wanderings, the México were led by four priests, who carried a great idol of Huitzilopochtli before the people. Through the idol, Huitzilopochtli spoke secretly to the priests, telling them to call themselves the México, advising them on the best route to take, and

promising them that, if the México honoured him, they would overcome all their enemies and receive riches in tributes of precious stones, coral, gold and quetzal feathers. When they arrived in the Basin of Mexico he gave the México the sign of the eagle (which was his representative) alighting on a *nopal* (prickly pear) cactus, clutching a serpent in his claw, on an island (*MEZTLIAPÁN*) to show them the spot where they should build their capital.

As Huitzilopochtli's chosen people, the México felt compelled to supply their wilful god with the life-giving blood of sacrificial victims, and they fomented ritual wars to secure captives for these tributes (see *XOCHIYAÓYOTL*, "Flowery War"). The prisoners were handed over to the priests at the foot of the Templo Mayor, from where they were dragged up the steps, stretched out across the sacrificial stone, and their chests then sliced open with an obsidian knife. Then the heart of the sacrificial victim was wrenched out, the corpse was skinned, and the limbs dismembered. It is thought that pieces of the flesh were then sent down for

HUITZILOPOCHTLI, the Aztec war god, was frequently depicted in the codices dressed for war and carrying his favourite weapons – atl-atl (spear-thrower), clutch of feather-tipped arrows and shield.

the rulers and nobility to eat, while the heart was allegedly sometimes consumed by the priests. The priests also made offerings of flowers, incense and food to Huitzilopochtli, and they adorned his idol with wreaths and lavish garlands of flowers.

In the codices Huitzilopochtli is usually depicted brandishing his favourite weapon, an *atl-atl* (spear-thrower) made in the shape of *XIUHCÓATL*, the "fire serpent". He has blue-painted arms and legs, hummingbird feathers on his left leg, and arrows tipped with featherdown. His calendrical name was *Ce Técpatl* ("1 Flint"), and his messenger was called Paynal. His malevolent aspects were summed up in the alternative name *YÁOTL*, "the enemy".

HUITZILOPOCHTLI is depicted here in warlike mode, carrying his serpent-shaped atl-atl (spear-thrower), his shield and feathered arrows.

HUIXTOCÍHUATL, or Uixt-oxíhuatl, was the "inventor" and *AZTEC* patroness of salt. A young woman in the guise of Huixtocí-huatl was one of four who served a warrior-youth, himself in the role of *TEZCATLIPOCA*, destined to be sac-rificed at the end of a year of honour and enjoyment. At the fes-tival of *TÓXCATL* young girls and old women performed a dance wearing special flower-headdresses. The cli-max of the dance ceremony was the sacrifice of Huixtocíhuatl and of her "sister-wives" – *ATLATONAN*, *XILONEN* and *XOCHIQUETZAL*.

HUN AHAU see *AH PUCH*.

HUN BATZ and Hun Chouen, described in the *POPUL VUH*, were the sons of *HUN HUNAHPÚ*, and half-brothers of the hero twins *HUNAHPÚ* and *XBALANQUÉ*, of whom they were jealous. Trained by their father and uncle, *VUCUB HUNAHPÚ*, Hun Batz and Hun Chouen were skilled at the Meso-american ball game, and were expert acrobats, dancers and musi-cians, while the twins favoured hunting and exploring the forest. The spoiled older boys took all the twins' game, leaving them only scraps. One day, the twins returned from the day's hunt empty-handed but told their brothers that the birds they had shot were caught in a tree. Hun Batz and Hun Chouen followed them into the forest and agreed to fetch the birds down. As the two climbed, however, the tree trunk miraculously grew taller. The older boys panicked and called out for help. Hunahpú and Xbalanqué advised their brothers to untie their loincloths and wrap them around their hips, leaving the long ends dangling like tails, so as to be able to move more freely. By this trick the older twins were changed into monkeys, but they were not forgotten. To the *MAYA*, because of their former skills, they became the patrons of the arts and crafts, and of musicians and dancers.

THE BALL GAME, a major Mesoamerican ritual, played an important part in the career of the hero twins. The stone ball court at Chichén Itzá, shown here, is the largest in Mesoamerica. (POSTCLASSIC PERIOD)

HUN CAME ("one death") and Vucub Came ("seven death") were the leaders of the Lords of *XIBALBA* (underworld) in the *POPUL VUH*. Annoyed at the noise made by the brothers *HUN HUNAHPÚ* and *VUCUB HUNAHPÚ* when they played the ball game, they challenged the brothers to a game in Xibalba, in which they and the other Lords of Xibalba defeated and sacrificed them. Later, the hero twins *HUNAH-PÚ* and *XBALANQUÉ*, sons of Hun Hunahpú, avenged their father's and uncle's deaths by travelling to Xibalba and defeating Hun Came, Vucub Came and the rest of the Lords, and cutting up their bodies.

HUN CHOUEN see under *HUN BATZ*.

HUN HUNAHPÚ (literally "one Hunahpú") and *VUCUB HUNAHPÚ* ("seven Hunahpú") were *MAYA* deities and the first-born of the human race: the twin sons of the "grandfather" creator god *XPIYACOC* and the "grandmother" creator god-dess *XMUCANÉ*. The twins and Hun Hunahpú's sons *HUN BATZ* and Hun Chouen were fond of the Mesoamer-ican dice game and, especially, the ball game, but the noise they made when playing the latter on the hard stone ball court annoyed the Lords of *XIBALBA* (underworld). The Lords tricked the Hun Hunahpú and Vucub Hunahpú into travelling to Xibalba, where they were challenged to a ball game. There, they were tricked, defeated and sacrificed.

Hun Hunahpú's head was cut off and was hung among the fruits of a calabash tree as a trophy. The fruit of the tree, which was forbid-den, tempted *XQUIC*, the maiden daughter of one of the underworld Lords. When she questioned aloud if she should pick some of the fruit the head overheard and spat into the hand of the unsuspecting girl. As a result she became pregnant and gave birth to the hero twins *HUNAHPÚ* and *XBALANQUÉ*, who later journeyed to Xibalba and avenged the deaths of their father and uncle.

HUNAB KU, an unusual *MAYA* deity, was a supreme, single, cre-ator god of the Yucatecan Maya – an apparent attempt to focus on an over-arching concept of divinity. His name means "one" (*hun*) "state of being" (*ab*) "god" (*ku*). Hunab Ku was thought to be the father of *ITZAMNÁ* himself and, in one ver-sion of the *CREATION MYTH*, was believed to have made the world and set *THE BACABS* at its four cor-ners to hold up the sky.

Unlike the other gods of the Maya pantheon, Hunab Ku was invisible, and therefore was not portrayed – or at least no represen-tation in the codices has positively been identified as Hunab Ku. He was, rather, an abstract concept preached about by priests in the early Postclassic Period, perhaps an early attempt to view the universe under a monotheistic philosophy (see also *TLOQUE NAHUAQUE*).

HUNAHPÚ was one of the hero twins of the Quiché *MAYA*. The sacred *POPUL VUH* describes how

Hunahpú and his brother *XBALAN-QUÉ* were conceived by the spittle of their father, *HUN HUNAHPÚ*, when his severed head spat into the hand of the unsuspecting *XQUIC*, maiden daughter of one of the Lords of *XIBALBA* (the underworld).

The twins went to Xibalba to avenge their father and uncle, *VUCUB HUNAHPÚ*, who had been defeated and slain by the Lords of Xibalba. In Xibalba they underwent several trials: they fought and destroyed the bird-monster *VUCUB-CAQUIZ* and his two giant sons, *CABRACÁN* and *ZIPACNÁ*; Hunahpú was beheaded with an obsidian knife by *CAMA ZOTZ* (the killer bat-god) in *ZOTZIHÁ* (the "House of Bats"); and they challenged the Lords of Xibalba to a ball game, in which Hunahpú participated by borrowing a turtle's head – or sub-stituting a squash in another version – and fooling the Lords. When the Lords threw the ball at Hunahpú's head, which was sus-pended over the court, the ball bounced away, startling a rabbit and causing it to bolt from its hole; in this distraction, Xbalanqué snatched Hunahpú's head and stuck it back on.

The twins defeated the Lords by a ruse: they showed them that they (the twins) were able to cut them-selves into pieces and reassemble themselves. The foolish Lords asked the twins to perform this feat on them too. So the twins dis-membered the Lords, but left them that way. After this final victory they were reborn and ascended into the sky as the sun (Hunahpú) and the moon (Xbalanqué).

Hunahpú is also the name for the last day of the 20-day month of Quiché Maya calendar, corre-sponding to Yucatecan Maya *AHAU*. (See also *TWINS & CULTURE HEROES*)

IJ ("reed") see under *QUIJ*.

IK ("breath" or "wind") was the second of the 20 *MAYA* day-names; it was associated with the rain god and with the number six. The *AZTEC* and *ZAPOTEC* equivalent days were *ÉHECATL* and *QUIJ* or *Laa*.

ILAMATECUHTLI, an ancient central Mesoamerican earth and sky goddess, was associated with the earth and with the corn (maize) crop (see also *CENTÉOTL*, *XILONEN*), as the goddess of the old, dried-up corn ear. She was honoured at the feast *TÍTITL* ("shrunken", "withered", or "wrinkled"). She was also the last of the 13 *LORDS OF THE DAY*.

IMIX ("earth monster") was the first of the 20 *MAYA* day-names; it was associated with earth, water, water lilies, crocodiles, plenty, vegetation, the number five and "the beginning". *AZTEC* and *ZAPOTEC* equivalents were *CIPACTLI* and *CHILLA*.

ITZAMNÁ ("iguana house"), *MAYA* God D, was a supreme deity, second only to *HUNAB KU*, but less abstract (see also the *OLD FIRE GOD*). In one sense Itzamná and Hunab Ku were the same, and thus embodied another aspect of Maya monotheistic–polytheistic duality. The Maya universe was conceptualized as a reptilian configuration, or house (*na*), whose four sides (or walls), roof (or sky) and floor (or earth) were formed by the huge bodies of iguanas (*itzam*). Unlike Hunab Ku, whose son he was thought to be, Itzamná was frequently portrayed in the codices and in wall-paintings and sculpture, along with his wife *IX CHEBEL YAX*. He was the father of creation and of the gods, of the earth and the sky, and so had both terrestrial and celestial manifestations.

He was a benign deity, and was never accompanied by symbols of death or destruction. He invented writing and taught it to humankind, and was the patron of the arts

ITZAMNÁ, or "iguana house", was the Maya creator god. He is depicted here, carved onto a stone tablet, as an old man with a prominent nose. He is holding the writhing form of a double-headed "sky" or "vision" serpent. (EARLY CLASSIC PERIOD.)

and sciences. His sons were the four *BACABS*, whom Itzamná (or, in another myth, Hunab Ku), at the time of creation, set at the four corners of the earth to support the heavens above it.

Itzamná was ruler of the Maya days *MULUC* ("water") and *AHUA* ("king, monarch, prince, or great lord"; the last and most important day of the Maya 20-day month). He can be identified by the sun glyph, *Kin*, and, more especially, by a glyph whose main element is *ahau*. Itzamná was invoked in several ceremonies during the Maya year: as the sun god Itzamná-*KINICH AHAU* the sacred books were consulted in his name in the month *Uo* for auguries of the coming year; in the month *Zip* he was invoked as the god of medicine, along with *IX CHEL* (the moon

goddess); in the month *Mac* he was worshipped by old men in a ceremony in which the four aspects of the rain god *CHAC* played a role. In the important ceremonies at the Maya New Year, Itzamná was invoked especially to prevent calamities in the coming year.

He was portrayed either as a wise old man with a distinctive "Roman" nose, sunken cheeks and a mouth with only a single tooth, or as the creator god, a giant double-headed iguana/serpent in the sky. As the great fiery two-headed serpent he represented the Milky Way (see also *MIXCÓATL*). His right head, which faced east, symbolized the rising sun and the morning "star" (Venus), and thus life itself, while his left head, which faced the west, symbolized the setting sun and death.

As the supreme Maya deity, Itzamná was the principal patron of Maya rulers. The kings of the great Maya city-states identified themselves with Kinich Ahau, the sun god, himself a manifestation of Itzamná as Lord of the Day. For example, Itzamná-Kinich Ahau was a patron deity of the city of Palenque, where the Temple of the Cross, representing the creation of the world and of the gods, is partly dedicated to him.

ITZCUINTLI ("dog") was the tenth of the 20 *AZTEC* day-names; it had a favourable augury and its patron deity was *MICTLANTECUHTLI*, the god of death. The *MAYA* and *ZAPOTEC* equivalent days were *OC* and *TELLA*.

In Mesoamerican belief, dogs would guide the dead across the river to the underworld, and so were often buried along with them. The breed known as *itzcuintli* was also a domesticated dog, raised and eaten by the Aztecs. Calendrical dates and deity associations for *Itzcuintli* included: 1 *Itzcuintli*, for the fire god *XIUHTECUHTLI*; 5 *Itzcuintli*, for Mictlantecuhtli; 9 *Itzcuintli*, for *CHANTICO*, patroness of metalworkers; and 13 *Itzcuintli*, as the morning and evening "star" (Venus) *TLAHUIZCALPANTECUHTLI*.

ITZPAPÁLOTL ("obsidian butterfly") was a goddess of *CHICHIMEC* origin. She was the earth goddess and the mother of *MIXCÓATL* ("cloud serpent"), the principal god of the Chichimecs. She ruled the 16th of the 20 *AZTEC* days, known as *COZCACUAUHTLI* ("vulture"), and, when portrayed with jaguar claws, she represents one of the *TZITZIMIME*, who were the "demons of darkness".

ITZTLACOLIUHQUI was an alternate name for, or manifestation of, the *AZTEC* god *TEZCATLIPOCA*. In this guise he was the "Black Tezcatlipoca", the god of ice and cold, sin and human misery. Itztlacoliuhqui was patron of the day *ÁCATL* ("reed").

ITZTLI ("obsidian knife", the sort used in Aztec ceremonial human sacrifices) was the deputy of *TEZCATLIPOCA*. He was the second of the nine *LORDS OF THE NIGHT*.

IX ("jaguar") was the 14th of the 20 *MAYA* day-names and one of the year-bearing days – there were 13 *Ix* years in a 52-year cycle (see also *CAUAC*, *KAN* and *MULUC*). It was associated with the west cardinal direction and the colour black. Also associated with the *JAGUAR GOD*, it was represented by a glyph of circles (like jaguar-skin spots). The *AZTEC* and *ZAPOTEC* equivalent days were *OCÉLOTL* and *GUECHE*.

IX CHEBEL YAX, or Chebel Yax, *MAYA* Goddess O, was a creator goddess, a supreme deity by proxy, as the wife of *ITZAMNÁ*. She was the mother of all the gods and goddesses. She was patroness of weaving and associated domestic arts – in the codices she was portrayed as an old woman, painted red and holding a hank of cotton or woven cloth – and of painting. She corresponds to *COATLÍCUE* and *TOCI* in the Méxica *AZTEC* pantheon.

IX CHEL, *MAYA* Goddess I, wife of the sun god *KINICH AHAU*, was

moon goddess and had a number of manifestations. She was "she of the rainbow", the benevolent mother goddess, patroness of childbirth and procreation; also of medicine and healing; and, as a water goddess, she displayed benevolence as life-giving rain and malevolence through destructive floods.

Ix Chel was sometimes portrayed as a female warrior standing guard with spear and shield and surrounded by symbols of death and destruction. In other portrayals she was shown as "the angry old woman" emptying her vials of wrath as rainstorms and floods upon humankind, or, even more primevally, as a clawed goddess with a writhing serpent on her head and embroidered crossbones on her skirt. She ruled the day *CABAN* ("earth"). There was a special shrine and place of pilgrimage dedicated to the worship of her on the island of Cozumel, off the east coast of Yucatán.

AZTEC counterparts of her manifestations are in included both *COATLÍCUE* and *COYOLXAUHQUI*.

IXCUINAN, probably of *HUASTEC* origin, was an aspect of the earth goddess *TLAZOLTÉOTL*, representing the earth and fertility.

IXTAB ("goddess of the gallows"), was the *MAYA* goddess of suicide who is usually portrayed in the codices suspended from the sky by a rope noose, her eyes closed in death, and with a black ring – the symbol of decomposition – on her cheek. The Maya believed that those who took their own lives by hanging, warriors killed in battle, women who died giving birth, the victims of human sacrifice (and the priests who killed them) and rulers were all taken directly to paradise by Ixtab. There, in the shade of the cosmic *Yaxché* tree (see *WORLD TREE*), they were free from further work, suffering and want. Consequently, death in battle or in

childbirth were considered to be honourable, and suicide by hanging was common amongst those who felt afflicted by sorrows, troubles or sickness. As a malevolent goddess, Ixtab may have been one aspect of *IX CHEL*.

IXTACCÍHUATL, a volcanic cone on the eastern rim of the Basin of Mexico, is sometimes identified in *AZTEC* myth with *TONACATÉPETL* ("sustenance mountain").

IXTLILTON was the *AZTEC* god of health and medical curing. He was the dark-hued brother of *MACUILXÓCHITL* and of *XOCHIPILLI*, the three together being different aspects of good health, pleasure and wellbeing. He was also associated with the dance, presumably because dancing formed a part of many medical cures.

IZCALLI ("resurrection") was the first (or, in some sources, the last) of the *AZTEC* 18 months in the solar year, in which the fire god *XIUHTECUHTLI* was honoured with

IXTLILTON, the Aztec god of health and medicine, taught the priests the use of herbal remedies to common ailments. Many such are still in use today, and the ingredients for them are widely sold in local markets.

the sacrifice, every four years, of his impersonators. Other names were *Huauhquiltamalcualiztli* ("eating of stuffed tamales"), *Xochitoca* ("plants, flowers"), *Xóchilhuitl* ("flower feast day") and *Pillahuanaliztli* ("intoxication of the children").

JAGUAR GODS appear widely in Mesoamerican mythology. The jaguar (*Felis onca*; *océlotl* in NAHU-ATL) figures prominently in art and iconography, along with its smaller cousin the ocelot (*Felis pardalis*; *tlacoocélotl* in Nahuatl). As symbols of the supernatural world, jaguar fangs, claws and other features are components of deities from OLMEC civilization onward: for example, as the were-jaguar of Olmec art, half-man, half-human, or in portrayals of Zapotec COCIJO or the Aztec TZITZIMIME. To the AZTECS, the océlotl was the NAHUAL (alter ego) of their god TEZCATLIPOCA.

The Jaguar god appears to have been a major deity in the ancient and powerful city of TEOTIHUACÁN from the first to the seventh centuries AD, and later became known by the Nahuatl name TLALCHITTO-NATIUH. It is depicted prominently

ONE OF a line of jaguars prowls along the top of a wall in the main precinct at Tollán (Tula), capital of the Toltecs.
(*EARLY POSTCLASSIC PERIOD.*)

in the Palace of the Jaguars, one of several palaces – perhaps places of cult worship (see also QUETZALPA-PÁLOTL) – around the Plaza of the Pyramid of the Moon.

From Teotihuacán, the cult of the Jaguar god spread south and east, probably as a by-product of Teotihuacán's extensive trade "empire" and perhaps through military conquest. It was disseminated to the highlands of Guatemala – where the architecture of the MAYA site of Kaminaljuyú also shows strong influence from Teotihuacán in the fourth to seventh centuries AD – and to other Yucatecan Maya cities.

Mythological texts dating from the Postclassic Period identify the jaguar as the night beast, signifying the earth, who devoured the sun each night. The Aztec god TEPEYOLOHTLI (literally "heart of the mountain") was the jaguar god who inhabited the interior of the earth, and possibly originated in the Olmec jaguar cult. Similarly, the Maya god KINICH AHAU was believed to turn into a jaguar at night for his journey through the underworld from sunset to sunrise. The name CHILAM BALAM (the Maya sacred texts) means "jaguar prophet", and the Maya Jaguar god ruled the day AKBAL ("darkness") and the number seven.

The 14th day of the Mesoamerican 20-day month was named after the jaguar/ocelot in the three great civilizations: those of the Maya (IX, "jaguar" or "jaguar skin"), Zapotec (GUECHE, "jaguar") and Aztec (OCÉLOTL, "jaguar"). Many

JAGUAR GODS and imagery featured in the iconography of every Mesoamerican culture, from the Olmecs to the Aztecs: this sculpted jaguar head decorates a wall at Classic Period Maya Copán, Honduras.

other jaguar calendrical references come from Aztec sources: XIPE TOTEC, the god of regeneration, was represented by the date *1 Océlotl*; *4 Océlotl* was the glyph for the First Sun in Aztec cosmology; *5 Océlotl* was patron god of the feather workers (*amentecas*); *8 Océlotl* was the birth date of Tepey-

olohtli; *9 Océlotl* represented the rain god, TLÁLOC; and *13 Océlotl* was a manifestation of the earth goddess, COATLÍCUE.

As a symbol of fierceness, courage and strength, the jaguar was highly revered by the cult or society of the "Jaguar Warriors". (See also CHACMOOL, TEZCATZONTÉCATL AND WARRIOR CULTS)

JONAJI BELACHINA was the Southern ZAPOTEC goddess of the underworld (see BENELABA).

KAN ("ripe corn/maize") was the fourth of the 20 MAYA day-names and one of the year-bearing days – there were 13 *Kan* years in a 52-year cycle (see also CAUAC, IX and MULUC). It was associated with the east cardinal direction, the colour red, and the number eight. The AZTEC and ZAPOTEC equivalent days were CUETZPALLIN and ACHE.

KAN PAUAHTUN
see THE PAUAHTUN.

DUALITY & OPPOSITION

DUALITY PERVADES DESCRIPTIONS OF the gods and goddesses, their world and the world of humans throughout Mesoamerica. Omeyocán, the 13th of the Aztec celestial levels, was literally "the place of the two". The concept of a "creator pair", male and female deities, and of a "first man" and a "first woman" was widespread. Most of the gods and goddesses had a counterpart, or male and female manifestations; for example, the name Ometeotl meant "twice god". More generally, duality – in terms of opposition – was a common feature in Mesoamerican cosmological and practical thought: such as celestial and underworld cosmic stratification, life and death, fertility and barrenness, good and evil, day and night (Day Sun and Night Sun), movement and stillness, sound and silence, order and chaos.

Many of the myths and legends illustrate such oppositions. For example, the Aztecs believed in the daily battle between the sun (Huitzilopochtli) and the moon (Coyolxauhqui) each dawn, and the Maya thought that the rain god Chac brought forth new shoots of corn (maize) and other plants each year, while the death god Ah Puch attempted to nip off the buds and tender new leaves. The opposition of conflict and peace, almost a daily affair, was expressed in the divine rivalry and occasional co-operation of Quetzalcóatl and Tezcatlipoca, and in the legendary history of the political struggles of Mixcóatl, Ce Ácatl Topiltzin Quetzalcóatl-Kukulkán, and Nezahualcóyotl.

THE COMPLEX DEITY *Ometeotl (above), "twice god", was the ultimate Aztec expression of duality and opposition – here represented as Tonacatecuhtli, the old man of fate. With both male (Ometecuhtli) and female (Omecíhuatl) manifestations he/she was perceived as a remote creator deity, the source of all creation and power in the universe. He/she represented all aspects of opposition and transcended the concepts of time and space on earth. Such an enigmatic deity was both respected and feared, but was too abstract for normal daily worship.*

QUETZALCÓATL (left) and his twin Xólotl, are divine representations of duality. One of Quetzalcóatl's principal roles was that of Venus as the morning "star", who rose from the jaws of the earth-monster, as depicted here in a stone stela from Azcapotzalco – a contemporary city on the mainland to the northwest of Aztec Tenochtitlán in the Basin of Mexico.

XÓLOTL (left) was in opposition to Quetzalcóatl. Hideous, distorted and burst-eyed, he was a disruptive god who, as Venus the evening "star", would force the sun down into the earth and darkness in the evening.

A TOTONAC STELA (left) from the Gulf Coast depicts Quetzalcóatl in his familiar conical cap. Here he is identifiable as Venus the morning "star" by his sun pendant.

A DIVINE DUALITY was incorporated in the god Tonatiuh (above), the ruler of the Fifth Sun. Like many of the other gods and goddesses, he was both a Lord of the Day and a Lord of the Night. As Tonatiuh, he ruled the day and was Cuauhtlehuánitl the "ascending eagle". His counterpart, Yohual-tecuhtli (or Yohualtonatiuh), was the Night Sun, who passed through the darkness of the underworld, and was Cuauhtémoc the "descending eagle". He is the central face in this Aztec "calendar stone", but scholars disagree about whether he represents Tonatiuh or Yohualtonatiuh on the stone.

L

KAN XIB CHAC
see *THE CHACS*.

KAPOK see under *WORLD TREE*; see also feature spread *COLOURS & THE CARDINAL DIRECTIONS*.

KAWIL, the name used in some Classic Period *MAYA* texts, was an alternative for *BOLON DZ'ACAB*, the god of lineage and descent.

KEDO was the *ZAPOTEC* god of justice, possibly an ominous permutation of *COQUI BEZELAO*, god of death. His *AZTEC* equivalent was *MICTLANTECUHTLI*.

KINICH AHAU, *MAYA* God G, also known as Ahau Kin and Ah Kinchil ("the sun-face one"), was the Maya sun god and husband of the moon goddess *IX CHEL*. He was closely associated with the supreme deity *ITZAMNÁ* and, in some ways, is regarded as a manifestation of the latter. Kinich Ahau was the day aspect of Itzamná and, as such, symbolized the life of the sun in its daily journey across the sky, a metaphor for life itself. After sunset, as he journeyed through the underworld overnight, he was believed to turn into a jaguar. He

KINICH AHAU, the Maya sun god/ God G, was a source of power and representative of the right to rule. Here, king "Stormy Sky" (upper left) cradles the sun god in his left arm (lower right).
(*STELA 31, CLASSIC PERIOD TIKAL.*)

was portrayed in Classic and Post-classic Period Maya art with a square eye and a stout nose. His head glyph was a personification of the number four.

Kinich Ahau was worshipped in particular by the rulers of the Maya city-states, who perceived themselves as his descendants, or even assumed his identity. For example, he was a patron deity of the city of Palenque, where the Temple of the Cross, representing the creation of the world and of the gods, is partly dedicated to him. The Maya date inscribed on the temple might refer to his mythical date of birth.

KUKULKÁN (sometimes Kukul-cán), or *GUCUMATZ*, was the *MAYA* translation of the central Meso-american "plumed-serpent" deity *QUETZALCÓATL*, and was introduced to Yucatán by the Putún Maya in the 10th century AD. Among the Quiché Maya of the Guatemalan highlands he was known as Gucu-matz (see also *TAMOANCHÁN* and *TEPEU*). He was prominent in the Postclassic Period, in keeping with the increasing influence from central Mesoamerica into Mayaland.

Kukulkán was the god of the winds, and of hurricanes. In the *Dresden Codex* he is associated with Venus which, in turn, is Quetzal-cóatl in the guise of morning "star"; and a birth date that is recorded on Palenque's Temple of the Cross, 9 *Ik*, appears to correspond to an alternative name for Quetzalcóatl, 9 *Wind* (*Ik*, which is the second day in the Maya 20-day month, means "life" or "breath").

In another interpretation Ku-kulkán is classified as one of the many manifestations of *ITZAMNÁ*, the supreme god. The two mani-festations, Kukulkán on the one hand and Quetzalcóatl on the other, appear to represent yet another expression of Mesoamer-ican duality – one aspect associated with good omens and the other with evil omens – paralleled in the life and death manifestations sym-bolized by the two-headed celestial serpent spirit of Itzamná.

In legend, Kukulkán was a crypto-historical Maya or Maya-*TOLTEC* leader or culture hero – the "Feathered Serpent". He invaded the Yucatán Peninsula and brought Mexican (that is, Toltec) civilization to the region, in particular to the ancient Maya city-state of Chichén Itzá. There, a temple-pyramid (the Temple of Kukulkán or "El Castillo") was dedicated to him in the Post-classic Period section of the city, which has many structures almost identical to structures in the Toltec capital city of Tollán (modern Tula).

Kukulkán was said to have come by sea, from the west, tradi-tionally in AD 987, having fled from an insurrection in his home city. About 30 years prior to this date, two factions in Tollán struggled for power, one faction lead by Kuk-ulkán (Quetzalcóatl) and the other (victorious) one by *TEZCATLIPOCA* ("smoking mirror"). Intriguingly, Toltec-Aztec sources record that, at about the same time, the legendary king, *CE ÁCATL TOPILTZIN QUETZAL-CÓATL*, was expelled from Tollán, also having been defeated by Tez-

KUKULKÁN, the "plumed serpent" (the Maya name for Quetzalcóatl), was especially important at Postclassic Period Chichén Itzá, where the Temple of Kukulkán was dedicated to him.

catlipoca. A further clue is provided by the legend of the Itzá, a Chontal Maya people in the Gulf Coast region of Tabasco, which records that they were led by Kuk-ulkán to resettle the more ancient city of Uucil Abnal ("Seven Bushy Place"), which they renamed Chi-chén Itzá – "[The place] at the rim (edge, mouth) of the well of the Itzás". Kukulkán might, therefore, be more a generic term for a leader than a personal name, and the two figures might have been one and the same.

(The association of Kukulkán the god and the man provides an interesting parallel in ancient Amer-ican mythology. In the central Andes, the legendary eighth Inca ruler of Cuzco, Viracocha Inca, was similarly identified with their cre-ator god Viracocha.)

LAA ("wind" and "reed") see under *QUIJ*.

LAMAT (Venus) was the eighth of the 20 *MAYA* day-names; it was associated with the number 12 and was the day of the planet Venus. The *AZTEC* and *ZAPOTEC* equivalent days were *TOCHTLI* and *LAPA*.

LANA ("blackness") was the sixth of the 20 *ZAPOTEC* day-names; the *AZTEC* and *MAYA* equivalent days were *MIQUIZTLI* and *CIMI*.

LAO ("flower") was the last of the 20 *ZAPOTEC* day-names; the *AZTEC* and *MAYA* equivalent days were *XÓCHITL* and *AHAU*.

LAPA ("rabbit") was the eighth of the 20 *ZAPOTEC* day-names; the *AZTEC* and *MAYA* equivalent days were *TOCHTLI* and *LAMAT*.

LAXEE, LAXOO see *PITAO XOO*.

THE LONG COUNT of the Maya recorded the dates of significant events depicted on stone monuments: here, Shield Jaguar of Yaxchilán is shown preparing for battle in 9.14.12.6.12 (the glyphs above the figures) or 12 February AD 724.

LERA ACUECA (OR ACUECE)

was the Southern ZAPOTEC god of sickness and healing.

LETA AHUILA was the South-

ern ZAPOTEC name for COQUI BEZELAO.

LETA AQUICHINO, or Lira-

aquitzino, was the Southern ZAPOTEC name for COQUI XEE.

LOCIYO was the Southern ZAP-

OTEC name for COCIJO.

LOCUCUY was the Southern

ZAPOTEC name for the corn (maize) god PITAO COZOBI.

THE LONG COUNT, or Initial

Series, was the Maya calendrical system that enabled them to reckon from a date "0", and thus to calculate the exact number of days since time, as they knew it, began. (The zero was invented independently by the Maya; the only two other inventors were the ancient Babylonians and Hindus.) To do this they used a number of cumulative numerical positions or place values: 1 *kin* = 1 day, 1 *uinal* = 20 days (20 *kins*), 1 *tun* = 360 days (18 *uinals*), 1 *katun* = 7,200 days (20 *tuns*), 1 *baktun* = 144,000 days (20 *katuns*) and 1 *piktun* = 2,880,000 days (20 *baktuns*). This system closely resembles a vigesi-

mal counting system, except that the *tun* was only 18 *uinals*, not 20 because, as 360 days, it was closer to the solar year. The Maya zero date was *13.0.0.0.0. 4 Ahau 8 Cumkú* – that is, 13 *baktuns* on the day *4 Ahau* of the month *8 Cumkú*, the day- and month-names being the beginning of the next *baktun*.

Although there are several systems for converting Maya dates to Christian dates, the most accepted system is the Goodman-Martínez-Thompson Correlation (GMT), which renders the Maya date "1" as 13 August 3114 BC.

The Short Count, related to the Long Count, was a shorter date reckoning system that had come into use in the Postclassic Period, long before the Spaniards arrived in Mesoamerica. Instead of counting from a year "1" of 13 *baktuns*, the Short Count began at the end of *katun 13 Ahau* and used only *tuns*, numbered consecutively, and *katuns*, which were named. The *katun* cycles thus established always finished on a day in *Ahau* in the sequence *katun 13 Ahau, katun 11 Ahau, katun 9 Ahau*, then 7, 5, 3, 1, 12, 10, 8, 6, 2 *Ahau*, and, after 256.43 years, back to *katun 13 Ahau*. The cyclical nature was important, and certain events were expected to be repeated.

THE LONG-NOSED GOD

see *BOLON DZ'ACAB*.

LOO ("dog"), or *Goloo*, was the 11th of the 20 ZAPOTEC day-names; the AZTEC and MAYA equivalent days were OZOMATLI and CHUEN. At the same time *Loo*, or *Guiloo* ("crow") was also the 16th of the 20 ZAPOTEC day-names; the AZTEC and MAYA equivalent days of this were COZCACUAUHTLI and CIB.

THE LORDS OF THE DAY

(NAHUATL, Tonalteuctin; MAYA, OXLAHUN TI KU) were the 13 deities especially associated with particular day signs, identities and "birds" (*volátiles*, or "flyers") in the Mesoamerican calendar, and with the 13 day-time "hours" of the Aztec day. In the Aztec TONALAMATL (translated as the "Book of the Days") each deity accompanies a day sign

SOME AZTEC SCULPTURES, such as this turquoise and shell inlaid mask, remain as enigmatic as the gods themselves. This might be Quetzalcóatl, ninth Lord of the Day, or Tonatiuh, fourth Lord of the Day.

and a number. The concept of 13 lords might also be related to the 13 heavens of the CREATION MYTH. Some of the gods were simultaneously Lords of the Day and LORDS OF THE NIGHT. Five of the lords presided over the five Aztec cosmic suns, in order of succession: TEZCATLIPOCA, QUETZALCÓATL, TLÁLOC, CHALCHIÚTLICUE and TONATIUH.

The Maya equivalent names of the Oxlahun ti Ku are unknown. However, the Nahuatl names and associated identities and "birds" were as follows:

Nahuatl name	Associated identity	Associated "bird"
1st Lord:	Xiuhtecuhtli/Huehuetéotl as god of fire	the blue hummingbird
2nd Lord:	Tlaltecuhtli as earth god	the green hummingbird
3rd Lord:	Chalchiútlicue as water goddess	the hawk
4th Lord:	Tonatiuh as sun god	the quail
5th Lord:	Tlazoltéotl as goddess of love	the eagle
6th Lord:	Teoyaomiqui/Mictlantecuhtli as god of fallen warriors	the screech owl
7th Lord:	Xochipilli-Centéotl as god of pleasure/of corn (maize)	the butterfly
8th Lord:	Tláloc as god of the rains	the eagle
9th Lord:	Quetzalcóatl as god of the winds	the turkey
10th Lord:	Tezcatlipoca as god of sustenance	the horned owl
11th Lord:	Mictlantecuhtli/Chalmecatecuhtli as god of the underworld	the macaw
12th Lord:	Tlahuizcalpantecuhtli as god of the dawn	the quetzal
13th Lord:	Ilamatecuhtli as goddess of the sky	the parrot

THE LORDS OF THE NIGHT

(*NAHUATL*, Yohualteuctin; *MAYA*, *BOLON TI KU*) were the nine gods and goddesses who were especially associated with particular day signs, identities and auguries as good or evil in the Mesoamerican calendar, and with the nine night-time "hours" of the Aztec day. In the Aztec *TONALAMATL* ("Book of the Days") each deity accompanies a day sign and a number. The concept of nine lords might also be related to the nine layers in the underworld in the *CREATION MYTH*. Some of the gods were simultaneously *LORDS OF THE DAY* and Lords of the Night.

The Maya equivalent names of ti Ku are unknown, but the Nahuatl names and associated identities and auguries were:

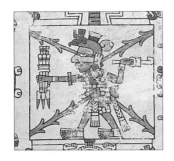

the sacred ball game (*NAHUATL tlachtli*; *MAYA pok-ta-pok*). Macuilxóchitl was identified with the calendrical day-name "5 flower" through his relation to *XOCHIPILLI*, but was also called Ahuíatl and *AHUIATÉOTL*, one of the five genies of the south (see *AHUIATETEO*). In general, the brothers Macuilxóchitl, *IXTLILTON* and Xochipilli together comprise three aspects of good health, pleasure and well-being,

Nahuatl name	Associated identity	Augury
1st Lord:	Xiuhtecuhtli/Huehuetéotl as god of fire	unfavourable
2nd Lord:	Itztli as god of obsidian/flint	unfavourable
3rd Lord:	Piltzintecuhtli-Tonatiuh/ as the youthful sun god Piltzintecuhtli-Xochipilli	excellent
4th Lord:	Centéotl as god of corn (maize)	excellent
5th Lord:	Mictlantecuhtli as god of the underworld	favourable
6th Lord:	Chalchiútlicue as water goddess	favourable
7th Lord:	Tlazoltéotl as goddess of love	unfavourable
8th Lord:	Tepeyolohtli-Tezcatlipoca as the heart of the mountain	favourable
9th Lord:	Tláloc as god of the rains	favourable

MACUILXÓCHITL

was one of several *AZTEC* gods devoted to pleasure. He was patron of games in general, for example the ancient board game of *patolli* (somewhat like modern pachisi), and of all the celebrations associated with them, but was especially associated with

Macuilxóchitl being the aspect given over more to excess or over-indulgence in pleasure. In this last capacity he was particularly associated with the name Ahuiatéotl.

MALINALLI

("grass") was the 12th of the 20 *AZTEC* day-names; it had an unfavourable augury and its patron deity was *PATÉCATL*, god of *PULQUE* drinking.

MACUILXÓCHITL, an Aztec god of pleasure and patron of games, watches over a patolli *game.* (EARLY POST-SPANISH-CONQUEST CODEX MAGLIABECCHIANO.)

THE "OLD FIRE GOD", Xiuhtecuhtli was pictured as part of the cosmic map on the title page of the Codex Fejérváry-Mayer.

The *MAYA* and *ZAPOTEC* equivalent days were *EB* and *PIJA*. Calendrical dates and deities associated with it included: *1 Malinalli*, for *TLAZOL-TÉOTL* as the earth goddess and goddess of love; and *8 Malinalli*, for the earth goddess *COATLÍCUE*.

MANIK

("hand") was the seventh of the 20 *MAYA* day-names; it was associated with the number 11. The *AZTEC* and *ZAPOTEC* equivalent days were *MÁZATL* and *CHINA*.

MATLALCUEITL

("lady of the green skirts"), or Matlalcueye, was the second wife of *TLÁLOC*, the *AZTEC* god of rain, after *TEZCATLIPOCA* had abducted his first wife *XOCHIQUETZAL*. She was the goddess of rain, Matlalcueye, and, in her honour, this name was given to an extinct volcano located between Puebla and Tlaxcala, to the east of the Basin of Mexico; the same volcano was renamed La Malinche during the Spanish colonial period.

THE MAYA

inhabited the eastern and southern regions of Mesoamerica, east of the Isthmus of Tehuantepec, including the Yucatán Peninsula (modern Campeche, Yucatán and Quintana Roo states), parts of modern Tabasco and Chiapas states, all of Guatemala and Belize, and western Honduras and El Salvador. They were part of a Macro-Mayan language group that migrated from North America to the Guatemalan highlands by about 2500 BC. During the next 1,000 years, various groups split off and migrated north

into the lowlands of Yucatán and northwest into the Gulf Coast region. More than 30 Maya languages are recognized, including, Quiché, Chontal/ Putún, Itzá and *HUASTEC*. The Huastecs of the central and northern Gulf Coast eventually became cut off.

Archaeologists traditionally recognize three main geographical and cultural Maya areas, with subdivisions based on architectural and other culturally distinctive styles. These divisions and their areas are: the Highland Maya, who occupied the Guatemalan and western Honduran and El Salvadoran highlands; the Southern Lowland Maya, who occupied the lowlands of central and northern Guatemala, and the adjacent regions of Belize and northwest Honduras and the southern Yucatán Peninsula from the Caribbean to the Atlantic; and the Northern Lowland Maya, who occupied the northern two-thirds of the Yucatán Peninsula. Major cultural subdivisions include the Quiché Maya of the Guatemalan highlands; the Classic Period Petén style of the Southern Lowland Maya in central and northern Guatemala; and the Classic Period Río Bec, Chenes and Puuc styles of the Northern Lowland Maya.

Distinctive Maya cultural traditions in architecture, sculpture, ceramics, wall-painting and other arts developed from the Preclassic Period, especially in the Highland area, into the great Classic Period city-state civilization of the Southern Lowland area and the southern part of the Northern Lowland area. Central Mesoamerican influence, especially on the architectural style of *TEOTIHUACÁN*, was also of great importance. During the Postclassic Period, the emphasis of Maya civilization shifted into the Northern Lowland area, where numerous city-states dominated the northern Yucatán Peninsula by the time the Spaniards arrived.

In addition to their distinctive urban, political, architectural,

THE MAYA SITE of Tikal in central Guatemala was one of the longest occupied, and had trade and diplomatic contacts throughout Mesoamerica, including with Teotihuacán in the Basin of Mexico.

artistic, and religious developments, other important Maya achievements include the development of a sophisticated calendrical system, a hieroglyphic writing system, vigesimal mathematics and the independent invention of the zero and place values in counting.

THE MAYA GODS were numerous.

Among the various Maya groups at least 166 named gods and goddesses are known. Some were universally worshipped, while others were special to particular regions or patrons of specific cities or city-states. In 1904, before linguists had begun to make progress in the decipherment of Maya writing, an alphabetical letter list of some of the principal Maya deities was proposed by P. Schellhaus: A = *AH PUCH* or Yum Cimil, B = *CHAC*, C = *XAMAN EK*, D = *ITZAMNÁ*, E = *AH MUN* or Yum Kaax, F = *BULUC CHABTÁN*, G = *KINICH AHAU*, H = *CHICCAN* god, I = *IX CHEL*, (J was not used), K = *BOLON DZ'ACAB*, L = *OLD BLACK GOD*, M = *EK CHUAH*, N = *PAUAHTUN*, O = *IX CHEBEL YAX*, (P was not used), Q = *ETZ'NAB*, R = formerly used for Buluc Chabtán. (See *GOD A* to *GODDESS O*).

A thematic classification of the Maya gods and goddesses is proposed by Linda Schele and Mary Ellen Miller, in which they all fall into one of four categories: worldly phenomena, anthropomorphs, zoomorphs and animals. A deity can be manifested in more than one form and, while the imagery of some deities appear to have remained fixed, others clearly changed, developed, or even "aged" through time.

CHAC, the god of rain, was of crucial importance to Maya daily life and agriculture; he was frequently featured in repetitive, stacks of masks, as at Classic Period Uxmal, on the corners of buildings.

MAYÁHUEL,

the *AZTEC* goddess of the *maguey* or *agave* plant (*Agave americana*), was "mother" of the *CENTZÓNTOTOCHTIN* (the numberless gods of drunkenness), and, by association, of the alcoholic drink, *PULQUE*, made from it. She was thought to have "400 breasts" to feed them – the *NAHUATL* root word *centzontli* means, literally, "without number". With her consort *PATÉCATL* she presided over drunken excess. She ruled the day *TOCHTLI* ("rabbit"), the eighth of the 20-day Aztec month, and was represented by the glyph *Ce Tochtli* ("one rabbit").

The origin of *pulque* is explained in the story of Mayahuél's abduction by the wind god *ÉHECATL*, which also relates the introduction of physical love to the world. Having helped to bring corn (maize) and other edible plants to the notice of humankind, the gods concluded that something further was needed to provide humans with pleasure and to cause them to sing and dance in honour of the gods. *QUETZALCÓATL*, in the guise of Éhecatl, persuaded the beautiful young virgin Mayáhuel to leave her abode in the sky, where she was guarded by the fierce "grandmother" goddess *TZITZIMITL*, and to descend to the earth with him. The two became lovers, embracing each other in the form of a tree with two entwined branches.

Tzitzimitl pursued the couple but arrived too late to prevent the union so, in her wrath, she split the tree in two, destroying the branch representing Mayáhuel and feeding the shreds to her demon servants, the *TZITZIMIME*. Éhecatl, however, remained unharmed; resuming his former shape, he gathered together Mayáhuel's bones and planted them in a field where they grew, and lived on, as the *maguey* used to produce the white "wine" known as *pulque*.

MÁZATL ("deer")

was the seventh of the 20 *AZTEC* day-names; it had a favourable augury and its patron deity was the rain god *TLÁLOC*. The *MAYA* and *ZAPOTEC* equivalent days were *MANIK* and *CHINA*. The deer was a symbol of fire and drought. Calendrical dates and deities associated with it included: *1 Mázatl*, for the creator deities; *4 Mázatl*, for *ITZTLACOLIUHQUI*; and *5 Mázatl*, for *XÓLOTL*.

THE MAZEHUALOB

were the *MAYA* peoples themselves, the inhabitants of the Third World in Maya creation (see *HUNAB KU* and *CREATION MYTHS*).

MBAZ

was a *ZAPOTEC* earth god/goddess and the Zapotec seventh or eighth *LORD OF THE NIGHT*. He/she was the equivalent of the Aztec deities *TEPEYOLOHTLI* and *TLAZOLTÉOTL*.

MDI

was a *ZAPOTEC* rain god and the Zapotec ninth *LORD OF THE NIGHT*, with aspects similar in nature to those of the Teotihuacano and *AZTEC* deity known as *TLÁLOC* (see also *COCIJO*).

MEN

("moon", "wise one", or "eagle") was the 15th of the 20 *MAYA* day-names; it was associated with the aged moon goddess, patroness of weaving. The *AZTEC* and *ZAPOTEC* equivalent days were *CUAUHTLI* and *NAA*.

MAYÁHUEL, goddess of the maguey or agave plant is seen here beside an octecomatl (pulque vessel). Note the serpent coiled around its base, and the stake piercing a human heart). The brew is being tasted by the figure on the left.

MÉXICA see *AZTEC*.

MEZTLI was the *NAHUATL* name for the "moon". In the *AZTEC CREATION MYTH*, the moon and the Fifth Sun were created in an assembly of the gods at *TEOTIHUACÁN*. The moon was the ascendant god *TECUCIZTÉCATL*, who leapt into the ceremonial fire after his brother *NANAHUATZIN*, who became the sun. The moon shone as bright as the sun until one of the gods threw a rabbit (*tochtli*) into its "face" – rather than a "man in the moon", Mesoamerican peoples perceived the outlines of a rabbit in the shadows and craters of the moon, crouching on its back legs with its ears prominent to the right.

The word is also an element in the Aztec names *Meztlipohualli* ("counting of the lunar months") and *MEZTLIAPÁN* ("Lake of the Moon"), and was the term applied to the Aztec god *TEZCATLIPOCA* in his nocturnal manifestation.

MEZTLIAPÁN ("Lake of the Moon") was Lake Texcoco, the central lake in the Basin of Mexico. Near its western shore lay the island where *HUITZILOPOCHTLI* gave the México *AZTECS* the sign of his representative, the eagle alighting on a nopal cactus (prickly pear), clutching a serpent in its claw, to show them where to build their capital, *TENOCHTITLÁN*.

MICCAILHUITONTLI ("small feast of the dead") was the tenth (or, in some sources, ninth) of the 18 months in the *AZTEC* solar year, in which the gods and goddesses in general were propitiated, but especially the war god *HUITZILOPOCHTLI*, whose image was covered in flowers, and the "smoking mirror" *TEZCATLIPOCA*. It was also called *Tlaxochimaco* ("the surrendering of flowers").

MICTECACÍHUATL was the wife of *MICTLANTECUHTLI*, god of the underworld.

MEZTLI was the Aztec name for the moon. The rabbit, thrown into its face to dull its brightness after creation, can be seen, with some imagination, in the light and dark features of the surface.

MICTLÁN ("that which is below us"), ruled by *MICTLANTECUHTLI* and *MICTECACÍHUATL*, was one of the *AZTEC* underworlds and part of the three-part Aztec universe, comprising Mictlán, *TLALTÍCPAC* and *TOPÁN*. As opposed to other abodes of the dead – for example the underworld of warriors who died in battle (east) or of women who died while giving birth (west) – Mictlán was the specific destination of the souls of those who died a natural death. It was believed that the spirits of the deceased passed through nine magical trials before finding repose. After four years, however, the soul was believed to disappear forever. The *MAYA* equivalents were *MITNAL* and *XIBALBA*.

MICTLANTECUHTLI, one of the most popular of the *AZTEC* pantheon, was honoured throughout central Mesoamerica. He was the god of death and, together with his wife Mictecacíhuatl, ruled the underworld, *MICTLÁN*, the place of silence and rest from the toils of the world. As the god of death, he was appropriately portrayed covered in bones, or as a skeleton, and wearing a skull mask with ear plugs of human bones. He had black, curly hair (unusual in a land of straight-haired people), star-like eyes that enabled him to see in the dark, and was sometimes depicted wearing a conical bark-paper hat and clothes made of bark-paper. Animals accompany him in the codices – owls (symbols of war and death), bats and spiders.

He was instrumental in the origin of humans in the account of the Fifth Sun of the Aztec *CREATION MYTH*, in which, being reluctant to relinquish the bones of the people of the previous world, he tried to delay *QUETZALCÓATL* by setting him several tasks to perform.

Mictlantecuhtli was the ruler of the day *ITZCUINTLI* ("dog"), the tenth day in the 20-day month, the fifth *LORD OF THE NIGHT*, and variously the sixth or 11th *LORD OF THE DAY*. Both in form and domain he was the equivalent to Maya god *YUM CIMIL* (see also *AH PUCH*).

When Hernán Cortés landed in Mexico, the Aztec ruler Moctezuma II Xocoyotzin was told by his priests that the news of inextinguishable fires, odd flights of birds and the appearance of comets in the night sky portended impending disaster, so

MICTLANTECUHTLI, *the god of death, was one* *of the most popular* *Mesoamerican deities.* *In this example he wears* *a bark-paper hat and sits* *with staring eyes, contemplating the futures of* *souls. (CLASSIC PERIOD* *TOTONAC.)*

he ordered human sacrifices and offered the flayed skins of the victims to Mictlantecuhtli. It was thought that, in his fear and uncertainty, he was seeking the peace of Mictlán, for the Spaniards' arrival appeared to be the return of Quetzalcóatl from the east, and the beginning of the end of the world of the Fifth Sun, as foretold in Aztec myth and legend. (See also *COLOURS & THE CARDINAL DIRECTIONS*)

MIQUIZTLI ("death") was the sixth of the 20 *AZTEC* day-names; it had an unfavourable augury and its patron deity was the moon god *TECCIZTÉCATL*. The *MAYA* and *ZAPOTEC* equivalents were *CIMI* and *LANA*.

In the codices, *Miquiztli* is shown as a skeleton or as a hollow-eyed skull with a hole in the side where the pole for the *TZOMPANTLI* rack would have been inserted. Calendrical dates and deity associations

included: *1 Miquiztli*, for *TEZCAT-LIPOCA* as the god of sustenance; *5 Miquiztli*, for the sun god *TONATIUH* or "flower prince" *XOCHIPILLI*; and *13 Miquiztli*, for the god of death.

MITNAL, the lowest of the nine Lowland *MAYA* underworlds, was ruled by *AH PUCH*. The word might be derived from the *AZTEC NAHU-ATL* word *MICTLÁN*, the northern Mesoamerican underworld. It was also the equivalent of the Quiché Maya underworld, *XIBALBA*.

MIXCÓATL ("cloud serpent") was the legendary leader of the *TOLTEC-CHICHIMEC* peoples – his full name was *CE TÉCPATL MIXCÓATL* – and the father of *CE ÁCATL TOP-ILTZIN QUETZALCÓATL*. After his murder by a rival faction he was deified as the god of the hunt, and in his deified state acquired several divine wives. The Chichimec goddess *ITZPAPÁLOTL* ("obsidian butterfly"), an earth goddess, was his mother, and, perhaps in the same guise as the earth goddess, *COATLÍCUE* ("serpent lady") was also said to be his wife. He was patron deity of the *TLAXCALTECANS*.

In Toltec legendary history, as interpreted by the Aztecs, the hero Ce Técpatl Mixcóatl led his people into the Basin of Mexico, where they established the city of Cul-huacán and founded the Toltec dynasty. In this account he took to wife a local Nahua woman named *CHIMALMAN*, whom he symbolically impregnated with an arrow from his bow. After his death she gave birth to Ce Ácatl Topiltzin Quetzalcóatl, the legendary founder and ruler of Tollán (Tula), a new Toltec capital to the northwest of the Basin of Mexico.

As the "cloud serpent" Mixcó-atl's name was also applied to the Milky Way (see also *ITZAMNÁ*).

(The leadership and the later deification of Mixcóatl provide an interesting parallel in ancient American mythology. The association of Viracocha, the creator god, and

Viracocha Inca, the eighth ruler of Cuzco, assumed deification of a sort after an encounter with the creator god in a time of tribulation.)

THE MIXTECS were the peoples who settled in the southern highlands and adjacent coast of central Mesoamerica, in and around the Valley of Oaxaca (in the present Mexican state of that name). The region is subdivided into the Mixteca Baja (western and northwestern Oaxaca), the Mixteca Alta (eastern and southern Oaxaca) and the Mixteca de la Costa (the Pacific coastal lowlands). They spoke one of the languages of the Oto-Zapotecan group in the region.

By about AD 1000, in the early Postclassic Period, they had established a highly developed urban civilization based on a loose confederation of city-states. Some of their most famous cities were Coixtlahuaca, Teozacoalco, Tilantongo, Tlaxiaco, Tututepec, Yanhuitlán, Mitla and Yagul, only the last two of which survive as well-preserved ruins. Having thus established themselves in the former territory of the Classic Period *ZAPOTEC* state, they made use of the ancient tombs in the Zapotec capital, Monte Albán, to bury their own rulers with rich trappings (the most famous of these is Tomb 7). They also built new cruciform tombs with polychrome murals at Mitla, which later became known as the "city of the dead". Their dynastic history can be traced back to AD 692 and includes the legendary ruler *EIGHT DEER TIGER CLAW* (AD 1011–63) of Tilantongo.

Although conquered and subjugated by the *AZTECS* in the 15th century, their culture had a strong influence on the latter, in particular the exquisite craftsmanship of their polychrome pottery, the mastery of Mixtec metalsmiths in gold-working and their skill and artistry in compiling painted codices (seven of the surviving pre-Spanish-conquest codices are

Mixtec). Mixtec deities were, for the most part, those of the central Mesoamerican pantheon, although they called their rain god *DZAHUI*.

THE MONKEY-FACED GOD was probably the *MAYA* god *XAMEN EK*, who was god of the North Star. As such he ruled the Maya day *CHUEN* ("monkey").

The two Maya brothers, *HUN BATZ* and Hun Chouen were also "monkey-faced gods", having been turned into monkeys in the forest by the trickery of their younger, twin brothers *HUNAHPÚ* and *XBAL-ANQUE*. The skills of Hun Batz and Hun Chouen were honoured by the Maya in the codices by depicting them as the patrons of the arts and crafts, and of artists, musicians and dancers.

MSE was a *ZAPOTEC* earth goddess and the Zapotec seventh *LORD OF THE NIGHT*; she resembled *MBAZ* and Aztec *TLAZOLTÉOTL*.

MULUC ("water") was the ninth of the 20 *MAYA* day-names and one of the year-bearing days – there were 13 *Muluc* years in a 52-year cycle (see also *CAUAC*, *IX* and *KAN*). It was associated with the north cardinal direction and the colour white. It was a favourable day, represented by the glyph of a fish head. The *AZTEC* and *ZAPOTEC* equivalents were *ATL* and *NIZA* or *Queza*.

MIXCÓATL, the legendary Toltec-Chichimec leader and god of the hunt, is shown here with raised atl-atl (spear-thrower) and a clutch of hunting darts, and is associated with the jaguar, whose hunting prowess was greatly admired. (CODEX VATICANUS B.)

NAA ("eagle") was the 15th of the 20 *ZAPOTEC* day-names; the *AZTEC* and *MAYA* equivalent days were *CUAUHTLI* and *MEN*.

NAHUAL was the *NAHUATL* word for "alter ego", used to describe the dual nature of many Mesoamerican deities and for alternative aspects or manifestations of the deities. Nahual or Nahualli was the soul companion of a person, that usually took the form of an animal (for example, the nahual of *ITZPA-PÁLOTL* was a deer). The term is still used among the present-day Maya.

NAHUATL, or Nauatl, a dialect of the Nahua language group (which also includes Nahual and Nahuat), is one of the Uto-Aztecan languages of ancient Mesoamerica and is still spoken by nearly 1.5 million people in central and western Mexico. "Classical" Nahuatl was the language of the *TOLTECS* and *AZTECS* of central Mesoamerica and became the *lingua franca* of ancient Mesoamerica, spread by Toltec and, later, Aztec conquest and trade.

O

NANAHUATZIN, the weak and syphilitic god, was the special deity of twins and physically deformed people. He played a key role in the story of the creation of the Fifth Sun in the Aztec *CREATION MYTH*.

The creation of the (present) Fifth Sun and of the moon was the result of the self-sacrificial deaths by cremation of the gods Nanahuatzin – the poor and syphilitic one, weak, humble and allegedly cowardly – and *TECUCIZTÉCATL*, his rich, healthy, haughty and headstrong twin brother. The gods had assembled at the ancient city of *TEOTIHUACÁN* after the destruction of the Fourth Sun and built a huge sacrificial fire. The proud and noble Tecuciztécatl boasted that he would sacrifice himself in the fire and rise again as the sun. When faced with the flames, however, he lost his nerve and only jumped after he was inspired by Nanahuatzin, who leaped into the fire first. Consequently, it was Nanahuatzin who rose as the sun, while Tecuciztécatl emerged as the moon. Nevertheless, both were equally bright until one of the gods threw a rabbit (*tochtli*) into the moon's face, dulling its shine (see also *MEZTLI*). Still motionless, the sun and moon were stirred, in one version of the story, by *ÉHECATL* (who blew on them) and, in another version by *TLAHUIZCAL-PANTECUHTLI* (who threw a dart at the sun in outrage at the latter's demand for human blood sacrifice).

Nanahuatzin also played a crucial role in bringing corn (maize) and other edible plants to humankind, when he was selected by the old diviners *OXOMOCO* and *CIPAC-TONAL* to split open *TONACATÉPETL* (literally "sustenance mountain"), which he accomplished with the help of the four *TLÁLOCS*.

NAPPATECUHTLI ("four times lord"), or Nappateuctli, was one of the four directional *TLÁLOCS* and the patron deity of Chalco, and of the artisans who wove reed matting.

He was particularly prone to produce draughts.

NAUAL see *NAHUAL*.

NAUATL see *NAHUATL*.

NDAN, the *ZAPOTEC* deity of oceans and one of the nine *LORDS OF THE NIGHT*, was depicted both as god and a goddess, or even as a bisexual being. His/her messenger was *NDOZIN*.

NDO'YET was a *ZAPOTEC* god of death and one of the nine Zapotec day names for sacred objects or natural forces.

NDOZIN, a *ZAPOTEC* god of death and justice, was one of the nine *LORDS OF THE NIGHT* and the messenger of *NDAN*.

NEMONTEMI, or Nentli ("worthless"), was the *NAHUATL* term for the five ill-omened days at the end of the *AZTEC* solar calendar year. With 18 months of 20 days each (that is, 360 days, the *XÍHUTL*), there were five days left over to complete the sun–earth cycle. These were considered a time to be wary and to avoid the chance of misfortune. The *MAYA* equivalent was the *UAYEB*.

NENE, first woman (see under *CREATION MYTHS*).

NENTLI see *NEMONTEMI*.

NEW FIRE CEREMONY see *TOXIUHMOLPILIA*.

NEZAHUALCÓYOTL ("Fasting Coyote") was a mid-15th-century king of *TEXCOCO* and advocate of the abstract concept of the deity *TLOQUE NAHUAQUE*. Nevertheless, in deference to his people, he was careful not to neglect the conventional gods and goddesses of the *AZTEC* pantheon. A ruler given to recondite, metaphysical thought on the nature of things, the pursuit

THE OCÉLOTL (*Nahuatl for "jaguar"*) *was an important figure in Mesoamerican religion and art. The* océlotl *was the mascot of the jaguar warriors and is frequently depicted on temple walls.*
(EARLY POSTCLASSIC PERIOD, TOLLÁN [TULA])

of peace and the rule of order, Nezahualcóyotl was wary of the increasing belligerence of the Méxica and tried to stem their aggression, condemning especially the *XOCHIYAÓYOTL* ("Flowery War"). He was a gifted poet, and sponsored and fostered the arts and crafts, music, poetry and history. He was the first to codify and set down the ancient laws of Texcoco and established what was probably Mesoamerica's first library. In partnership with the rulers of neighbouring city-states, he also carried out public works, including building a dyke across Lake Texcoco and an aqueduct to bring fresh water from Chapultepec (west of *TENOCHTITLÁN*) to the Aztec capital. In and around Texcoco he built a magnificent ten-level temple-pyramid to represent the heavens, a special temple dedicated to Tloque Nahuaque, and a summer palace at Texcotzingo (in the foothills east of Texcoco) that included numerous temples, fountains, aqueducts from mountain springs, and baths.

NIZA, or Queza, ("water") was ninth of the 20 *ZAPOTEC* day-names; the *AZTEC* and *MAYA* equivalent days were *ATL* and *MULUC*.

NOÇANA see *COZAANA*.

NOHUIÇANA see *NOHUICHANA*.

NOHUICHANA, an alternative name for *HUECHAANA*, especially in relation to childbirth and creation.

OC ("dog") was the tenth of the 20 *MAYA* day-names; it was associated with Venus as the evening "star". The *AZTEC* and *ZAPOTEC* equivalent days to *Oc* were *ITZCUINTLI* and *TELLA*.

OCÉLOTL ("jaguar") was the 14th of 20 *AZTEC* day-names; it had an unfavourable augury and its patron was the earth goddess *TLAZ-OLTÉOTL*. The *MAYA* and *ZAPOTEC* equivalents were *IX* and *GUECHE*.

In Mesoamerican myth it was the *océlotl* (as the earth) that devoured the sun at the end of the day, and therefore represented the night (see also *JAGUAR GODS*). It was also the mascot of the Jaguar *WARRIOR CULT* (see also *THE RITUAL BALL GAME*). Calendrical dates and deity associations included: *1 Océlotl*, for *XIPE TOTEC*, the "flayed god"; *4 Océlotl*, for the First Sun of the Aztec *CREATION MYTH*; *5 Océlotl*, as patron of featherworkers (*amantecas*); *8 Océlotl*, the mythical birth date of *TEPEYOLOHTLI*; *9 Océlotl*, for the rain god *TLÁLOC*; and *13 Océlotl*, for the earth goddess *COATLÍCUE*.

OCHPANITZTLI ("road sweeping") was the 12th (or, in some sources, the 11th) of the 18 months in the *AZTEC* solar year, in which a harvest festival was held to worship the old earth goddess and mother of the gods *TETEOINNAN-TOCI* and her corn- (maize-) goddess manifestation as *CHICOMECÓATL*. Rituals included the slaying of honoured war captives in the *TLACALILIZTLI* arrow sacrifice.

Ochpanitztli was also called *Tenahuatiliztli* ("clearing up and putting in order").

THE OLD BLACK GOD, *MAYA* God L, a rather enigmatic deity, was a lord of the Maya underworld, *XIBALBA*, a god of death and ruler of the day *AKBAL* ("darkness"),

THE OLMEC *civilization of the Gulf Coast was the first in Mesoamerica to build ceremonial precincts. Olmec rulers were portrayed by colossal stone heads, each with distinctive facial features and head gear, such as at San Lorenzo Tenochtitlán (left); and La Venta (far left).*

THE OLMEC GODS have no names that have come down to us, so anthropologists have designated them by numbers (see *GOD I* to *GOD X*). No Olmec deities can be categorically defined as male or female, but many of their attributes and much of their imagery can be seen in the gods and goddesses of later Mesoamerican civilizations, and they are therefore regarded as the sources of many aspects of pan-Mesoamerican mythology and religion, and as prototypes of later gods and goddesses.

OMÁCATL, a manifestation of the *AZTEC TEZCATLIPOCA*, presided over banquets and feasting. His name *Two ÁCATL* means "Two Reed".

OMECÍHUATL, or *CITLALÍCUE*, Citlalinícue or Tonacacíhuatl, was the female counterpart of *OMETE-CUHTLI*, and therefore the female aspect of the androgynous duality *OMETEOTL*. She was a primitive central Mesoamerican creator deity.

third day of the 20-day Maya month. He is usually associated with *AH PUCH*, possibly as his predecessor or as one of his companions. The codices show him smoking a rolled-leaf cigar and wearing a *Muan*-bird (or *Moan*-) headdress, but also sometimes with a merchant's bundle, which associates him with *EK CHUAH* and *XAMEN EK*.

THE OLD FIRE GOD was a primitive deity whose worship began early in Mesoamerica with the *OLMECS*. Their *GOD I* is thought to have been his prototype. He was later included in the Maya pantheon as *ITZAMNÁ* and in the Aztec pantheon as *HUEHUETÉOTL* and *XIUHTECUHTLI* (his weapon and sign of office was the *XIUHATLATL* spear-thrower). At *TEOTIHUACÁN*, he might have been the consort of the *TEOTIHUACÁN SPIDER WOMAN*.

OLLIN ("movement" or "earthquake") was 17th of the 20 *AZTEC* day-names; it had a neutral augury and its patron was *XÓLOTL*, Venus the evening "star". The *MAYA* and *ZAPOTEC* equivalents were *CABAN* and *XOO*.

Calendrical dates and deity associations for this day included *1 Ollin*, for Xólotl and *4 Ollin*, for the Fifth Sun of the Aztec *CREATION MYTH*, which was destined to end in catastrophic earthquakes.

THE OLMEC civilization of the Mexican Gulf Coast region, known as the Olmec Heartland, was the first to arise in Mesoamerica and to build monumental temple mounds and ceremonial precincts. Their antecedents are unknown, nor do we know what they called themselves – the word Olmec means "rubber people" in *NAHUATL*, the language of the *AZTECS*.

Olmec civilization flourished in the Preclassic Period, their most famous Gulf Coast sites being occupied in an overlapping sequence: first at San Lorenzo Tenochtitlán (occupied *c*. 1450–400 BC; flourished *c*. 1150–900 BC) and at La Venta (occupied *c*. 2250–500 BC; flourished *c*. 900–500 BC), then at Tres Zapotes (occupied *c*. 1000–50 BC; flourished *c*. 600–50 BC).

At these sites, in addition to monumental precincts, they carved and erected 17 colossal stone heads (including one found at the site of Cobata), often using stone that had been brought from considerable distances away, and each one so distinct in its facial features and its head-gear that they are thought to be the portraits of actual Olmec rulers. Other distinguishing monuments that have survived include carved stone altars and stelae and turquoise mosaic floor masks, as well as a wealth of stone and ceramic figurines.

The Olmec art style and architectural organization of ceremonial spaces were exported in the early stages of long-distance trading networks and, possibly, empire-building. Their influence spread north along the Gulf Coast and inland to the Basin of Mexico and the present states of Morelos, Guerrero and Oaxaca south of it.

That they exercised a certain amount of power in these areas is indicated by the existence of "gateway" ceremonial communities, such as Chalcatzingo, which was sited at a pass giving access into the Valley of Morelos and where they carved the faces of numerous boulders with feline beings and figures of power and rulership, and Teopantecuanitlán, 300 miles (480 km) west of La Venta, where four huge Olmec feline faces were carved on stone blocks. In Guerrero they painted mythological beings onto the walls of the caves of Oxtotitlán and Juxtlahuaca. (See also *COLOURS & THE CARDINAL DIRECTIONS, THE RITUAL BALL GAME*)

THE OLMECS *were the first to adopt the Mesoamerican reverence for jade and turquoise as the most precious stones. Long-distance trade routes were established to obtain them, and control of their sources became an important feature of the politico-economic structure. (PRECLASSIC PERIOD CEREMONIAL JADE MASK.)*

COLOURS & THE CARDINAL DIRECTIONS

T HE MESOAMERICAN WORLD, all living things, and the gods and goddesses were grouped according to the four cardinal directions on earth, and personified by special colours that were assigned to these directions. The Mesoamerican fifth (or fifth/sixth) cardinal direction was the centre, and went up to the heavens or celestial layers of the universe, and down into the earth and the underworld layers. The numbers four (representing the four horizontal directions) and five (for the fifth direction) were thus especially important in Mesoamerican cosmology. The Maya centre was a *Ceibe* tree (*Bombax pentandra*), called either *Yaxché* or *Kapok*, whose roots penetrated the underworlds, and whose branches spread into the celestial levels. The Aztec centre was ruled by the god and goddess Ometecuhtli and Omecíhuatl, unified as Ometeotl, literally "twice god".

The colour–direction combinations varied from one region to another. In addition to colours, the Aztecs also associated particular trees, birds or animals, day and year signs, deities, and favourable or unfavourable auguries with each direction. For the Maya, death ruled from the south; for the Aztecs, death ruled from the north.

MAYA DIRECTIONS AND COLOURS

	North	South	East	West
Name	*Xamen*	*Nohol*	*Likin*	*Chikin*
Colour	zac (white)	kan (yellow)	chac (red)	ek (black)
Year-bearing day-name	*Muluc*	*Cauac*	*Kan*	*Ix*

AZTEC DIRECTIONS, COLOURS AND ASSOCIATIONS

	North	South	East	West
Name	*Mictlampa*	*Huitzlampa*	*Tlapcopa*	*Cihuatlampa*
Colours	black (or red, or white)	blue (or red, or white)	red (or yellow, or blue-green)	white (or yellow, or blue-green)
Sky-bearing deity	a fire god	Mictlantecuhtli	Tlahuizcalpantecuhtli	Éhecatl-Quetzalcóatl
Trees	*ceibe* or *mesquite*	willow or palm	*ceibe* or *mesquite*	cypress or *maguey* (*agave*)
Birds/animals	eagle or jaguar	parrot or rabbit	quetzal or eagle	hummingbird or serpent
Days	Océlotl, Miquiztli, Técpatl, Itzcuintli, Éhecatl	Xóchitl, Malinalli, Cuetzpalin, Cozcacuauhtli, Tochtli	Cipactli, Ácatl, Cóatl, Ollin, Atl	Mázatl, Quiáhuitl, Ozomatli, Calli, Cuauhtli
Year	*Técpatl*	*Tochtli*	*Ácatl*	*Calli*
Augury	unfavourable	indifferent	favourable	"too humid"

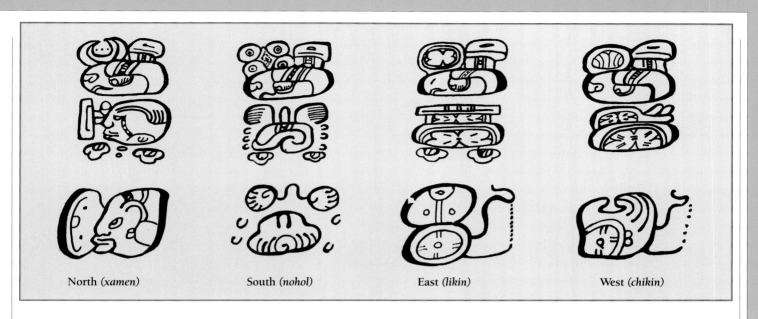

North (*xamen*)   South (*nohol*)   East (*likin*)   West (*chikin*)

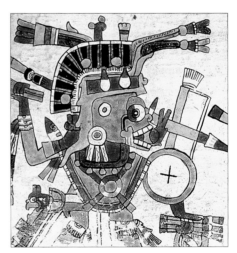

THE FOUR CARDINAL DIRECTIONS (above) were recognized by the Maya, who had established colour associations for them by the early Classic Period. Their fascination with them possibly originated with the Olmecs, to whom the directions clearly formed an important part of their ideas regarding the cosmos – for example, at La Venta they laid out jade and serpentine celts in crosses oriented to the four directions. At early Classic Period Maya Río Azul, Guatemala, directional glyphs painted on the walls of Tomb 12 (top row) were confirmed by well-known Postclassic Period glyphs from, among other sources, the Dresden Codex (bottom row).

THE AZTECS and other central Mesoamericans were equally convinced of the importance of the directions, but were less uniform and consistent in their colour associations. The Aztecs, however, assigned four sky-bearing gods to the four quadrants of the earth: the Old Fire God (above left) supporting the north (here represented in the Codex Borbonicus), Mictlantecuhtli (left) supporting the south (in the Codex Magliabecchiano), Tlahuizcalpantecuhtli (above) supporting the east (in the Codex Cospi) and Éhecatl (far left) supporting the west (in a buccal-masked and conical-capped stone figurine).

P

OMETECUHTLI, also called Citlatona and Tonacatecuhtli, was the male counterpart of *OMECÍHUATL*, therefore the male aspect of the androgynous duality *OMETEOTL*. He was a primitive central Mesoamerican creator god, perceived as a remote power. With his consort Omecíhuatl he lived in the 13th level of the *AZTEC* heaven, *OMEYOCÁN* and was patron of the day *Cipactli* ("crocodile"), representative of the earth and the first day of the Aztec 20-day month.

The sons of Ometecuhtli and Omecíhuatl were the four corners of the earth, the cardinal directions, and their associated colours: north=Black *TEZCATLIPOCA*; south =Blue Tezcatlipoca (or *HUITZILOPOCHTLI*); east=Red Tezcatlipoca (or *XIPE TOTEC* or *CAMAXTLI*); and west=White Tezcatlipoca (alternatively *QUETZALCÓATL*).

As Tonacatecuhtli ("Lord of Sustenance"), he rewarded the gods Quetzalcóatl and Tezcatlipoca for helping to create the Fifth Sun (see *CREATION MYTHS*), making them lords of the heavens and the stars.

OMETEOTL, literally "twice god" or "dual lord" in *NAHUATL*, was a primordial central Mesoamerican "notional" deity, two gods in one, but indivisible, a bisexual divinity expressive of androgynous duality.

The source of all existence and the creative energy from which all the other gods and goddesses descended, he/she was above the events of the world, beyond the heavens and the stars, and outside of space and time. His/her realm was *OMEYOCÁN*, the "place of the two". Ometeotl was the supreme being, the unity of opposites: male (*OMETECUHTLI*) and female (*OMECÍHUATL*), light and dark, action and inaction, movement and stillness, sound and silence, order and chaos. Such a concept of "first principle" was too abstract for daily, active cult worship, and was used only by *AZTEC* (and presumably earlier) priests in their cosmic definition and divinations. (See also *DUALITY & OPPOSITION* and *TLOQUE NAHUAQUE*)

OMETOCHTLI ("two rabbit") was a generic calendrical term for *THE CENTZÓNTOTOCHTIN* ("400 rabbits") or for *TEPOZTÉCATL* (a *PULQUE* god of the city of Tepoztlán).

OMEYOCÁN (literally "place of the two") was the supreme, 13th, heaven in the *AZTEC* (central Mesoamerican) cosmos and the realm of *OMETEOTL*, the supreme expression of androgynous duality. It was the abode of *OMETECUHTLI* (maleness) and *OMECÍHUATL* (femaleness), and of light/dark, action/inaction, movement/stillness, sound/silence, order/chaos and all other dualities and oppositions.

In the Aztec world of the Fifth Sun (their present) the two great opposed spirits of world – represented by *TEZCATLIPOCA* and *QUETZALCÓATL* – were in temporary exile from Omeyocán. They were associated with the four corners of the earth as the cardinal directions and their associated colours: north=Black Tezcatlipoca; south=Blue Tezcatlipoca; east=Red Tezcatlipoca; and west=White Tezcatlipoca. Alternatively, they were Quetzalcóatl, who would return from the east to inaugurate a new religion and world order.

OPA ("cold") was the 18th of the 20 *ZAPOTEC* day-names; the *AZTEC* and *MAYA* equivalent days were *TÉCPATL* and *ETZ'NAB*.

OPOCHTLI ("left-handed one") one of the *Tlálocs*, was a manifestation of the rain god *TLÁLOC*. He was identified with the south, and the particular deity of those who lived on or near water. He invented and

PACHTONTLI, or Ecoztli, and Panquetzaliztli were two Aztec months during which their patron god Huitzilopochtli was offered sacrifices.

gave to such people the tools of their trade: fishing net, bird net or snare, three-pronged fisherman's harpoon, spear-thrower (*atl-atl*) and the boatman's pole.

THE OTOMÍ, called in one legend the Otontlaca, were a group of people of *CHICHIMEC* origin who settled the region to the north and west of the Basin of Mexico. Following the late 13th- or 14th-century Chichimec invasion of central Mesoamerica under the legendary leader Xólotl, they moved into the Basin itself, and their own leader married one of Xólotl's daughters. They established the kingdom of Xaltocán and were later incorporated into the Tepanec Empire, contemporary with the México *AZTECS*. The Tepanecs-Otomí were Aztec allies at first, but were subjugated by them in the 15th century.

OTONTECUHTLI, also called Xócotl, was the primitive fire god and patron god of the *OTOMÍ* and their neighbours the Tepananeca and Mazahua (see also *HUEHUETÉOTL* and *XIUHTECUHTLI*).

THE OXLAHUN TI KU were the 13 *MAYA* Lords of the Heavens/upper world, identified as glyphs but whose names are otherwise unknown. They were the arch rivals of, and overcame, the nine

Lords of the Underworld (*THE BOLON TI KU*) at the creation (see *CREATION MYTHS*). Their *AZTEC* equivalent were the Tonalteuctin (see *LORDS OF THE DAY*).

OXOMOCO was the "first woman" in the *TOLTEC* and *AZTEC* *CREATION MYTH* and the wife of *CIPACTONAL*. Together they were regarded as the first sorceress and sorcerer, and the inventors of astrology and of the calendar. Her *MAYA* equivalent was *XMUCANÉ*.

OZOMATLI ("monkey") was the 11th of the 20 *AZTEC* day-names; it had a neutral augury and its patron deity was *XOCHIPILLI*, the "flower prince". The *MAYA* and *ZAPOTEC* equivalent days were *CHUEN* and *LOO* or *Goloo*.

In Mesoamerica, the monkey was a frolicsome animal, representing pleasure, and associated with lust. Calendrical dates included: *1 Ozomatli*, as one of the *CIHUAPIPILTIN*; *2 Ozomatli*, for the feast day of merchants; *6 Ozomatli*, for the moon god *TECCIZTÉCATL*; *8 Ozomatli*, also for the moon; *9 Ozomatli*, for *ITZPAPÁLOTL*, the "obsidian butterfly"; and *12 Ozomatli*, for *HUEHUECÓYOTL* as god of music and dance.

PACHTONTLI ("a bit of hay") was the 13th (or, in some sources, the 12th) of the 18 *AZTEC* months,

a month of general deity worship, but especially of the war god *HUIT-ZILOPOCHTLI*, the "smoking mirror" *TEZCATLIPOCA* and the patron of merchants *YACATECUHTLI*.

It was also called *Ecoztli* ("letting of blood") and *Teotleco* ("the coming of the gods").

PANQUETZALIZTLI ("raising of banners") was the 16th (or, in some sources, 15th) of the 18 *AZTEC* months, in which honours and sacrifices were made to the war god *HUITZILOPOCHTLI*.

PATÉCATL, one of *THE CENT-ZÓNTOTOCHTIN*, was chief *AZTEC* god of drinking and of drunkenness. His consort, *MAYÁHUEL*, was goddess of the *maguey* or *AGAVE* plant (*Agave americana*), and it was Patécatl who cured the fermenting juice of the plant to turn it into *PULQUE*. *Pulque* was consumed in quantity at many ceremonies and festivals to worship the gods, and was believed to possess magical powers. (See also *COQUIHUANI*, *QUIABELAGAYO*, *TEPOZTÉCATL* and *TEZCATZONTÉCATL*)

Patécatl was ruler of *MALINALLI* ("grass"), the 12th day of the 20 *AZTEC* day-names, and god of medicine and curing. In the latter capacity he was associated with herbs and narcotic plants, including *peyote* and various mushrooms.

THE PAUAHTUN, *MAYA* God N, were the four winds of the cardinal points. As *THE BACABS* or *CHACS* they were also associated with rain. Each was associated with a colour and a direction, thus: *Zac* Pauahtun (white and north), *Kan* Pauahtun (yellow and south), *Chac* Pauahtun (red and east) and *Ek* Pauahtun (black and west).

PAYNAL was the messenger of *HUITZILOPOCHTLI*, the *AZTEC* god of war.

PECALA, or Pixee Pecala, was the Valley *ZAPOTEC* god of love.

PETELA was the name applied to the deified ruler of the Southern *ZAPOTEC* city of Ocelotepec. Curiously, the element *tela* in the name is thought to mean "dog".

PEZALAO see *COQUI BEZELAO*.

PICHANA GOBECHE was the principal deity of Valley *ZAPOTEC* Chichicapa. He was the god of healing, but nevertheless had to be constantly appeased and appealed to through a female intermediary called Pichanto.

PICHANTO see under *HUE-CHAANA* and *PICHANA GOBECHE*.

PIJA ("draught") was the 12th of the 20 *ZAPOTEC* day-names and one of the year-bearing days – there were 13 *Pija* years in a 52-year cycle (see also *CHINA*, *QUIJ* and *XOO*). The *AZTEC* and *MAYA* equivalent days were known as *MALINALLI* and *EB*.

PIJE XOO, ("the source of time"), was an alternative name for Zapotec *COQUI XEE*.

PIJETAO ("great time") was an alternative name for the Zapotec *COQUI XEE*.

PILALAPA CAACHE see *BENELABA*.

PILLAHUANA see *HUEYPACHTLI*.

PILLAHUANALIZTLI see *IZCALLI*.

PILTZINTECUHTLI was the youthful manifestation of *TONA-TIUH* – appropriately referred to as "the young (sun) god" – and a manifestation of the *XOCHIPILLI*. He was the third of the nine Aztec *LORDS OF THE NIGHT*.

PITAO COCHANA was an alternative name for *HUECHAANA*.

PITAO COCIJO see *COCIJO*.

PITAO COPIJCHA see *COPIJCHA*.

PITAO COZAANA see *COZAANA*.

PITAO COZOBI ("abundant sustenance"), or Betao Yozobi, or Locucuy, was the Valley *ZAPOTEC* god of corn (maize). His Southern and Sierra Zapotec names were Locucuy and Betao Yozobi. He was sometimes represented as a *BAT-GOD*. On collecting the first ears of corn at harvest time, special ceremonies were held in which native

PILTZINTECUHTLI was the youthful manifestation of Tonatiuh the sun god. (CODEX VATICANUS B.)

fowl were sacrificed and the blood sprinkled on 13 pieces of *copal* incense (in honour of the principal deities), and on the house patio. The *copal* was then burned while incantations for a good harvest were recited. He was equivalent to Aztec *CENTÉOTL*.

PITAO HUICHAANA see *HUECHAANA*.

PITAO PEZALAO see *COQUI BEZELAO*.

PITAO XICALA (OR ZICA-LA) was the Valley *ZAPOTEC* god of dreams.

PITAO XOO, or Laxee, or Laxoo, was the Valley *ZAPOTEC* god of earthquakes, which were a frequent occurrence in their homeland. He was known as Laxoo among the Sierra Zapotec and Laxee among the Southern Zapotec.

PIXEE PECALA see *PECALA*.

POCHTECA see under *YACATE-CUHTLI*.

Q

THE POPUL VUH was one of the most sacred books of the Quiché *MAYA* of highland Guatemala, written between 1554 and 1558. Its tells the stories of the creation by the "grandfather" god *XPIYACOC* and the "grandmother" goddess **XMUCANÉ**, and the adventures in *XIBALBA* (the underworld) of the hero twin brothers, and gives the chronology of the Quiché rulers down to 1550. The first set of twins were *HUN HUNAHPÚ* and *VUCUB HUNAHPÚ*, the sons of Xpiyacoc and Xmucané, and the second were *HUNAHPÚ* and *XBALANQUÉ*, the sons of Hun Hunahpú and *XQUIC*.

The manuscript was discovered by Fray Francisco Jiménez in the early 18th century, but is now lost. However, he both copied and translated it into Spanish, now in the Newberry Library, Chicago, US. (See also *CREATION & THE UNIVERSE, TWINS & CULTURE HEROES*)

PULQUE, the *AZTEC* (and Mexican) alcoholic drink made from the *maguey* or *agave* plant (*Agave americana*), was consumed in large quantities at ceremonies and festivals (see *CENTZÓNTOTOCHTIN*) and was believed to possess magical powers. It was drunk to excess, for example, at ceremonies devoted to Aztec *XOCHIPILLI* and *MACUIL-XÓCHITL* and to Zapotec *QUIA BELAGAYO*, god of pleasure, and *COQUIHUANI*, god of light. In ancient Tepoztlán, Morelos, the patron deity was *TEPOZTÉCATL*, a moon god and god of *pulque*. Another god of *pulque*, possibly the *CHACMOOL* figure, was *TEZCATZONTÉCATL*. (For the mythical origins of *maguey* and *pulque* see *MAYÁHUEL* and *PATÉCATL*.)

QUAXOLOTL ("split at the top") was a goddess related to the earth goddess *CHANTICO*. Her image parted into two heads, and represented twins. She signified flame bifurcated into tongues and, by extension, was concerned with duality. (See also *OMETEOTL*)

PULQUE was made from the juice of the maguey *cactus (Agave americana).*

QUECHOLLI ("valuable feather") was 15th of the 18 *AZTEC* months, in which the hunting gods *MIXCÓ-ATL* and *CAMAXTLI* and their female consorts were honoured.

It was also called *Tlacoquecholli* ("half-*Quecholli*") and *Tlamiquecholli* ("end-*Quecholli*").

QUERENDA-ANGAPETI, literally "the stone that is in the temple", was the *TARASCAN* god of corn (maize), a manifestation of the sun god *CURICAUERI*. His cult was at Zacapu, where Tarascan lords offered the first fruits of the harvest to his idol. His *AZTEC* equivalent was *CENTÉOTL*.

THE QUETZAL (*Pharomachrus mocinno*) is the brilliant green bird of the humid mountain forests of Chiapas and Guatemala. Mesoamerican rulers and nobility coveted its tail feathers and obtained them through long-distance trade. (Strong *TEOTIHUACANO* influences at *MAYA* Kaminaljuyú and Tikal demonstrate this contact.) Its rarity made it a symbol of value and preciousness, along with jade, and the element *quetzal* in numerous *NAHUATL* words means "plumed" or "feathered".

QUETZALCÓATL was a deity venerated throughout Mesoamerica and one of the most ancient and fundamental gods; he might have been descended ultimately from *OLMEC GOD VII*. His *NAHUATL* name means "plumed serpent", but he was known by other names in different parts of Mesoamerica:

QUETZALCÓATL is pictured enthroned and holding a plumed serpent opposite the goddess Chantico. (CODEX BORBONICUS.)

Quetzalcóatl to central Mesoamericans; *KUKULKÁN* to the *MAYA*; *GUCUMATZ* to the Guatemalan Quiché; and *ÉHECATL* to the Gulf Coast *HUASTECS*. Like his brother *TEZCATLIPOCA*, he was a child of *OMETEOTL* and played a vital role in the *CREATION MYTHS*. His *AZTEC* brothers were Tezcatlipoca, *HUIZILO-POCHTLI* and *XIPE TOTEC*, and he was frequently associated with the rain god *TLÁLOC*. He was ninth of the 13 *LORDS OF THE DAY*.

The mystery and duality of Quetzalcóatl was manifest in his many guises and roles, both divine and human. He was a creator god and a father of the gods, the god of learning, science, arts and crafts. He was a god of agriculture, who gave humankind corn (maize), the inventor of the calendar and god of the winds and cardinal directions. He was patron of priests, who often assumed his name.

In contrast to the destructive gods *XIUHCÓATL* and Tezcatlipoca, Quetzalcóatl was benevolent, and brought knowledge and prosperity to humankind. He was Éhecatl the wind god (represented by the four colours: black=north, blue=south, red=east, and white=west); *TLA-HUIZCALPANTECUHTLI*, the morning "star", and his twin *XÓLOTL*, the

THE PYRAMID OF THE SERPENT, *at Xochicalco, depicts Quetzalcóatl face-on, alternating with images of the rain god Tláloc. Quetzalcoátl, the "plumed serpent", was portrayed on architecture, sculpture, portable objects and in the codices. He is also depicted, more famously, on the Pyramid of Quetzalcóatl at Teotihuacán*

evening "star"; *CE ÁCATL TOPILTZIN QUETZALCÓATL*, the legendary *TOL-TEC* leader and founder of Tollán (Tula); and *KUKULKÁN*, the Maya-Toltec founder of Chichén Itzá.

As one of the five world rulers (Tezcatlipoca, Quetzalcóatl, Tláloc, Chalchiútlicue and Tonatiuh) he played a key role in the *CREATION MYTH* of the five suns – he ruled the Second Sun, having overthrown his brother Tezcatlipoca. He featured prominently in the Classic Period *TEOTIHUACÁN*, where a six-tiered pyramid was dedicated jointly to him and to Tláloc, and it was here that Mesoamericans believed that the gods assembled and created the world of the Fifth Sun.

QUETZALCÓATL was often sculpted by the Aztecs as free-standing stone pieces and as architectural embellishment.

In the Postclassic Period, Quetzalcóatl was portrayed with many attributes in numerous combinations: wearing a conical hat (*copilli*), divided vertically and painted half dark, half light; with a hat-band holding the tools of autosacrifice (*ómitl* and *huitzli*); with a flower to symbolize blood; with a fan of black crow and yellow macaw feathers at his neck; wearing a bird-beak mask and beard; with a black body and with his face divided vertically, and painted black on the front and yellow on the back, with a dark, vertical band through the eye; wearing jade-disc or spiral-shell ear ornaments (*epcololli*); wearing a breast plate cut from a conch shell (*ehecailacacózcatl*); or holding a spear-thrower (*atl-atl*), the symbol of the fire god.

Quetzalcóatl played several roles in the creation of the Fifth Sun. *NANAHUATZIN* and *TECUCIZTÉCATL*, having sacrificed themselves in the fire and risen as the sun and moon, remained motionless. Nanahuatzin, now *TONATIUH*, demanded blood sacrifice. Outraged at such arrogance, Quetzalcóatl-Tlahuizcalpantecuhtli hurled a dart at him but missed. Tonatiuh retaliated, and his dart pierced Tlahuizcalpantecuhtli through the head and transformed him into stone (the god of coldness *ITZTLACOLIUHQUI*). To get the sun and moon into motion, therefore, the gods were forced to sacrifice themselves, calling upon Quetzalcóatl to cut out their hearts with an obsidian blade, establishing the manner in which humans were to sacrifice and be sacrificed to feed Tonatiuh with blood.

Quetzalcóatl also played a vital role in peopling the world and providing them with sustenance. As Éhecatl-Quetzalcóatl, they sent him to *MICTLÁN* (the underworld) to bring back the bones of the people of the Fourth Sun. After overcoming challenges from *MICTLANTECUHTLI* and *MICTECACÍHUATL* (Lord and Lady of Mictlán), he escaped and brought the bones back to the old goddess *CIHUACÓATL*, who ground them up and mixed them with divine blood to mould men and women. In the search for food for these humans, Quetzalcóatl noticed the red ant *AZCATL* and persuaded it to lead him to *TONACATÉPETL* ("sustenance mountain"), where it kept its store of grain. He brought corn (maize) and other seeds back to the gods, who chewed them and fed them to the infant humans. Quetzalcóatl also attempted to drag Tonacatépetl to a more convenient place but, failing, the gods called upon Nanahuatzin, who enlisted the help of the four *TLÁLOCS* to split the mountain open and scatter the grains and seeds where the rain could water them and the sun cause them to grow.

Finally, Éhecatl-Quetzalcóatl created the *maguey* (Agave americana) and alcoholic *PULQUE* to cause humans to sing and dance in honour of their creators. He abducted the virgin sky goddess *MAYÁHUEL*, and on earth they embraced as the intertwining branches of a tree. Mayáhuel's guardian *TZITZIMITL* pursued them but, when she saw that she had arrived too late to prevent their union, she splintered the branches apart and fed Mayáhuel's shreds to her demon servants. Éhecatl, who remained unharmed, collected Mayáhuel's bones and planted them in a field, where they grew into the *maguey*.

Quetzalcóatl the man was the legendary ruler of the Toltecs, Ce Ácatl Topiltzin Quetzalcóatl, whose memory was perpetuated by the Aztecs in reverence for all things Toltec. The quasi-historical leader was the son of *CE TÉCPATL MIXCÓATL*, born after his father's murder by a rival faction, raised in exile and brought up to avenge his father. This relatively straightforward legend was mystified by the Aztecs, however, in variations on the tale and its characters. Ce Ácatl Topiltzin's father was deified as the god of the hunt, *MIXCÓATL*, and his mother elevated in some versions to the goddess *CHIMALMAN*. His mother's impregnation became symbolic (accomplished with an arrow from Mixcóatl's bow), and his upbringing was consigned to the goddess *QUILAZTLI*, herself a manifestation of the goddess Cihuacóatl, the "serpent woman".

In a further permutation, again interweaving divine and human affairs, the young Ce Ácatl Topiltzin led the Toltecs out of the Basin of Mexico (where his father had established their dynasty) and founded Tollán (Tula) to the northwest (in AD 968, according to Aztec tradition). Later, like his father, he got caught up in political rivalry: as Quetzalcóatl, he required only peaceful sacrifices involving offerings of jade, birds, snakes and butterflies. His political rivals, however, were resolved on expansion by conquest – symbolized by Tezcatlipoca ("smoking mirror", patron of warriors and Quetzalcóatl's perpetual rival) – and demanded human sacrifice to appease the gods. The contest ended with Quetzalcóatl being expelled from Tollán and leading his followers east, to the Gulf of Mexico, where he immolated himself on a pyre and was reborn as the "star" Venus. In a formal, divine version, Tezcatlipoca plied Quetzalcóatl with drink and, inebriated, he slept with his own sister. His subsequent anguish and shame led him to burn his palace, bury his treasures and sacrifice himself on a funeral pyre, from which his ashes rose as rare birds. In another variation, he left on a raft of serpents and disappeared over the eastern horizon, vowing to return one day for revenge and to build a new, peaceful world order.

In the Maya version, Kukulkán invaded Yucatán by sea to found the Maya-Toltec dynasty at Chichén Itzá (traditionally in AD 987, which coincides roughly with the Aztec dates for the departure of Quetzalcóatl from Tollán). See also *TEPEU*.

The significance of these legends was grasped, and taken advantage of, by Hernán Cortés in 1519, and recognized by the 16th-century Spanish historian Bernadino de Sahagún, who wrote: "In the city of Tollán reigned many years a king called Quetzalcóatl. . . He was exceptional in moral virtues. . . [and] the place of this king among the natives is like [that of] King Arthur among the English."

QUETZALCÓATL the ruler and hero in the post-Spanish conquest Codex Florentine, *holding an* atl-atl *(spear-thrower), and wearing a feathered cloak and conical feathered hat.*

T

QUETZALPAPÁLOTL ("quetzal butterfly", "plumed butterfly" or – because of the Mesoamerican value of *quetzal* feathers – "precious butterfly") was a mythical creature revered in the ancient city of *TEOTIHUACÁN*. A palace at the southwest corner of the Plaza of the Pyramid of the Moon appears to have been dedicated to her and has decorations that undoubtedly represent religious symbolism; but, apart from obvious water symbols and the mythical Quetzalpapálotl, neither the significance nor the role of this creature is known.

QUEZA ("water") see *NIZA*.

QUEZELAO was "provider of the seasons" (probably a permutation of *COCIJO*), a Sierra *ZAPOTEC* god of agriculture and principal deity of the city of Atepec.

QUIABELAGAYO ("five flower"), or Quiepelagayo, was Valley *ZAPOTEC* god of pleasure, music and flowers, the equivalent of Aztec *MACUILXÓCHITL* and *XOCHIPILLI*. Curiously, in the worship of Quiabelagayo there were periods of fasting lasting from 40 to 80 days, during which the devotee was only allowed to use a certain tobacco every four days to stem hunger. He also pierced his tongue and ears to let blood as an offering. Other, luckier, devotees consumed much *PULQUE*, and feasted and danced.

QUIÁHUITL ("rain") was the 19th of the 20 *AZTEC* day-names; it had an unfavourable augury and its patron deity was the sun god *TONATIUH* or *CHANTICO*, goddess of the hearth. *MAYA* and *ZAPOTEC* equivalents were *CAUAC* and *APE*.

Calendrical dates included: *4 Quiáhuitl*, for the Third Sun of the Aztec *CREATION MYTH*; and *9 Quiáhuitl*, for the rain god *TLÁLOC*.

QUIJ, or *Laa*, ("wind") was the second of the 20 *ZAPOTEC* day-names and a year-bearing day –

QUETZALPAPÁLOTL was a mythical creature, portrayed in bas-relief on the square stone pillars of the Palace of Quetzalpapálotl at Teotihuacán. The eyes and other shallow circles, perhaps representing coloured spots on its wings, were filled with obsidian and other polished stones.

there were 13 *Quij* years in a 52-year cycle (see also *CHINA*, *PIJA* and *XOO*). The *AZTEC* and *MAYA* equivalents were *ÉHECATL* and *IK*. *Quij*, or *Ij*, or *Laa*, ("reed") was also the 13th of the 20 *ZAPOTEC* day-names; the *AZTEC* and *MAYA* equivalent days of this were *ÁCATL* and *BEN*.

QUILAZTLI, an aspect of the goddess *CIHUACÓATL*, was the goddess of pregnancy and childbirth, and patroness of the sweat bath (*NAHUAL temescal*). She raised the legendary ruler *CE ÁCATL TOPILTZIN QUETZALCÓATL*, founder of the Toltec capital at Tollán (Tula), after

his mother, *CHIMALMAN*, died when giving birth to him. Thus, through her association with Cihuacóatl, she was patroness of the *CIHUATETEO* (spirits of woman who died in childbirth).

THE QUINAMETZIN were the giants who inhabited the *AZTEC* world of the First Sun (see *CREATION MYTHS*), and the servants of *TEZCATLIPOCA*. This world ended when Tezcatlipoca's brother, *QUETZALCÓATL*, caused them to be eaten by jaguars.

THE RITUAL OF THE BACABS is a Yucatecan *MAYA* codex of medicinal incantations, rich in symbolism and with frequent mythological allusions to stories about plants, birds and insects. However, without the text of these stories, the meanings cannot be fully understood.

SACRED FIRE CEREMONY see *TOXIUHMOLPILIA*.

SAIYAM UINICOB ("adjuster men") were the dwarf inhabitants of the first world in the *MAYA CREATION MYTH*. They were believed to have built the great ruined Maya cities, working in darkness because the sun had not yet been created. When the sun rose on the first dawn, they were turned to stone, and their world was destroyed in the first great flood called *haiyococab* ("water over the earth").

SERPENTS see *CÓATL*.

THE SHORT COUNT see under *LONG COUNT*.

SICUINDIRO was a *TARASCAN* ceremony honouring the deities *CURICAUERI* and *CUERAUÁPERI*, the masculine and feminine aspects of creation, in which Tarascan priests dressed and danced in the flayed skins of human sacrificial victims (see also *XIPE TOTEC*). The hearts of the victims were thrown into the thermal springs of Araró, while the body parts were reserved for ritual cannibalism. From the springs, Cueraupéri created the clouds to water the crops.

SKY-BEARER see under *WORLD TREE*, and see also *COLOURS & THE CARDINAL DIRECTIONS*.

SPIDER WOMAN see *TEOTIHUACÁN SPIDER WOMAN*.

TAJÍN was the *TOTONAC* god of rain and associated elements, including thunder, lightning and coastal hurricanes. He was equivalent to Aztec *TLÁLOC*, Maya *CHAC*, Zapotec *COCIJO* and Mixtec *DZAHUI*, and probably also to Tarascan *CHUPITHIRIPEME*.

Tajín is also the name of a Classic Period ceremonial centre in the central Gulf Coast (Veracruz state), believed to have been the Totonac capital. It was occupied from the

first century BC to the 13th century AD and had several building phases in which pyramid-platforms and ball courts were built around numerous plazas. Its architecture and iconography show a combination of OLMEC, HUASTEC, TEOTIHUACANO and Maya influences but it also has its own characteristic style of stone slab niches, flying cornices and other elements. It was the most powerful Gulf Coast city after the demise of Teotihuacán.

Its two most famous monuments are a 12th-century ball court (one of seven) with six panels carved with ball-game scenes and associated ritual sacrifice, and the Pyramid of the Niches (begun in the fifth century AD), which has 365 stone-panelled niches in its six tiers and temple (88 on the base, 76 on the second tier, 64 on the third, 52 on the fourth, 40 on the fifth, 28 on the sixth and 17 on the temple). These probably correspond to the days of the solar year.

TAMOANCHÁN, a terrestrial paradise, was where, in one account of the CREATION MYTH, the gods convened and decided to repopulate the world of the Fifth Sun. They sent QUETZALCÓATL (the "plumed serpent") to MICTLÁN (the underworld) to fetch the bones of the beings who had inhabited the world of the Fourth Sun. After a struggle with MICTLANTECUHTLI and MICTECACÍHUATL (the rulers of Mictlán), he brought the bones to the old goddess CIHUACÓATL, who ground them to powder and mixed them with the blood of the gods to mould men and women.

Tamoanchán was a pan-Mesoamerican concept, spread by the TOLTECS/México AZTECS, and probably of HUASTEC origin. The word itself derives from a MAYA toponym meaning "land of the plumed serpent" (ta=prefix for "of", moan=a tropical bird, chán=an older form of can, "serpent"), that is, Quetzalcóatl himself. This interpretation associates Tamoanchán with the

TAJÍN, the Totonac rain god, is thought to be represented by a double, angular scroll motif set into the niches of Structure C and other buildings at El Tajín.

legend of CE ÁCATL TOPILTZIN QUETZALCÓATL, the fabled Toltec hero and founder of Tollán (Tula) who, after he was ousted by his political rivals, travelled east from Tollán to the Gulf Coast – through the southern territory of the Huastecs – and, in one version, put out to sea on a raft of serpents. In Maya legend, the founder/hero of the later Maya-Toltec city of Chichén Itzá was KUKULKÁN, the Maya name for Quetzalcóatl. He arrived in Yucatán by sea from the west, presumably having crossed the Gulf of Mexico.

THE TARASCANS lived in a state in western Mesoamerica, north and west of the Basin of Mexico, which was focused around ceremonial centres – Pátzcuaro, Ihuatzio and Tzintzuntzan – on the shores of Lake Pátzcuaro in present-day Michoacán. Their capital was shifted to Tzintzuntzan in the 15th century, where a five-fold complex of temples known as YÁCATAS was built.

Sworn enemies of the México AZTECS, the Tarasacans vigorously resisted Aztec attempts to conquer them in the 15th and early 16th

centuries. Although not as extensively as the Aztecs, they practised both human and autosacrifice, particularly blood-letting from the ears, to their gods CURICAUERI, CUERAUÁPERI and others. Since the two states were almost constantly at war, captives were a ready source of sacrificial victims. Blood sacrifice was accompanied by ritual cannibalism at special feasts. Having drugged or intoxicated them, the king and higher nobles cut open victims' chests before the temple fires; the heads were severed and put aside in a special place, and the hearts were extracted and offered to the gods. The remainder of the body provided the feast.

Whether war captives or honoured Tarascan citizens, the victims were believed to take on the personality of Curita-caheri, the messenger of the gods, and such a death was considered to be as glorious as death in battle. In one ceremony, the feast of SICUINDIRO, Tarascan priests dressed and danced in the flayed skins of the victims (see also XIPE TOTEC), and threw the hearts into the thermal springs of Araró, from which the rain god Cuerauáperi caused the clouds to form to water the crops.

The principal Tarascan gods were the creator and sun god Curicaueri, his creator consort Cuerauáperi and the moon

goddess XARATANGA, CHUPITHI-RIPEME the god of rain, TIHUIME the god of death, QUERENDA-ANGAPETI the god of corn (maize), and XIPE TOTEC the flayed god of sacrifice and springtime. TARIÁCURI, the Tarascan king and founder of the dynasty, was deified as a wind god. Associated with the gods were the messenger Curita-caheri and the reclining deity CHACMOOL, the alleged receptacle of sacrificial hearts and blood.

TARIÁCURI was the culture hero who founded the TARASCAN state. According to legend he consolidated the Tarascan peoples into a kingdom in the late 14th century, and established a capital city at Pátzcuaro; his successors later moved the capital to Tzintzuntzan. He was deified after his death as god of the winds and the patron of learning and wealth.

TATA was the first man (see under CREATION MYTHS).

TECCIZTÉCATL was the central Mesoamerican "old moon god", in both masculine (see also TECU-CIZTÉCATL) and feminine forms. He was also a deity of fertility. In male form he was portrayed as an old man carrying a huge white seashell on his back as a representation of the moon.

141

TÉCPATL ("flint knife") was the 18th of the 20 AZTEC day-names and a year-bearing day – there were 13 *Técpatl* years in a 52-year cycle (see also *ÁCATL*, *CALLI* and *TOCHTLI*). It had a favourable augury and its patron was *CHALCHIUHTOTOLIN-TEZCATLIPOCA*; its orientation was north. MAYA and ZAPOTEC equivalent days were *ETZ'NAB* and *OPA*.

Calendrical dates and deity associations included: *1 Técpatl*, for *HUITZILOPOCHTLI-CAMAXTLI*; *4 Técpatl*, for the moon god *TECCIZTÉCATL*; *7 Técpatl*, for *CHICOMECÓATL*; *8 Técpatl*, for the *maguey* plant (see *PULQUE*); and *12 Técpatl*, for the earth or death god.

TECUCIZTÉCATL, the AZTEC moon god of the world of the Fifth Sun, was the haughty, healthy and headstrong twin brother of the weak, humble and allegedly cowardly *NANAHUATZIN*, whom he followed in leaping into the ceremonial fire lit by the gods at *TEOTIHUACÁN* (see also *CREATION MYTHS*). The brightness of his radiance was diminished when one of the gods threw a rabbit (*tochtli*) into his face, which explains the Aztec belief in the "rabbit in the moon." He was ruler of *MIQUIZTLI* ("death"), sixth of the 20 Aztec days-names.

TECUILHUITONTLI ("small feast of the lords") was the eighth of the 18 AZTEC months, in which *HUIXTOCÍHUATL*, goddess of salt, was honoured.

TELLA ("dog") was the tenth of the 20 ZAPOTEC day-names; the AZTEC and MAYA equivalent days were *ITZCUINTLI* and *OC*.

TENAHUATILIZTLI
see *OCHPANITZTLI*.

TENOCH, TENOCHCA
see under *TENOCHTITLÁN*.

TENOCHTITLÁN was the México-ica AZTEC capital, built on an island near the west shore of the central

THE MÉXICA *Aztecs built a magnificent city on an island just off shore from the western edge of Lake Texcoco. They carved out first a kingdom within the Basin of Mexico and then beyond, eventually to conquer and exact tribute from a vast empire. (*WOODCUT FROM LETTERS OF HERNÁN CORTÉS TO EMPEROR CHARLES V, 1524.*)*

lake in the Basin of Mexico. The México also called themselves the Tenochca, after the semi-legendary priest and leader Tenoch associated with the founding of the city.

According to legend, the sun and war god *HUITZILOPOCHTLI* led the México from a cave in *AZTLÁN*, a land in the deserts of the northwest, into central Mesoamerica. In their wanderings the México were led by four priests, who carried a great idol of Huitzilopochtli before the people. The god spoke secretly to them through the idol, telling them to call themselves the México-ica, advising them on the best route to take and promising them victory and riches if they honoured him. In the Basin of Mexico, he gave the México the sign of the eagle (his representative) alighting on a *nopal* cactus (prickly pear), clutching a serpent in its claw, on an island in the "Lake of the Moon" (*MEZTLIAPÁN*), to show them where to establish their capital.

The Great Temple-Pyramid that dominated the ceremonial precinct supported the twin temples of Huitzilopochtli and the rain god *TLÁLOC*. From these temples, the priests could survey the entire city and see far across the lakes of the basin in all directions.

THE TEOMAMAQUE (singular "Teomama") were the chosen bearers of the tribal idols during the early

AZTEC migrations from *AZTLÁN* into the Basin of Mexico, one of whom was *CHIMALMAN*. After the Aztecs had settled in the Basin, the title continued to be used for those chosen to carry out this honour symbolically by carrying the idols on their shoulders at state festivals.

TEOTIHUACÁN ("city of the gods") was the largest and most powerful state in central Mesoamerica during the Classic Period, and flourished from the first to the eighth century AD in the Teotihuacán Valley off the northeast of the Basin of Mexico. Later, its dilapidated and overgrown pyramid-platforms were believed by the Aztecs to be the burial mounds of giants and of the gods (see *CREATION MYTHS*). At its apogee it covered more than 20 sq kilometres (8 sq miles) and supported a population of as many as 200,000.

The core of the city was a huge ceremonial precinct, divided into hundreds of smaller compounds and precincts along a ritual avenue more than 2 km (1 mile) long. Aligned north–south, this so-called Avenue of the Dead ran from the Ciudadela compound at the south end to the Pyramid of the Moon at the north. Roughly halfway along, on the east side, stood the Pyramid of the Sun, the largest pyramid-platform in the city, buried beneath which was a sacred cave and spring. Around this religious core, the residential and industrial suburbs stretched in all directions, and beyond these, were the irrigated fields of the farmlands that were needed to support the city's dense population.

The influence of Teotihuacán was spread throughout Mesoamerica, as far south as the MAYA cities of Tikal and Kaminaljuyú and as far north as the northern deserts. Its influence was manifestly artistic and architectural, in particular the spread of the *talud–tablero* profile of an upright plate (*tablero*) cantilevered on a sloping plate

THE VAST CITY *of Teotihuacán dominated much of Mesoamerica economically, and perhaps politically as well, throughout much of the Classic Period. Its ceremonial core alone included an avenue, more than 2 km (1 mile) long, lined with pyramids, temples and palaces.*

(*talud*), used to clad the rubble cores of the pyramid-platforms.

Diplomatic relations were apparently long-standing with the kingdom of the ZAPOTECS at Monte Albán in the Valley of Oaxaca. Each maintained an enclave of its own citizens in the other's city. However, scholars continue to debate the exact nature of their political or military control over the rest of Mesoamerica. What is certain is that the city and its ruler commanded a vast network of trade in manufactured goods and raw materials, for example, jade and other precious stones, obsidian (black volcanic glass), ceramics and *quetzal* feathers.

The reasons for Teotihuacán's collapse are uncertain. There is clear evidence for worsening climatic conditions and for invasions or migrations coming in from the north in the seventh and eighth centuries. Simultaneously, several central Mesoamerican city-states – Cholula, Teotenango, Xochicalco and El Tajín – reasserted regional control. Another factor may have been a decline in relations with the Zapotecs. There was widespread economic implosion, vast population migrations and a rise in city-state rivalry in the ensuing century of the early Postclassic Period.

THE PYRAMID OF THE SUN at Teotihuacán mimics the bulk of the surrounding mountains.

TEOTIHUACANO GODS are

well-documented. A principal temple-pyramid of *TEOTICHUACÁN*, on the west side of the great sunken plaza of the Ciudadela, comprised six diminishing tiers (of which only four now survive) with alternating sculptured images of *QUETZALCÓATL* and *TLÁLOC* around the upright faces (*tablero*) of the tiers. Each outward-facing serpent head – in high relief – is surrounded by a feathered collar, and a scaly serpent body in low relief writhes to the left of each head and ends in a vertebrae-like section representing a rattle. In ancient times the sculptures would have been smoothly plastered, and remnants still retain traces of the brilliant colours with which they were originally painted, with red jaws, white serpent fangs, green *quetzal* plumes on their collars, red, yellow and blue shells around the bodies, and blue side ramps to the central, ceremonial staircase.

Palatial structures in the city testify to the other major deities that were worshipped at Teotihuacán. In the Tepantitla palace murals, a mythical world is depicted, once thought to represent *TLALOCÁN* (the Paradise of Tláloc). It has more recently been interpreted as the world of the *TEOTIHUACÁN SPIDER WOMAN* or Great Goddess, who was the supreme Teotihuacano deity and creator goddess. Other palace murals depict various birds, especially owls, and jaguars and other feline creatures. Stone statuary attests to the worship of *CHALCHIÚTLICUE* ("she of the jade skirt"), and the wealth of incense burners representing the *OLD FIRE GOD* confirms his importance, possibly as the consort of the Spider Woman/Great Goddess. A Sun God and a Moon Goddess, who were otherwise nameless, were also important at Teotihuacán, and the flayed god of springtime, *XIPE*

TOTEC represented the renewal of vegetation during the all-important rainy season.

TLALCHITONATIUH ("land of *TONATIUH*"), the later *NAHUATL* name for the Jaguar or Falling sun, was a major god from the first to the seventh centuries AD, and his cult was disseminated to Kaminaljuyú, Tikal and other Maya cities in the fourth to seventh centuries. At Teotihuacán, near the Plaza of the Pyramid of the Moon, the Jaguar Palace complex might have been the temple of *JAGUAR GOD* worship. The complex is comprised of three chambers on the north, south and west sides of a courtyard and an open platform on the east. A central staircase is flanked by ramps decorated with bas-relief serpents, their rattles at the bases of the ramps. The main chamber contains a mural depicting two "plumed jaguars" wearing fancy feather headdresses and with a row of shells running down each of their backs to the tips of their tails; each is blowing a plumed *Strombus*-shell trumpet (the sound is symbolized by small scrolls) from which fall drops of blood or water. Above the figures is a row of masks representing Tláloc, that alternate with year-sign glyphs. A narrow passage leads from the northwest corner of the courtyard to several more rooms decorated with murals

THE PYRAMID-TEMPLE of Quetzalcóatl and Tláloc at Teotihuacán is decorated with alternating near full-relief sculptures of the plumed serpent and the rain god, both of whom were vital to the wellbeing of the city and its inhabitants.

depicting pairs of human hands clutching feline-like animals caught in a net; scrolls representing their roars issue from their mouths. These murals undoubtedly represent religious symbolism that attached importance to water and/or blood, but we have no idea of the significance, or of the role played by the creatures, or of what ceremonies might have been performed in the rooms.

Another palace complex (also near the Plaza of the Pyramid of the Moon), aptly named the Palace of *QUETZALPAPÁLOTL* ("quetzal butterfly" or "plumed butterfly"), might also have been a place of worship and/or priestly quarters for a cult of that being. The rooms sit beyond a wide staircase entrance, flanked by carved serpent heads. Within a portico, the entrance hall walls are decorated with abstract "half-eyes" and symbols representing rippling water. In an inner patio beyond the hall, stout stone pillars around the open court have bas-reliefs of the mythical "plumed butterfly" and other symbols. Obsidian discs are

still set in some of the symbols, and other semi-precious stones might also have been set into the eyes of the creatures and other symbols. The walls of the patio have the remains of what were once brilliantly painted murals, the most complete of which (the north wall) depicts various geometric designs and what appears to be the cross-section of a huge seashell. Small circles remain around the walls where discs of polished mica were once set into the plaster. Around the roof of this gallery are crenellations carved with the Teotihuacano year-signs. As with the Jaguar Palace, the symbolism in these rooms was important, but its meaning is now lost.

That these palaces had long histories as places of religious importance is indicated by an earlier palace beneath the base platform of the Palace of the Quetzalpapálotl. Called the Palace of the Caracoles Emplumados ("plumed shells"), it was also approached by a staircase, which, in this case, is decorated with green parrots out of whose yellow beaks flow streams of blue water. The façades of this building had bas-reliefs of "plumed seashells", painted various colours, and what appear to be the mouthpieces of musical instruments. Two pilasters are decorated with bas-reliefs of four-petalled flowers, also painted. A narrow tunnel from the west side leads to a small chamber containing an "altar" painted with red circles on a white background.

DEATH & SACRIFICE

MESOAMERICANS LEARNED TO control their environment to some extent through agriculture and city living. Nevertheless, death was ever-present. To the Aztecs and other central Mesoamericans, death in battle (for men), in childbirth (for women) and in human sacrifice were considered particularly honourable. The Maya, in contrast, feared death greatly, even though warfare and conquest were frequent, and the bereaved expressed extreme mourning, weeping silently by day and giving out shrieks of grief during the night. The Aztec underworld was called Mictlán; the Maya equivalent was Mitnal or Xibalba.

Sacrifice – in terms of time given to participating in special ceremonies, as autosacrifice, and as offerings of flowers, animals and humans – was congenital in Mesoamerican culture. Human sacrifice began in the Preclassic Period, but its institutionalization was a Toltec and, in particular, an Aztec speciality. As in the case of death, the Maya and Aztec views on sacrifice differed. For the Maya, the

victim's blood was needed to replenish and ensure the smooth progress of cyclical events, and sacrifice demonstrated obeisance to the deities. To the Aztecs, the sacrifice of humans was necessary on an ever-increasing scale, in order to hold the universe together, and to strengthen the sun for its nightly journey and battle against the forces of darkness. In practice, Aztec human sacrifice also became a means of political coercion and social control.

AUTOSACRIFICE – as penance and as an offering of blood to the deities – was an important method of appeasing the gods and goddesses, and of ensuring the smooth progress of the world. Bloodletting from the ears was common and, for Maya men, a favoured organ was the penis, while for women it was the tongue (above): a worshipper kneels before her lord and ruler, Shield Jaguar, and draws a spiked cord through her tongue. (LINTEL 24, LATE CLASSIC PERIOD YAXCHILÁN.)

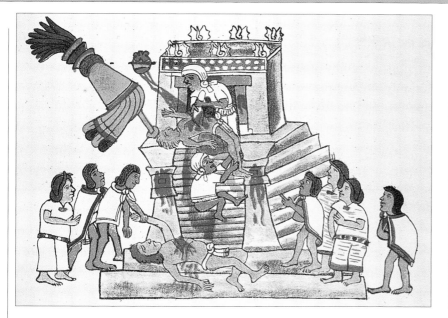

HUMAN SACRIFICE (far left) was a necessity of life to the Aztecs – the victim's life blood fed and sustained the sun god Tonatiuh and thus ensured that their world survived. Such sacrifices were frequently depicted in the codices, as here, in the early post-Spanish conquest Codex Magliabecchiano. At major festivals, the sacrifices were allegedly in the

thousands, according to Spanish chroniclers. Here there seems to be something of an assembly line operating, the victims being thrown down the steps of the pyramid after being dispatched. Parts of the victims might also have been eaten by priests in ritual feasts, and their skulls displayed on the municipal tzompantli (skull rack) (left), here represented as a stone sculpture.

FIRE (right) played an important part in sacrifice, as the ultimate fate of the human hearts torn from victims' bodies – possibly placed and burnt on the abdomens of Chacmools – and as a medium in its own right and for burning incense and tobacco in ritual ceremonies.

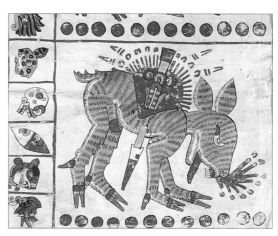

A DEER (above) is sacrificed by killing it with an atl-atl (spear-thrower) dart, depicted in the pre-Spanish conquest Codex Vaticanus B. As well as humans, all manner of animals and plants – and even objects – were sacrificed and/or offered to the gods and goddesses. Quetzalcóatl, as the ruler/hero of Tollán (Tula), went so far as to advocate that sacrifices should be limited to offerings of jade, birds, serpents and butterflies. This policy led to his undoing when his political rivals – supporters of Tezcatlipoca and human sacrifice – defeated and banished him from the city.

THE SHROUD-ENCASED body (above) of a young man, perhaps one who died in battle, has been prepared for cremation and is accompanied by beans and tamales for his journey. Death was not feared by the Aztecs, but was recognized as inevitable, ever-present and often sudden. One's fate after death was unrelated to conduct on earth, although warriors who died in battle and women who died giving birth went straight to eastern and western paradises, respectively. (ILLUSTRATION FROM THE CODEX MAGLIABECCHIANO.)

AUTOSACRIFICE (above) was also used to induce sacred visions. Lady Wak Tun, one of the wives of Prince Yaxun Balam, experiences a serpent vision, rising from an incense burner, presumably after a ritual auto-sacrificial bloodletting. (LINTEL 15, LATE CLASSIC PERIOD, YAXCHILÁN.)

THE TEOTIHUACÁN SPIDER
WOMAN, or Great Goddess of the Classic Period, whose ancient name we do not know, is thought to have been the supreme Teotihuacano deity, and to have been the creator of the present universe.

She is depicted in the murals of the palatial residence of Tepantitla, 500 m (545 yds) to the east of the Pyramid of the Sun and its ceremonial precinct. The most famous of the murals of Tepantitla was long thought to depict Tlalocán, the "Paradise of the rain god" *TLÁLOC*, and to include the dominating figure of Tláloc himself. More recently, however, careful examination of the figure's details has revealed that it is almost certainly female, and that its mouth has the fangs and palps of a spider; hence its revised attribution.

The place depicted in the murals appears, therefore, to be the setting of the Teotihuacano origin myth. It includes a sacred mountain with springs gushing forth at its base, and might well have been inspired by the looming presence of Cerro Gordo, which dominates the horizon to the north of the ancient city. Around the figure of the Spider Woman, human figures – who are tiny in comparison to the

THE TEOTIHUACÁN SPIDER WOMAN, or Great Goddess, was the city's supreme deity and creator goddess, depicted both on palatial murals and in stone, as carved blocks that fit together to make up her image. (DRAWING AFTER KARL TAUBE)

goddess – engage in a happy, frolicsome scene: they dance, sing (speech scrolls come from their mouths) and play games amid the butterflies and flowering trees.

Spider Woman dominated the Teotihuacano pantheon and ruled in her own world; she might well have been the precursor to Aztec *TOCI*, "our grandmother", and her consort was probably the *OLD FIRE GOD*, also evident at *TEOTIHUACÁN*.

TEOTLECO see *PACHTONTLI*.

TEOYAOMIQUI, or Huahuantli, was a god specific to the *AZTECS*, honoured by warriors as the patron and protector of those who died in the *XOCHIYAÓYOTL* ("Flowery War"), initiated specifically to capture victims for sacrifice to the war god *HUITZILOPOCHTLI*. In some calendar representations Teoyaomiqui replaced *MICTLANTECUHTLI* as the sixth of the 13 *LORDS OF THE DAY*.

TEPEÍLHUITL see *HUEYPACHTLI*.

TEPEU ("conqueror"), despite his central Mesoamerican name, was a creator god of the Quiché *MAYA* of the highlands of Guatemala. The Quiché sacred text, the *POPUL VUH*, describes how Tepeu and *GUCUMATZ* created the earth and all living things on it, but were only able to create satisfactory humans after many failed attempts (see *CREATION MYTHS*).

Interestingly, the Tepeu were also one of the tribes of *TOLTEC* origin from northwest of Mesoamerica. In the Postclassic Period they emigrated across north-central Mesoamerica and then down the Gulf Coast. From there they moved into the Guatemalan highlands, where they are known as the Yaqui-Tepeu – who were the ancestors of the Quiché Maya. This accumulation of connections in the word "Tepeu" – a creator god with a *NAHUATL* name meaning "conqueror" as companion to Maya Gucumatz (himself the equivalent of the "feathered serpent" *KUKUL-KÁN*), and a Toltec tribe as the ancestor of the Quiché Maya – gives further tantalizing clues to the legendary events in ancient Tollán (Tula) and the journeys of the Toltec hero *CE ÁCATL TOPILTZIN QUETZALCÓATL* (or Yucatecan Maya

Kukulkán). (For further information, see *MIXCÓATL, QUETZALCÓATL* and *TAMOANCHÁN*.)

TEPEYOLOHTLI ("heart of the mountain") was a fundamental and primitive central Mesoamerican earth deity: the *JAGUAR GOD* who inhabited the interior of the earth. He might have been the successor to the *OLMEC* jaguar cult. He was one of the many manifestations of *TEZCATLIPOCA* and was eighth of the nine *LORDS OF THE NIGHT*. His calendrical glyph was 8 *OCÉLOTL* (the jaguar) and he was patron of *CALLI* ("house"), the third day of the Aztec 20-day month.

THE TEPICTOTON, the little *TLÁLOCS*, were the gods of the mountain rains. They dwelt in recesses in the mountain and were perceived as dwarfs by the *AZTECS*.

TEPOPOCHTLI see *TÓXCATL*.

TEPOZTÉCATL was the patron deity of ancient Tepoztlán, a *TLAL-HUICA* and later *AZTEC* town in the present-day Mexican state of Morelos. He is identified as a moon god through his calendrical name, *OMETOCHTLI* ("2 rabbit"; ancient central Mesoamericans saw a rabbit in the moon, rather than a man), and as a *PULQUE* god and god of drunkenness through association with *PATÉCATL*.

His shrine – Tepozteco – stood on a clifftop overlooking the town. Begun by the *TLALHUICA* in about 1250, a small pyramid-platform and other structures were built on an artificially levelled space on the summit. After the Aztec ruler Ahuitzotl had conquered the town in the late 15th century, the shrine was rebuilt as a three-tiered pyramid-platform that supported a two-chambered temple, the back and side walls of which were lined with carved stone benches. The carvings include a glyph to Ahuitzotl, "ten rabbit", and it was probably at this time that the

TEPOZTÉCATL was the patron deity and culture hero who relieved the city of Tepoztlán from the burden of sacrificial tribute to Xochicalco. (ILLUSTRATION FROM THE CODEX MAGLIABECCHIANO.)

shrine was dedicated (or perhaps rededicated) to the honour of Ometochtli-Tepoztécatl.

As the moon god, and god of darkness, Tepoztécatl was often portrayed with a crescent-moon nose, and with half his face painted red and the other half painted black. It was believed that he helped to bring the earth out of its winter hibernation and assisted in the spring rebirth, and for this reason he was worshipped, with much revelry and consumption of *pulque*, in an autumn festival in which the seeds of his work were planted symbolically.

Tepoztécatl was also a Tlalhuica culture hero. In legend he delivered them from the onus of providing the ancient city of Xochicalco – west of Tepoztlán – with an annual sacrificial victim. The victim had to be an old man, who was to be eaten by a dragon – the Pyramid of the Plumed Serpents at Xochicalco, one of the principal pyramid-platforms, has a main panel around which are carved eight writhing feathered serpents. The young Tepoztécatl, disguising himself as an old woodcutter, volunteered himself as that year's sacrificial offering and, when the dragon appeared, he slew it, thus ending the dreadful tribute. (Rivalry between the various city-states was a common feature of Mesoamerican history, especially in the Postclassic Period, and it is conceivable that this tale contains a kernel of truth relating to a war or battle in which Tepoztlán defeated Xochicalco and threw off its domination.) (See also *TWINS & CULTURE HEROES*)

TETEOINNAN ("mother of the gods") was a central Mesoamerican earth-mother concept, more primitive than, but certainly related to, *CIHUACÓATL, COATLÍCUE, TLAZOL-TÉOTL* and *TOCI*. The earth-mother cult was particularly strong in the late Postclassic Period, especially in the Gulf Coast cultures and among the *CHINAMPA*-dwellers who lived on the "floating islands" (really artificially-created rectangular fields built out from the shores of lakes) in the Basin of Mexico. Teteoinnan was worshipped at the feast of *OCHPANITZTLI*.

TEXCOCO, which was a city on the eastern shore of Lake Texcoco in the central Basin of Mexico, was a joint foundation of the *CHICHIMECS* of Tenayuca and the Acolhua *AZTECS*. Its mid-15th-century king, called *NEZAHUALCÓYOTL*, joined with the México Aztec king, Moctezuma I Ilhuicamena, to form the Triple Alliance with the cities of *TENOCHTITLÁN* and Tlacopán against the states of Tlaxcala and Huexotzingo east and southeast of the Basin. Although the México were soon feeling less in need of the alliance, Texcoco remained powerful and autonomous, and the rulers of the city co-operated with the Aztec emperors in major construction projects, such as building bridges to link the island of Tenochtitlán with the mainland, an aqueduct to bring fresh water to the island and the extension of the *CHINAMPA* style of agriculture from the lake shores.

TEYOLLOCUALOYÁN was the name used by the *AZTECS* for their own universe. (See *CREATION & THE UNIVERSE*)

TETEOINNAN, "mother of the gods" and primeval earth-mother, was especially honoured by rural people and the chinampa-dwellers around the lakes of the Basin of Mexico.

TEZCATLIPOCA ("smoking mirror") was one of the major deities of the Postclassic Period. His worship was prominent among the *TOLTECS* from the 10th century AD onwards, and the México *AZTECS*, in their reverence for everything Toltec, adopted him and gave him his Nahuatl name. He was a special god in the city of *TEXCOCO*, in the Basin of Mexico across the lake from the Aztec island capital *TENOCHTITLÁN*, and was probably also important to the México for that reason. He was the tenth of the 13 *LORDS OF THE DAY*, and central Mesoamericans honoured him, especially the México, in the month *TÓXCATL*, the sixth of the 18 months of the solar year.

His brothers in the Aztec pantheon were *HUITZILOPOCHTLI*, *QUETZALCÓATL* and *XIPE TOTEC*. Like Quetzalcóatl, Tezcatlipoca was a child of *OMETEOTL* and played a prominent role in the *CREATION MYTHS*: he ruled the world of the First Sun until he was defeated by Quetzalcóatl, who caused the giants who inhabited that world to be eaten by jaguars. Later, however, the two brothers co-operated in the creation of the Fifth Sun when, as serpents, they defeated and dismembered the great Earth Monster *TLALTECUHTLI* and used the body parts to create the earth and the heavens. The perpetual tension between Tezcatlipoca and Quetzalcóatl is also reflected in the quasi-historical legend of *CE ÁCATL TOPILTZIN QUETZALCÓATL*, for it was the followers of Tezcatlipoca who defeated Ce Ácatl Topiltzin and the followers of Quetzalcóatl, and exiled them from the Toltec capital Tollán (Tula).

Tezcatlipoca was portrayed with a polished black obsidian mirror in place of his left foot, which had been ripped off in his mythological battle with the Earth Monster. Another accoutrement was often a turquoise serpent. His alter ego (or *NAHUAL*) was the *OCÉLOTL* (see *JAGUAR GODS*), the night beast who

TEZCATLIPOCA, the "smoking mirror" creator god. This mosaic-decorated skull, which possibly represents him, is covered with tiny chips of polished black lignite and bright blue turquoise. The eye sockets are filled with large, shining orbs of impenetrable black iron pyrite ringed in brilliant white shell – staring, all-seeing, all-knowing. (SKULL FROM THE BRITISH MUSEUM.)

fought a daily battle against the sun. He was also associated with the cardinal points and colours – for each direction his colours and affiliations changed: for the north he was Black Tezcatlipoca, the "smoking mirror", god of Texcoco and of the day *ÁCATL* ("reed"); as the south he was Blue Tezcatlipoca, who was the "hummingbird sorcerer", god of Tenochtitlán and associated with the sun and war god Huitzilopochtli; as the east he was blood Red Tezcatlipoca, the "flayed one" as the god *XIPE TOTEC*, god of the *TLAXCALTECANS*, and associated also with *CAMAXTLI* and with *MIXCÓATL*, and ruler of the day *CUAUHTLI* ("eagle"); and finally, as

the west he was White Tezcatlipoca, or the "plumed serpent" Quetzalcóatl, who was the god of Cholula, as well as of education and the priesthood.

Tezcatlipoca was thus a creator god of many forms and aspects. Some authorities regard all other creator gods and goddesses in the Aztec creation myths as manifestations of his omniscience and omnipotence, and the Aztecs certainly called him by more names and gave him more manifestations than any other deity. He was conceived of as invisible, ever-present and lord of the shadows, wielding his magic mirror to see into, and manipulate, the lives of humans. He was capricious in nature, and was capable of dispensing evil and misery or valour and good fortune with equal unpredictability.

He was the god of conflict and, because of this association, he was – along with Huitzilopochtli – a special god to warriors. One of his many names was *YÁOTL* ("enemy" in Nahuatl) and he was patron of

the *telpochcalli* ("houses of war", that is, military training colleges). As *Yáotl-ÉHECATL* ("night wind") he was associated with warfare, death and the realm of darkness, and it was believed that he could appear at crossroads during the night to challenge warriors – surely an evil omen. He was sometimes also referred to as *MEZTLI* ("moon") and, in jaguar imagery, he was *TEPEYOLOHTLI*, the jaguar at the heart of the mountain of the earth.

His Nahuatl name represented simultaneously the penetration of the mirror and the cloud-like haze of smoke. He was seen as "black" Tezcatlipoca – *CHALCHIUHTECÓLOTL* ("precious owl") or *CHALCHIUHTOTOLIN* ("precious turkey") – the god of night and mystery, the representative of evil, destruction and death, but he could just as easily wreak revenge on one's behalf as bring personal misery. He was also *ITZTLACOLIUHQUI* – the god of ice and cold, sin and misery. He was the patron of the Toltec and Aztec nobility – as *OMÁCATL* he presided over banquets and feasting – but, at the same time, was the patron of sorcerers, thieves and those generally up to no good. In keeping with his malevolent nature, Tezcatlipoca is credited with the corruption of his virtuous brother Quetzalcóatl – by intoxicating him and inducing him to seduce his own sister – and with abducting *XOCHIQUETZAL*, the first wife of *TLÁLOC*. These malevolent aspects were summed up best in one of his many alternative names: *Yáotl*. He was the "adversary", and his "justice" was inescapable; an epithet applied to his worshippers – *titlacauan* ("we are his slaves") – was not unjustified. (See also *CREATION & THE UNIVERSE, DEATH & SACRIFICE*)

TEZCATZONTÉCATL was one of the many Mesoamerican *PULQUE* gods and one of the *CENTZÓNTOTOCHTIN*. His image might have been represented by the numerous *CHACMOOL* figures found both in

TEZCATZONTÉCATL was one of the Centzóntotochtin – the pulque gods of drinking and drunkenness. (ILLUSTRATION FROM THE CODEX VATICANUS B.)

central Mesoamerican and MAYA cities. For related deities, see MAYÁHUEL and PATÉCATL.

TEZCOCO see *TEXCOCO*.

TIANQUIZTLI (the Pleiades) see under *TOXIUHMOLPILIA*.

TIHUIME was the TARASCAN god of death and of the underworld. His AZTEC counterpart was called *MICTLANTECUHTLI*.

TÍTITL ("shrunken" or "wrinkled") was the last of the 18 months in the AZTEC solar year. It occurred during the winter solstice (by this time of the year, any stored corn/maize ears would indeed be dry), and the principal ritual was in honour of the ancient moon goddess *ILAMATECUHTLI*.

TITLACAUAN ("we are his slaves"); see *TEZCALIPOCA*.

TLACALILIZTLI, a special sacrifice of war captives to ensure a good harvest, was a widespread Mesoamerican practice, and was the highlight of the AZTEC ceremonies of OCHPANITZTLI honouring the corn (maize) goddess CHICOMECÓATL and the old earth mother

TETEOINNAN. The victims were bound, spread-eagled, on an upright wooden frame as a target, and shot with arrows. The custom was also practised by the MAYA, as depicted in graffiti on Temple II at the Guatemalan site of Tikal. For a related ritual, see *TLAHUAHUANALIZTLI*.

TLACATZINACANTLI see *BAT-GOD*.

TLACAXIPEHUALIZTLI ("flaying of men") was the third (or, in some sources, second) of the 18 months in the AZTEC solar year, occurring in spring. Ancient fertility rites were observed, possibly of HUASTEC origin, in which the spring god XIPE TOTEC was propitiated with sacrificial victims who were slain and then flayed. Priests donned the bloody skins and performed frenzied dances wearing them. (These ceremonies were completed in the next month – see *TOZOZTONTLI*.) The bravest of the prisoner victims was honoured with death by the TLAHUAHUANALIZTLI. It was also known as *Coaílhuitl* ("snake festival"), presumably in recognition of the snake's shedding of its skin.

TLACOQUECHOLLI see *QUECHOLLI*.

TLAELQUANI ("eater of excrement") was the manifestation of the goddess *TLAZOLTÉOTL* as the

source of, and force behind, all manner of "unclean" behaviour; she was also associated with witchcraft and the purging of sin. The literal meaning of her NAHUATL name expresses her association with confession and purification, and she acted as a delegate for the penitent to the god *TEZCATLIPOCA*. She was often portrayed with a blackened mouth to symbolize this unpleasant but unavoidable duty.

She was especially associated with the darker side of sex and, in this capacity, was the patroness of a special corps of military prostitutes: young girls recruited, as an obligation, from among the ordinary citizenry of the AZTEC capital TENOCHTITLÁN, whose purpose was allegedly to sustain the fanaticism of Aztec warriors. They were maintained in special quarters where they worshipped Tlaelquani, and groups of them were periodically brought to the military barracks for a "festival" of licentiousness, at the culmination of which they were ceremonially sacrificed.

TLAHUAHUANALIZTLI was the height of the ceremonies at the feast of *TLACAXIPEHUALIZTLI* in honour of the god of springtime, *XIPE TOTEC*. In addition to other human sacrifices, those war captives judged to have been the most valorous in avoiding capture were sacrificed in a special "gladiatorial"

contest. However, since the object was to honour the god by offering him human blood as a symbol and supplication for a good future harvest, the outcome of the combat was hardly in doubt. The captive, bound in order to restrict his movements, stood atop a large circular stone platform known as a *temalacatl* (for example, the "Stone of Tizoc" in the Museo Nacional de Antropología, Mexico City might have been one such platform, used in TENOCHTITLÁN.) Upon this, he was forced to defend himself against the onslaughts of successive Eagle and Jaguar "knights" of the Aztec warrior cult, armed with the dreaded *macuauhuitl*, a flat-sided hardwood war sword that had edges of long, razor-sharp blades made of obsidian (volcanic glass). The victim's *macuauhuitl*, however, had had its obsidian blades removed and replaced by somewhat less effective cotton tufts or feathers. The contest appears to have been of ZAPOTEC origin, from the Oaxaca or Guerrero region. (For details of a related ritual, see *TLACALILIZTLI*; see *WARRIOR CULTS* for more information about the Jaguar and Eagle "knights".)

TÍTITL was the month during which a feast was celebrated at the winter solstice, at which the dead and the moon goddess Ilamatecuhtli were honoured. (ILLUSTRATION FROM THE CODEX MAGLIABECCHIANO.)

TWINS & CULTURE HEROES

MANY CITIES IN ANCIENT Mesoamerica had special patron deities and, for some, it is difficult to separate the god from a legendary hero of the same name who benefited the city in some way. The stories in the highland Quiché Maya sacred book *Popul Vuh* of the twins Hun Hunahpú and Vucub Hunahpú, and of the hero twins Hunahpú and Xbalanqué, and of their journeys and conflicts with the underworld lords and involvement with creation, are just two examples of culture heroes who provided an exemplar to Maya rulers in their relations with the gods. Other heroes, who provided inspiration or who embodied tribal and legendary history and claims to lineage, might have been the end product of conflated histories that originally included several rulers or heroes.

Such might have been the case with Mixcóatl, the Toltec founder of Culhúa, and with his son Ce Ácatl Topiltzin and the man-god Quetzalcóatl/Kukulkán, founder of Tollán (Tula) and of Chichén Itzá. The México Aztecs deliberately sought marriage alliance with the Culhúa, accepted rule by a Culhúa prince in order to secure their claim to Toltec ancestry and lineage, and subsequently rewrote Toltec history to suit and support their claim. In another example, to the Tlalhuica Aztecs of the Valley of Morelos, south of the Basin of Mexico, the god/hero Tepoztécatl delivered the people of Tepoztlán from the dominance of the city of Xochicalco.

THE HERO TWINS *Hunahpú (above) and Xbalanqué of the Quiché Maya sacred text, the Popul Vuh, who played the ball game for their lives, were perhaps the most well-known heroes of ancient Maya Mesoamerica. Maya vases and other ceramic vessels depicted a wealth of such figures. (CLASSIC PERIOD POLYCHROME VASE FROM HIGHLAND GUATEMALA, POSSIBLY SHOWING HUNAHPÚ.)*

THE MOST CELEBRATED hero of both central and southern Mesoamerica, and of both Toltec-Aztec and Maya civilizations, was the legendary leader and god Quetzalcóatl/Kukulkán. His politically and religiously charged peregrinations led him to found two cities, and the prophesy of his triumphant return, seized upon by Hernán Cortés, made inevitable the downfall of the Aztec Empire. At the two cities that he allegedly established – Tollán (ancient Tula) (top left and top right) and Chichén Itzá (above and right) – there are pyramid-temples dedicated to his honour, and nearly identical palatial structures.

A PRINCIPAL structure at Xochicalco is the Pyramid of the Plumed Serpents (left), whose bodies coil around the base of the pyramid-platform. According to local legend, the town of Tepoztlán was obliged to offer an annual sacrificial victim – an old man – to its rival Xochicalco, to be devoured by the latter's dragon. Tepoztécatl disguised himself as an old woodcutter and, presenting himself as the sacrificial victim, slew the dragon, thus ending the tribute. The story is possibly a long folk memory and metaphor for a time when Xochicalco dominated Tepoztlán but was eventually defeated and its domination overthrown.

TLAHUIZCALPANTECUHTLI,

a manifestation of *QUETZALCÓATL* and of *XÓLOTL*, was the twin deity of the planet Venus, as both morning and evening "star": as the former, he was Quetzalcóatl; as the latter, he was Xólotl, the twin brother. As the morning star he was Lord of the Dawn, 12th of the 13 *LORDS OF THE DAY*. The dual nature of the Venus "star" was represented in the codices as a living man (the morning) and as a skull (the evening).

The movements of Venus were of considerable importance in the Mesoamerican calendar and religion. Not only were its movements calculated and monitored with great accuracy in day-to-day life through the seasons of the year, but the grand coincidence of the Venusian and other celestial cycles was also of supreme importance in the "Calendar Round" (that is, the commencement, on exactly the same named day and month, of several calendrical cycles: the Venusian orbit of 584 days, the solar year of 365.25 days, the shorter day-and-month cycle of 260 days, and two 52-year ritual cycles). The eve of the day of this coincidence was felt to be a time of apprehension, fear and foreboding by the Aztecs; it was a period of evil and of immense potential for menace and destruction. Consequently great sacrifices, offerings and strict adherence to ritual were required at these times (see *TOXIUHMOLPILIA*).

In the Aztec *CREATION MYTH* Tlahuizcalpantecuhtli was ultimately responsible for setting the sun and the moon into motion. The two bodies had ascended into the sky as the spirits of *NANAHUATZIN* and *TECUCIZTÉCATL*, but they remained motionless. Nanahuatzin (the sun) demanded blood sacrifice (see also *TONATIUH*) and, for such arrogance, Tlahuizcalpantecuhtli hurled a dart at him with his *atl-atl*. It missed its mark, and he received in return a dart through the head, transforming him into stone – the god of coldness, *ITZTLACOLIUHQUI*. The gods and goddesses concluded that only their own sacrifice would persuade the sun and moon to move, so Tlahuizcalpantecuhtli (as Quetzalcóatl) cut out their hearts one by one with an obsidian knife. (See also *ORDERING THE WORLD, COLOURS & THE CARDINAL DIRECTIONS*)

TLAHUIZCALPANTECUHTLI, Venus, whose cycle ruled the social orders throughout the year, is depicted here attacking a Jaguar Warrior, piercing his heart with a dart thrown from an atl-atl (spearthrower). (ILLUSTRATION FROM THE CODEX COSPI.)

TLALCHITONATIUH ("land,

or place, of *TONATIUH* – the sun") was a later *NAHUATL* name for an early Mesoamerican deity worshipped at the ancient city of *TEOTIHUACÁN*. He was the Jaguar sun or Falling sun and, as such, became the special deity to the later *TOLTEC, MAYA*-Toltec and *AZTEC* Jaguar and Eagle *WARRIORS CULTS*.

A major god at Teotihuacán during the first to the seventh centuries AD, his cult was disseminated into the highlands of Guatemala – where the art and architecture of the Maya highland site of Kaminaljuyú shows strong Teotihuacano influence in the fourth to seventh centuries AD – and into other Maya cities in the Yucatán.

At Teotihuacán itself, the Jaguar god might have been worshipped in the Palace of the Jaguars, one of several palaces around the Plaza of the Pyramid of the Moon.

The Jaguar Palace complex comprises three chambers on the north, south and west around a central courtyard, and an open platform on the east. The central staircase has flanking ramps decorated with bas-relief serpents, their rattles at the bases of the ramps. The main chamber is decorated with a mural depicting two "plumed jaguars" – they wear fancy feather headdresses – with rows of shells running down their backs to the tips of their tails. Each is shown blowing on a plumed *Strombus*-shell trumpet – the sound of which is symbolized by small scrolls that issue from the shells. Drops of blood or water also fall from the shells. Above the figures is a row of masks representing *TLÁLOC*, alternating with year-sign glyphs. A narrow passage, leading from the northwest corner of the courtyard, enters several more rooms, in which there are further murals. These depict pairs of human hands, clutching feline-like animals caught in a net, with scrolls representing their roars issuing from the animals' mouths.

These murals undoubtedly represent religious symbolism. Apart from the obvious importance of water and/or blood, however, and of the surreal beasts, we have no idea of their significance, of the role played by the creatures, or of what ceremonies might have been performed in the rooms.

THE TLALHUICA were one

of the original seven *AZTEC* tribes from the legendary caves of *CHICOMOZTOC*. These people migrated from northwestern Mesoamerica, in the 12th century AD, into the Valley of Morelos south of the Basin of Mexico. There, they established a loose confederation of city-states based around Cuernavaca. They were eventually conquered by the México Aztecs in the latter's 15th-century expansions, and the ceremonial centre of Teopanzolco was built in Cuernavaca. The city became a favourite vacation retreat for Aztec rulers.

TLALCHITONATIUH, who was the patron god of the Aztec Eagle and Jaguar Warrior cults, presides over the initiation of Eagle Warriors. (CARVING ON A STONE PANEL OF THE SOUTH BALL COURT AT THE GULF COAST SITE OF EL TAJÍN.)

TLÁLOC (*tlalli* "earth", *oc* "something on the surface") was the *AZTEC* name for one of the most ancient and fundamental of Mesoamerican gods, a giver of life and a source of destruction, but, first and foremost, the god of rain. Images of him were made from at least the second or third century AD at *TEOTIHUACÁN*, and he is probably descended from the more "primitive" Olmec *GOD IV*. He is directly equivalent to Maya *CHAC*, Mixtec *DZAHUI*, Totonac *TAJÍN* and Zapotec *COCIJO*, and possibly also to Tarascan *CHUPITHIRIPEME*.

In the Aztec capital of *TENOCHTITLÁN*, Tláloc was given equal status with the exclusively Aztec god *HUITZILOPOCHTLI*. Their twin temples stood atop the Templo Mayor pyramid-platform, with a magnificent double staircase leading up to them – Tláloc's plastered and painted in brilliant blue (representing water) and white, and Huitzilopochtli's plastered and painted blood red, for war. The priests of both gods were afforded equal rank in Aztec society.

Associations with other deities include his sister-consort *CHALCHIÚHTLICUE* – alongside whom he governed Tlaloque (literally, the Tlálocs), his two wives *XOCHIQUETZAL* (abducted by *TEZCATLIPOCA*) and *MATLALCUEITL*, as well as the plumed serpent *QUETZALCÓATL*. Tláloc was the ruler of the seventh day, *MÁZATL* ("deer"), and his calendrical name was *9 OCÉLOTL* ("9 jaguar") in the 365-day calendar cycle; he was eighth of the 13 *LORDS OF THE DAY* and ninth of the nine *LORDS OF THE NIGHT*. He ruled over the Third Sun of the Aztec *CREATION MYTH*.

Tláloc was associated with all forms of precipitation and their related events and conditions: rain, hail, ice, snow, clouds, floods, drought, thunder and lightning. Presumably on account of these attributes, he was also associated with mountains (for example, on the appropriately named volcanic

TLÁLOC, god of rain and agriculture, was an ancient and fundamental Mesoamerican deity (his carved head alternates with that of Quetzalcóatl on the Pyramid of Quetzalcóatl at Teotihuacán) and he appears frequently in the codices, as here, with bespectacled eye. (ILLUSTRATION FROM THE CODEX MAGLIABECCHIANO.)

peak of Tláloc, southeast of Mexico City, the ruins of a long pair of walls mark a processional way approaching the artificially flattened summit, where there are two quadrangular structures, a courtyard and various other mounds). He was also frequently depicted with serpents, as at Teotihuacán, where his sculpted images alternate with those of Quetzalcóatl on the tiers of the Pyramid or Temple of Quetzalcóatl.

He was most spectacularly portrayed with rings or "spectacles" around his eyes, and with fangs, and often also with a volute across his mouth; at Teotihuacán and other sites, his importance to agriculture is shown by a symbolic corn- (maize-) cob-shaped mouth. Elsewhere he was represented in free-standing sculptures, and he was also depicted in pre-Spanish-

conquest and post-conquest codices. His Maya counterpart, Chac, was depicted singly and repeatedly in stacks of heads at Copán and Chichén Itzá and elsewhere in the Petén and Puuc regions of Yucatán.

In ritual, Tláloc presided over numerous other fertility gods and goddesses, and was celebrated in regular rites. Frequent human sacrifices were offered to him and to these associated deities, symbolically bringing together the blood and the water of human existence. Less violently, corn ears and stalks were kept and venerated in households and were used as decoration by warriors. Particular rituals and festivities were held in Tláloc's honour in the months of *ATLCAHUALO* and *TOZOZTONTLI*, at which time children were sacrificed on mountain tops; if the child cried it was considered a good sign, as the tears were a symbol of rain and moisture in a dry land.

Tláloc received victims of death by drowning, lightning and contagious diseases, including leprosy, into an earthly paradise called Tlalocán. In keeping with his more benevolent side, this "Place of Tláloc", was believed to be a garden of abundance and pleasure and, instead of being cremated (the normal death rite), such victims were buried with a piece of dry wood, which was believed to sprout abundantly with leaves and blossom in Tlalocán. (For an alternative interpretation, see *TEOTIHUACÁN SPIDER WOMAN*.) Tláloc's importance to agriculture and climate were further represented in his fourfold conception as the four world colours and cardinal directions. He was believed to keep four great clay jars, one for each earthly direction: from the jar for the east he dispensed life-giving rains to fertilize the soil, and from the other jars he poured forth death-dealing drought, frost and disease. (See also *CREATION & THE UNIVERSE*)

THE MASSIVE carved block of the rain god Tláloc (or of his female counterpart or sister – the water goddess Chalchiúhtlicue) stands in front of the Museo Nacional de Antropología, Mexico City.

TLALOCÁN, the mythical paradise of the rain god *TLÁLOC*.

THE TLÁLOCS, the gods of the four directional winds and cardinal points (two of whom were *NAPPATECUHTLI* and *OPOCHTLI*), were the dispensers of sustenance to humankind. At the beginning of time they had played a crucial role in bringing corn (maize) and other edible plants to humankind (see *TONACATÉPETL*) and continued to do so in the cycle of the seasons.

The *TEPICTOTON*, another manifestation, were the "little Tlálocs", gods of mountain rains.

TLALOQUE see *TLÁLOCS*.

TLALTECUHTLI ("earth lord") was one of the many central Mesoamerican deities to have dual gender (see *OMETEOTL*). Although perceived as having both male and female aspects, Tlaltecuhtli was usually referred to as female. She was the Earth Monster, portrayed as a huge, fat, toad-like beast possessing a wide mouth with two great protruding fangs, and feet armed with sharp claws. The Yucatecan *MAYA* pantheon included a similar earth beast, and the monster-toad image was frequently merged with another earth monster in the form of a colossal crocodile, whose wide, ridged back formed the world's mountain ranges. She was also the second of the 13 *LORDS OF THE DAY*.

Tlaltecuhtli swallowed the sun every evening as it set and regurgitated it in the morning at sunrise. She was said to consume the hearts of sacrificial victims and was therefore frequently carved on the undersides of the stone boxes called *cuauhxicalli* (literally "eagle house" or "eagle box") in which the heart and blood of the victims were placed after being torn from their opened chest cavities.

In the creation – or more correctly the re-creation – of the earth, it was Tlaltecuhtli who provided

TLALTECUHTLI, the fat toad-monster and foundation of the earth, is suitably placed to support the base of a Totonac pyramid-platform. (POSTCLASSIC PERIOD GULF COAST TOTONAC SITE OF EL TAJÍN.)

the raw materials. The process began when *QUETZALCÓATL* and *TEZCATLIPOCA* descended from their abode in the sky to see Tlaltecuhtli astride the world ocean. She greeted them ferociously and craved flesh to eat; not only were her jaws equipped with fangs, but her elbows, knees and other joints also had gnashing mouths. The appalled Quetzalcóatl and Tezcatlipoca concluded that the new world of the Fifth Sun could not possibly exist while such a monster survived, so they plotted to destroy her. Transforming themselves into two great serpents, one seized her by the right hand and left foot while the other seized her by the left hand and right foot and, in the ensuing struggle, they eventually succeeded in ripping her asunder – but not before she had torn Tezcatlipoca's left foot off his leg. The upper portion of her body became the earth and the remaining portions were thrown into the sky to create the heavens.

The other gods were not pleased with such summary action, however, and, in order to console the spirit of the dismembered earth

monster, they decreed that all the plants of the earth that are essential to the well-being of humans must arise from the parts of her body. Thus, her hair became the trees, flowers and herbs, while her skin provided the materials for the grasses and smaller flowers. Her eyes were transformed into sources for springs, wells and caves, while her mouth was the source of large caverns and the great rivers. Her nose was transformed into the mountains and valleys.

Mesoamericans declared that the sounds of the earth were sometimes the screams of Tlaltecuhtli in her death throes, or alternatively the sounds of her demands for human flesh and blood. Only the sacrifice of humans could quell her anger and ensure that the earth would continue to provide its sources of human sustenance; so, as with the demands of *HUITZILOPOCHTLI* and *TONATIUH*, the *AZTECS* were provided with more reasons to pursue their wars of conquest (see *XOCHIYAÓYOTL*).

TLALTÍCPAC ("earth"), in the tripartite *AZTEC* universe, represented the here and now, the visible, tangible present, the surface of the earth. It stood in juxtaposition to *TOPÁN* – "that which was above" – and to *MICTLÁN* – "that which was below".

TLAMIQUECHOLLI see *QUECHOLLI*.

TLAUIXCALPANTECUHTLI see *TLAHUIZCALPANTECUHTLI*.

THE TLAXCALTECA, also sometimes called the Teochichimeca, were one of the original seven *AZTEC* tribes from the legendary caves of *CHICOMOZTOC*. They migrated from northwestern Mesoamerica in the 12th century AD and eventually settled in the eastern Basin of Mexico, in Alcoluacán. Their patron deity was the god *MIXCÓATL-CAMAXTLI*.

In the 14th century they were driven to the south by the Tepanec, Culhua and México Aztecs, some migrating to Chalco and others over the eastern rim of the Basin into Tlaxcallán, the area of the present-day state of Tlaxcala. The México continued to attack them but never succeeded in conquering them and incorporating them into their empire. When the Spaniards arrived, the Tlaxcalteca eagerly joined them in their attack on the Aztec Empire.

TLAXOCHIMACO see *MICCAILHUITONTLI*.

TLAZOLTÉOTL, a central Mesoamerican earth goddess related to *CIHUACÓATL* and *COATLÍCUE*, was the goddess of desire and carnal love, and therefore of fertility. Her *NAHUATL* name translates literally as "goddess of filth", and in that sense she represented the consequences of lust and licentiousness, and, by extension, the purification and curing associated with diseases of sexual excess; in this aspect she had the alternative name of *TLAEL-QUANI*, which literally means "eater of excrement". She was patroness of the day *OCÉLOTL*, the 14th of the 20 days, was the fifth of the 13 *LORDS OF THE DAY*, and seventh of the nine *LORDS OF THE NIGHT*. She was also sometimes associated with the more primitive earth goddess *TOCI*. Other manifestations or associations for Tlazoltéotl were with *IXCUINAN* and *HUIXTOCÍHUATL* and, in certain aspects, her *MAYA* counterpart was *IX CHEL*.

Tlazoltéotl was portrayed in the codices with a band of raw cotton and with two spindles or bobbins decorating her headdress. Sometimes, like the god *XIPE TOTEC*, she would wear the flayed skin of a human sacrificial victim, possibly to represent new birth from the womb. She was worshipped during the festival of *OCHPANITZTLI* along with *CHICOMECÓATL* (goddess of corn/maize) and *TETEOINNAN* (the old earth goddess).

Her ultimate origin was *HUA-STEC*, and she appeared in the *AZTEC* pantheon after their conquest of the northern Gulf Coast.

TLOQUE NAHUAQUE ("lord of everywhere"), an abstract concept, was a deity advocated by the *TEXCOCAN* king *NEZAHUALCÓYOTL* ("Fasting Coyote"). He/she was a representation of infinity ("he – or it – without beginning or end"), and the unknowable. In spirit he/she was genderless, a creator deity and the supreme force of the cosmos. He/she was invisible and, although worshipped like other gods and goddesses, there were no idol images of him/her in the temples.

Such an over-theoretical deity was far ahead of its time compared to the rest of the Mesoamerican pantheon, and Tloque Nahuaque was the closest approach ever made to monotheism in Mesoamerica (see also *COQUI XEE*, *HUNAB KU* and *OMETEOTL*). In deference to his people's feelings and beliefs, Nezahualcóyotl was careful not to neglect the conventional gods and goddesses. Acceptance and veneration of Tloque Nahuaque was not widespread, nor did it survive long after the king's death.

TOCHTLI ("rabbit") was the eighth of the 20 *AZTEC* day-names and one of the year-bearing days – there were 13 *Tochtli* years in a 52-year cycle (see also *ÁCATL*, *CALLI* and *TÉCPATL*). It had a favourable augury and its patron deity was *MAYÁHUEL*, associated with the moon and fertility; its orientation was south. The *MAYA* and *ZAPOTEC* equivalents were *LAMAT* and *LAPA*.

Calendrical dates and deity associations included: *1 Tochtli*, for Mayáhuel as goddess of *PULQUE*; *2 Tochtli*, for *OMETOCHTLI* ("two rabbits"); *7 Tochtli*, for the earth goddess *COATLÍCUE*; and *400 Tochtli*, for the *pulque* gods in general (see *CENTZÓNTOTOCHTIN*).

TOCI, "our grandmother", was an ancient earth goddess. It is possible that she was originally a goddess of the *HUASTECS*. A major *AZTEC* deity, she was closely associated with *TETEOINNAN* ("mother of the gods") and was sometimes called *Tlallilyollo* ("heart of the earth"). She was worshipped at the harvest festival of *OCHPANITZTLI*.

As an earth goddess Toci was the patroness of midwives and curers, and was also closely associated with the Mesoamerican sweat bath (*temescal*; see also *QUILAZTLI*). She was also clearly related to *TLAZOL-TÉOTL-TLAELQUANI*, and was often depicted with black facial markings and a cotton-spool headdress similar in appearance to those worn by these goddesses.

Toci was also associated with war. According to Aztec legend, when they were offered a daughter of the ruler of Culhuacán in a marriage alliance, the Aztecs sacrificed the unfortunate girl to their war god *HUITZILOPOCHTLI*, and flayed her as Toci. As a result of this act they incurred the wrath of the Culhua, who banished them to the marshes of the western lake shores.

TOHIL was a major deity of the highland Quiché *MAYA* of Guatemala, who was described in the sacred *POPUL VUH* text as the god who guided the Quiché during their migrations through Mesoamerica to the highlands. He made great demands for blood sacrifice of his people, and the Quiché obliged him by sacrificing some of their own as well as war captives. Tohil's principal temple was situated at Utatlán, the Quiché capital city.

TOLLÁN
see *TOLTECS*.

TLAZOLTÉOTL ("goddess of filth") or Tlaelquani ("eater of excrement"), originally a Huastec deity, was the goddess of sexual desire, excess and sin – the consequence of overindulgent lust.

(ILLUSTRATION FROM *CODEX VATICANUS B.*)

TONACATECUHTLI or Ometecuhtli, seen here as the male part of duality – Ometeotl. A remote concept, he dwelt with his female counterpart Omecíhuatl in Omeyocán, the highest of the13 heavenly levels. (ILLUSTRATION FROM CODEX VATICANUS B.)

THE TOLTECS were a mingled group of *CHICHIMECA* tribes from the northwest of Mesoamerica who migrated into central Mesoamerica and ultimately into the Yucatán Peninsula in the ninth and tenth centuries AD. Their culture became a combination of more ancient *TEOTIHUACANO* (and other central Mesoamerican city-states), Gulf Coast and *MAYA* elements, mixed with distinctive Toltec elements.

According to *AZTEC* legend, the Toltec dynasty was founded by their heroic leader *CE TÉCPATL MIX-CÓATL* ("One Flint Cloud Serpent"), who led his people from somewhere in northwest Mesoamerica into the Basin of Mexico, where they established the city of Culhuacán. He married a local Nahua woman and, shortly after his murder by a rival political faction his son, the future king *CE ÁCATL TOPILTZIN* ("One Reed Sacrificer"), was born. Although the mother died in childbirth, Ce Ácatl Topiltzin was raised in exile to avenge his father, which he did upon coming of age.

As leader of the Toltecs, Ce Ácatl Topiltzin led them out of the Basin of Mexico to found a new capital to the northwest at Tollán (Tula). Again, according to legend, renewed political rivalry developed between factions supporting the peaceful plumed-serpent god *QUET-ZALCÓATL* and the war advocate *TEZCATLIPOCA*. Renamed as Ce Ácatl Topiltzin Quetzalcóatl, the king was driven into exile and led his followers east to the Gulf Coast, and, according to *MAYA* legend, became *KUKULKÁN*, the heroic founder of Chichén Itzá.

Toltec religion included most of the major central Mesoamerican gods and goddesses, and was centred on human sacrifice to honour and appease the deities. Their war-like tendencies were greatly revered and emulated by the Aztecs, who clearly altered the histories to establish a dynastic relationship with the Toltecs. The Aztecs, as well as many other central Mesoamerican peoples, regarded the Toltecs as the inventors of almost all civilized things, from writing, art and medicine to metallurgy.

Archaeological evidence at Tollán and Chichén Itzá bears out an astonishingly close relationship between the architecture of the two sites, but also reveals much longer sequences of settlement and development at both sites than the legendary histories would indicate. Nevertheless, the connections between the two cities and the peregrinations of the Tolteca-Chichimeca and their leaders seem to have some basis in fact. The very name Tollán, meaning "place of the rushes", was also applied by Mesoamericans to Teotihuacán and to the Aztec capital *TENOCHTITLÁN*; and the Quiché Maya sacred *POPUL VUH* text recounts the story of journey from their highland Guatemalan kingdom, east to "Tulan", by which it seems they actually meant Chichén Itzá (whose ancient name, Uucil Abnal, means "Seven Bushy Place"). (See also *THE RITUAL BALL GAME*)

TONACACÍHUATL

see *OMECÍHUATL*.

TONACATECUHTLI

see under *OMETECUHTLI*.

TONACATÉPETL

("sustenance mountain") was where, in the *CREATION MYTH*, corn (maize) and other grains were stored. According to the *ANALES DE CUAUHTITLÁN*, after the creation of the Fifth Sun and of humans, the gods realized that they needed to supply the new race with sustenance. They therefore set about searching for a source of food for humans, and it was *QUETZALCÓATL* who espied a red ant running along the ground carrying a grain of corn. He asked the ant, *AZCATL*, where such a wonderful food was to be found, but the ant at first refused to tell. After much threatening, however, Azcatl agreed to show Quetzalcóatl the source, and led him to Mount Tonacatépetl. Quetzalcóatl changed himself into a black ant and followed Azcatl through a narrow entrance and deep into the mountain, to a chamber filled with not only corn, but also with many other seeds and grains. Quetzalcóatl took some of the corn kernels back to *TAMOANCHÁN*, where the gods chewed the corn and fed some of the resulting mash (*maza*) to the infant humans, whereupon they gained in strength and grew.

The gods then asked, "What is to be done with Tonacatépetl?" Quetzalcóatl tried to sling a rope around the entire mountain and haul it to a more convenient place on earth, but it proved too heavy even for him to move. So, rather than try to move the mountain, with its grains and seeds, to humankind, it was decided to scatter the grains and seeds from the mountain. The old diviners *OXOMOCO* and *CIPACTONAL* cast lots to determine how to do this, and the signs told them that the weak and diseased god *NANAHUATZIN* should break Tonacatépetl open. To do so he called upon the help of the four *TLÁLOCS*, the directional gods of the winds and the rains, and, crucially, of lightning. Tonacatépetl was duly split asunder, and the black, blue, red and white (or yellow) winds blew the grains and seeds across the land, while the rains watered them so that they grew where they fell. Humans were quick to take advantage of these renewable sources of food.

The Aztecs sometimes identified Iztaccíhuatl, a lofty volcanic cone on the southeastern rim of the Basin of Mexico, as Tonacatépetl.

TONALAMATL

a Mexican *Book of the Days*, was a ritual calendrical text written to record a *Tonalpohualli* or cycle of 260 named days and months. The text and pictures, known as a codex, were painted on deerskin or bark paper and folded as a screen-fold. For the elements of the *Tonalamatl* and *Tonalpohualli*, see the feature spread *ORDERING THE WORLD*, and *LORDS OF THE DAY* and *LORDS OF THE NIGHT*.

THE TONALTEUCTIN were the 13 Aztec *LORDS OF THE DAY*.

TONANTZIN ("little mother") was the *AZTEC* name for the benevolent manifestation of the goddess *CIHUACÓATL* in her role as earth goddess and mother of humankind (see *CREATION MYTHS*). In Aztec *TENOCHTITLÁN* a temple dedicated to Tonantzin stood on the site of the present-day Basilica of Tepeyac in Mexico City, the church that contains the shrine of the Virgin of Guadelupe, patron saint of Mexico.

TONATIUH, the central Mesoamerican sun god, was manifested as *Cuauhtlehuánitl* ("ascending eagle") and as *Cuauhtémoc* ("descending eagle"). His counterpart was *YOHUALTECUHTLI* (or *Yohualtonatiuh*), meaning the "night sun". Especially for the México *AZTECS*, he was associated with the god of

war, *HUITZILOPOCHTLI*, as the young warrior. In another manifestation he was *PILTZINTECUHTLI*, the youthful Tonatiuh and third of the nine *LORDS OF THE NIGHT*. His Zapotec equivalent was *COPIJCHA*.

Tonatiuh, the life-giving sun, was the present, the Fifth Sun of central Mesoamerican creation. He ruled the day *QUIÁHUITL* ("rain") and was fourth of the 13 *LORDS OF THE DAY*. Through his heat and thirst for human blood he gave strength and courage to warriors. It was to him – as well as to *TLALTECUHTLI* and to Huitzilopochtli – that frequent human sacrifice, carried to extremes by the México Aztecs, was required, and to whom the hearts and blood of the victims were offered. Daily he battled against the dark and was swallowed by the Earth Monster Tlaltecuhtli. Daily he accepted the spirits of slain warriors and escorted them across the sky to his paradise.

Tonatiuh himself was born as a result of the personal sacrifices of the gods: first *NANAHUATZIN*, who heroically leapt into the ceremonial fire and rose again as the sun – at first stationary – at the meeting of

the gods and goddesses at *TEOTIHUACÁN*; then the other gods and goddesses, who appeased Tonatiuh's demands for sacrificial blood by allowing *QUETZALCÓATL-TLAHUIZCALPANTECUHTLI* to cut out their hearts and create *Nahui Ollin* (literally "four movement"), the sun of motion (see *CREATION MYTHS*).

The huge, intricately carved stone popularly known as the "calendar stone", discovered at the site of the Templo Mayor (Great Temple) in Mexico City (*TENOCHTITLÁN*) in 1790, is believed by some scholars to represent Tonatiuh. Others hold that the central image represents his counterpart, the night sun Yohualtecuhtli or Yohualtonatiuh. Whichever aspect is portrayed, the symbolism of the sun and the cosmic forces of Mesoamerican mythology are manifest. The sculpted face of the stone is made up of a centre and series of ring-panels. In the centre is the sun, carved as a stylized human face. From his mouth protrudes the sacrificial knife and, in the first ring, to right and left of the face, two rounded arms form claws clutching human hearts. Some scholars have

suggested that the stone was used flat, as a sacrificial platform upon which to stretch victims.

The remaining concentric ring-panels are filled with hieroglyphic signs. The first ring, framing the face, is the predicted date (*Nahui Ollin*) of the end of the Fifth Sun. The dates of the preceding suns – Jaguar, Wind, Rain (of Fire) and Water – are carved in boxes to upper left and right, and lower left and right, of the face. The second ring contains glyphs of the 20 *NAHUATL* day-names. Starting at top left, reading anti-clockwise, these are: *CIPACTLI* ("crocodile"), *ÉHECATL* ("wind"), *CALLI* ("house"), *CUETZPALLIN* ("lizard"), *CÓATL* ("serpent"), *MIQUIZTLI* ("death"), *MÁZATL* ("deer"), *TOCHTLI* ("rabbit"), *ATL* ("water"), *ITZCUINTLI* ("dog"), *OZOMATLI* ("monkey"), *MALINALLI* ("grass"), *ÁCATL* ("reed"), *OCÉLOTL* ("jaguar"), *CUAUHTLI* ("eagle"), *COZCACUAUHTLI* ("vulture"), *OLLIN* ("movement", or "earthquake"), *TÉCPATL* ("flint knife"), *QUIÁHUITL* ("rain") and *XÓCHITL* ("flower"). Next, a narrow ring has repetitive, decorative designs, and the final ring contains repeated symbols of turquoise and jade, the colours of the heavens, and symbols of the equinoxes and solstices. The outer border comprises two *XIUHCÓATL* (turquoise or fire snakes) that symbolize cosmic order, cyclicity and the present world. Their heads, adorned with appropriately elaborate headdresses, meet at the base, and at the top their tails flank a boxed glyph of the ritual date "13 Reed" – AD 1011, the "official" date of the start of the Fifth Sun. (*See ORDERING THE WORLD*)

TONATIUH "ascending eagle", the Aztec sun god and ruler of the Fifth Sun. On his back is the symbol for ollin (earthquake), which the Aztecs believed would destroy the world of the Fifth Sun. His image also occupies the central part of the great "calendar stone" (see ORDERING THE WORLD and DUALITY & OPPOSITION).

TOPÁN ("that which is above us") was part of the *AZTEC* tripartite universe, comprising *TLALTÍCPAC*, *MICTLÁN* and Topán. Topán included the skies and the heavens – the dwelling place of the gods and goddesses.

THE TOTONACS were a people of Postclassic Mesoamerica who inhabited the area of the present-day Mexican states of northern Puebla and northern and central Veracruz. The powerful early Post-classic Period city-state of El Tajín might have been their early capital but, by the 16th century, it was at Cempoala, more than 150 km (93 miles) to the south. They spoke a language belonging to the Macro-Mayan group.

Cempoala was among the first cities visited by the Spaniards and the Totonac were the first allies to Hernán Cortés in his campaign against the *AZTECS*.

TÓXCATL ("dry thing") was the sixth (or, in some sources, the fifth) of the 18 months in the *AZTEC* solar year, during which special ceremonies were held to honour *TEZCATLIPOCA* ("smoking mirror"). Preparations for the ceremony began a year in advance, when a young warrior, captured in battle, was chosen to impersonate the god Tezcatlipoca. For a year Aztec priests taught him how to conduct himself at court as a noble. He was given his own entourage to attend to his needs, including four chosen maidens who were themselves impersonating the goddesses *ATLA-TONAN, HUIXTOCÍHUATL, XILONEN* and *XOCHIQUETZAL*. He was taught to play the clay flutes and allowed to stroll the streets of *TENOCH-TITLÁN* carrying a bouquet of flowers and smoking tobacco from a gilded reed pipe.

At the beginning of *Tóxcatl* his dress was changed for that of a warrior captain and he was symbolically married to the four goddesses. On the ceremonial day

he was praised by the king and nobles as a great man, and honoured with bouquets of flowers and ritual dances. Then, on the appointed day, he was taken with his wives and court by royal canoe to a small temple on the lake shore, where all but a few attendants abandoned him. He walked towards the temple playing his clay flutes and, as he mounted the temple steps, broke a flute on each step. At the top, where the priests awaited him, he was spread across the sacrificial stone, a priest holding each limb, while a fifth cut open his chest with an obsidian knife and extracted his heart. This month is also called *Tepopochtli* ("hill of little moisture").

The "Battle of Tóxcatl" or "Massacre of Tóxcatl" occurred in Tenochtitlán in 1520. Hernán Cortés had been welcomed somewhat reluctantly into the city by Moctezuma II Xocoyotzin, but had returned to the coast to confront an expedition, led by Pánfilo de Narváez from Cuba, that had been sent to arrest him. He left his lieutenant, Pedro de Alvarado, in command. As this was the month of *Tóxcatl*, the Aztecs proceeded

with the festival. The Spaniards, uneasy at the noise and activities around their quarters, interpreted – or used as an excuse – the enthusiasm and exuberance of the gathered crowds of Aztecs as a threat, and impetuously attacked the ceremony as idolatry. According to Spanish chronicles, more than 8,500 unarmed Aztecs were slain in the ensuing fight.

TOXIUHMOLPILIA ("the tying of the years"), also referred to as the New Fire Ceremony or Sacred Fire Ceremony, was the intense and auspicious ceremony of the renewal and/or securing of the continuance of the present sun. It was the eve of the end of one 52-year calendrical cycle and the beginning of the next, a time of mixed fear and hope: unless the sun could be induced to rise again the next day, and the new fire could be rekindled, the end of the world was nigh.

All temple and household fires were extinguished and the idols of the gods in the temples were doused with water. Household effigies, cooking pots and implements, and the three traditional household hearth stones were discarded.

AT THE END of a successful Toxiuhmol-pilia *or "New Fire Ceremony", priests lit torches for runners to carry the renewed fire – and hope – to temples and households in* Tenochtitlán. (*CODEX BORBONICUS.*)

Houses, courtyards and streets were swept free of debris. As darkness approached, people climbed onto rooftops and walls. Pregnant women and children covered their faces with *maguey*-leaf masks for protection against the demons of darkness; some sources state that women and children were confined indoors, and that pregnant women were hidden in huge corn (maize) storage jars. Children were kept awake for fear that if they were permitted to fall asleep they would be transformed into mice as a result of failing to witness the critical rite.

Priests, dressed as gods, climbed Mount Uixachtecatl (Uixachtlán) or Citlaltepec (the Cerro de la Estrella in the Mexico City precinct of Ixtapalapa) near the ceremonial centre of *TENOCHTITLÁN*, the *AZTEC* capital. At midnight, when the Pleiades (*Tianquiztli*) passed through the zenith and the star *YOHUALTECUHTLI* appeared in the centre of the sky, a selected captive

V

– no doubt intoxicated and feeling especially honoured – was sacrificed by opening his chest with a ceremonial obsidian knife and extracting his still-pulsating heart. In his opened chest cavity, a fire was kindled, and, if lit successfully, the cry went up – doubtless accompanied by huge relief and release from the tension of the moment – and runners with torches were despatched to dispense the new flame throughout the land in relays. Autosacrifice by ear-piercing and blood-letting was offered by all as penance and, as dawn broke, general rejoicing followed, including the renewal of discarded articles, the rekindling of the household hearths and temple fires, and even the start of new building projects.

If the fire in the sacrificial victim's chest should have failed to light, it was believed that darkness would engulf the earth, and that celestial monsters – the *TZITZIMIME* – would descent to devour it and all humankind.

TOZOZTONTLI ("short watch") was the fourth (or, in some sources, the third) of the 18 months in the *AZTEC* solar year, in which various rain, water and corn (maize) deities were propitiated, especially *TLÁLOC* (to whom flowers were offered) and *CHALCHIÚHTLICUE*, and *CENTÉOTL* and *CHICOMECÓATL*. Also in this month, the "flayed skin" ritual (see *TLACAXIPEHUALIZTLI*) was completed when the skins of human sacrificial victims were deposited in the "cave" Temple of *XIPE TOTEC* by alms-begging priests. It is also called *Xochimanalo* ("offering of flowers").

TYING OF THE YEARS see *TOXIUHMOLPILIA*.

TZAHUI see *DZAHUI*.

THE TZITZIMIME ("demons of darkness") were the stars visible only during a solar eclipse (see also *ITZPAPÁLOTL*). Naturally, to a

people to whom the sun god *TONATIUH* was a principal and life-giving god, they were seen as harbingers of dread and evil. According to the Aztec *CREATION MYTH*, one day the Tzitzimime would descend to the earth and devour humankind, thus ending the (present) age of the Fifth Sun. Ever-present and always threatening, although unseen, they engaged in a daily battle against the sun at sunrise and sunset.

TZITZIMITL, the *AZTEC* "grandmother" goddess in the sky, was the jealous guardian of the beautiful young virgin *MAYÁHUEL*, who became goddess of the *maguey* plant. She pursued Mayáhuel and the wind god *ÉHECATL*, who had abducted Mayáhuel down to the earth, and, finding the two lovers already united as the entwined branches of a tree, split the tree in two in her rage. This destroyed the branch representing Mayáhuel, the shreds of which Tzitzimitl fed to her demon servants, the *TZITZIMIME*. Éhecatl, however, was unharmed, and he resumed his former shape, gathered Mayáhuel's bones and planted them in a field, where they grew into plants. These were the *maguey* or *agave* (*Agave americana*), from which the white "wine", known as *PULQUE*, is made.

TZOMPANTLI, the skull rack, was a framework supporting poles for displaying the skulls of sacrificial victims – the skulls were aligned along poles inserted through holes drilled in their sides. Stone blocks were also carved in facsimile of these racks.

UAYEB GOD, a *MAYA* deity of misgivings and mishaps, was associated with the five ill-omened days (the *uayeb*) at the end of the solar calendar year (see *NEMONTEMI*). The Uayeb god was portrayed as an old man and also as the small atlante figures, made of stone, that supported stone shelves, plinths and benches, and he was associated with the *BACABS* and with the *PAUAHTUN*. His symbols included, of course, the number five, and he can be identified by a snail or turtle shell on his back. He was also a god of the underworld.

UEUECÓYOTL see *HUEHUECÓYOTL*.

UIXACHTECATL, or Uixachtlán, was one of the *AZTEC* names for Cerro de la Estrella in the Mexico City precinct of Ixtapalapa, near to the ceremonial centre of *TENOCH-TITLÁN*, and the venue for the *TOXIUHMOLPILIA*, "the tying of the years", ceremony.

THE SKULLS of sacrificial victims were stacked on tzompantli (skull racks) in rows, and also represented on huge block stone sculptures – as seen here at Tenochtitlán/Mexico City.

UIXACHTLÁN see *UIXACHTECATL*.

UIXTOXÍHUATL see *HUIXTOCIHUATL*.

THE VEINTANAS were the 18 annual 20th-day feasts and religious ceremonies held over the course of the Mesoamerican 365-day solar year. Every eight years, an extra set of rituals known as the *Atamalcualiztli* was held, and every 52 years the New Fire Ceremony – *TOXIUHMOLPILIA* – was celebrated. Within the 260-day calendar cycle – *Tonalpohualli* (see under *TONALAMATL*) – were still more ceremonies. These were the "movable ceremonies", so called because they did not occur at the same time each year but changed their dates according to the seasons. (See also the feature *ORDERING THE WORLD*, and the individual entries for each month)

VUCUB CAME ("seven death"), was one of the leaders of the Lords of *XIBALBA*, the Quiché *MAYA* underworld (see *HUN CAME*).

X

VUCUB HUNAHPÚ ("seven Hunahpú") was one of the first-born of the human race – born of the "grandfather" *XPIYACOC* and of the "grandmother" *XMUCANÉ* – and the twin brother of *HUN HUNAHPÚ*.

VUCUB-CAQUIZ was a bird-monster in the Maya *POPOL VUH*. At the creation of the world he proclaimed himself both the sun and the moon. Along with his evil giant sons *ZIPACNÁ* and *CABRACÁN*, he was slain by darts from the blowguns of the hero twins *HUNAHPÚ* and *XBALANQUÉ* in *XIBALBA*.

WARRIOR CULTS were an important feature of *AZTEC* society. The Eagle (sun) and Jaguar (earth) "knights" were two Aztec military orders or cults, though they had originated, or had first been formally organized, by the *TOLTECS*, whose military prowess was legendary, and revered by the Aztecs. Members of the orders were selected, high-ranking members of society. Eagle and Jaguar warriors worshipped the rising sun – *TONATIUH* – and the setting sun – *TLALCHITONATIUH*, respectively. Members of each cult dressed in appropriate costumes of feathered helmet and/or shirt, or jaguar skin. The rites of each mystical order involved special knowledge and initiation procedures, in which, according to the 16th-century chronicler Diego Muñoz Camargo, an aspirant was confined in the temple for 30–40 days to practise fasting and autosacrifice. One privilege was the right to take part in the gladiatorial sacrifice of princely war captives, called the *TLAHUAHUANALIZTLI*.

WORLD TREE was a concept closely allied to the Mesoamerican recognition of the terrestrial cardinal directions and the perceived directions of the Mesoamerican universe, together with assignments of colours, birds, animals, trees, types, day- and year-signs,

EAGLE AND JAGUAR warriors, once chosen for membership, underwent elaborate initiation ceremonies. These were usually held in special temple complexes, often in remote mountain-top locations. One of the most intact of these is the cult site of Malinalco on a cliff top near Tenancingo, northwest of Cuernavaca in the State of Mexico. Steps carved out of the living rock lead up to the main temple, inside which the floor is sculpted with a central eagle, and a jaguar is carved on the bench that runs around the room.

and auguries to the cardinal directions. The *MAYA* assigned particular day-names as "year-bearers" whereas the *AZTECS* assigned particular deities as "sky-bearers", and in both cultures these were linked to the cardinal directions.

In Aztec myth, *TEZCATLIPOCA* and *QUETZALCÓATL* transformed themselves into trees to support the sky (see *CREATION MYTHS*).

The Maya world tree, *Yaxché* or *Kapok*, was the *Ceibe*. *Yaxché* itself signifies "first" or "green" tree, both terms being appropriate: first in terms of a cosmic centre and green as the Maya colour associated with a central place. The great world tree was perceived to link the parts or levels of the universe, with its roots anchored in the underworld, its trunk linking the earth to underworld and heavens, and its

branches spreading into the sky. A similar image prevailed among the cultures of central Mesoamerica, and similar association with the underworld, the earth and the sky are described in several Aztec codices. Throughout Mesoamerica, the world tree was regarded as the central, or fifth, direction, and of equal, if not greater, importance than north, east, south and west.

XAMEN EK, or Ah Chicum Ek, *MAYA* God C, was the god of the North Star (*xamen* means "north"). He was often associated in the codices with *EK CHUAH*, the "black star" or "black warrior". He was portrayed with a distinctive snub-nose and black markings on his head, and is thus frequently associated with, or identified as, the *MONKEY-FACED GOD*; as such, he ruled the Maya day *CHUEN* ("monkey"). His glyph resembles the head of a monkey, and signifies "north". He was a benevolent deity, often depicted alongside *CHAC*.

As the North Star he was the patron and guide of merchants, whose long-distance trading networks were of such importance to Maya civilization (see also *THE OLD BLACK GOD*). In the latitudes of the Yucatán and Petén regions of Maya culture, the North Star is the star that holds its position throughout the year. Xamen Ek's intercession and goodwill were invoked by prayers and offerings of *pom* incense (the resin from the *copal* tree) at special roadside altars. His *AZTEC* counterpart was *YACATECUHTLI*.

XAQUIJA, the Valley *ZAPOTEC* sun god, was an alternative name for *COPIJCHA*.

XARATANGA, the *TARASCAN* moon goddess, was the daughter of *CURICAUERI* and *CUERAUÁPERI*. She was the goddess of the new moon, and of germination, fertility, growth and sustenance. An ancient goddess of agriculture, her cult was centred on the island of Jarácuaro in Lake Pátzcuaro. Her mother, Curicaueri, was the goddess of the old moon.

XBALANQUÉ was one of the hero twins of the Quiché *MAYA* of Guatemala. The sacred *POPUL VUH* text describes how he and his twin brother *HUNAHPÚ* were conceived by the spittle of their father, *HUN HUNAHPÚ*, and how they journeyed to the underworld to avenge the deaths of their father and uncle. (See also *TWINS & CULTURE HEROES*)

XIBALBA, derived from the root word *xib* (meaning "fear, terror, trembling with fright"), was the Quiché *MAYA* underworld (the Lowland Maya and *AZTEC* equivalents were *MITNAL* and *MICTLÁN*). In the sacred *POPUL VUH*, Xibalba was the scene of the adventures of the twin brothers *HUN HUNAHPÚ* and *VUCUB HUNAHPÚ*, who are defeated by the Lords of Xibalba, and then of the revenge taken by the hero twins *HUNAHPÚ* and *XBALANQUÉ*, who succeeded in defeating the lords.

Xibalba had many different levels or worlds within it, including the House of Gloom, the House of Knives, the House of Cold, the House of Jaguars, the House of Fire and the House of Bats. In the last of these, *Zotzihá*, the hero twins faced and passed a series of tests, and Hunahpú was temporarily beheaded by the bat-god *CAMA ZOTZ*. (See also *TWINS & CULTURE HEROES*)

XÍHUTL was the Nahuatl term for the 18 months of 20 days each (that is, 360 days) of the *AZTEC* solar calendar. The remaining five days were called the *NEMONTEMI*.

XIPE TOTEC, the "flayed god" of spring, was probably of Olmec origin. Priests performed ritual dances in his honour wearing the flayed skins of sacrificial victims to symbolize renewal.

XILOMANALIZTLI

see *ATLCAHUALO*.

XILONEN,

an adolescent goddess, was a central Mesoamerican fertility deity, the goddess of young corn (maize) – both the plant and the cob. As such, she was closely related to the fertility goddess *CHICOMECÓATL* and in some ways a manifestation of the latter, or a continuity within the concept of fertility. Together with *CENTÉOTL* and *ILAMATECUHTLI* she formed part of the cycle from young and tender corn, through mature and ripe corn, to the old and withered plant. Xilonen was served by a special cult of young virgins in the *AZTEC* capital, *TENOCHTITLÁN*.

Xilonen was one of four Aztec goddesses – with *ATLATONAN*, *HUIXTOCÍHUATL* and *XOCHIQUETZAL* – who were impersonated by virgins and who were wed for a year to a chosen young warrior, impersonating *TEZCATLIPOCA*, until his sacrifice at the festival of *TÓXCATL*.

XIPE TOTEC

("flayed one") was the central Mesoamerican god of springtime, an agricultural deity and patron of seeds and of planting. He was the Red *TEZCATLIPOCA* and was associated with the east cardinal direction. He was patron of *CUAUHTLI* ("eagle"), the 15th of the 20 *AZTEC* day-names, and was represented by the date *1 OCÉLOTL*. His three brothers in the Aztec pantheon were *HUITZILOPOCHTLI*, *QUETZALCÓATL* and *TEZCATLIPOCA*.

Xipe Totec seems to have been of southern highland Mesoamerican origin, possibly ultimately derived from the ancient *OLMEC GOD VI*, or possibly among the *YOPE* of the southern highlands of Guerrero. He was especially honoured by the *TLAXCALTECANS*, and was also honoured by the *ZAPOTECS* and *MIXTECS* of the southern highlands and by the *TARASCAN* state. He was introduced to, and taken up by, only in Late Postclassic times, a few of the *MAYA* city-states, where his imagery appeared in the cities of Oxkintok, Chichén Itzá and Mayapán. Perhaps because of the long tradition of superb craftsmanship – especially metalwork – in the southern highlands of Oaxaca–Guerrero, he was also the patron god of metalsmiths and lapidaries.

He was a god closely associated with torture, and demanded a heavy toll in human sacrifice for his services in giving each year's crops a good prognosis. In the spring festival of *TLACAXIPEHUALIZTLI*, in the third month of the 365-day solar year, ceremonies to supplicate his favour were held in which sacrificial victims were flayed (skinned) and priests then donned the skins to performed a dance (see also *TLAZOLTÉOTL*); the victims were war captives from the *XOCHIYAÓYOTL*, and the purpose was to evoke ancient fertility rites. The "bravest" captive was selected for the honour of being slain in the one-sided "gladiatorial sacrifice" called the *TLAHUAHUANALIZTLI*.

Statuary and masks of Xipe Totec are easily recognizable by their puffy appearance, with double lips and sunken eyes showing a priest in the hideous stretched skin of a victim; on full-body representations the skin is tied with string at the back. The act of donning the sacrificial victim's flayed skin symbolized the regeneration of plant life – the skin was regarded as analogous to the seed husk of the living plant – and flaying the sacrificed victim was considered a re-enactment of the plant's own yearly self-sacrifice of shedding its skin in the act of renewal. The victim's sacrifice was an act of penitential torture, a spiritual liberation, for in the Mesoamerican mindset, death by sacrifice was widely regarded as an honourable death, on a par with death in battle.

Through this association with death, Xipe Totec was linked with the underworld, *MICTLÁN*, and, by extension, it was he who sent dreadful illnesses to humankind, such as smallpox, the plague, skin diseases, scabs and blindness.

XIUHATLATL

("turquoise spear-thrower") was the weapon and sign of office of the *OLD FIRE GOD* and related deities, such as *HUITZILOPOCHTLI*.

XIUHCÓATL

("turquoise serpent") was the coil of fire, the counterpart of *XIUHTECUHTLI*. In contrast to the benevolent serpent god, *QUETZALCÓATL*, Xiuhcóatl represented the power of fire and the dangerous forces of aridity and drought. In *AZTEC* mythology, the turquoise serpent carried the sun from its rise in the east to its zenith at noon, and, indeed, two such serpents are found encircling the great Aztec "calendar stone" discovered at *TENOCHTITLÁN* in 1790 (see *TONATIUH* and *ORDERING THE WORLD*). Turquoise serpents were also seen as an accoutrement of the deities *HUITZILOPOCHTLI* and *TEZCATLIPOCA*.

In their form as an "endless" circle, huge stone sculptures of Xiuhcóatl formed a wall (*coatepantli*) or boundary around the sacred precinct of Tenochtitlán. A continuous row of them also forms the base of three sides of the great pyramid-platform of the Tenayuca, a city north of Tenochtitlán; and beside the north and south sides, two great coiled serpents are depicted sitting on platforms.

XIUHCÓATL, the fire serpent, could be represented in several forms: such as an endless ring of two serpents around the "calendar stone" of Tonatiuh, or as a double-headed turquoise serpent, as here.

XIUHPILTONTLI, literally "turquoise shield", was the general *NAHUATL* word for the sun.

XIUHTECUHTLI, or *HUE-HUETÉOTL*, was the *AZTEC* name for the primitive Mesoamerican deity, the "Old One" and *OLD FIRE GOD*, who possibly originated in the Preclassic Period cultures of the Basin of Mexico and among the *OLMECS* of the Gulf Coast as *GOD I*. Among the *OTOMÍ* he was called *OTONTE-CUHTLI* and Xócotl. He was usually depicted as an old man, with wrinkled skin and toothless mouth, supporting a brazier on his head for burning incense. Patron of the day *ATL* ("water") and first of the nine Aztec *LORDS OF THE NIGHT* and of the 13 *LORDS OF THE DAY*, he was associated with the number three, symbolic of the three hearthstones of the tradi- tional

XIUHTECUHTLI, the "Old One" and the centre of the universe, was portrayed as an old man with a toothless mouth. His flattened head supported a ritual brazier.

Mesoamerican household. His counterpart was *XIUHCÓATL*, the serpent of fire.

He was perceived as the great, ancient pillar of the world. His fire ran through the entire universe, beginning in *MICTLÁN* ("that which is below us") to *TOPÁN* ("that which is above us"), via the realm of the serpent goddess *COATLÍCUE* and the home fires of all the peoples of the earth. It was Xiuhtecuhtli who presided over the New Fire Ceremony (the *TOXIUHMOLPILIA*), when all household fires had to be extinguished and kindled anew, and who assisted the spirits of the dead in being absorbed into the earth. (See also *COLOURS & THE CARDINAL DIRECTIONS*)

XMUCANÉ was the highland Quiché *MAYA* creator goddess in the *POPUL VUH*, wife of *XPIYACOC* and the "grandmother" of the human race. Her sons were the twins *HUN HUNAHPÚ* and *VUCUB HUNAHPÚ*. Her Aztec equivalent was the goddess *OXOMOCO*.

THE XMULZENCAB were the *MAYA* bee gods of the *CREATION MYTH* in the sacred text of the *CHILAM BALAM*. Each was assigned to a cardinal direction and associated with a specific colour. A deity depicted in the murals at the fortified site of Tulum, on the east-

XOCHIPILLI, the Aztec "flower prince", was a youthful, benign god of pleasure and representative of summer. He is portrayed here bedecked with flowers, singing and accompanying himself with rattles (now lost).

ern coastal cliffs of Yucatán, and designated "the descending god", is interpreted by some scholars as a representation of a Xmulzencab. (See also *AH MUCEN CAB* and *THE BACABS*)

XÓCHILHUITL see *IZCALLI*.

XOCHIMANALO see *TOZOZTONTLI*.

XOCHIPILLI ("flower prince") was a benevolent central Mesoamerican deity. As the god of flowers and souls, and the symbol of summer, he was the benign and amiable manifestation of the young sun god *PILTZINTECUHTLI* – the youthful representation of *TONA-TIUH*, and the third of the nine *LORDS OF THE NIGHT*. He was closely associated, as well, with *CENTÉOTL* and, in the guise of Centéotl-Xochipilli ("corn-flower prince"), was seventh *LORD OF THE DAY*. He was the flayed flower god of souls, the red-faced personification of the spirit. Thus, penitence to Centéotl-Xochipilli was thought to ensure a regular supply of corn (maize). *AHUIATÉOTL*, the *AZTEC* god of voluptuousness, was another of his manifestations.

With his brothers *IXTLILTON* and *MACUILXÓCHITL*, Xochipilli formed a triumvirate of general good health, pleasure and wellbeing. He represented masculine fecundity and youth in terms of general gaiety, frolicking, playful mischievousness and even poetry. Little wonder, then, that he ruled the day *OZOMATLI* ("monkey"). *PULQUE* was consumed in large

quantities at ceremonies and festivals held to worship him and other gods of like mind. Alongside his sister/female counterpart *XOCHIQUETZAL*, he was popular among the *CHINAMPA*-dwellers of the southern and western lakes of the Basin of Mexico, especially Xochimilco. Statuary of him was decorated with flowers, garlands and butterflies.

Xochipilli appears to have superseded an earlier pan-Mesoamerican deity of the Preclassic to Classic Period, known as *THE FAT GOD*, who was worshipped especially in the Classic Period city of *TEOTI-HUACÁN*. His *ZAPOTEC* equivalent was *QUIABELAGAYO*.

XOCHIQUETZAL, the sister/female counterpart of *XOCHIPILLI*, was the *AZTEC* goddess of flowering and of the fruitful earth. Her name literally means "feathered flower", "richly plumed flower" or, more poetically, "precious flower".

Xochiquetzal was the personification of love and beauty, of domesticity and flowers, and epitomized female sexual power. As the goddess of physical love, the Aztecs saw her as the giver of children. She was patroness to the *anianime* or *maqui*, the courtesans and lady companions of unwed Aztec warriors, and of silversmiths, sculptors, painters and weavers. In some regards she was related to *TOCI* and to *TLAZOLTÉOTL*, but unlike those goddesses, she remained ever young and beautiful. In the codices, she is depicted with two large plumes of quetzal feathers. She ruled the day *XÓCHITL* ("flower").

In myth she was the first wife of *TLÁLOC*, but was abducted by *TEZCATLIPOCA*. She was also associated with the underworld and was celebrated at festivals of the dead with offerings of marigolds. In legend she graced the earth with beauty and with the gifts of flowers and lush growth during the peaceful reign of *QUETZALCÓATL* and the world of the Second Sun.

Xochiquetzal was also one of four Aztec goddesses – along with *ATLATONAN*, *HUIXTOCÍHUATL* and *XILONEN* – who were impersonated by virgins and who were wed for a year to a chosen young warrior, impersonating *TEZCATLIPOCA*, until his sacrifice at the festival of *TÓXCATL*. The human Xochiquetzal was herself sacrificed and flayed, and her skin put on by a priest who pretended to weave at a loom while craftspeople dressed in monkey, jaguar, puma, dog and coyote costumes danced around him. The worshippers completed this gruesome ritual by confessing their sins

to Xochiquetzal's idol through bloodletting from their tongues and achieved atonement through a ritual bath.

XÓCHITL ("flower") was the last of the 20 *AZTEC* day-names; it had a neutral augury and its patron deity was *XOCHIQUETZAL*, the "precious flower". The *MAYA* and *ZAPOTEC* equivalent days were *AHAU* and *LAO* or *Loo*.

Calendrical dates and deity associations included: *1 Xóchitl*, for the corn (maize) god *CENTÉOTL*; *2 Xóchitl*, for the feast day of merchants; *5 Xóchitl*, for *MACUILXÓCHITL*, god of pleasure; *7 Xóchitl*, for the sun; and *10 Xóchitl*, for the war god of the city of Huaxtepec, in the present-day state of Morelos, south of the Basin of Mexico.

XOCHITOCA see *IZCALLI*.

THE XOCHIYAÓYOTL ("Flowery War"), initiated by Tlacaélel, the *CIHUACÓATL* (co-ruler) of Moctezuma I Ilhuicamina in the 15th century, was a ritual tournament set up especially to supply victims for sacrifice. They were mock combats, not intended to kill, although warriors often did die. An ongoing state of belligerence between the México *AZTECS* of *TENOCHTITLÁN* and their neighbours, especially against the stubborn and recalcitrant *TLAXCALTECAN* state to the east of the Basin of Mexico, provided captives for sacrifice to *HUITZILOPOCHTLI*, god of war and of the sun, who demanded regular, frequent

XOCHIQUETZAL, "feathered flower" or "precious flower", personified beauty, physical love, female sexual power and fertility. She was the first wife of Tláloc and the sister/female counterpart of Xochipilli.

blood sacrifice as nourishment. His chosen people seem to have gone out of their way to secure regular supplies of sacrificial victims (as well as for empire-building and economic domination). Indeed, it was considered more honourable to capture an enemy for sacrificial purposes than to kill him outright in battle. The souls of warriors who died in these "wars" were taken and protected by the god *TEOYAOMIQUI*.

The bound and hapless victims were handed over to the priests at the foot of the Templo Mayor (the Great Temple) in Tenochtitlán, from where they were dragged up the steps, stretched across the sacrificial stone and their chests sliced open with an obsidian knife. The heart of the victim was wrenched out, the corpse flayed and the limbs dismembered. Allegedly, pieces of the flesh were sent down to the rulers and nobility to eat, while the heart was sometimes consumed by the priests. As well as human sacrifices, priests offered Huitzilopochtli flowers, incense and food, and adorned his idol with wreaths and garlands.

XÓCOTL see *OTONTECUHTLI*.

XOCOTLHUETZI see *HUEYMICCAILHUITL*.

XÓLOTL ("dog animal") was the *AZTEC* name for the god of Venus as the evening "star", who pushed the sun down into the darkness each night. He was a manifestation or twin of *QUETZALCÓATL-TLAHUIZCALPANTECUHTLI* (Venus as the morning "star"). He ruled *OLLIN* ("movement" or "earthquake"), 17th of the 20 day-names, and was often portrayed with a dog's head with a burst eye, set on a human body with backward-turned feet. By extension, he was thus the god of deformity and misfortune (his burst eye has been interpreted as a sign of penitence). In one version of the *CREATION*

XÓLOTL, the "dog animal", represented Venus as the evening "star", who pushed the sun down into darkness at the end of each day.

MYTH, Xólotl acted as Quetzalcóatl's companion and dog guide to the underworld, when he visited *MICTLÁN* to collect the bones of the people of the world of the Fourth Sun. In another variation, it was Xólotl who brought back a bone to the gods, who sprinkled it with blood and caused it to give birth to a boy and a girl. Xólotl then raised the children on thistle milk, and they peopled the world of the Fifth Sun.

Xólotl was also the name of a legendary *CHICHIMEC* leader (see *CHICHIMECA* and *OTOMÍ*). (See also *DUALITY & OPPOSITION*)

XONAXI GUALAPAG see *XONAXI QUECUYA*.

XONAXI HUILIA see *XONAXI QUECUYA*.

THE RITUAL BALL GAME

HE MESOAMERICAN BALL GAME was as much a ritual as it was a sport, and features in both myth and legend – for example in the tale of Hun Hunahpú and Vucub Hunahpú. Stone-clad ball courts formed an integral part of ceremonial complexes, and many cities had several courts. Versions of the game, using dirt ball courts, spread to native cultures beyond Mesoamerica – northwards into the US Southwest, and eastwards to the Caribbean Antilles. The game originated in the Preclassic Period and, by the middle Classic Period, it had become a state cult in which human sacrifice played a vital part, with the losing team or captain as the victim. It was especially important to the Warrior Cults.

BALL PLAYERS were frequently portrayed in several media, including ceramics (left) and stone (above). Ceramic models of players come from the Island of Jaina in the Gulf Coast region and the Maya frequently included sculptured stone panels of players on the their ball courts and other buildings. Both players shown here are Early Postclassic Period in date and show the typical gear worn by players for protection – belts, waist and hip pads, knee and wrist pads, and fancy headdresses.

ALMOST EVERY Mesoamerican city had one or more ball courts. One of the most famous ball courts, and one of the largest, is that of the Maya-Toltec city of Chichén Itzá (above). On either side of the court, mounted vertically in the walls were two stone rings – the goals. The earliest known ball court was at the Olmec site of San Lorenzo, and the Olmec are thought to have invented the game. Rules varied from culture to culture, area to area, and through time; in most games, the object was to knock the rubber ball through the ring using only the body – not the hands – to manoeuvre and hit the ball.

A FAMOUS SCENE of ritual sacrifice (above), at the culmination of a Classic Period ball game, is one of six bas-relief carved panels lining the two sides of the South Ball Court at El Tajín (one of seven courts in the city). It depicts two priests on either side of the unfortunate victim (probably the captain of one of the teams), holding him down and ready to slice his chest open with an obsidian sacrificial knife. To the left of the scene rises death, represented by a skeleton.

Z

XONAXI PEOCHINA COYO
see *BENELABA*.

XONAXI QUECUYA
was the Valley *ZAPOTEC* goddess of the dead and the underworld who, along with her husband *COQUI BEZELAO*, was special to the city of Mitla. Her Sierra Zapotec and Southern Zapotec names were respectively Xonaxi Gualapag and Xonaxi Huilia.

XOO
("earthquake") was the 17th of the 20 *ZAPOTEC* day-names and one of the year-bearing days – there were 13 *Xoo* years in a 52-year cycle (see also *CHINA*, *QUIJ* and *PIJA*). The *AZTEC* and *MAYA* equivalent days were *OLLIN* and *CABAN*.

XPIYACOC
was the highland Quiché *MAYA* creator god in the *POPUL VUH*, husband of *XMUCANÉ* and the "grandfather" of the human race. His sons were the twins *HUN HUNAHPÚ* and *VUCUB HUNAHPÚ*. His *AZTEC* equivalent was the god *CIPACTONAL*.

XQUIC
the ill-fated daughter of one of the Lords of *XIBALBA* (the underworld), was the mother of the hero twins *HUNAHPÚ* and *XBALANQUÉ*. After the brothers *HUN HUNAHPÚ* and *VUCUB HUNAHPÚ* had been defeated by the Lords, and Hun Hunahpú's severed head hung in a calabash tree, she came to see the tree and asked herself aloud if she should pick one of the fruits. The head, overhearing her, informed her that the "fruits" were only a crop of skulls. Nevertheless, Xquic requested a fruit, whereupon Hun Hunahpú spat into her hand, thereby impregnating her. When her father demanded to know the identity of her lover, she denied any sin and escaped his wrath by travelling up to the surface to her mother-in-law *XMUCANÉ*. Xmucané rejected her at first, but then tested the truth of her claim to be Hun Hunahpú's wife by bidding her to collect corn (maize) from the field

THE TARASCAN YÁCATA, like their language, was unique in Mesoamerica, emphasized here in the round base of the temple platform.

of her half-brothers-in-law, *HUN BATZ* and Hun Chouen, knowing that there was only a single corn plant in the field. Xquic nevertheless returned with a great load of ears, which proved her claim to Xmucané. Despite this, Xquic's twin sons Hunahpú and Xbalanqué were not well received by Xmucané, and their half-brothers remained jealous. (See *TWINS & CULTURE HEROES*)

YÁCATA
was the name for a *TARASCAN* temple. In the Yácatas, perpetual fires to the sun god *CURICAUERI* were kept burning by specially designated priests. The centre of the cult, the great temple complex at the capital Tzintzuntzan, comprised a huge rectangular platform, some 425 by 250 m (465 by 273 yards), upon which stood five *yácata* platforms, each one T-shaped in plan, with a large circular extension at the base of the stem.

YACATECUHTLI
or Yiacatecuhtli, ("he with the pointed nose") was the *AZTEC* patron of merchants, and the god of their "guild", the *pochteca*. He was portrayed with, and symbolized by, a bamboo staff and a fan. He was worshipped especially by the citizens of Cholula and Tlatelolco, both city-states in the Basin of Mexico before the founding of the Aztec capital at *TENOCHTITLÁN*. Tlatelolco later became the home and great central marketplace of the

Aztec Empire. His *MAYA* equivalents were *EK CHUAH* and *XAMEN EK*.

YÁOTL
was the general *AZTEC NAHUATL* word for "enemy", or the malevolent aspect of certain Aztec gods. (See *HUITZILOPOCHTLI* and *TEZCATLIPOCA*)

YAQUI-TEPEU
see under *TEPEU*.

YAXCHÉ
see under *WORLD TREE*, and *COLOURS & THE CARDINAL DIRECTIONS*.

YEAR-BEARER
see under *WORLD TREE*, and *COLOURS & THE CARDINAL DIRECTIONS*.

YIACATECUHTLI
see *YACATECUHTLI*.

YOHUALTECUHTLI
or Yohualtonatiuh, literally "Lord of the Night", was the counterpart to the sun god *TONATIUH*, and therefore the "night sun". He was the representative of both the sun and Venus as they joined in the underworld to end each daily cosmic cycle. Yohualtecuhtli was identified as the star appearing in the centre of the sky at midnight among the Pleiades, initiating the crucial sacrifice of the *TOXIUHMOLPILIA*. In general he represented darkness, midnight and cyclic completion, and was regarded as the central world direction (as opposed to the four cardinal directions).

believed by some scholars to represent the night sun Yohualtecuhtli rather than Tonatiuh.

THE YOHUALTEUCTIN
were the nine Aztec *LORDS OF THE NIGHT*.

YOHUALTONATIUH
see *YOHUALTECUHTLI*.

THE YOPE
or Yopi, were a people in the southern highlands region known as Yopitzingo, in what is now the Mexican state of Guerrero. The cult of the "flayed one", *XIPE TOTEC*, possibly began in this region.

YUM CIMIL
("Lord of Death"; *cimi*, "death"), was an alternative name, used especially in Yucatán, for the *MAYA* god *AH PUCH*.

YUM KAAX
("Lord of the forests") was an alternative name for the *MAYA* agricultural deity known as *AH MUN*.

ZAC CIMI
see *THE BACABS*.

ZAC PAUAHTUN
see *THE PAUAHTUN*.

ZAC XIB CHAC
see *THE CHACS*.

THE ZAPOTECS
("Cloud People") were the peoples who settled in the southern highlands of

The huge, intricately carved stone popularly known as the "calendar stone", discovered at the site of the Templo Mayor in Mexico City in 1790, is

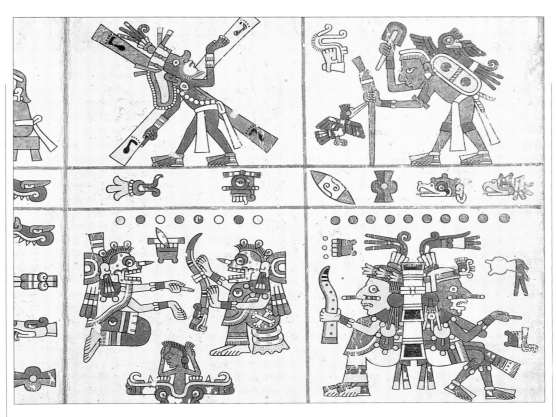

central Mesoamerica, in and around the Valley of Oaxaca (in the present Mexican state of that name). Their civilization was centred on the mountain plateau site of Monte Albán, which dominated three converging valleys below it (collectively called the Valley of Oaxaca). They spoke one of the variations of the Oto-Zapotecan language groups.

In the Preclassic Period, agricultural communities in the valleys grew to a point where there was increasing competition for control of the region and its resources. Long-distance trade links had been established with the *OLMECS* of the Gulf Coast. A deliberate alliance appears to have been established among the local élite, which resulted in the construction and maintenance over several hundred years of a huge ceremonial "capital" and centre on the plateau overlooking the three principal valleys of the region. This site, Monte Albán, was begun about 500 BC and endured as a ritual centre, residential city and burial place for Zapotec kings for more than 1,000 years until the Zapotec state crumbled and the site was all but abandoned by about AD 800. The site was later recognized as a sacred place by the *MIXTEC* inheritors of power in the region, and used as a burial place for Mixtec kings as well.

At the height of Zapotec power, the rulers of Monte Albán commanded a kingdom that enjoyed long-distance trade networks throughout Mesoamerica and included diplomatic relations with the *TEOTIHUACÁN* "empire" in the Basin of Mexico and with several *MAYA* city-states. Throughout the Classic period, the Zapotecs domi-

nated the southern highlands, while the Teotihuacanos dominated the central and northern regions of Mesoamerica, and also penetrated beyond the Zapotecs, to establish relations with several Maya cities themselves. Each site maintained an enclave of its own citizens as merchants and artisans in the other's city.

Zapotec civilization supported a large population in towns and villages throughout the Valley of Oaxaca and in and around Monte Albán itself on terraced residential suburbs, including at least 15 elite palaces around their own plaza compounds. At its most populous, from c. AD 400 to 700, it has been estimated that 25,000 people lived in Monte Albán. The reasons for Monte Albán's collapse are uncertain, but its coincidence with the collapse of Teotihuacán indicates that there was widespread economic implosion and a rise in city-state rivalry.

THE ZAPOTEC GODS present a bewildering verbal maze of names. Although it is as full as the pantheons of other Mesoamerican cultures, it includes gods and goddesses for the same purposes and

natural forces. In one view, all the deities of the Zapotecs represent parts of one great wholeness, comprising one god with numerous manifestations. Although the names vary, the creator deities and gods and goddesses of earth, sun, rain, war, love and death can be grouped into those of the Valley Zapotec (in the Valley of Oaxaca and its environs), the Sierra Zapotec (to the north of the Valley) and the Southern Zapotec (to the south and east, towards the Isthmus of Tehuantepec). Many cities had their own patron deities, and the characters of most Zapotec gods resembled those of deities for similar forces occurring elsewhere in Mesoamerica.

ZEE, or *Zij*, ("serpent") was the fifth of the 20 *ZAPOTEC* day-names; the *AZTEC* and *MAYA* equivalent days were *CÓATL* and *CHICCHAN*.

ZIJ ("serpent") see *ZEE*.

ZIP was the Yucatecan *MAYA* god of the hunt, particularly associated with the hunting of deer.

ZIPACNÁ, an evil giant in the Maya *POPOL VUH*, was the first son

of *VUCUB-CAQUIZ* and brother of *CABRACÁN*; he was destroyed with them by the hero twins *HUNAHPÚ* and *XBALANQUÉ* in *XIBALBA*. Zipacná was so mighty that he could lift mountains. He once fooled 400 warriors into thinking that they had killed him, but, as they celebrated their victory, he rose and destroyed their house around them, crushing them to death (after which the warriors became stars in the night sky). He suffered poetic justice at the hands of the hero twins, who lured him deep into a mountain cave by offering him his favourite dish, a succulent crab, and then pulled the mountain down and buried him within it.

ZOTZ ("bat") was represented by the *MAYA* glyph of the leaf-nosed vampire bat. He was a main feature of the name glyph for the Maya city of Copán, and also the name for the royal house of the Cakchiquel Maya in the Guatemalan highlands (for example, King Ahpozotzil, literally "Lord Bat"). (See also *CAMA ZOTZ*)

ZOTZIHÁ ("House of Bats") was one of the levels of *XIBALBA*, the Quiché *MAYA* underworld.

SOUTH AMERICAN MYTHOLOGY

INTRODUCTION

THE ANCIENT PEOPLES OF the vast continent of South America never formed a coherent cultural unit. They cannot, therefore, be treated as such in describing their religions and mythologies.

Ancient urban-based societies were confined to the Andes mountains and adjacent western coastal valleys and deserts. Cultures with ceremonial centres, political organizations governing large areas, and advanced technology – including metallurgy – developed in present-day western Venezuela, Colombia, Peru, Bolivia, the northern half of Chile and the northwestern part of Argentina. Peoples elsewhere in South America developed sophisticated societies, but did not build monumental ceremonial centres or cities, or develop technology of quite the same complexity, or build kingdoms and empires. Mythologies varied throughout the continent, but seem less complex and had fewer deities in some areas.

The concentration of civilizations was in part due to geographic stimuli. Within a relatively small area, there is a range of contrasting landscapes, from Pacific coastal plains and deserts, to coastal and foothill valleys, to high mountain valleys and plateaux, to the eastern slopes on the edges of the rain forests and *pampas*.

A key factor in the development and endurance of these civilizations was control of water, which became important functionally, symbolically and religiously. Geographical contrasts fostered and nurtured the development of sophisticated agriculture based on complex irrigation technologies and a wide variety of crops within and between the lowland and highland regions. This development opened the way for economic specializations that enabled cultures to develop social hierarchies and complex divisions and distributions of labour and rulership, trading contacts across long distances, and sophisticated religious beliefs and structures, both theoretical and architectural.

THE INITIAL PERIOD site of Cerro Sechín featured a distinctive style of low-relief carvings of grimacing warriors and severed heads on large stone slabs.

South American cultures can be "classified" into three groups. First, the Northern, Central and Southern Andean Areas, where civilizations evolved in the mountains and adjacent foothills and coastal regions, north to south from the Colombian–Ecuadorian border to the northern half of Chile and east to west from the rain forests to the Pacific coast. Second, the Intermediate Area comprised the southern half of Central America, Colombia and western Venezuela, plus the Caribbean islands and adjacent South American mainland. Third, areas inhabited by tribal societies: the Amazonian–Orinoco drainages (Amazonian Area), the eastern highlands (East Brazilian Area), the *pampas* (Chaco and Pampean Areas) and Tierra del Fuego (Fuegian Area).

City-states, kingdoms and empires evolved within the Andean Areas, based on corn (maize) and potato agriculture and the herding of camel-family animals (llamas, alpacas and vicuñas). In the Intermediate Area, economies were based on maize/corn agriculture, but societal organization remained at the chiefdom level. Rain forest peoples thrived on manioc agriculture rather than maize/corn, plus hunting and gathering; and in some fringe groups, where agriculture was impossible, solely on hunting, gathering and fishing.

Within these simple frameworks of society, cultures developed on different timescales and at different paces, yet they interacted through trade, political alliance and conquest, and the diffusion of ideas.

Language and Sources

Thousands of languages and dialects were spoken throughout South America, but there were no writing systems before the Spanish conquest. The sources of ancient myths are therefore native oral records transcribed by Europeans or European-trained natives in Spanish, Portuguese and other European languages, or in a few cases, Quechua (the language of the Incas) or Aymará (in the Titicaca Basin) using the European alphabet, accounts by contemporary chroniclers and modern anthropological studies. Chronicles written during the century or so after the Spanish conquest were fraught with opportunities for misinterpretation, elision, embellishment, amendment and reinterpretation, and are therefore more difficult to interpret for their ancient mythological content.

These oral sources are supplemented by archaeological, artistic and architectural evidence, and much of the religious content of the transcribed oral sources can be projected back on earlier civilizations. Archaeological evidence shows how the deities were depicted and the physical spaces within which religion was practised. Gods, goddesses and ceremonial practices and rites were depicted in free-standing and architectural stone and wooden sculptures, on ceramics and in jewellery, in murals, feather-work, textiles and metalwork, and, by western

Peruvian coastal cultures, as geoglyphs – large-scale line drawings on the ground. Temples and ceremonial precincts tell us something about the nature of religious worship through their layout, divisions, and the use of spaces – open and enclosed, sunken and raised, between and within them.

The Incas were particularly enthusiastic about, and adept at, incorporating the religious practices and deities of subject peoples into their own religion in their attempt to create a cohesive empire. Knowing this Inca propensity – and the manifest continuity of many iconographic symbols, characters and themes – provides a sound basis on which to reconstruct Andean religion, beginning with the ancient civilization of Chavín.

Although not written, one recording device – the *quipu*, a system of tied bundles of string – served as an aide-mémoire to designated *quipucamayoqs* ("knot makers or keepers"). Many of the first records of Inca culture transcribed by Spanish priests were based on the memories of *quipucamayoqs* and the *amautas*, officially appointed Inca court poet-philosophers responsible for memorizing, recounting, interpreting, reinterpreting, amplifying, reciting and passing on the legends, history and genealogies of the Inca kings and queens.

About two dozen chroniclers' works provide information on the Incas and their contemporaries. Pedro Cieza de León's *Crónica del Peru* (1553 and 1554) contains much on Inca myth, as does Juan de Betanzos' *Narrative of the Incas* (1557), from the Inca nobility's point of view. Another record is Garcilasco de la Vega's (known as "El Inca") *Comentarios reales de los Incas* (1609–17), a complete history of the Inca Empire. A late pretender to the Inca throne, Melchior Carlos Inca, recorded the Inca origin myth, according to him, from interviews with four aged *quipucamayoqs* who had served the last emperor, in his *Relación de los Quipucamayoqs* (1608).

The exceptionally important Huarochirí Manuscript – written in Quechua – *Dioses y Hombres de Huarochirí* (c. 1608), records the myths of the central highlands of Peru. Accounts of the mythology of the peoples of the north Peruvian coast are Cabello de Balboa's *Miscelánea Antártica* (1586) and Antonio de la Calancha's *Crónica moralizada del Orden de San Augustínen el Perú* (1638). Accounts written by Spanish-trained native Quechua-speakers include Felipe Guaman Poma de Ayala and Juan de Santacruz Yamqui Salcamaygua. The former wrote his *Nueva Corónica y Buen Gobierno* between 1583 and 1613; the latter produced his *Relación de Antiguedades deste Reyno del Pirú* about 1613. Other documents, known as *idolatrías*, are records by Spanish priests attempting to stamp out idolatrous practices known to persist among local people under Spanish rule. These 17th-century documents are rich in information on local myth based on interrogations of local authorities, native curers, "witches" and other local diviners.

Lastly, the Jesuit priest Bernabé de Cobo, drawing principally from earlier chronicles, compiled the most balanced and comprehensive synthesis of Inca history and religion in his monumental work *Historia del Nuevo Mundo* (completed in 1653), books 13 and 14 of which are on Inca religion and customs.

Society and Religion

The term "mythology" reveals a cultural bias on the part of the user, for the legendary and mythological accounts, together with deductions based on archaeological evidence, constituted the religions of South American societies.

Their religious beliefs and deities were those of the forces of nature. Like all peoples, they felt compelled to explain the important things in their universe, beginning with where they came from and their place in the larger scheme of things. They developed accounts of their observable cosmos to help them to understand what things were important, and

THE EARLY INTERMEDIATE period north Peruvian coastal kingdom of the Moche was particularly rich in ceramic representations of warriors, such as this spouted bottle in the shape of a seated warrior wearing an eagle mask.

how and why things were the way they were. Explanations of these concepts were functional. They did for these ancient peoples what science and/or religion does for society today: they provided a conceptual framework for living and for comprehending and relating to the mysteries of their observable universe. Their myths sanctified the universe and humankind's place within it, at the same time educing or inciting direct experience of the sacred.

Common Beliefs

Despite the regional and cultural diversity of South America, there were common elements, some almost universal. In most regions, for example, there was a named creator god. Among the Late Intermediate Period and Late Horizon Andean civilizations Viracocha, with many variations, was the creator. Although his worship was prevalent among coastal civilizations, there was also confusion and/or rivalry with the supreme god Pachacamac. Viracocha prototypes appear in the imagery of earlier civilizations, for example Early Horizon Chavín and Middle Horizon Tiahuanaco. Among the Intermediate Area cultures, the Chibcha god Bochica, to name but one, fulfilled a similar role. In contrast, while most rain forest tribes acknowledge the existence of a creator deity, he was believed to have little interest in day-to-day human and earthly matters after creating the cosmos.

The religious iconography of cultures in the Andean and Intermediate areas, and therefore presumably their beliefs and mythology, was influenced from the earliest times by rain forest animals (jaguars, serpents, monkeys, birds) and composite anthropomorphic beings. In particular, both Andean civilizations and Amazonian cultures shared a fascination with the power and influence of jaguars. Iconographic motifs that persisted through the cultures of the Andes, in addition to the jaguar, were feline-human hybrids, staff deities (often with a composite feline face and human body), winged beings, and falcon-headed or other bird-headed warriors.

Andean Themes

The religions of Andean peoples share several common themes. As well as their creator Viracocha, almost all their rituals had a calendrical organization. There was a liturgical calendar based on the movements of heavenly bodies, including solar solstices and equinoxes, lunar phases, the synodical cycle of Venus, the rising and setting of the Pleiades, the rotational inclinations of the Milky Way, and the presence within the Milky Way of "dark cloud constellations" (stellar voids). Consultation of auguries concerning these movements were considered

THE EARLY INTERMEDIATE Period Nazca culture, on the southern Peruvian coast , known for its textiles and the "Nazca lines" (geoglyphs), also produced highly painted pottery, in this example depicting a fierce-looking staring deity, perhaps in the tradition of the Paracas Oculate Being.

vital at momentous times of the year, such as planting time, harvest time and the beginning of the ocean fishing season.

Sacrifice, both human and animal, and a variety of offerings were practised. Strangulation and beheading were early ritual practices, and were depicted in ceramics, murals, architectural sculpture, textile decoration and metalwork – and are also well attested from remains in burials and tombs.

Another theme, the recognition of special places as sacred, endured for centuries, regardless of the rise and fall of political powers. One of the most famous is the shrine and oracle of Pachacamac, but there were tens of thousands of others. Called *huacas*, such places could be springs (emphasizing the importance of water), caves (prominent in human origin mythology), mountains, rocks or stones, fields or towns where important events had taken place, lakes or islands in them, or artificial objects such as stone pillars erected at specific locations.

Hallucinogenic and other drugs were frequently used in ritual. *Coca (Erythroxylon coca)* leaves were chewed in a complex and many-staged ritual connected with war and sacrifice, and certain cacti were also employed. Tobacco was used in ritual by the cultures of the Intermediate Area.

Ancestor reverence and worship was widespread, and charged with its own special ritual. The mummified remains of ancestors – themselves considered *huacas* – were kept in special buildings, rooms or chambers, or in caves. They were brought out on ritual occasions to participate in the festivals and were offered delicacies of food and drink, as well as objects and prayers. Another Andean preoccupation concerned death and the underworld. Skeletal figures, depictions of priests imitating the dead in order to visit the underworld, skeletons with sexual organs and the dead embracing women were associated with beliefs in fertility.

Four common elements were associated with Andean accounts of cosmic origin and the creation of humankind. First was the belief that humanity originated at Lake Titicaca, and that Viracocha was the creator god. Second was the concept that each group recognized a particular place or feature in their landscape as the place from which they emerged. Third was a dual relationship between local people and a

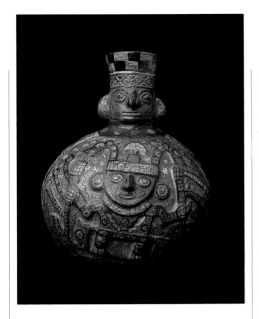

THE MIDDLE HORIZON *Huari Empire continued the tradition of the Staff Deity (depicted on this effigy bottle dated from 800 AD) after its highland predecessor, Chavín.*

group of outsiders; the relationship could be portrayed as one of co-operation or of conflict, but the relationship always defined the nature of the political arrangement that prevailed. Fourth was the conviction that there was a correct ordering of society and place in terms of rank.

Amazonia

Among Amazonian tribes, four almost universal themes can be recognized. First is the presence and power of shamans, and the associated use of hallucinogenic drugs to gain access into the spirit world for the wellbeing and guidance of humankind. Second is belief in the power and ancient divinity of jaguars. Third is the practice of cannibalism: both endocannibalism, to perpetuate the power and character of a dead relation, and exocannibalism, to entrap the power of an enemy and inflict insult and revenge on an enemy's relations. And fourth, less widespread, is headhunting, a practice steeped in supernatural and ritual significance for the purpose of capturing an enemy's soul.

Ancient Andean History

No single chronological scheme can be applied to the whole of ancient South America, for technology, social and political organization, and the

pace of development varied greatly from region to region. Archaeologists employ several broad chronological schemes to define development within large areas of general cultural cohesion, and which can be used to compare the areas through time.

The earliest pottery was made by peoples in the Intermediate Area and Amazonian Area in the late sixth and fifth millennia BC. In the other areas – except the Fuegian, which remained aceramic until Europeans arrived – ceramics were developed from about 1500 BC or later. Corresponding roughly to the Andean Initial Period, the Intermediate Area chronology is divided into the Early Ceramic Period and the Formative (or Initial) Period; similarly, the far Southern Andean Area had Early Ceramic and Initial Periods from about 1500 BC.

Ancient Andean chronology is subdivided into eight major periods, each characterized primarily by emphases on technological development and political organization. Much of the artistic expression and iconography of these civilizations endured for long periods, through political changes, but distinctive styles arose and were copied, changed, embellished and interpreted by successive cultures.

People migrated into South America in the Archaic Period – hunter-gatherer, stone-, bone-, wood- and shell-tool-using cultures reaching the tip of Tierra del Fuego by at least 9000 BC. The term Preceramic Period (from *c.* 3500 BC to the development of ceramics, which varies by region), is applied to the first agricultural societies, which by 3000 BC had mastered the domestication of plants and animals – a process that had begun several millennia earlier – and constructed the first monumental architecture in the form of platform compounds. These cultures were initially aceramic, but during the third and second millennia BC, pottery technology spread throughout the Andes.

In the Initial Period (*c.* 1800–900 BC), irrigation agriculture was developed into a sophisticated technology. Constructions of monumental

architecture included much more ambitious projects, such as a tradition of U-shaped ceremonial centres at Sechín Alto/Cerro Sechín, Garagay, Los Reyes and other sites on the northern Peruvian coast, and sunken courts and other constructions at Chiripa in the Titicaca Basin and at Kotosh and La Galgada in the sierras.

In the Early Horizon (*c.* 900–200 BC), the earliest civilization of the central Andes, Chavín, dominated much of the area, both artistically and religiously, if not politically. Chavín imagery was distributed (east–west) from the upper Amazon drainage across the Andes mountains to the north Pacific coastal valleys. Its iconography comprised animal and anthropomorphic figures with feline, serpentine, harpy eagle and falcon heads, and humanoid bodies. Canine teeth protrude menacingly from wide, grimacing mouths. The Staff Deity (male or female) was portrayed ubiquitously, and endured into the 16th century. He or she was shown frontally, with outstretched arms holding two staffs or corn stalks, and was depicted on architecture and portable objects of all kinds. The exact significance or meaning of the Staff Deity is unknown, but his/her importance is without doubt. It seems likely that the Staff Deity was a creator being, and that the principal city, Chavín de Huántar, was a place of cult pilgrimage.

The Paracas culture, contemporary with Chavín, flourished on the southern Peruvian coast, where the mainland population used the peninsula as a necropolis for burials rich in grave goods, especially textiles – both woven and embroidered – wrapped around mummified bodies. Paracas textiles and ceramics display a wealth of iconographic symbols and deities in rich colours. One deity, known as the Oculate Being, was particularly prominent.

The Early Intermediate Period (*c.* 200 BC–AD 500) followed the Early Horizon. The cohesion of Chavín disintegrated, and several regional chiefdoms developed in the coastal and mountain valleys. Despite this political fragmentation, some remarkable advances were achieved in urbanization and in political, social, economic and artistic expression. Prominent among the kingdoms that developed were the Moche in the north Peruvian coastal valleys, and the Nazca in the southern coastal valleys. Rich iconographies are displayed in both cultures on architecture, pottery and textiles, and as geoglyphs.

Moche iconography is rich in painted figures – humans, anthropomorphized animals, birds and marine animals – and in set scenes showing rituals and sacrifices. Archaeological evidence from élite burials of Moche Sipán lords bears out the real-life practices depicted. On the south coast, the Nazca and contemporary cultures practised an apparently common religious tradition focused on burials of mummified bodies wrapped in rich textiles, on sacred ceremonial and pilgrimage sites – such as Cahuachi – separate from urban settlements, and on ground drawings including lines, outlined areas, and geometric and animal figures representing supernatural images and sacred ritual pathways.

In the Intermediate Area, contemporary cultures developed ceremonial sites and rich and sophisticated traditions of metal technology in gold, silver and alloys – Tumaco, San Agustín, Tierradentro, Calima, Tolima – in the Regional Development Period (c. 200 BC–AD 900).

In the Andean Area, the Middle Horizon (c. AD 500–1000) followed the Early Intermediate. The wealth of cultures and political entities that had existed continued to develop but, during the course of the next 500 years, two political centres built empires that unified the northern and southern Andes and adjacent western coastal regions.

In the north was Huari (or Wari), in the south-central Peruvian highlands. Through military and economic conquest, Huari rulers built an empire that eventually extended to the Pacific coast and engulfed the Nazca and Moche areas. A powerful central Peruvian coastal kingdom, Pachacamac, although conquered by the Huari, remained a pre-eminent shrine and pilgrimage site throughout the Middle Horizon and after.

In the Titicaca Basin, the city of Tiahuanaco (or Tiwanaku) was built, and Tiahuanacan rulers expanded their state throughout the Basin and beyond. At their northwest border, they confronted the Huari Empire at the pass of La Raya near Cuzco. Tiahuanaco included a large ceremonial centre with monumental architecture, enclosed compounds and monumental freestanding stone sculpture.

Although distinct politically, Huari and Tiahuanaco shared numerous cultural features. Their rich iconographic traditions drew from earlier developments in their respective areas. Much of their religious imagery was shared: staff deities, winged figures, feline and serpentine beings, bird-headed figures and decapitated heads. The importance of the Staff Deity emphasized its almost certain role as a creator god and possible precursor to the gods Viracocha and Pachacamac. Tiahuanaco became an important religious shrine, and later cultures believed Lake Titicaca to be the place of creation.

Following the demise of Huari and Tiahuanaco, the Late Intermediate Period (c. AD 1000–1400) was a new era of political fragmentation. As before, numerous local and regional city-states were established, which, towards the end of the period, were being unified into larger kingdoms. The Kingdom of Chimor (or Chimú) arose in the valleys of the north Peruvian coast (the ancient Moche area). Its capital, Chan Chan, surrounded an imperial precinct of compounds dedicated to the perpetuation of the memory of the kings of Chimor. Chimú iconography had obvious roots right back to Chavín and yet the culture was distinctive for its monumental architecture, vast administrative quarters, carved *adobe* wall friezes depicting repeated birds and marine animals, and a distinctive arched, double-headed beast called a rainbow serpent.

In the Intermediate Area, in the Integration Period (c. AD 900–1450), the rich metallurgic traditions continued – in addition to those listed above, the Nariño, Popayán, Quimbaya, Tairona, Sinú and Chibcha (also known as Muisca).

IN THE TITICACA BASIN, the city of Tiahuanaco, Huari's Middle Horizon rival, specialized in monumental stone sculptures, such as the Ponce Stela depicting a noble figure holding a beaker and short sceptre.

In the final Andean period, the Late Horizon (c. AD 1400–1532), the Incas established their capital at Cuzco and built their immense empire – from Colombia to mid-Chile and from the rain forest to the Pacific – in a little over 130 years. They conquered and subjugated the peoples throughout this vast area. In an attempt to unify religious belief, Inca emperors and priests emphasized the supremacy of the sun god Inti and continued to honour the all-powerful creator god Viracocha/Pachacamac, while incorporating local beliefs, pantheons and *huacas*.

Perhaps inevitably, the strains and tensions of holding together such a vast and diverse empire led to rivalry over the throne. When the Spanish adventurer Francisco Pizarro landed on the north coast of the empire in 1532, a civil war had been raging for more than six years between the half-brothers Huascar and Atahualpa. Exploiting this situation, appearing to support one side, then the other, and recruiting native allies, Pizarro played the king-maker, and proceeded to conquer the Inca Empire and strip its wealth, both material and cultural.

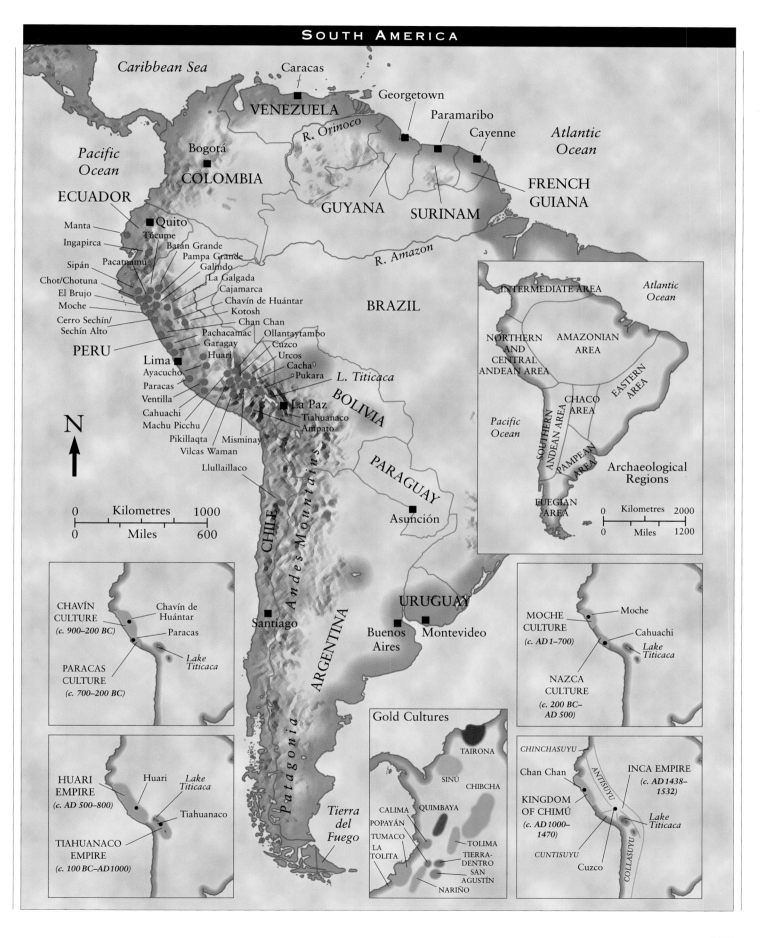

SOUTH AMERICA

Caribbean Sea

Caracas

VENEZUELA

Georgetown

Paramaribo

Cayenne

Atlantic
Ocean

R. Orinoco

Pacific
Ocean

Bogotá

COLOMBIA

GUYANA

SURINAM

FRENCH
GUIANA

ECUADOR

Manta

Quito

Ingapirca

Túcume

Batán Grande

Sipán

Pacatnamú

Pampa Grande

Chot/Chotuna

Galindo

El Brujo

La Galgada

Moche

Cajamarca

Cerro Sechín/
Sechín Alto

Chavín de Huántar

Kotosh

Chan Chan

Pachacamac

Ollantaytambo

Garagay

Cuzco

PERU

Huari

Urcos

Lima

Cacha

Ayacucho

Pukara

Paracas

L. Titicaca

Ventilla

Cahuachi

La Paz

BOLIVIA

Machu Picchu

Tiahuanaco

Ampato

Pikillaqta

Misminay

Vilcas Waman

Llullaillaco

PARAGUAY

Asunción

R. Amazon

BRAZIL

N

Archaeological
Regions

INTERMEDIATE AREA

Atlantic
Ocean

NORTHERN
AND
CENTRAL
ANDEAN AREA

AMAZONIAN
AREA

CHACO
AREA

EASTERN
AREA

Pacific
Ocean

SOUTHERN ANDEAN AREA

PAMPEAN AREA

FUEGIAN
AREA

0   Kilometres   2000

0   Miles   1200

0   Kilometres   1000

0   Miles   600

CHILE

Andes Mountains

ARGENTINA

Patagonia

URUGUAY

Santiago

Buenos
Aires

Montevideo

Tierra
del
Fuego

CHAVÍN
CULTURE
(c. 900–200 BC)

Chavín de
Huántar

Paracas

PARACAS
CULTURE
(c. 700–200 BC)

Lake
Titicaca

MOCHE
CULTURE
(c. AD 1–700)

Moche

Cahuachi

Lake
Titicaca

NAZCA
CULTURE
(c. 200 BC–
AD 500)

HUARI
EMPIRE
(c. AD 500–800)

Huari

Lake
Titicaca

Tiahuanaco

TIAHUANACO
EMPIRE
(c. 100 BC–AD 1000)

Gold Cultures

TAIRONA

SINÚ

CHIBCHA

CALIMA

QUIMBAYA

POPAYÁN

TUMACO

LA
TOLITA

TOLIMA

TIERRA-
DENTRO
SAN
AGUSTÍN

NARIÑO

CHINCHASUYU

Chan Chan

ANTISUYU

INCA EMPIRE
(c. AD 1438–
1532)

KINGDOM
OF CHIMÚ
(c. AD 1000–
1470)

Lake
Titicaca

CUNTISUYU

Cuzco

COLLASUYU

A

ABE MANGO was the daughter of the *TUKANO* creator god *PAGE ABE*. After her father had created humans, she descended to the earth and personally taught humans how to use fire and to cook, how to build huts for shelter and how to weave cloth and make pottery.

ACLLAHUASI see under *ACLLAS*.

ACLLAS ("chosen women") were hand-picked *INCA* girls trained to serve in the cult of *INTI*, the sun god, and destined to become the concubines of the Inca ruler. They were sometimes referred to as the "Virgins of the Sun". The maidens were chosen at the age of eight, and kept in special cloisters called *acllahuasi* in the Inca capital at *CUZCO*, where they were super-

ACLLAS, the "chosen women" of the Inca emperor and sometimes referred to as "Virgins of the Sun", kept the sacred fires alight in the Temple of the Sun (Inti).

vised by elderly women called Mama Cunas. Here their tasks were to guard and keep the sacred fire of Inti burning, to weave and sew special clothing, and to prepare food and *CHICHA* (corn/maize beer) for state ceremonial occasions and the ceremony of *INTI RAYMI*. As concubines at the command of the emperor, they were also used by

him to bestow favours on high-ranking foreign officials and to secure arranged marriages with foreign rulers for political alliances.

AI APAEC was a *MOCHE* and later *CHIMÚ* sky god and creator god (or, alternatively, the son of the sky god) in the Early Intermediate Period. Fanged-being images depicted on *CHAVÍN* pottery of much earlier date might have been his prototype.

The archaeological evidence suggests that the Moche worshipped a creator god who was a remote and somewhat mysterious deity, a mountain god who paid little attention to the daily affairs of humankind. His throne was usually placed on a mountain top, beneath which Ai Apaec, perhaps a manifestation of the creator, was more active in terrestrial affairs. Moche military conquest and/or ritual combat provided prisoners for sacrifice to the gods, usually by slitting the victim's throat and offering his blood and body to the sky gods.

The image of Ai Apaec is conspicuous among a host of minor deities depicted on Moche pottery vessels. He is portrayed with a fanged mouth, wears snake-head earrings and sometimes a jaguar headdress, and snakes almost invariably form part of his belt. Sometimes he is shown in combat with a monster being, which he always overcomes. His role as a sky god appears to be implied by his association with a tableau of two scenes separated by a two-headed serpent. In the upper part appear

AI APAEC was the fanged creator god of the Moche and later Chimú cultures. A somewhat remote deity, his fanged nature stems from a long tradition going back to Chavín imagery.

gods, demonic beings and stars, while in the lower part there are musicians, lords or slaves; and rain falls from the serpent's body, implying a celestial/terrestrial division.

According to some authorities, Ai Apaec was also the principal god of the Chimú of the Late Intermediate Period, derived from the Moche cult. Others argue that Ai Apaec simply means "to make", and was therefore an invisible creator comparable to later Inca *VIRACOCHA*.

AKAPANA TEMPLE see under *TIAHUANACO*.

ALCAVICÇA was the pre-*INCA* Lord of the Valley of Cuzco. His existence establishes two links between Lake *TITICACA*, the place of origin of *VIRACOCHA*, and *CUZCO*, the Inca capital. From

URCOS, Viracocha travelled to the Cuzco Valley during his wanderings northwest from Lake Titicaca. At the site that would become the Inca capital he created, or summoned up from the earth, a great lord and named him Alcavicça. Alcavicça became the ruler of a people of the same name who occupied part of the valley when the Incas arrived. When Viracocha left the valley to continue northwest, his last act was to command that the *OREJONES*, a Spanish nickname for the Inca nobility, should rise out of the earth after his departure. This act gave Cuzco and the Incas a divine precedent for claiming rulership of the valley.

In another, more elaborate, version of Inca state origin, six of the four brothers and sisters/wives of "the ancestors", including *MANCO CAPAC* and *MAMA HUACO*, travelled from *HUANACAURI* into the Valley of Cuzco and to the town of Cuzco, where Alcavicça ruled. They went to Alcavicça and declared that they had been sent by their father, the sun, to take possession of the town. The Alcavicça people agreed to this and provided the six ancestors with accommodation. Manco Capac then took corn (maize) kernels, which he had brought with him from the cave of *TAMBO TOCO*,

ALCAVICÇA, according to legend, was taught to plant corn (maize) by Manco Capac. Corn and the potato were the staple crops that sustained ancient Andean populations.

and taught the Alcavicças how to plant it, thus introducing the first corn crop into the valley. In yet another permutation of the story, it was Mama Huaco who planted the first corn field.

Thus, the takeover of Cuzco by divine command, after travelling from Titicaca (place of the world's birth) and teaching local people the art of agriculture, established the Incas' right to rule. Viracocha's very creation of Alcavicça hints at a divine master plan; and these acts established and justified the pattern of Inca expansion and their hierarchical political relationships with the peoples they conquered: foreign invaders (the Incas) subordinating local peoples and taking control of their destinies. Nevertheless, things did not always work out as smoothly as was anticipated, for MAYTA CAPAC, the fourth legendary Inca emperor, was forced to put down a rebellion by the Alcavicças, who were apparently dissatisfied with Inca overlordship.

ALUBERI, among the Orinoco River ARAWAK tribe, is a sort of supreme being – a "first cause". He/it is remote and indifferent towards humankind, and did not create men and women. Instead, humans were created by Aluberi's "agents" on Earth, KURURUMANY and Kulimina.

AMAUTAS were INCA court poet-philosophers – colleagues of the QUIPUCAMAYOQS – responsible for keeping the state histories alive through oral remembrance. In addition to recording in song the deeds of the present emperor, they had to remember the official histories of the founding and history of CUZCO, which inevitably were bound up with myth and the legendary exploits of former leaders and state heroes. They created songs to document royal genealogies and to chronicle the deeds of the Incas, their queens, coronations, battles, and important state events, per-

forming them for the emperor and his court at state ceremonies.

As the Inca Empire continued to expand, the *amautas* were tasked with reconciling (through recasting) the myths, legends, histories, dynastic ties and religious tenets of the conquered peoples, incorporating them into the official Inca version of events and state religion. For example, the reconciliation of the shared name and visionary connection between VIRACOCHA the man and the god, and the usurpation of Viracocha's throne by PACHACUTI INCA YUPANQUI must have occupied the talents of successive generations of *amautas*. The official account of the Inca conquest of the CHIMÚ is a classic example of how they recorded the defeat and incorporation of a people to the advantage of both the state and the conquered peoples (see MINCHANÇAMAN).

After the Spanish conquest, the *amautas* were a principal source for Spanish chroniclers, who recorded the myths, legends, histories and beliefs of the Incas and other peoples of the empire.

AMPATO is a mountain peak in the southern Peruvian Andes near Arequipa, the site of several ritual CAPACOCHA child sacrifices discovered in 1995 (see LLULLAILLACO). The victim, a young teenage girl who has come to be known as the "ice maiden", was found near the summit at about 6,300 m (20,670 ft). Her sacrifice was probably an offering to the sun god INTI or VIRACOCHA.

The frozen state of the body, hidden until volcanic ash from

nearby Mount Sabancaya and an earth tremor freed the body from its covering of snow, preserved a wealth of archaeological evidence. The girl was dressed in the style of a CUZCO noblewoman, in finely woven llama-wool garments, including a red and white shawl clasped about her with a silver *tupu* pin. A computer-tomography scan of her body showed a fracture, 5 cm (2 in) long, on her right temple, implying that she was clubbed to death, or had been finished off with a final blow. Accompanying her was a small female figurine, similarly dressed, made of shell. Also nearby were woven woollen bags containing corn (maize) kernels and a corn cob. Another bag contained *coca* (Erythroxylon coca) leaves and was covered with feathers. The bodies of two other child sacrifices were excavated below the summit.

At 4,890 m (16,040 ft) a camp, presumably used by the performers of the rituals, was excavated, included the bases of rectangular and round stone structures and a llama corral. Remains of a second camp were found at 5,670 m (18,900 ft) and, just below the summit, excavations revealed an area strewn with *ichu* grass, wooden tent posts and a stone-walled platform, suggesting that Mount Ampato was used repeatedly for sacrifices.

ANACONDA see YURUPARY.

APACHETAS, a special type of sacred huaca, were believed to be inhabited by local deities, whose protection travellers sought by leaving offerings on them.

ANTISUYU, the northeast quadrant of the Inca Empire, stretched from the Andes to their eastern foothills on the edge of the Amazon rainforests.

ANAN YAUYOS see HUAROCHIRÍ MANUSCRIPT.

THE ANCESTORS, INCA, see MANCO CAPAC.

THE ANDEAN TRIAD comprised the "three Viracochas" (see CON TICCI VIRACOCHA).

"ANGELS" were winged, running beings that accompanied the STAFF DEITY in the iconography of HUARI and TIAHUANACO.

ANTISUYU was the northeast quarter of the INCA Empire (see TAHUANTINSUYU). It comprised the Andes mountain regions north, east and southeast of CUZCO, as far as the foothills overlooking the Amazon forests.

APACHETA was the Inca name for a particular type of HUACA (sacred place), that comprised a pile of stones set at the top of a mountain pass or at a crossroads. Apachetas were believed to hold the spirits of local deities, and travellers would seek their favour by leaving offerings of *coca* (Erythroxylon coca) or clothing. Another method of obtaining their aid was to add a stone to the heap before continuing on a journey. (Compare APU, CEQUE and HUANCA)

APU was the Inca name for a type of *HUACA*, or sacred place. In a land dominated by the high peaks and volcanoes of the Andean cordillera, the mountains were believed to have supernatural spiritual powers. In particular, the mountain tops were regarded as the abodes of the gods – and long-standing tradition, which continues to the present day, regards especially prominent peaks as sacred and powerfully imbued. These were (and still are) venerated as *apu* (literally "lord") and were believed to have a direct influence on animal and crop fertility. Sacred pilgrimages, made to these mountain tops to seek the favour of the spirits of the *apus*, were a regular feature of Andean traditional religion. (Compare *APACHETA*, *CEQUE* and *HUANCA*)

AQLLA see *ACLLAS*.

AQLLA WASI see *ACLLAHUASI*.

ARAVATURA was the culture hero of the tribes of the *XINGU RIVER* region, and the discoverer of the fate of the spirit after death. Following the death of his best friend, Aravatura went to seek for his spirit in the forest. He eventually found it, along with many other spirits of the departed, all preparing to do battle against the birds. The ultimate fate of the spirit, if it were defeated, was to be devoured by a huge eagle. Because of his discovery, Aravatura was afflicted with the stench of death when he returned to his village, but he was cured through the intervention of the tribal *SHAMANS*.

THE ARAWAK were a rain forest tribe of the Orinoco River drainage in South America, and, before the arrival of the Spaniards, also the prehistoric culture/people of Haiti, Cuba and other islands of the Greater Antilles. (For their mythological concepts, see *ALUBERI*, *KURURUMANY*, *THREE-CORNERED IDOL*, *ZEMÍ*)

AROTEH and Tovapod are the creators of the Tupi of southeastern Brazil: two magicians who lived at the beginning of time, when humans lived beneath the earth and had little food to eat. The magicians jealously guarded the edible plants and animals on the surface so, when some humans climbed up through a tunnel one night, and stole food from them, Tovapod dug up the hole. Out tumbled hordes of ugly, web-footed people, with boars' tusks growing from their mouths. Undeterred, Aroteh and Tovapod reshaped these creatures into the humans of today by breaking off the tusks and remoulding their webbed feet into toes (see also *VALEJDAD*).

APUS, another aspect of ancient Andean sacred landscape, were mountains believed to be the abodes of the gods. Mount Ausangate in central Peru is a typical example.

ARUTAM see *HEADHUNTING*.

ATAHUALPA was the 14th and last pre-Spanish conquest *INCA* ruler (ruled AD 1532–3). When Francisco Pizarro and his followers landed on the Peruvian coast in 1532, a civil war between Atahualpa and his half-brother *HUASCAR* had been raging for more than six years since the death of their father, *HUAYNA CAPAC* and his chosen heir, in 1526. Different court factions had backed each of the rival brothers' claims to the succession, and Atahualpa had only recently captured his brother and secured the throne when Pizarro arrived.

Atahualpa's pivotal place in Inca legend rests with the fact that he was beheaded by Pizarro following his defeat and capture at Cajamarca in 1533. From that point onwards, the legend of the "future return of the king" developed – known as the *INKARRÍ* – in which the severed and buried head of Atahualpa was believed to be slowly growing a new body for the ruler's eventual return and overthrow of the Spaniards and the reinstatement of the Inca world order.

YOUNG GIRLS of the Wapisana, one of the Arawak tribes of Guyana, whose dress might indicate considerable acculturation away from ancient mythological beliefs.

ATUN-VIRACOCHA ("great creator") was the *INCA* name given to *VIRACOCHA* by the people of *URCOS*, and to the statue of him erected by them – described by the 16th-century Spanish chronicler Cristobal de Molina.

THE AUCA peoples of northern Chile were some of the fiercest opponents of the *INCA*s' expansion into the southern Andes (see *GUECUFU*, *GUINECHEN*, *PILLAN*).

AUCA see *AYAR AUCA*.

AUCA RUNA were the people of the *INCA* Fourth Sun (see *PACHACUTI*).

AYAHUASCA SNUFF see *SHAMAN*.

AYAR stems from the *QUECHUA* word *aya* ("corpse") (see *MANCO CAPAC* and *MALLQUIS*).

AYAR AUCA, also Cuzco Huanca, the brother/husband of *MAMA HUACO*, was one of the original eight *INCA* ancestors (see *MANCO CAPAC*). The name of the Inca capital, Cuzco, is derived from the alternative form of his name.

His alternate name reflects his importance in the Inca state foundation myth as the stone pillar (see *HUACA* and *HUANAYPATA*).

AYAR CACHI was the brother/husband of *MAMA IPACURA* (although one chronicler names *MAMA HUACO* as his wife) and one of the original eight *INCA* ancestors (see *MANCO CAPAC*).

AYAR MANCO see *MANCO CAPAC*.

AYAR UCHU, the brother/husband of *MAMA RAUA*, was one of the original eight *INCA* ancestors (see *HUACA* and *MANCO CAPAC*).

AYLLU ("family", "lineage" or "part") is the *QUECHUA* term for

B

social and economic groupings within the *INCA* Empire. In pre-Inca times they were blood lineages, but in the time of the Inca Empire they could be blood lineages or local administrative groupings unrelated to actual kinship.

There were tens of thousands of *ayllus* throughout the empire, each discontinuously distributed across the land. Members of the same *ayllu* lived in different ecological zones, some up in the high montane *puna* (tundra), some at mid-altitudes, and some in intermontane valleys, coastal lowlands or tropical forest lowlands. This distribution of each socially and economically closely tied group ensured that there was a regular redistribution among the *ayllu* members of agricultural produce and man-made goods and commodities from each zone. Exchange occurred both through the regular movement of *ayllu* members

among the zones and at annual gatherings and festivals, at a central settlement.

In addition to this internal co-operation, each *ayllu* was obliged to render tribute to the Inca Empire – to the regional administrator sent out from *CUZCO*. This took the form of public labour called *MIT'A* (literally "turns of service"), which included working lands and herding the llama flocks in the region that belonged to the emperor and the gods, and performing a quota of work at a state installation, such as a redistribution warehouse.

As with so many Inca state institutions, this official organization was interwoven with mythical and ritual overtones. The origin of the *ayllu* concept was grounded in the creation myth of the empire and of the royal line of rulers. Upon their emergence from the cave of *TAMBO TOCO* in *PACARITAMBO*, the Inca ancestors conquered the locals and organized them into ten *ayllus*.

REMAINS of an ayllu field system are seen at Carangas, Bolivia. From such designated lands, members of the kinship group could supply crops for redistribution among ayllu members in other ecological zones.

ATAHUALPA Inca was one of two claimants to the Inca throne when Francisco Pizarro arrived and began the Spanish conquest. (PAINTING FROM THE 18TH-CENTURY "CUZCO SCHOOL".)

These became the ten groupings of commoners at Cuzco, to complement the ten royal *ayllus* called *PANACAS*. In addition, *ayllus* kept the mummified bodies of ancestors, to be venerated by all the members of the group on ceremonial occasions, and to provide a setting for the recital of the *ayllu* creation myth. Each *ayllu* also recognized and maintained one or more *HUACAS*, or sacred places, within their lands, at which regular offerings were made. A larger group, of several *ayllus*, was the *MOIETY*.

AYMARÁ was once a major ancient Andean language. It now survives mainly in northern Bolivia.

BACHUE ("large breasted") was the *CHIBCHA* earth goddess and mother goddess, symbol of fertility and protector of crops. According to Chibcha myth, shortly after the world had been created by *CHIMINIGAGUA*, she emerged from a sacred lake in the mountains bearing her three-year-old son with her. She waited for the boy to grow to manhood, then "married" him and proceeded to people the world with their offspring. Once the earth was populated, the two were transformed into serpents and returned to the sacred lake.

THE BARASANA were a rain forest tribe of the Colombian Amazon (see *YURUPARY*).

BATÁN GRANDE was the largest Middle Horizon religious centre of the *SICÁN*

BACHUE, who was the "large breasted" fertility goddess of the Chibcha peoples, is possibly represented in this handled effigy vessel from Ecuador.

culture in the *LAMBAYEQUE* Valley. The site had been occupied from the Early Horizon, from as early as 1500 BC, and was finally abandoned about AD 1100. The Sicán religious precinct comprised 17 *adobe* brick temple-mounds, surrounded by shaft tombs and multi-roomed enclosures filled with rich burials and furnishings reminiscent of Early Intermediate Period *MOCHE* burials. The mummy bundles and the iconography of the Sicán culture's metalwork, ceramics and architecture also drew on, and continued, those of *CHAVÍN* and Moche.

Batán Grande was abandoned, apparently owing to economic disaster accompanying an El Niño weather event. Piles of wood were deliberately placed against the temple walls and set alight. The survivors established a new religious centre at *TÚCUME*.

BENNETT STELA
see *TIAHUANACO*.

BIRD PRIEST
see *DECAPITATOR GOD*.

BOCHICA was the legendary founder hero of the *CHIBCHA*. In Chibcha myth he arrived in Colombia from the east and travelled through their world as a bearded sage, teaching them civilization, moral laws and the sophisticated technology of metalworking.

Not all accepted his teaching, however. A woman named Chie challenged him by urging men and women to ignore Bochica and make merry, whereupon Bochica transformed her into an owl. Even so, she was able to help the god *CHIBCHACUM* to flood the earth. Bochica appeared as a rainbow then, as the sun, sent his rays to evaporate the waters and also created a channel by striking the rocks with his golden staff for the water to drain into the sea. For this role he is sometimes worshipped as the sun god Zue, while Chie is known as the moon goddess. When he disappeared into the west, he left his footprints, literally in stone.

(Compare *NEMTEREQUETEBA* and, for Central Andean cultures, *CONIRAYA VIRACOCHA*, *ROAL*, *THUNUPA VIRACOCHA* and *VIRACOCHA*)

BOIUNA, a fearsome goddess described by many tribes along the Amazon and its tributaries, takes the form of a snake. She will eat any living creature, and a mere glance from her flashing eyes can, it is believed, make a woman pregnant.

BORARO ("the white ones") are rather fearsome Amazonian *TUKANO* tribal forest spirits. They are tall, hairy creatures, with huge penises, ears that point forwards and feet that point backwards. Their legs are not jointed at the knee so, if one falls down, he has great difficulty in rising again. The Tukano believe that if a Boraro is seen carrying a stone hoe, he is searching for a human to eat!

BOTOQUE, the legendary culture hero of the Kayapo tribe of the central Brazilian rain forest, was

responsible for bringing knowledge to humankind. At the beginning of time, the people of the earth did not know how to use fire. The edible plants that they collected were eaten raw, and they only warmed their meat on rocks in the sun. Then one day the young man Botoque and his brother-in-law were in the forest and saw a macaw's nest high up on a cliff-side. Botoque climbed up to the nest, using a crude ladder that he made on the spot, and threw down two eggs to his brother-in-law. On the way down, however, the eggs turned to stone and broke the brother-in-law's hand when he tried to catch them. Angered, the brother-in-law pushed the ladder away, so that Botoque was stranded on the cliff ledge, and left him.

After several days, Botoque spotted a *JAGUAR* walking through the forest, carrying all sorts of dead game as well as a bow and arrows. When the jaguar noticed Botoque's shadow, he pounced on it, but then realized his mistake. The jaguar spoke to Botoque, promising him that, if he would come

down, the jaguar would not kill and eat him. Instead, he said, he would adopt Botoque as his son and teach him to hunt. Botoque agreed, and the jaguar replaced the ladder for Botoque to climb down.

The jaguar's wife was not at all pleased with the idea of having to raise a human son, and feared that it would lead to trouble, but she was overruled by her husband. Botoque observed, and so learned, how it was that the jaguars made fire and cooked their meat. The next day, when the jaguar went out hunting and left Botoque with his wife, Botoque asked her for cooked tapir, but she refused him and bared her claws. The frightened Botoque took refuge up a tree. When the husband returned and heard about what had happened, he warned his wife to leave Botoque alone, but she was very reluctant to do so, so much did she resent Botoque's imposition.

Next, the jaguar taught Botoque how to make a bow and arrows. When the jaguar went off hunting again, his wife once more threatened Botoque, and so Botoque

THE REVERSAL of the rulership of the earth, taken from the jaguar by Botoque, is celebrated by the Kayapo of central Brazil after the killing of a jaguar.

fired an arrow from his bow and killed her. He knew he had to flee, so he gathered up some roasted meat, a burning ember and his bow and arrows, and found his way through the forest back to his village.

When his fellow humans saw these amazing things, and realized their meaning and use, they too went to the jaguar's house. From it they stole the fire, all the cooked meat, bows and arrows, and even the jaguar's cotton string. (In some versions of the story, they dropped some embers as they ran from the house, and birds caught them up to keep the forest from catching fire – those that were singed became the species with flame-coloured beaks, legs and feet.) When the jaguar returned, he was enraged at Botoque's ingratitude and disloyalty, but, now outnumbered and weaponless, was forced to begin eating his meat raw and to hunt with his claws and teeth, while men could hunt with bows and arrows and cook their food on the fire. To this day, the jaguar's lost fire can be seen, especially at night, in the gleam of its eyes.

CABILLACA see *CAVILLACA*.

CACHA, a pre-*INCA* and Inca city/ceremonial centre about 100 km (62 miles) southeast of *CUZCO*, was the site of a temple to *VIRA-COCHA*. Its religious significance was revealed when excavations, which uncovered dense occupation of the site from at least the late Middle Horizon, demonstrated the antiquity of belief in Viracocha. The temple itself, a massive building with interior columns, was unlike many other Inca constructions in being made of *adobe* bricks rather than stone.

Myth and legend form a significant part of the city's pre-Inca history. After the creation at *TITICACA*, Viracocha travelled widely, teaching and performing miracles, and soon came to Cacha. When they saw him approach, the people came out of the town in a hostile mood and threatened to stone him. Several of them rushed at him with weapons. Viracocha fell upon his knees and raised his arms to the skies as if in supplication. The skies were immediately filled with fire, and the people of Cacha, terrified and cowed, asked for Viracocha's forgiveness and begged him to save them. According to one source, he extinguished the fires with three strokes of his staff, but not before they had scorched the huge rocks of the area such that they became "light as cork".

The people of Cacha thereafter revered the stones and regarded them as *HUACAS*. They gave the god the name *CONTITI VIRACOCHA PACH-AYACHACHIC* ("god, the maker of the world") and carved and erected a large stone sculpture on the spot where they had met him. They brought offerings of gold and silver both to the stones and to the representation of Viracocha.

The 16th-century chronicler, Juan de Betanzos, described his visit to the site, where he saw the statue (he also records having seen a similar one at *URCOS*). He questioned the people of the town, who described Viracocha's appearance: tall, dressed in a pure white robe that fell to his ankles, belted at the waist; he was bare-headed and had short-cropped hair, tonsured like a priest's; and in his hands he carried an object that was said to resemble a priest's breviary.

It is easy to suspect Christian influence and overtones in this description, particularly since the Inca had no writing system and were under heavy proselytizing pressure from Spanish priests. But what is mythology to Europeans was firm religious belief to Andean peoples, and their description was undoubtedly sincere, and might well have been accurate. It might be that the Spanish words and interpretations transform the Inca description into an image familiar to European understanding.

CACHI see *AYAR CACHI*.

CAHUACHI, in the *NAZCA* Valley of southern Peru, comprised a vast complex of ceremonial mounds and associated plazas scattered over 150 ha (360 acres). Its location was deliberately chosen in the middle section of the valley, where, for geological reasons, the Nazca River disappears underground (it re-emerges below Cahuachi). The mounds were built of *adobe* bricks to enhance the tops of a cluster of about 40 natural hills in the middle of the valley. The earliest mounds were constructed before AD 100, by which time Cahuachi was the most important site in the region, but later mound-building ceased rather abruptly, and by about AD 550 the site was abandoned – although it continued to be recognized as sacred, and remained a mortuary ground and place of votive offerings long after that date.

Cahuachi faced north, towards the desert of San José, and a virtually straight "road" leads from it across the desert to the site of Ventilla, thought to have been a Nazca "capital". Few architectural or artefactual elements found at Cahuachi indicate permanent residence. There was no domestic refuse, and storage buildings were mostly for ritual paraphernalia or workshops. Two-thirds of the ceramics are special wares for offerings, rather than Nazca household wares. The burials and artefacts associated with the mounds show conclusively that the entire site was a place of pilgrimage and ritual burial in family plots, each kin group building its own mound. The largest of the mound structures, known as the "Great Temple", was a 30 m (98 ft) high modified hillock made up of six or seven terraces formed by *adobe*-brick retaining walls. At its base, excavations have revealed small storage rooms filled with caches of clay panpipes used in Nazca ritual ceremonies.

As with so many other cultures in the Andean and adjacent western lowland regions, the focus appears to have been on ancestor worship alongside a pantheon of gods who are now nameless.

Although most of the burials have been looted over the past centuries, excavations of unlooted tombs in the 1980s and 1990s uncovered mummified burials accompanied by exquisitely decorated, multicoloured woven burial coats and pottery, and sometimes by animal sacrifices. By virtue of their treatment, some of the burials appear to be sacrificial victims – not captured enemies, but men, women and children of the Nazca themselves. Some of the skulls had excrement placed in their mouths; some had been perforated and a cord inserted for carrying; some had blocked eyes, cactus spines pinning the mouth, tongues removed and placed in pouches: all indicative of ritual practices.

On the textiles and pottery were images of the gods: half-human, half-animal figures – felines with long, ratcheted tails, spiders with human faces, birds, monkeys, lizards. The fringes of some of the textiles display rows of dangling heads/mummified skulls with staring eyes, and even lines of full figures wearing short tunics, dancing above round-eyed deities who appear to be flying. In general the figures resemble those depicted in the Nazca "lines", the geoglyphs on the *pampa* desert nearby.

As the coastal plains and lower valleys of southern Peru became more arid, through changes in the weather patterns in the mountains to the east (perhaps coupled with disastrous earthquakes), Cahuachi was abandoned – deliberately, for the mounds were systematically covered with layers of dirt, as the Cahuachi people believed that the power of the gods had abandoned them. At the same time, there was an increase in the number and elaboration of Nazca "lines" and ground markings on the desert between Cahuachi and Ventilla.

EXQUISITELY PRESERVED textiles *from Nazca burials in the ritual city of Cahuachi depict mythological symbols and figures in vivid colour.*

C

CAJATAMBO, an *INCA* and Spanish colonial town in the highlands of central Peru, was remarkable for the strength of *IDOLATRÍAS* recorded there by the Spanish "extirpator of idolatries" in the early 17th century. It serves as an exemplar of the intimate connections that persisted between Inca provincial communities and their local *HUACAS*, or sacred objects and places, in the countryside around them, both in Inca and post-Spanish-conquest times.

The peoples of Cajatambo, like most provincial inhabitants of the Inca Empire, were grouped into lineage *AYLLUS* and *MOIETIES*. Here they were divided into two perceived "types" of people, the Guari and the Llacuaz. The Guari, the original inhabitants of the region, had established the earliest towns throughout the lowland valleys, and their economy was based primarily on corn (maize) cultivation. The other group, the Llacuaz, were not indigenous, but had come from the *puna*, or highlands, and cultivated the potato, as well as herding flocks of llamas and alpacas; they were later arrivals, having migrated into or invaded the region probably shortly before it was conquered by the Incas in the 15th century, and had established dominance over the Guaris.

Each group had its own principal deity. The patron god of the Guaris was a giant referred to as "Huari" who lived among the caves. Another important Guari deity was the "night-time sun" (the sun after sunset, when it was believed to pass through a hidden, watery passage into the underworld until the next day's sunrise). Guari myth recounted how their ancestors came into the region in the distant past, either from the west, across the ocean, or from the south, from Lake *TITICACA*. The principal god of the Llacuazs was Llibiac, the god of thunder and lightning, and they also worshipped, in contrast to the Guaris,

the "daytime sun" (that is, the sun from sunrise to sunset), as well as the stars.

The religious ritual of the two groups celebrated the conquest and domination of the Guaris by the Llacuazs, and also their reconciliation and confederation into what might be termed a symbiotic relationship. Each group would perform rituals to commemorate the other moiety, and there were also certain rituals that were performed jointly. Both of the groups maintained and revered common *huacas* and sacred objects, and the Guaris worshipped special amulets called *canopas*, which they believed to control the fertility of their corn (maize) crops. Each group recognized sacred places throughout the region where *CAPACOCHA* sacrificial victims were buried. At the time that the Spaniards recorded the "idolatries" that the people of Cajatambo believed these sacrificial burials to be the link between themselves and the Inca overlords, and that the Incas were the rightful owners of the land.

In addition, each group maintained exclusive bonds with special *huacas* (mountain-tops, springs and caves in the surrounding countryside) and *HUANCAS* (particularly prominent boulders) that they believed held the spirits of one or more of the group's ancestors. Particular focus was given to the numerous caves in the region, called *machay*, for it was from these that the *ayllus* believed that their ancestors had come, and it was in these that they stored the mummified bodies (*MALLQUIS*) of the ancestors. They dressed the mummies in new clothes at ceremonies marking the agricultural turning-points of the year, especially planting and harvest times, and offered them food and drink so as to assure the prosperity of the community. The importance of the *mallquis* is shown by the *idolatría* accounts for 1656–8, which record 1,825 mummies among four towns

around Cajatambo alone. The beliefs of the Guaris and Llacuazs thus included myths recounting the events that led to the establishment of these sacred places and how the ancestors came to be incorporated into the landscape and to interact with it.

(For another source of comparable "idolatries" see *HUAROCHIRÍ MANUSCRIPT.*)

CANNIBALISM was a widespread feature of many cultures, both "civilized" and "primitive", throughout the ancient Americas. Among the Aztecs of Mesoamerica it was a regular ritual practice of the nobility and priests following human sacrifice, and in South America the practice was widespread among rain forest tribes, and was documented historically to recent times.

The practice was always associated with ritual, rather than with nourishment in the physical sense. It was bound up with sacrifice, warfare, death and regeneration, with social identity and kinship relations, and with the transference of

"Exocannibalism" was a form that involved the eating of the flesh of an enemy in order to prove one's power, to confirm and finalize martial triumph and the humiliation of the defeated foe, and to take revenge on his companions. Cannibalistic warriors were thought to have the spirits of *JAGUARS*, whose behaviour was seen as not dissimilar.

"Endocannibalism" had a more respectful motivation. The dead person's bones were ground to dust and then mixed into manioc "beer" to be drunk by the family and other relatives in order to preserve within the kinship groups the essence of the dead person. By this means, his or her qualities were believed to be perpetuated in the bodies and spirits of the cannibals.

CANOPAS see under *CAJATAMBO*.

CAPAC RAYMI was the December summer solstice, the occasion of one of the two most crucial, and, it was hoped, propitious ceremonies of the year in honour of the *INCA* sun god, *INTI*. It was a royal feast and a ceremony that focused

the soul or essence of being from the eaten to the eater. It was an act intended to transfer the power, prowess, accomplishments and skills of the dead person.

CANNIBALISM, when discovered by Europeans among Amazonian tribes, was abhorred and therefore depicted in an exaggerated fashion. (GOTTFRIED'S *HISTORIA ANTIPODUM*, 1665.)

HUANAYPATA PLAZA, in present-day Cuzco, is thought to be where Capac Usnu – "the navel of the universe" of the Inca world – stood, and from which astronomical observances took place.

on the initiation rituals for boys of royal lineage (see also *INTI RAYMI*). Plotting and confirmation of the date of the ritual was done by observations taken from the *CORICANCHA*.

CAPAC TOCO, *INCA*, literally

"rich window", was one of the caves of *TAMBO TOCO*, the central "window" from which *MANCO CAPAC* and the Inca ancestors emerged.

CAPAC USNU, or Capac Ush-

nuo, ("navel of the universe"), stood in the sacred *CORICANCHA* in *CUZCO*, at the centre of the *INCA* Empire (*TAHUANTINSUYU*). It was the first *HUACA* on a sacred *CEQUE* line that linked it to two stone pillars on the skyline west of the city, and to the *huaca* at *CATACHILLAY* spring.

The Capac Usnu comprised a multifaceted, finely carved stone dais with a carved seat and the vertical pillar of Usnu itself. The seat was the throne of the *SAPA INCA* ("Son of the Sun") from which he refreshed and maintained the order of the world. The emperor sat on this throne to review processions of the mummified ancestors – the *MALLQUIS* – and to placate them with offerings. From the dais, he toasted the gods, especially *INTI* and *VIRACOCHA*, with copious libations of *chicha* (corn/maize beer), which were poured down the "gullet of the sun": a stone basin, lined with sheet gold, that was set at the foot of the Usnu.

The Usnu pillar served as a sighting point for astronomical observations. From it, both the sunset on 26 April and the setting of the Pleiades on or about 15 April were observed through the distant pillars on the skyline. Astronomical observations of *MAYU* (the Milky Way) and other celestial groups, and of the southern constellations,

were made from this and other positions around the Coricancha plaza, including from a tower of finely fitted stone blocks. The time of the zenith could be predicted precisely from a window in the tower by viewing at sunrise a marker point set up on the skyline to the east of the city.

CAPAC YUPANQUI was the

legendary fifth *INCA* ruler of *CUZCO*, probably ruling at some time in the first half of the 13th century. Like all Inca rulers, he was considered to be a direct descendant of the ancestors, *MANCO CAPAC* and *MAMA OCLLO*.

CAPACOCHA, or Qhapaq Hu-

cha, were ritual practices that involved taking specially selected individuals, usually children, from among the high-ranking *AYLLU* kinship lineages of the provinces of the *INCA* Empire and bringing them to the capital at *CUZCO* to be trained and prepared for the ritual. The selection was made annually and those chosen were destined to become sacrificial victims following ritual ceremonies in the capital. Such sacrifices were offerings to the sun god *INTI*, to the creator god *VIRACOCHA*, or to both. Momentous events – war, pestilence, famine or other natural disasters – could also provoke such sacrifices.

Having been brought to Cuzco, the chosen ones were sanctified by the priests in the *CORICANCHA*

precinct, who offered them up to the supreme god, Viracocha, and then marched back to their home provinces along the sacred *CEQUE* lines that linked those provinces to the capital. There, the victims were sacrificed by being clubbed to death, strangled with a cord or having the throat slit, before burial, or by being buried alive in a specially constructed shaft-tomb. Children were sometimes drugged with *chicha* (corn/maize beer). Votive offerings usually accompanied the victim in death, such as elaborate clothing, human figures made of gold, silver, bronze or shell and dressed in miniature garments, llama figurines and miniature sets of ceramic containers.

The victims were sometimes carried up and left on high mountain tops regarded as sacred *HUACAS*, where their bodies sometimes became preserved in the cold, dry conditions that prevailed in such places; some famous examples include Cerro el Plomo in the Chilean Andes, Mount Aconcagua on the Chilean–Argentinian border, Puná Island off the coast of Ecuador, the "ice maiden" at Mount *AMPATO* and

CAPAC YUPANQUI, the fifth Inca emperor, depicted in an imaginary sketch. (NUEVA CORÓNICA Y BUEN GOBIERNO BY FELIPE GUAMAN POMA DE AYALA, 1583–1613.)

the sacrifice of two girls and a boy on Mount *LLULLAILLACO*.

Such practices served two purposes: to renew or reconfirm the bond between the Inca state and the provincial peoples of the empire, and to reassert Inca overlordship and reaffirm the heirarchy between the Inca centre and the provincial *ayllus*.

CARANCHO see *CHACO*.

CARI and Zapana were legendary

rulers of city-states in the *TITICACA* Basin in the Bolivian highlands. According to an *INCA* legend, Cari sought the help of the Incas in the valley of Cuzco to the northwest, against his rival Zapana. The Incas, however, saw this as an opportunity (or invitation) to invade the region and subjugate both cities. Although long after the civilization of *TIAHUANACO* had flourished, the Incas were conscious of the powerful empire that had obviously created the ruined city and its huge stone statues, and were keen to legitimize their own empire as its heir, as well as to justify their incursions into other regions. This legend therefore seems to be another example of the Inca rewriting history to suit their own purposes.

183

CATACHILLAY was the name of an *INCA* sacred spring on a ritual *CEQUE* line radiating from the *CORICANCHA* in *CUZCO*. The line led west and linked the spring to the *HUACAS* of the *CAPAC USNU* and to two upright sighting stones on the horizon between the spring and the pillar.

Because the alignment was used for observations of the April setting of the Pleiades, Catachillay was also an alternative name for that star group (see *COLLCA*).

CAVILLACA, in pre-*INCA* and Inca legend, was a beautiful female virgin *HUACA* wooed by *CONIRAYA VIRACOCHA*. The tale is related in the *HUAROCHIRÍ MANUSCRIPT*.

CAYLLA VIRACOCHA, the *INCA* name of a creator worshipped by the *Wari Wiracocharuna* of the "first age" (see *PACHACUTI*), was one of many variations of *VIRACOCHA*.

THE CEQUE system was an *INCA* concept interwoven with myth, astronomical observation, architectural alignment, and the social and geographical divisions of the empire.

Ceques were sacred "lines" that radiated from the *CORICANCHA* precinct, *CUZCO*, each line linking numerous sacred locations (*HUACAS*) along its length. There were 41 *ceques* uniting 328 *huacas* and survey points within and around Cuzco. It is perhaps significant that the 328 *huacas* and stations equal the number of days in 12 sidereal lunar months (328 ÷ 12 = the 27.3-day period of the rotation of the moon around the earth–moon centre of mass). They were grouped according to *HANAN* (upper) and *HURIN* (lower) Cuzco and thus according to the four quarters (*TAHUANTINSUYU*) of the empire. Points along the lines also served to regulate landholdings, water distribution, labour divisions, and ritual and ceremonial activities. *Ceque* lines also served as processional paths to be followed by the *CAPA-*

COCHA victims before being sacrificed. Similarly, the combination of *ceques* and their *huacas* were used to distinguish the different *PANACA* kin-group landholdings. Sunset on 26 April and the setting of the Pleiades on or about 15 April were observed from the pillar in the *CAPAC USNU* between two stone pillars, together regarded as a *huaca*, erected on the skyline west of the city. Along the same *ceque*, beyond the horizon, was a further *huaca*, the spring of *CATACHILLAY* (a name for the Pleiades). The 16th-century chronicler Juan de Betanzos describes the sixth *ceque* of *ANTISUYU*, on which lay the sixth *huaca*, known as "the house of the puma". Here, the richly dressed and mummified body of the wife of the emperor *PACHACUTI INCA YUPANQUI* was kept, to whom child sacrifices were offered.

Similarly, the movements of *MAYU*, the Milky Way, were linked to the *ceque* system by a division separating the four quarters of the empire along the intercardinal axis of the Milky Way and the southernmost point of the Milky Way's movement in the night sky.

CETERNI was the wife of the *LAMBAYEQUE* ruler *NAYAMLAP*.

CEUCY was the virgin woman of the Brazilian *TUPI* tribe, instrumental in the domination of humans by men (see *JURUPARI*).

THE FANGED GOD, or stylized jaguar, along with the Staff Deity, was typical of Chavín imagery. Numerous representations adorned the Old Temple.

SACRED CEQUE LINES of Inca ritual and astronomical sighting radiated from the Temple of the Sun (Inti) in the Coricancha precinct in Cuzco, on the Inca base of which now stands the church of Santo Domingo.

CHACO and Chaco tribes were the region and peoples of the *pampas* of northern Argentina and Chile, Paraguay and southeastern Bolivia (see also *TOBA*). The hunting peoples of this area seem to have lacked a consistent cosmology or supreme being. Variations include Kasogonaga, the sky goddess who brought rain, and a red anteater and a giant beetle as the creators of the first man and woman. There were also ancestor deities referred to as the "grandfather" and the "grandmother", and various benevolent spirits who aided the hunt. Different tribes recounted stories of rival brothers to explain duality; of the rainbow that brought death by its tongue; of killer stars; and of a culture hero – "the hawk" – whom they called Carancho, who was confronted by a fox, but overcame him.

CHAN CHAN see *CHIMÚ*.

CHANCA was a powerful political unity west of the *INCA* capital, *CUZCO*. The Chancas attacked Cuzco in the early 15th century but were defeated by the tenth Inca ruler, *PACHACUTI INCA YUPANQUI*.

CHASCA see *CHASKA-QOYLOR*.

CHASKA-QOYLOR ("shaggy star") was the *INCA* goddess of Venus, one of the luminaries recognized within *MAYU*, the Milky Way. She was the guardian of young maidens and flowers.

CHAVÍN, the first great civilization of the central Andean region, defines the period known as the Early Horizon (900–200 BC). Its principal "city" and ceremonial centre was Chavín de Huántar.

Although not the largest ceremonial centre, Chavín de Huántar was one of the most elaborate sites, and the focus and source of a pan-Andean religious cult, together with its accompanying iconography. It also played a crucial role in the dissemination of technology. The site would appear to have been strategically located in the Andes roughly midway between the coast (west) and the tropical lowlands (east). Although not truly urban in layout and proportions, Chavín de Huantar's size and importance implies that it housed a resident population of priests, officials, artisans, servants and pilgrims to support and serve the cult.

At its greatest extent the site covered about 42 ha (104 acres) and had between 2,000 and 3,000

inhabitants. The Old Temple is a U-shaped platform wrapped around a circular sunken courtyard. Projecting from its four-storey high stone walls are scores of sculpted heads. Inside the temple itself there is a labyrinthine series of interconnecting narrow passages and chambers. The southern wing, later doubled in size as the site flourished, is known as the New Temple, although both temples were used simultaneously after the expansion.

In one of the interior galleries stands the stone idol known as the *Lanzón* (so called because of its lance-like shape) or Great Image, probably the earliest pan-Andean oracle: a carved granite monolith 4.55 m (15 ft) high. The idol faces east and portrays a humanoid, but overall monstrous visage. Its right hand is raised, its left lowered by its side, and both feet and hands end in claws. Its mouth is thick-lipped, drawn in a hideous snarl and punctuated by long, outward-curving canine teeth (see *FANGED GOD*). Its eyebrows and hair end in serpent-heads; its earlobes hang heavy with pendants. It wears a tunic and headdress, both decorated with feline heads. The notched top of the idol protrudes through the ceiling into the gallery above, where it is thought that priests sat in secrecy projecting their voices as the voice of the god.

That Chavín de Huántar was the site of a cult seems indisputable. In a gallery next to the sunken circular plaza, excavators found some 800 broken ceramic vessels decorated in a variety of styles from cultures spread as far apart as the northern coast and the central highlands. There were bowls and bottle-like containers and, scattered among them, the bones of llamas and other camelids, deer, guinea pigs and fish. The pots and bones are thought to have been either offerings or stored ritual trappings for ceremonies.

Chavín iconography drew its inspiration from the natural world – animals and plants – and from a

THE RUINS of Chavín de Huántar, the first great cult centre and pilgrimage site of ancient Andean religion.

gamut of ecological zones – the ocean, the coast, the mountains and the tropical lowlands. The Tello Obelisk, found buried at Chavín de Huántar, is a low-relief granite monolith, 2.52 m (99 in) high, carved in the shape of a supernatural crocodile. Notched at the top like the *Lanzón*, it probably also stood upright in a gallery. Additional carvings on and around the crocodile depict various plants and animals, including peanuts and manioc from the tropical lowlands and *Strombus* and *Spondylus* shells of species native to the Ecuadorian coast, attesting to the wide net spread by the Chavín cult. In addition there are *JAGUARS*, *SERPENTS* and harpy or crested eagles.

As the fame of the cult spread and the site was enlarged, ceramic styles and further exotic foods, plants, and animals continued to inspire the cult iconography. There is evidence from the domestic buildings for the development of social hierarchy among the citizenry, in the form of unequal distribution of goods, and for craft specialization. The religious cult supported artisans who applied its symbolism to portable artefacts as well as to monumental sculpture, and the distribution of these artefacts by exchange expanded and entrenched the spread of the cult.

With the expansion of the south wing of the temple complex, the iconography began to grow still more elaborate. The relief of a new supreme deity was set up in the patio of the New Temple. Like the *Lanzón*, this depicts a humanoid figure with a fanged mouth, who is shown wearing multiple bracelets, anklets and ear pendants. It is holding a *Strombus* shell in its right hand and a *Spondylus* shell in its left hand. This deity may be the precursor for the late *MOCHE/CHIMÚ* god *AI APAEC*.

Another huge carved stone slab, the Raimondi Stela (1.98m/6½ ft long), depicts a hallmark of the Chavín cult: the *STAFF DEITY*. This figure, ubiquitous in Chavín iconography, was portrayed with male or female attributes as a full-frontal, standing figure of composite animal and human characteristics. Like other Chavín deities, the hands and feet end in claws, the mouth displays huge, curved fangs, and the ears are bedecked with ornaments. The arms are outstretched to either side and clutch staffs in one form or another, themselves elaborately festooned with spikes and plume-like decorations.

The significance and meaning of the Staff Deity is uncertain. His/her importance is attested by the appli-

cation of the image all over Chavín de Huántar, and throughout the central Andes and coast. His/her potency is likewise demonstrated by the fact that the imagery of a full-frontal, staff-bearing deity endured from the Early Horizon to Late Horizon times. Given this exceptional importance, it seems certain that the Staff Deity was a supernatural being with a distinct "personality", possibly a primeval creator god (see also *HUARI*, *TIAHUANACO*).

A final aspect of the labyrinth of galleries and passages in the Chavín de Huántar temples is the ritual use of water. A system of conduits in the chambers could literally be made to roar when water was flushed rapidly through the drains and the sound vented around the chambers. What this sounded like, and what other-worldly feelings it evoked in the minds and hearts of worshippers, can only be imagined (see also *MACHU PICCHU*, *PARACAS*, and *SACSAHUAMAN*).

CHAVÍN DE HUÁNTAR
see *CHAVÍN*.

CHECA YAUYOS
see *HUAROCHIRÍ MANUSCRIPT*.

CHEQO HUASI (WASI)
see *HUARI*.

THE TELLO OBELISK, carved in the shape of a crocodile, is covered with images of animals and plants from mountains, coast and rain forest, attesting to the widespread influence of the Chavín cult.

CREATION MYTHS

CREATOR DEITIES AND CREATION myths feature in all the ancient South American cultures. Among the ancient civilizations of the Andes and the adjacent western coastal valleys, two supreme creator gods were particularly prominent: Viracocha and Pachacamac. The former had numerous manifestations and names, but most accounts portray him as a creator who once walked among the people and taught them. Pachacamac was somewhat more remote, more an oracle to be consulted than a missionary. Common features were the creation of the sun and moon, and the emergence of humankind from underground. Most myths name the Titicaca Basin as the place of creation; indeed, so all-pervading was its importance that the Inca sought to link their own origin to Tiahuanaco in Titicaca, and went to great lengths to embrace the accounts of all the peoples they conquered.

Among the rain forest tribes of the Amazon drainage, eastern coasts, *pampas* and Patagonia, accounts of creation are more discursive. All tribes have beliefs about where people came from and how they came into being, but there is less emphasis on detail, and wider variation in the place of origin. For example, humans came either from underground or from the sky. After creating the world, however, rain forest gods take little further interest in humankind's day-to-day existence. A prominent theme is that jaguars were the masters of the earth before humans, and that the jaguars' powers were acquired by humans after they had been adopted by jaguars and had betrayed them.

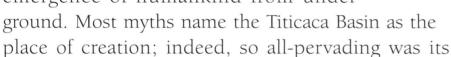

VIRACOCHA (above) was perhaps the most universally recognized Andean god. He was known by numerous additional names, and his character varied in detail from culture to culture. In general, he was described as a benevolent god who created the earth, sun, moon and humankind at Lake Titicaca and travelled throughout the land teaching the arts of civilization before departing across the ocean. Variously described in Inca accounts as wearing a white robe or in the rags of a beggar, and having a long beard, numerous stone statues – assumed from their contexts to represent him – present a different image, such as this angular Tiahuanaco stone idol.

LAKE TITICACA (above) was a place of reverence for most of the ancient cultures of the Andes, and almost universally believed to be the place where the world began. The sun and the moon were believed to have risen from islands named for them, created by the act of Viracocha. The islands became places of pilgrimage, and the nearby ancient site of Tiahuanaco was revered by the Incas, who recognized the power of the civilization that must have ruled there.

THE IMPORTANCE and power of the jaguar (above) was a prominent theme among rain forest tribes east of the Andes. The jaguar was believed to have originally been the possessor of fire and of hunting weapons, both of which were obtained by humans through trickery or theft. The roles were then reversed, and jaguars had to hunt by stealth, kill their prey with their fangs and claws and eat their meat raw. Nevertheless, reverence for the jaguar's power and ancient knowledge endured, for example through shamans.

THE EMERGENCE of humans from underground (left), usually from caves, was a common theme in Andean creation myths. The Incas identified the caves of their own origin in the mountain Tambo Toco ("window house") in Pacaritambo, about 26 km (16 miles) south of Cuzco. Acknowledging the importance and power of the ancient site of Tiahuanaco in the Titicaca Basin, however, they sought to link their origins – and right to rule – to Titicaca by claiming that the Inca ancestors were led by Manco Capac underground from the lake to emerge at Tambo Toco.

THE CHIBCHA, or Muisca, of the Colombian central highlands were one of several skilled metalworking peoples who developed distinctive cultures in the cordilleran and western coastal regions from about the 1st century AD to the Spanish conquest. They worked primarily with gold and copper (individually, or alloyed as *tumbaga*) but also with silver and platinum. The Chibcha were less interested than others in making finely finished objects, but focused on making multiple versions of an object. Other metal-working cultures included Tairona and Sinú (northern Columbia); Tolima, Tierradentro and San Agustín (in the eastern cordillera); Quimbaya, Calima, Popayán and Nariño (western cordillera); and Tumaco (coastal lowlands).

According to Chibcha myth, the sun and moon created the first man from clay and the first woman from reeds. All these cultures held the afterlife as an important realm, judging by the richness of their graves, in which intricately worked gold and alloyed metal diadems, pectorals, masks and pendants, as well as stone and ceramic items were placed beside the mummified bodies. It was from the Chibcha ritual of the gilded heir to the throne that the legend of EL DORADO was born. (See BACHUE, BOCHICA, CHIBCHACUM, CHIE, CHIMINIGAGUA, HUITACA, NEMTEREQUETEBA)

CHIBCHACUM, the CHIBCHA patron deity of workers and merchants, was important among a people whose metalworking skills were highly valued. That honour notwithstanding, in Chibcha myth he once attempted to destroy humankind with a flood, enlisting the help of a woman called CHIE, to spite the founder hero BOCHICA. The people appealed to Bochica for help, and Chibchacum was unsuccessful. He fled underground in fear, and from that day on was burdened with having to support the world on his shoulders.

CHICHA

was the fermented corn (maize) beer that was offered to the mummified bodies (MALLQUIS) of ancestors and drunk by priests and attendants in ritual worship and ceremony.

CHIE was the CHIBCHA moon goddess who helped CHIBCHACUM in an attempt to defy BOCHICA.

CHIMINIGAGUA was the CHIBCHA so-called creator god. He created the large black bird that carried the light (probably of the sun) over the mountains, but left the rest of creation up to others. The goddess BACHUE was responsible for the procreation of humans.

CHIMO CAPAC ("Lord Chimú") invaded the LAMBAYEQUE VALLEY following the death of FEMPELLEC of the NAYAMLAP dynasty. According to myth, he came from the south by sea. As with the earliest INCA kings, this myth appears to be an early account, handed down the generations, recording the early days of the CHIMÚ Kingdom. Chimo Capac probably came up from the MOCHE Valley, the centre of Chimor, in the 14th century, conquered the Lambayeque Valley and incorporated it into his kingdom. The account of this says that he appointed a man named Pongmassa as local CURACA, and that Pongmassa was succeeded by his son and then by his grandson. During the rulership of the grandson, the Incas conquered the valley, established their alliance with the Kingdom of Chimor and continued to administer the valley through five further *curacas*.

THIS PECTORAL

of hammered and repoussé gold is in the Calima style and depicts a deity. The cultures of Colombia probably shared similar beliefs and deities, although we know the names of only a few Chibcha gods.

CHIMOR see CHIMÚ.

CHIMÚ, or Kingdom of Chimor, emerging in the Late Intermediate Period, was a state-level society that established its dominance in the northern coastal valleys and adjacent Andean region of Peru, and later came into conflict with the INCA Empire. Like the MOCHE before them, the Chimú conquered north and south over a period of about 400 years. The Chimú are second only to the Incas in importance in the study of Andean mythology, as their culture is the only other one for which we have written accounts of the myths and cosmology, although these have reached us primarily through the Incas (see AMAUTAS and QUIPUCAMAYOQS). Much of Chimú religion appears to have been influenced by the Moche; certainly the Chimú were the inheritors of Moche

CHICHA beer was drunk on ritual occasions in most ancient Andean cultures. This Moche stirrup-spouted vessel is in the shape of a noble holding a chicha cup.

power in the region, although they seem to have come from outside, a possibility recorded in their mythology (see CHIMO CAPAC, TAYCANAMU).

Chan Chan, their capital, was founded *c.* AD 1000 and endured until the Inca conquest of the region in the 1470s by TUPAC INCA YUPANQUI, overcoming MINCHANÇAMAN. It comprised an extensive complex of individual compounds covering 6 sq km (1,480 acres), around which domestic and workshop suburbs spread over 20 sq km (4,940 acres). Each walled compound (known as a *ciudadela*) of the central core was rectangular, its long axis oriented north–south, and made of thick walls up to 9 m (30 ft) high of poured *adobe* mud. Most had only one entrance, on the north side, guarded by painted wooden human figures set in niches on each side. Each court contained the residences of the reigning Chimú king, and his officials. Around other courtyards within the compounds were storerooms, U-shaped structures (called *audiencias*) and burial platforms. Adjacent wings

contained rooms for service and maintenance retainers, and walled-in wells.

Burials were placed in and near the U-shaped structures, which were possibly meant to reflect reverence for the ancient U-shaped ceremonial complexes of the area (see CHAVÍN). They represented "cosmic niches", and served a ritual purpose. They were also centres for the redistribution of goods, part of a tightly controlled social structure for collection and distribution of wealth, foods and commodities, according to social rank. Along the

THE FUNERARY ciudadela compounds, each surrounded by massive adobe walls, form the core of the ruins of Chan Chan, the ancient capital of Chimú.

that might have housed the mummified dead body (see MALLQUIS) of the king. The Chimú king list, which was recorded by the Incas, names ten kings.

There are also five monumental *adobe* brick mounds at Chan Chan, possibly temple platforms, but they have been so destroyed by treasure-seekers that we cannot now be sure of their function.

More generally, Chimú iconography appears to be a merging of Moche and HUARI styles and mythological beings, and Chimú ritual architecture reveals Huari influence. The FANGED GOD, JAGUARS and JAGUAR-HUMANS, and SERPENTS (all elements that ultimately stem from Chavín) figure prominently. On the other hand, the Chimú repertoire seems more limited than Moche, and composed ritual scenes were rarely portrayed. In general, the Chimú religion and pantheon seem more remote.

The nature of Chimú ceremonies is uncertain, so filtered was their history by the Inca record keepers. A huge burial platform next to one of the *ciudadelas*, however, held more than 200 bodies, including those of young women who might have been sacrificed to accompany the Chimú king into the afterlife.

More informative is a painted wooden model excavated in a Chimú tomb inserted into the Moche Huaca de la Luna. It appears to represent an episode of the periodic

reopening of a Chimú tomb for the addition of bodies and/or replenishment of offerings. It is 410 x 480 mm (16 x 19 in) and comprises a rectangular, miniature *ciudadela*. On its diminutive walls is a painted frieze of fish in yellow, brown, black, and white ochre. The compound has just a single, narrow entrance, and wooden human figurines stand within, carved and inlaid with mother-of-pearl and *Spondylus*-shell ornament. The figures all face a ramped platform, some standing on benches along the sides of the enclosure, others serving CHICHA beer. At the rear, partly covered by a tiny gable supported by two columns, is a sunken chamber, within which were three miniature mummy bundles, two females and one male.

HUACA EL DRAGON, a funerary compound northwest of Chan Chan, includes well-preserved examples of Chimú images, including repeated staff-bearing figures, a variety of creatures and repeated arched, double-headed "rainbow serpents".

THE WALLS of the Tschudi ciudadela at Chan Chan show characteristic Chimú carved friezes of repeated figures and geometric patterns, and storage niches.

south walls of the compounds, sloping ramps led to burial platforms for the royal family. There are ten compounds, nine of which have a truncated pyramid in the southeast corner. Entered from above through a court, each pyramid contains a suite of cells and a larger room

We know the names of only a few Chimú gods. Chief among them appear to have been AI APAEC (a sky/creator god), the moon goddess SI, and the sea god NI.

The walls and other aspects of the *ciudadelas*, however, and artefacts from these and other Chimú sites, give some insights into the nature of Chimú religion. The walls of the compound were carved and sculpted with repetitious friezes: of geometric patterns, images of birds and marine animals, and of the double-headed rainbow serpent (considered to be associated with the moon goddess Si).

CHIMÚ CERAMICS depicted everyday objects, as well as zoomorphic, anthropomorphic and ritual scenes. This stirrup-spout bottle of polished blackware (left) shows a small figure on a reed fishing raft (c. AD 1000).

CHINCHASUYU, the north-west quarter of the *INCA* Empire, comprised the Andes mountain regions and the coast west and north of Cuzco, encompassing most of modern Ecuador and stretching as far north as southern Colombia. Its western limit was the Pacific Ocean (see *TAHUANTINSUYU*).

CHOCO is a region of the Colombian rain forest inhabited by tribes whose cosmological belief is typical of the cyclicity that imbues the religion of most peoples of South America in some form. Their myths tell the story of a first race of humans that was ultimately destroyed by the gods because the people practised cannibalism. A second race was transformed into the animals, while the present race of humans had been created by the gods from clay.

THE CHOCO tribes of the Colombian rain forest believe that the present-day human race was made by the gods from clay.

CHOT was the capital city that was established by *NAYAMLAP* in the *LAMBAYEQUE VALLEY*.

CIUM, the eldest son of *NAYAMLAP*, was the second legendary ruler of the *LAMBAYEQUE* dynasty in north coastal Peru. Unlike his father, who had invaded the valley with his wife, Cium married a local woman named Zolzoloñi – the myth refers to her by the Spanish

CHINCHASUYU, the northwest quadrant of the Inca Empire, stretched from the central Andes of modern Peru and Ecuador west to the fertile Pacific coastal plains.

word *moza*, "commoner" or "outsider" in a specified group, that is, the descendants of Nayamlap. They had 12 sons, each of whom married and also produced a large family. As the population grew, each son left the capital, Chot, and founded a new city within the valley.

COCA see *MAMA COCA*.

COLLARI was the first woman in a central Andean *Q'ERO/INCA* variation of the creation myth (see *ROAL*).

COLLASUYU, the southeast and largest quarter of the *INCA* Empire, encompassed the entire *TITICACA* Basin of modern Peru and Bolivia as well as the vast Atacama Desert of northern Chile. It stretched from *CUZCO* in the northwest, south as far as, or even beyond, modern Santiago in central Chile. Its eastern and western limits were the tropical forests of the southern Amazon drainage and high *pampas* of northern Argentina, and the Pacific Ocean (see *TAHUANTINSUYU*).

COLLCA ("granary"), or Catachillay, was one of the star groups the *INCA* saw within *MAYU*, the Milky Way, identified as the Pleiades. It was believed to be the guardian of stored seeds and of agriculture.

COLLASUYU, the southeast quadrant of the Inca Empire, encompassed the high Andes and alti-planos of modern southern Peru and Bolivia, including numerous rich, high-altitude valleys.

CON see *PACHACAMAC*.

CON TICCI VIRACOCHA (central Andean/pre-*INCA*/Inca) was, at the simplest, another of the many names for *VIRACOCHA*. He was the creator god of the peoples of the Colloa region of southern highland Peru, possibly predating the Inca supreme god Viracocha and later conflated within the mythology centring on Viracocha and his travels from the *TITICACA* Basin northwest towards *CUZCO*.

Among the Colloas, he was believed to have created the sun and then made stone figures of the various peoples of the Andes, which he placed throughout the valleys. Then he travelled around bringing the stone models to life and instructing them in his worship.

One version of the Inca creation myth, related by the 16th-century chronicler Cristobal de Molina, begins at a time when the world was already full of people. A great flood rose to the tops of the mountains, destroying all except one man and one woman, who were cast up on land at the ancient site of *TIAHUANACO*. Con Ticci Viracocha appeared to them and

ordered them to remain where they were as *MITIMAES*. He repopulated the land by making the Inca ancestors out of clay and painting them with the regional dress by which they were to become known, and also made a second race of people at Tiahuanaco. He also made the birds and animals (two of each, male and female) and spread them among their habitats, designated what each was to eat, and gave each bird its song.

In Inca mythology, this dispersal of the models of the new humans was crucial to their legitimization of conquest, state creation and empire-building. Scattering humans across the regions as distinctive peoples or "nations" was regarded as a "seeding" of the land in preparation for the "coming into being". They were ordered by Viracocha to descend into the ground and re-emerge out of caves, mountains and springs when called upon.

Con Ticci Viracocha kept two of his creations with him, naming them *IMAYMANA VIRACOCHA* and *TOCAPO VIRACOCHA*. The inclusion of "Viracocha" in their names imbued them with divinity and supernatural power, as well as identifying them with Viracocha himself. In some versions, they are said to be Con Ticci Viracocha's sons.

After these creations, Viracocha began his pilgrimage from Lake Titicaca. He commanded his elder son, Imaymana Viracocha, to travel northwestwards along a route bordering the forests and mountains,

THE RICH, intensive agriculture carried out on terraces in the Andes was believed to come under the protection of Collca, or the Pleiades, one of many star groups that were recognized in the Milky Way.

and his younger son, Tocapo Viracocha, to journey northwards along a coastal route, while he went along a route between them, northwestwards through the mountains. As they passed through the land, they called out the people created by Viracocha, named the trees and the plants, established the times when each would flower and bear fruit, and instructed the people on which were edible and which medicinal.

They continued to what would become the northwesternmost edge of the Inca Empire, in modern Ecuador, to the coastal site of *MANTA*, then continued across the sea, walking on water until they disappeared.

The trinity implied by the three Viracochas suggests that there was an element of Christian persuasion in the relations of the Spanish chroniclers, but it is an argument that cannot be concluded. The Incas had no writing system and were under heavy pressure from proselytizing Spanish priests. Their religion, written as mythology by the chroniclers, brought them favour if it could be shown to have an element of the "truth" by being a warped version of Christian belief. One 16th-century Inca chronicler, Juan de Santa Cruz Pachacuti Yamqui, even believed that the creator, known as *THUNUPA VIRACOCHA* to him, was the apostle St Thomas; and the Inca chronicler, Felipe Guaman Poma de Ayala, identified Viracocha with St Bartholomew.

On the other hand, triadism is a general concept, and was held by many ancient cultures throughout the world. The specific "Andean Triad" of a tripartite Viracocha had several variations, and only in some of them does the triad comprise a father and two sons – which in itself is not a configuration characteristic of Christian trinitarianism.

CONAPA see *TONAPA*.

CONCHA YAUYOS see *HUAROCHIRÍ MANUSCRIPT*.

CONIRAYA VIRACOCHA, a pre-*INCA* deity named in the early 17th-century *HUAROCHIRÍ MANUSCRIPT,* was described as a creator god by its compilers, but they reach no conclusion as to whether Coniraya Viracocha was the same deity as the pan-Andean *VIRACOCHA*, who created the world at Lake *TITICACA*. The significant point is that the adventures of Coniraya Viracocha, some of which parallel those of Viracocha, were recounted to the compilers by highland Andean dwellers even though the legendary events take place in the coastal lowlands. The reality of ancient coastal and Andean cultural interrelationships and interdependencies, and Inca efforts to integrate and reconcile the peoples and religious beliefs throughout its empire, appears to be reflected in the mythology.

The story in the Manuscript begins when the god *HUALLALLO CARHUINCHO* had ruled Huarochirí for some time. The authors are unclear as to whether Coniraya Viracocha lived before or after this time. Still he was a powerful deity who, by his word alone, could create towns and villages, agricultural lands, and terraces across the hillsides. To water the lands, he created irrigation canals by tossing the flower of the *pupuna* reed down into the ground to form channels.

Like Viracocha, Coniraya Viracocha was a wandering teacher. He travelled around dressed in the rags of a beggar and was often taken for one. Those who failed to recognize him often treated him with abuse.

During his journeys, Coniraya Viracocha learned of a beautiful female virgin *HUACA*, Cavillaca. He became enamoured and desperate to sleep with her, but she would have nothing to do with him. One day he observed Cavillaca weaving beneath a *lúcuma* tree (a coastal tree that bears yellow-orange fruit). Changing himself into a bird, he flew to the tree and put his semen into one of the ripened fruits, then caused it to fall beside Cavillaca. She ate the fruit, thus becoming impregnated. Nine months later she gave birth to a boy, still unaware of who had made her pregnant.

When the child was a year old, Cavillaca grew determined to discover the father. She called upon the aid of the *VILCA* and *huaca* male spirits of the surrounding landscape, who came, dressed in their finery, each hoping to "claim" the fatherhood and love of Cavillaca. Conspicuous among them stood Coniraya Viracocha, dressed in his usual rags. Cavillaca asked the assembled company which one of them was the father of her child, but none spoke. Cavillaca then placed her son on the ground to see which god the boy would crawl to; the child crawled along the line-up until he came to Coniraya Viracocha and promptly climbed into his true father's lap.

Cavillaca, furious at the idea of such a despicable-looking being as her husband, seized her son from his father's lap and raced for the western sea. There, near the site of *PACHACAMAC* (just south of present-day Lima), she continued straight into the water, where she and her son were turned into stones which, the manuscript claims, could still be seen offshore.

Coniraya Viracocha was so distressed by Cavillaca's disappearance that he set off to find her. He asked every creature he encountered after her whereabouts. Depending on whether the animal gave him encouraging or discouraging news, he gave it good or bad traits. Thus, for example, the condor told him that he would surely soon find Cavillaca, and so Coniraya Viracocha declared that the condor would enjoy long life and always have plenty to eat, and that anyone who killed a condor would also die. In contrast, the skunk told him that Cavillaca had gone far away and that he would never find her, so he gave the skunk its stink in order that people would hate it, and confined its activities to the night-time. (Clearly, this part of the myth resembles Viracocha's journeys from Lake Titicaca.)

Coniraya Viracocha continued his search for Cavillaca until he too reached Pachacamac. There he saw the two daughters of the god Pachacamac guarded by a snake, as their mother, *URPAY HUACHAC*, was away. He seduced the elder sister and tried to sleep with the younger as well but, before he could do so, she turned herself into a dove and flew off. Coniraya Viracocha was enraged at this rejection and, as a result, became the cause of the presence of fish in the ocean. At the time, the only fish in existence were those raised by Urpay Huachac in a special pond near Pachacamac, the site; he sabotaged her operation by smashing the pond and scattering her fish into the oceans.

He continued his search for Cavillaca and his son but never found them. The manuscript says that he travelled far up the coast, playing many more tricks on the peoples and *huacas* whom he met.

CONTITI VIRACOCHA PAC-HAYACHACHIC (meaning "god, creator of the world") was the name given to the central Andean/*INCA* god *VIRACOCHA* by the people of *CACHA,* and recorded by the 16th-century Spanish chronicler Juan de Betanzos.

CORI OCLLO see *MAMA OCLLO*.

THE CORICANCHA ("golden enclosure" or "building of gold"), the main square of the *INCA* capital at *CUZCO,* was the perceived centre of the Inca world and cosmos on earth. Together with the royal palaces and shrines, it served a multitude of religious and official functions. It was the "centre" of the city itself – and, by extension, of *TAHUANTINSUYU,* the four quarters of the empire – and was the supreme sacred ceremonial precinct of the city. From the Coricancha, sacred *CEQUE* lines were projected from the capital to the provinces, partitioning the empire, as well as the capital; and the movements of the Milky Way (see *MAYU*) across the night sky were keenly observed and plotted from points within the precinct. (One such was the pillar of the *CAPAC USNU,* from which sightings of Mayu were taken between two pillars on the distant horizon.)

The complex itself was in the tail of the image of a puma, as seen in profile by linking with lines the various edifices of the Inca city, and lay at the confluence of Cuzco's two rivers, the Huantanay and the Tullamayo. The head of the puma

was formed by *SACSAHUAMAN,* another sacred precinct. The Coricancha consisted of an enclosure known as a *cancha,* constructed of fitted stone blocks. Within this were six *wasi,* or covered chambers, arranged around a square courtyard. (In some cases the entire complex is referred to as the "Temple of the Sun". In fact, the temple to the sun god, where the sacred fires of *INTI* were guarded by the *ACLLAS,* was only one of the several temples making up the complex, although the increased emphasis on Inti by the later emperors led to a certain focus on that cult.)

The walls of the buildings were covered with sheet gold, referred to as "the sweat of the sun", and silver. Specific rooms within the group of buildings were designated for the six principal Inca state gods, guardians of the official religion. Each room housed the images and idols of its appropriate deity, plus lesser objects of worship. There were *VIRACOCHA,* the supreme creator, Inti the sun god, *QUILLA* the moon goddess, *CHASKA-QOYLOR* the god of Venus as the morning and evening "stars", *ILLAPA* the god of weather, and *CUICHU* the god of the rainbow, ranged hierarchically in that order, although the relative positions of Viracocha and Inti are thought to have been equivocal.

The intimate mythological connection between Inti and gold was

THE INTERIOR of the Temple of Inti (the sun) in the Coricancha includes the large niche in which was displayed the golden mask or image of the god.

THE SACRED CORICANCHA precinct in Cuzco comprised the temples of the principal Inca deities, including those of Inti (the sun) and Quilla (the moon).

further borne out by images in the temple garden. Here Inca goldsmiths and craftsmen created cast gold and silver models of all the creatures known to them. There were butterflies and other insects, *JAGUARS,* llamas, guinea pigs and many others.

One room of the complex was reserved for the storage and care of the mummies of past Inca emperors (see *MALLQUIS*). On special ritual days, these formed a focus for the sacred ceremonies (see, for example, *CAPAC RAYMI* and *INTI RAYMI*). The mummies were dressed in rich garments and placed upon royal litters, which were carried in procession around the capital. In the precinct, too, sanctification and incantations to the *CAPACOCHAS* – specially selected sacrificial victims – took place before their ritual journey along the *ceque* lines back to their provinces for sacrifice.

Other rooms within the complex were used to store sacred objects taken from the conquered provinces, including a sacred *HUACA* from each subjugated population. The *huaca* was required to remain in perpetual residence as a sort of "hostage", and selected members of the nobility of each subject population were forced to

live in the capital for several months of each year.

The tenth emperor, *PACHACUTI INCA YUPANQUI,* reorganized the Coricancha into this final form in his rebuilding of the city. His actions, it is argued, were taken in order to formalize his defiance of his father, *VIRACOCHA INCA,* and brother, *INCA URCO,* from whom he had usurped the throne.

Alongside the oracle temple of *PACHACAMAC* and the *ISLAND OF THE SUN* in Lake *TITICACA,* the Coricancha was one of the most revered places in the Inca Empire. Something of its splendour is captured in the words of conquistador Pedro de Cieza de León, who recorded his experiences in his *Crónica del Peru* (Seville, 1550–3): "The temple was more than 400 paces in circuit. . . [and the finely hewn masonry was] a dusky or black colour. . . [with] many openings and doorways. . . very well carved. Around the wall, halfway up, there was a band of gold, two *palmos* wide and four *dedos* in thickness. The doorways and doors were covered with plates of the same metal. Within [there] were four houses, not very large, but with walls of the same kind and covered with plates of gold within and without. . .

"In one of these houses. . . there was the figure of the sun, very large and made of gold. . . enriched with many precious stones. . .

"They also had a garden, the

D

clods of which were made of pieces of gold; and it was artificially sown with golden corn [maize], the stalks, as well as the leaves and cobs, being of that metal. . . Besides all this, they had more than 20 golden sheep [llamas] with their lambs, and the shepherds with their slings and crooks to watch them, all made of the same metal. There was [also] a great quantity of jars of gold and silver, set with emeralds; vases, pots, and all sorts of utensils, all of fine gold."

The golden wealth of the Coricancha formed the basis of the ransom with which Inca *ATAHUALPA* attempted to secure his freedom from Francisco Pizarro at Cajamarca in 1533.

COYA see *MAMA OCLLO*.

CRYSTAL TABLET see under *PACHACUTI INCA YUPANQUI*.

CUICHU was the *INCA* god of the rainbow. His idol was one of the images of the gods kept in the sacred *CORICANCHA* in *CUZCO*.

CUNA see *MAMACUNA*.

CUICHU, the Inca rainbow god, was among the deities honoured with a temple in the Coricancha precinct in Cuzco.

modern central and southwestern Peru; see *TAHUANTINSUYU*.

CURA see *MAMA CURA*.

CURACA was a member of the *INCA* provincial nobility (see also *HATUNRUNA*). In the first century after the Spanish conquest, the *curacas* became an important source of information on local belief and legend for Spanish and Spanish-trained native chroniclers, in their attempts to root out local idolatry (see *IDOLATRÍAS*). In the legend surrounding the foundation of the Inca state by *MANCO CAPAC*, he was said to have been the son of a local *curaca* of *PACARITAMBO*. Similarly, according to legendary histories which narrate the foundations of the *CHIMÚ* and *PACHACAMAC*, *CHIMO CAPAC* installed Pongmassa as his *curaca* in the former, and the god Pachacamac named several *curacas* to rule the local peoples of the coastal lowlands.

CUSCO see *CUZCO*.

CUZCO, the *INCA* capital in the Valley of Cuzco in central Andean

CUNTISUYU, the southwest quadrant of the Inca Empire to the south of Cuzco, encompassed the dry desert regions bordering the Pacific Ocean.

CUNTISUYU, the southwest and smallest quarter of the *INCA* Empire, comprised a triangular region whose borders diverged from a point at the capital at *CUZCO* to points in the Pacific coast in

Peru, was the "navel" of the Inca world. From it radiated the highways and politico-religious tendrils of the vast Inca Empire (*TAHUANTINSUYU*). Within its *CORICANCHA* ceremonial precinct and élite residential structures were planned and executed the administration of the empire, through its extensive network of provincial capitals and local rulerships.

The final plan of the city was established by *PACHACUTI INCA YUPANQUI*, the tenth emperor, and, seemingly deliberately, forms the shape of a puma profile if viewed

from above. Principal compounds included the sacred Coricancha temples and the *SACSAHUAMAN* complex, the latter of which formed the shape of the puma's head. Precincts of the city were grouped into *HANAN* (upper) and *HURIN* (lower) Cuzco to reflect the hierarchical social divisions of the capital's citizens.

CUZCO HUANCA see *AYAR AUCA*.

THE "DARK CLOUD" CONSTELLATIONS see *MAYU* and *PACHATIRA*.

DAY-TIME SUN, that is, the sun as it passed across the sky from sunrise to sunset, was an object of worship of the *LLACUAZ* lineage of *CAJATAMBO*.

THE FINAL PLAN of the Inca capital, Cuzco, was established by the tenth emperor, Pachacuti Inca Yupanqui. His addition of the Sacsahuaman temple precinct completed the outline of a puma's profile.

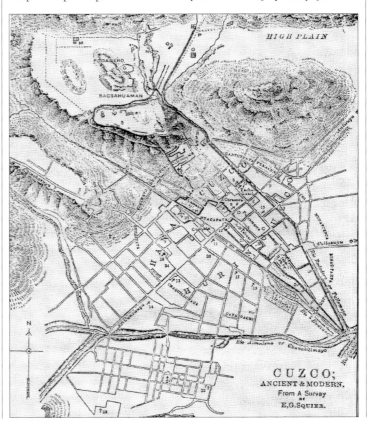

E

DECAPITATOR GOD, a *MO-CHE* deity, was a fearsome half-human, half-*JAGUAR* being depicted on ceramics, metalwork, friezes and murals at Moche (on the Huaca de la Luna and in temples), at *SIPÁN* in the *LAMBAYEQUE VAL-LEY*, and at other sites. He was frequently portrayed holding a crescent-shaped *tumi* ceremonial knife in one hand and a severed human head in the other, but appeared in several other guises as well. Elaborate plaster friezes at the Huaca de la Luna depict a fearful face framed in a diamond. In black, white, brown and shades of red and yellow ochre, a grimacing mouth bares four long fangs, eyes stare menacingly, and the face is embellished with double ear-ornaments and curling hair and beard.

He is shown in an elaborate bloodletting rite painted on pottery vessels and on temple and tomb walls. His role, acted out by priests, embodied a gruesome sacrificial ritual. It was once thought such scenes were merely representational imagery of a mythical event, but archaeological evidence at several sites attests to its reality.

At the Huaca de la Luna, an enclosure at the back of the platform contained the buried remains of 40 men, aged 15 to 30. They appear to have been pushed off a stone outcrop into the enclosure after having been ritually mutilated and killed. The structure, outcrop and enclosure seem to mirror nearby Cerro Blanco. Some skeletons were splayed out as if they had been stretched when tied to stakes; some had their femurs torn from the pelvis; skulls, ribs, finger-, arm- and leg-bones all have cut marks. Several severed heads, their lower jaws ripped off, were scattered among the bones.

The skeletons and scattered bones were covered in a layer of sediment that had been deposited during heavy rains, indicating that the ceremony took place in response to an El Niño weather event

that might have disrupted the economic stability of the realm – some victims being offered to the gods in a plea for them to stop the rains and flooding, others in gratitude when the rain did finally cease.

Detailed combat scenes were painted on Moche ceramics and walls. Friezes show opposing warriors in combat, usually both wearing Moche armour and bearing Moche arms. Pairs of combatants are shown in narrative sequences. Instead of being killed in battle, the loser is shown stripped and tied with a rope round the neck, being marched off for arraignment. Finally, the captives are shown naked, having their throats slit, and then their blood presented in goblets to four presiding figures. The most elaborate is the Warrior Priest, wearing a crescent-shaped metal plate to protect his back, and rattles suspended from his belt; to his right sits the Bird Priest, wearing a conical helmet bearing the image of an owl and a long beak-like nose-ornament. Next to the Bird Priest is a priestess, identified by her long, plaited tresses, dress-like costume, and plumed and tasselled head-dress. The final figure wears a headdress with serrated border and long streamers, decorated with a *FELINE* or similar face.

The fact that most of the combatants in these scenes are Moche seems to indicate that they repre-

sent not battles but ritual combats among the fields near Moche cities for the purpose of "capturing" victims for sacrifice to the gods.

In keeping with these scenes, the Sipán tombs contained bodies and artefacts that verify the practices depicted. Several unlooted tombs (dated *c.* AD 300) contain rich burial goods – including gold, silver, turquoise and other jewellery, and textiles – and bodies dressed in costumes similar to those in the ritual scenes on pottery and murals. The principal body, possibly a noble, personified the Warrior Priest. He wore a crescent-shaped back plate and had rattles suspended from his belt. Both plate and rattles are decorated with the image of the Decapitator, in this case an anthropomorphized spider, with the characteristic Decapitator fangs and double ear-ornaments, perched on a golden web. The spider is thought to reflect the parallel between bloodletting and the spider's sucking of the life juices from its prey. Offerings to the Decapitator God consisted of three pairs of gold and turquoise ear-spools (one of which depicts a Moche warrior), a crescent-shaped gold headdress, a crescent-shaped nose-ornament, and one gold and one silver *tumi* knife. At the Warrior Priest's side lay a box-like sceptre of gold, embossed with combat scenes.

THE FEARSOME DECAPITATOR GOD was depicted in every medium by Moche craftsmen – here as a gold disc showing the god with a fanged mouth and crescent-bladed ceremonial tumi *knife.*

Near this tomb was another, not quite as rich, containing the body of a noble with a gilded copper headdress decorated with an owl with outspread wings – clearly the Bird Priest of the friezes. Sealed rectangular rooms near the tombs contained other offerings – ceramic vessels, copper goblets, miniature war gear – and, tellingly, the skeletal remains of severed human hands and feet, probably from sacrificed victims.

Further confirmation of the accuracy of the Moche friezes was discovered at San José de Moro in the Jequetepeque Valley, where the tombs (dated *c.* AD 500–600) of two women were found to contain silver-alloyed copper headdresses with plume-like tassels and other accoutrements of the Priestess. Finally, at El Brujo in the Chicama Valley, a terrace frieze shows a life-size warrior leading a procession of ten life-size nude prisoners tied by a rope around their necks. On a terrace above this (later destroyed by looters) a huge spider or crab with fanged mouth and double ear-ornaments was depicted, identifying it as the Decapitator. It had segmented legs, one of which was brandishing a *tumi* knife.

EKKEKO, the household god, is a traditional Andean deity still honoured today. This silver example has a pre-Spanish conquest "feel" while displaying a modern guitar and umbrella.

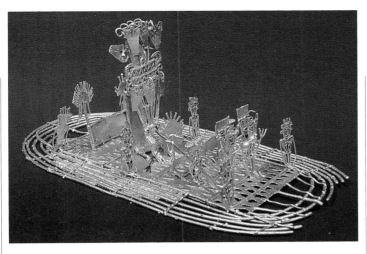

EKKEKO, a Late Horizon, central Andean deity, was a household god, thought to bring good fortune if looked after properly. Like a good-luck charm, he was portrayed as a little man with a round stomach, festooned with tiny household utensils. He was thought to rule a miniature city. Ekkeko figurines are still bought today in the Andes as good-luck charms.

EL DORADO ("Gilded Man" in Spanish) was the legendary king of the chiefdom of the *CHIBCHA* or Muisca of the far northern Andes in Colombia. El Dorado was a person, city, entire kingdom and in time, a myth. The Spanish myth or legend is a product of their lust for gold. Once tales of untold wealth from the northern "kingdoms" reached their ears, the Spaniards began to associate the legend with the entire region of central Colombia. In reality, the quest for gold and riches beyond belief turned out to be a chimera: El Dorado was always just one more range of mountains away, but was never found.

The most reliable sources of the legend focus on the Chibcha/Muisca and their chiefdom around Lake Guatavita in central Colombia. Gold was extremely important to the chiefdoms of the far northern Andes, and several distinctive styles of goldworking developed throughout the region from the 1st century BC/AD; the Muisca style itself dates from the 8th century AD. The Spaniards learned the story of the golden king from many sources, including Chibcha who had actually witnessed the ceremony before the Spaniards arrived. Every conquistador and chronicler of this area mentions the Golden Man, but the most complete account is that of mid-17th-century chronicler Rodríguez Freyle, who was told the legend by his friend Don Juan, the nephew of the last independent lord of Guatavita.

The ritual that gave rise to the legend was performed at the

inauguration of a new king. The heir to the throne spent the days before the ceremony secluded in a cave. During this time, he was required to abstain from women and was forbidden to eat chilli peppers or salt. Then, on the appointed day, he made his first official journey to Lake Guatavita, to give offerings to the gods. At the lakeside, a raft of rushes was prepared and bedecked with precious decorations and treasures. Four lighted braziers were placed on the raft, in which *moque* incense and other resins were burned. Braziers of incense were also lit on the shore, and such a quantity of smoke was produced that the light of the sun was said to be obscured.

The king-to-be was then stripped naked and his body smeared with sticky clay or resin. Over this he was entirely covered with glittering gold dust, shown being blown from a tube in an engraving of 1599. He then boarded the raft, accompanied by four principal subject chiefs, all of whom were richly attired in "plumes, crowns, bracelets, pendants and earrings all of gold", but also otherwise naked. The king remained motionless on the raft while at his feet was placed a great heap of gold ornaments and precious stones (referred to as "emeralds" by Freyle).

The raft was pushed off across the lake, whereupon musicians on shore struck up a fanfare of trumpets, flutes and other instruments, and the assembled crowd began to sing. When the raft reached the centre of the lake, a banner was raised as a signal for silence. The gilded king then made his offering to the gods: one by one, the treasures were thrown into the lake by the king and his attendants. Then the flag was lowered again, and the raft paddled towards shore to the accompaniment of loud music, singing and wild dancing.

Upon reaching the shore, the new king was accepted as lord and master of the realm.

THE SPANISH LEGEND of El Dorado ("the gilded man") (above) originated with tales of the investiture ceremonies for a Chibcha chief. The ruler-to-be was dusted with fine gold dust, then paddled out into the middle of Lake Guatavita on a raft laden with gold objects (top left), to be offered into the lake waters.

THE CEREMONY of El Dorado took place on Lake Guatavita, Colombia (below left). So convinced were the Spanish that a fortune in gold lay beneath the waters of the lake that several attempts, all incompletely successful, were made to drain it. In the 1580s the merchant Antonio de Sepúlveda tried by cutting a huge notch to drain the water out (still visible to the left of the picture).

EL-LAL was the legendary culture hero of the *ONA* and *YAHGAN* tribes of Patagonia, and was regarded as the teacher of mankind.

When he was about to be born, his father, Nosjthej, snatched him from his mother's womb because he wanted to eat him. El-lal was saved by a rat, who carried him off to his nest, fostered him and taught him the sacred lore. Having learned well, El-lal came back to the surface and made himself master of the earth through his invention of the bow and arrow. With this weapon he fought Nosjthej, and the giants who dwelt on the earth long ago, overcoming them all.

Eventually, he tired of the earth and decided to leave it behind. As he departed, he declared that humans would thenceforth have to look after themselves.

ENDOCANNIBALISM
see *CANNIBALISM*.

EXOCANNIBALISM
see *CANNIBALISM*.

UNIVERSALITY, CONTINUITY & CYCLICITY

OR THE PEOPLES OF ANCIENT ANDEAN and coastal civilizations the endless cycle of time began with the daily movement of the sun across the sky and then progressed through seasonal change to repetitious decades to the religious concept of *pachacuti*, or the "revolution of time and space". Andean and western coastal peoples believed in the existence of an overall supreme power, and that the course of history and civilization formed an inevitable succession of repetition and renewal. Collecting and collating their own beliefs and those of the peoples they conquered, the Incas believed in an elaborate succession of worlds or creations, inhabited by different races of beings and/or civilizations. Each "Age" was referred to as being ruled over by a sun, and the general course of development was from the more primitive to the sophisticated. Each world ended in its destruction by some catastrophic event. Naturally, they considered the Inca Empire to be the supreme achievement in this progression, and manipulated the creation myths to convince themselves and their subjects of their divine right to rule. That the Spanish conquest has merely interrupted this course of events is embodied in the concept of *Inkarrí*, the return of the Inca king.

THE ENDLESS daily cycle of the sun was considered vital in Inca religion. The sun god Inti was special to the Inca and in the later empire began to rival even the creator god Viracocha in importance. The movement of the sun through the year was carefully charted by Inca priests, and two of the most important annual festivals were the summer and winter solstices, known respectively as Capac Raymi (December in the southern hemisphere) and Inti Raymi (June).

TWO VITAL ELEMENTS in the economies of Andean and coastal civilizations were corn (maize) (silver representation, top) and the llama herds (above). It was important to chart the seasons carefully, relating them to botanical and zoological cycles so that steps could be taken during the agricultural year and herding seasons to ensure the wellbeing of the people.

THE CYCLE of the seasons was carefully plotted from the movements of the sun, and of the Milky Way (Mayu) and other stars and celestial bodies from observation posts carefully placed in relation to marker pillars at strategic points on local horizons. As well as in the capital Cuzco itself, there were observation platforms in several Inca cities. For example, at Kenko near Cuzco there was an intihuatana or "Hitching Post of the Sun" (above), perhaps less well known than its monolithic brother at the Inca mountain retreat at Machu Picchu.

INKARRÍ, the return of the Inca king, is the ultimate extension of Inca pachacuti or "revolution of time and space". This post-Spanish conquest development of Inca mythology or religion believes that the interlude of Spanish rule will ultimately end when the Inca return to power with the arrival of a new Sapa Inca (emperor). The festival of the sun celebrated today (right) is perhaps a wistful rehearsal for that time, as well as a revival of the ancient solstice rituals.

G

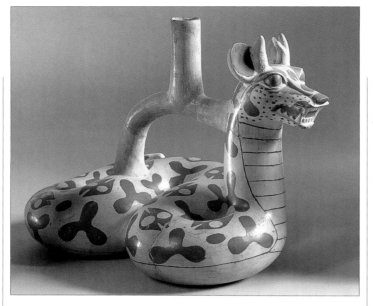

THE FANGED GODS, represented from before the Early Horizon, were especially favoured by Moche craftspeople, as here, in a composite fanged feline/deer/serpent.

FANGED GOD, a general term, is sometimes used for beings depicted by several Andean cultures. Even before the Early Horizon religious prominence of CHAVÍN, many U-shaped ceremonial centres in the coastal valleys of Peru demonstrated an apparently widespread religious coherence, displaying fanged beings and painted figures on sculptured architecture at many sites, for example at Garagay, Sechín Alto and Cerro Sechín.

Faces with grimacing mouths and protruding fangs were especially prominent in Early Horizon Chavín and in later MOCHE art of the Early Intermediate Period. For example, a being with thick, upturned lips and fangs was a common image in the Chavín pantheon. The DECAPITATOR GOD of Moche, identifiable by his distinctive protruding fangs and double ear-ornaments, was depicted in numerous painted scenes on pottery and walls, and on the contents of tombs; and the sky or creator god AI APAEC of the Moche (and later the CHIMÚ) also had a distinctive fanged FELINE mouth.

Farther south, in the Early Intermediate Period NAZCA culture, fanged creatures were also frequently depicted on pottery. Such common imagery no doubt reflects a certain basic animism and naturalism in Andean iconography, which prevails through centuries of religious practice. At the same time, the variations of detail in the fanged beings portrayed belies a wealth of imagination in conjuring up fearful gods/goddesses to strike awe in the intended worshippers.

FELINES, like SERPENTS, were pan-Andean. JAGUARS in particular, inspired a ubiquitous imagery used by many Andean cultures from the very earliest times. The most prominent aspect was long, curved canine teeth. (See also CHAVÍN, DECAPITATOR GOD and FANGED GOD)

FEMALE DOMINATION is a widespread mythological theme, recounted with many variations among South American tribes, from the Amazon rain forests to Tierra del Fuego (see JURUPARI, TEMAUKEL, WATAUINEIWA). For various reasons, the situation was reversed by the gods. In general, among the rain forest tribes, women are associated with natural fertility, ignorance of spiritual matters, and chaos; in contrast, men are associated with cultural fertility, sacred knowledge and order.

FEMPELLEC was the 12th ruler in the legendary line of NAYAMLAP in the LAMBAYEQUE VALLEY dynasty of northern coastal Peru. In myth, he is remembered as the king fated to bring disaster on the kingdom.

RECOGNIZABLE FELINES, especially jaguars, were depicted in all media, including metals, as here, in a gold and copper jaguar head from the Lambayeque Valley.

He insisted on moving the stone idol of YAMPALLEC, symbol of the dynasty, from the capital at CHOT to another city – an act of which his priests heartily disapproved. Before he could accomplish this sacrilege, however, a demon appeared to Fempellec in the form of a beautiful woman. She seduced him, after which it began to rain heavily, an event all too rare in this arid region of the coastal valleys. It rained for 30 days, and then followed a year of drought and – inevitably – hunger, as the crops failed. By this time, the priests had had enough. They seized Fempellec and tied his hands and feet; then they carried him to the sea, threw him in, and left him to his fate, thus ending the dynasty of Nayamlap.

GATEWAY GOD see under TIAHUANACO.

GATEWAY OF THE SUN see under TIAHUANACO.

GENTE BRUTA ("brutish/ignorant folk") were the "stupid folk" taken in by a ruse to lay the foundations for MANCO CAPAC's claim to rule CUZCO in the INCA state foundation myth.

"GOLDEN ENCLOSURE" see CORICANCHA.

GRAN CHACO see CHACO.

GREAT IMAGE see CHAVÍN.

GUACA BILCAS, supernatural devils (see PACHACUTI).

THE GUARI were one of the legendary lineage AYLLUS of CAJATAMBO. They were conquered by, then confederated with, the LLACUAZ *ayllu* and shared ritual beliefs with them.

GUASCAR see HUASCAR.

GUAYNA CAPAC see HUAYNA CAPAC.

GUECUFU was the evil spirit of the AUCA peoples of northern Chile, the ultimate source of misfortune. It was Guecufu who sent the floods that could destroy humankind.

GUINECHEN ("master of men") was the supreme god of the AUCA peoples of northern Chile. Guinechen was a deity of all natural

phenomena: animals, plants, humans, crops, flocks and their fertility. Because of this, he was also known as Guinemapun (literally "master of the land").

GUINEMAPUN see *GUINECHEN*.

HANAN AND HURIN CUZ-CO (*INCA*) literally "upper *CUZCO*" and "lower Cuzco" were the two groups or social divisions of the populace of the city. In Inca legend, the division was believed to have been ordered by the first ruler, *MANCO CAPAC*, and the two groups prevailed up to the time of the arrival of the Spaniards. The two parts of Cuzco were also associated with a similar division of the system of *CEQUE* lines that regulated sacred ritual and astronomical observations. An upper set of *ceques* was associated with Hanan Cuzco, and with the quarters of *CHINCHASUYU* and *ANTISUYU*, while a lower set was associated with Hurin Cuzco, and with the quarters of *COLLASUYU* and *CUNTISUYU*.

Divisions into *hanan* and *hurin* were also generally used among the *MOIETY* groupings of *AYLLUS*. The division was based on locally important topographic features in the area inhabited by the group, and on distribution rights to water.

HATUNRUNA (meaning "the great people") were the *INCA* commoners. They were of lower social rank than the royal *PANACAS* and lesser nobility and made up the majority of the populace, especially in the provinces of the empire. They were organized into tens of thousands of *AYLLUS*, or kinship lineages. Members of higher-ranking lineages of the *hatunruna*, called *CURACAS*, held hereditary lordships and served the Inca state as imperial agents and local authorities to supervise provincial affairs.

The value of the *hatunruna* in the study of Andean mythology lies in the fact that their religious beliefs were recorded in the *IDOLATRÍAS*

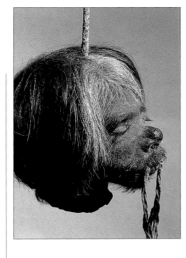

("idolatries"), which comprised a multitude of local traditions, legends and beliefs.

The Inca practice of redistributing large groups of *hatunrunas* as *MITIMAES* throughout the empire not only resulted in a stabilizing economic, ethnic and social mix, but also served to transfer, alter and amalgamate *hatunruna* notions of geographic identity and religious/ mythological concepts.

Although there are fewer sources for local religion and mythology than for official Inca state religion, one particular text, the *HUAROCHIRÍ MANUSCRIPT*, provides a detailed record of such provincial beliefs in the western Andes of central Peru, to the east of Lima.

HAYSQUISRRO was the *INCA* ancestors' fourth place of sojourn during their wanderings related in the Inca state foundation myth, and where the plot to get rid of Ayar Cachi was conceived (see *MANCO CAPAC*).

HEAD-HUNTING was a ritual practice among several tribes of the Amazonian rain forest, persisting, for example, among the Ecuadorian-Amazon Jivarro tribe into the 1960s. The taking and keeping of human heads was restricted to a select group of especially fierce male warriors, who became feared killers.

The Jivarro head-hunter was thought to possess two souls in conflict. The first, called *Arutam*, gave the owner permission and power to kill and head-hunt, but not without impunity, for the second soul,

AFTER HEAD-HUNTING, to prevent revenge, the head was shrunk in order to block the power of the Muisak, *or second soul of the victim.*

Muisak, was meant to avenge the death of the hunted. To prevent it from taking revenge, the head was shrunk, thus drawing *Muisak* into it, from which it was believed to be powerless to escape.

"HITCHING POST OF THE SUN" see *INTIHUATANA*.

HUACA (*INCA* and, more generally, central Andean) was a sacred place or object in the landscape (see also *ZEMÍ*). As well as the powerful central deities of the Inca pantheon, each of which was given a special temple in the *CORICANCHA* in *CUZCO*, the Andean peoples recognized a host of lesser nature gods, spirits and oracles throughout the land.

Huacas were hallowed places where significant mythological events had taken place and/or where offerings were made to local deities. They were frequently natural objects such as mountain tops (*APU*), caves, springs, and especially stones or boulders (*APACHETA*, *HUANCA*), but could also be locations along a sacred *CEQUE* line or man-made objects, such as the pillars erected on the western horizon above Cuzco for viewing the sunset from the *CAPAC USNU* for special astronomical observations. Other examples include the stones (the *PURURAUCAS*) around Cuzco that rose up to help *PACHACUTI INCA YUPANQUI* defend Cuzco against the *CHANCAS*, and the sacred shrines and statues of *VIRACOCHA* at *CACHA* and *URCOS*. In some cases, the *huaca* was a combination of the natural and the miraculous. One example was the stone of the ancestor brother *AYAR UCHU* atop *HUANACAURI* mountain, a principal Inca *huaca* believed to be the lithified body of that ancestor; another example was that of *PARIACACA*,

who seems to have been simultaneously a mountain and a mobile deity/culture hero.

Most Andean "nations" and towns had a particular place that they recognized as their own *huaca*, as did most of the *AYLLUS*, or kinship groups. It was their belief that the spirit of the *huaca* exerted a special and beneficial influence over the lives and destinies of the members of the group.

Huacas continue to be recognized by local peoples in the Andes today, in a mixture of pre-Christian and Catholic belief.

HUACA CHOTUNA, an archaeological site in the *LAMBAYEQUE VALLEY*, was almost certainly the *CHOT* of *NAYAMLAP*.

HUACAS, both natural and man-made, were a common aspect of ancient Andean landscapes. As well as using natural features, stone pillars were also frequently erected by the Incas for use in astronomical sightings, such as the ones shown here at Kenko near Cuzco.

HUACA DE LA LUNA see *DECAPITATOR GOD* and *MOCHE*.

HUACA DEL SOL see *MOCHE*.

HUACA FORTALEZA see *MOCHE*.

HUACO see *MAMA HUACA*.

HUALLALLO CARHUINCHO

(pre-*INCA*) was the principal god of the indigenous people of the Huarochirí region described in the *HUAROCHIRÍ MANUSCRIPT*.

He was a fierce, fire-breathing, volcanic god of ancient origin, long predating the Inca conquest of this region in the western Andes east of Lima. The manuscript refers to the people of Huarochirí as *Lurin* (lower) and *Anan* (upper) *Yauyos*, a kinship *AYLLU* dichotomy implying that there were also "outsiders" among the indigenous population. The manuscript is principally concerned with the *Lurin Yauyos*.

According to the Huarochirí creation myth, Huallallo Carhuincho was present at the beginning of time, and exercised unchallenged power and control over the daily lives of the people. At that time, Huarochirí province had a climate that was comparable to the adjacent warm coastal lowlands. The land was filled with snakes, toucans, *JAGUARS* and other animals normally associated with warmer coastal regions. It was presumably during this early time that agriculturalist *Yauyos* migrated into or invaded the area.

The story itself begins some time after Huallallo Carhuincho had been ruling his people in this autocratic manner. At the beginning of the Huarochirí Manuscript he was challenged by another god, *PARIACACA*, a five-fold being who had been born on a distant mountain. Pariacaca was the principal deity of the *Checa* portion of the *Yauyos*, the pastoralists, and is described as the ancestor(s) of these more recent immigrants to the region. In the end, Huallallo Carhuincho was defeated, despite the help he received from *MAMA ÑAMCA*, and fled to the low country to the north, called Antis (that is, *ANTISUYU*). He left behind him a huge two-headed snake, which Pariacaca transformed into stone.

Huallallo Carhuincho also had a penchant for cannibalism. He

issued the command that the *Lurin Yauyos* be allowed to have only two children per household, one of which was to be handed over to him for his meals.

HUANACAURI

or Huana Cauri, was the mountain at Quirirmanta described in the *INCA* state foundation myth. It was from this place that the Inca ancestors first viewed the Valley of *CUZCO* after their wanderings. Huanacauri was also the name of *MANCO CAPAC*'s father's principal idol.

HUANAYPATA

was the final stopping place of the *INCA* ancestors in their wanderings, where the centre of *CUZCO* was established and where *AYAR AUCA* was turned into a stone pillar (see *MANCO CAPAC*).

HUANCA

was the *INCA*/central Andean term for a particular type of *HUACA*. As opposed to obvious mountains, springs or caves, these were especially prominent or large boulders in the landscape, which were believed to incorporate the essence of an ancestor of one or more local *AYLLU* kinship groups. (See also *APACHETA*, *APU*, *CEQUE*)

HUARI

(*INCA* and Spanish colonial) was the principal deity of the *GUARI AYLLU* of *CAJATAMBO*.

HUARI

or Wari, an ancient site and kingdom in the Andes of south-central Peru, dominated the highlands and coastal regions of Peru and in due course, during the

HUALLALLO CARHUINCHO, the fire-breathing, volcanic god of the Huarochirí Manuscript, was no doubt inspired by the presence of nearby active volcanoes.

Middle Horizon, expanded into the regions to the north, almost to the Ecuadorian border. One of its northernmost outposts was the city of Cajamarca in northern Peru; its southernmost was Pikillaqta near Cuzco. Although major constructions in Huari began earlier – not long after those at its chief rival *TIAHUANACO*, to the south near Lake *TITICACA* – its main period of expansion and imperial power lasted from about AD 600 to 800. The two empires confronted each other across the mountain pass of La Raya, south of Cuzco, and appeared to agree to make this region a buffer zone between them. Despite their obvious military and political rivalry, both cultures shared a religious iconography and mythology.

The city of Huari occupied the plateau of an intermontane valley at some 2,800 m (9,180 ft) above sea-level between the Huamanga and Huanta basins. Serving as a civic, residential and religious centre, it grew rapidly to cover more than 100 hectares (247 acres), expanding to 300 hectares (740 acres), with an additional periphery of residential suburbs occupying a further 250 hectares (620 acres). From *c*. AD 600, alongside its military expansion, Huari spread a religious hegemony that was characterized by a distinctive iconography, much of which shows continuity with the ancient traditions of *CHAVÍN*, which survived the political fragmentation of the Early Intermediate Period. Shortly before AD 800, however, there appears to have been a political crisis that caused building within the capital to abate rapidly and then cease. At the same time, *PACHACAMAC*, a political centre and religious shrine on the central Peruvian coast, which had flourished since the later Early Intermediate, and which had been recently occupied by the Huari, began to reassert itself and possibly even to rival Huari power. Huari expansion ended abruptly, and the capital was abandoned by AD 800.

The architecture of the site, although megalithic, has not lasted well. Some of it approximates to the ceremonial architecture at Tiahuanaco, although more crudely, including several rectangular compounds. In contrast to Tiahuanaco, however, the rapid expansion of Huari appears to have occurred at random, without the deliberate and preconceived planning of its competitor. The huge enclosure of Cheqo Huasi (or Wasi) included dressed stone-slab chambers. Two of the most important temple complexes were Vegachayoq Moqo and

HUANAYPATA, the central plaza of Inca Cuzco, was the site where Ayar Auca was turned into a stone Huaca.

THE HUARI military empire of central Peru conquered as far south as Pikillaqta (above), near Cuzco, where its fortress confronted its rival Tiahuanaco, beyond the La Raya Pass to the south.

Moraduchayoq, the latter a semi-subterranean compound similar to that at Tiahuanaco. In keeping with the comparatively frenetic pace of Huari's development, the Moraduchayoq Temple was dismantled in about AD 650.

Much of the religious and mythological iconography of Huari and Tiahuanaco was virtually identical, and originated in Early Horizon and Early Intermediate times. Despite the two capitals' obvious military opposition, scholars think it possible that religious missionaries from one city visited the other. It may have been that the priests were willing to let religious beliefs transcend politics.

Shared religious imagery included, in particular, the *STAFF DEITY* image, winged beings (sometimes referred to as "angels") in profile – sometimes with falcon and condor heads – and severed trophy heads. Winged beings appear both accompanying the Staff Deity and on their own; and are shown running, floating, flying or kneeling. The frontal Staff Deity – with mask-like face, radiating head rays (sometimes ending in serpent heads) and tunic, belt and kilt – appears on pottery and architecture and might have been the prototype for the creator god *VIRACOCHA*.

HUARI CULTURE shared many features with other Andean cultures that flourished both before and afterwards, including ancestor worship through mummy bundles (below) of dead forebears.

Yet, despite this apparent religious unity, the focus of the imagery at Huari differed from that at Tiahuanaco. At Huari it was applied primarily to portable objects, particularly ceramics; at Tiahuanaco it was applied to monumental stone architecture, but rarely appeared on pottery. Thus, while Huari ceramics spread the word far and wide, Tiahuanaco imagery was confined to standing monuments at the capital and a few other sites. Religious ceremony at Huari appears to have been quite private, confined to small groups, judging by the architecture, while at Tiahuanaco it seems to have been more public, taking place within large compounds designed for the purpose.

Given such differences within the similarities, the exact nature of the relationship between the two powers remains a keenly debated subject. What is indisputable is that religious imagery and concepts continued through politically divided times as well as more unified imperial times, as states, kingdoms and empires rose and fell during the fragmented Middle Horizon.

THE HUAROCHIRÍ MANU-SCRIPT,

a post-Spanish-conquest *INCA* document, composed in the early 17th century (*c.* 1608), was one of the most valuable and detailed sources of pre-Spanish conquest religious belief among the *HATUN-RUNA* commoners of the Inca Empire. Written in *QUECHUA*, it was almost certainly the work of a native chronicler and, like the *IDOL-ATRÍAS*, compiled at the instigation of the local "extirpator of idolatries", Francisco de Avila (see also *CAJATAMBO*).

Huarochirí was an Inca province in the western Andes, east of present-day Lima. The inhabitants were of the *AYLLU* kinship lineage of *Yauyos*, and, reflecting Inca imperial practice in the capital, were divided into two groups – *Anan* (or "upper") *Yauyos* and *Lurin* (or "lower") *Yauyos* (see also *HANAN* and *HURIN* Cuzco). The information recounted in the manuscript concerns two subgroups of the *Lurin Yauyos*, called the *Checa* and *Concha*, who were respectively pastoralists and agriculturalists. The label "*Yauyos*" was a general social classification for "outsiders", implying that at least part of the *ayllu*, the pastoralists, came into the region only relatively recently, probably from the south, and established themselves in complementary opposition to the indigenous lowland agricultural population. The

HUASCAR was the Inca emperor who seized power after the death of his father Huana Capec. (NUEVA CORÓNICA Y BUEN GOB-IERNO, FELIPE GUAMAN POMA DE AYALA, 1583–1613.)

agriculturalists, however, also *Yauyos*, had probably themselves moved into the region much earlier and become integrated with the people already there.

The principal deities of the Huarochirí *Yauyos* were *HUALLALLO CARHUINCHO*, a fierce, powerful, fire-breathing god, and his *Checa* rival *PARIACACA*, who was "born" on a distant mountain top.

HUASCAR, or Huascaran, was the 13th Inca emperor (ruled 1526–32), having seized the throne after the sudden death of his father *HUAYNA CAPAC* and the heir-apparent from smallpox. Although some sources indicate that he had a more legitimate claim to the throne, his rule was contested by his half-brother *ATAHUALPA*, who captured him and took control in 1532.

HUATHIACURI was a lesser deity/culture hero of the pre-*INCA Yauyos* of the Huarochirí region in the western Andes of central Peru. He was the son of *PARIACACA*, god of rain, thunder and lightning. He met a rich man whose wife had committed adultery. Because of her impiety, two *SERPENTS* were slowly eating away the jilted husband's life; Huathiacuri confronted the wife and forced her to confess, thereby causing the serpents to die and saving the husband's life.

HUAYNA CAPAC was the 12th *INCA* emperor, who ruled from 1493 to 1526. He died suddenly of smallpox in 1526 along with his heir apparent. The Spanish sources leave some doubt as to whether he had actually designated his successor, whether he favoured his son *HUASCAR*, or whether he secretly hoped that another son, *ATAHUALPA*, would use his own control of the army to supplant Huascar – or whether he had planned to divide the empire among several sons.

Huayna Capac's place in Inca "myth" lies in the fact that, as smallpox spread rapidly south from Mesoamerica, where it had been introduced to the Americas by the Spaniards, he received reports from traders from the north of bearded strangers who sailed in strange ships. These reports coincided with of a series of ill omens, and his priests prophesied evil and disaster when they witnessed the death of an eagle, which fell out of the sky after being mobbed by buzzards during ceremonies in honour of the sun god *INTI*.

HUAYNA PICCHU see under *MACHU PICCHU*.

HUITACA was the *CHIBCHA* goddess of evil, and the patroness of misbehaviour and drunkenness. She challenged the work of the preacher hero *NEMTEREQUETEBA*. In one version of the myth, he transformed her into the moon, and she is therefore sometimes confused with the moon goddess *CHIE*.

HURIN CUZCO see *HANAN AND HURIN CUZCO*.

IAE was the *KAMAIURA* moon god (see *KUAT*).

IAMURICUMA WOMEN, among the tribes of the Brazilian *XINGU* River region, were a tribe of female warriors who, like the Amazon warriors of Greek myth, cut off their right breasts so that they

HUAYNA CAPAC, the 12th Inca emperor, was the last to rule a relatively peaceful empire before civil war and the arrival of the Spaniards. (IMAGINARY SKETCH BY FELIPE GUAMAN POMA DE AYALA IN HIS NUEVA CORÓNICA Y BUEN GOBIERNO WRITTEN BETWEEN 1583 AND 1613.)

could draw their bows and shoot arrows more effectively. They could transform themselves into spirits and could capture anyone who looked upon them. When 16th-century Europeans heard these stories, they thought they had discovered the land of the Amazons and thus gave the area its name.

IDOLATRÍAS ("idolatries") are the records of the investigations of Spanish priests into idolatrous practices in the countryside. In the first few decades after the Spanish conquest, the conversion of the peoples of the *INCA* Empire to Catholicism appeared, on the surface, to be successful. In reality, however, for more than a century Spanish priests continued to discover, and struggle with, a wealth of ingrained local belief and ritual practice "behind the altar" and, in fact, many local legends and "beliefs" continue to the present day.

This conflict of religions was particularly fierce during the late 16th and early 17th centuries, and knowledge of the struggle, and thus of provincial Inca religious belief among the *HATUNRUNA* commoners, comes mostly from the local nobility, the *CURACAS*, who were interviewed and enlisted by Spanish priests. Through them, the priests were able to interrogate local curers, "witches", diviners, and communal leaders about the persistent worship of ancestral mummies (*MALLQUIS*) and celestial bodies (see *MAYU*), and reverence for the spirits of local *HUACAS* (sacred places).

Another important source for pre-Spanish Andean provincial religion, and one of the most detailed,

INCA BELIEF in and practice of their ancient religion well into the 17th century prompted the Spanish authorities to attempt to extirpate such practice. This Idolatría records their efforts.

is the work of the Spanish-trained native acolyte Felipe Guaman Poma de Ayala from Huamanga, an Inca town in the central Peruvian Andes. Guaman Poma claimed to be the son of a *curaca* who had served as an emissary of Inca *HUASCAR* to Francisco Pizarro at Cajamarca. His monumental work, *Nueva Corónica y Buen Gobierno*, written over the course of 30 years, was completed in 1613. Perhaps prompted by the descriptions in myth of *VIRACOCHA* as a bearded white god, Guaman Poma was convinced that the Andean peoples knew the God of Christianity before the conquests of the Inca state, and thus were practising Christians until corrupted by Inca religion. He even identified Viracocha as St Bartholomew.

Yet another important and detailed source is the *HUAROCHIRÍ MANUSCRIPT*, which came from a town in the western Andes east of Lima, the nature of which has been used to argue that it was written by a native under the guiding hand of the local "extirpator of idolatries", Francisco de Avila.

As well as the information on religious beliefs and practices, these sources relate detailed information

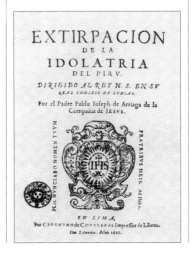

A FANCIFUL reconstruction of an Inca procession, which attempted to convey the near-divine status of the Inca emperor. (PAINTING BY ALBERTO FEBALLOS FRANCHI, 1905.)

on everyday *hatunruna* life. This detail provides valuable contextual background for interpreting the myth and legend of the official Inca state religion and for understanding the intricacies and permutations of local pre-Inca beliefs. The most revealing aspect of the *idolatrías* is their demonstration of the intimate bond between the peoples of local communities and their "personal" sacred *huacas* and local deities. Although few *idolotrías* have been published, those of Huarochirí province and *CAJATAMBO* are particularly informative.

The *idolatrías* show us the mythology of Inca commoners – how they believed their communities were created, how they regarded the relationship between the living and the dead, their sense of how the supernatural regulated and influenced daily life, and their integration, both religious and social, into official Inca state religion. At the same time, they show the relationships between religion and the social structure, the opposition and co-operation between highland and lowland communities, and the relationships among *AYLLU* kinship groupings, and between pastoralists and agriculturalists. Local legends have been, and continue to be, recorded by anthropologists. One of the most enduring, universal themes in the Andes is that of the return of the Inca, the *INKARRÍ* legend.

ILLA see *ILYA*.

ILLAPA was the *INCA* weather god of thunder, lightning and rain. One of the temples in the sacred *CORICANCHA* in *CUZCO* was dedicated to him, and he was offered prayers and gifts to bring fertilizing rain for the crops. The Incas appear to have modelled him on the thunder god *THUNUPA* of *TIAHUANACO*.

Illapa was usually portrayed holding a war club in one hand and a sling in the other (perhaps corresponding to the spear-thrower and spears of Thunupa). He drew water from *MAYU*, the Milky Way, which was regarded as a "celestial river". The water was kept in a clay jar owned by his sister, and when Illapa wanted to send down rain to earth he would shatter the jar with a stone from his sling. Thus the whir and crack of his slinging made the whistle of the winds and the thunder, while his brisk movements caused the shining garments he wore to flash as lightning.

ILLMA was a pre-*INCA* name for *PACHACAMAC*.

ILYA ("light") was one of the many epithets used by the *INCA* to refer to *VIRACOCHA*.

ILYAP'A see *ILLAPA*.

IMAYMANA VIRACOCHA was the elder son or special aide of *CON TICCI VIRACOCHA* in different versions of the central Andean creation myth. After the creation of the world by *VIRACOCHA* at Lake *TITI-CACA*, Imaymana Viracocha set off northwestwards along a route bordering the forests and mountains. He called forth the clay models of people made by his father, named the trees and plants and established when they would flower or bear fruit, instructing the people on which were edible or medicinal. He

eventually rejoined his father and brother, *TOCAPO VIRACOCHA* at *MANTA* on the Ecuadorian coast, where they disappeared out to sea by walking across the waters.

INCA was the name of one of the peoples of the Valley of Cuzco, who rose to prominence and eventually built a vast empire throughout the Andes, and the adjacent western coastal regions and eastern rain forests. Their empire, traditionally founded by *MANCO CAPAC* and the ancestors, began about 1100 and lasted until the Spanish conquest of the 1530s. They called their lands *TAHUANTINSUYU*, literally "the land of the four quarters".

The two principal gods of the Inca were *VIRACOCHA* and *INTI*, although the latter became increasingly favoured shortly before the arrival of the Spaniards. Other important deities included *QUILLA*, *CHASKA-QOYLOR*, *ILLAPA* and *CUICHU*. The two principal temple complexes in *CUZCO* were the sacred *CORICANCHA* precinct and the imposing *SACSAHUAMAN* edifices. *SAPA INCA* was the honorary title given to the Inca emperor.

INCA ROCA was the legendary sixth *INCA* ruler of *CUZCO*, probably sometime in the 13th century.

INCA ROCA was the sixth legendary Inca emperor, who ruled at some point in the 13th century. (IMAGINARY SKETCH BY FELIPE GUAMAN POMA DE AYALA IN HIS NUEVA CORÓNICA Y BUEN GOBIERNO, WRITTEN BETWEEN 1583 AND 1613.)

Like all Inca rulers, he was considered to be a direct descendant of the ancestors, *MANCO CAPAC* and Mama Ocllo.

INCA URCO, or Urcon, the ninth *INCA* ruler of *CUZCO*, had the shortest reign of any pre-Spanish-conquest Inca king, traditionally less than a year in 1438. He had been chosen by his father, *VIRA-COCHA INCA*, to be his successor but had fled from Cuzco with his father at the approach of the army of the rival city-state of *CHANCA*, leaving his brother, *PACHACUTI INCA YUPANQUI*, to defend the city.

INCA YUPANQUI see *YAHUAR HUACAC*.

INKARI was the name of the first man in the *Q'ERO/INCA* central Andean variation of the creation myth (see *ROAL*).

INKARRÍ was/is the central character in a post-Spanish conquest *INCA* millenarian belief in the "dying and reviving Inca". The derivation of the name itself is a combination of *QUECHUA Inca* and Spanish *rey*, meaning both king or ruler. The myth foretells a time when the current sufferings of the original peoples of the Andes will be ended in a cataclysmic transformation of the world, in which Spanish overlords will be destroyed. The true Inca will be resurrected and reinstated in his rightful place as supreme ruler, and prosperity and justice will return to the world.

Many slightly different versions of the Inkarrí myth were collected and recorded by the Peruvian anthropologist Josémaria Arguedas in the 1950s in southern Peru. A typical example recounts how Inkarrí was the son of a savage woman and Father Sun. Inkarrí was powerful; he harnessed his father and the very wind itself. He drove stones with a whip, ordered them around, and founded a city called K'ellk'ata, probably *CUZCO*. Then he threw a golden rod from a mountain top, but found that Cuzco did not fit on the plain where it had landed, so he moved the city to its present location. When the Spaniards came, however, they imprisoned Inkarrí in a secret place, and his head is all that remains. But Inkarrí is growing a new body and will return when he is whole again.

Such belief is clearly in keeping with the Andean concept of *PACHA-CUTI*, the revolution of time and space, and understandably arose from a sense of oppression and injustice to the native populations by the Spaniards. It probably harks back to events of the first few decades after the Spanish conquest, during which the last Inca emperor *ATAHUALPA* was beheaded by Francisco Pizarro, and to the beheading of *TUPAC AMARU*, a claimant to the Inca throne who led an unsuccessful revolt against Spanish rule in the 1560s and 1570s. In different

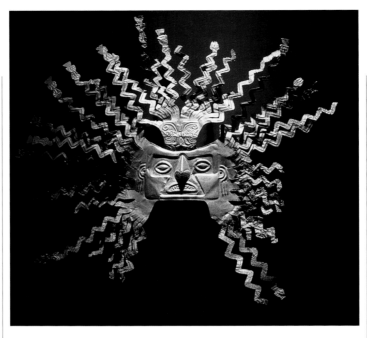

INTI *the sun god rivalled even the creator Viracocha in importance among the Inca peoples. A golden mask of him, similar to this one, was probably displayed in his temple in the Coricancha in Cuzco.*

accounts, the heads were taken to Lima or to Cuzco, but in both cases the belief is that, once buried in the ground, the head becomes a seed that regrows its body in anticipation of Inkarrí's return.

INTI, the *INCA*/pan-Andean manifestation of the sun, was the life-giving force universally recognized by Andean peoples, undoubtedly from earliest times and by numerous, now lost, names. The sacred *CORICANCHA* precinct in *CUZCO* was the centre of the official state cult dedicated to his worship. By Inca times, Inti rivalled in importance the creator god *VIRACOCHA* himself, owing in particular to his special relationship with the Inca emperor, the *SAPA INCA*, and to the splendour and importance of his temple within the Coricancha. So powerful and important was Inti that an incident witnessed by the priests during ceremonies in his honour appeared to foretell the downfall of the empire. The event – the ill omen of an eagle, mobbed by buzzards, falling from the sky – occurred in the reign of *HUAYNA CAPAC*, the 12th emperor (1493–1526), and coincided with reports of the spread of an unknown and deadly menace from the north – now known to have been smallpox spreading from Mesoamerica.

The universality of the sun notwithstanding, the sun god as Inti was in many respects a uniquely Inca deity; the emperor became regarded as the manifestation of the sun on earth. Although regarded with awe because of his power, Inti was believed to be a benevolent and generous god. Nevertheless, solar eclipses were regarded as signs of Inti's anger.

The image of Inti was most frequently a great mask of sheet gold, moulded as a human-like face, wide-eyed and showing a toothy grin. Surrounding the face were rays of sheet gold, cut in zig-zags and ending in miniature human-like masks or figures.

By the second half of the 15th century, when the Inca Empire was reaching the limits of its expansion and power, Viracocha had become a somewhat remote deity. Inti came to be regarded as his intermediary, with the weather god *ILLAPA* and others. This relationship was carefully emphasized by the Sapa Incas, and it became the basis for their own intimate association with Inti, putting forth themselves as the intermediary between the sun and the people. The Sapa Inca's presence was regarded as essential to assure the light and warmth of the sun to make the world habitable. Ritual ceremonies and offerings to Inti served to reinforce this melding of god and king, and to legitimize Inca power and right to rule. The Incas were painstaking in their

efforts to establish, and to permute as necessary, an elaborate mythology to support this close association of Inti, the emperor and power.

Historical and archaeological evidence shows that expansion of the empire beyond the Valley of Cuzco began in earnest with *PACHACUTI INCA YUPANQUI*, the tenth ruler of Cuzco (1438–71), and his son *TUPAC INCA YUPANQUI* (1471–93). Much of the appearance of the capital described by the Spanish conquistadors was the work of these rulers. It also appears that development of the Inti–Sapa Inca bond and perfection of the state foundation myth took on increasing importance during their reigns. It became necessary for the Incas to demonstrate their right to rule, and to unify the empire, by proving that all peoples were descended from the same ancestors, namely the Inca ancestors. The beliefs and cosmologies of those they conquered needed to be incorporated into a universal state religion, and to do this alongside continuous acquisition of territories and peoples required an equally unremitting campaign of addition to and alteration of the state mythology (for example, see *MINCHANÇAMAN*). It was also important to extend this continuity back to the first ruler of Cuzco, Ayar *MANCO CAPAC*, and even to link the state foundation myth with creation mythology itself. This was the task allocated to the *AMAUTA* and *QUIPUCAMAYOQ* record-keepers.

In the official mythology of the ancestors' wanderings after their emergence from the cave at *TAMBO TOCO*, Manco Capac was given divine sanction when his brother Ayar Uchu flew up and spoke to the sun. The message he brought back was that Ayar Manco should thenceforth be called Manco Capac and rule Cuzco in the name of the sun.

In other versions of the state creation myth, Inti is named as the father of Ayar Manco Capac and Mama Coya (otherwise known as *MAMA OCLLO*) and of the other Ayars and their sister/partners, collectively known as the ancestors. Manco Capac and Mama Ocllo were sent down to earth specifically to bring the gifts of civilization to humankind, namely corn (maize) and potato cultivation, and this myth established the Incas' right to rule on the basis of their benevolent influence. In a somewhat more sinister variation on this theme, however, interpreted by some as an attempt by disgruntled members of the empire to discredit Inca rule, "Son of the Sun (Inti)", was the nickname given to Manco Capac by his (human) father in a ruse to trick the populace of Cuzco into handing over power and the rulership of the city. This and another

THE INCAS built temples to Inti throughout the empire. One of the best preserved is at Ingapirca, Ecuador, one of the most northerly sites of the empire.

rendition describe how Manco Capac bedecked himself in gold plates to lend credibility to his "divine" dawn appearance to the people of Cuzco.

Further elaborate permutations and details are given in other myths, especially those involving Pachacuti Inca Yupanqui. His discovery of the crystal tablet, with its image of Viracocha, at the spring of *SUSUR-PUQUIO*, together with his renewed construction and rearrangement of the sacred Coricancha to give

A MODERN MURAL in Lima depicts the honouring of Inti with the offer of a herd of llamas. (CHAVEZ BALLON COLLECTION.)

greater prominence to Inti, can be interpreted as an attempt to bond the creator, the sun and the emperor in one stroke. This appears to be the beginning of the "solarization" of Inca religion and of the empowerment of a state cult meant to accommodate and include all the peoples of the empire. The construction of *SACSAHUAMAN* at the northwest end of the capital (probably begun by Pachacuti Inca Yupanqui), its use as a sacred precinct and place of sacrifice to Inti, and the probability that it was used for cosmological observations (see *MAYU*) further link Inti, the Sapa Inca and the people in a clear hierarchy. Further still, the mountain fortress and sacred estate of *MACHU PICCHU*, also begun by Pachacuti Inca Yupanqui, held the *INTIHUATANA* or "Hitching Post of the Sun".

After the death of Pachacuti Inca Yupanqui, his body was embalmed and mummified. Along with the mummified body of his principal consort, he was kept in a special palace tomb, where both were looked after by a dedicated cult of young women called the *ACLLAS* ("chosen women"). In biannual official state celebrations of the

THE INTIHUATANA, literally the "Hitching Post of the Sun", at Machu Picchu, comprised two "shadow clocks" for Inca priests to observe and record the movements of the sun.

summer and winter solstices, *CAPAC RAYMI* and *INTI RAYMI*, the royal *MALLQUIS* were carried in procession on gold-covered seats from the tomb into the Coricancha, to the Temple of Inti, where they were offered food and drink.

Incorporation of "foreign" mythologies as conquests increased is well illustrated by the Inca Empire's encounter with the ancient and powerful kingdom of *PACHACAMAC* on the central Peruvian coast. Here the Incas met an ancient culture and polity with its own long-standing religious entity. It was a coastal religion, and thus more alien than, for example, that of *CHIMÚ* which, as an Andean culture, shared most of the basic tenets of Inca beliefs. To reconcile the traditions and ease potential tension between them – while insuring that Inca belief remained primary and all-inclusive – the *quipucamayoqs* and *amautas* included the ancient oracle site of Pachacamac in the story of *CONI-RAYA VIRACOCHA* (thus probably identifying him with *VIRACOCHA*),

demonstrating that the creator was already associated with Pachacamac and recognizing a connection in all but name between the two creator-god centres – Pachacamac and the *ISLAND OF THE SUN* in Lake *TITI-CACA*. Significantly, the shrine of Pachacamac was allowed to continue functioning but, to strengthen the link, the Incas established a temple to Inti alongside it.

Provincial peoples were continually reminded of their bond with Inti and the Sapa Inca by *CAPA-COCHA* sacrifices to Inti. Annually, the chosen victims were brought to the capital, then marched back out to their respective provinces again for ritual immolation.

INTI RAYMI, the *INCA* winter solstice festival in honour of the sun god *INTI*, was held in June (see also *CAPAC RAYMI*).

INTIHUATANA (the "Hitching Post of the Sun") was a stone pillar at *MACHU PICCHU*, carved atop a massive stone block. This and other stone pillars were used as "shadow clocks", from which *INCA* priests observed and recorded the regular movements of the sun in order to understand the cycles of cosmic events and to predict the future. At solstices, they would symbolically tie the sun to the pillar with a cord to prevent it from disappearing.

STAFF DEITY
& FANGED GODS

THE RELIGIOUS BELIEFS OF ancient Andean and western coastal civilizations imagined the gods in many forms, and as possessing different powers and rulership in different spheres. Thus a pan-Andean pantheon included a creator deity, a sun god, a moon god or goddess, a rain and weather deity, a sea god and a less universal collection of other deities of more specific natural phenomena, such as the rainbow or thunder, or of specific cultural commodities, such as crops or metalworking.

Running through the sequence of Andean civilization is the persistence of several iconographic themes and imagery. From earliest times, architecture, ceramics, textiles and even geoglyphs repeatedly used images of composite beings incorporating serpentine, feline and avian features. From at least as early as the Chavín civilization, the Staff Deity – a deity portrayed frontally, with outstretched arms holding staffs – and fanged, clawed, winged and bird-headed beings were depicted in various culturally distinctive styles. The jaguar also features prominently in Amazonian mythology, and many rain forest animals, including the jaguar, strongly influenced Andean art from the earliest times.

ONE OF THE MOST enduring iconoclastic images used from the Chavín culture of the Early Horizon (c. 900–200 BC) to the Late Horizon (15th–16th century AD) Inca was the Staff Deity. Male (left) or female (above), he/she was represented on every medium – stone, ceramics, paint on cloth, wood and metal. Although details of the imagery varied greatly from one culture to another, the essential elements were always included: a frontal stance and outstretched arms holding staffs or corn stalks. The imagery was clearly associated with fertility.

FANGS were applied to all manner of creatures and imagery – singular or composite – in ancient South American cultures. The jaguar (left) was particularly revered, and jaguar faces or fangs were added to realistic and abstract images on all media:

A FANGED STONE mask with jaguar snout and mouth, human head and ears (centre left) comes from the La Tolita culture of Ecuador (c. 500 BC–AD 500).

FROM THE CHAVÍN culture of the Early Horizon (c. 900–200 BC) is a pugnacious-looking stone bowl or mortar (below left) in the form of some type of feline.

A 15TH-CENTURY Inca ceramic painted kero, or drinking cup, (above) is in the form of a jaguar.

J

IPACURA see *MAMA IPACURA*.

IRIN-MAJE see *MONAN*.

IRMA, a pre-*INCA* name for *PACHACAMAC*.

THE ISLAND OF THE MOON is an island in Lake *TITICACA* in the highland Andean Titicaca Basin. In many versions of pan-Andean mythology describing the creation of the contemporary world, it was the place from which the moon first rose into the sky and was set into motion at the command of *VIRACOCHA*. (In other versions, the moon arose, along with the sun and the stars, from the *ISLAND OF THE SUN*.)

THE ISLAND OF THE SUN is an island in Lake *TITICACA* in the highland Andean Titicaca Basin. In pan-Andean mythology it was the

THE ISLAND OF THE SUN (right) and the island of the Moon (above) in the middle of Lake Titicaca were two of the most sacred sites of Andean religion. It was believed that the sun, moon and stars rose from the islands over the lake waters and were set in motion by the creator god Viracocha.

place from which the sun – and, in some versions, the moon and the stars as well (see also *ISLAND OF THE MOON*) – first rose into the sky and was set into motion at the command of *VIRACOCHA*. The *INCAS* identified and named the island, and built a shrine to Viracocha there, which was the focus of an annual pilgrimage by the Inca emperor and nobility. This shrine, along with that of *PACHACAMAC*

and the *CORICANCHA* in *CUZCO*, was one of the most sacred in the Inca realm until it was sacked by the Spaniards.

In one version of the origins of the Inca state, *MANCO CAPAC* and his sister/wife *MAMA OCLLO* were associated with the Island of the Sun in a deception meant to justify Inca conquest of the local peoples. In another rendering, Manco Capac was said to have led the "ancestors" underground from Lake Titicaca to the cave of *PACARITAMBO*.

JAGUARS AND JAGUAR-HUMANS were universal sources of imagery and mythology among the peoples of South America, as they were in ancient Mesoamerica. Among the cultures of the Andes and the west coast, the jaguar face has clearly inspired much of the

FANGED GOD imagery from the earliest times to the *INCA* Empire. The beast itself was depicted frequently in wall paintings and stone carvings, on ceramics and textiles, and in metalwork and other portable artefacts. The beast-like monster gods of *CHAVÍN*, the *MOCHE*, the *CHIMÚ* and other cultures incorporate features and characteristics of the jaguar or felines in general, such as fangs and claws.

Such general recognition of the ferocity and power of the jaguar was, and still is, also prominent among Amazonian, Orinoco and *XINGU RIVER* peoples. There they regard the jaguar as the spirit of the rain forest, and their mythology refers to jaguars as the first beings to inhabit the world, in much the same role as later occupied by humans (see *BOTOQUE*). The jaguar represents power, fertility and an ambivalent force that needs to be mastered, or controlled and kept in check, by *SHAMANS*. Among the rain forest peoples of eastern Bolivia, men, in order to win their warrior status, must go into the forest alone and armed only with a wooden spear to kill a jaguar.

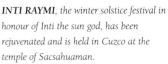

INTI RAYMI, the winter solstice festival in honour of Inti the sun god, has been rejuvenated and is held in Cuzco at the temple of Sacsahuaman.

Shamans and spiritual healers of the rain forest tribes don jaguar skins, wear necklaces of jaguar canine teeth (see also *KUAMUCUCA*) and, in their ritual trances, even growl like jaguars. The jaguar is regarded as their alter ego so that,

THE POWERFUL IMAGE of the jaguar was used from the earliest times by Andean cultures on everyday objects, such as this Chimú wooden vessel, as well as for architectural embellishment.

when a shaman dies, it is believed that his soul becomes a jaguar – a prowling jaguar seen at night near a village or burial ground is greatly feared because it is believed to be the metamorphosed body and soul of a dead shaman.

THE JIVARRO are an Ecuadorian rain forest tribe (see *HEAD-HUNTING*).

THE JURUNA are a rain forest tribe of the *XINGU RIVER* region of Brazil; see *SINAA* and *UAICA*.

JURUPARI is the central character in the Brazilian *TUPI* tribal myth, accounting for the present dominance of men in their society. The myth typifies the widespread belief among many South American tribes of original female dominance.

The Tupi believe that the sun became angered at the domination of the earth by women, and decided to reverse the situation. First, he caused Ceucy, a young female virgin, to become pregnant from the sap of the *cucura* tree. When she gave birth to a boy named Jurupari, the precocious child took power away from women by teaching men to hold ritual feasts in order to gain and keep knowledge and power. Women were forbidden to attend the feasts on pain of death. A precedent was set when Jurupari caused the death of his own mother as punishment.

Jurupari's other task was to find a perfect woman to be the wife of his father the sun but, so far, he has not succeeded in finding one.

KALASASAYA see *TIAHUANACO*.

THE KAMAIURA are a *XINGU RIVER* tribe of central Brazil (see *KUAT* and *MAVUTSINIM*).

KANASSA is a creator god of sorts to the Kuikuru of the *XINGU RIVER* region of central Brazil.

At the beginning of time, in the darkness, Kanassa could not see what he was doing. He traced the outline of a ray in the mud of the river bank but, in the darkness, stepped on it and was stung by it. The ray then plunged into the water and swam away. Thus was the alligator given its flat tail.

Kanassa blamed all on the firefly, because it refused to give light for him to see by. Then he recalled that the vulture king, Ugwvucuengo, was also the master of fire. Kanassa went to him and seized him by the leg, refusing to let go until the vulture brought down an ember from the sky. When Kanassa used the ember to create fire, the frogs tried to squirt water on it to put it out, but Kanassa, with the help of the serpent, moved the fire

THE KAYAPO of the central Brazilian rain forest believe themselves to have been the original "beasts" of the forest until they stole the jaguar's knowledge of fire and the bow and arrow for hunting.

safely away from the water's edge. Thus was fire brought from the sky to humankind (see also *KUAT*).

Kanassa also taught ducks how to swim and gave the curassow bird its brilliant feathered headdress.

KASOGONAGA was a sky goddess (see *CHACO*).

KASPI are the souls of the Tierra del Fuegan *ONA*, who join their creator *TEMAUKEL* after death.

THE KAYAPO are a rain forest tribe of central Brazil (see *BOTOQUE*).

K'ELLK'ATA was the legendary city founded by *INKARRÍ*.

KHUNO, the storm god of the high Andes, brought rain and snow to the high mountain valleys when humans began to clear the forests for agriculture.

KHUNO was a storm god of the peoples of the high Andean valleys, where snow was frequent. According to myth, when people began to clear the highest valleys for farming by burning the trees, Khuno became angry because of the smoke and smut that blackened his snow. In retaliation, he sent a flood to wipe out the people, but some survived by hiding in caves. When the waters subsided and they came out there was nothing to eat. It was then that humans discovered the

coca plant (*Erythroxylon coca*) and found that, when they chewed its leaves, they lost all sense of hunger, cold and unhappiness.

KILLA see *QUILLA*.

KILYA see *QUILLA*.

KONONATOO ("our maker") is the creator god of the Warao tribe of the lower Orinoco River. The Warao believe that they originally lived in heaven with their maker, who desired that they stay there with him. One day, however, the Warao descended to earth, when a young hunter discovered a hole in the sky and led the people through it. Later they were unable to return because a fat woman got lodged in the hole and blocked it up. As well as this, Kononatoo was disappointed in the Warao's disobedience, and so

he refused to create another entrance for them to return to the sky (see also *TOBA*).

The Warao are reluctant to bathe in lakes and rivers because, on earth, two girls once swam in a lake forbidden by Kononatoo and became pregnant by a water god, thus creating snakes.

KOYLLUR see *QOYLOR*.

KUAMUCUCA is a culture hero of the tribes of the Brazilian *XINGU RIVER* region. With the help of the sun and the moon, he invaded the village of the *JAGUARS* and killed them all, after which Kuamucuca and his fellow warriors collected the jaguars' claws as trophies with which to make necklaces. They were warned by the sun, however, not to eat the meat, and so the people of the Xingu tribes never eat jaguars when they kill them.

KUARUP is the name given to the rituals performed among the *XINGU RIVER* tribes when a person of importance has died (see *MAVUTSINIM*).

KONONATOO, the creator god of the Orinoco River Warao tribe, refused to allow them to rejoin him in the sky after a young warrior led them through a hole down to the earth.

L

KUAT is the sun god and culture hero of the *XINGU RIVER KAMAIURA* tribe. His brother Iae is moon god.

At the beginning of time, humankind lived in a world of total darkness, for it was always nighttime. Humans lived near termite hills, and their lives were wretched. The birds, however, lived in a kingdom of shining light ruled by the vulture king, Urubutsin. Kuat and Iae wanted to make life better for their fellow humans but could not think what to do, for they could not make light. So they plotted, and decided on a ruse to steal the birds' daylight and bring light into the world of humans.

They made an effigy in the form of a rotting corpse, buzzing with flies and crawling with maggots, and sent it to Urubutsin. But Urubutsin could not understand the flies' humming until one of his subjects interpreted the effigy as an offering and the maggots as a gift for the vulture king to eat. Then Urubutsin understood that the flies were inviting him to visit Kuat and Iae, who would give him more maggots to eat.

Meanwhile, Kuat and Iae had made another effigy corpse, and concealed themselves inside it. The vultures shaved their heads and made their way to Kuat's and Iae's village. The very moment that Urubutsin alighted on the corpse

THE LAMBAYEQUE VALLEY was ruled by a succession of powerful kingdoms – Moche, Sicán and Chimú. Each left monuments of their power, such as the Sicán pyramids at Túcume.

to feast, however, Kuat leaped out and caught hold of his leg. The other birds flew off in fright. Kuat refused to release Urubutsin until he promised to share the light of day with humans, so the secret of daylight was bought as a ransom. Urubutsin explained that day and night must alternate, promising that day would always return. So it was that humans began to live in the endless cycle of day and night (see also *KANASSA*).

THE KUIKURU are a *XINGU RIVER* tribe of central Brazil (see *KANASSA*).

KULIMINA was the *ARAWAK* creator of women (see *KURURUMANY*).

KURURUMANY is one of two Orinoco River *ARAWAK* tribal creator deities (see also *ALUBERI*). Kururumany created men, while the goddess Kulimina created women. He was also responsible for introducing death to humankind when he saw that his creations were not

KUAT and his brother Iae, the culture heroes of the Kamaiura Xingu River tribe, wanted to better the life of their fellow humans, so they stole the sunlight of the forest birds from the vulture king Urubutsin. Kuat became the sun god and Iae the moon god, thus initiating the endless cycle of night and day.

perfect. To plague humans, he also created serpents, lizards, mosquitoes, fleas and other biting creatures.

LAKE TITICACA see *TITICACA*.

LAMBAYEQUE VALLEY, in northern coastal Peru, was one of several valleys in this region where the *MOCHE*, *SICÁN* and *CHIMÚ* kingdoms developed from the Early Intermediate Period to the Late Horizon. In myth and legend, the Lambayeque Valley was invaded and settled by *NAYAMLAP*, with his idol *YAMPALLEC*, and his descendants, and later invaded by *CHIMO CAPAC* from the Moche Valley. It came under *INCA* rule after the conquest of Chimú in the 1470s.

LANZÓN IDOL see *CHAVÍN*.

THE LLACUAZ were one of the legendary lineage *AYLLUS* of *CAJATAMBO*. They conquered the *GUARI ayllu*, and shared ritual beliefs.

LLASCA CHURAPA was one of the five selves that made up the pre-*INCA* god *PARIACACA* in the *HUAROCHIRÍ MANUSCRIPT*.

LLAUTO was a common *INCA* headdress; one was worn by the image of *VIRACOCHA* seen by *PACHACUTI INCA YUPANQUI*.

LLIBIAC see under *CAJATAMBO*.

LLOQUE YUPANQUI was the legendary third *INCA* ruler of *CUZCO*, probably sometime in the 12th century AD. Like all Inca rulers, he was considered to be a direct descendant of the ancestors, *MANCO CAPAC* and *MAMA OCLLO*.

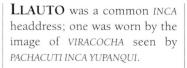

LLOQUE YUPANQUI was the third legendary Inca emperor. (IMAGINARY SKETCH BY FELIPE GUAMAN POMA DE AYALA IN HIS NUEVA CORÓNICA Y BUEN GOBIERNO, WRITTEN BETWEEN 1583 AND 1613.)

LLULLAILLACO, a mountain peak in the northern Argentinian Andes, was the site of the *INCA* ritual sacrifice of two young girls and a boy between the ages of 8 and 14. Two of the bodies were buried about 2 m (6 ft) deep in the ground, possibly alive, in a child sacrifice (see *CAPACOCHA*) to the sun god *INTI*, or perhaps to the creator *VIRACOCHA*. Conditions at the site, discovered in 1999 at 6,700 m (22,000 ft) froze the bodies in near-perfect condition, and this has enabled scientists to study their diet and any genetic relationships (see also *AMPATO*).

MACHU PICCHU, a remote mountain retreat north of Cuzco, was one of the Incas' most sacred sites. The even more remote retreat of Huayna Picchu was perched on a rocky outcrop above the main site.

LURIN YAUYOS see *HUAROCHIRÍ MANUSCRIPT*.

MACAW see *YURUPARY*.

MACHAY (caves) see under *CAJATAMBO*.

MACHU PICCHU was a remote *INCA* mountain retreat above the Urubamba Valley, north of *CUZCO* – possibly of military significance to commemorate the conquest of the eastern provinces, but certainly much more important as a sacred site and Inca royal estate. Its construction was begun by *PACHACUTI INCA YUPANQUI*, and it served as an estate for his descendants until it was abandoned shortly before the Spaniards arrived. Its vast natural and polygonal stone construction incorporates several ritual locations, including the *INTIHUATANA* or "Hitching Post of the Sun", the Torreón Sun Temple and the Temple of Three Windows, all significant for ritual and astronomical observation. An even more isolated retreat, Huayna Picchu, is reached by a flight of stone steps from Machu Picchu to a rocky outcrop above it. In addition, a chain of 16 spring-fed water catchments supplied water and may have been used in the ritual control and manipulation of water (see also *CHAVÍN*, *SACSAHUAMAN* and *TIAHUANACO*).

MASSIVE polygonal stone structures such as the Intihuatana ("Hitching Post of the Sun") and numerous other temples and ritual locations were incorporated at Machu Picchu, as well as natural Huacas.

MAIRE MONAN see *MONAN*.

MALLQUIS (*INCA* and pre-Inca) were the mummified remains of the ancestors of a kinship or lineage *AYLLU*, including the mummies of Inca emperors and their queens. The care and veneration of *mallquis* were a central and essential part of Andean religious practice. They were usually stored in caves seen as sacred places, and at festivals for the gathering of *ayllu* members they were dressed in rich clothing, put on display, and offered food and

MALLQUIS, the carefully preserved mummified remains of ancestors, formed an important element in the religious structure and played a vital role in the rituals of Inca and earlier cultures.

drink. The *mallquis* were the focus of veneration and provided a setting for the recounting of the clan's origin myths, thus passing the knowledge down the generations. Such ceremonies were regarded as crucial in order to ensure the fertility of crops and herds, and to maintain cosmic order.

Judging from archaeological finds of well prepared and cared for mummies in the Andes and among the southern coastal cultures of Peru, the practice appears to have begun as early as the Early Horizon. Mummies also played an early and important role in the myth of the creation of the Inca state. The name *Ayar* itself, given to each of the male brothers/husbands of the Inca founders/ancestors, means "corpse", linking the ancestors and the mummified bodies of the deceased Inca rulers. According to the late 16th-century chronicler Cristobal de Molina, *MAMA HUACO*, the sister/wife of the founder/ancestor *AYAR AUCA*, was embalmed and mummified, and *chicha* (corn/maize beer), fermented from the corn of a special field believed to have been planted by her, was drunk by the keepers of her cult. Emperor *PACHACUTI INCA YUPANQUI* and his main consort were similarly honoured.

Although the *mallquis* of the Inca emperors were destroyed by the Spaniards in Cuzco, reverence for *mallquis* lasted into the 17th century in the provinces, much to the consternation of Spanish priests. Special "extirpators of idolatries" appointed to search out and destroy them discovered hundreds hidden in caves near provincial towns (see *IDOLATRÍAS, CAJATAMBO*).

MAMA COCA was the *INCA* goddess of the sea. She was a lesser deity in the Inca pantheon. As a highland people, the Incas had less to do with the sea than did the coastal cultures, except to trade with the latter for their products.

MAMA COYA see *MAMA OCLLO*.

MAMA CUNAS see under *ACLLAS*.

MAMA CURA see *MAMA IPACURA*.

MAMA HUACO was the sister/wife of *AYAR AUCA* (although one chronicler names *AYAR CACHI* as her husband) and one of the original *INCA* ancestors (see *MANCO CAPAC*).

MAMA IPACURA was the sister/wife of *AYAR CACHI* and one of the original eight *INCA* ancestors (see *MANCO CAPAC*).

MAMA KILYA see *QUILLA*.

MAMA ÑAMCA (pre-*INCA*) was the female ally of *HUALLALLO CARHUINCHO*. Both fought *PARIACACA* (see *HUAROCHIRÍ MANUSCRIPT*).

MAMA OCLLO, also Cori Ocllo, Mama Coya, or Ocllo Huaco, was the sister/wife of *MANCO CAPAC* and mother of *SINCHI ROCA*. She was one of the eight *INCA* ancestors.

MAMA RAUA was the sister/wife of *AYAR UCHU* and one of the original eight *INCA* ancestors (see *MANCO CAPAC*).

MAMACUNA was the *INCA* Temple of the Sun at *PACHACAMAC*.

MAMA OCLLO, wife of the first Inca ruler, holds a symbol of Quilla (the moon), which she represents. (ILLUSTRATION FROM THE GENEALOGY OF THE 18TH-CENTURY "CUZCO SCHOOL".)

M

AS "SON OF THE SUN" Manco Capac, leader of the Inca ancestors, was depicted holding a sun 'mask' and ceremonial axe-staff of office. (ILLUSTRATION FROM "CUZCO SCHOOL" GENEALOGY, 18TH CENTURY.)

MANCO CAPAC, or Ayar Manco, was the legendary first *INCA* ruler and founder of the Inca dynasty, known as Hurin Cuzco (see *HANAN AND HURIN CUZCO*). His alternative name was in keeping with his brothers' names, all of which had Ayar as the first element. Manco Capac was the principal character in Inca mythology surrounding the origins of the state and in Inca hegemony. Manco Capac was also the name of one of the four kings who figure in the myth of the *UNNAMED MAN*, concerning the origin of the four-fold division of the Inca Empire.

The Incas vigorously promoted their own political agenda. They were particularly keen to establish their origins as special, and to convince others that their own place of origin was the same as that of the Incas. In the words of the 17th-century Jesuit priest, Bernabé Cobo, this official line was "caused by the ambition of the Incas. They were the first to worship [at] the cave of *PACARITAMBO* as the [place of the] beginning of their lineage. They claimed that all people came from there, and that for this reason all people were their vassals and obliged to serve them."

Permutations of the state creation myth seem to have prevailed simultaneously. The most prominent version, in outline, described how four brothers and four sisters came forth from the central one of three "windows" or caves in the mountain of *TAMBO TOCO* ("window mountain"). These were "the ancestors", and their leader (the eldest brother) was Manco Capac or Ayar Manco. The ancestors led the people who lived around Tambo Toco in search of a new land to settle. After much wandering, they came to a hill overlooking the Valley of Cuzco. Certain miraculous signs informed them that here was where they should settle, so they came down from the mountain, overcame any local resistance, and took possession of the land.

This standard version comes from the 16th-century chronicler Sarmiento de Gamboa's *Historia de los Incas* (1572), an early source and one that relied heavily on interviews with keepers of the Inca state records, the *QUIPUCAMAYOQS*.

Pacaritambo was the "inn, or house, of dawn", the "place of origin". According to the chroniclers it was six leagues (about 33 km/20 miles) south of Cuzco; in fact, it is closer to 26 km (16 miles). The mountain there, Tambo Toco, had three windows, the central one of which was called Capac Toco ("rich window"). From this window stepped the four ancestral couples, the brother/sister–husband/wife pairs: Ayar Manco Capac with Mama Ocllo, Ayar Auca with Mama Huaco, Ayar Cachi with Mama Ipacura or Mama Cura, and Ayar Uchu with Mama Raua. From the flanking windows, Maras Toco and Sutic Toco, came the Maras and Tambos, both allies of the Incas. A divine link was immediately established in the promotion of the myth by the claim that the ancestors and their allies came out of the caves at the urging of *TICCI VIRACOCHA*.

Ayar Manco declared that he would lead his brothers and sisters, and the allies, in search of a fertile land, where the local inhabitants would be conquered and their land seized. He promised that he would make the allies rich. Before setting out, the ancestors and allies were formed into ten lineage groups called *AYLLUS*. (This was the origin of the ten *ayllus* of commoners at Cuzco, as opposed to the *PANACA*, the ten royal *ayllus*, who were the descendants of the Inca emperors.)

Ayar Manco led his followers north, towards the Valley of Cuzco. He had a golden bar, brought from Tambo Toco, with which he tested the ground for fertility by thrusting it periodically into the soil.

Progress was slow, and there were several stops. At the first stop Ayar Manco and Mama Ocllo conceived a child. At the second stop a boy was born, whom they named *SINCHI ROCA*. A third stop was made at Palluta, where they lived for several years, but eventually became dissatisfied with the fertility of the land, and so moved on to a place called Haysquisrro. It was here that the first breaking up of the company occurred.

Ayar Cachi was known to be unruly and sometimes cruel. Wherever the ancestors passed through or stopped he caused trouble with the local inhabitants. He was also a powerful slinger and could hurl stones hard enough to split mountains open, causing dust and rocks to fly up and obscure the sun. The other ancestors began to consider him a liability and a hindrance to their prospects, so the brothers and sisters formed a plan to dispense with him. Ayar Manco told him that several important objects that should have accompanied the golden rod had been left in Pacaritambo: a golden cup (*topacusi*), a miniature llama figurine (called a *napa*) and some seeds. Ayar Cachi at first refused to return to Capac Toco, but agreed to do so when his sister, Mama Huaco, herself a forceful character, chided and accused him of laziness and cowardice.

Ayar Cachi journeyed back to Capac Toco with a Tambo companion called Tambochacay (literally, "the window entrance-bearer"). He was unaware, however, that Ayar Manco and the others had convinced Tambochacay to dispose of him. So, when Ayar Cachi went into the cave to retrieve the forgotten items, Tambochacay sealed the entrance, trapping Ayar Cachi inside forever. The site, later known as *MAUQALLAQTA*, became an important Inca *HUACA* and place of pilgrimage.

The ancestors' next stop was at Quirirmanta, at the foot of a mountain called Huanacauri. They climbed the mountain and, from the top, saw the Valley of Cuzco for the first time. From the summit, Ayar Manco threw the golden rod into the valley to test the soil. To their amazement the entire rod vanished into the earth, and a rainbow appeared. Taking these as propitious signs, they decided this was the place that should become their homeland.

Before they could descend the mountain, however, Ayar Uchu became the second to depart from the company. He sprouted huge wings and flew up into the sky, where he met the sun. The sun told Ayar Uchu that thenceforth, Ayar Manco, the eldest brother, should be called Manco Capac ("supreme rich one"), and that they should go into the valley to the place of Cuzco, where the ruler of that place, *ALCAVICÇA*, would welcome them. Ayar Uchu returned to his brothers and sisters, told them this news, and was transformed into stone. A stone, identified by the Incas as Ayar Uchu, became another of their principal *huacas*.

The remaining ancestors did not, however, proceed straight to Cuzco and Alcavicça. They stopped first at a place called Matao, near Cuzco, where they remained for two years. During this period another strange event occurred. Mama Huaco, like Ayar Cachi, was also an expert slinger. She hurled a stone at a man in Matao and killed him. Splitting open his chest, she removed his heart and lungs, and blew into the lungs to make them inflate. When she displayed these to the people of the town, they fled in terror.

Finally, Manco Capac led the ancestors to Cuzco. They met Alcavicça and declared that they had been sent by their father, the sun. This news convinced Alcavicça, who allowed them to take over the town. In return, the ancestors "domesticated" the inhabitants by teaching them to plant corn (maize). (In one version it was Manco Capac who planted the first field; in another it was Mama Huaco.) At the place that would become the centre of the Inca city of *CUZCO* – the plaza called Huanaypata – the last remaining brother ancestor, Ayar Auca, was turned

MANCO CAPAC *was founder ancestor and first ruler of the Incas. (CONCEIVED AND SKETCHED BY FELIPE GUAMAN POMA DE AYALA IN HIS NUEVA CORÓNICA Y BUEN GOBIERNO, WRITTEN BETWEEN 1583 AND 1613.)*

into a stone pillar, which, like the stone of Ayar Uchu on Huanacauri, became a revered *huaca*.

This left Manco Capac, his four sisters and his son Sinchi Roca to organize the building of Cuzco: a convenient outcome, and in keeping with later Inca imperial practice of sister/wives, and leaving only one descendant to the leadership.

This was the "standard" version. It contains all the necessary elements of Inca legend, including the wandering, conquering, alliances and divine intervention needed to telescope the folk memory of a long and complex history of a people.

So ambitious were the Incas, however, that they felt the need to link this lineage creation myth to the world creation myth, and thus gain the ultimate divine sanction. And in variations, the Incas appear openly devious in their determination to rewrite and shape history to fit their self-image as the supreme and only people fit to rule.

In one version, the ancestors deliberately tricked the inhabitants of the Valley of Cuzco into believing them to be the descendants of the sun itself. Manco Capac made two golden discs, one for his front and one for his back. He then climbed the hill of Huanacauri before dawn so that at sunrise he appeared to be a golden, god-like being. The populace of Cuzco was so awed that he had no trouble in descending the hill and taking over their rule.

In yet another version, Manco Capac achieved rulership, but the account, given by four elderly *QUIPUCAMAYOQS*, contains an undercurrent of the resentment that local valley inhabitants might have harboured, even years after ancestors of the Inca had invaded and conquered them. The story can be interpreted as a suggestion that the whole fabric of Inca rule was illegitimate.

In this variation, Manco Capac was the son of a local valley *CURACA* or official in Pacaritambo. His mother had died giving birth to him, so he grew up with his father, who gave him the nickname, "Son of the Sun [*INTI*]". The father died when Manco Capac was about 10 or 12, never having explained to his son that the nickname was just that, and not the truth. What is more, the commoners of the town – referred to as *gente bruta* ("stupid folk") in the chronicle – appear also to have been convinced that Manco Capac was actually the son of the sun. Two old men, the priests of Manco Capac's father's household gods, continued to encourage this belief. As Manco Capac reached early manhood, the priests further promoted Manco Capac's own conviction that he was the son of a god and that he had a natural right to rule on earth. With these ideas in his head, he set off for Cuzco with several relatives and the two old priests; also with his father's principal idol, named Huanacauri. In this version also, Manco Capac wins the rule of the people of Cuzco by appearing at dawn on the mountain of Huanacauri, bedecked in gold as a divine being and dazzling them.

THE TRADITION *of the Sapa Inca and the founding of the Incas nation by Manco Capac has recently been revived, and is celebrated annually in Cuzco with a representative, symbolism and ritual attire.*

In a final variation, Manco Capac and his sister/wife Mama Ocllo were associated with the *ISLAND OF THE SUN* in Lake *TITICACA*, a deception meant to justify Inca conquest of local peoples. This version provides another example of Inca efforts to reconcile the beliefs of the local peoples with creation in general and with the origins of the Inca state – efforts whose ulterior motive was to justify and secure divine sanction for Inca rule. As in the other renditions, Manco Capac, as the legendary first Inca "emperor" and founder of the state to be, identified himself as the son of the sun. Titicaca Basin myth described a great deluge that had destroyed the previous world, and told that the sun of the present world first shone on the Island of the Sun. In this version, therefore, a fable was concocted that, after his creation, the sun placed his two children, a male and a female, on the island with the task of teaching the "barbarous" people of the region how to live in a civilized manner. Undoubtedly these two must have been Manco Capac and Mama Ocllo.

A further connection with the Titicaca Basin was given in an account in which it was claimed that Manco Capac led the "ancestors" underground from Lake Titicaca to the cave of Pacaritambo. In this case, it was even claimed that the creator *VIRACOCHA* bestowed a special headdress and stone battleaxe upon Manco Capac, and prophesied that the Incas would become great lords and conquer many other nations. Both of these renditions have the great advantage of linking Manco Capac and the Inca state with Titicaca and *TIAHUANACO*, which the Incas knew to be revered throughout the Andes as the place where the world began.

MAYTA CCAPAC YNCA IV.

MAYTA CAPAC, *fourth Inca emperor, is holding an axe-staff of office. (DEPICTED IN THE 18TH-CENTURY "CUZCO SCHOOL" GENEALOGY.)*

MANIOC STICK ANACONDA see *YURUPARY*.

MANTA was the site on the northernmost coast of the *INCA* Empire where, in pre-Inca creation myth, *CON TICCI VIRACOCHA*, *IMAYMANA VIRACOCHA* and *TOCAPO VIRACOCHA* rejoined each other after their journeys and disappeared by walking northwest out across the ocean.

THE MARAS were allies of the *INCA* ancestors (see *MANCO CAPAC*.)

MARAS TOCO was one of the caves of *TAMBO TOCO* in the *INCA* state foundation myth (see *MANCO CAPAC*).

MATAO was the sixth place of sojourn of the ancestors on their wanderings in the *INCA* state foundation myth (see *MANCO CAPAC*).

MAUQALLQTA ("old town") is the modern name for the ruins of an *INCA* site 26 km (16 miles) south of *CUZCO*. It has been identified as *PACARITAMBO/TAMBO TOCO*, the place of origins of the Inca ancestors (see *MANCO CAPAC*).

MAVUTSINIM was the "first man" of the peoples of the *XINGU RIVER* region. He wanted to bring the dead back to life, so he collected logs (*kuarup*) and brought them to the village, where he dressed them up as people. His plan failed, however, because one member of the village did not complete Mavutsinim's exact instructions, so the logs remained wooden.

According to *KAMAIURA* tribal myth, in the beginning only Mavutsinim existed, and was thus the creator. He transformed a shell into a woman, and with her produced the first boy child. He took the child for himself, away from its mother, who returned tearfully to a lagoon, where she became a shell again. Thus the Kamaiura declare themselves to be the "grandchildren of the son of Mavutsinim".

A variant myth describes how, one day, Mavutsinim was caught in the forest by *JAGUARS*. In exchange for his life, he promised the jaguars his daughters in marriage, but sent wooden figures instead. Two of Mavutsinim's daughters did actually marry jaguars, and one of them became pregnant. Her jealous jaguar mother-in-law, however, killed her, but let her twin boys live. When they grew up, the twins hunted jaguars in revenge and became the sun and the moon.

MAYTA CAPAC was the legendary fourth *INCA* ruler of *CUZCO*, probably sometime in the later 12th century. Like all Inca rulers, he was considered to be a direct descendant of the ancestors, *MANCO CAPAC* and *MAMA OCLLO*.

MAYU (*QUECHUA*, "celestial river") was the Milky Way, the movements of which across the night sky were keenly observed by the *INCA* from points within the sacred *CORICANCHA* precinct in *CUZCO*.

In Inca religion, the observation of this celestial river was the starting point for calendrical correlations with natural changes in terrestrial conditions and seasons. (This is in notable contrast to the calendrical calculations of most other cultures, which proceed from observations of the movements of the closest single celestial bodies, namely the sun and the moon. By contrast, the observation of the Milky Way is of galactic proportions.) This starting point provided a scheme with which to chart the correlations of heavenly positions and terrestrial change, and to organize daily, seasonal and annual labour and ritual.

Observation of the Milky Way is of vast galactic rotation: the plane of rotation inclines noticeably from the plane of the earth's rotation by between 26° and 30°. When the movements are plotted from the southern hemisphere, the broad band of the "river" divides the sky into three sections (above, below, and Mayu itself), and follows a sequence that rocks it slowly through the course of the year, such that during half the year it tilts from right to left, and during the other half from left to right. In the course of 24 hours, Mayu crosses its zenith in the sky, and, in doing so, forms two intersecting or inter-cardinal axes oriented northeast/southwest and southeast/northwest.

Thus the divisions of the sky provided a celestial grid against which all other astronomical observations could be plotted, including not only the obvious luminated planets and stars, but also immense stellar voids or "dark clouds". To the Incas, these voids were constellations, which they named after animals: adult llama, baby llama, fox, *tinamou* (a partridge-like bird), toad and *SERPENT*. Luminary bodies included *COLLCA* ("granary" – the Pleiades), *ORQO-CILAY* ("multi-coloured llama" – another star group) and *CHASKA-QOYLOR* ("shaggy star" – Venus as the morning "star").

The movements of these celestial bodies were used by the Inca to predict zoological and botanical cycles, wild and domestic, and to regulate the care of their crops and llama flocks. Practical observations and applications were interwoven with myth. For example, the solstices of Mayu coincide with the Andean wet and dry seasons, and thus the celestial river was used to predict seasonal water cycles. The "dark cloud" llama (*YACANA*) disappears at midnight, when it was believed to have descended to earth to drink water and thus prevent flooding. (In contrast, black llamas were starved during October, in the dry season, in order to make them weep, regarded as a supplication to the gods to water the crops with rain.)

The sun's movements were used to calculate the two most important ritual dates in the year – the summer and winter solstices, *CAPAC RAYMI* and *INTI RAYMI*. Similarly, the first appearance of the Pleiades before sunrise was correlated with the regular sidereal lunar months (the 27.3-day period of the rotation of the moon around the earth–moon centre of mass), beginning on 8–9 June and ending on 3–4 May. In *Ayrihua* (the month of April), as this lunar-plotted year ended, ceremonies in Cuzco honoured the royal insignia, and a white llama was dressed in a red tunic and fed *coca* and *CHICHA* (corn/maize beer) to symbolize the first llama to appear on earth after the great flood.

As well as regulating daily and seasonal life, Mayu's movements were reflected in the Inca organization of their empire into four quarters (*TAHUANTINSUYU*), and oriented the routes of the four principal highways out of Cuzco to the quarters: the routes approximated the intercardinal axes of the Milky Way. Mayu's axes were also associated with sacred *CEQUE* ritual alignments, at least one of which correlated to the southernmost point in the Milky Way's movements. (see also *MISMINAY*).

THE MINATA-KARAIA were

a mythical race of beings whom the tribes along the *XINGU RIVER* of Brazil believe existed in the remote past. Minata-Karaia men had a hole in the top of their head, through which they could whistle, and bunches of coconuts grew beneath their armpits. This latter convenience meant that whenever they were hungry, they could simply take a coconut, crack it open against their head and eat it (see also the *OI*).

MINCHANÇAMAN, or Minch-

ancamon, was the pre-*INCA*, partially legendary, king of the *CHIMÚ* dynasty of *TAYCANAMU* in the *MOCHE* valley, the sixth or seventh ruler in that line. During the course of his reign, the valley was conquered by *TOPA YUPANQUI* (or *TUPAC INCA YUPANQUI*) in the 1470s. The Inca account of this (in Garcilaso de la Vega's *Comentarios Reales de los Incas*, 1609–17) demonstrates their method of incorporating new kingdoms into the fabric of their empire, firmly establishing their overlordship while at the same time recognizing the integrity and power of the ruling dynasty: "The brave Chimú [Minchançaman], his arrogance and pride now tamed, appeared

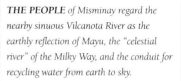

before the prince [Tupac Inca Yupanqui] with as much submission and humility, and grovelled on the ground before him, worshipping him and repeating the same request [for pardon] as he had made through his ambassadors. The prince received him affectionately in order to relieve [his] grief . . . [and] bade two of the captains raise him from the ground. After hearing him, [Tupac Inca Yupanqui] told him that all that was past was forgiven . . . The Inca had not come to deprive him of his estates and authority, but to improve his idolatrous religion, his laws and his customs."

MISMINAY is a town in Peru

situated 25 km (16 miles) south of *CUZCO*. Anthropological research has revealed that the people of the town and region continue to observe the night sky and *MAYU*, the Milky Way, in the manner of the ancient *INCA*, and to apply mythological and cosmological meaning to what they see. The nearby Vilcanota River is regarded as the reflection of Mayu, the "celestial river", and the two are regarded as conduits for recycling water from earth to sky and back again as rain.

MAYU, the Milky Way, was regarded as the "celestial river". Star clusters within it were considered to be celestial signs, one of the most important of which was the Pleiades, called Collea *("the granary").*

THE PEOPLE of Misminay regard the nearby sinuous Vilcanota River as the earthly reflection of Mayu, the "celestial river" of the Milky Way, and the conduit for recycling water from earth to sky.

As the Milky Way rotates through the sky over a 24-hour period, its zenith traverses two axes that the people of Misminay use to divide the heavens into four quadrants. This grid provides a template for the town itself, which is similarly divided by intersecting footpaths along the two principal irrigation canals, all of which meet at the chapel of Crucero, the name also used for the celestial intersection of Mayu's axes.

The beliefs of the people of Misminay perpetuate ancient Inca perception that all earthly animals and birds have a celestial equivalent, and that the sky beasts govern procreation and sustenance on earth. "Dark Cloud" constellations – stellar voids collectively called *Pachatira* – include llamas, a fox, a toad, a *tinamou* bird and a *SERPENT*, and their influence over their earthly equivalents reflects the concept of the earth mother *PACHAMAMA* and fertility in general. For example, when the "eyes of the llama" – the stars Alpha and Beta Centauri – rise before dawn in November and December, llamas give birth; and the serpent constellation, seen in the sky during the rainy season, brings rain, but is below ground (that is, below the horizon) during the dry season. Rainbows (see *CUICHU*), perceived as multicoloured serpents, rise from the ground after rain showers.

MIT'A ("turns of service") was an

INCA state institutional organization of labour for service to the royal household and for the redistribution of goods; see also *AYLLU*. It could take the form, for example, of tending royal lands and llama flocks, and performing a quota of work at state installations, such as redistribution warehouses.

CULTURE HEROES

THE IDEA OF A LEGENDARY figure as culture hero was an important part of Andean mythology, and continues to be so among rain forest peoples in South America. Among the Andean civilizations, such figures include both divine heroes and teachers, such as Viracocha and his sons, or Bochica in Colombia, and the founders of dynasties, kingdoms and empires, such as Manco Capac and the Ayars, Chimo Capac or Nayamlap. Each of these heroes brought the gifts of civilization, such as agriculture and monumental architecture, to humans and taught them the arts and moral codes by which to live.

A common feature in all of these stories is the eventual departure of the divine or human hero from the world, across the seas or into the sky, leaving humankind to fend for itself. In some cases, the hero existed on the fringes of history and appears to be an inflated version of a real person – for example, Pachacuti Inca Yupanqui. In other cases, the divine nature of the teacher and his description tempted Spanish chroniclers into equating him with a Christian saint.

Among the rain forest tribes, a common belief throughout the vast Amazonian and *pampas* regions is of a hero who learns how to use fire, weapons and tools after having been adopted by jaguar beings, the first masters of the earth who behaved like humans.

Shamans are the tribal spiritual leaders. With the use of hallucinogenic drugs, they gain access to the spiritual "other" world in order to intermediate on behalf of the tribe. Such practice appears to have been a long-standing tradition among ancient Andean cultures as well.

THE ANCIENT USE of hallucinogens to induce trance and gain access to the spiritual world for religious purposes is attested by numerous images on ancient pottery, such as this Moche stirrup vase (left) in the shape of a noble (with large ear discs) and cocaine-induced expression. Similarly, a much later Chimú painted textile (above) depicts a priest or shaman wearing an axe headdress who is apparently in a spirit world. The two anthropomorphized plants in the lower corners are cacti whose hallucinogenic juices induce visions.

A KAYAPO warrior/hunter (above) of the Xingu River region of central Brazil with a jaguar he has killed – ancient Andean cultures and rain forest tribes alike universally revered the jaguar for its power and cunning. Among rain forest tribes, fire and hunting weapons were stolen from the jaguar, thus reversing the roles of the jaguar and man. Shamans imitate jaguars as part of their ritual communication with "other" worlds.

THE CREATOR GOD Viracocha (in some versions accompanied by his sons) travelled throughout the land teaching humankind the arts of civilization. Later inhabitants of alleged stopping places on his legendary journeys honoured him with temples, as at Rachi (or Raqchi), Peru (above).

COCA continues to be used among Andean peoples for divination (above), for example, among the Chipaya people of Bolivia.

PRIESTS AND SHAMANS were/are healers as well as religious leaders – this Moche ceramic model (above) shows a priest with ear discs and a feline headband praying over a sick or deceased person.

MITIMAES was the *INCA* term for groups of people of one province whom they had moved to and settled in another part of their empire.

The practice was used in order to exercise demographic and social control and for economic reorganization. By shifting large groups of people around within the empire, the Incas could redistribute labour and the commodities grown and produced by different groups, as well as mixing peoples' notions of geographic identity and religious/mythological concepts.

The practice undoubtedly had a significant impact in rearranging and conflating the details of creation myth, especially, such that a more generalized pan-Andean/pan-Inca version was propagated. The result provided the Incas with a means of legitimizing their right to rule as a "chosen" people, whose semi-divine ruler had sanction by descent from the creator god *VIRA-COCHA* (see also *VIRACOCHA INCA*). The term itself was even established in myth, for it was used in some versions of the creation myth: *CON TICCI VIRACOCHA* ordered the two survivors of the great flood, thrown up on land at *TIAHUANACO*, to remain there as *mitimaes*.

THE MOCHE, or Mochica, were a culture and people who dominated the northern coastal valleys of Peru through the Early Intermediate Period, succeeding *CHAVÍN* cultural influence in that region and roughly contemporary with the *NAZCA* culture in the southern coastal valleys. A powerful kingdom was developed over several hundred years through conquest and domination of the local valleys to the north and south of the "capital" city at Moche in the valley of the same name (see also *FEMPEL-LEC* and *NAYAMLAP*).

By AD 450, two huge pyramidal structures, each made of millions of *adobe* bricks, had become the focus of political and religious power. The Huaca del Sol, 40 m

(130 ft) high, comprised a four-tiered, cross-shaped platform whose summit was reached by a north-side ramp; 500 m (1,650 ft) away, across an area occupied by dwellings and workshops, the Huaca de la Luna, at the foot of Cerro Blanco, was a three-tiered structure whose walls were richly decorated with friezes depicting mythological scenes and deities. The two ceremonial platforms sat within a sprawling urban setting that, at its maximum size, occupied as much as 300 hectares (740 acres).

About 100 years later, evidence indicates that the impingement of a huge sand sheet around Moche choked the canal system and stifled agriculture, and caused the inhabitants to move away. Some of Moche's inhabitants were probably responsible for the settlement of Galindo, farther up the valley, but from this time onwards the focus of Moche politics and religion shifted northwards, to the *LAMBAYEQUE VALLEY* and the sites of Pampa Grande and *SIPÁN*. As well as the element of natural disaster, these movements appear also to have been influenced by the early expansion of *HUARI* power from the southeast, out of the Andes.

Pampa Grande covered an area of some 600 ha (1,485 acres) and lasted about 150 years. Its most imposing structure, the Huaca Fortaleza, appears to have served a similar function to the Huaca del Sol at Moche as a ritual platform. It rose 38 m (125 ft), and its summit was reached by a 290-m (950-ft) ramp. At the very top,

columns supported the roofs of a complex of rooms, one containing a mural depicting *FELINE* beings. The Huaca Fortaleza appears to have been the élite sector of the city, while the residences of the lower classes of Moche society were spread around it.

Like Moche, Pampa Grande was abandoned abruptly, owing to a combination of agricultural disaster caused by an El Niño weather event and the continued expansion of the Huari state. Fierce internal unrest may also have been a factor, for the archaeological evidence shows intense conflagration in the centre of the city – so hot that *adobes* of the Huaca Fortaleza were fired into brick.

Like the Chavín cult before it, Moche imagery reflected a potent religion, with its own distinctive iconography and pantheon, albeit much derived from Chavín. Like Chavín de Huántar, at least one Moche pilgrimage centre has been recognized in the cliff-top site of *PACATNAMÚ*. Moche iconography was characterized by humans and anthropomorphized animal figures, *SERPENTS* and frogs, birds (owls in particular) and sea animals (crabs and fishes), and by standardized groups and ceremonial scenes, including a *coca* ritual recognizable by distinctive clothing and ritual combat. Murals, friezes and vignettes on pottery depict the capture and sacrifice of "enemies", drink offerings by subordinates to lords and gods, and persons passing through the night sky in moon-shaped boats. Rich tombs at

Sipán (some of the few unlooted tombs of the Andes) contain burials and artefacts, and mural scenes that confirm the images on the walls, ceramics, textiles and metalwork that have been excavated from other Moche sites.

Although we do not know the names of all the Moche deities directly, *AI APAEC* and *SI*, a sky/creator god and a moon goddess respectively, appear to have been prominent, if extended back in time from the later *CHIMÚ* pantheon. In a similar manner, a *MOCHE MOUNTAIN GOD* has been named by some from the many feline-featured beings depicted on Moche ceramics and textiles. Especially prominent, however, were the *FANGED GODS* and the complex ceremony and ritual of the *DECAPITATOR GOD*. In later Moche imagery, there was a mingling with Huari style, presumably imposed, and subtle changes in the depiction of eyes and headdress ornaments suggest the beginnings of the influence of Chimú.

THIS MOCHE CERAMIC bottle reflects the rich tradition of anthropomorphized animal figures and fierceness, with a fanged feline head, human hands, serpents and warrior insignia.

MOCHE MOUNTAIN GOD
was a remote and nameless deity with *FELINE* features depicted on *MOCHE* pottery and textiles. He seems to have been a creator god and sky god, but played little part in the affairs of humankind. He was closely associated with *AI APAEC*, who might have been his son.

MOCHICA see *MOCHE*.

MOIETY,
an anthropological term borrowed from the French word for "half" (*moitié*), describes two-part divisions for groups of *AYLLUS*. The organizational device was used throughout the Inca Empire and in precursor cultures. In Inca times, the two moieties were called *hanan* ("upper") and *hurin* ("lower"). The parts were frequently used in recognition of locally important land and water distribution rights, and/or in memory and respect for more ancient complementary oppositions within local or regional social and economic structures – for example pastoralists and agriculturalists, indigenous peoples and invaders, or highlanders and lowlanders.

MONAN
is the creator god of the Tupinambá tribe in Brazil, who live around the mouth of the Tocantins River, southeast of the mouth of the Amazon. He made the sky, the earth and the animals. Then he made humans, but they behaved so badly that Monan destroyed them in a huge fire. Only one man,

named Irin-Maje, survived the flames when Monan sent water, which became the ocean, to put out the fire.

After Monan came Maire Monan, who gave names to all the animals and taught the Tupinambá agriculture and the art of civilization.

MORADUCHAYOQ TEMPLE
see *HUARI*.

MUISAK see *HEADHUNTING*.

MUISCA see *CHIBCHA*.

ÑAMCA see *MAMA ÑAMCA*.

NAPA
was a miniature llama figurine alleged by *MANCO CAPAC* to have been left behind unintentionally in the cave of *TAMBO TOCO*.

NASCA see *NAZCA*.

NAYAMLAP
was the principal character in a myth concerning the *LAMBAYEQUE VALLEY* on the north coast of Peru, one of the few accounts of legendary heroes known from outside the Andean highlands. He was the leader of the primordial sea peoples who invaded the valley in a time that seems to have stretched far back in the folk memories of the region.

Nayamlap led a "brave and noble company" of men and women on a fleet of balsawood rafts from somewhere south of the Lambayeque Valley. He was accompanied by his wife, Ceterni, his

NAPA was the miniature llama figurine forgotten by Manco Capac in the cave of Tambo Toco. (BRITISH MUSEUM; GOLD)

harem and 40 followers, among whom the legend lists a trumpeter, a guardian of the royal litter, a craftsman whose task it was to grind conch shells into powder for ritual purposes, a cook and other special attendants and servants. Nayamlap also brought with him a special green stone figurine, the idol known as Yampallec (which is regarded as the origin of the name of the valley). The visage, stature and figure of the idol was a double of the king.

Nayamlap and his men invaded the valley and built a palace at the place called Chot, which archaeologists have identified as the site of Huaca Chotuna in the Lambayeque

Valley. The conquest of the local peoples was successful, and the invaders and invaded settled down together in peace. After a long life, Nayamlap died and was buried in the palace; he had arranged in secret with his priests, however, that they should tell his people that upon his death he had sprouted wings and flown away into the sky.

Nayamlap was succeeded by his eldest son, *CIUM*, and by ten other kings in his dynasty, which lasted until the last ruler, *FEMPELLEC*, brought dishonour and disaster to the kingdom.

NAYAMLAP led his band of followers to invade the Lambayeque Valley, bringing with him the green stone idol Yampallec, a deity perhaps represented by this Chimú tumi ceremonial knife handle, made of gold and inlaid with turquoise.

THE NAZCA were a people and culture that flourished in the south coastal region of Peru, in the Nazca and adjacent valleys, from about 200 BC to AD 500 through the Early Intermediate Period; the Nazca were roughly contemporary with the MOCHE culture in the northern coastal valleys. Two of the most important Nazca settlements were CAHUACHI and Ventilla, the first a ritual "city", the second an urban "capital". Ventilla, by far the largest Nazca site recorded, covered an area of at least 200 hectares (495 acres) with terraced housing, walled courts, and small mounds. It was linked to its ceremonial and ritual counterpart by a "Nazca line" across the intervening desert.

Over the centuries, increasing drought in the highlands to the east caused an ever-growing aridity in the coastal plains. Such was the pressure to obtain water that the Nazca people invented an ingenious system of subterranean aqueducts and galleries to collect and channel the underground waters around Cahuachi, to minimize evaporation and to provide at least a small amount of water in the dry season. Access to the galleries is down spiral paths, whose sides were immaculately terraced using smooth river cobbles.

The characteristic artefacts of Nazca culture were textiles and ceramics, the styles of both of which carried on in similar traditions from those of the preceding PARACAS culture in the same general area. Both of these media were decorated with mythical beings and deities in a society that was apparently highly preoccupied with and motivated by religious iconography and ceremonial ritual. Effigy vessels were decorated with SERPENT beings, monkeys and other animals, and some were made in the shapes of trophy heads. These last were a feature of a trophy-head cult that collected caches of the trepanned, severed skulls of sacrificial victims in Nazca cemeteries.

The dominance of daily life by ritual was further emphasized across the desert *pampa* floor in the form of geoglyphs. These Nazca "lines" began to be made as early as the settlements at Cahuachi, Ventilla and other sites, but increased in number and complexity as Cahuachi was abandoned. They were made by scraping aside the darker surface gravel to expose the underlying lighter rock, and the region's aridity itself has been instrumental in preserving them. (Experimental archaeology has shown that it would have taken little effort and time to create the geoglyphs. In one experiment, nearly 1.6 hectares/4 acres of desert was cleared in about a week.)

There are two principal types of geoglyph: figures on hillsides, placed in such a way that they are obvious to travellers on the plains below; and lines, both straight and curving. Various lines and sets of lines form numerous geometric patterns, clusters of straight lines, and also sometimes recognizable figures, such as animals or birds. Individual straight lines of different widths stretch for long distances across the *pampa* desert, some for more than 20 km (12½ miles). Altogether there are some 1,300 km (808 miles) of such lines. One famous set forms a huge arrow, approximately 490 m (1,600 ft)

THE WEALTH of Nazca geoglyphs, especially ritual lines and cleared spaces crossing and overlapping each other, shows that they were used over a long period of time and often abandoned.

long, pointing towards the Pacific Ocean, and is thought to be a symbol to invoke rains.

Figures include a hummingbird, a duckling, a spider, a killer whale, a monkey, a llama, several plants and anthropomorphic figures, as well as trapezoids and triangles of cleared areas, zig-zags and spirals. The patterns and figures often resemble those used to decorate Nazca textiles and ceramic vessels. Although the lines frequently cross, individual patterns or figures are each made of a single, continuous line. Altogether there are some 300 such figures, and, combined with the lines, about 360 hectares (890 acres) of *pampa* floor have been scraped away to create them.

Argument has raged for more than 60 years over the meaning

THE NAZCA culture was associated in particular with geoglyphs and textiles. Geoglyphs could be figures, lines or cleared areas. The famous hummingbird is formed by a single, continuous ritual line.

and purpose of the geoglyphs. Among the theories that have been put forward are proposals ranging from their having been made by beings from outer space – for which there is categorically no evidence – to their use in the making of astronomical observations – which seems quite plausible but which has not been conclusively demonstrated as yet.

The most convincing, and indeed obvious, explanation of their meaning is linked to the very nature of the landscape, climate and accompanying features of Nazca settlement and material culture. The lines were associated with the Nazcas' necessary preoccupation with water and the fertility of their crops, together with the worship of mountains – the ultimate source of irrigation waters – and a pantheon of deities or supernatural beings, who were believed to be responsible for bringing or withholding the rains. Sets of lines frequently radiate from "ray centres"

P

on hills – 62 such nodes have been identified so far – and some of the lines lead to irrigated oases. The animal and other figures each comprise a single line with different beginning and ending points.

The sheer number of lines and the fact that they were made over a period of some seven to eight hundred years, over-marking each other in great profusion, shows that they were not conceived in any grand overall plan. As with the profusion of ceremonial kin-group mounds at their sacred "city" at Cahuachi, the Nazca lines and figures appear to have been made by and for small groups – or perhaps even individuals – each for a separate but confederately agreed purpose. "Solid" cleared areas might have been for congregations of participants, while "outlines" of figures probably formed the routes of ritual pathways to be walked with specific resolutions and outcomes in mind, by a people and culture attempting to farm their landscape, practise their specialized crafts and make sense of the deeper meanings of their lives through ritual communion with their gods.

Although we do not know the names of Nazca deities, their images appear on pottery and textiles as well as in the geoglyphs. Anthropomorphic and composite beings abound, and, in particular, the Oculate Being (see PARACAS) was inherited from the preceding Paracas culture.

NEMTEREQUETEBA, a legendary culture hero of the CHIBCHA, was believed to have come from a distant land. He was an old man with a long beard and hair, who travelled around the land teaching the Chibcha and others the art of weaving and civilized behaviour.

His rival was the goddess HUITACA (see also BOCHICA, CONIRAYA VIRACOCHA, ROAL, THUNUPA VIRACOCHA and VIRACOCHA).

NEW TEMPLE see CHAVÍN.

NI was the CHIMÚ deity of the western sea (that is, the Pacific Ocean) over which the supreme deity, SI, travelled.

NIGHT-TIME SUN (that is, the sun after sunset, when it was thought to pass through a hidden, watery passage into the underworld until the next sunrise) was a deity of the GUARI lineage AYLLU of CAJATAMBO.

NOSJTHEJ see EL-LAL.

NYAMI ABE (TUKANO), literally the "Night Sun", that is, the moon (see PAGE ABE).

OCLLO see MAMA OCLLO.

OCLLO HUACO see MAMA OCLLO.

OCULATE BEING see under PARACAS.

THE OI were a legendary or mythical race of beings from the remote past whom the tribes along the XINGU RIVER of Brazil believe existed until quite recently. The Oi were tall people who sang in chorus as they travelled through the forest. Because they were frequently heard by the tribes, and only died out lately, their chants

became known and are still sung by the Xingu tribes (see also the MINATA-KARAIA).

OLD TEMPLE see CHAVÍN.

OMAM is the YANOMAMI creator god, a beneficent deity who made the earth, the sky, sun and moon, humans, all the animals and plants on the earth and everything else that exists.

In the beginning the earth had two layers, but now there are three layers because the upper layer of the original two became worn and a large section fell away. There were two men on the part that became detached, one of whom was Omam. One day while he was fishing, Omam hooked and pulled a woman from the river, but she had no genitalia – only a hole the size of a hummingbird's anus. So Omam took piranha teeth and made sexual organs for the woman. With her, he then proceeded to father many children, the ancestors of the Yanomami. The other races of humans are believed by the Yanomami to have been made of river mist and foam, fashioned into humans of different colours by a huge bird.

ONA are a tribe of Tierra del Fuego (see EL-LAL, KASPI and TEMAUKEL).

OREJONES ("big ears" in Spanish) was an epithet applied to the INCA nobility, owing to their practice of piercing their ears and enlarging them by inserting golden

spools. When VIRACOCHA summoned ALCAVICÇA from the earth at CUZCO, he also commanded the orejones to rise from the ground, and gave them his divine sanction for rulership.

ORQO-CILAY ("multicoloured llama") was one of the luminary star groups that the INCA recognized within MAYU, the Milky Way. It was believed to protect the royal llama herd.

PACARITAMBO, also Pacari Tambo, Pacaritampum or Pacariqtambo, was the land in which lay the TAMBO TOCO caves, the legendary place of origin of the INCA ancestors (see MANCO CAPAC, MAUQALLQTA).

PACATNAMÚ, a spectacularly cited ceremonial centre on the cliffs above the Jequetepeque River in northern Peru, was a MOCHE religious pilgrimage centre in the Early Intermediate Period and later. It has been compared in importance to the coastal pilgrimage centre at PACHACAMAC, and, like that site, retained its ceremonial importance into much later periods, and even after its abandonment as a place of residence around 1370.

DIVINE KINGSHIP &
ANCESTOR REVERENCE

THE INCAS regarded their emperor, Sapa Inca, as the divine sun's representative on earth, and his principal wife, the Qoya, as the moon's. Persistent iconography and religious imagery makes it logical to interpret these beliefs as the culmination of attitudes in earlier Andean civilizations. One pre-Inca example is the ruler Nayamlap in the Lambayeque Valley, who contrived with his priests to convince his subjects of his divine nature after death. Rich Moche, Sicán and Chimú burials similarly indicate the development of the idea of divine kingship.

INTI THE SUN GOD, *the official deity of Inca rulership and the Sapa Inca – the emperor was regarded as the sun's representative on earth. Niches in the walls of the Coricancha Temple to Inti held sheet gold masks, such as this example, which would have formed part of the emperor's accoutrement on ceremonial occasions.*

Despite the official state view, however, rulership of the Inca Empire began and ended in rivalry – in the conflict between Urco and Pachacuti Inca Yupanqui over the succession to Viracocha Inca, and, when the Inca ideal of rulership by divine right of descent went awry, in a bloody civil war, less than a decade before the Spanish conquest.

Ancestor worship was widespread among Andean civilization. Physical manifestations of such reverence are well documented among the Inca in the mummified remains – *mallquis* – of Inca rulers and queens. Dedicated cults cared for *mallquis*, housed in the Coricancha Temple in Cuzco and accorded them special honours at ceremonies. Similarly, the *mallquis* of rulers and ancestors of provincial towns were kept in special buildings or in caves and honoured at ceremonies. The care for and elaborate nature of Nazca burials at Cahuachi and the rich burials of Moche lords, in the Moche and Lambayeque valleys, to cite just two examples, show that reverence for ancestors was a theme that began in the earliest Andean civilizations. In the 15th century, at Chan Chan, the Chimú made a substantial industry of ruler worship.

EARLY EVIDENCE of Andean ancestor reverence comes from the hundreds of burials (left) now decaying on the desert floor at Nazca. Nazca burials were accompanied by rich ceramics and textiles wrapped around the mummy.

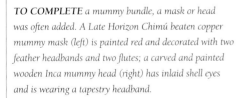

THE CHIMÚ, the Incas and other Late Horizon peoples wrapped honoured ancestors in mummy bundles (above) and stored them for regular ceremonial display rather than burying them. Numerous whole mummies have been found, as well as parts from mummy bundles. A typical, probably 15th-century, example is this Chimú mummy bundle wrapped in woven textiles and given a "head".

TO COMPLETE a mummy bundle, a mask or head was often added. A Late Horizon Chimú beaten copper mummy mask (left) is painted red and decorated with two feather headbands and two flutes; a carved and painted wooden Inca mummy head (right) has inlaid shell eyes and is wearing a tapestry headband.

NUMEROUS chullpa *burial towers (right) were used as the mausoleums of ruling families in the "Aymara kingdoms" of the Titicaca Basin in the Late Intermediate Period (c. AD 1000–1400) and later, after the Inca conquest of the region. Chullpas were single structures near settlements or separated groups. One of the largest groups is at Sillustani, west of Lake Titicaca. It includes square and round towers, containing as many as 20 or more adult and child bodies.*

PACHA KAMAQ

see PACHACAMAC.

PACHACAMAC, or Pacha Kamaq, ("Earth-maker", "Maker of Earth/time" or "He who embraces the entire Earth") was the ancient creator deity of the peoples of central coastal Peru and adjacent Andes, and a coastal site – a shrine and place of pilgrimage – and city-state. Archaeological evidence shows ceramic and architectural links with the central-southern Andes, and linguistic studies indicate association through the spread of QUECHUA from the region into the highlands.

The site became important in the latter half of the Early Intermediate Period, when the first phases of the pyramid-platform to the sun and adjoining Temple to Pachacamac were built. It was the centre of an important political power during the Middle Horizon, and later became an outpost of HUARI power from the central-southern Andes. The site's continued religious importance is implied by a wooden post carved with figures of Huari divinities, as well as stone figurines. The upper part of the post depicts a man holding a *bola* and wearing a chest ornament; the lower part has double-headed SERPENTS, JAGUARS, and a figure with attributes like those of the "angels" on the Gateway of the Sun at TIAHUANACO.

Pachacamac was the only serious rival to VIRACOCHA for the title of creator god. His following was very ancient and widespread in the central coastal region. The site remained a shrine and potent oracle into INCA times. Like Tiahuanaco, the shrine drew visitors from throughout the central lowland plains and valleys, and from the adjacent Andes. After their con-

THE SITE of Pachacamac became perhaps the most famous pilgrimage site in South America, drawing pilgrims from Andean and coastal peoples alike to the temple built atop a huge artificial mound of adobe bricks.

quest of this region, the Incas went out of their way to reconcile this potential conflict, since the power of feeling for, and longevity of worship of, Pachacamac presented a potential threat to the official state cult of the sun god INTI.

The cult of Pachacamac lasted for more than a millennium and, alongside the sacred CORICANCHA in CUZCO and the ISLAND OF THE SUN in Lake TITICACA, the site was one of the most revered places in the Inca Empire. The Pachacamac–Viracocha–Inti rivalry constituted a mythical manifestation of the distinctions and liaisons between the worlds of the highlands, represented by Viracocha, the coastal lowlands, represented by Pachacamac, and the newcomer official

PACHACAMAC was the "Earth-maker" to whom humankind owed all existence, and to whom continual sacrifices were offered.
(FELIPE GUAMAN POMA DE AYALA, FROM THE NUEVA CORÓNICA Y BUEN GOBIERNO, 1583–1613.)

state cult, represented by Inti.

The potency of Pachacamac, and Inca deference to him and to his temple and idol, was described by the 16th-century chronicler Pedro de Cieza de León in his *Crónica del Peru* (Seville, 1550–3): "They say . . . that . . . aside from those at Cuzco . . . there was [no temple] to compare with this at Pachacamac, which was built upon a small, man-made hill of *adobes* and earth, and on its summit stood the temple, [with] many gates, that, like the walls, were adorned with figures of wild animals. Inside, where the idol stood, were the priests who feigned great sanctimoniousness. And when they performed their sacrifices before the people, they kept their faces toward the door of the temple and their backs to the figure of the idol, with their eyes to the ground, and [were] all trembling and overcome. . . Before this figure of the devil they sacrificed many animals, and [offered the] human blood of

persons they killed; and that on the occasion of their most solemn feasts they made utterances which were believed and held to be true. . . The priests were greatly venerated. . . and beside the temple there were many spacious lodgings for those who came in pilgrimage. . . And the Incas, powerful lords that they were, made themselves the masters of the kingdom of Pachacamac, and, as was their custom in all the lands they conquered, they ordered temples and shrines to be built to the sun. And when they saw the splendour of this temple [to Pachacamac], and how old it was, and the sway it held over the people of the surrounding lands, and the devotion [that] they paid [to] it, holding that it would be very difficult to do away with this, they agreed with the native lords and the ministers of their god or devil that this temple of Pachacamac should remain with the authority and cult it possessed, provided [that] they built another temple to the sun, which should take precedence."

The voice of Pachacamac's oracle was sought from near and far, to the extent that devotees petitioned the priesthood there to establish

sibling shrines in their homelands, where Pachacamac was added to their own pantheons. Reciprocally, and in addition to the main temple and oracle, secondary shrines were established at Pachacamac as "wives", "sons" and "daughters" to the "father", some of which were dedicated to the foreign deities of pilgrims. Prophesy from the oracle was sought for everything from health, fortune and the wellbeing of crops and flocks, to the weather, and the prognosis of Inca battle plans.

Clearly, the Incas recognized Pachacamac's influence in the coastal region, and knew that they needed his oracle to achieve their imperial aims. Several Inca emperors adopted Pachacamac's name and included it in their titles, just as others included Viracocha's name. The Temple of the Sun, or *Mamacuna*, at Pachacamac was an Inca construction, acknowledging the site's potency, but also establishing ultimate authority of the state cult in the region.

There are many threads to the mythology of Pachacamac. His cult developed much earlier than and independent of the Inca cult of Inti, but the predominance of ancient contact between coastal lowlands and Andean highlands inevitably brought the two creator gods, Viracocha and Pachacamac, into "contact" long before the Inca compulsion to incorporate all myths and pantheons into their official state religion. At times, the two gods seem to have had distinct identities, at other times they appear to have been identical. The mythology recorded in the *HUARO-CHIRÍ MANUSCRIPT*, from a people living midway between highlands and coast, complicates the matter further by substituting the sun for Viracocha in opposition to Pachacamac, as if in recognition of the Inti cult of their new overlords.

To scholars, these conflicts seem confusing yet important. To the Inca, the imposition of all-inclusiveness was paramount, yet they

imposed it by mixing, combining, recognizing the similarities, and acknowledging the variety and nuances of the gods of all the peoples of their empire. In essence, lowland Pachacamac and highland Viracocha have retained a core of similarities. They created the world; they held control over the creation and destruction of the first people; they travelled throughout the land and taught, often in the guise of a beggar; and they met, named and gave their characters to the animals and plants.

In the principal myth of Pachacamac, he was the son of the sun and the moon. An earlier deity known as Con had created the first people, but Pachacamac challenged and overcame him, and transformed the first people into the monkeys.

Pachacamac then created a man and a woman, but because he did not provide them with food, the man died. The woman solicited the sun's help (or in another version accused the sun of neglecting his duty) and in return was impregnated by the sun's rays. When she bore a son, the woman taught the child how to survive by eating wild plants. Pachacamac, jealous of his father the sun's powers, and angered by the woman's independence and apparent defiance, killed the boy and cut his corpse into pieces. Pachacamac then sowed the boy's teeth, which grew into corn (maize); planted the ribs and other bones, which grew into yucca, or manioc, tubers; and planted the flesh, which grew into vegetables

and fruits – an apparent mythical précis of the discovery of cultivation among coastal peoples.

Not to be outdone, the sun took the penis and navel of the boy, and with these created another son for himself, whom he named Vichama (Wichama) or Villama. Pachacamac wanted to kill this child too, but could not catch him, for Vichama had set off on his travels, so he slew the woman/his mother instead, and fed her body to the vultures and condors.

Next, Pachacamac created another man and woman, and these two proceeded to repopulate the world. Pachacamac appointed certain of these people as *CURACAS* (leaders) to rule the rest. In the meantime, Vichama had returned. Miraculously, he found the bits and pieces of his mother, and reassembled her. Pachacamac was in fear of Vichama's reprisal, and rightly so, for the formerly pursued became the pursuer, and Pachacamac was driven, or fled, into the sea, where he sank in front of the place of the temple of Pachacamac/Vichama. In a further act of revenge, Vichama transformed the people of Pachacamac's second creation into stone, but later partly repented and changed the ordinary stone of the *curacas* into sacred *HUACAS*.

Finally, Vichama turned again to his father the sun and asked him to create another race of people. The sun sent three eggs, one of gold, one of silver and one of copper. The gold egg developed into the *curacas* and nobles, the silver became women,

and the copper egg became commoners. (A variation of the story of the final peopling of the earth, from another coastal group, states that it was Pachacamac who did the deed by sending four stars to earth. Two of these were male, and generated kings and nobles; and the other two were female and generated commoners.) Thus this second part of the tale seems to be a mythical précis of the creation of the social order of humankind.

These variations in the Pachacamac–Vichama myth demonstrate the mutability and interchangeability of the creator Pachacamac and the creator sun.

In recognition of the power of Pachacamac exhibited in these myths, defiance of his will was believed to provoke earthquakes. Offerings to him in solicitation of his oracular predictions – and no doubt of much use to the cult priests – included cotton, corn (maize), coca (*Erythroxylon coca*) leaves, dried fish, llamas, guinea pigs, fine textiles, ceramic drinking vessels, and gold and silver.

The Incas' need to alleviate the potential conflict between Pachacamac and Viracocha was accomplished in two ways. First, they believed that the primitive peoples of the First "Age" or Sun named their creator variously *TICCI VIRACOCHA, CAYLLA VIRACOCHA* or Pachacamac (see *PACHACUTI*) – there was no conflict of interest. Secondly, they incorporated the shrine of Pachacamac and his wife and daughters into their own mythology in the story of the central Andean deity *CONIRAYA VIRACOCHA*. Both amalgamations were presumably attempts to show that the two deities had in fact always been inseparable.

PACHACUTI (*QUECHUA*), a "revolution" or "turning over or around" (*cuti*) of "time and space" (*pacha*), was a millenarian *INCA*/Quechua/ *AYMARÁ* concept of succession and renewal that formed a core belief in Andean and Peruvian coastal cosmology and mythology. The Incas thought of themselves as the final stage in a succession of creations and destructions, a notion of cyclicity that has interesting parallels with Aztec and Maya mythology in Mesoamerica. The term was used frequently by the 16th- and 17th-century Spanish and Spanish-taught native chroniclers and, because of its nature, fuelled the fires of Spanish priestly enthusiasm to read Christian sparks of inspiration within ancient native beliefs.

The Incas and many other Andean peoples regarded themselves as living in the world of the Fifth "Age" or Fifth Sun. Each previous Age was thought to have lasted 1,000 years.

The First Age was embryonic, a time of primordial, metaphorical darkness. The people living at that time were called the *Wari Wiracocharuna*, a name whose Quechua

PACHACUTI, *the revolution of time, included a cycle of "ages", the first of which was the primordial time when the primitive Wari Wiracocharuna lived.* (ILLUSTRATION FROM THE NUEVA CORÓNICA Y BUEN GOBIERNO BY FELIPE GUAMAN POMA DE AYALA, 1583–1613.)

base words mean a camelid hybrid (*wari*); from the crossing of a llama and an alpaca), and "folk" (*runa*). (The element *Wiracocha* is the name of the creator god – *VIRACOCHA* – but in this case was used by the chroniclers to refer to Europeans or Spaniards, who regarded these ancient pre-Incas as related to the people of Noah's ark.) These people were primitive, wore clothing of leaves, and ate only the wild plants that they could collect. They called their creator Ticci Viracocha, Caylla Viracocha or *PACHACAMAC*. It is unclear how the First Age ended.

The Second Age was more advanced, because its people practised rudimentary agriculture. They were called the *Wari Runa* (also hybrids), and they wore clothing of animal skins. They lived simply and peacefully, and recognized Viracocha as their creator. The age of the Second Sun ended in cataclysmic deluge.

The Third Age was inhabited by the *Purun Runa*, the "wild folk". Despite the name, civilization was increasing in complexity: people had learned to spin, dye and weave llama and alpaca wool; they practised more sophisticated agriculture, with a wider variety of crops; and they mined and worked metals to make jewellery. The population of the world increased, and people found it necessary to migrate from the Andes into the lowlands. They lived in towns, each with its own king, and there was conflict between towns and regions. The people generally called their creator Pachacamac in this age.

The Fourth Age was that of the *Auca Runa*, the "warlike folk". In some variations, this age included the beginnings of the Inca Empire, but more tidily, most versions excluded the Incas. At this time the world was divided into four parts. There was increased warfare, and people were forced to live in stone houses and in fortified towns. Like the land divisions, people were divided in this age into *AYLLU* lineages. Technology and standards of

PACHACVTIC YNGA IX.

PACHACUTI INCA YUPANQUI is depicted here with the ceremonial axe-staff of office. ("CUZCO SCHOOL" GENEALOGY, 18TH-CENTURY.)

living were more advanced and more complex. How the Third and Fourth Suns ended is not specified.

The Fifth Age was that of the Incas, and it came to an end when the Spaniards arrived. In their belief that a theoretical "Sixth Age" included the inauguration of true beliefs among the people of the Andes, the chroniclers refer to the *Guaca Bilcas*, or supernatural "demons of *CUZCO*", as the corrupters of the people during the Fifth Age – who, it was perceived, must have originally believed in the one true Christian God.

The notion of cyclicity was also endemic in the Inca post-colonial belief in the myth of the return of the Inca (see *INKARRÍ*).

PACHACUTI INCA YUPANQUI, the tenth *INCA* ruler, emerges from legend into history as a real person and Inca leader, and as the

effective founder of the empire. It was he who began the Inca conquest of neighbouring cities within the Huantanay (Cuzco) Valley and expansion beyond the valley. The traditional dates of his reign are 1438 to 1471.

The rival city-state of *CHANCA*, to the west of *CUZCO*, attacked in the early 15th century during the reign of *VIRACOCHA INCA*. In one version of Inca history, Viracocha Inca repulsed the attack. But the stronger tradition declares Yupanqui to be the saviour of Cuzco, perhaps influenced by selective rewriting of Inca history by the latter. Viracocha Inca had already chosen as his successor his son *INCA URCO*, but when the Chanca

attacked the city, much of the populace and both father and son decided to flee into the hills to a distant redoubt. Yupanqui, a somewhat recalcitrant younger prince, stayed behind with a few companions, rallied those who remained and repulsed the first two Chanca assaults. In a third attack, when the fate of Cuzco seemed to hang in the balance, Yupanqui called upon the gods for help and received the assistance of the very rocks and stones, which arose transformed into Inca warriors. Thereafter, these *PURURAUCAS* became Inca objects of worship.

Yupanqui thus began his reign as Inca emperor by usurping his brother Urco and taking the name Pachacuti ("Earth-shaker King"). His subsequent mission of conquest was, as a result of these events, believed to have received divine sanction; and from this time Inca history becomes somewhat less legendary. The chronicles seem less mythical and more purely factual, simply recounting events in the history of Inca conquest. Yupanqui first won over the Valley of Cuzco and made all *QUECHUA*-speakers there honorary Inca citizens. (It is important, however, to bear in mind that, to date, archaeological evidence cannot corroborate any specific events in these Inca legendary histories.)

Pachacuti next turned his attention southeast, to the *TITICACA*

Basin, where he conquered and incorporated the Lupaqa, Colla and other kingdoms around the lake. He then returned to Cuzco and turned his armies over to his son and chosen heir, *TUPAC INCA YUPANQUI*, to pursue further expansion of the empire while he devoted his own energies to developing the state and organizing the institutions and systems that would become the hallmarks of Inca rule: national taxation and labour levies, roadways and an imperial communication network, and extensive warehousing of food and other commodities for redistribution throughout the empire.

Pachacuti was further enshrined as an Inca legendary hero, and confirmed as receiving divine help and inspiration, by a legendary event that probably preceded the Chanca war. One day, as Yupanqui drew near to the spring called Susurpuquio near Cuzco, en route to visit his father Viracocha Inca, he saw a crystal tablet fall into it. At the spring, he peered into the waters and saw on the tablet the image of a man wearing a headdress (a *LLAUTO*), ear spools and a tunic like those worn by Inca men. From the headdress shone three sun rays, and snakes coiled around the figure's shoulders; from between his legs jutted the head of a puma, and another puma stood behind him with its paws on the man's shoulders, while a *SERPENT*

THE STONE TOMB at Kenko near Cuzco is claimed by some to be the tomb of Pachacuti Inca Yupanqui.

stretched from the bottom of his back to the top of his head.

Pachacuti retrieved the tablet from the spring, and found that he could use it to see into the future. The Incas believed that he identified the image on the tablet with the creator god *VIRACOCHA PACHAY-ACHACHIC*, and that this inspiration prompted him to begin a programme of religious reform among the Inca peoples following the defeat of the Chanca and the commencement of his reign. He reorganized the main temple, the *CORICANCHA*, in Cuzco to accommodate and display six principal gods, ranged in the following hierarchy: first *VIRACOCHA* himself, then *INTI* the sun god, *QUILLA* the moon goddess, *CHASKA-QOY-LOR* the god of Venus, *ILLAPA* the god of weather, and *CUICHU* the god of the rainbow. Because of his association of the crystal tablet's image with Viracocha, Pachacuti appears, in one interpretation of

PACHACUTI INCA YUPANQUI, the empire builder, was the first Inca emperor of historical credibility. Here he is seen brandishing a sun symbol and warrior's sling. (SKETCH BY FELIPE GUAMAN POMA DE AYALA FROM THE NUEVA CORÓNICA Y BUEN GOBIERNO, 1583–1613.)

these events, to have "promoted" the creator god to a position of superiority, above that of the sun god. On the other hand, this rearrangement of the Coricancha has also been interpreted as increasing the emphasis on Inti's status as a deity of near equal importance to Viracocha, and thus triggering the beginning of a "solarization" of Inca religion. Indeed, according to some sources, Inti also appeared to the young Pachacuti in visions, these apparitions inspiring him to perform great deeds and to strive for the betterment of humankind.

Despite a lack of specific corroborative archaeological evidence, its seems fair to credit Pachacuti with the beginning of the Inca Empire. It also appears justified to associate these myths and legends with the basic, and apparently correct, "facts" that are available involving the Inca state's rise to prominence in the Valley of Cuzco. The essential events of the war with the Chancas (disregarding the supernatural elements) might quite possibly represent the deep-seated oral history of the Incas, recording their overthrow of the final remnants of *HUARI* power in the valley – because the chronicled location of the Chanca state and the homeland of the Huari people coincide. Similarly, the reorganization of Inca religion and of the Coricancha might have been a practical way to record the effective usurpation of the throne by Yupanqui, defying his father, who bore the name of the creator god, and overthrowing his brother, whom his father had chosen as his heir.

There can be no doubt that it was Pachacuti's social manipulations, and his reorganization and formalization of the state religion, as well as his reconstruction of Cuzco, that formed the basis of the vast Inca Empire that was created by him and his successors over the next 90 years, until the arrival of Francisco Pizarro and his Spanish followers.

PACHAMAMA, or Pacha Mama, the *INCA* earth goddess, was a primeval deity responsible for the wellbeing of plants and animals. Her worship is thought to date back to the first constructions of sunken courts at Chavín de Huántar and other Andean sites, and continues to the present day in the form of offerings of *coca* (*Erythroxylon coca*) leaves, *chicha* corn (maize) beer and prayers on all major agricultural occasions. She is sometimes identified as the Virgin Mary of Christianity.

In one myth, the Inca ancestors (see *MANCO CAPAC*) sacrificed and offered a llama to Pachamama before they entered Cuzco to take it over. One of the sister/wives, *MAMA HUACO*, sliced open the animal's chest, extracted the lungs, inflated them with her own breath and carried them into the city alongside Manco Capac, who carried the golden emblem of the sun god *INTI*.

PACHATIRA was the *INCA* collective name used for the "dark cloud" constellations within *MAYU*, the Milky Way, particularly by the people of *MISMINAY*.

PAGE ABE ("Father Sun") was the name of the creator god of the Amazonian *TUKANO*.

According to Tukano cosmology, at the beginning of time there was Page Abe, the sun, and Nyami Abe, the moon (or "Night Sun"). Nyami Abe had no wife and was lonely, so he attempted to force himself on the wife of Page Abe. When Page Abe learned of this, he deprived the moon of his fancy feathered headdress and banished him from the family. Thus never again will the sun and the moon share the same quarter of the sky.

After this incident, Page Abe made the earth and all the plant life and creatures on it, including humans. He was helped in this creation, although not very usefully it seems, by the god *PAMURI-MAHSE*,

and later by his daughter, *ABE MANGO*, who taught humankind many useful skills.

PAHMURI-MAHSE
see *PAMURI-MAHSE*.

PALLUTA was the third place of sojourn of the ancestors during their wanderings as recounted in the *INCA* state foundation myth (see *MANCO CAPAC*).

PAMPA GRANDE see *MOCHE*.

PAMURI-MAHSE was the name of the divine, but not particularly useful, helper of the *TUKANO* creator-god *PAGE ABE*.

According to the myth, among the animals being created, Pamuri-mahse brought down to earth the dangerous beasts, including the large snakes that live along the Amazon. One of these snakes, which had seven heads, fell in love with a young human girl and tried to carry her off with him, but a dog and a medicine man interceded. They fought a fierce battle with the snake, and succeeded in defeating all of the heads. The medicine man lit a fire and burned the snake's carcass, but the smoke and ashes rose into the sky and were blown by the wind out to sea. Over the sea the smoke and ashes fell as rain, and the fearsome snake was reborn.

A variant of the myth tells how the sun god ordered Pamuri-mahse to paddle a huge canoe, shaped like an anaconda snake, up river. At

every place where Pamuri-mahse stopped, a village was established, and the spirit beings taught the people of that village how they should conduct their lives, and instructed them in their customs.

PANACA was the term for the dozen or so royal *AYLLU* kin groups of the *INCA* imperial household. They were considered the direct descendants of the first ten kings of *CUZCO*, and complemented the original ten *ayllus* of the Tambos at *TAMBO TOCO*.

PAQCHA was a carved and painted wooden staff-like device with a bowl on one end, that was used in divination ceremonies by *INCA* priests.

PARACAS, a group of sites and a culture in the southern coastal region of Peru, was one of the first Early Horizon cultures to develop mummification and, probably, ancestor worship, a characteristic of virtually all later Andean and western coastal cultures. Mummies were "bundled" in tight, foetal positions, placed in baskets, and wrapped in multiple layers of high-quality woven and embroidered cotton and llama-wool textiles, displaying a wealth of natural imagery and supernatural mythological iconography that was clearly part of a rich mythology and associated with ritual practices. The burials were accompanied by richly decorated and plainer ceramic vessels, many in the shapes of animal effigies, and by sheet gold ornaments.

THE PARACAS CULTURE Oculate Being was the most prominent deity depicted on burial textiles – here it is depicted as a serpent-tongued, feline-faced anthropomorphic figure with staring eyes.

Among and between sprawling areas of habitation remains around the Paracas peninsula, special sites had been chosen as necropolises for hundreds of burials, each possibly the focus of a family cult. As the numbers of burials appear to exceed the requirements of the immediately adjacent settlements, it is thought that the Paracas necropolises might also have been pilgrimage centres, like the contemporary Chavín de Huántar and the later *PACHACAMAC* ceremonial centres farther north.

Because we lack written accounts for this early period, we can only surmise the names and details of any Paracas deities and ceremonial practices. The imagery shows strong influence from *CHAVÍN*, but soon developed its own regional flavour. Among the images depicted on the textiles, one is especially prominent and has been named the Oculate Being. This deity was portrayed horizontally (as if flying), upside down (perhaps looking down on humankind) and crouching.

THE PARACAS *Oculate Being was often depicted repeatedly on textiles, as here, both upright and upside down on an embroidered burial mantle.*

"He" has a characteristic, frontal face with large, circular, staring eyes. Long, streaming appendages originate from various parts of his body and end in trophy heads or small figures. The Oculate Being appears to have been a cult image that continued to form an important part of the succeeding NAZCA iconography in the same region. The face is often heart-shaped, and sometimes sprouts a smaller head from its top. On other figures, the Oculate Being wears a headband identical to actual sheet gold headbands found in some of the burials.

PARIACACA was the principal god of the pre-INCA *Checa Yauyos* of the Huarochirí region, in the western Andes of central Peru east of Lima, described in the *HUAROCHIRÍ MANUSCRIPT*. The *Checa* were pastoralist invaders or immigrants, who formed part of the *Lurin* (or "lower") *Yauyos* kinship group.

Pariacaca is described in the manuscript as a high mountain peak, regarded as a sacred HUACA whose spirit was able to move about the landscape in the simultaneous manifestation of a patron deity and culture hero. Among the Huarochirí *Lurin Yauyos*, his rival was the fierce, fire-breathing god *HUALLALLO CARHUINCHO*.

According to the myth, Huallallo Carhuincho had held sway over the people of Huarochirí for some time. Pariacaca was born on the mountain top of that name in the

PUKU is the name of this typical Inca Pucara *or hill fortification. It is situated near Cuzco.*

form of five eggs. Each egg became a falcon, and these were then transformed into five men, who became ancestors of the pastoralist *Yauyos*.

In this five-fold existence, Pariacaca arrived at Huarochirí and challenged Huallallo Carhuincho's supremacy. He prophesied that he would defeat Huallallo Carhuincho and drive him from the land. In the battle that ensued, each god used his most potent weapon – fire for Huallallo Carhuincho, and water for Pariacaca.

As five persons, Pariacaca rained down on Huallallo Carhuincho from five directions. He sent yellow rain and red rain, then flashes of lightning from all five directions. In his defence, Huallallo Carhuincho blazed up in the form of a gigantic fire across the countryside, thwarting Pariacaca's every effort to extinguish him. The battle continued from dawn to sunset. The waters of Pariacaca rushed down the mountainsides towards a lake called Ura Cocha. One of Pariacaca's five selves, called Llacsa Churapa, was too big to fit into the basin of the lake, so he swept away an entire mountain in order to block the waters from lower down and form a new, larger lake. As Llacsa Churapa's waters filled this lake, they rose up over the land and quenched Huallallo Carhuincho's fires. However, Huallallo Carhuincho refused to give up. Pariacaca continued to hurl lightning bolts at him from all directions, never allowing him a moment's rest, until

finally Huallallo Carhuincho gave in and fled north to the lowlands of Antis (*ANTISUYU*).

Huallallo Carhuincho was not without allies, however, and the fight was not over. A female *huaca* called *MAMA ÑAMCA* attacked Pariacaca, and he was forced to defeat her as well, driving her west into the ocean.

These mythical battles appear to contain the historical kernel of a much telescoped history of the region. It can be argued that they strongly reflect what might have been a campaign of several battles, in which mountain pastoralist *Checa Yauyos* invaded Huarochirí, defeating the agriculturalist *Concha Yauyos* and driving at least some of them away. Perhaps allies of the latter arrived too late and were driven back into the sea. Nevertheless, there does not appear to have been a complete displacement of the peoples, since the Huarochirí Manuscript was written from the point of view of both of the *Lurin Yauyos* subgroups – pastoralists and agriculturalists.

More generally, the character and powers ascribed to Pariacaca in the manuscript reveal him to have been the god of rain, storms and floods, who was worshipped by the peoples of ancient western Peru (see also *HUATHIACURI*).

PERIBORIWA is the *YANOMAMI* moon spirit. The Yanomami call themselves "the fierce people", according to their belief that in the beginning the moon spirit spilled on to the earth and changed into

men as it touched the ground. Thus born of "blood", the Yanomami regard themselves as naturally fierce and aggressive, and must thus make continual war on one another.

A later descendant of Periboriwa gave birth to more docile men and to women.

PIKILLACTA was a Middle Horizon *HUARI* regional religious and political centre. It was established in about AD 650, and remained a ceremonial centre for the élite for about 300 years. Its vast complex of more than 700 rigidly planned structures with few doorways and corridors suggests a centre of special purpose and strictly controlled access and movement.

PILLAN, a deity of the *AUCA* peoples of northern Chile, was the god of sudden natural catastrophe, who sent storms, floods and volcanic eruptions to menace humankind.

PIPTADENIA SNUFF see *SHAMAN*.

PONCE STELA see under *TIAHUANACO*.

PONGMASSA see under *CHIMO CAPAC*.

PUCARA, or Pukara, was a general *INCA* term for a stone house or fortification in the mountains. The people of the Fourth Age, the *Auca Runa* (see *PACHACUTI*) had particular need of them in that period of increasing warfare.

229

Q

THIS STONE serpent carving is typical of the Early Intermediate Period site of Pukara near Lake Titicaca.

PUKARA was an Early Intermediate Period ceremonial centre in the *TITICACA* Basin, a precursor to the rise of *TIAHUANACO*. It was occupied from *c.* 200 BC to *c.* AD 200 and displayed numerous stone stelae carved with *FELINE*, *SERPENT*, fish and lizard iconographic imagery. Its influence extended some 150 km (90 miles) to the north.

PUMAPUNKU TEMPLE see *TIAHUANACO*.

PURUN RUNA were the people of the Third Sun (see *PACHACUTI*).

PURURAUCAS were the stones miraculously metamorphosed by the gods into warriors at the eleventh hour during the siege of *CUZCO*. In *INCA* legendary history, *PACHACUTI INCA YUPANQUI* called upon divine help in the war against the *CHANCAS*, whereupon the stones in the fields rose up as armed men to fight beside the Incas. After the battle, Pachacuti ordered that the stones be gathered up and distributed among the city's shrines. As objects of worship the stones became *HUACAS*, sacred places.

Q'ERO was a town and people in the Valley of *CUZCO* (see *ROAL*).

QOCHA see *MAMA COCA*.

QORI KANCHA (literally "building of gold") see *CORICANCHA*.

QOYA, the *INCA* "queen" or "empress", was the principal wife of the *SAPA INCA*. In late imperial times and at the time of the Spanish arrival, she would also have been the Inca's sister. She was regarded as the earthly embodiment of the moon, *QUILLA* and, in that role, she regulated the tempo of ritual activity in *CUZCO*, in keeping with the lunar cycles.

QOYLOR was the general *QUECHUA* term for the stars (see, for example, *CHASKA-QOYLOR*).

QUAPAQ HUCHA see *CAPACOCHA*.

QUECHUA was the language of the *INCA* and, more generally, of central Peru. It served as the *lingua franca* of the Inca Empire, and is still spoken in Andean regions of Peru, Ecuador and Bolivia.

QUILLA was the *INCA* moon goddess. Just as the *SAPA INCA*, the emperor, was regarded as the earthly embodiment of the sun, his primary wife, the *QOYA*, was regarded as the embodiment of the moon on earth. One of the temples in the sacred *CORICANCHA* precinct in *CUZCO* was dedicated to her, and held her image, made of silver. The mummified bodies (*MALLQUIS*) of former *Qoyas* were kept in the temple and brought out on ritual occasions (for example, an October spring moon festival), when they were dressed in sumptuous clothes and jewellery, offered food and drink, and, like the mummies of the former emperors, carried on biers in processions.

QUILLA, the moon goddess, was represented by the Qoya, principal wife of the Sapa Inca. As well as her temple in the Coricancha in Cuzco, she was also honoured with a temple at Machu Picchu (right).

QOYA was the Inca empress as well as being the representative of the moon on earth. (ILLUSTRATION BY FELIPE GUAMAN POMA DE AYALA, FROM THE NUEVA CORÓNICA Y BUEN GOBIERNO, 1583–1613.)

An eclipse of the moon was believed by the Inca to be an attempt by a huge celestial *SERPENT* or mountain lion to eat Quilla. During such events, they would gather in force in their sacred precincts and make as much noise as possible in order to scare off the creature.

QUIPUCAMAYOQS ("knot-makers") were the keepers of the *QUIPUS*. They were charged with recording official information of a statistical nature and also with tying the coded knots that served, in a manner not yet fully understood, as aids to recalling and narrating *INCA* myth, legend and history. Alongside their colleagues, the *AMAUTAS*, they were a principal source of Inca history, religious belief and social organization to Spanish chroniclers. Like the *amautas*, the *quipucamayoqs* must have struggled continually to keep the official state records straight

and to reconcile the histories and beliefs of conquered peoples.

One document in particular, the *Relación de los Quipucamayoqs*, provides an example of their role. It was written in Spain in 1608, but was composed of materials assembled to support the claims of a hopeful late pretender to the Inca throne, one Melchior Carlos Inca. In his claim, he attempted to add depth and weight to his legitimacy by incorporating a version of the early foundation of *CUZCO*. His source was the manuscript of an inquest held in 1542, the informants at which were four elderly *quipucamayoqs* who had served the Inca before the Spanish conquest; their information provides some of the earliest known versions of the Inca state origins. Likewise, in his *Historia de los Incas* (1572) the Spaniard Sarmiento de Gamboa asserts that he interviewed more than 100 *quipucamayoqs*, and actually names 42 of them. This, too, is one of the earliest sources for Inca myth and legend.

QUIPUS (*INCA*), from the *QUECHUA* word for "knot", were linked bundles of knotted and dyed string, usually of twisted cotton, but sometimes also of wool. They were used to record, and served as

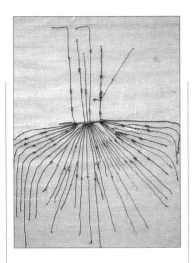

A QUIPU (above left) was a bundle of knotted string that a quipucamayoq *(above right) used to record information and Inca narratives. (FELIPE GUAMAN POMA DE AYALA, THE NUEVA CORÓNICA Y BUEN GOBIERNO, 1583–1613.)*

aide-mémoires for official Inca statistical information (for example, censuses and tribute accounts) and historical information, including their myths and legends.

QUIRIRMANTA was the fifth place of sojourn of the Inca ancestors during their wanderings, as recounted in the state foundation myth (see *MANCO CAPAC*).

RAIMONDI STELA see *CHAVÍN*.

RAUA see *MAMA RAUA*.

ROAL was a creator god of the Q'ero in the Valley of Cuzco. Their account of creation has elements in common with the creation story of *VIRACOCHA* and with the legend of *MANCO CAPAC*. The world was a dark place, unlit by the sun and inhabited by a race of powerful primeval beings. Roal, the creator, offered the gift of his power to these people, but they boasted that they were so mighty that they had no need of the god's power. This angered Roal, so to punish them he created the sun, which blinded the people and dried them up, but did not destroy them. The Q'ero believed that these beings still came out from their hiding places at sunset and at the time of the new moon.

According to the myth, the *APUS* (mountain spirits) then brought forth a man and a woman, and named them Inkari and Collari. They gave Inkari a golden bar and instructed him to establish a city where the bar, when he hurled it into the sky, would come down and stand upright in the earth. The first time that Inkari threw the bar, it landed badly and did not stick. A second attempt ended with the bar lodged in the earth at an angle, but despite this Inkari built the town of Q'ero. The Apus regarded this as disobedience and attempted to punish Inkari by resurrecting the primeval men, who attempted to kill Inkari by rolling huge stone blocks at him. Inkari fled in terror to the *TITICACA* Basin.

Later he returned to the Valley of Cuzco and threw the golden bar into the air a third time, and this time it fell straight. So, at this site, Inkari founded *CUZCO*. He sent his eldest son to nearby Q'ero to re-populate that community, while the rest of his descendants became the *INCAS*. Along with Collari, Inkari then travelled throughout the Andes teaching the art of civilization until the two of them finally disappeared into the rain forest to the east.

SACSAHUAMAN ("royal eagle") forms the northwestern end of the *INCA* imperial capital at *CUZCO*. The city was planned by *PACHACUTI INCA YUPANQUI*, and from an aerial perspective the outline of the Inca

SACSAHUAMAN, overlooking Cuzco, forms the head of the feline plan of the city, and was the sacred precinct built by Pachacuti Inca Yupanqui.

buildings and wall along the edge of the city forms the image of a puma in profile. The redoubt of Sacsahuaman forms the "head" of the cat, while the sacred *CORICAN-CHA* precinct forms the "tail".

One side of the Sacsahuaman complex runs along a cliff edge and overlooks the rest of the capital. The opposite side, sloping more gently, was encased in three successive tiers of zig-zag terracing. The huge polygonal stone blocks used in the walls were shaped and fitted together precisely; each one weighed between 90 and over 120 tonnes, and some came from as far as Rumiqolqa quarry 35 km (22 miles) southeast. The hilltop thus enclosed was flattened to accommodate a complex of ashlar buildings, including two huge towers, one circular and one rectangular, linked by alleys and staircases, incorporating a sophisticated system of stone channels and drainage chambers. The 16th-century Spanish chronicles record that 30,000 *MIT'A* workers were employed in its construction.

The imposing nature of Sacsahuaman has led some observers to conclude that it was built primarily as a fortress. The 16th-17th-century chronicler Garcilaso de la Vega said that it was a depository of "arms, clubs, lances, bows, arrows, axes, shields, heavy jackets of quilted cotton [armour] and other weapons of different types", but also declared that only Inca royalty and nobility were allowed to enter the precinct because it was the house of the sun, *INTI*, a temple for priestly prayer and a place for sacrifice. The 16th-century Spanish conquistador and chronicler, Pedro de Cieza de León, however, stated in his *Crónica del Peru* (Seville, 1550–3) that from the start of its construction Pachacuti Inca Yupanqui planned it as a temple complex.

This information, written not long after its construction in the mid- to late 15th century, seems to support both interpretations. The manner in which Pachacuti gained his throne – by usurping his half-brother *INCA URCO*, who had been the chosen successor of his father *VIRACOCHA INCA* – also tends to support both arguments: the position of the complex would certainly have been advantageous for defence; equally, the site was ideal for the observation of the Milky Way (see *MAYU*) and other celestial bodies so important in Inca cosmology, calendrical calculations and the confirmation of mythological concepts. A wide esplanade forms a levelled space between the terraces or ramparts and a large, carved stone outcrop opposite. It has been suggested that this was a venue for staged ritual battles similar to those recorded by the chroniclers to have taken place in the capital's square below. Finally, the elaborate system constructed for channelling water through the precinct suggests its ritual manipulation, which appears to have been an ancient and common Andean practice (see *CHAVÍN*, *MACHU PICCHU*, *TIAHUANACO*).

HUMAN SACRIFICE
& CANNIBALISM

HUMAN SACRIFICE was widespread in ancient Andean culture. It was regarded as a sacred ritual to secure the favour of the gods, and appears to have been practised from the earliest of times. Evidence for strangulation, throat-slitting, clubbing to death and trepanning (penetrating the skull) has been found in the burials at Cahuachi, Moche Sipán and in the high mountain *capacocha* (child-sacrifice) sites, apparently often used, of Ampato, Llullaillaco and others. The Incas held annual ritual sacrifices of children and adults from all over their empire.

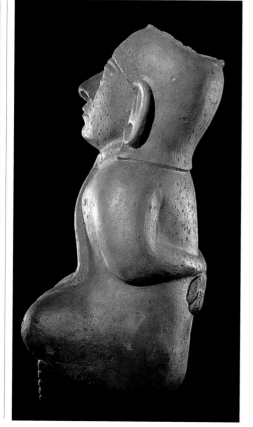

Among the tribes of the rain forest, ritual cannibalism was, until fairly recently, practised as a form of ancestor reverence: preserving the powers and character of an ancestor through "endo-cannibalism" or, through head-hunting and "exo-cannibalism", of capturing and holding, out of fear, the power of enemies.

THE MOCHE were particularly graphic and prolific in their representations of human sacrifice. Scenes were painted on pottery and on temple and tomb murals, frequently featuring the Decapitator God. Portable objects served as constant reminders of the practice, as in this redware (with traces of white paint) figurine (left and above) showing a sacrificial prisoner with his hands bound behind his back, while a second cord is tied around his neck and to his penis.

THE FRIGHTENING SCENE *of a sacrifice in progress is shown on this Moche stirrup-spout ceramic bottle (above). Gripping the victim's hair to yank the head back, the priest/executioner, wearing a fierce-looking stag helmet, is about to slit the victim's throat – one of several common methods of execution. It is impossible to tell whether the victim's visage represents fear, resignation or a drugged state.*

THE WEAPON *normally used in execution by slitting the throat was the sacrificial tumi knife (left). Their characteristic, workman-like crescent-shaped copper blades were frequently elaborately decorated with exquisite gold handles, particularly in the Late Intermediate Period (c. AD 1000–1400) Sicán culture. This example has the large earspools, elaborate headdress and winged shoulders of the Sipán Lord.*

SEVERED HEADS, *a public reminder of sacrifice, were displayed in many ancient Andean cultures. For example, decapitated heads feature in early Chavín low-relief stone wall decoration and as stone heads tenoned into temple walls at Tiahuanaco. Portable examples are also found, such as this otherwise unprovenanced ceramic example (above), made as a container, from Peru.*

SAPA INCA ("sole" or "unique" Inca) was the title of the ruling *INCA* emperor. He was believed to be the direct descendant of the founder of the dynasty, *MANCO CAPAC*, and the manifestation on earth of the sun, *INTI*. In this capacity, his presence brought light and warmth to make the world habitable.

SEMI-SUBTERRANEAN TEMPLE see *TIAHUANACO*.

SERPENTS, like *FELINES*, *JAGUARS* and fanged beasts, were a pan-Andean source of religious iconography. They figure frequently in all media: wall painting, stone carving, ceramic decoration, textiles and metalwork. They were a frequent element in the imagery of the deities of almost all the major cultures of the Andes and western coast, from Early Horizon *CHAVÍN* and *PARACAS*, via Early Intermediate Period *MOCHE*, *NAZCA* and *PACHACAMAC*, and Middle Horizon *HUARI* and *TIAHUANACO*, to the empires of *CHIMÚ* and the *INCA*.

SHAMAN (plural: shamans) is the anthropological term for a person who is in possession of special powers, usually aided by the use of hallucinatory plant drugs, which enable the shaman to gain access to the spirit world.

A YANOMAMI SHAMAN is seen taking hallucinogenic snuff in order to induce a trance and to enter the spirit world.

The tropical rain forest tribes of Central and South America believe that everything that happens on earth has a spirit-world cause and/or consequence. But the spirits are ambivalent, even fickle, in their relationships with humankind, and their powers must therefore be harnessed and channelled, even if only temporarily, and interpreted by an intermediary or medium. Thus the shaman is a combination

SERPENTINE and fanged figures pervaded Andean and coastal religious imagery in all media, such as this serpent-man figure from the coastal site of La Tolita, Ecuador.

of sorcerer, curer, spiritual interpreter and diviner, and also the upholder of the codes of the social moral order and the dispenser of justice.

Through the use of hallucinatory plant drugs – for example *ayahuasca*, *vihoo* or *Piptadenia* snuff mixed with tobacco or in drink – the shaman can temporarily enter

the spirit world on behalf of the tribe and negotiate with the spirits on equal terms. Through this "window", he is able to understand the true nature of things, to explain events past and present, and even to divine the future and suggest appropriate courses of action. He can rid the village of pestilence and illness or send such ailments to enemies; or ensure the success of the hunt.

Entering of the spirit world is frequently done at night, when the shaman is believed to become transformed into another body. Those who become a *JAGUAR* are the most feared of all; to accomplish this feat, the shaman dons a jaguar skin and necklace of jaguar teeth or claws – often from animals he has slain himself – and in a trance growls and howls like a jaguar. Among the northwestern Amazon and Orinoco tribes, the shaman's drugs are sometimes referred to as "the jaguar's drug", or even "the jaguar's sperm", and are kept in a hollowed-out jaguar bone.

The shaman's visions are imbued with religious significance and give the tribe knowledge of the "mythological" past of "the ancestors". Connection with the past is believed by many to continue after the death of the shaman, who then becomes one of the ancestors, and whose powers continue to protect the village and tribe from the malevolent spirits and from the malicious intentions of shamans from other villages or tribes.

SI was the *MOCHE* and (later) *CHIMÚ* moon goddess, or god, and overlord of the Moche and Chimú pantheons. S/he was the supreme deity, omnipresent, and held sway over the gods and humankind due to her/his control of the seasons, natural elements and storms, and therefore agricultural fertility. Her/his origins have been traced to an earlier unnamed radiant and armoured goddess/god of war, who was related to or replaced *AI APAEC* in importance. One source refers to Si-an, a Chimú temple dedicated to Si, interpreted as Huaca Singan in the Jequetepeque Valley, possibly the structure known today as Huaca del Dragón.

The Moche and Chimú peoples became aware that the tides and other motions of the sea, as well as the arrival of the annual rains, were linked to the phases of the moon. For these reasons they allocated great power to Si, because their food supply and the wellbeing of their flocks were dependent upon her/his beneficence; in contrast, the sun was considered by them to be a relatively minor deity. Si was also regarded as more powerful than the sun because s/he could be seen by both night and day. Eclipses were believed by them to be battles between the moon and sun. An eclipse of the moon was considered a disastrous augury to be regarded with fear, while an eclipse of the sun was treated as a joyful occasion.

Si was also regarded as the protector of public property, for s/he could reveal thieves in the night. Given the tightly controlled redistribution mechanisms of Chimú society, revealed in the organization of the royal compounds at their capital Chan Chan, the importance of property and a protector thereof is understandable.

SICÁN was a later Middle Horizon-Late Intermediate Period culture in the *LAMBAYEQUE* Valley (see *BATÁN GRANDE* and *TÚCUME*).

SINAA is the *FELINE* ancestor of the people of the Brazilian Juruna tribe in the *XINGU RIVER* region. He was born of a huge jaguar father and a human mother. Although very old, Sinaa regains his youth every time he bathes, when he is said to "pull his skin over his head like a sack". Another of his traits is that, like his father, his eyes are in the back of his head. The Juruna believe that the end of the world will come when Sinaa decides to remove an enormous forked stick that they believe holds up the sky (see also *UAICA*).

SINCHI ROCA was the son of *MANCO CAPAC* and *MAMA OCLLO*, and the legendary second ruler of *CUZCO*. According to different versions of the myth of *INCA* state foundation he was born at the ancestors' second stopping place after leaving *PACARITAMBO*, before reaching the town of *PALLUTA*, or in Cuzco itself. With his father, mother and aunts, he established and organized the construction of the capital. He was also credited with having commanded the people of the Valley of Cuzco to cultivate potatoes – the staple crop when the Spaniards arrived.

SIPÁN is an Early Intermediate Period site in the *LAMBAYEQUE VALLEY*, with rich burials of *MOCHE* lords (see *DECAPITATOR GOD*).

SMILING GOD is an epithet sometimes applied to a deity of the Early Horizon. Like many other images of the *CHAVÍN* culture, its

SINCHI ROCA was the second Inca ruler, credited with encouraging his people to cultivate potatoes. (ILLUSTRATION BY FELIPE GUAMAN POMA DE AYALA, NUEVA CORÓNICA Y BUEN GOBIERNO, 1583–1613.)

upturned mouth has fangs, but whether it was a distinct deity or one of the many manifestations of the *FANGED GOD* is difficult to say.

THE STAFF DEITY was a pan-Andean deity of either gender portrayed as a frontal figure with outstretched arms holding staffs. The image originated in the Early Horizon *CHAVÍN* cult and endured through to the Late Horizon.

SUNKEN COURTYARD TEMPLES see under *CHAVÍN, FANGED GOD* and *PACHAMAMA*.

SUSURPUQUIO was the name of the spring outside *CUZCO* where *PACHACUTI INCA YUPANQUI* found a crystal tablet bearing the image of *VIRACOCHA*.

SUTIC TOCO, *INCA*, was one of the caves of *TAMBO TOCO* (see *MANCO CAPAC*).

SUYU was the *INCA* word for a "quarter" in terms of a division of territory. The Inca Empire was divided into four *suyus* (see *TAHUANTINSUYU*).

TAHUANTINSUYU, or Tawantinsuyu, was the *INCA* name for their empire, and literally means "land of the four united quarters". *CUZCO*, the capital, was the focal point from which the four, unequal, quarters were oriented. The four quarters were Antisuyu (northeast), Chinchasuyu (northwest), Cuntisuyu (southwest) and Collasuyu (southeast). Their boundaries were linked to sacred *CEQUE* lines radiating from the *CORICANCHA* in Cuzco, and were thus also associated with four great highways to the provinces, each of which departed from Cuzco along a route approximating an intercardinal axes of *MAYU*, the Milky Way.

Encompassing a vast territory, from modern Ecuador to central Chile north to south, and from the Pacific coast to the eastern flank of the Andes mountain chain west to east, it was inhabited by a great variety peoples and languages. In Inca myth, this diversity was explained by the deliberate actions of *VIRACOCHA*: when he had created the second world of humans from clay, he dispersed them after imbuing them with the accoutrements and languages of the different tribes and nations.

The division of the empire into the four quarters was as such virtually ignored in Inca mythology. One myth, however, recounted in Garcilaso de la Vega's *Commentarios Reales de los Incas*, described this

SUSURPUQUIO spring near Cuzco is the place where Pachacuti Inca Yupanqui found a crystal tablet.

TAHUANTINSUYU was the name of the Inca Empire, of which Cuzco was the capital. In an aerial view of present-day Cuzco (north is upper left), it is possible to see the Plaza de Armas, the site of the Inca Haunaypata (above centre), and the Coricancha (shadowed area right of plaza).

division as being the work of an *UN-NAMED MAN* who appeared at *TIAHUANACO* after the destruction of a previous world by deluge. This dearth of explanation is especially curious given the emphasis in Inca legendary history on the progress of state creation from Lake *TITICACA* (near the actual geographical centre of the empire) to the north and west. The direction of this progression makes sense for Antisuyu, Chinchasuyu and Cuntisuyu, but not for Collasuyu, which lies almost entirely to the south of Lake Titicaca. One explanation might be that the Incas recast the origin mythology of the peoples of this quarter in order to bolster their own claims to have originated from the Titicaca Basin and to legitimize their right to rule the region, for the ruins of Tiahuanaco and of other great cities of the region must have been recognized as an existing and former power base.

TAMBOCHACAY ("Tambo entrance-bearer") accompanied Ayar Cachi on his return to the *TAMBO TOCO* cave (see *MANCO CAPAC*).

THE TAMBOS were allies of the Inca ancestors (see *MANCO CAPAC*).

235

TAMBO TOCO

TAMBO TOCO ("window house") was the mountain with three caves, from the central one of which the *INCA* ancestors emerged; see *MANCO CAPAC, MAUQALLQTA*.

TARAPACA was one of many names for *VIRACOCHA*.

TAWANTINSUYU see *TAHUANTINSUYU*.

TAYCANAMU was the founder of a new *CHIMÚ* dynasty in the *MOCHE* Valley in the 14th century. Like so many pre-*INCA* rulers in the kingdoms eventually subjugated by the Incas, knowledge of him is meagre and cloaked in legend. He was said to have arrived at Moche on a balsawood raft, "sent" from afar with the express mission of governing the valley peoples. Several unnamed kings succeeded him until the conquest of the valley, then under the rulership of *MIN-CHANÇAMAN*, by the Incas.

TEMAUKEL is the supreme being worshipped by the *ONA* of Tierra del Fuego. He is the all-powerful creator, and is believed to be without body, wife or child. Prayer and initiation rites to him are the preserve of men, who take the dominant role on earth now, after an initial period when women dominated.

TEMPLE OF THE SUN see *CORICANCHA, INTI, MACHU PICCHU, PACHACAMAC, TIAHUANACO*.

TEMPLE OF THE THREE WINDOWS see *MACHU PICCHU*.

TAMBO TOCO, the mountain in Pacaritambo with three windows, is mirrored by the Temple of Three Windows at Machu Picchu (above).

THE THREE-CORNERED IDOL

IDOL was a common deity, or *ZEMÍ*, of the prehistoric *ARAWAK* of the Greater Antilles, the giver of *MANIOC* to humankind. Carved of stone or conch shell, he is thought by archaeologists to derive from the observed form of the volcanic cone.

THE THREE VIRACOCHAS

see *CON TICCI VIRACOCHA*.

THUNUPA VIRACOCHA

THUNUPA VIRACOCHA was ostensibly one of many names for the *INCA* creator god *VIRACOCHA*, but it seems to be more ancient.

The central figure on the Gateway of the Sun at *TIAHUANACO* has been interpreted as portraying Thunupa, a sky god and weather deity worshipped in the *TITICACA* Basin. He brought rain, thunder and lightning, but the rays projecting from the head of the figure are likely to represent the rays of the sun. Written sources for him are few and come from much later chroniclers, making it hard to imagine exactly how the Tiahuanacos perceived him. But it is known that the Incas acknowledged the ancient power of Tiahuanaco and revered its very ruins. The most ancient Andean myths emanated from Titicaca, and the world itself was believed to have been created there by Viracocha. Thus, according to the mid-17th-century Jesuit priest Bernabé Cobo, the Incas modelled their own god of weather, *ILLAPA*, on Thunupa.

The 16th-century Inca chronicler Juan de Santa Cruz Pachacuti Yamqui also relates the legend of Thunupa Viracocha, portraying him as a white man with a long grey beard and hair. Thunupa travelled about the land preaching and teaching, even performing miracles to impart moral behaviour to the people. In the enthusiasm of his own conversion to Christianity, and probably to please his new Spanish masters, Pachacuti Yamqui, was convinced that Thunupa was the apostle St Thomas. According to Pachacuti Yamqui, the Incas, by forcing their official state cult of the sun (*INTI*) on their subjects, corrupted them and turned them away from the true God of Christianity.

TIAHUANACO, or Tiwanaku, an ancient site and kingdom in the *TITICACA* Basin, dominated the southern Andes in the Middle Horizon. It lies near the southern shore of Lake Titicaca and, in its heyday, occupied 445 hectares (1,100 acres). The earliest major constructions at the site were begun by AD 200 and, by AD 500, Tiahuanaco was the capital of a considerable empire, stretching to the Bolivian lowlands, the Peruvian coast, and into northern Chile. Its cultural and religious influence extended even farther. Its chief rival to the north was the *HUARI* Empire, and the two empires "met" at the La Raya pass, south of *CUZCO*, which became a sort of buffer zone between them. The prosperity of Tiahuanaco endured for roughly a millennium, matching the 1,000-year periods of the five "Ages" or Suns of Andean cosmology (see *PACHACUTI*).

The core of the city was formed by ceremonial–religious–civic structures, displaying religious motifs and gods whose iconography shows affinities to earlier *CHAVÍN* imagery

THE MONOLITHIC Gateway of the Sun at Tiahuanaco focuses on the central figure of the Staff Deity, probably Thunupa or Thunupa Viracocha, also called the "Weeping God", flanked by running "angels".

and indicates the continuity or resurgence of ancient religious beliefs. This core was aligned east–west, was confined within a moat, and was surrounded by residential compounds built of *adobe* bricks.

Tiahuanaco was a culmination of religious and mythological antecedents that appear to have united the peoples of the Titicaca Basin from as early as 1000 BC; ceremonial architecture at earlier sites such as *PUKARA* herald that at Tiahuanaco. The site chosen for the capital was in the midst of fertile land, enhanced by a sophisticated system of dykes, canals, causeways and aqueducts. The choice of location seems to have been deliberate, within a landscape itself perceived as sacred, in which natural features were worshipped: the sacred waters of Lake Titicaca to the west and the snow-capped mountain peaks to the east. The ceremonial centre was planned on a grid pattern, with all structures oriented on cardinal directions. The moat segregated it from the residential sections of the city, and reflected the sacred *HUACAS* of the *ISLAND OF THE SUN* and the *ISLAND OF THE MOON* in the lake.

Construction of the major elements of the religious centre had begun by *c.* AD 300. It comprised an area of stone temples, sunken courts, gateways and architraves. Some buildings were probably residential palaces, but the gateways and sculptures were the focuses of

open spaces clearly meant for civic participation in ritual and ceremony. Traces of gold pins within the stone blocks and remains of paint show that the sculptures were decorated and/or clothed.

At the island's core was the Akapana Temple, an artificial mound 17 m (56 ft) high, created from the excavation of the moat. It is roughly T-shaped (with a double bar across the top, one bar shorter than the other), about 200 m (650 ft) each side, composed of seven tiers clad in sandstone slabs. At the top is a sunken court in the shape of a quadrate cruciform, of an andesite base paved with sandstone slabs. Two staircases climb the east and west sides of the terraces, either side of which were rooms that might have been priests' quarters. Stone-lined channels and subterranean canals drained water down the terraces into the Tiahuanaco River, indicating ritual use of the sounds of rushing water (see also *CHAVÍN*, *MACHU PICCHU*, and *SACSAHUAMAN*). Lake Titicaca and Mount Illimani are visible from the top of Akapana.

Near the Akapana Temple are other monuments, principally the Semi-subterranean Temple to the north. This comprises a sunken court 28.5 x 26 m (94 x 85 ft), entered by a staircase on its south side. Its surrounding interior walls are adorned with carved stone heads, and at its centre stand several carved stone stelae, originally

THE FITTED *stone block walls of the Semi-subterranean Temple at Tiahuanaco are adorned with carved stone heads.*

including the "Bennett Stela" (after its discoverer, Wendell Bennett; now in the plaza of La Paz). The largest stone sculpture discovered in the Andes to date (7.3 m/24 ft tall), it portrays a richly dressed human thought to be one of Tiahuanaco's rulers or a divine ruler. In his/her hands are a *kero* beaker and a staff-like object, perhaps a snuff tablet.

Also north of the Akapana Temple, and west of the Semi-subterranean Temple, is the Kalasasaya, a low-lying rectangular platform 130 x 120 m (427 x 394 ft). It defines a large ceremonial precinct for public ritual, whose walls are made up of sandstone pillars alternating with smaller ashlar blocks. It is ascended by a stairway carved from stones set between two gigantic stone pillars.

At the northwest corner of the Kalasasaya stands the Gateway of the Sun. It seems to comprise two monolithic stone slabs supporting a third, carved, slab across the top, but is a single huge block of andesite whose top section is a panel completely covered with carving. The central figure portrays the "Gateway God", an anthropomorphic figure standing on a stepped platform resembling the tiered mounds of the sacred precinct. The figure has a squarish head adorned in a headdress with sun rays radiating from the top and sides; the eyes have large drops below them, giving rise to the name "Weeping God". Its outstretched arms hold two "staffs" – one has been interpreted as a spear-thrower and the other a quiver for spears, a clear resemblance to the *STAFF DEITY* of Chavín times. Flanking it are three rows, each of eight smaller winged figures in profile – sometimes called "angels" – running towards it, each of which also bears a staff. Below it is a row of carved heads.

The Gateway God is most likely a portrayal of *THUNUPA*, the god of thunder, lightning and rain. His sun-ray headdress also fits the character of a weather god, as do his spear-thrower and cluster of

spears, common metaphors for thunder and lightning.

Just within the Kalasasaya is the giant Ponce Stela (after archaeologist Carlos Ponce), 3.5 m (11 ft 6 in) tall. It portrays a ruler or deity, richly clothed, and with a mask-like face and staring eyes, thin trapezoidal nose, rectangular mouth and cheek panels. His/her hands hold a *kero* beaker and a staff-like object or snuff tablet.

Southeast of the Akapana Temple is the separate, much lower mound of the Pumapunku Temple, and ceremonial area. This is a T-shaped mound 5 m (16 ft) high, covering 150 sq m (179 sq yds), made up of three sandstone slab-covered tiers. The sunken courtyard at its summit, with carved stone doorways and lintels, was possibly the original site of the Gateway of the Sun.

The shared religious iconography of Tiahuanaco and Huari demonstrates that religious continuity prevailed from the Early Horizon through the Early Intermediate Period, despite political fragmentation in the Early Intermediate. Similarities include the Staff Deity image, winged and running falcon- and condor-headed creatures, often wielding clubs, and also decapitated heads. Priests might have kept contacts in the two capitals.

The Incas held the ruins at Tiahuanaco in reverence and regarded the Titicaca Basin as the place of the origin of the world. So great was their regard for the primacy of

IN COMMON *with other Andean cultures, Tiahuanacan imagery includes bird, serpent, feline and other animal motifs, as exemplified in this painted ceramic drinking cup.*

A MONUMENTAL *staircase leads up to the western entrance of the Kalasasaya at Tiahuanaco, a monumental compound with monolithic sculptures, including the Ponce Stela just within the arched gateway.*

the site that they linked their own state foundations myth to it (see *MANCO CAPAC*) and regarded the huge stone statues at Tiahuanaco to be an ancient race of giants. In one variation of the deluge myth, the *UN-NAMED MAN* at Tiahuanaco divided the world into the four *SUYUS* and designated their rulers.

Despite such similarities, however, religious imagery at Tiahuanaco concentrated on stone sculpture at the ceremonial capital, which was built for public ceremony and with a preconceived plan. At Huari, by contrast, structures were private, more intimate, and development appears to have been haphazard. Also, religious imagery was concentrated on ceramics, textiles and other portable objects, and was therefore personal and perhaps more widespread.

TIAHUANACO GIANTS
see *TIAHUANACO* stone figures.

TICCI, or Tiqsi, ("the beginning of things") was one of the many epithets used by the *INCAS* to refer to *VIRACOCHA*.

TICCI VIRACOCHA was the *INCA* name for a creator worshipped by the *Wari Wiracocharuna* of the First "Age" and one of many name variations for *VIRACOCHA* (see *MANCO CAPAC*, *PACHACUTI*, *CON TICCI VIRACOCHA*).

TIQSI see *TICCI*.

TITICACA, the lake in the central Andes on the borders of modern Peru and Bolivia, was the centre of the Titicaca Basin and the location of the ancient city of *TIAHUANACO*. Both the lake and the city maintained a pan-Andean importance during the dominance of the region by Tiahuanaco and afterwards as the legendary place of the origin of the cosmos, including the sun, moon, stars and humankind.

Peoples throughout the Andes created myths and legendary historical links to establish their origin at Titicaca/Tiahuanaco, including (and especially) the *INCAS*. The creator was invariably *VIRACOCHA*

ON LAKE TITICACA, *Aymará fishermen continue to use reed boats like those made by the inhabitants of ancient Tiahuanaco more than 1,200 years ago.*

who, in the episodic story of creation, was believed to have called forth the sun, moon and stars from islands in the lake, specifically the *ISLAND OF THE SUN* and the *ISLAND OF THE MOON*. The waters of the lake were said to be the tears of the creator, that he shed in acknowledgement of the sufferings of the beings he created.

Lake Titicaca also plays an important role in several versions of the origins of the Inca state. In these versions, *MANCO CAPAC* and his sister/wife *MAMA OCLLO* were associated with the Island of the Sun, and after their creation the "ancestors" were said to have made their way underground from Lake Titicaca to the

THE TOBA PEOPLE *of Paraguay and northern Argentina believed that humans once dwelt in the sky.*

cave of *PACARITAMBO*. Similarly, a strong link between Titicaca and the Inca capital at Cuzco was established by the travels of Viracocha. Temples dedicated to him were established at *CACHA* and *URCOS*, in the Vilcanota (or Urubamba) Valley to the northwest of the Basin, shortly after the creation.

TIWANAKU see *TIAHUANACO*.

THE TOBA, a tribe of the Gran *CHACO* of Paraguay and northern Argentina, believed that humans once dwelt in the sky. When they came down to earth to hunt animals, however, they became trapped here and have had to remain for ever (see also *KONONATOO*).

TOCAPO VIRACOCHA was the younger son or special aide of *CON TICCI VIRACOCHA* in different versions of the central Andean creation myth. After the creation of the world by *VIRACOCHA*, Tocapo Viracocha travelled northwards along a coastal route from Lake *TITICACA*, calling forth the clay models of people made by his father, naming the trees and plants, allocating their flowering and fruiting seasons and instructing the people in their uses

for food or medicinal purposes. He rejoined his father and brother, *IMAYMANA VIRACOCHA*, at *MANTA* on the Ecuadorian coast, and disappeared out to sea by walking across the waters.

TONAPA, or Conapa, was the divine assistant of the creator god *VIRACOCHA*. In one of many myths about Viracocha, Tonapa disobeyed Viracocha, and for this was set adrift on Lake *TITICACA*. His symbol was a cross, which over-enthusiastic Spanish priests took to be clear evidence of a pre-Spanish-conquest Christian connection.

TOPA YUPANQUI, almost certainly *TUPAC INCA YUPANQUI*, was a name for the conquering *INCA* lord cited in the histories of the dynasty of *TAYCANAMU* and *MINCHANÇA-MAN* at *MOCHE*.

TOPACUSI was a golden cup alleged by *MANCO CAPAC* to have been left behind unintentionally in the cave of *TAMBO TOCO*.

TORREÓN SUN TEMPLE see *MACHU PICCHU*.

TOVAPOD see *AROTEH*.

TUPAC INCA YUPANQUI,

probably the same as *TOPA YUPAN-QUI*, was the 11th *INCA* emperor, succeeding his father *PACHACUTI INCA YUPANQUI*, and ruling from 1471 to 1493. Like his father, he is less a legendary ruler and more a known historical figure. Less interested in developing the state than his father, he was mainly responsible for the second great wave of Inca imperial expansion, extending beyond the Valley of Cuzco and the *TITICACA* Basin, to encompass some 4,000 km (2,500 miles) of land north to south between modern central Ecuador and central Chile. The Inca manner of dealing with local kingdoms after conquest, incorporating local rulers and religious beliefs into their own systems, is demonstrated in the legendary account of the conquest of the *CHIMÚ* in the *MOCHE* Valley ruled by *MINCHANÇAMAN*.

THE TUPI

are a rain forest tribe of southeastern Brazil (see *AROTEH*, *CEUCY*, *JURUPARI* and *VALEJDAD*).

TUPAC INCA YUPANQUI, the 11th emperor, continued the expansion of the Inca Empire after his father Pachacuti Inca Yupanqui. (SKETCH BY FELIPE GUAMAN POMA DE AYALA FROM THE NUEVA CORÓNICA Y BUEN GOBIERNO, 1583–1613.)

TRIAD see *ANDEAN TRIAD*.

TÚCUME, a late *SICÁN* site, was successor to *BATÁN GRANDE* in the *LAMBAYEQUE VALLEY* of northern coastal Peru. The largest concentration of monumental and ceremonial architecture ever constructed in the Andes, it covered some 150 hectares (370 acres). It served as the regional religious centre until the arrival of *CHIMÚ* conquerors in the 14th century.

THE TUKANO are a rain forest tribe from the upper reaches of the Colombian and Brazilian Amazon (for their myths, see *ABE MANGO*, *BORARO*, *PAGE ABE*, *PAMURI-MAHSE*, *VAI-MAHSE*, *YAJE WOMAN*).

TUMI knife, see *DECAPITATOR GOD*.

TUPAC AMARU, who was the last claimant to the *INCA* throne after the Spanish conquest, "ruled" from 1571 to 1572. His place in continuing post-Spanish-conquest Inca myth, discovered by anthropologists in the 1950s, derived from the fact that he was beheaded after leading a revolt against Spanish rule, and was/is therefore a candidate for the Inca millenarian belief in the *INKARRÍ*, or revival of the king.

TUPAC CUSI HUALPA is an alternative name for the *INCA* ruler *HUASCAR*.

SACRED SKIES

EVERY ANCIENT CULTURE OF the Andes worshipped the sun; most also worshipped the moon; and a few, for example the Chimú, considered the moon to be superior to the sun (*Inti*). It was the Incas who institutionalized worship of the sun, above almost all other deities, in their promotion of *Inti* throughout their empire. Their founding ancestor, Manco Capac, was regarded as having been the sun's representative on earth, and this epithet was applied to each emperor in the line of succession that

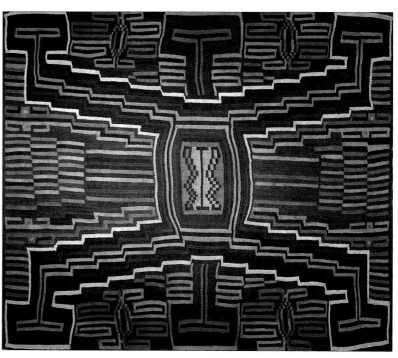

THE IMPORTANCE *of the sun in ancient Andean cultures is manifest from the earliest times. Temples and gold sun discs are obvious representations of this. Less evident is this stylized sun symbol woven into a cotton mantle from the desert Nazca culture of southern coastal Peru.*

followed. Observation and recording of the sun's movements were considered to be vital to the health of the empire, and were performed from distinctive carved stone platforms called *intihuatana*.

As well as the recognition of the importance of solar and lunar cycles, and their effects on the weather and seasons, the night sky – and in particular *Mayu*, the Milky Way – was regarded as a vast source of inspiration and mythological meaning. *Mayu* was seen as the celestial river, and its progression of positions through the night sky, tallied with the seasons, was the starting point for all calendrical correlations. In this vast galactic body, the Incas recognized not just points and regions of light, but also the dark bodies of stellar voids, the "dark-cloud constellations" which, to them, were just as important.

As with other major themes in Andean civilization, imagery and iconography reveal the antiquity of sun worship, from deities with haloed radiations emanating from their heads (for example, on the Gateway of the Sun at Tiahuanaco) to the sheet-gold sun masks of the Incas.

NORTHWEST *of Cuzco, in Antisuyu – in the area first brought under Inca rule – the fortress and sacred retreat of Machu Picchu (above) includes the massive Sun Tower, carved from solid granite and used for astronomical observation.*

AT SACSAHUAMAN *(top left), Emperor Pachacuti Inca Yupanqui's fortress-like sacred precinct on a prominent hill just northwest of Cuzco, massive polygonal monumental masonry required intensive labour, and undoubtedly served to impress upon his subjects the fullness of his power and the supremacy of Inti and the state religion.*

AT THE CONFLUENCE *of the Urubamba and Patakancha rivers, the ceremonial centre and administrative seat of Ollantaytambo (centre left), built for more than 1,000 residents, includes the Sun Temple, which was still under construction when the Spanish invasion began.*

AT THE FARTHEST *northerly provinces of the empire, the administrative centre and Temple of Inti at Ingapirca (bottom left) in Ecuador underscored Inca power and control.*

THE HEAVENS *at night and the movements of celestial bodies, star groups and the entire Milky Way (right) were equally important in Inca religion and cosmography, and were carefully charted. Without the "light pollution" of modern cities it is easier to imagine the immensity of the night sky and to see the dark bodies between stars, as well as the star clusters.*

U

THE TUPINAMBÁ are a coastal rain forest tribe located in south-eastern Brazil (see *MONAN*).

TUTUJANAWIN, a general and somewhat enigmatic pan-Andean deity, was an all-embracing concept of "the beginning and end of all things". He/she/it was a supreme power that gave life and energy to everything in the cosmos.

UAICA was a culture hero of the Juruna rain forest tribe of the *XINGU RIVER* region of Brazil, and a famous medicine man and teacher.

One day, when out hunting in the forest, he came upon a large number of dead animals piled beneath a tree. As he approached the heap of animals, he became dizzy and collapsed into a deep sleep. In his sleep he dreamed about the Juruna *JAGUAR* ancestor *SINAA*, who spoke to him. This dream occurred several times, until finally Sinaa ordered Uaica to stay away from him, a command that Uaica obeyed.

As the tribal medicine man, Uaica made a drink from the bark of a certain tree, which gave him special knowledge and powers. For example, Uaica could take away a disease simply with the touch of his hands. In his dreams, Sinaa gave him answers and instructions to supply all the needs of the Juruna people.

The Juruna urged Uaica to take a wife, but when he finally consented, the wife proved to be unfaithful to him. The lover even attempted to kill Uaica with a club, but, as Uaica had eyes in the back of his head (like the jaguar ancestor), he was able to dodge the blow, and subsequently disappeared down the hole made when the club struck the ground. Thus, through these events, the Juruna lost their medicine man, who declared, "I will not return. You will have to use arrows and clubs. I tried to teach you the wishes of Sinaa, but now I go." The Juruna claim that Uaica

A TUPINAMBÁ ceremonial dance.
(ILLUSTRATION BY JEAN DE LERY, 1556.)

beckoned them to follow him beneath the ground but, in their grief, they were too confused and afraid to follow him.

UCHU see *AYAR UCHU*.

UGWVU-CUENGO was the *KUIKURU* vulture king; see *KANASSA*.

THE "UNNAMED MAN", who appeared at *TIAHUANACO* after the waters of the great world deluge receded, is the principal character in the only substantial account in *INCA* myth of the division of the four *SUYUS*. His great power enabled him to create the four quarters of *TAHUANTINSUYU* and to designate a king for each, although the quarters assigned do not quite conform to the actual directional distribution around *CUZCO*, nor are three of the four kings otherwise known. To the northern quarter (*CHINCHASUYU*?) he appointed *MANCO CAPAC*; to the southern quarter (*COLLASUYU*?), Colla; to the

eastern quarter (*ANTISUYU*?), Tocay; and to the western quarter (*CUNTISUYU*?), Pinahua. He commanded each king to conquer the lands assigned and govern the people who lived there.

URA COCHA was the lake that figured in the battle between *PARIACACA* and *HUALLALLO CARHUINCHO*, as described in the *HUAROCHIRÍ MANUSCRIPT*.

URCO, or Urcon, see *INCA URCO*.

URCOS, a pre-Inca and *INCA* city and ceremonial centre about 35 km (22 miles) southeast of *CUZCO* in the Vilcanota (or Urubamba) Valley, was the setting for the second significant encounter between *VIRACOCHA* and the peoples northwest of the *TITICACA* Basin, shortly after the creation of the world.

According to the myth told to and related by the 16th-century Spanish chronicler Juan de Betanzos, Viracocha arrived at the site and immediately ascended to the

top of a nearby mountain. He sat down there and called upon the ancestors of the Urcos people, whose spirits were believed to inhabit the mountain (were buried there), to come out. The summit where Viracocha sat became a sacred *HUACA* to the people of Urcos and, on that spot, they set up a bench of gold upon which they placed a statue of the god. The contemporary chronicler Cristobal de Molina describes the image of Viracocha as that of a white man dressed in a white robe that hung down to his feet (see also *CACHA*).

The people of Urcos gave Viracocha the name Atun-Viracocha, meaning "great creator".

URPAY HUACHAC was the wife of *PACHACAMAC*, with whom she had two daughters. She was also the creator of fish, which she bred in a pond at Pachacamac, the site. As recounted in the text of the *HUARO-*

V

CHIRÍ MANUSCRIPT, CONIRAYA VIRA-COCHA seduced one daughter, and tried to seduce the other. When she escaped his clutches by transforming herself into a dove and flying away, he smashed the pond in rage, thus releasing fish into the oceans.

URUBUTSIN was the KAMAIURA vulture king (see KUAT).

U-SHAPED CEREMONIAL CENTRES see under CHAVÍN and FANGED GOD.

USHNUO see CAPAC USNU.

USNU PILLAR see under CAPAC USNU.

VAB see VALEJDAD.

VAI-MAHSE ("the master of animals") is the TUKANO tribal spirit of the forest and of the hunt. He is perceived to be a dwarf, with his body

painted red, and certain hills within the forest are sacred to him. His weapon is a highly polished stick, also painted red. He controls all of the game of the forest and all of the

fishes in the rivers, and even the herbs that grow around the bases of trees. Great care must therefore be taken not to offend him, lest in his displeasure he were to bring disaster on the people by withholding the game and the catch or by curtailing the fertility of the animals. He is a jealous god, and his concern with fertility extends to women, to whom he gives sickness and pain in pregnancy because he was not the cause of their condition.

VALEJDAD, and his brother Vab, were the first men according to the TUPI of southeastern Brazil. At the beginning of time, the brothers were born or created from a large rock, which was female. Valejdad was the wicked one of the two and, because of this, was banished to the north. When he becomes angry he sends torrential rains down south, where the Tupi live. (See also AROTEH)

VEGACHAYOQ MOQO TEMPLE see HUARI.

URCOS became a sacred site after being visited by Viracocha on his travels from Lake Titicaca. This is the Temple of Viracocha at Rachi in the Vilcanota Valley, southeast of Cuzco.

VILCAS WAMAN, like Cuzco, had an Usnu platform for making astronomical observations and to ensure cosmic order.

VENTILLA see under CAHUACHI and NAZCA.

VICHAMA
see under PACHACAMAC.

VILCA, a HUAROCHIRÍ term, was a general name for the powerful male deities who play a role in the myth of the young virgin CAVILLACA and CONIRAYA VIRACOCHA, who seduced and impregnated her by concealing his semen in the fruit of a *lúcuma* tree.

VILCAS WAMAN, located about 50 miles (80 km) southeast of Ayacucho, Peru, was one of the Incas' earliest conquests as they began to expand beyond Cuzco. In common with the Inca capital it had an Usnu platform (see CAPAC USNU) and a Sun Temple of finely fitted monumental masonry architecture that rivalled those at the capital. The Sun Temple sits upon a three-tiered platform with trapezoidal doorways and niches for idols.

VILLAMA
see under PACHACAMAC.

VIRACOCHA, or Wira Qocha, the supreme god of the *INCAS*, was the creator of the universe, of the human race and of all things on earth. In concept he became a rather remote and inaccessible deity, although his presence was ubiquitous and inescapable. Nevertheless, he was often represented as an old man with a long beard or as a man wearing a sun crown, holding thunderbolts in his hands and shedding tears from his eyes to represent rain. In the Inca capital at *CUZCO*, Viracocha was represented in his own shrine by a golden statue about three-quarters of the height of a grown man. He was white-skinned, bearded and wore a long tunic, as described by the Spaniards who first saw him there. In legend, Viracocha travelled south to *CACHA*, about 100 km (62 miles) south of Cuzco, where a statue was erected and a temple dedicated to his worship was built. *URCOS* was another important place of worship where a shrine and statue of Viracocha was erected.

In practice, Viracocha, as an immanent but primordial creator, remained nameless to the Incas. Instead, he was referred to by descriptive terms befitting his role in the various permutations of the creation myth. Thus he was known as Ilya (meaning "light") and as Ticci ("the beginning of things"), as Viracocha Pachayachachic or Wiraqoca Pacayacaciq ("great lord, instructor of the world"), and as Tarapaca. Spanish chroniclers, perhaps perplexed by this seeming confusion, gave him the general title of Viracocha. Possible meanings, or glosses, of the name Viracocha itself were "the lake of creation", "sea fat" and "sea foam".

Many Andean cultures, especially in the central Andes, believed that Lake *TITICACA* on the Peruvian–Bolivian border was the site of the creation of the sun, moon and stars, and that the waters of the lake were the tears of the creator god acknowledging the sufferings of the

VIRACOCHA, the supreme pan-Andean creator god, created a race of giants – sometimes associated with the giant stone statues of Tiahuanaco – in the Second Age but later destroyed them when they displeased him.

beings he had created. Viracocha first created a world of darkness, which he populated with humans fashioned from stone. In one version, these beings were giants. These people, however, disobeyed Viracocha, and he had to punish them, destroying them by a flood, or by transforming them back into stones, which could be seen, it was believed, at ruined cities such as *TIAHUANACO* and *PUKARA*. Only one man and one woman survived, and were magically transported to Tiahuanaco, where the gods dwelt. Next Viracocha created the present race of humans, and animals, out of clay. On the humans he painted distinctive clothes and gave them customs, languages, songs, arts and crafts and the gift of agriculture to distinguish the different peoples and nations. Having breathed life into these humans, Viracocha instructed them to descend into the earth and disperse, then to

re-emerge on to the earth through caves and from lakes and hills. These places became sacred, and shrines were established at them in honour of the gods. The world was still dark, so Viracocha next ordered the sun, moon and stars to rise into the sky from the islands in Lake Titicaca.

It was thus from the Titicaca Basin that, in legend, Viracocha set out to preach and to spread civilization to the people, but he did so as a mendicant beggar dressed in rags, and under many names, such as *ATUN-VIRACOCHA*, *CON TICCI VIRACOCHA* and *CONTITI VIRACOCHA PACHAYACHACHIC*. In certain other accounts, he was described as a tall white man. Many of those he encountered reviled him, but Viracocha taught humankind the ways of civilization, as well as working miracles among them. This initial active role with the earth and people gave Viracocha affinities in

common with the other preacher heroes so prominent in Andean theology, and he is therefore sometimes confused with similar heroes/deities such as *NEMTEREQUETEBA* and Thunupa (see *THUNUPA VIRACOCHA*). To the Incas, however, he remained remote and only interacted with humans through other gods, particularly through *INTI*, the god of the sun, and *ILLAPA*, the god of thunder, lightning and rain.

The supreme Inca deity Viracocha was the final title for an ancient creator god who figured in the pantheons of many pre-Inca cultures in the central Andes (see also *CONIRAYA VIRACOCHA*). As with many other Andean religious concepts, he was partly adopted by the Incas from the cultures they conquered. For example, his portrayal with weeping eyes was a characteristic almost certainly adopted from the *WEEPING GOD* of Tiahuanaco. In the Inca legend of the creation of their people, Viracocha called out to them as the sun and moon rose at his command. He bestowed a special headdress and stone battle axe upon *MANCO CAPAC*, the Inca leader, and prophesied that they would become great lords and conquer many other nations. Manco Capac led his people back into the earth, from which they re-emerged at the cave of *PACARITAMBO*. A further connection with pre-Inca traditions was provided when Viracocha entered the Valley of Cuzco during his wanderings and created Lord *ALCAVICÇA*, also the name of a people living in the valley when the Incas entered it.

Although he later lost popularity, Viracocha was never neglected by the Incas, in spite of their elevation of Inti to near-equal status in their pantheon. He was accorded

ELOTABO ÍNGA
VIRACOCHA·INGA

his own temple in Cuzco, and human sacrifices were offered to him on the most important and solemn occasions, such as the investiture of a new emperor. He was especially honoured with child sacrifices, CAPACOCHAS, before which the Inca priests recited a specific prayer to him. Several such sacrifices have been discovered high up on Andean peaks and volcanoes, believed to be the abodes of the gods, and where the dry and frozen conditions have preserved the bodies and artefacts in a near pristine state at several sites.

A late Inca cosmology comprised a five-fold sequence of the creation of the Inca world (see PACHACUTI). The First "Age" was ruled by Viracocha and the other gods, and death was unknown. The Second Age was that of the giants, created by Viracocha, who worshipped him, but who displeased him and were destroyed by flood. The Third Age was inhabited by the first humans, again created by Viracocha, but they lived on a primitive level and lacked even the rudiments of civilization. The Fourth Age was that of the *Auca Runa* ("the warriors"), to whom Viracocha presumably imparted the arts of civilization, for these were creators of the early civilizations, such as the MOCHE. The Fifth Age was that of the Incas themselves, who spread civilization far and wide through conquest. Vira-

VIRACOCHA INCA was the eighth Inca ruler, depicted here in an imaginary sketch.
(ILLUSTRATION BY FELIPE GUAMAN POMA DE AYALA, FROM THE NUEVA CORÓNICA Y BUEN GOBIERNO, 1583–1613.)

cocha himself ended his travels and teachings when he reached MANTA in modern Ecuador, from which he departed to the west, across the Pacific Ocean, "walking across the waters as if they were land", or on a raft, or by walking on his cape, in various versions. The Fifth Age ended with the coming of the Spaniards and with the downfall of the Inca Empire, but upon their arrival, the Spaniards were hailed as the returning emissaries of the creator and were referred to as *viracochas*, a term still used as one of respect among QUECHUA speakers.

The only serious rival for the title of creator was the coastal deity PACHACAMAC. After their conquest of the central Peruvian coastal peoples, the Incas went out of their way to reconcile this potential conflict. The ancient site and shrine of Pachacamac was included in the itinerary of Viracocha, which included the seduction and attempted seduction of Pachacamac's daughters. In a general way, the "rivalry" constituted a mythical manifestation of the distinctions and links between the two worlds of the highlands, represented by Viracocha, and the coastal lowlands, represented by Pachacamac.

Viracocha was also the name of the eighth Inca ruler (see VIRACOCHA INCA).

VIRACOCHA INCA was the eighth, semi-legendary, INCA ruler, who traditionally ruled in the early 15th century. At this time, CUZCO was a small city among several

THE DEITY represented on the Gateway of the Sun at Tiahuanaco represents a combination of pan-Andean beliefs. Clearly in the tradition of the Staff Deity, he is variously assumed to represent Viracocha, Thunupa or the Weeping God.

in the Huantanay (Cuzco) Valley. This is a case where the shared name has caused blurring and confusion concerning the relationship between the god and the man, which has vexed scholars and remains unresolved. In one legend, the Inca (Viracocha the man) claimed that Viracocha the god appeared to him one night during troubled times. The creator calmed his fears. When the Inca reported this event to his people the next morning, he was unanimously proclaimed the creator and renamed Viracocha Inca. The troubled times were undoubtedly the result of the rivalries that existed among the various cities of the valley. In the war against the CHANCAS, a significant milestone in the beginning of Inca empire-building, some versions of Inca history record Viracocha Inca as the saviour of Cuzco. More traditionally, however – and no doubt owing to his recasting of Inca history during his reign – the saviour of Cuzco from the Chanca onslaught was Viracocha's son PACHACUTI INCA YUPANQUI, who became tenth ruler following on from the brief reign of another son, INCA URCO.

The person, kingship and divinity of Viracocha Inca provide a fascinating Andean parallel with the interlinked figures of Mixcóatl, Quetzalcóatl/Ce Ácatl Topiltzin Quetzalcóatl and Kukulkán in Mesoamerica, in whom mythology and historicity are also seen to overlap and become blurred. Mixcóatl was the founder of the Toltec nation, and was later deified; his son was the deity and legendary Toltec ruler, and founder, of the city of Tollán in central Mesoamerica; Kukulkán was the god and legendary leader of the Maya-Toltec city of Chichén Itzá in Yucatán, Kukulkán being the Maya translation of the name Quetzalcóatl. In all four cases, scholars are challenged with trying to separate the god from the man, although in Viracocha's case, the two are more distinct because, in the Inca example, the ruler assumed the divine name after his vision of the god.

VIRACOCHA PACHAYACHA-CHIC, or Wiraqoca Pacayacaciq, (meaning "great lord and instructor of the world") was one of several terms that were used by the INCAS to refer to VIRACOCHA.

SACRED PLACES
& RITUAL LINES

AN INTEGRAL PART OF ancient Andean religion was the designation of features and objects throughout the landscape as sacred sites. Known as *huacas*, such locations could be as large as a mountain or as small as a boulder; or a cave, spring, field or other place in which an important event had occurred, or an artificial object such as a stone pillar.

Sacred places were individually significant and collectively linked by ritual lines, one elaborate system of which – the *ceques* – was used by the Incas. Ritual lines could be conventional terrestrial routes between *huacas*, or virtual networks – for example, lines of sight from one *huaca* to another on the horizon for astronomical observations. The cardinal *ceques* radiating from the Inca capital at Cuzco were the four great highways of the empire, leading to the four quarters, the *Tahuantinsuyu*. In addition to their practical purpose, they metaphorically bound the parts of the empire, and

SACRED PLACES and the sacred skies were intimately linked through natural and deliberately erected sacred stones, sited on prominent horizons for use in astronomical observations, as here at Horca del Inca in Bolivia.

served as ritual routes for the progression of sacrificial victims. Similarly, in earlier cultures among the coastal valleys from Nazca in the south to Moche in the north, lines marked out in the desert landscape to form anthropomorphic animal, plant and geometric figures – called geoglyphs – were used as ritual pathways for ceremonial progressions. They appear to be lineage or kinship routes, some used for a single occasion, others over generations.

Pilgrimage sites – some of them used for hundreds, even thousands, of years – were also important, and demonstrate the continuity of religious belief. Two of the most important were Pachacamac and Tiahuanaco.

VIRTUALLY THE ENTIRE landscape (above) was sacred in one way or another to ancient Andean cultures. Entire mountains were designated apus, as was Mount Ausangate in the central Peruvian cordillera near Cuzco.

PROMINENT ROCKS (huancas) in the landscape were named and regarded as sacred (huaca). The antiquity of their status as sacred places can only be guessed at in most cases, but when carved and well worn, as at Nusta Ispana, Yuruk Rumi in the Vilcabamba Mountains (above), it must have been great.

THE LANDSCAPE of the desert in southern coastal Peru has the greatest concentration of sacred lines (above) of anywhere in ancient South America. With long-distance straight lines, cleared areas and animal images, these geoglyphs knit together several aspects of ancient American religion: the sacredness of the landscape itself, the use of ritual pathways in the experience of religious ceremony and the expression of animal imagery to envision the deities. This example depicts a monkey, an animal of the Amazonian rain forest, far to the east of the Nazca culture whose people made the sacred pathway.

LAKE TITICACA (above) was perhaps the most sacred site of all, and one of the most famous places of pilgrimage for ancient Andean peoples, for it was here that Viracocha created the world, caused the sun and moon to rise, and created humankind.

THE LONG-STANDING use of the desert for individual ritual pathways and cleared spaces for ceremonial gatherings (above) is emphasized by the density of crossing and overlapping lines.

Y

WANADI is the sun god of the Yekuana, a Venezuelan rain forest tribe. The architectural details of the Yekuana's houses reflect the structure of their cosmological beliefs. The central support post links the underworld of lost souls with the earth of humans and the heavens above. At the top of it sits a carved crimson-crested wood-pecker, the animal reincarnation of Wanadi. The main entrance faces east, to permit the rising equinoctial sun to shine on the central post, while the two crossbeams supporting the roof are oriented north–south, mimicking the way the Milky Way supports the "roof" of the sky.

THE WARAO, or Warau, are a tribe of the Venezuelan–Guianan Orinoco River (see *KONONATOO*).

WARI see *HUARI*.

THE WARI RUNA were the people of the *INCA* Second Sun (see *PACHACUTI*).

THE WARI WIRACOCHA-RUNA were the *INCA* people of the First Sun (see *PACHACUTI*).

WARRIOR PRIEST see *DECAPITATOR GOD*.

WATAUINEIWA (meaning "the most ancient one") is the benevolent sky god of the *YAHGAN* people of Tierra del Fuego, who they believe created and continues to sustain the world. Initiation rites and prayer to Watauineiwa are the sole preserve of men, who now dominate the affairs of the earth after an initial period when women were dominant.

WAYNA CAPAC see *HUAYNA CAPAC*.

WEEPING GOD was an epithet applied to the god portrayed on the Gateway of the Sun at *TIAHUANACO*, possibly a manifestation of *VIRACOCHA*.

WICHAMA see *PACHACAMAC*.

WINGED BEINGS/CREATURES see under *HUARI* and *TIAHUANACO*.

WIRA QOCHA see *VIRACOCHA*.

WIRAQOCA PACAYACACIQ see *VIRACOCHA PACHAYACHACHIC*.

THE XINGU RIVER, which runs through central Brazil, is the homeland of a group of tribes, including the Juruna, Kamaiura and

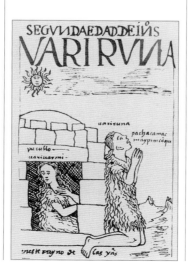

THE WARAO *of the Orinoco River delta (left) believe that they had originally dwelt in the sky with their creator Kononatoo.*

WATAUINEIWA *was the benevolent sky god of the Yahgan people of Tierra del Fuego (below).*

Kuikuru, who share similar beliefs and deities and who have been studied extensively by anthropologists (see *ARAVATURA, IAMURICUMA WOMEN, KANASSA, KUAMUCUCA, KUARUP, KUAT, MAVUTSINIM, MINATA-KARAIA, OI, SINAA, UAICA*).

YACANA, the llama, was one of the "dark cloud" constellations that the *INCA* recognized within *MAYU*, the Milky Way. In myth, when the llama disappeared at midnight it was believed to have descended to earth to drink and thereby prevent flooding during the rainy season.

THE YAHGAN are a tribe of Tierra del Fuego (see *EL-LAL* and *WATAUINEIWA*).

YAHUAR HUACAC, or Inca Yupanqui, was the legendary seventh Inca ruler of *CUZCO*, probably reigning sometime in the 14th century. Like all *INCA* rulers, he was considered to be a direct descendant of the ancestors, *MANCO CAPAC* and *MAMA OCLLO*.

YAJE WOMAN, according to *TUKANO* belief, was the person indirectly responsible for providing the

IN THE SECOND AGE *of Pachacuti or cycle of creation, the Wari Runa (left) were created. They wore only animal skins but recognized Viracocha, their creator.*

THE NUMEROUS *rain forest tribes of the Xingu River (above) of central Brazil have been some of the most intensely studied by anthropologists.*

YAHUAR HUACAC, the seventh Inca ruler, is shown holding a ceremonial axe-staff of office. (ILLUSTRATION FROM THE 18TH-CENTURY "CUZCO SCHOOL" GENEALOGY.)

rain forest tribes with the hallucinatory plants that they use to gain visions and knowledge. She was impregnated by the sun and, when her baby boy was born, she rubbed him with leaves taken from special plants until he shone bright red. Then she took him to the first men, each of whom claimed fatherhood and tore a piece from the child. In this way, each tribe acquired the distinctive plant used by its *SHAMANS* to gain access to the spirit world.

YAMPALLEC was the green stone idol in his own image brought by *NAYAMLAP* to the *LAMBAYEQUE VALLEY* when he invaded it.

THE YANOMAMI are a rain forest tribe of the Venezuelan Amazon who call themselves "the fierce people" (see *OMAM, PERIBORIWA*).

YAUYOS see *HUAROCHIRÍ MANUSCRIPT*.

THE YEKUANA are a Venezuelan rain forest tribe (see *WANADI*).

YURUPARY brought fire to the human race by stealing it from the underworld, but killed both himself and his brother with it in the process.

YLLAPA see *ILLAPA*.

YUPANQUI see *PACHACUTI INCA YUPANQUI, TUPAC INCA YUPANQUI*.

YURUPARY is the principal character in the Colombian Barasana tribal myth about how humans acquired fire. According to this myth, Yurupary – in some versions known as "Manioc Stick Anaconda" – obtained fire from the underworld and brought it back to humankind on earth.

Yurupary used the fire to kill his own brother, Macaw, but was himself also burned to death. His bones are the charred logs that are the result of the slash-and-burn method of creating a garden plots in the rain forest, and provide nourishment for the cultivated plants grown there by humans.

YUTU-YUTU the *tinamou* (the name of a partridge-like bird), was one of the "dark cloud" constellations or stellar voids that the *INCA* people recognized within *MAYU*, the Milky Way.

ZAPANA see *CARI*.

ZEMÍ was the general term used by the prehistoric *ARAWAK* of the Greater Antilles for their gods, and for anything else sacred. Spanish sources record that this term was applied to both the deity and to the idol representing it; to the concept of the idol's oracular powers; and

also to the powers of the sun, the moon, the earth, the sky, the wind and even the remains of the dead. *Zemís* were carved out of wood and stone, and were painted. In the conduct of rituals connected with the predictive abilities of such idols, *SHAMANS* would paint them-

selves in a similar fashion and were then granted visions by means of the use of an hallucinatory plant snuff. (See also *THREE-CORNERED IDOL, HUACA*.)

ZOLZOLOÑI was the wife of *CIUM*.

YANOMAMI WARRIORS relate their mythical origins by using the blood of Periboriwa, the moon spirit, and practise an elaborately graded system of intergroup violence.

ZUE was the name of the *CHIBCHA* sun god (see *BOCHICA*).

BIBLIOGRAPHY

GENERAL READING

Brotherston, Gordon (1979) *Image of the New World: The American Continent Portrayed in Native Texts*. Thames and Hudson, London and New York.

Coe, Michael, Dean Snow and Elizabeth Benson (1986) *Atlas of Ancient America*. Facts on File, New York and Oxford.

Willis,Roy (ed.), *World Mythology: An Illustrated Guide*. Duncan Baird, London.

NORTH AMERICA

Alexander, Hartley Burr (1969) *The World's Rim; Great Mysteries of the North American Indians*. University of Nebraska Press.

Asatchaq (1992) *The Things That Were Said of Them: Shaman Stories and Oral Histories of the Tikigaq People* (transl. by Tukummiq and Tom Lowenstein). University of California Press.

Bahr, Donald (1994) *The Short, Swift Time of Gods on Earth: The Hohokam Chronicles*. University of California Press.

Barnouw, Victor (1977) *Wisconsin Chippewa Myths and Tales and Their Relation to Chippewa Life*. University of Wisconsin Press.

Bierhorst, John (1985) *The Mythology of North America*. Morrow, NY.

Boas, Franz (1969) *The Religion of the Kwakiutl Indians*. AMS Press, NY.

Boas, Franz (1970) *Tsimshian Mythology*. Johnson Reprint Corp, New York.

Burland, Cottie Arthur (1968) *North American Indian Mythology*. Hamlyn, UK.

Callicott, J. Baird and Overholt, Thomas W. (1982) *Clothed-in-fur, and Other Tales: An Introduction to an Ojibwa World View*. University Press of America, Washington, DC.

Clark, Ella Elizabeth (1966) *Indian Legends from the Northern Rockies*. University of Oklahoma Press.

Coffin, Tristram Potter (1961) *Indian Tales of North America; An Anthology for the Adult Reader*. American Folklore Society, Philadelphia.

Coleman, Bernard, Sister (1971) *Ojibwa Myths and Legends*. Ross and Haines, Minneapolis.

Courlander, Harold (1982) *Hopi Voices: Recollections, Traditions, and Narratives of the Hopi Indians*. University of New Mexico Press.

Davis, Mary B. (ed.) (1994) *Native America in the 20th Century: An Encyclopedia*. Garland. New York.

de Laguna, Frederica (ed.) (1995) *Tales from the Dena: Indian Stories from the Tanana, Koyukuk, and Yukon Rivers*. University of Washington Press.

Dorsey, George Amos (1903) *Traditions of the Arapaho*. Chicago.

Dorsey, George Amos (1904) *Traditions of the Arikara*. The Carnegie Institution of Washington.

Dorsey, George Amos (1904) *The Mythology of the Wichita*. Carnegie Institution of Washington.

Dorsey, George Amos (1969) *Traditions of the Skidi Pawnee*. Kraus Reprint, NY.

Edmonds, Margot (1989) *Voices of the Winds: Native American Legends*. Facts on File, New York.

Erdoes, Richard and Ortiz, Alfonso (eds.) (1984) *American Indian Myths and Legends*. Pantheon Books, New York.

Gill, Sam D. (1992) *Dictionary of Native American Mythology*. Santa Barbara, California.

Grinnell, George Bird (1892) *Blackfoot Lodge Tales; The Story of a Prairie People*. Scribner's Sons, New York.

Highwater, Jamake (1977) *Ritual of the Wind: North American Indian Ceremonies, Music, and Dances*. Viking Press, New York.

Hitakonanulaxk (Tree Beard) (1994) *The Grandfathers Speak: Native American Folk Tales of the Lenape People*. Interlink Books, New York.

Howard, James Henri (1984) *Oklahoma Seminoles: Medicines, Magic, and Religion*. University of Oklahoma Press.

Hultkrantz, Ake (1981) *Belief and Worship in Native North America*. Syracuse University Press, New York.

Johnston, Basil (1995) *The Manitous: The Spiritual World of the Ojibway*. HarperCollins, New York.

Josephy, Jr., Alvin (1991) *America in 1492: The World of the Indian Peoples Before the Arrival of Columbus*. Knopf, New York.

Judson, Katharine Berry (1911) *Myths and Legends of Alaska*. A.C. McClurg & Co., Chicago.

Kroeber, Alfred Louis (1978) *Yurok Myths*. University of California Press.

Kroeber, A.L., E.W. Gifford (comp.) (1980) *Karok Myths*. University of California Press.

LaPointe, James (1976) *Legends of the Lakota*. Indian Historian Press, San Francisco.

Leeming, David Adams (1998) *The Mythology of Native North America*. University of Oklahoma Press.

Levy, Jerrold E. (1998) *In the Beginning: The Navajo Genesis*. University of California Press.

Lomatuway'ma, Michael (1993) *Hopi Ruin Legends: Kiqotutuwutsi*. Published for Northern Arizona University by the University of Nebraska Press.

Lowie, Robert Harry (1975) *The Assiniboine*. AMS Press, New York.

Lowie, Robert Harry (1976) *The Religion of the Crow Indians*. AMS Press, New York.

Marriott, Alice Lee (1968) *American Indian Mythology*. Crowell, New York.

Merkur, Daniel (1991) *Powers Which We Do Not Know: The Gods and Spirits of the Inuit*. University of Idaho Press.

Molyneaux, Brian Leigh (1995) *The Sacred Earth*. Macmillan, London.

Opler, Morris Edward (1942) *Myths and Tales of the Chiricahua Apache Indians*. NY.

Penn, W.S. (ed.) (1996) *The Telling of the World: Native American Stories and Art*. Stewart, Tabori & Chang, New York.

Radin, Paul (1948) *Winnebago Hero Cycles: A Study in Aboriginal Literature*. Waverly Press, Baltimore.

Ridington, Robin (1988) *Trail to Heaven: Knowledge and Narrative in a Northern Native Community*. University of Iowa Press.

Schoolcraft, Henry Rowe (1980) *Legends of the American Indians*. Crescent Books, New York.

Shipley, William (ed. and transl.) (1991) *The Maidu Indian Myths and Stories of Hanc'ibyjim*. Heydey Books in conjunction with Rick Heide, Berkeley, CA.

Smith, Anne M. (coll.) (1992) *Ute Tales*. University of Utah Press.

Smith, Theresa S. (1995) *The Island of the Anishnaabeg: Thunderers and Water Monsters in the Traditional Ojibwe Lifeworld*. University of Idaho Press.

Thompson, Stith, (1967) *Tales of the North American Indians*. Indiana University Press.

Trafzer, Clifford E. (ed.) (1996) *Blue Dawn, Red Earth: New Native American Storytellers*. Anchor Books, New York.

Waldman, Carl (1985) *Atlas of the North American Indian*. Facts on File, NY.

Williamson, Ray A. (1984) *Living the Sky: The Cosmos of the American Indian*. Houghton Mifflin, Boston.

Williamson, Ray A. and Farrer, Claire R. (eds.) (1992) *Earth and Sky: Visions of the Cosmos in Native American Folklore*. University of New Mexico Press.

Zimmerman, Larry and Brian Leigh Molyneaux (1996) *Native North America*. Macmillan, London. (Repub. 2000): University of Oklahoma Press.

MESOAMERICA

Aveni, Frank (1980) *Skywatchers of Ancient Mexico*. University of Texas Press.

Benson, Elizabeth P. (ed.) (1981) *Mesoamerican Sites and World Views*. Dumbarton Oaks, Washington, DC.

Berdan, Frances F. (1982) *The Aztecs of Mexico: An Imperial Society*. Holt, Rinehart & Winston, New York.

Berrin, Kathleen, and Esther Pasztory (eds) (1993) *Teotihuacan: Art from the City of the Gods*. Thames and Hudson, London and New York/The Fine Arts Museums of San Francisco.

Bierhorst, J. (1990) *The Mythology of Mexico and Central America*. Harper & Row, New York.

Bierhorst, J. (1992) *History and Mythology of the Aztecs: The Codex Chimalpopoca*. University of Arizona Press.

Blanton, Richard E., Gary M. Feinman, Stephen A. Kowalewski and Linda M. Nichols (1999) *Ancient Oaxaca: The Monte Albán State*. Cambridge University Press.

Boone, Elizabeth H. (ed.) (1970) *Ritual Human Sacrifice in Mesoamerica*. Dumbarton Oaks, Washington, DC.

Bray, Warwick (1968) *Everyday Life of the Aztecs*. Batsford, London.

Broda, Johanna, David Carrasco and Eduardo Matos Moctezuma (1987) *The Great Temple of Tenochtitlan: Center and Periphery in the Aztec World*. University of California Press.

Brotherston, Gordon (1982) *A Key to Mesoamerican Reckoning of Times: The Chronology Recorded in Native Texts*. British Museum Occasional Papers, 38, London.

Brotherston, Gordon (1995) *Painted Books from Mexico: Codices in UK Collections and the World They Represent*. British Museum Press, London.

Brundage, Burr Cartwright (1979) *The Fifth Sun: Aztec Gods, Aztec World*. University of Texas Press.

Burkhart, Louise M. (1985) *The Slippery Earth: Nahua Christian Moral Dialogue in Sixteenth-Century Mexico*. University of Arizona Press.

Carrasco, David (1990) *Religions of Mesoamerica: Cosmovision and Ceremonial Centers*. Harper & Row, San Francisco.

Carrasco, David (1991) *To Change Place: Aztec Ceremonial Landscapes*. University of Colorado Press.

Caso, Alfonso (1958) *The Aztecs, People of the Sun* (trans. Lowell Dunham). University of Oklahoma Press.

Clendinnen, Inga (1991) *Aztecs: An Interpretation*. Cambridge University Press.

Collis, John, and David M. Jones (1997) *Blue Guide Mexico*. A & C Black, London/W. W. Norton, New York.

Conrad, Geoffrey W., and Arthur A. Demarest (1984) *Religion and Empire: The Dynamics of Aztec and Inca Expansionism*. Cambridge University Press.

Diehl, Richard A. (1983) *Tula: The Toltec Capital of Ancient Mexico*. Thames and Hudson, London and New York.

Durán, Fray Diego (1971) *Books of the Gods and Rites* (trans. Fernando Horcasitas and Doris Heydon). University of Oklahoma Press.

Durán, Fray Diego (1971) *The Ancient Calendar* (trans. Fernando Horcasitas and Doris Heydon). University of Oklahoma Press.

León-Portilla, Miguel (1963) *Aztec Thought and Culture*. University of Oklahoma Press.

León-Portilla, Miguel (1980) *Native American Spirituality: Ancient Myths, Discourses, Stories, Doctrines, Hymns, Poems from the Aztec, Maya, Quiche-Maya, and other Sacred Traditions*. Paulist Press, New York.

McEwan, Colin (1994) *Ancient Mexico in the British Museum*. British Museum Press, London.

Matos Moctezuma, Eduardo (1988) *The Great Temple of the Aztecs: Treasures of Tenochtitlan* (trans. Doris Heydon). Thames and Hudson, London and NY.

Miller, Mary Ellen, and Karl Taube (1993) *The Gods and Symbols of Ancient Mexico and the Maya: An Illustrated Dictionary of Mesoamerican Religion*. Thames and Hudson, London and NY.

Muser, Curt (1978) *Facts and Artifacts of Ancient Middle America*. Dutton, NY.

Nicholson, Henry B. (1971) "Religion in Pre-Hispanic Central Mexico", in Robert Wauchope, Gordon Ekholm and Ignacio Bernal (eds.), *Handbook of Middle American Indians*, vol. 10, pp.395–446, University of Texas Press.

Nicholson, Henry B. (ed.) (1976) *Origins of Religious Art and Iconography in Preclassic Mesoamerica*. University of California Press.

Pasztory, Esther (1983) *Aztec Art*. Harry N. Abrams, New York.

Porter Weaver, Muriel (1993) *The Aztecs, Maya, and their Predecessors: Archaeology of Mesoamerica* (3rd ed.). Academic Press, San Diego.

Rostas, Susanna (1992) "Mexican Mythology", in C. Larrington (ed.), *The Feminist Companion to Mythology*. Pandora Press, London.

Sahagún, Fray Bernadino de (1950–69) *General History of the Things of New Spain* (trans. Arthur O. J. Anderson and Charles F. Dibble). University of New Mexico Press.

Saunders, Nicholas J. (1993) 'Mesoamerica', in Roy Willis (ed.), *World Mythology: An Illustrated Guide* pp.234–49. Duncan Baird, London.

Scarborough, Vernon, and David R. Wilcox (eds) (1991) *The Mesoamerican Ballgame*. University of Arizona Press.

Schele, Linda, and Mary Ellen Miller (1986/1992) *The Blood of Kings: Dynasty and Ritual Maya Art*. Kimbell Art Museum & George Braziller, Fort Worth, Texas/Thames and Hudson, London and New York.

Sharer, Robert J. (1994) *The Ancient Maya*. (5th ed.), Stanford University Press, California.

Siméon, Rémi (1885/1984) *Diccionario de la Lengua Nahuatl o Mexicana* (trans. from French Josefina Oliva de Coll), Siglo Veintiuno, México, DF.

Soustelle, Jacques (1955/1961) *Daily Life of the Aztecs on the Eve of the Spanish Conquest* (trans. Patrick O'Brian). Stanford University Press, California.

Soustelle, Jacques (1979/1985) *The Olmecs: The Oldest Civilization in Mexico* (trans. Helen R. Lane). Oklahoma University Press.

Spence, Lewis (1923) *The Gods of Mexico*. T. Fisher Unwin, London.

Spores, Ronald (1984) *The Mixtecs in Ancient and Colonial Times*. Oklahoma University Press.

Taube, Karl (1983) "The Teotihuacan Spider Woman". *Journal of Latin American Lore*, 9 (2), pp.107–89.

Taube, Karl (1992) *The Major Gods of Ancient Yucatan*. Dumbarton Oaks, Washington, DC.

Taube, Karl (1993) *Aztec and Maya Myths*. British Museum Press, London.

Tedlock, Dennis (trans.) (1985) *Popul Vuh: The Definitive Edition of the Mayan Book of the Dawn of Life and the Glories of Gods and Kings*. Simon and Schuster, NY.

Townsend, Richard F. (1992) *The Aztecs*. Thames and Hudson, London and New York.

Townsend, Richard F. (ed.) (1992) *The Ancient Americas: Art from Sacred Landscapes*. The Art Institute of Chicago.

Whitecotton, Joseph W. (1977) *The Zapotecs: Princes, Priests, and Peasants*. Oklahoma University Press.

SOUTH AMERICA

Alva, Walter, and Bill Ballenberg (1988) "Discovering the New World's Richest Unlooted Tomb." *National Geographic*, 174 (4), pp.510–49.

Alva, Walter, and Nathan Benn (1990) "The Moche of Ancient Peru: New Tomb of Royal Splendor." *National Geographic*, 177 (6), pp.2–15.

Alva, Walter, and Christopher B. Donnan (1993) *Royal Tombs of Sipán*. Fowler Museum of Cultural History, University of California.

Ascher, Marcia, and Robert Ascher (1981) *Code of the Quipu: A Study in Media, Mathematics, and Culture*. University of Michigan Press, Ann Arbor.

Aveni, Frank (ed.) (1990) *The Lines of Nasca*. American Philosophical Society, Philadelphia.

Aveni, Frank (2000) *Nasca: Eighth Wonder of the World?* British Museum Press, London.

Bonavia, Duccio (trans. P. J. Lyon) (1985) *Mural Painting in Ancient Peru*, University of Indiana Press.

Bray, Warwick (1978) *The Gold of El Dorado*. Times Newspapers, London.

Burger, Richard L. (1995) *Chavín and the Origins of Andean Civilization*. Thames and Hudson, London and New York.

Cobo, Bernabé de (transl. Roland Hamilton) (1653/1983) *History of the Inca Empire*. University of Texas Press.

Cobo, Bernabé de (transl. Roland Hamilton) (1653/1990) *Inca Religion and Customs*. University of Texas Press.

Conrad, Geoffrey W., and Arthur A. Demarest (1984) *Religion and Empire: The Dynamics of Aztec and Inca Expansionism*. Cambridge University Press.

Cordy-Collins, Alana (1992) "Archaism or Tradition: The Decapitation Theme in Cupisnique and Moche Iconography". *Latin American Antiquity*, 3 (3), pp.206–20.

Demarest, Arthur A. (1981) *Viracocha – The Nature and Antiquity of the Andean High God*. Peabody Museum Monographs, 6, Cambridge.

Donnan, Christopher B. (1976) *Moche Art and Iconography*. University of California at Los Angeles Latin American Center, Los Angeles.

Donnan, Christopher B. (1988) "Iconography of the Moche: Unravelling the Mystery of the Warrior Priest". *National Geographic*, 174 (4), pp.550–55.

Donnan, Christopher B. (1988) "Moche Funerary Practices". *Tombs for the Living: Andean Mortuary Practices*, pp.111–59, Dumbaton Oaks, Washington, DC.

Donnan, Christopher B., and Nathan Benn (1990) "The Moche of Ancient Peru: Masterworks of Art Reveal a Remarkable Pre-Inca World". *National Geographic*, 177 (6), pp16–33.

Donnan, Christopher B., and Luis Jaime Castillo (1992) "Finding the Tomb of a Moche Priestess". *Archaeology*, 45 (6), pp38–42.

Donnan, Christopher B., and Carol J. Mackey (1978) *Ancient Burial Patterns of the Moche Valley, Peru*. University of Texas Press.

Hadingham, Evan (1987) *Lines to the Mountain Gods: Nazca and the Mysteries of Peru*. Random House, NY.

Harner, J. (1971) *The Jivaro*. University of California Press.

Hugh Jones, S. (1979) *The Palm and the Pleiades: Initiation and Cosmology in North West Amazonia*. Cambridge University Press.

Isbell, William (1997) *Mummies and Mortuary Monuments*. University of Texas Press.

Lumbreras, Luis G. (1969) (trans. Betty J. Meggers) (1974) *The Peoples and Cultures of Ancient Peru*. Smithsonian Institution Press, Washington, DC.

Kolata, Alan L. (1993) *Tiwanaku: Portrait of an Andean Civilization*. Blackwell, Oxford and Cambridge.

Kolata, Alan L. (1996) *Valley of the Spirits: A Journey into the Lost Realm of the Aymara*. John Wiley, New York.

Morrison, Tony (1979) *Pathways to the Gods*. Harper and Row, New York.

Morrison, Tony (1987) *The Mystery of the Nasca Lines*. Nonesuch Expeditions, Woodbridge, UK.

Moseley, Michael E. (1992) *The Incas and Their Ancestors: The Archaeology of Peru*. Thames and Hudson, London and NY.

Moseley, Michael E, and Kent C. Day (eds) (1982) *Chan Chan: Andean Desert City*. University of New Mexico Press.

Paul, Anne (1990) *Paracas Ritual Attire: Symbols of Authority in Ancient Peru*. University of Oklahoma Press.

Reichel-Dolmatoff, Gerardo (1971) *Amazonian Cosmos: the Sexual and Religious Symbolism of the Tukano Indians*, University of Chicago Press.

Reinhard, Johan (1985) "Chavín and Tiahuanaco: A New Look at Two Andean Ceremonial Centers". *National Geographic Research*, 1, pp.395–422.

Reinhard, Johan (1988) *The Nazca Lines: A New Perspective on their Origin and Meaning*. Editorial Los Pinos, Lima.

Reinhard, Johan (1992) "Sacred Peaks of the Andes". *National Geographic*, 181 (3), pp.84–111.

Reinhard, Johan (1996) "Peru's Ice Maidens: Unwrapping the Secrets". *National Geographic*, 190 (6), pp.62–81.

Rostworowksi de Diez Canseco, María, and Michael E. Moseley (eds.) (1990) *The Northern Dynasties: Kingship and Statecraft in Chimor*. Dumbarton Oaks, Washington, DC.

Rowe, John H. (1946) "Inca Culture at the Time of the Spanish Conquest", in Julian H. Steward (ed.), *Handbook of South American Indians*, pp.183–330, Washington, DC.

Rowe, John H. (1979) "An Account of the Shrines of Ancient Cuzco", *Nawpa Pacha*, 17, pp.2–80, Berkeley, CA.

Salles-Reese, Verónica (1997) *From Viracocha to the Virgin of Copacabana: Representation of the Sacred at Lake Titicaca*. University of Texas Press.

Saunders, Nicholas J. (1993) 'South America', in Roy Willis (ed.), *World Mythology: An Illustrated Guide* pp.250–63. Duncan Baird, London.

Shobinger, Juan (1991) "Sacrifices of the High Andes". *Natural History*, 4, pp.63–9.

Shimada, Izumi (1994) *Pampa Grande and the Mochica Culture*. University of Texas Press.

Silverman, Helaine (1993) *Cahuachi in the Ancient Nasca World*. University of Iowa Press.

Urton, Gary (1981) *At the Crossroads of the Earth and the Sky*. University of Texas Press.

Urton, Gary (1990) *The History of a Myth: Pacariqtambo of the Origin of the Inkas*. University of Texas Press.

Urton, Gary (1999) *Inca Myths*. British Museum Press, London.

von Hagen, Adriana, and Craig Morris (1998) *The Cities of the Ancient Andes*. Thames and Hudson, London and New York.

Zuidema, R. Tom (1964) *The Ceque System of Cuzco: The Social Organization of the Capital of the Inca*. Leiden-anford University Press, Stanford CA.

PICTURE ACKNOWLEDGEMENTS

The publishers are grateful to the agencies, museums and galleries listed below for kind permission to reproduce the following images in this book:

NORTH AMERICA

AKG: 23br; 60br

Brian and Cherry Alexander: 77bl; 82tr; 82bl; 83bl

Art Resource: 19br National Museum of American Art, Washington, DC; 50br; 52tc; 75tr National Museum of American Art, Washington, DC

Artemis Picture Research: 22br

Bancroft Hunt: 17bl; 19tc; 26tr; 26bl; 33tl; 34tr; 40tr; 40bl; 41cr; 44bc; 45tl; 46tl; 46bc; 48tl; 53tr; 53tl; 55bc; 60tc; 61tr; 61bc; 66bc; 67tc; 73tl; 81tl; 84c; 84cl; 85bl; 87br

Bridgeman Art Library: 27tr Library of Congress, Washington, DC; 28br Princeton Museum of Natural History, New Jersey; 63t Royal Ontario Museum, Toronto; 63cr Private Collection; 73br Private Collection

Bruce Coleman: 12tl; 25tl; 29t; 34br; 41bl; 57t; 83br; 86bl

Sylvia Cordaiy: 16br; 18tc; 31br; 57bl; 87tc

Ecoscene: 20b; 35br; 38br; 47tl; 49br

Mary Evans Picture Library: 35bl; 41tc

Favell Museum, Klamath Falls, Oregon: 65tr

Galaxy Picture Library: 25br; 29bl; 62br; 67br; 68bl; 75bl

Gibson Photo: 36c; 36bl; 37t; 37c; 37b

The Granger Collection: 51tl; 70bl; 71tl

Michael Heron: 13tr

Indian and Northern Affairs, Canada: 23c

Brian L. Molyneaux: 29br; 43cl; 43br; 64ct; 71bl; 77t

Peter Newark Pictures: 17tr; 21tc; 44tl; 45cr; 47cr; 47bc; 51cr; 63bl; 68tr; 71cr; 71br; 72tl; 74ct; 76br; 80tl; 81br; 85tr; 87bl

North Wind Pictures: 21cr; 24tr; 27bl; 30br; 34tl; 43tl; 48tr; 48bc; 51cl; 65br; 69ct

Phoebe Hearst Museum of Anthropology, University of California: 51b

Prema Photos: 66tr

Rochester Museum and Science Center: 70tr; 86tr

Santa Barbara Mission Archive-Library: 11br

Smithsonian Institution, Department of Anthropology: 59br

Smithsonian Institution, National Museum of the American Indian: 59tl

Superstock: 24br; 58tl National Museum of Natural History, Smithsonian Institution, Washington, DC; 69br Lowe Art Museum, University of Miami

Travel Ink: 18br; 24cl; 32tr; 38tc; 63br

VBC Museum of Anthropology: 13bl

Werner Forman Archive: 16tc Sheldon Jackson Museum, Alaska; 20tr, 23t, 33br Provincial Museum, Victoria, British Columbia; 35tr National Museum, Denmark; 39tc Arizona State Museum; 42cr; 42bl; 43cr; 49tl Museum of Anthropology, University of British Columbia, Vancouver; 55tr Provincial Museum, Victoria, British Columbia; 58bc Schindler Collection, New York; 72br Field Museum of Natural History, Chicago; 74cl; 77br Haffenreffer Museum of Anthropology, Brown University, Rhode Island; 78tl; 78br; 79tl Provincial Museum, Victoria, British Columbia; 79br; 80br Provincial Museum, Victoria, British Columbia

MESOAMERICA

AKG: 98cl Biblioteca Nacional, Madrid; 98tl, 103cl Museum für Völkerkunde, Berlin; 105cl Austrian Nationalbibliothek, Vienna; 112bc; 132tr; 135bl SMPK Museum für Völkerkunde, Berlin; 135c; 142tcl; 145tr; 145bl British Museum, London; 158 Bibliotheque Nationale, Paris; 164r National Museum of Anthropology, Mexico

Ancient Art and Architecture: 100br; 107br; 108; 113tl; 113br; 123bc; 130br; 147r; 148; 162tr; 163tr

Andes Press Agency: 99br National Museum of Anthropology, Mexico; 123tl; 141; 152bc; 154

The Bridgeman Art Library: 90 Museo Casa Diego Rivera, Mexico; 103tr Museo Nacional de Antropologia, Mexico; 104bl Royal Geographical Society, London; 105tr Museo Casa Diego Rivera (INBA), Guanajuato, Mexico; 115tr Royal Geographical Society, London; 122br; 133br, 144 British Museum, London; 145cr Biblioteca Apostolica Vaticana; 161tl National Museum of Anthropology, Mexico; 165t

Grażyna Bonati: 93bl; 143br

Sylvia Cordaiy: 101bl; 110br; 120tc; 129cl; 151cl;

ET Archive: 91, 97br National Library, Mexico; 98br Archaeological Museum, Copan, Honduras; p100tc, 101cr National Library, Mexico; 101tl; 102tr; 105br Anthropological Museum, Merida, Spain; 119tc National Library Mexico; 119br Antochiw Collection; 122tl National Library, Mexico; 123tr Archaeological Museum, Copan, Honduras; 126bl; 129br, 131tr National Library, Mexico; 133tl; 135b; 136br, 137tr National Library, Mexico; 138br; p139tl Archaeological Museum Mexico; 139br Antochiw Collection; p145tl; 145cl; 145br; 149tl, 153tc, 155, 156 National Library, Mexico; 163bl Archaeological Museum, Mexico; 164l Archaeological Museum, Copan, Honduras

Michael Holford: 117br Anthropological Museum, Mexico City

Hutchison Library: 118tr Anthropological Museum, Mexico City

David M. Jones: 142tr; 151tl; 151tr; 151cr; 160

Panos Pictures: 129tl

South American Pictures: 92; 93tr, 94; 97tl; 106br; 107tl; 109tl; 109br; 110tc; 125br; 126tc; 138tcl; 138tr; 140; 143tc; 150; 151bl; 153br; 159; 165b; 166

Mireille Vautier: 102tl, 102bl, 106tc, 116bl, 128bl, 149br National Library Mexico City

Werner Forman Archive: 96 British Museum, London; 99tl Private Collection, New York; 104r St. Louis Art Museum, US; 111br Liverpool Museum, Liverpool; 114 National Museum of Anthropology, Mexico City; 115cr; 115cl Biblioteca Universitaria, Bologna, Italy; 117tl Dallas Museum of Art; 121 David Bernstein, New York; 124 Museum für Völkerkunde, Basel; 125tl National Museum of Anthropology, Mexico; 125tr Anthropology Museum, Veracruz University, Jalapa; 125bl Museum für Völkerkunde, Berlin; 127tl National Museum of Anthropology, Mexico; 127tr British Museum, London; 133ct Anthropology Museum, Veracruz University, Jalapa; 135r; 152tl Biblioteca Universitaria, Bologna, Italy; 157bl, 157bc Museum für Völkerkunde, Basel; 161br British Museum, London; 162bl National Museum of Anthropology, Mexico City; 167 Liverpool Museum, Liverpool

SOUTH AMERICA

AKG: 194tc Linden-Museum, Stuttgart; 195tc Gold Museum, Bogotá; 195tr

Andes Press Agency: 209br; 211tl; 217tl

Bridgeman Art Library: 182br The Stapleton Collection; 203tr Phillips, The International Fine Art Auctioneers, UK; 207br Museo de America, Madrid; 207tbl Museo Nacional de Anthropologia y Arqueologia, Lima; 216bl Freud Museum, London; 223tr Bolton Museum and Art Gallery, UK

Sylvia Cordaiy: 189br; 223tl

ET Archive: 171bc Archaeological Museum, Lima; 173tl, 176tc Larco Herrera Museum, Lima; 179tl Pedro de Osma Museum, Lima; 198br Bruning Museum, Lambayeque, Peru; 205tc Chavez Ballon Collection, Lima; 211br 212tc, 214tl Pedro de Osma Museum, Lima; 218br, 219tl Archaeological Museum, Lima; 226tr Pedro de Osma Museum, Lima; 239tl, 249tl Museo Nacional de Historia, Lima

Hutchison Library: 197br; 222tr

Panos Pictures: 176br; 187t; 200tcl; 249br

Nick Saunders: 218tc; 231br; 237t; 241tl; 247br

South American Pictures: 170tc; 172c; 174tr; 177tc; 177br; 178tl; 178bc; 179bl; 180tr; 181br; 183tc; 183br; 184tc; 184br; 185tr; 185br; 187bl; 187cr; 188tc; 189tr; 189cl; 189bl; 190tc; 190cl; 190br; 191tc; 192tl; 192br; 193tc; 193bl; 193br; 194br; 195c; 196br; 197tl; 197cr; 199cr; 200br; 201tl; 201c; 201br; 202ct; 202br; 203br; 204tc; 205cl; 205br; 207cl; 208tc; 208cr; 208cl; 208bc; 209tr; 209c; 210tl; 210tc; 210cr; 210bc; 211tc; 211bl; 213tc; 213bl; 215tr; 217tr; 217bl; 219br; 220ct; 220br; 221br; 221tc; 223br; 224tc; 224br; 225tc; 226bl; 227tl; 227br; 228tc; 229tl; 229br; 230tr; 230tl; 230br; 231tc; 231tl; 234cl; 234bc; 235tl; 235tr; 235br; 236tl; 236br; 237bl; 237br; 238tr; 238bl; 239br; 241tr; 241cl; 241bl; 242tr; 243tr; 243bl; 244tc; 245tl; 245br; 246tr; 247bl; 247cr; 247tl; 247tr; 248tl; 248tr; 248bc; 248br; 249cr

Mireille Vautier: 199tl

Werner Forman Archive: 176cl Museum für Völkerkunde, Berlin; 179br; 186tr Museum für Völkerkunde, Berlin; 188br British Museum, London; 197tr, 198tl Museum für Völkerkunde, Berlin; 207tl Dallas Museum of Art; 216tr Private Collection; 217br Museum für Völkerkunde, Berlin; 223cl Dallas Museum of Art; 223c Museum für Völkerkunde, Berlin; 228br David Bernstein Fine Art, New York; 232tr British Museum, London; 232bl British Museum, London; 233l, 233tr Museum für Völkerkunde, Berlin; 233br British Museum, London; 240tr David Bernstein Gallery, New York.

INDEX